Andreas Zeman
The Winds of History

Africa in Global History

Edited by
Joël Glasman, Omar Gueye, Alexander Keese and
Christine Whyte

Advisory Board:
Joe Alie, Felicitas Becker, William Gervase Clarence-Smith, Lynda Day,
Scholastique Diazinga, Andreas Eckert, Babacar Fall, Toyin Falola, Matt Graham,
Emma Hunter, Erin Jessee, Isabella Kentridge, Colleen Kriger, Kristin Mann,
Patrick Manning, Conceição Neto, Vanessa S. Oliveira, Lorelle Semley,
Ibrahim Sundiata

Volume 7

Andreas Zeman

The Winds of History

―

Life in a Corner of Rural Africa since the 19th Century

DE GRUYTER
OLDENBOURG

This book is a revised version of the author's dissertation, which was accepted by the Faculty of Humanities of the University of Bern in 2019.

The open access publication of this book has been published with the support of the Swiss National Science Foundation.

ISBN 978-3-11-163209-4
e-ISBN (PDF) 978-3-11-076500-7
e-ISBN (EPUB) 978-3-11-076505-2
ISSN 2628-1767
DOI https://doi.org/10.1515/9783110765007

This work is licensed under the Creative Commons Attribution-NonCommercial-NoDerivatives 4.0 International License. For details go to https://creativecommons.org/licenses/by-nc-nd/4.0/.

Creative Commons license terms for re-use do not apply to any content (such as graphs, figures, photos, excerpts, etc.) not original to the Open Access publication and further permission may be required from the rights holder. The obligation to research and clear permission lies solely with the party re-using the material.

Library of Congress Control Number: 2023938854

Bibliographic information published by the Deutsche Nationalbibliothek
The Deutsche Nationalbibliothek lists this publication in the Deutsche Nationalbibliografie; detailed bibliographic data are available on the internet at http://dnb.dnb.de.

© 2024 the author(s), published by Walter de Gruyter GmbH, Berlin/Boston.
This volume is text- and page-identical with the hardback published in 2023.
This book is published open access at www.degruyter.com.

Cover image: Chingomanje's Village. George H. Swinny, "With Chingomanje," *Central Africa* (*CA*) 5, no. 56 (1887): 113.

www.degruyter.com

Nkholongue Village, Eastern Shores of Lake Malawi, 1887. Source: George H. Swinny, "With Chingomanje," *Central Africa* (*CA*) 5, no. 56 (1887): 113.

Nkholongue Village, Niassa Province, Mozambique, 2009. Photograph taken during my first visit to Nkholongue in January 2009.

Contents

Acknowledgments —— XI

Abbreviations —— XV

Foreword —— XVII

1 Introduction: Ways and Arguments Towards a "Global" Microhistory —— 1
1.1 The Starting Point of My Research —— 1
1.2 Microhistory: My Approach, Its Antecedents and Particularities —— 3
1.3 On the Traces of an "Unknown" Matrilineal Village: Methods and Sources —— 23
1.4 The Winds of History: Life in a Corner of Rural Africa since the 19th Century —— 36
1.5 Topics and Key Findings of the Chapters —— 48
1.6 Notes on Spelling and Terminology —— 52

2 Linking the Global with the Local: A Village Crafted by the Slave Trade —— 54
2.1 "When our parents came here, it was not themselves who wanted to come here" —— 54
2.2 The Lake Malawi Region in the 19th Century —— 59
2.3 The Formation of Nkholongue —— 70
2.4 The Slave Trade and Slavery in Nkholongue —— 74
2.5 Conclusion —— 82

3 Christianity's Double: Islamization as Slave Emancipation —— 85
3.1 Chiefs as Key Players? —— 85
3.2 The Anglican Mission in Nkholongue —— 89
3.3 The Spread of Islam —— 94
3.4 Conclusion —— 101

4 One Village, One People? The Colonization of Masters and Slaves —— 104
4.1 "They let them enter": Looking Beyond Resistance in Mozambique —— 104
4.2 Chief Chingomanje bin M'ponda: One Who Knows How to Speak and Act with Strangers —— 109
4.3 Changing Settlement Patterns as a Sign of Emancipation —— 130
4.4 Conclusion —— 135

5 The Grandmother of Poverty: A (Local) Periodization of Colonialism —— 138
5.1 The Colonial State on the Periphery: A History of Absence? —— 138
5.2 The Ruins of the *Companhia* in Metangula —— 143
5.3 Colonial Exploitation along the Lakeshore —— 151
5.4 Reactions: Resistance, Accommodation, and Intermediaries —— 172
5.5 Conclusion —— 189

6 Uncaptured Again: History and the Subsistence Mantra of Development Studies —— 192
6.1 A Déjà-Vu of Economic Transformation —— 192
6.2 The Rise and Fall of Nkholongue's Pottery Manufacture in the 1940s and 1950s —— 202
6.3 From Sorghum to Cassava to Maize to Cassava: Complicating the History of Subsistence Food Production —— 229
6.4 Fishing *Ussipa*: A History of Capitalism from Below —— 239
6.5 Conclusion —— 247

7 Being Resettled: A Social History of the Mozambican War of Independence —— 252
7.1 How "Loyalty" Became a Viable Option —— 252
7.2 Buying History with Money: Frelimo's Fake Veterans —— 258
7.3 From Fighting for the Nationalist to Supporting the Portuguese War Effort —— 262
7.4 Zooming Out: Nkholongue's Experience in the Broader Perspective —— 286
7.5 Conclusion —— 300

8 At the Margins of the Nation: Malawians at Heart in Mozambique —— 302
8.1 "Aah! Even I was afraid": Mozambican Independence on the Ground —— 302
8.2 "We even fled to Malawi": The Moment of Independence in the Biographies of People from Nkholongue —— 307
8.3 From Taxing Natives to Taxing Citizens: The New Government on the Ground —— 315
8.4 Conclusion —— 336

9 From Victims to Voters: Renamo's Delayed Supporters —— 338
9.1 Renamo, or How to Evade the Blame —— 338
9.2 The Local History of the War —— 342

9.3 How Renamo Victims Became Renamo Supporters —— **354**
9.4 Conclusion —— **360**

10 Tourism and the Return of Tradition and Custom: How to Find the Chief? —— 362
10.1 The Re-Emergence of the Customary Institutions —— **362**
10.2 Mozambican Legislation and the Customary —— **367**
10.3 Tourism and Leisure Projects in Nkholongue since 2000 —— **372**
10.4 Finding the "Community" (Representative) —— **380**
10.5 Conclusion —— **395**

11 From Slave Trade to Tourism: Towards a Local History of Matriliny —— 397
11.1 Matriliny: Resilient, but Not Ahistorical —— **397**
11.2 Matrilineal Resilience against the Virilocal Shift —— **401**
11.3 Conclusion —— **414**

12 Conclusion: The World and a Really Small Place in Africa —— 417

13 Bibliography —— 422

List of Maps —— 469

List of Figures —— 470

List of Tables —— 471

Index —— 472

Acknowledgments

This work grew out of my PhD thesis at the University of Bern, which I defended in 2019. However, the first steps of research for it were already taken in 2010 when I was still an undergraduate. During this long period of learning, erring, researching and (re)writing, many have provided me with invaluable support and helped to make this work possible.

First and foremost, my thanks go to all the people from Nkholongue and Malango and elsewhere who gave me their time and taught me so much about the processes and events that are analyzed in this book. Without their readiness to share insights into their life experiences and trajectories, this book would never have been written. The biggest *zikomo* ('thank you') therefore goes to them! Undoubtedly, as is the danger with every encounter of historians and contemporary witnesses, this book also discusses certain complicated local "realities" that some interviewees may have portrayed somewhat differently. Still, I hope that this book will on the whole help to deepen the understanding of the different and common perspectives of all my interviewees and, in this way, also give a little something back to all of them.

Fieldwork would not have been possible the way it was without the assistance of various translators and assistants. My thanks go to Lourenço Thawe, Arturo Stambuli, Assane G. Ambali, Andrew Chingani, and especially Mustafa Mamboia. Mustafa was a very valuable research companion, not only while interviewing people in and around Nkholongue, but also on our joint journeys through Mozambique and Malawi. Even after fieldwork, his assistance in transcribing and translating was invaluable. His interest in history and his always critical stance were of great benefit to my research. It was a pleasure to work with you.

For this project, I enjoyed working in many different archival collections. I am grateful for the support of the staff and directors of these different archives. A special thank goes to Lucy McCann (Bodleian Library), Catherine Wakeling (Archives of the United Society Partners in the Gospel), Simão Jaime, Calbrito Jaime, Joel das Neves Tembe (all *Arquivo Histórico de Moçambique*), Isabel Beato (*Arquivo Histórico da Marinha*), P. Pedro Louro (Consolata Mission), Conceição Casanova, Ana Canas, Ana Roque (all *Instituto de Investigação Científica Tropical*), Paulo Tremoçeiro (*Arquivo Nacional Torre do Tombo*) and the staff of the administrations of the Governor's office of Niassa, the District of Lago, and the administrative posts of Meluluca and Maniamba. António Sopa (*Arquivo Histórico de Moçambique*) once gave me a very generous lift, peppered with importants hints, when I was still a very young and inexperienced researcher (and he will hardly remember me). Many thanks also go to Ludwig Deuss, who provided me with many photos from his late father's collection, and to Robert Layng and Manuel António Lima Torres Ribeiro who allowed me to use their photos in this book. I also thank the University of Wisconsin Press for permission to reprint a figure from one of their publications.

Without the support and motivation of many people and institutions, I would not have made it to Mozambique and Niassa in the first place. My thanks go to Fritz Wenzinger, Stefan Frei, Darco Cazin, *Schweizer Jugend Forscht* and the Swiss Ministry of Foreign Affairs. Maya and Thomas Litscher gave me the best welcome to Mozambique that I could have imagined and opened up a whole new world to me. I am very grateful for their generosity and openness. For company and support during my different stays in Mozambique, I thank Nina Pfaff, Dominic Schuppli, and Arsénio Matavele. Gerd Roscher proved to be a very pleasant travel companion on our common quest to learn more about the fate of Albrecht Roscher.

A large number scholars have given me important backing and advice. Christian Gerlach has supported this project from the beginning. Without his encouragement, I probably would never have made my research about Nkholongue a full-time endeavor. His empirical and analytical rigor, as well as his way of asking unconventional questions, were a great inspiration and fascinated me already as an undergraduate. Gesine Krüger was willing to support my application for a grant of the Swiss National Science Foundation and act as co-supervisor. Many thanks to her for this. Alexander Keese has been tireless in his support and help for my project, and has provided me with countless opportunities to present my research. I am very grateful for this and always happy to exchange our ideas. The same goes for Moritz Feichtinger, who not only gave me countless pieces of advice and read many of my drafts, but also kept listening to my concerns and problems. Jonas Flury has always been an excellent conversation partner and has helped me to sharpen my arguments and also to solve many riddles of the English language.

During my time at the University of Bern, many gave me important ideas and hints in many good discussions and exchanges. They include Christian Hadorn, Lena Joos, Felix Frey, Fabian Lüscher, Andreas Stucki, Julia Richers, Michael Volkart, Robert Heinze, Stephan Scheuzger, Michael Offermann, Tanja Bührer, Matthias Ruoss, Moritz von Brescius, Vera Blaser, Franziska Zaugg, John Ly, Philipp Horn, Francesca Fuoli, and Melina Teubner. The members of the reading group of global history read and extensively discussed the introduction of this book. Thanks to all of them and especially to Agnes Gehbald, who initiated the group.

Many specialists of Mozambique and Africa provided me with most valuable suggestions and resources. At the Eduardo Mondlane University in Maputo, the support of the late Gerhard Liesegang proved crucial in enabling my principal fieldwork stay in Mozambique. James Brennan shared archival material with me like no other. David Bone helped me better frame my discussion of the spread of Islam, and Jonna Katto that of matriliny. Raquel Soeiro de Brito was kind enough to go through her fieldwork notes from the 1960s and share them with me. Arianna Huhn facilitated my entry to fieldwork in Mozambique and her oral history collection at the local museum of Metangula was a great addition to my work. Malyn Newitt read the entire manuscript and gave me very generous and valuable feedback at a moment when I was once again in doubt about the path to finishing this book. Others I would like to thank for support, conversations and exchanges at many moments and in many places around the world include James Amanze, Pedro Cerdeira, Justin Roborg-Söndergaard, Miguel Bandeira Jerónimo, Ricarda Stegmann, Frank Schubert, Eric Allina, Beatriz Valverde Contreras, Philip Havik, Alan Thorold, Adolphe Linder, Christoph Kalter, Rosemary Galli, René Pélissier, Didier Péclard, and Benoît Henriet, as well as all those who tried to help me find the whereabouts of Robert Carl Greenstein.

Several institutions lent important support to make this project possible. Among them are the History Department of the University of Bern and the Center for Policy Analysis at the Eduardo Mondlane University in Maputo. The Swiss National Science Foundation generously funded the research for this project for three years (funding scheme no. 162216) and also made possible the open access publication of this book. The Field Work Expenses Committee of the Faculty of Humanities of the University of Bern provided financial support for my first research trips. Many thanks to all of them.

For the production of the book, I thank Rabea Rittgerodt and Jana Fritsche at De Gruyter and Christine Whyte and the other editors of the Africa in Global History series. It is a pleasure to see my book published in a series that I believe fits so well with the objectives of my book. Two anonymous reviewers gave me valuable feedback and suggestions. Many thanks to them and to John Ryan and Ian Copestake for proofreading my English. Adriana Stroe and her many colleagues had to fix far too many errors and inconsistencies in the final stages of the book's production, and I am very grateful to them for this tedious work.

My thanks also go to my family, friends and neighbors. They were not only willing to listen to many stories from Mozambique, but also supported me in my work in manifold ways, not least by caring for my children during times of work and absence. I would especially like to thank Annemarie, Susanne, Margaretha and Hans Reber for their manifold support at many stages of this project. Christian Zeman has been an extraordinary brother and I thank him for the many good moments. My parents Johanna and Jaroslav Zeman have always been there for me, and enabled me to study what I wanted to study. And no doubt they have also both in their own way contributed a lot to this being history. I thank them with all my heart for everything they have done for me. Last but not least, I thank Marianne for all her support and especially for her readiness to travel with me to Mozambique and stay there for an extended period of time with our children, who were still very young at the time. I would also like to thank her and our children Moritz, Felix, and Matis for their patience, their flexibility and all their positive energy and creative talents, with which they have created an outstanding and enjoyable balance to my everyday worries with academic life.

Abbreviations

ADL	Administração do Distrito de Lago
ADN	Arquivo da Defesa Nacional
AGMAfr	Archives de la Société des Missionnaires d'Afrique
AHD	Arquivo Histórico Diplomático
AHM	Arquivo Histórico de Moçambique
AHMar	Arquivo Histórico da Marinha
AHMil	Arquivo Histórico Militar
AHU	Arquivo Histórico Ultramarino
AIMC	Arquivo Geral Instituto Missionário da Consolata
ANTT	Arquivo Nacional Torre do Tombo
APAM	Administração do Posto Administrativo de Maniamba
APGGN	Arquivo Permanente do Gabinete do Governador de Niassa
ASM	Archives of the Society of Malawi
AUMCA	Archives of the Universities' Mission to Central Africa
AUNHCR	Archives of the United Nations High Commission for Refugees
AUSPG	Archives of the United Society Partners in the Gospel
CA	Central Africa (periodical)
CJ	S.S. Charles Janson (steamship)
CM	S.S. Chauncy Maples (steamship)
DFE	Destacamento de Fuzileiros (Portuguese navy unit)
DGS	Direcção-Geral de Segurança (successor organization of PIDE)
DML	Deposito Museológico de Lichinga
DUAT	Direito do Uso e Aproveitamento da Terra (Land title in Mozambique)
FMS	Fundação Mario Soares
LDQP	Likoma Diocesan Quarterly Paper (periodical)
MLM	Museu Local de Metangula
MNA	Malawian National Archives
NDC	Nyasaland Diocesan Chronicle (periodical)
NDQP	Nyasaland Diocesan Quarterly Paper (periodical)
PA	Personal archives
PIDE	Polícia Internacional e de Defesa do Estado (Portuguese secret police)
SFA	Swiss Federal Archives
TNA	The National Archives (UK)
TNN	The Nyassa News (periodical)
UMCA	Universities' Mission to Central Africa

Foreword

This book is about the history of a village on the eastern shores of Lake Malawi. Maybe, it is also the history of two villages. For there is no doubt that the settlement of Malango, a 30-minute walk north of the original center of Nkholongue, can today be considered a distinct village. In 2015, Nkholongue and Malango had 548 and 400 inhabitants respectively. Compared to other lakeside villages, they are small settlements. Nkholongue and Malango stretch along the main trail that follows the shore of Lake Malawi. From Malango it is about a two-hour walk to Metangula, the capital of Lago District. If the winds and waves on the lake permit, the trip is made faster by boat, taking about 30 minutes. From Metangula, minibuses reach Lichinga, the capital of Niassa, in about three hours. From here it is another road trip of 2,300 kilometers to Mozambique's capital Maputo. Few of Nkholongue's inhabitants have ever made this journey.

"The end of the world" is what Niassa is often called in Mozambique. I certainly shared this sentiment when I first arrived in Nkholongue in the rainy season of 2008/9 as a 19-year old student from Europe with only a very scant knowledge of African history, encountering the mud huts with thatched roofs, the women with their hoes in their fields, the fishermen in their dugout canoes and a more than 90-year-old village chief, who did not speak any Portuguese, Mozambique's only official language. For me, it seemed that little had ever happened in this out-of-the-way place. This image was further reinforced by the impressive scenery of this seemingly endless lake, given the contours of opposite Malawi were usually only visible when the sun disappeared behind them.

But doubtlessly, there was also considerable change going on. In the hills behind the lake, on Niassa's *planalto*, a Swedish company was busy drawing up large plantations of pine trees along the road to Lichinga. The road itself had been asphalted only a few years prior to my arrival. In 2006, Metangula had been connected to the national power network or *Cahora Bassa*, as people use to call it in Mozambique after the large dam on the Zambezi river. Connection to Cahora Bassa was quickly followed by the installation of the first mobile phone antenna. The first petrol station and bank were to follow in the years to come. And in Nkholongue, a small "upmarket lodge" was about to receive its first tourists from Europe.

In many ways, I arrived in Niassa as part of this change, even if I had never intended to do so. I had originally come to Mozambique to do a short internship at the Swiss Embassy in Maputo. The internship was a prize I had won in a science competition for Swiss high school students. I had initially rejected the idea of my chemistry teacher Fritz Wenzinger to participate in it, because I doubted the scientific value of my high school thesis (it was a conceptual work for a network of mountain bike trails). He finally persuaded me to participate. How I finally won the prize I can only guess. The prize message read something like "an internship at a Swiss embassy of my choice." As generous as this may sound, the range of possible embassies turned out to be much more limited than initially thought. I had wanted to go to Russia because I was learning Russian. However, for certain reasons this was not possible. The same was true for the other former republics of the Soviet Union. So I had to resort to my third option: somewhere in Africa. The Swiss Ministry of Foreign Affairs proposed either Kenya or Mozambique. I chose Mozambique for the sole reason that I had never heard of the country before.

Having arrived in Maputo, I made the acquaintance of Thomas and Maya Litscher, the Swiss ambassador at the time and his wife. It was Maya who had set up the lodge mentioned above. When I arrived in Maputo, the lodge called Mbuna Bay was still lacking a proper website. Since I had been working as a web designer in Switzerland, I offered to build one. When it was ready, she urged me to visit the place, which until then I had known only virtually. It was an extremely fascinating trip and I undoubtedly came back with the feeling that I had learned more about life in a few days than in an entire year at home. I later returned to Niassa to work as a volunteer for Mbuna Bay for three months in 2010 and almost a year in 2011. It was during my free time that I started to delve into the history of Nkholongue, the nearby village.

I consider it important to highlight this rather unprofessional beginning of my research, first, to show how the object of my study was initially chosen, or rather "not chosen," and, second to critically point out my initial involvement in Nkholongue.

Map 1: Nkholongue and the larger region including the borders of the modern day district of Lago (Please note that this map only shows a selection of roads, places, and rivers). Map by the author. Small map based on a template by GeoCurrents Customizable Base Map.

Map 2: The lakeshore area around Nkholongue. Map by Dominic Schuppli and the author.

1 Introduction: Ways and Arguments Towards a "Global" Microhistory

1.1 The Starting Point of My Research

As I have tried to highlight in the foreword, the region around Nkholongue seemed to me to be quite untouched by history when I came here for the first time. In line with long-held clichés about rural Africa, it seemed to me as if little had ever changed in this small village with its seemingly traditional appearances. If anything, I thought it was only now, with the advent of international tourism, that life in the village was about to change. But at the same time, I felt a distinct unease about combining what I thought I saw in Nkholongue with my scant knowledge of African history. This unease was certainly what drove me to do my first interviews. And the histories people told me quickly put an end to my initial ahistorical ideas.

They showed that Nkholongue, far from being an isolated place in history, had been a surprisingly global spot from the beginning. The village came into being when the ancestors of the present chief settled here around 1880. They belonged to the Wayao and originally came from a place called Unango in the highlands east of the lake. Their motivation for founding the village was twofold: first, the village served them as a trading point on the eastern shores of the lake for slaves and ivory on the way to the Indian Ocean. Second, the village served its chief, Chingomanje, to expand his status and power base by purchasing and settling slaves for his personal use. These slaves came from the other side of the lake, namely the town of Nkhotakota. It is their descendants who today make up the majority of Nkholongue's population.

My early research also showed that the village, now almost entirely Muslim, had been an early "target" of Anglican missionaries, whose large steamships made regular stops here until the early 1950s. Furthermore, I realized that the village had even ceased to exist twice during the last 60 years, first when its population was resettled by Portuguese troops during the Mozambican War of Independence (1964–1974), and then during the Mozambican Civil War (1977–1992), when repeated attacks by the South African-backed rebels of Renamo (*Resistência Nacional Moçambicana*, Mozambican National Resistance) forced people to abandon their homes.

Hence, what looked so "traditional" to me was actually quite "modern," with most of the houses of the village only having been built in the last 20 years. And, despite the village's seeming remoteness, Nkholongue's history had in reality been connected to global and supra-regional developments ever since. It was this insight that led me to examine the history of Nkholongue from the time of its formation around 1880 until the present day. But while the combination of the seeming remoteness of the village and the simultaneous global embeddedness of its history was thus certainly the initial raison d'être of my research, I later found many other reasons why my initial approach could make a valuable contribution to historiography. It was these reasons that also helped me to steer my project into new directions.

The result of this research process is in many ways a typical microhistorical study that is characterized by the belief that "[p]henomena previously considered to be sufficiently described and understood assume completely new meanings by altering the scale of observation."[1] However, the present study differs from the majority of microhistorical studies in various ways. These include, first, its embrace of social rather than cultural history; second, the ambition to relate local processes to global history; third, the aspiration to think consistently about the generalizability of local findings by placing analyses in historiographical discussions that go beyond regional or national levels; and, last but not least, the number and variety of topics examined. In ten chapters, the book discusses such diverse topics as the slave trade, the spread of Islam, colonization, subsistence production, counter-insurgency, decolonization, civil war, ecotourism, and matriliny and shows in what ways the experience of the small village of Nkholongue can be placed within existing historiography and in what ways this experience urges us to re-evaluate and reassess previous conceptions and narratives about the course of certain processes and events. In this way my study challenges explanations that do not stand up to the "lived reality" of ordinary villagers.

Although the chapters of the book deal with very different topics and can also stand by themselves, they are united by a common interest in the history of rural Africa in what most people would call the *longue durée*.[2] The book as a whole shifts the focus to the agency, perspective, and experiences of the inhabitants of a seemingly insignificant village and highlights how people's room for maneuver changed over time. It aims to underline the historical changeability of social conditions and relations as a result of changes at various levels, spanning a wide spectrum from the local to the global.

---

[1] Giovanni Levi, "On Microhistory," in *New Perspectives on Historical Writing*, ed. Peter Burke (Cambridge: Polity Press, 1991), 98.

[2] My hesitation with the term stems from the fact that Braudel originally meant something quite different than most people do today. According to Braudel's three-level time scheme, this book certainly looks at events and conjunctures rather than the *histoire quasi immobile* ('almost motionless history'). See: Fernand Braudel, *La méditerranée et le monde méditerranéen à l'époque de Philippe II*, 2nd ed., vol. 1, 2 vols. (1949; Paris: Armand Colin, 1966).

The central goal of this book as a whole is to demonstrate that it is not possible to analyze the lives of people in this corner of rural Africa in any meaningful way without emphasizing the frequent and often violent ruptures they were confronted with during their lifetimes. As will still be elaborated in Section 1.4, these dynamics are what I call the Winds of History. The book highlights how the Winds of History repeatedly forced the inhabitants of Nkholongue to readapt their lives to new conditions, and thus seeks to counter long-standing ahistorical clichés about rural Africa that still dominate many Western public perceptions and also continue to be echoed in academic debates.

On a methodological level, this book addresses current discussions about the relationship between micro- and global history and hopes to show how the two scales can be fruitfully combined. Furthermore, this book attempts to demonstrate how the past of a small village which seems to have little history and documentation at first glance can in fact be discovered from various angles based on a solid empirical foundation, by drawing on numerous interviews and documents from more than 20 archives worldwide.

In what follows in this introduction, I will first explain my microhistorical approach in detail and then provide an overview of my methods and sources. This will be followed by a discussion of the cross-chapter contributions that I seek to make to (African) historiography through the Winds of History. The introduction concludes with outlines of the contents of each chapter and the findings on the various topics they address.

1.2 Microhistory: My Approach, Its Antecedents and Particularities

Microhistory's origin is usually linked to the Italian *microstoria* movement and its most prominent practitioners, Giovanni Levi and Carlo Ginzburg. But while French and American versions of microhistory were certainly influenced by *microstoria*, similar historiographical developments have happened simultaneously in different academic environments around the world. So, the German *Alltagsgeschichte* ('history of everyday life') and what was become known as historical anthropology or ethnohistory in different (geographical) contexts have shared many methodological considerations and practices with microhistory, to such an extent that the terms are sometimes used interchangeably.[3]

---

[3] For examples, see: Georg G. Iggers and Q. Edward Wang, *A Global History of Modern Historiog-*

Commonalities have included an interest in the small and ordinary,[4] a drive to challenge the grand political and economic narratives of history, and a desire to bring agency and people into the structure obsessed social history of the time—all characteristics that microhistory and history of everyday life also shared with simultaneously emerging approaches to history around the globe, such as the subaltern studies group, the history from below, and feminist history. This global push to do history against the grain was related to a growing exhaustion of belief in modernization and progress and a growing recognition of the social costs of modernization. History-from-below approaches specifically aimed at making these costs visible.

While the debates of Europeanists on microhistory or history of everyday life were rarely taken up explicitly by Africanists, African historiography has by no means stood apart from these global developments. One has only to think about the early recognition of the need for fieldwork and oral history.[5] Compared to their Europeanist colleagues, historians of Africa had "long been obliged to come to terms with the data and interpretations of anthropologists and sociologists," as Terence Ranger put it in 1976.[6] Correspondingly, there have also been many studies from and about the African continent that could be (and less frequently were) labeled as microhistories even though they have only rarely found their way into the anthologies of microhistories.[7] Furthermore, the issue

---

raphy (London: Routledge, 2008), 275–277; Stefan Jordan, *Theorien und Methoden der Geschichtswissenschaft* (Paderborn: Ferdinand Schöningh, 2009), 152–160.

4 It has been argued that Italian *microstoria* in particular was precisely not interested in the ordinary, but rather in the idiosyncratic. While there was certainly a focus on such figures and phenomena, this was in my view primarily owed to the availability of sources. Their "exceptionality" was still seen as a key to the normal and ordinary, as Edoardo Grendi's notion of the "exceptional normal" suggests. See: Francesca Trivellato, "Is There a Future for Italian Microhistory in the Age of Global History?," *California Italian Studies* 2, no. 1 (2011); Levi, "On Microhistory," 109.

5 On this point, see as well: Klaas van Walraven, "Prologue: Reflections on Historiography and Biography and the Study of Africa's Past," in *The Individual in African History: The Importance of Biography in African Historical Studies*, ed. Klaas van Walraven (Leiden: Brill, 2020), 34.

6 Terence O. Ranger, "Towards a Usable African Past," in *African Studies Since 1945: A Tribute to Basil Davidson*, ed. Christopher Fyfe (London: Longman, 1976), 28. On this point, see as well: Andreas Eckert and Adam Jones, "Historical Writing about Everyday Life," *Journal of African Cultural Studies* 15, no. 1 (2002): 7. One might in this respect also think of the early importance that was given to "life history" approaches in African historiography. On this point, see: Lisa A. Lindsay, "Biography in African History," *History in Africa* 44 (2017): 11–26.

7 Landeg White, *Magomero: Portrait of an African Village* (Cambridge: Cambridge University Press, 1987); E.S. Atieno-Odhiambo, "The Movement of Ideas: A Case Study of Intellectual Responses to Colonialism among the Liganua Peasants," in *History & Social Change in East Africa*, ed. Bethwell A. Ogot (Nairobi: East African Literature Bureau, 1976), 165–85; David William Cohen,

of subalternity played an eminent role in inscribing African agency (back) into history and in countering both colonialism and colonial historiography.

My own approach follows the footsteps of previous microhistorical practice and theory in- and outside the African continent on the premise that a narrowly defined research subject can grasp otherwise hardly discovered meanings and processes. It fully agrees with various history-from-below approaches about the importance of bringing the perspectives, actions and experiences of ordinary, marginalized or subaltern people to the center of history.

However, my approach also stands out from many previous microhistorical studies and history-from-below approaches in different ways. Five areas demand special attention to understand the particularities of my own approach. They are 1) the problematization of the (African) village as a unit of research, 2) the ambition to do global history, 3) the explorative character of my research, 4) the perspective on the category "agency," and 5) the centrality of social history.

The (African) Village as a Problematic Unit of Microhistorical Research

The "village" is probably the category most people will think about when they hear the term "microhistory." In fact, several well-known microhistories have been village histories, such as Emmanuel Le Roy Ladurie's *Montaillou, village occitan de 1294 à 1324* (1975) or Hans Medick's *Weben und Überleben in Laichingen 1650– 1900: Lokalgeschichte als allgemeine Geschichte* (1996). With Landeg White's *Magomero: Portrait of an African Village* (1987) and Tom McCaskie's *Asante Identities: History and Modernity in an African village 1850–1950* (2000), village histories

---

"Doing Social History from Pim's Doorway," in *Reliving the Past: The Worlds of Social History*, ed. Olivier Zunz (Chapel Hill: University of North Carolina Press, 1985), 191–235; David William Cohen and E.S. Atieno-Odhiambo, *Siaya: The Historical Anthropology of an African Landscape* (London: James Currey, 1989); Belinda Bozzoli, *Women of Phokeng: Consciousness, Life Strategy, and Migrancy in South Africa, 1900–1983* (Portsmouth: Heinemann, 2002); Charles van Onselen, *The Seed Is Mine: The Life of Kas Maine, a South African Sharecropper 1895–1985* (New York: David Philip, 1996); Tom C. McCaskie, *Asante Identities: History and Modernity in an African Village 1850–1950* (Edinburgh: Edinburgh University Press, 2000); Kenda Mutongi, *Worries of the Heart: Widows, Family, and Community in Kenya* (Chicago: University of Chicago Press, 2007); James A. Pritchett, *Friends for Life, Friends for Death: Cohorts and Consciousness among the Lunda-Ndembu* (Charlottesville: University of Virginia Press, 2007); Geert Castryck, "'My Slave Sold All of Kigoma': Power Relations, Property Rights and the Historian's Quest for Understanding," in *Sources and Methods for African History and Culture: Essays in Honour of Adam Jones*, ed. Geert Castryck, Silke Strickrodt, and Katja Werthmann (Leipzig: Leipziger Universitätsverlag, 2016), 317–335. For further works, see as well: Nancy R. Hunt, "Whither African History?," *History Workshop Journal* 66, no. 1 (2008): note 2, 263.

also figure prominently among the most frequently cited examples of African microhistories.[8]

The prominence of the "village" as a microhistorical unit seems obvious since the term embodies various concerns of microhistory. It evokes smallness, ordinariness, and, combined with rurality, also marginality. However, the "village" is also a problematic category. This has to do, on the one hand, with its vagueness, and, on the other, with the Eurocentric conception behind it. For, while the village seems to be a category that can be applied universally nowadays, at least part of this universality owes to the role of the "village" in the European expansion project. We cannot ignore this historical function of the concept as an element of (colonial) order.

This is particularly true in the case of the "African village." Villages of and in Africa have long dominated the (European) imagination of rural Africa.[9] We can, thereby, discern two different currents of thought. The first, and certainly dominant one in the public perception, has seen the "village" as the archetypal place of Africa, Africa as a collection of individual villages headed by their chiefs. In this current of thought, the "village" has been identified as the place that represents "traditional" Africa, whether in the positive sense of "authenticity" or in the negative sense of "backwardness." This notion of the village as the archetypal place of Africa can be found in the descriptions of European explorers and missionaries, as well as in the colonial administrative organization.[10] It has long been popularized in Europe, with a striking example being the exhibitions of "African villages" in the "human zoos" of the late nineteenth and early twentieth centuries.[11] It has also been perpetuated by countless ethnological and socio-economic village studies conducted by anthropologists and sociologists.[12] Furthermore, much explanatory and symbolic power has been invested in it in Africa itself in both arts and politics, a prominent example being Chinua Achebe's world-famous novel

---

[8] Emmanuel Le Roy Ladurie, *Montaillou, village occitan de 1294 à 1324* (Paris: Gallimard, 1975); Hans Medick, *Weben und Überleben in Laichingen 1650–1900: Lokalgeschichte als allgemeine Geschichte* (Göttingen: Vandenhoeck & Ruprecht, 1996).
[9] Ellen Hurst provides an example how the African village can also dominate African imaginations of rural Africa: Ellen Hurst, "Local Villages and Global Networks: The Language and Migration Experiences of African Skilled Migrant Academics," *Globalisation, Societies and Education* 15, no. 1 (2017): 50–67.
[10] Achim von Oppen, "Village Studies: Zur Geschichte eines Genres der Sozialforschung im südlichen und östlichen Afrika," *Paideuma* 42 (1996): 17.
[11] For another example, see: Wanjiru Kinyanjui, "Über Filme und Dörfer," in *Filmwelt Afrika: Retrospektive des panafrikanischen Filmfestivals FESPACO in Ouagadougou, Burkina Faso*, ed. Haus der Kulturen der Welt (Berlin, 1993), 17–22.
[12] Biplab Dasgupta, ed., *Village Studies in the Third World* (Delhi: Hindustan, 1978); Oppen, "Village Studies."

Things Fall Apart, in which he narrates the process of colonization in a Nigerian village. A recent example of rural Africa as a collection of villages is the Millennium Villages Project, which aimed at demonstrating that the realization of the Millennium Development Goals can be achieved "village by village."[13]

The second current of thought stands in contrast to the first even though they have co-existed at times. This current perceived the problem to lie precisely in the fact that people in Africa did not live together in villages, or at least not in villages big enough, and that villages in Africa were not sufficiently stable. Colonial administrations tried to concentrate dispersed settlements from the early colonial period onward.[14] Later, numerous villagization schemes of both colonial and post-colonial governments equally tried to move people into villages, promising modernization and facilitating control.[15]

There are thus many reasons for a microhistorical study to treat the unit of the village with skepticism, both because of its symbolism of a "traditional" Africa and because of its historical role as a place of and for development. The two existing microhistories of "African villages" have not reflected their use of this unit. Referring to their villages as "African villages," they merely made use of the perspective that the village is the archetypal place of rural Africa and, thus, also perpetuated the idea that something like an "African village" actually exists. White was very explicit in this respect in his preface by writing the following:

> The majority of people in Malawi, as indeed in much of Africa, continue to live in such villages or to maintain strong rural ties. What I have tried to recover, working so far as I could from the inside, is the experience of living in such a place since the mid-nineteenth century.[16]

For both McCaskie and White, the village was in many ways a mere microhistorical container to narrate history. They used the term without much reflection and, in White's case, quite randomly. In fact, *Magomero* is not the history of the same vil-

---

[13] "Millennium Villages: A New Approach to Fighting Poverty," UN Millennium Project, accessed December 10, 2014, http://www.unmillenniumproject.org/mv/.
[14] For examples, see: Iva Peša, *Roads through Mwinilunga: A History of Social Change in Northwest Zambia* (Leiden: Brill, 2019), 4–5; MNA, S1/1150/28: Note on Concentration of Native Huts and Villages by the Acting Assistant Chief Secretary, 1928. Such attempts were also made around Nkholongue. See Footnote 133 on p. 133.
[15] Nicole Sackley, "The Village as Cold War Site: Experts, Development, and the History of Rural Reconstruction," *Journal of Global History* 6, no. 3 (2011): 481–504; Achim von Oppen, "The Village as Territory: Enclosing Locality in Northwest Zambia, 1950s to 1990s," *The Journal of African History* 47, no. 1 (2006): 57–75. See also Chapter 7 in this book.
[16] White, *Magomero*, xii.

lage over time. Rather, it tells, in two parts, the history of two very different "communities" that happened to live in the same place at different points of time. Neither of them was actually called Magomero. And, if we follow the book, the village of the second part was in reality not one but eight villages, which were called the "Lomwe Village" in the table of contents and the "Lomwe Villages" in the actual contents. White's vague usage of the term had its antecedents in various village studies. Polly Hill, for example, called "her" famous Hausa village of Batagarawa indiscriminately a "village," a "hamlet," a "town," and even a "district capital" within the space of only five pages.[17] Being in fact the seat of a district, Batagarawa hardly corresponds to the common notion of a "village." The development industry practices a similar lighthearted handling of the term. Thus, the "Sauri village" of the Millennium Villages Project is in reality a "village cluster" with about 70,000 inhabitants.[18]

In this book, the term "village" is used despite its misleading symbolism, problematic historical role, and vagueness. I hope that the explicit and reflective use of the term, coupled with the analysis of the significantly changing composition and nature of the settlement of Nkholongue, best serves the goal of challenging its non-specificity and the clichés associated with it. In the end, the term still seems to me to be the best option for describing a group of people who 1) identify themselves as belonging to that group, 2) live in a rural environment and in a certain proximity to one another, and 3) share certain political and/or religious institutions. The term also seems to be able to reflect local terminology, the equivalent in Chinyanja being *mudzi*. Still, while village as defined above seems to be the principal meaning of *mudzi* in Nkholongue in the 21st century, it must be emphasized that the word has been used to cover a different semantic range than the English "village." For, it can also simply mean "home" or be used as a term for what we would call "neighborhood."[19] There is no doubt that local ideas of what a *mudzi* is

---

[17] Polly Hill, *Rural Hausa: A Village and a Setting* (Cambridge: Cambridge University Press, 1972), 8–12.

[18] The Earth Institute (Columbia University), Millennium Promise, and UNDP, "The Millennium Villages Project: 2009 Annual Report," 53, accessed October 27, 2021, https://irp-cdn.multiscreensite.com/6fae6349/files/uploaded/MVP%202009%20Annual%20Report%20-%20EIMPUNDP%20-%20General%20Public%20Version%20-%20FINAL.pdf; Joyce Chen, Kumbukani Chirwa, and Sonia Ehrlich Sachs, "Fortification with Micronutrient Powder to Address Malnutrition in Rural Kenya," *Sight and Life* 29, no. 1 (2015): 129–131.

[19] The use of the word is similarly flexible as in the case observed by Jaap van Velsen's for the lakeside Tonga, where—depending on the context—the word *mudzi* could refer "to a hamlet of one hut or to a large village of one hundred huts, or for that matter, to Johannesburg, London or Chicago." See: Jaap van Velsen, *The Politics of Kinship: A Study in Social Manipulation among the Lakeside Tonga of Malawi* (Manchester: Manchester University Press, 1964), 29.

have changed over time and in interaction with conceptions introduced from outside.

If this book thus employs the term "village" as a signifier for the microhistorical lens used, it does not do so without underlining its changing characteristics and delimitations. It will also reflect in what ways the subject of our study has in fact become two villages over time. Indeed, as already announced in the Foreword, many people would say that Nkholongue nowadays consists of two villages (or *midzi*) even if they still somehow belong together. Or, in the words of one interviewee:

> We, here, do have two *midzi*, the *mudzi* of Malango and the *mudzi* of Nkholongue, but the people of Malango and Nkholongue are one.[20]

This separation goes back to the emigration of the majority of Nkholongue's population in the 1950s to the creek of Malango, a good 30 minutes' walk from the center of Nkholongue. While both parts "continue" to be under the same chief, today they have their own village secretaries, their own schools, and their own mosques (although the mosque of Malango did not have an imam at the time of fieldwork, so its inhabitants were forced to go to Nkholongue for Friday Prayers).[21] As we will see in this book, the question of how strongly Nkholongue and Malango still belong together has also been an issue of (local) political struggles (see Chapter 10).

This book thus hopes to show that history did not just happen in the village, but that history also changed and challenged the village. While I agree with the credos of Levi and Geertz that microhistorians/anthropologists "do not study villages, they study in villages" in principle, I consider it essential to also reflect the (changing) characteristics and delimitations of the village in which one studies, particularly if one studies in an "African village," a category filled with clichés of rural inertia.

---

20 "Ife pano tili ni midzi yawili: mudzi wa malango, mudzi wa nkholongue, koma wanthu amalango ni ankholongue ndi amodzi." PA, I124: interview with *P0376 (♂, 1968)* (Nkholongue, April 26, 2016), min 00:05:47–00:05:58.
21 The practice was however not very widespread during my fieldwork. I can only think of two persons (P1102 and P1193) from Malango who regularly went to Nkholongue for the Friday Prayer. "Continue" is written in quotation marks to highlight that the chiefs were not officially recognized by the post-colonial government between 1975 and 2000.

Micro in a Global World: A Village on the Shores of Global History

The accusation of descriptive isolation was one of the earliest and most pronounced points of criticisms against microhistory and history of everyday life. In Germany, where the exchange was more heated than elsewhere, critics such as Hans-Ulrich Wehler blamed the "small is beautiful" approach for its hostility to theory and its lack of ability to contextualize.[22] Jürgen Kocka spoke of the microhistorical "small-small" ("klein-klein").[23]

Practitioners of microhistory reacted differently to this criticism. Some, in line with the linguistic turn, seemed content with the supposedly self-explanatory narrative value of their studies, sometimes explicitly denying the need to connect their findings to larger contexts or discussions. Some reflected actively on the relationship between micro- and macrohistory such as a group around Jacques Revel, proclaiming their "playing with the scales" (*jeux d'échelles*).[24] Others, such as Giovanni Levi, stressed in a similar vein that there was no contradiction between microhistory and macro-questions, since the "micro" was not the object but the scale of research.[25] Consequently, they underscored the potential of microhistorical research "to draw far wider generalizations although the initial observations were made within relatively narrow dimensions[.]"[26]

The extent to which the bulk of microhistorical studies have indeed aspired to this goal of generalization or achieved it is debatable. Arguably, the initial concern of Italian *microstoria* for theoretical reflection and broader analysis was lost when

---

[22] Hans-Ulrich Wehler, "Aus der Geschichte lernen?," in *Aus der Geschichte lernen? Essays*, by Hans-Ulrich Wehler (München: Beck, 1988), 11–18; Hans-Ulrich Wehler, "Alltagsgeschichte: Königsweg zu neuen Ufern oder Irrgarten der Illusion?," in *Aus der Geschichte lernen? Essays*, by Hans-Ulrich Wehler (München: Beck, 1988), 130–151.
[23] Jürgen Kocka, "Sozialgeschichte zwischen Strukturgeschichte und Erfahrungsgeschichte," in *Sozialgeschichte in Deutschland: Entwicklungen und Perspektiven im internationalen Zusammenhang. Band 1: Die Sozialgeschichte innerhalb der Geschichtswissenschaft*, ed. Wolfgang Schieder and Volker Sellin (Göttingen: Vandenhoeck & Ruprecht, 1986), 81; Jürgen Kocka, "Perspektiven für die Sozialgeschichte der neunziger Jahre," in *Sozialgeschichte, Alltagsgeschichte, Mikro-Historie*, ed. Winfried Schulze (Göttingen: Vandenhoeck & Ruprecht, 1994), 34.
[24] Jacques Revel, ed., *Jeux d'échelles: la micro-analyse à l'expérience* (Paris: Gallimard, 1996). For other reflections about this relationship, see the contributions in: Jürgen Schlumbohm, ed., *Mikrogeschichte – Makrogeschichte: Komplementär oder inkommensurabel?* (Göttingen: Wallstein, 1998).
[25] Levi, "On Microhistory," 96.
[26] Levi, 98. Medick and Trivellato argued similarly. However, they attributed such reflective qualities more to (Italian) microhistory than to the history of everyday life. See: Hans Medick, "Mikro-Historie," in *Sozialgeschichte, Alltagsgeschichte, Mikro-Historie*, ed. Winfried Schulze (Göttingen: Vandenhoeck & Ruprecht, 1994), 40–44; Trivellato, "Is There a Future for Italian Microhistory in the Age of Global History?"

microhistory traveled abroad.[27] I think that Jan de Vries is right in associating the dominant form of microhistory with empathetic storytelling and postmodernism.[28] Explicit analysis was neglected in such approaches in an effort to let their subjects speak for themselves. Not scholarly reflection but people's voices and experiences should explain historical developments. African examples of microhistories in my eyes resonate with this form of microhistory, tending to do so consciously without much analytical contextualization and reflection. This is also true of the most prominent "African microhistory," Landeg White's oft-cited *Magomero*, whose story is "portrayed" in a novelistic style.[29] While Tom McCaskie undoubtedly pursued a different agenda in his study, he too emphasized his attempt "to portray African lives in detail, over an extended historical period, on their own terms, and in their own words"[30] and saw no reason or point in "summing up" the lives of "his" villagers.[31] Moreover, his reflections remained mostly within the confinements of historiography on the Asante.

In recent years, the old micro-macro debate has been resurrected under a new label. Using the term "global microhistory," various scholars have considered how microhistorical approaches can be linked to the global turn in historiography.[32] In

---

[27] Jan de Vries, "Changing the Narrative: The New History That Was and Is to Come," *The Journal of Interdisciplinary History* 48, no. 3 (2017): 320. See also Sewell's comments on the lack of studies that have actually realized the theoretical ambition of bringing together the analysis of micro- and macroprocesses: William Hamilton Sewell, *Logics of History: Social Theory and Social Transformation* (Chicago: University of Chicago Press, 2005), 75–76.

[28] Jan de Vries, "Playing with Scales: The Global and the Micro, the Macro and the Nano," *Past & Present* 242, Supplement 14 (2019): 25.

[29] White, *Magomero*. The same goes for Charles van Onselen's famous biography of Kas Maine. See: Onselen, *The Seed Is Mine*.

[30] McCaskie, *Asante Identities*, 22.

[31] McCaskie, 238.

[32] Hans Medick, "Turning Global? Microhistory in Extension," *Historische Anthropologie* 24, no. 2 (2016): 241–52; Giovanni Levi, "Globale Mikrogeschichte als 'Renaissance'? Ein Kommentar zu Hans Medick," *Historische Anthropologie* 25, no. 1 (2017); Trivellato, "Is There a Future for Italian Microhistory in the Age of Global History?"; Angelika Epple, "Globale Mikrogeschichte: Auf dem Weg zu einer Geschichte der Relationen," in *Im Kleinen das Grosse suchen: Mikrogeschichte in Theorie und Praxis*, ed. Ewald Hiebl and Ernst Langthaler (Innsbruck: StudienVerlag, 2012), 37–47; Angelika Epple, "Lokalität und die Dimensionen des Globalen: Eine Frage der Relationen," *Historische Anthropologie* 21, no. 1 (2013): 4–25; Tonio Andrade, "A Chinese Farmer, Two African Boys, and a Warlord: Toward a Global Microhistory," *Journal of World History* 21, no. 4 (2011): 573–591; Melvin E. Page, "Up from the Farm: A Global Microhistory of Rural Americans and Africans in the First World War," *Journal of Global History* 16, no. 1 (2021): 101–21; Harald Fischer-Tiné, "Marrying Global History with South Asian History: Potential and Limits of Global Microhistory in a Regional Inflection," *Comparativ: Zeitschrift für Globalgeschichte und vergleichende Gesellschaftsforschung* 29, no. 2 (2019): 52–77.

2019, *Past & Present* dedicated a special issue to the topic.[33] The renewed interest in microhistory seems to mirror the original microhistorical motivation, with the new target being global rather than social history. Thus, Tonio Andrade, who coined the term, promoted his approach with the need to "populate" the "powerful models of global historical structures and processes" with "real people."[34] John-Paul Ghobrial criticized global history's downgrading of place-based knowledge and expertise and the ineffectiveness of explaining change in specific contexts and "small spaces."[35]

While various historians have underlined the potentials of an encounter between micro- and global history, the ways in which this combination can or should be reached have differed. Some have, in line with Levi's conceptualization of microhistory, pointed to its inherent potential to reflect on the micro-scale about general (global) questions. But others such as Francesca Trivellato and Angelika Epple have stressed that, for fruitful encounters, microhistorical approaches would need to become less narrativistic and more reflective in style.[36]

This book shares the concerns of Trivellato and Epple, and aims to overcome microhistorical descriptive isolation. It tries to link microhistory to global history in two ways, first by looking at connections and disconnections and second by systematically reflecting on comparability and generalizability.[37] Thus, it hopes to make a significant contribution to the debate and practice of "global microhistory."

Connections, flows and entanglements have become central objects of global-historical research. "Global" thereby often does not mean global in the sense that the adjective refers to the entire planet, but rather constitutes what Stephan Scheuzger has characterized as "a distant horizon denoting the ultimate container of processes and structures that cross spatial boundaries of all kinds."[38] Frederick Cooper has called this the "soft" version of global history, an explicit critique of the fact that this endeavor could just as accurately be defined as "interconnected his-

---

[33] *Past & Present*, Volume 242, Issue Supplement 14, November 2019, Global History and Microhistory.
[34] Andrade, "Toward a Global Microhistory," 574.
[35] John-Paul A. Ghobrial, "Introduction: Seeing the World like a Microhistorian," *Past & Present* 242, Supplement 14 (2019): 6–8.
[36] Trivellato, "Is There a Future for Italian Microhistory in the Age of Global History?"; Epple, "Globale Mikrogeschichte."
[37] Thus, I follow Chris Baily's global-historical agenda of "increasing historians' alertness to global or international connections and comparisons […]" See: Christopher A. Bayly, *The Birth of the Modern World, 1780–1914: Global Connections and Comparisons* (Malden: Blackwell, 2004), 469.
[38] Stephan Scheuzger, "Global History as Polycentric History," *Comparativ: Zeitschrift für Globalgeschichte und vergleichende Gesellschaftsforschung* 29, no. 2 (2019): 142.

tory" or *histoire croisée*.³⁹ Another shortcoming of this (arguably) dominant form of global history is its fetish of mobility. As different scholars have argued, the previous central focus on mobile actors, on long-distance movements, and on central hubs of connections has come at the expense of neglecting the analysis of the significance and role that connections and movements played in local events and processes.⁴⁰

This is where my book comes in. Beginning with Nkholongue's formation in the slave trade era, it will focus on how connections and movements of different scales interacted with the local throughout this book. It analyzes how processes and events at different political, economic and societal levels were entangled with local developments. The microhistorical focus on (global) connections is also aimed at challenging tempting notions that associate the global with change and dynamism and the local with constancy and stability.⁴¹ As already pointed to above, the local was also no fixed container, rather the village itself changed considerably over time. This focus will also reveal that Nkholongue's "global history" was not a one-way-street of growing connections, but one that also involved processes and phases of disconnections (on this point, see also my comments under 1.4).

The second way this study attempts to combine microhistory with the global is by facilitating (global) comparability. While a microhistorical study itself cannot by definition offer what Cooper has called "hard" versions of global history,⁴² it can analyze, reflect and present findings from the local level so that they can be easily linked to discussions from places around the world. My book attempts to offer what Levi has called a microhistorical study that addresses "general questions."⁴³ All chapters of this book discuss topics and processes that have operated on levels far beyond the boundaries of the village. Many of them were undoubtedly "global phenomena" such as, for example, the village's strategic resettlement during the

---

39 Frederick Cooper, "How Global Do We Want Our Intellectual History to Be?," in *Global Intellectual History*, ed. Samuel Moyn and Andrew Sartori (New York: Columbia University Press, 2013), 283–284. On this point, see as well: Frederick Cooper, "What Is the Concept of Globalization Good for? An African Historian's Perspective," *African Affairs* 100, no. 399 (2001): 189–213; Debora Gerstenberger and Joël Glasman, "Globalgeschichte mit Maß: Was Globalhistoriker von der Akteur-Netzwerk-Theorie lernen können," in *Techniken der Globalisierung*, ed. Debora Gerstenberger and Joël Glasman (Bielefeld: transcript Verlag, 2016), 11–40.
40 Scheuzger, "Global History as Polycentric History," 129; Ghobrial, "Seeing the World like a Microhistorian," 6–8; Fischer-Tiné, "Marrying Global History with South Asian History."
41 The danger of this association has been highlighted by: Epple, "Lokalität und die Dimensionen des Globalen," 7–8, 16.
42 Cooper, "How Global Do We Want Our Intellectual History to Be?"
43 Levi, "Globale Mikrogeschichte als 'Renaissance'?," 117.

Mozambican War of Independence. The potential for comprehensive discussions of different topics at the global level is certainly limited, both quantitatively and qualitatively. It is already difficult to strive for a "global coverage" of the state of research with respect to one topic. Furthermore, some issues are better contextualized on more circumscribed levels (supra-regional, national, trans-national, imperial or continental). Still, it is at least the aspiration of this study to reflect its findings as broadly as useful and possible on the one hand, and to present them in such a way that they are easily connectable to results from elsewhere on the other.

Looking at 1) how (global) entanglements materialized in a local setting, and 2) how findings gathered from research in Nkholongue compare to results from other places in other (world) regions, this book also hopes to take up the central concern of global history to decenter or, rather, recenter our perspectives.[44] Nkholongue has undoubtedly been a marginal place of modern history. But, this book hopes to show that Nkholongue was in many ways a village on the shores of global history, seemingly marginal from a geographical perspective, but in reality not such a completely unimportant node for the understanding of our complicated and connected past.

In this regard, we also have to highlight Nkholongue's geographical location on the shores of a lake. This undoubtedly resonates with global history's preference for coastal settlements. In fact, in this regard my study can be seen to stand in the tradition of other works, including Maria Candido's history of Benguela, Robin Law's book on Ouidah, and Martin Dusinberre's research on the Japanese town of Kaminoseki.[45] Being a port on the shores of a lake, Nkholongue has also been at times a hub, even if a peripheral one compared to these sea towns.[46] Furthermore, as will be pointed out in this book, Nkholongue's location on the lake might have contributed considerably to its stability as a spatial settlement.

---

[44] Scheuzger claims that the aspiration to systematically decenter historiographical perspectives has so far largely remained a theoretical desideratum. See: Scheuzger, "Global History as Polycentric History," 126–127.

[45] Mariana P. Candido, *An African Slaving Port and the Atlantic World: Benguela and Its Hinterland* (Cambridge: Cambridge University Press, 2013); Martin Dusinberre, *Hard Times in the Hometown: A History of Community Survival in Modern Japan* (Honolulu: University of Hawai'i Press, 2012); Robin Law, *Ouidah: The Social History of a West African Slaving "Port" 1727–1892* (Athens: Ohio University Press, 2004).

[46] Its setting is in this regard more comparable to Geert Castryck's ongoing study of Kigoma-Ujiji: Castryck, "'My Slave Sold All of Kigoma.'"

The Wager of Microhistory: History as Exploration

Stephan Scheuzger has criticized the term "global microhistory" for a certain redundancy, since in his eyes a substantive global-historical approach has to consider an appropriate sample of cases covering developments in a variety of contexts, and necessarily includes empirically grounded research in form of micro-level scrutiny.[47] Scheuzger rightly points out that the microhistorical claim to microscopic accuracy is in many ways not so different from the empirical rigor that should always accompany historical research.

Still, this view ignores a central characteristic that can (and in my eyes should) differentiate a microhistorical approach from a standard case study. The case study seeks to examine a more or less narrowly defined phenomena for a particular case. The case is chosen because it seems especially suitable to answer certain specified questions or to test certain generalizations. Microhistory constitutes a more open, more explorative research process. It explores the history of a micro-unit as broadly as possible with the goal of discovering relevant questions and topics.[48] This is what some microhistorians have described as the experimental character of microhistory or, in Revel's words, as "the wager of micro-social analysis."[49] Certainly, not all microhistorians have followed such an open and explorative research process. Many may have had narrower goals in their mind when they started their research.[50] Furthermore, critics have rightly objected that questions and interpretations can never be generated from the sources alone. They are always also (pre-)determined and limited by a researcher's world of ideas and thoughts. Sources can only give answers to questions.[51]

Nevertheless, the explorative character is a distinctive feature of my microhistorical approach. My research in Nkholongue did not begin with a clearly defined

---

47 Scheuzger, "Global History as Polycentric History," 138.
48 For this difference, see as well: Richard D. Brown, "Microhistory and the Post-Modern Challenge," *Journal of the Early Republic* 23, no. 1 (2003): 18; Dusinberre, *Hard Times in the Hometown*, 14.
49 Levi, "On Microhistory," 98; Ruth W. Sandwell, "History as Experiment: Microhistory and Environmental History," in *Method and Meaning in Canadian Environmental History*, ed. Alan MacEachern and William J. Turkel (Toronto: Nelson, 2009), 124–138; Jacques Revel, "Micro-analysis et construction du social," in *Jeux d'échelles: la micro-analyse à l'expérience*, ed. Jacques Revel (Paris: Gallimard, 1996), 30.
50 This can be exemplified by Oppen's study on villagization in Zambia, which specifically focused on processes of territorialization, but which he called a "micro-history." See: Oppen, "The Village as Territory," 61.
51 On this point, see especially: Wehler, "Aus der Geschichte lernen?," 16–17; Wehler, "Alltagsgeschichte," 141–142.

research topic. Rather, a large part of the research process revolved more around grounded theory than a closed system of questions. The design of my research was to define meaningful themes and issues during rather than before the research. I have made use of the advantage that the reduction of scale allows one to adapt research questions more flexibly to new findings. Within the microhistorical realm of the village of Nkholongue, I initially tried to put out feelers as far as possible. It was only in the course of my research that the topics that form the contents of the chapters of this book took shape.

The explorative character of my research is further underlined by the fact that my work did not dispose of an unusually rich and dense fund of written sources as many prominent other microhistorical works did.[52] Rather, in this respect it followed in the footsteps of Charles van Onselen's *The Seed is Mine* (1996) and his Europeanist counterpart, Alain Corbin's *Sur les traces d'un inconnu* (1998), by reconstructing the history of an unknown and seemingly undocumented village.[53] In terms of sources, Nkholongue could at first glance have been any village of the region. As will be discussed in detail below, it was only the combination of numerous interviews, three village surveys, and extensive research in more than 20 archives in six different countries that enabled me to compile the sources for this book like pieces of a jigsaw puzzle.

While the lack of an exceptional rich corpus of sources limits the potential for detailed historical reconstruction in many ways, it also comes with some methodological advantages, as usually the "stories which historians can tell in details are exceptional."[54] It is thus the exceptional rather than the exemplary that tends to produce more evidence. It is no coincidence that idiosyncratic figures have appeared prominently in microhistories. Ginzburg, Le Roy Ladurie and Zemon Davies could tell their stories in such a detailed manner because their subjects had stood out in history. This exceptionality complicates the generalization of their findings. A study of an "unknown" person or village offers a better prerequisite

---

52 This applies for example to Emmanuel Le Roy Ladurie's *Montaillou* (1975), Carlo Ginzburg's *The Cheese and the Worms* (1976), Tom McCaskie's *Asante Identities* and also Natalie Zemon Davies' *The Return of Martin Guerre*. See: Le Roy Ladurie, *Montaillou*; Carlo Ginzburg, *The Cheese and the Worms: The Cosmos of a Sixteenth Century Miller*, trans. John Tedeschi and Anne Tedeschi (Baltimore: Johns Hopkins University Press, 1980); McCaskie, *Asante Identities*; Natalie Zemon Davis, *The Return of Martin Guerre* (Cambridge: Harvard University Press, 1983).
53 Onselen, *The Seed Is Mine*; Alain Corbin, *Le monde retrouvé de Louis-François Pinagot: sur les traces d'un inconnu, 1798–1876* (Paris: Flammarion, 1998).
54 Robert Ross, "Transcending the Limits of Microhistory," *The Journal of African History* 42 (2001): 126.

to finding and thinking about both ordinariness and representativeness. This is even more so when a study can draw on oral history.

The explorative character of my work is also reflected in the state of historical research on the region where Nkholongue is located. While microhistorical research often begins where the state of research seems to be saturated,[55] my own research certainly did not begin in a historiographical land of plenty. Rather, Niassa Province has long been neglected by Mozambican historiography.[56] Very little historical in-depth research has been accomplished about the province. Gerhard Liesegang's regional study on Niassa remains unpublished and largely inaccessible.[57] The works of Richard Stuart and Charles Good are more about Anglican missionaries than the people who lived in the region.[58] The anthropologist Arianna Huhn has conducted considerable historical research along the lakeshore for a museum project (more on that below), but the historical dimension does not figure prominently in her publications on cultural and social aspects of nutrition in Metangula.[59] Recent exceptions of historical works on Niassa include two publications on the Mozambican War of Independence, namely Sayaka Funada-Classen's study

---

[55] Thus, Tom McCaskie's book undoubtedly addresses a region that has been much studied. On this point, see: Richard Reid, "Past and Presentism: The 'Precolonial' and the Foreshortening of African History," *The Journal of African History* 52, no. 2 (2011): 145.

[56] Just recently, Malyn Newitt, one of the most prominent experts of Mozambican history, complained about the lack of research on northern Mozambique. I was repeatedly approached at conferences and elsewhere by colleagues who showed their delight with the fact that, finally, somebody was working on Niassa. For Newitt's complaint, see: LUSA, "British Historian Malyn Newitt Calls for More Studies on Northern Mozambique," Club of Mozambique, June 21, 2018, accessed June 10, 2019, https://clubofmozambique.com/news/british-historian-malyn-newitt-calls-for-more-studies-on-northern-mozambique/.

[57] One draft chapter is available on Liesegang's Academia page: Gerhard Liesegang, "A história do Niassa, ca. 1600–1920. Cap. VI: A estrutura politica, a estratificação social e o lugar dos chefes na estrutura económica e religiosa antes da conquista colonial," 2014, accessed January 11, 2018, https://www.academia.edu/8133173/Hist%C3%B3ria_do_Niassa_precolonial_Ch._VI_Estrutura_Politica.

[58] Richard Stuart, "Os Nyanja, o U.M.C.A. e a Companhia do Niassa, 1880–1930," *Revista Internacional de Estudos Africanos* 3 (1985): 9–44; Richard Stuart, "Christianity and the Chewa: The Anglican Case 1885–1950" (PhD thesis, University of London, 1974); Charles Good, *The Steamer Parish: The Rise and Fall of Missionary Medicine on an African Frontier* (Chicago: University of Chicago Press, 2004).

[59] Arianna Huhn, *Nourishing Life: Foodways and Humanity in an African Town* (New York: Berghahn Books, 2020); Arianna Huhn, "The Tongue Only Works Without Worries: Sentiment and Sustenance in a Mozambican Town," *Food and Foodways* 21, no. 3 (2013): 186–210; Arianna Huhn, "Enacting Compassion: Hot/Cold, Illness and Taboos in Northern Mozambique," *Journal of Southern African Studies* 43, no. 2 (2017): 299–313.

on the district of Maúa and Jonna Katto's work on Frelimo's female combatants, and Benedito Machava's work on Niassa's reeducation camps.[60]

It is hoped that the explorative research process in a seemingly undocumented village located in an under-researched region helped to limit my expectations of what I would or should find in Nkholongue, thus allowing voices from the village to inform the direction of the analysis in the best possible way, even though questions and interpretations can certainly never be extracted from the sources (or the past) alone.

The Wide Spectrum of Agency: History from below beyond Romanticization

The ambition of bringing people and their agency into history has been a central tenet of microhistory and related research practices. Microhistorians have rightly argued that history is not made by great men or structures alone. As Lev Tolstoi already mockingly noted in *War and Peace*, Napoleon's cold had little impact on the outcome of the Battle of Borodino.

The way agency has been handled by scholars has, however, not always done the cause for complexity a favor. Or, as Lynn Thomas has argued, it has "made African history far less interesting and far more predictable [...] than it should be."[61] In relation to the African continent, agency has often been applied in two different problematic, and sometimes oddly combined, ways. The first glorifies resistance, the second underpins—sometimes unconsciously—a neo-liberal agenda, highlighting for example the innovative potential of African entrepreneurship. What both have in common is that they tend to exaggerate the room for people's maneuver and to underestimate structural constraints and that they endow agency with decidedly positive connotations. Agency often appears in tandem with creativity or resilience.[62] In resistance studies, the good agency is usually contrasted with the

---

60 Sayaka Funada-Classen, *The Origins of War in Mozambique: A History of Unity and Division*, trans. Masako Osada (Somerset West: African Minds, 2013); Jonna Katto, *Women's Lived Landscapes of War and Liberation in Mozambique: Bodily Memory and the Gendered Aesthetics of Belonging* (London: Routledge, 2019); Benedito Machava, "The Morality of Revolution: Urban Cleanup Campaigns, Reeducation Camps, and Citizenship in Socialist Mozambique (1974–1988)" (PhD thesis, University of Michigan, 2018).
61 Lynn M. Thomas, "Historicising Agency," *Gender & History* 28, no. 2 (2016): 329.
62 The editors of *Strength beyond Structure* use the word stem "creativ-" ten times in their introduction: Mirjam de Bruijn, Rijk van Dijk, and Jan-Bart Gewald, eds., *Strength beyond Structure: Social and Historical Trajectories of Agency in Africa* (Leiden: Brill, 2007). For other examples, see: Allen Isaacman, *Cotton Is the Mother of Poverty: Peasants, Work, and Rural Struggle in Colonial*

bad structure. Sherry Ortner has described this opposition with "a heroic individual—The Agent—up against a Borg-like entity called 'Structure.'"[63] Some scholars tend to credit agency for decisions they like and to blame structural pressures for decisions they disapprove of.

The generally positive notion of agency is problematic for various reasons. Resistance, for example, rarely takes an idealistic form, rather it is "often messy and contradictory."[64] The romanticization of resistance has also often resulted in a (cultural) essentialization of "small people." Their internal differentiation and conflicts tend to be ignored, their perspectives and goals to be unified.[65] The popularity of resistance has further led to an over-representation of resisters in historiography. The liberation fighters are certainly no longer those who are shut out of history. This applies rather to the bulk of people who adapted to their situation at various points in history. It is often ignored that accommodation also involved decisions and intentions, also entailed agency.

The "romance of resistance"[66] (Lila Abu-Lughod) has been repeatedly criticized by various scholars.[67] Moreover, historians have undoubtedly also begun to analyze the role of African agency in making structures, such as for example in the making of the colonial state.[68] Still, it seems to me that, in regard to the African continent, the potential to use agency as a tool to lay open the various responses of different people to the same or similar chances and constraints has not been

---

Mozambique, 1938–1961 (Portsmouth: Heinemann, 1996), 240; Peša, *Roads through Mwinilunga*, 116, 166, 180.

63 Sherry B. Ortner, *Anthropology and Social Theory: Culture, Power, and the Acting Subject* (Durham: Duke University Press, 2006), 130. See as well Bernstein who, in relation to farming, speaks of the "morally charged dualism of peasant virtue and state viciousness": Henry Bernstein, "Taking the Part of Peasants?," in *The Food Question: Profits versus People?*, ed. Henry Bernstein et al. (London: Routledge, 1990), 77.

64 Angela VandenBroek, "Agency and Practice Theory," in *21st Century Anthropology: A Reference Handbook*, ed. H. James Birx (Thousand Oaks: SAGE, 2010), 481.

65 Sherry B. Ortner, "Resistance and the Problem of Ethnographic Refusal," *Comparative Studies in Society and History* 37, no. 1 (1995): 176–177. For an orthodox Marxist critique on that point, see: Tom Brass, "Who These Days Is Not a Subaltern? The Populist Drift of Global Labor History," *Science & Society* 81, no. 1 (2017): 10–34.

66 Lila Abu-Lughod, "The Romance of Resistance: Tracing Transformations of Power through Bedouin Women," *American Ethnologist* 17, no. 1 (1990): 41–55.

67 For another example, see: Eric Allina, "Resistance and the Social History of Africa," *Journal of Social History* 37, no. 1 (2003): 187–198.

68 This applies for example to the analysis of the role of African intermediaries. See: Benjamin N. Lawrance, Emily Lynn Osborn, and Richard L. Roberts, eds., *Intermediaries, Interpreters, and Clerks: African Employees in the Making of Colonial Africa* (Madison: University of Wisconsin Press, 2006).

fully appreciated. A microhistorical approach even allows for quantification of the importance of people's different (re)actions even if only within the limits of a tiny unit.

This is precisely the way this book wants to employ "agency." Thereby, my approach has been guided by three basic considerations. First, it is crucial to not overemphasize people's room for maneuver. Precisely in a context such as that of Nkholongue, agency has often been limited, options few and choices difficult. It has been what John Lonsdale called "agency in tight corners."[69] Inequality permeates all aspects of social, economic and cultural life on our planet, and it would be naive to disregard the implications of this constellation.

Second, this study tries to take the perspective of its subjects seriously. This implies, in my view, the need to consider that people do not usually "live their lives on high with the analytical overview and scholarly hindsight of the historian or the anthropologist," as James Pritchett has put it.[70] Their basis for decision making often differs markedly from what a scholar can know today about processes and outcomes. Furthermore, decisions often have to be made quickly. Even in retrospect, people do not always see their circumstances in the same way as these circumstances are assessed by professional scientists. Their judgment of certain historical processes or events does not always correspond to the ideas that professional scientists have about these processes. Taking people seriously also means not pressing them into one's own political ideology and convictions. The "oppressed," the "poor," or the "voiceless" are not always as progressive as is often claimed or assumed.[71] The right question, in my eyes, is not whether the subaltern can speak (Spivak), but rather whether the theorist can listen (Cooper).[72] Klaas van Walraven has convincingly pointed out that one advantage of microhistory is that it facilitates the capacity to "dissociate subjects (specific events, things or persons) from the ideological packages of structural metanarratives and gain insight into the complex relation between human being and their environment."[73]

---

[69] John Lonsdale, "Agency in Tight Corners: Narrative and Initiative in African History," *Journal of African Cultural Studies* 13, no. 1 (2000): 5–16.
[70] Pritchett, *Friends for Life, Friends for Death*, 5.
[71] Nor are they usually a homogeneous group. For a Marxist critique of such idealizations, see: Tom Brass, *Marxism Missing, Missing Marxism: From Marxism to Identity Politics and Beyond* (Leiden: Brill, 2021).
[72] Gayatri Chakravorty Spivak, "Can the Subaltern Speak?," in *Marxism and the Interpretation of Culture*, ed. Cary Nelson and Lawrence Grossberg (Urbana: University of Illinois Press, 1988), 271–312; Frederick Cooper, "Conflict and Connection: Rethinking Colonial African History," *The American Historical Review* 99, no. 5 (1994): 1528.
[73] Walraven, "Prologue: Reflections on Historiography and Biography and the Study of Africa's Past," 33.

In my view, our task as scholars is to understand people's perspective and to analyze why these people came to the conclusion they did even if we do not agree with their position and decisions.[74] Taking people's perspectives and considerations seriously will also help us reveal the complex relationship between intentions and outcomes.

Last but not least, structures, constraints, hegemonies and circumstances are not realities outside history. They are also changing, often as a result of (collective) human action, even if the part played by individuals is usually difficult to reveal empirically. It is an advantage of the diachronic approach of this book to expose these changes and their causalities most clearly. Individuals might display especially great amounts of agency, when they oppose structures and when they rebel against hegemonies. But considering the changing nature of circumstances—the Winds of History—, it is imperative to reflect that the great actors of yesterday can easily become the pale conformists of today and vice versa. As we will see for example in Chapter 7, the local perspective on the prospects of the outcomes of War of Independence changed considerably within a short time period. Frelimo (*Frente de Libertação de Moçambique*, Mozambique Liberation Front) undoubtedly dominated the scene at the beginning of the war. Those who joined Frelimo in 1965 did not show special signs of agency. This was the mainstream choice of the time. The local situation was, however, completely different two or three years later after Frelimo had lost the momentum of the war to the Portuguese forces. Now, it needed either coercion or considerable political conviction for someone to still join Frelimo.

In line with these considerations, this book hopes to show how inhabitants from Nkholongue used their agency differently at various points in history. It will also try to lay open the constraints they encountered and how these constraints changed over time. It will try to demonstrate how different people came to the decisions they made and how they judged historical processes and why they did so.

Back to Social History

The growth and development of microhistory has been strongly linked with the cultural turn in historiography. This also applies to other (related) fields that have been mentioned in this introduction, such as for example historical anthro-

---

74 For similar arguments, see: Mutongi, *Worries of the Heart*, 197–198; William Cunningham Bissell, "Engaging Colonial Nostalgia," *Cultural Anthropology* 20, no. 2 (2005): 215–248.

pology or also subaltern studies, even though the association with the cultural turn might not always reflect the initial concerns and contents of these historiographical practices adequately.[75] My previous remarks, especially the importance given to (global) contextualization and comparability and the way I handle "agency," might have already pointed to the fact that I follow this turn only partly. In many ways, my approach can be considered a move back to social history, much in line with the current revival in social and economic questions in historical research[76] and the calls for a revival of social theory.[77]

Undoubtedly, various scholars have used the terms "social" and "cultural" in this context rather vaguely. There has also been what Patrick Joyce has called an "indiscriminate merging of culture and the social."[78] Still, I consider it important to demarcate my approach from certain directions taken under the banner of cultural history, especially the more linguistic ones among them. The style of my book is more one of empirical rigor than narrative storytelling. This book is guided by the expectation of the existence of an extra-narrative reality, without hopefully falling prey to a naive objectivism.[79] This book is more concerned with social relations and dynamics than with meanings and symbols. It is more about actions and processes than about identities, beliefs, values, or norms. The analysis of rituals, festivals, carnivals, cultural expressions and representations, symbolic acts and discursive strategies do not figure prominently in this study. Rather, my central interest lies in socio-economic questions, with social conflicts, social cohesion, social forces and social stratification.

This does not mean that my book ignores the perspectives, experiences, lifeworlds and beliefs of Nkholongue's inhabitants. On the contrary, my central interest in socio-economic questions is precisely guided by my observation that they have been central to the daily preoccupations of my interviewees. Cultural values and norms certainly directed people in their decisions, but just as often people reworked the meaning attached to these things because of (new) economic or political facts they were confronted with.

---

75 Sumit Sarkar has for example argued that subaltern studies began with a distinctive social-historical stance, and only later internalized the cultural turn: Sumit Sarkar, "The Decline of the Subaltern in Subaltern Studies," in *Writing Social History* (Delhi, 1997), 84.
76 For this revival, see: Frederick Cooper, "From Enslavement to Precarity? The Labour Question in African History," in *The Political Economy of Everyday Life in Africa*, ed. Wale Adebanwi, (Woodbridge: James Currey, 2017), 140.
77 Vivek Chibber, *The Class Matrix: Social Theory after the Cultural Turn* (Cambridge: Harvard University Press, 2022).
78 Patrick Joyce, "What Is the Social in Social History?," *Past & Present* 206, no. 1 (2010): 220.
79 In this regard, I am inspired by Sewell's advocacy to name an "'extratextual' social": Sewell, *Logics of History*, 51.

William H. Sewell Jr. noted in his *Logics of History* that the "preference of cultural historians for symbolically rich artifacts—usually texts—has also tended over time to displace our gaze from the poor and powerless [...] to those more favored categories who were likely to commit their thoughts to paper and whose papers were more likely to be conserved."[80] With its embrace of social history, this book also intends to distance itself from this tendency. Like Sewell, I believe that structural thinking does not necessarily lead to economic determinism but rather is fully compatible with an emphasis on culture, contingency and agency.[81] In this book, I hope to demonstrate that the history of the world's economic realities and structures are in fact crucial to understand the lives of the inhabitants of a small village on the eastern shores of Lake Malawi. In short, my microhistory strives to be a social history with people in it.

1.3 On the Traces of an "Unknown" Matrilineal Village: Methods and Sources

As I mentioned above, Nkholongue was not chosen as a research site and object because a particularly dense corpus of sources was available about it. Rather, I started my work on the traces of an "unknown" village. By combining intensive oral history interviewing with quantitative village surveys and extensive research in numerous archives, I was however able to turn an apparent lack of sources into a comparatively rich base, offering material for analysis for almost all periods of Nkholongue's history. In addition, I benefited greatly from my repeated and prolonged stays in Nkholongue (almost two years in total), during which I gathered countless impressions and insights. During my stays in Nkholongue, I never lived in a proper "mud hut" like an "innocent anthropologist"[82] but always resided on the premises of the Mbuna Bay lodge, through which I had originally come to Nkholongue. Still, I was in constant exchange with people from the village, strolled through it almost daily, and participated in a great variety of different village events and also, at times, joined people in their daily activities. My observations from these experiences have certainly helped me to open my eyes to the vantage points of Nkholongue's inhabitants and also helped me better understand the way of life in Nkholongue.

---

80 Sewell, 52.
81 Sewell, 80.
82 Nigel Barley, *Adventures in a Mud Hut: An Innocent Anthropologist Abroad* (New York: Vanguard Press, 1984).

As regards my "hard" sources, I make use of a very broad and diverse collection. They include: 1) a corpus of more than 160 interviews conducted for this study, 2) three village surveys, 3) documentary material from more than 20 archives from six different countries, and 4) various kinds of published sources. In what follows, I will first describe and discuss the characteristics of each of these sets of sources and then offer some general observations about my corpus of sources as a whole.

Interviews

The interviews were conducted over an extended period between 2010 and 2016. Consequently, the settings and contents of different interviews varied widely. Most of my interviews were conducted with a single person at a time, but a substantial number also involved two or more persons. The first interviews were conducted with older people only (the youngest interviewee of this group was born in 1952); later interviews included younger individuals, with the youngest person being born in 1992. Still, the older age cohorts represent the majority in the sample. Although I have tried to include both sexes equally, the sample of informants shows a slight male bias, with only about 40 percent of the interviewees being female. The bias is mostly caused by a disproportionate selection of the younger interviewees, who are predominantly male. This not the case for the group of older interviewees, where both sexes are equally represented. The interviews vary greatly in length, with the shortest lasting about 15 minutes and the longest four hours. My interview partners fall into three main groups:
1. Current residents: this group includes almost all the "old" people (born before 1950) who lived in Nkholongue and Malango at the time of my fieldwork, as well as a wide selection of younger people.
2. Emigrants: this group includes people who are originally from Nkholongue or have lived there in the past but have emigrated from the village for various reasons. Most of these interviews were conducted in the vicinity of Nkholongue (mainly in Metangula), but several also took place in quite distant locations. The latter group includes 13 interviews conducted in Malawi, two in Lichinga, and one in Nampula. The interviews of this group are supplemented by written communication with James Amanze, who was not formally interviewed but responded to my questions via email. Amanze is from Nkholongue on his father's side and, although he did not grow up in Nkholongue, he visited the village frequently during his childhood. Today he is a professor of theology at the University of Botswana.

3. Residents of neighboring villages or of the larger region: this group consists of people who have never lived in Nkholongue. They were contacted either for comparative reasons or because they were thought to be able to provide important information on topics related to the history of Nkholongue.

In my interviews, I usually did not follow a clearly defined sequence of questions, nor did I have a fixed set of questions. Rather, I adapted my questions very much to the specific interview, although many similar/identical questions were posed to many of my interviewees. Interviews usually began with an explanation of my project. Then, interview partners were asked to tell their "life history," after which concrete questions were phrased. However, many interviews deviated from this ideal form. On the one hand, this was because several people were interviewed more than once. In these cases, I usually had several concrete questions or topics to address. On the other hand, the way I conducted interviews also changed (and hopefully improved) over the course of my research with my growing awareness of the importance of letting people speak freely, but also with my growing knowledge of the village's and region's history, which allowed me to ask better questions and depend less on interrupting people when I did not understand something. The flow of the interviews improved further with my growing knowledge of Chinyanja, the local main language.

The languages used in the interviews varied. In the beginning, my knowledge of Chinyanja was virtually non-existent and even my Portuguese was very basic. Therefore, the first 15 interviews were all conducted with a translator, translating Chinyanja into English and vice versa. Later interviews included a variety of languages. The most common form was Chinyanja translated into Portuguese. Other forms included direct Portuguese (predominantly with younger men), Chiyao translated into Portuguese, and direct English (for some interviews conducted in Malawi).

While I did six interviews on my own (without translator/assistant) in 2013, I counted on the presence of an assistant for all others. In later interviews, this was even the case when no translator was needed, as I could communicate directly with the interviewee(s). This was mainly because myself and Mustafa Mamboia, my principal assistant, worked together very effectively in my eyes. We discussed problems and open questions beforehand and also both asked questions during the interviews.

Mustafa Mamboia was born in Malango in 1992. He grew up in Malango and partly in Metangula, where he attended secondary school. When I first met him in 2010, he was living in Malango next to his parents' house and still going to school in Metangula. He later worked as a fisherman and petty trader to earn a living. He translated for me for the first time in 2011 and then worked as one of the data collectors of the first village survey in 2012. He was subsequently my translator and assistant in almost all the interviews in 2013 and in all of the interviews in 2016. Of course, his role as an "insider" might have discouraged certain people from telling certain things. Still, I am sure that his presence also helped to make people less inclined to tell me just anything. On the whole, I am convinced that the advantages of his presence clearly outweighed possible methodological problems. Furthermore, he himself began to take a great interest in the project. He also conducted five interviews alone and on his own initiative (Interviews 88–92) with members of his family after I had discussed some of my hypotheses with him. After I left Mozambique, he conducted four more interviews alone to clarify certain aspects and take into account more recent developments in Nkholongue's history.[83]

With one exception (Interview 60), where the interviewee declined to do so, all interviews were recorded. Most of them were afterwards transcribed. All interviewees have been anonymized for this book. This decision was not easy for me. Highlighting the historical importance of previously under-represented actors and then erasing their names is not without contradictions. However, sensitive topics with potentially negative effects for the interviewees came up in many conversations. These included for example the question of war pensions for (alleged) veterans of the War of Independence, the involvement of interviewees on the side of the Portuguese military discussed in Chapter 7, and the participation of interviewees in the opposition discussed in Chapter 9. Furthermore, many interviewees—especially those not currently in positions of power on the local level—were indeed afraid to talk openly about certain topics. The issue of anonymity was not addressed in the early interviews, but beginning in 2013, all interviewees were told that I would not use their real names in the book. In cases, where individuals hold or played a specific position or role, absolute anonymity cannot be guaranteed. This is especially the case in Chapter 10 when discussing the role of local political elites. I consider this to be reasonable since the conflicts addressed have been debated relatively openly inside the village and have also been presented to the government on various occasions. Furthermore, by the time of the publication of this book, those most involved had all already either passed away or resigned from their posts, and thus had little to lose.

Thus, while the interviewees appear without names, the participants of each interview are identified by a personal ID number that corresponds to their ID number from the data of the village surveys (see below). This allows for easy identification if the same person also participated in another interview. Consistent with this book's emphasis on the importance of periodization, I also provide the age of

---

[83] Only one of them is used in this book.

each interviewee, or an estimation thereof. Furthermore, my references to the interviews in the footnotes include the exact time frame from which the respective piece of information was obtained.[84] As we all use page numbers for our written sources, I consider this important to allow for the legibility and verifiability of my arguments. Still, it must be emphasized that an interview is not only an audio or a transcript that can be listened to or read, but also a process that teaches you more than just words.

Interviews 17 to 31 have to be treated somewhat separately. These interviews were produced in cooperation with the German film-maker Gerd Roscher. The cooperation was the result of our common interest in the biography of the German explorer Albrecht Roscher. As I will discuss in Chapter 2, Albrecht Roscher was one of the first Europeans to reach Lake Malawi in 1859. He stayed at the lake about nine miles south of the point where Nkholongue is located. Roscher was killed in 1860 under circumstances that cannot be fully determined. My primary interest in Roscher's biography was twofold: first, it happened to be an ancestor of Nkholongue's chief who guided Roscher on the last stretch of his journey to the lake and who was also involved in "clearing up" the killing. Second, there was a distant, certainly somewhat naive hope that we could still find documents of Roscher somewhere, since all his diaries and other documents were lost when he was killed. Gerd, for his part, was interested in these questions because he was making a film about the history of his namesake.[85] The Roscher interviews were conducted in Nkholongue, Lussefa (the place where Roscher stayed at the lake), and in various locations on Niassa's *planalto* where Roscher might have passed through during his journey and where the ancestors of Nkholongue's chiefs had lived before coming to the lake. The interview constellation was different to most other interviews conducted for this research, because not only would myself and my respective assistant be present at the interview, but also Gerd and in some cases even more Europeans.[86] These interviews were also filmed. Many of them have not been used extensively as explicit sources in this book. However, the traveling that they involved provided me with a better sense of the geography of the 19th-century trade network. Furthermore, the interviews conducted with Chingo-

---

84 I have rarely seen this elsewhere. An exception is Julia Seibert: Julia Seibert, *In die globale Wirtschaft gezwungen: Arbeit und kolonialer Kapitalismus im Kongo (1885–1960)* (Frankfurt: Campus Verlag, 2016).
85 The first showing of the film was in 2013. See: *Kurze Schatten*, directed by Gerd Roscher (2013), 58 min.
86 In some interviews this included Roswitha Ziegler, who for her part was making a film on Gerd Roscher.

manje's relatives in Unango gave me a better understanding of the relationship between the two places.

Village Surveys

Inspired by the earlier village studies, I not only conducted interviews but also three extensive standardized village surveys. All surveys were carried out by assistants from the village.

The first survey was conducted in 2012. It included three questionnaires, one to record households, their members, and various factors concerning the economy of the household, another to record information about ancestors and relatives of adults living in the household, and a third to record the language skills of the respondents. The second and third surveys were carried out in 2016. The second focused on the economics and included a census of all agricultural fields farmed by each household. A key objective of this survey was to record land ownership and inheritance practices in relation to land. The third survey was an attempt to ask a standardized series of closed-ended questions about one's past to many different people. These included questions such as "When did you practice Ramadan?" with options to check off specific time periods, such as "1966–1974" (the time of the War of Independence) or "1975–1986" (the socialist period before the Civil War). The idea was that the quantitative data collected in this way could reveal possible trends of continuity and change in people's everyday lives, which in turn could be further explored using qualitative approaches. However, this intention was only partially realized, mainly due to time constraints. I was unable to be personally responsible for the data collection, which in retrospect would have been essential to allow for a critical interpretation of much of the data collected. These doubts about the scientific value of some of the data collected contributed to my decision to spend my time otherwise than on reviewing the data collected. Therefore, much of it remains unanalyzed.

The first survey included, with few exceptions, all households of the village. However, the questionnaires on relatives and language skills were in many cases answered by only one adult person of the household. Nevertheless, since many people have relatives within the village, the data on kinship relations could often be completed from different sides. Where necessary, this data was also supplemented with information from interviews.

To analyze the data collected in both the surveys and interviews, I designed a MySQL database and programmed a PHP-based database management system that allowed for the entry and analysis of the collected data. As most households are geo-referenced, the software has also allowed for spatial analysis and representation (mapping) of, for example, family relations (see Chapter 11). The software has not only served as a post-fieldwork digital history tool, but, filled with the data from 2012 survey on family relationships, was also used during the 2015 to 2016 fieldwork to identify potential new interviewees and to recognize connections between different interviewees.

Archival and Published Sources

Initially, I did not expect to find many—if any—written sources about Nkholongue. However, in the course of my research I was able to piece together relevant materials from more than 20 archives in six different countries (Mozambique, Malawi, United Kingdom, Portugal, Italy, Switzerland) and even find various publications with information on the village. In what follows, I will describe the most important collections. I will first present the archives and publications of the missionary society Universities' Mission to Central Africa (UMCA) and its members. Then, I will discuss the situation of the colonial and post-colonial state archives in Portugal and Mozambique. Third, I will point out some more specialized collections and sources.

One of the most important sets of sources comes from the Anglican High Church missionary society UMCA. Coincidentally, the UMCA is another link between Landeg White's *Magomero* and this book. The founding of the UMCA was a direct result of David Livingstone's campaign to combat the slave trade in "Central Africa" by introducing "Christianity and commerce."[87] The UMCA made its first attempt to establish a mission in the early 1860s in what is today southern Malawi. There, about 200 miles from Nkholongue, they founded a community of freed slaves, and it is this community that forms the starting point for Landeg White's village history. After only a few years, the missionaries' attempt ended abruptly when they became involved in local wars. They retreated, and instead of settling near Lake Malawi set up headquarters in Zanzibar. Their dream of fulfilling Livingstone's call remained, however, and they came to Nkholongue as part of their second attempt to establish themselves by the lake. Nkholongue was even the first place where the missionaries settled on the mainland of the eastern shores of the lake in 1886. While they later quickly moved on to focus on other lo-

---

[87] The slogan "Christianity and commerce" (or at times "commerce and Christianity") is now mainly associated with Livingstone but was in fact a widely used phrase to describe the (desired) nature of Britain's civilizing mission. See: Brian Stanley, "'Commerce and Christianity': Providence Theory, The Missionary Movement, and the Imperialism of Free Trade, 1842–1860," *The Historical Journal* 26, no. 1 (1983): 71–94; Andrew Porter, "'Commerce and Christianity': The Rise and Fall of a Nineteenth-Century Missionary Slogan," *The Historical Journal* 28, no. 3 (1985): 597–621.

cations, this coincidence has the fortunate consequence that the early history of Nkholongue is comparatively well documented.

Archival materials of the UMCA can be found in three main collections. One is held at the Bodleian Library in Oxford, UK, a second at the National Archives of Malawi in Zomba, and a third remains with UMCA's successor society *United Society Partners in the Gospel* (USPG) in London. The UMCA collection at Oxford is the densest for the early period of the mission's presence on the lake (1880s to 1910s) and contains a large amount of private and official correspondence. The one at Zomba is richer for later periods but is mainly limited to official correspondence about administrative matters. Also to be found in Zomba is the material of the Anglican Diocese of Nyasaland, to which the region on the Portuguese shore of the lake belonged until it was transferred to the Diocese of Lebombo in 1958.

In addition to these archival materials, there are several publications by the UMCA and its members that served as important sources for this book. Among these are the writings of William Percival Johnson (1854–1928) and several periodicals published by the UMCA and the Anglican Church. These periodicals include *Central Africa* (CA) (1883–1964), the *Nyasaland Diocesan Chronicle* (NDC)[88] (1903–1961), the *Lebombo Leaves* (1899–1980), the *The Nyassa News* (TNN) (1893–1895), and the Chinyanja "newspaper" *Mtenga Watu* (1893–1894).[89]

These periodicals focus mainly on describing missionary work, and since Nkholongue quickly lost importance in this regard it is hardly mentioned in later issues. However, they—the NDC in particular—constitute a very important source for those later years as well since they report regularly from and on a region for which documentary evidence is otherwise fragmentary at best for long periods. Even though the NDC's remarks on political and economic developments are brief and infrequent it thus serves as an important indicator of the socio-political atmosphere in the region.

Another advantage of the Anglican sources is that they are sources from a "foreign" mission in a Catholic country. While the UMCA was also part of the European colonizing project, its position brought it into conflict with the Portuguese colonial government at several points in history. Therefore, the observations and reports of its members can be read as a somewhat independent check on the local policies and practices of the colonial government.

---

[88] The name of the NDC was *Likoma Diocesan Quarterly Paper* (LDQP) from 1903 until 1908 and *Nyasaland Diocesan Quarterly Paper* (NDQP) from 1909 until January 1911.

[89] Note that the circulation of most of these periodicals was limited. Most of them are available at the Bodleian Library in Oxford. Copies of the NDC can also be found in the National Archives of Malawi in Zomba.

As far as state archives are concerned, the region around Nkholongue is a challenging case. While the holdings of *Arquivo Histórico de Moçambique* (AHM) on the colonial past are relatively dense for most provinces, there is very little material on Niassa.[90] The archives of the *Companhia do Nyassa*, the chartered company that colonized and administered the territory from 1900 to 1929 have either been lost or destroyed.[91] Unindexed holdings for later periods are said to exist, but a search I conducted in March 2016 in the AHM's storage rooms on the *Av. Samuel Filipe Magaia* revealed none.[92]

This means that archival documents from Niassa's colonial period are as a rule only available if they were sent to a hierarchically higher entity in the administration. Beyond that, we dispose of various inspection reports from the Portuguese inspection services, and some individual annual district/province reports. Copies of these can be found in the AHM, the *Arquivo Histórico Ultramarino* (AHU) or the *Arquivo Histórico Diplomático* (AHD) in Lisbon.

My research was able to partially alleviate this situation by looking for archives in Niassa itself. The greatest success was realized in the case of the *Arquivo Permanente do Gabinete do Governador do Niassa* (APGGN). These archives are not prepared to receive visitors, but I was able to get permission to work in them. At the time of my research in 2016, the APGGN comprised two parts. One was on the ground and the other on the first floor of Niassa's central government building in Lichinga. Newer documents tended to be on the first floor, older ones on the ground floor. But there was no visible order, let alone possible inventories. Some documents were well arranged in clearly separated and labeled dossiers, others were simply bound together as a pile of papers without any sense of sequence or thematic coherence. Still others were just stored as loose sheets in boxes. Several documents on the ground floor room were in a critical condition, threatened

---

90 The exception is, of course, the great collection of interviews in the *Secção da História Oral*. See: Jaime Simão, João Paulo Borges Coelho, and Gerhard Liesegang, "Collection and Administration of Oral History Records in the Arquivo Histórico de Moçambique and Problems with Research and Publication Encountered with Projects in the Social and General History of the War of Liberation (1964–1975) and the Post-Liberation Wars (1975–1992) in Mozambique," *Esarbica* 21 (2002): 91–104.
91 Gerhard Liesegang, "The Arquivo Histórico de Moçambique and Historical Research in Maputo," *History in Africa* 27 (2000): 474.
92 These storerooms are normally not accessible. The storage conditions are very precarious. Many of the floors are under water. I was in the rooms for about three hours, using a torch to search for documents from Niassa. The countless boxes I could find were labelled "Cabo Delgado," "Tete," "Manica e Sofala," "Chembe," "Caminhos de Ferro," "Cimentos de Moçambique," "Instituto Cereais de Moçambique," "Instituto Algodão de Moçambique," and "Concelho de Marromeu," among others, but none "Niassa."

by humidity, insects, and other hazards; and all were covered by thick layers of dust (see Figure 1). Despite these difficult working conditions, I was able to locate much relevant material. Most of it dated from the first decade after independence, some also from the last decade of colonialism. By using the sources from the APGGN, this book also contributes to highlighting the hitherto little exploited potential of regional and post-colonial archives in Africa.[93]

Another set of government sources can be found in the archives of Portuguese military and intelligence services in Portugal. They are particularly valuable for the time of the War of Independence (1964–1974). They include the files of the SCCIM (*Serviços de Centralização e Coordenação de Informações de Moçambique*) and those preserved of PIDE/DGS (*Polícia Internacional e de Defesa do Estado*, renamed *Direcção-Geral de Segurança* in 1969) at the *Arquivo Nacional da Torre do Tombo* (ANTT), the files of the army at the *Arquivo Histórico Militar* (AHMil), the files of the Ministry of Defence at the *Arquivo da Defesa Nacional* (ADN), and the files of the navy at the *Arquivo Histórico da Marinha* (AHMar).

My research could also draw on two collections of already existing interviews. These are the collection at the Oral Section of the AHM and a collection of interviews at the *Museu Local de Metangula* (MLM).

The collection at the AHM dates back to the early 1980s when the AHM collected oral history testimonies throughout Mozambique.[94] While no interviews were conducted in Nkholongue, several interviews were obtained in the larger region, including two in Metangula and six in Unango. Although this is a small sample, these interviews are valuable. Since they were conducted about 30 years earlier than my own, they tell of personal experiences that reach back correspondingly further. They thus not only allow for a shift of what Jan Vansina has called the "floating gap," but also facilitate comparisons about the relationship between memory and history. They have so far been used only rarely in scholarly works.

The collection at the MLM is the result of an initiative of the archaeologist Julio Mercader and the anthropologist Arianna Huhn, who together established a small Museum in Metangula.[95] The collection consists of 95 interviews, songs, and dances recorded by Arianna Huhn in 2007 at various sites along the Mozambican shore of

---

[93] On this point, see: Benedito Machava and Euclides Gonçalves, "The Dead Archive: Governance and Institutional Memory in Independent Mozambique," *Africa* 91, no. 4 (2021): 553–574; Alexander Keese and Brice I. Owabira, "Rescuing, Interpreting, and, Eventually, Digitizing Regional Postcolonial Archives: Endangered Archives and Research in Pointe-Noire, Republic of Congo," *History in Africa* 47 (2020): 143–165.
[94] Simão, Borges Coelho, and Liesegang, "Collection and Administration of Oral History Records."
[95] For more information on the museum, see: "Exhibition @ Museu Local: Metangula, Mozambique," accessed June 8, 2019, http://www.ariannahuhn.info/museu-local-exhibition.html.

1.3 On the Traces of an "Unknown" Matrilineal Village: Methods and Sources

Figure 1: *Arquivo Permanente do Gabinete do Governador do Niassa*: the ground floor room. Photograph taken by the author in 2016.

the lake. Three of the interviews were conducted in Nkholongue. These and other interviews conducted in neighboring villages provide an important source for my work, both in comparative and complementary terms.

Given the difficult archival situation, I have also consulted other archives that may have seemed less promising at first glance. These include the British National Archives (TNA) in Kew, the archives of the UNHCR (AUNHCR) in Geneva, and the archives of the Catholic missionary society Consolata (AIMC) in Rome. As Nkholongue lies in a border region, the British archives in London and in Zomba, for example, have proved valuable for the period of colonization. In the archives of the UNHCR, I was able to find important information about people who fled to Tanzania during the Mozambican War of Independence. And in the AIMC, I was able to uncover significant material on the everyday climate for religious folk in Niassa in the first years after Mozambican Independence.

General Observations about My Corpus of Sources

As should be apparent from this description of my various sources, my work can draw information from a wide range of materials. However, in many cases these sources are also very fragmentary. In addition, the availability of sources for different periods of the village's history varies considerably. This availability limits the ways in which different periods can be analyzed and portrayed. For example, while more recent periods include voices from various individuals, sexes and groups within the village, earlier periods require some imagination to articulate such voices and depend heavily on the perspective of male outsiders and their interpretation of the village's male elite voices.

The latter issue requires particular attention, as Nkholongue lies in what anthropologists used to call the "matrilineal belt" of Africa, in which property and social attributes have historically usually been transmitted by the female and not the male line. Scholarly opinion has varied with regard to the question of whether matriliny contributes positively to women's authority in society. Older research on matriliny tended to claim that matriliny is in reality just male authority in another guise, arguing that the authority is simply the mother's brother rather than the father. More recent research has however emphasized that matriliny in fact contributes positively to women's position in society.[96] It has criticized older

---

[96] Jessica Johnson, "Matriliny," Cambridge Encyclopedia of Anthropology, September 1, 2016, accessed May 17, 2019, http://www.anthroencyclopedia.com/entry/matriliny. Please note that the opinion that matriliny was linked to matriarchy was quite widespread in the 19th century, but was refuted in the early 20th century, among others by Malinowski. See: Christine Saidi, *Women's*

research for the patriarchal biases in their analyses and sources. In fact, in Section 2.4, I will offer an example of an episode in which one of the earlier European visitors to the region seems to have clearly misunderstood and misrepresented local female authority.[97] We should thus certainly be aware of the danger that, above all for the early periods of the village's history, the available sources might steer us too far in the direction of ignoring female authority in particular and female agency in general. However, there is little evidence to justify questioning the findings that male actors from the village played central roles in the processes of Nkholongue's early history analyzed in this book (slave trade, Islamization, colonization). The historicization of matriliny will still be addressed in various chapters of this book and, starting from a discussion of matriliny's present condition in Nkholongue, Chapter 11 will try to trace the history of matriliny in the village.

Other limitations of my corpus of sources will still be discussed and become visible at various points in this book. However, I am also convinced that the initial lack of sources has been overcome surprisingly well and in such a way that the documentary situation allows for a critical analysis and interpretation, which even has its methodological advantages over other studies that, at first glance, can rely on a more extensive body of sources. I would like to highlight three areas where the need for an extensive and creative search of sources has yielded particularly fruitful results.

First, this need has led me to seek specific sources on Nkholongue for all periods of the village's history, with the result that even the early period is now covered by evidence that explicitly refers to the village. This differs from other cases where more recent developments are investigated for specific locations, but the more distant past is described in much more general, often ethnic, terms, usually supported by references to earlier works on larger contexts.

Second, the extensive fieldwork on the micro-level of Nkholongue has proven most useful for the interpretation of my interviews. The "thick" work with many different informants from the same social environment has allowed me to cross-check and contextualize information from individual interviews in a very productive and critical way. Furthermore, it has allowed me to bypass the "target bias" of oral history: researchers practicing oral history often look for very specific informants, such as plantation workers, labor migrants, or liberation fighters. This necessarily entails some limitations, as those who look for the liberation fighters will find them. Likewise, those who search for the forcibly resettled will find them.

Authority and Society in Early East-Central Africa (Rochester: University of Rochester Press, 2010), 7–19.
97 For other such examples from other places, see: Pauline Peters, "Revisiting the Puzzle of Matriliny in South-Central Africa: Introduction," *Critique of Anthropology* 17, no. 2 (1997): 134–135.

But in this way, knowledge about the quantitative and qualitative importance of the liberation fighters or those resettled within local society will always remain limited, and worse, researchers will tend to exaggerate their importance. My approach was not to contact possible interviewees because of their historical role. It therefore allows the importance of different life trajectories to be quantified and qualified, albeit of course only for a tiny part of society.

Last but not least, the combination of oral and written sources has created important synergies that improve the critical interpretation of both types of sources. It has also allowed me to address the "problem bias" of state archives. This issue is rarely discussed, but from my experience I have no doubt that "problems" tend to be over-represented in archives. Local populations have tended to enter the colonial bureaucracy above all when they did not behave as desired by the colonial authorities, and especially when "they posed a threat to the colonial administration and the colonial order."[98] This "problem bias" is likely to be magnified in contexts such as that of this research, where local government documents and information have often survived only if they have found their way up the administrative hierarchy. Through the extensive inclusion of oral history, I was also able to uncover those periods that were characterized by an absence of confrontations with the state, when people posed no problems to the colonial administration.

1.4 The Winds of History: Life in a Corner of Rural Africa since the 19th Century

While the chapters of this book deal with very different topics and can also stand on their own, they are united by a common interest in the social history of rural Africa in the *longue durée*. Arranged chronologically, the chapters of this book document, in the style of a historical ethnography, "how things came to be the way they are now"[99] in a seemingly insignificant corner of rural Africa. The central argument of the book as a whole is that the circumstances of everyday reality in Nkholongue changed time and again considerably and often abruptly as a consequence of processes and events usually beyond people's control. These are what I call the Winds of History. They have repeatedly forced the village's inhabitants

---

98 Romain Tiquet, "Challenging Colonial Forced Labor? Resistance, Resilience, and Power in Senegal (1920s–1940s)," *International Labor and Working-Class History* 93 (2018): 140.
99 Marilyn Silverman and P.H. Gulliver, "Historical Anthropology through Local-Level Research," in *Critical Junctions: Anthroplogy and History beyond the Cultural Turn*, ed. Don Kalb and Herman Tak (New York: Berghahn, 2005), 152.

to re-adapt their lives to new conditions. By highlighting the historical changeability of social conditions and relations as a result of these changes, I hope to challenge and complicate three problematic ways of perceiving and portraying the course of history in Africa. I call them:
1. The Aboriginal Delusion, mainly marked by ideas of rural inertia, isolation and harmony.
2. The Legacy Mode, which is the way of explaining both the present and history through simplified references to an abstracted and essentialized past (often for example "legacies of colonialism").
3. The One-Way-Analysis, which is based on the premise of the linearity of historical processes (such as for example modernization, globalization, and urbanization).

These are ways of relating to the history of rural Africa which are all to be found in both public and academic discourses and, to varying degrees, are also still (or again!) practiced by historians. My critique of these ways does not claim to be original; many others have challenged them previously. Nevertheless, it is hoped that by highlighting them for a concrete and illustrative case in the *longue durée*, the message will come across more effectively than before.

In what follows, I will first explain my metaphor of the Winds of History in more detail, and then go on to elaborate on these three problematic ways of (not) doing history and explore how my book can contribute to overcome them.

The Winds of History

Those who live on the shores of Lake Malawi have to come to terms with its winds. The chief wind of the lake is a wind called *Mwera*. This is a very strong southern wind. Its main season is from April to September. Often, it blows for days without interruption with peaks in the afternoon and calmer periods only at night-time. Even my own fieldwork was considerably constrained by *Mwera* as the sound quality of many of my early interviews suffered due to the constant blast of air. On the lake, *Mwera* raises waves as high as two to three meters. Fishing is severely limited during *Mwera* time. When *Mwera* is blowing, many fishermen move to Malango with their boats as the bay of Malango promises somewhat calmer waters. Wind generally determines the pace of fishing, and sudden changes in wind and weather are a significant danger for fishermen and fishing material alike and, unfortunately, too often end in tragedy.

The winds seem to be an appropriate metaphor to describe life in Nkholongue since the 19th century. Throughout history, the circumstances of life in Nkholongue changed frequently and often abruptly, forcing the villagers to adapt to new conditions. Every chapter of this book deals with such fundamental changes in the everyday reality of Nkholongueans. Starting with the changes brought to the region by the slave trade (Chapter 2), followed by colonization (Chapter 4), independence (Chapters 7 and 8), the Civil War (Chapter 9) and finally the arrival of tourism companies (Chapter 10), ruptures of circumstances have been a constant feature of village life. Changes from outside reconfigured people's possibilities and barriers repeatedly and often profoundly. In the 1890s and 1900s, the end of the slave trade compelled the village chief to conform to the new situation and opened up new opportunities for the (former) slaves (Chapters 3 and 4). In the 1920s, the colonial state's presence in the region was significantly reduced by the relocation of the center of the colonial administration from nearby Metangula to more distant Maniamba, while shortly before forced labor on cotton plantations had caused widespread famine (Chapter 5). In the 1930s, rising lake levels destroyed homes and flooded cemeteries (Chapter 6). In the 1950s, the rhythm of life in Nkholongue was altered considerably when the Anglican mission sold its steamship S.S. Chauncy Maples, which previously stopped in the village twice a month. As a result, many villagers moved north to live in Malango (also Chapter 6). In the 1970s, the dearth of consumer goods such as salt or soap pushed people to look for subsistence alternatives (Chapter 8). In the 1980s, the repeated attacks by Renamo led to severe insecurity in the village and forced everyone to seek refuge in Metangula or abroad (Chapter 9). And in the early 2000s, the planned relocation of part of the village for the realization of a large game reserve seemed to leave Nkholongue once again subject to the Winds of History (Chapter 10).

The forced resettlement of the village in the 1960s by Portuguese troops (Chapter 7) was certainly one of the most disruptive moments in its history, but considering this long list of formative experiences, it also appears as just another such moment. The winds of change in Nkholongue rarely breathed the air of the gentle breezes of change invoked by the British Prime Minister Harold Macmillan during his historic visit to South Africa in 1960 or sung about by the Scorpions at the height of *perestroika*. More often, they came in the guise of storms, whirlwinds, or hurricanes.[100] In Nkholongue's history, moments of hope for political and social

---

100 This terminology is partly taken from Stuart Ward, who has however used it in a different context. Ward's article is still of interest for my argument, as he highlights the fact that "Macmillan's message was not meant for Africans, but for a 'stubborn and race-blinded white oligarchy'." See: Stuart Ward, "Whirlwind, Hurricane, Howling Tempest: The Wind of Change and the British World," in *The Wind of Change*, ed. L.J. Butler and Sarah Stockwell (London: Palgrave Macmillan, 2013), 64.

renewal were not prominent, and when they did occur, they rarely appeared entirely without clouds.

This does not mean that the inhabitants of Nkholongue were simply whirled through history. People still had room to handle the challenges and appropriate the chances brought upon them. For example, the chiefs of the region responded to colonization with very different attitudes, some cooperating, others resisting (see Chapters 3, 4, 5). In the 1960s, people reacted very differently to the Portuguese counter-insurgency strategy, some accepting resettlement and even volunteering as colonial troops, some fleeing abroad, and some staying loyal to the nationalist cause (Chapter 7). And since the 1990s, villagers have used their democratic rights in a variety of ways, some actively campaigning, others just voting, and many abstaining (Chapter 9). Similarly, the planned game reserve was actively supported by some and opposed by others (Chapter 10).

Nor does it mean that the inhabitants of Nkholongue could simply react to the course of things. People were able to show initiative themselves. In the 1890s, it was people from the village who brought Islam to Nkholongue (Chapter 3). During World War One, Muslims from Nkholongue were involved in a plot by German forces against the British steamships (Chapter 5). In the 1940s, women and men created handicraft to sell them on the S.S. Chauncy Maples (Chapter 6). And in the 2010s, it was my future research assistant who approached me to help him record some of his music, and, thus, made the first step to becoming my assistant and interpreter.

However, people's room for action was undoubtedly often limited. Moreover, initiatives and plans did not always come out as intended, and this was not rarely the consequence of new changes outside the reach of most villagers. "The magics of tomorrow" were rather often reversed by yet another blow of history. It is the central goal of this book as a whole to demonstrate that it is not possible to analyze the lives of people in this corner of rural Africa without spotlighting the frequent and often violent ruptures they were confronted with during their lifetimes.

The Aboriginal Delusion

The Aboriginal Delusion appears in different forms in a variety of contexts ranging from journalism to politics and academia. It assumes, consciously or not, that there was a static existence in Africa before history began. This existence is associated with having only cyclical time. The Aboriginal Delusion was in many ways the entry point for the professional study of rural Africa. Anthropologists studied villages in order to get to the original structure of African societies. Proper history was only what happened since the appearance of Europeans. And this change was often seen as so limited that it was still regarded as possible to reconstruct the pre-colonial existence.[101]

No doubt, the Aboriginal Delusion later faced strong opposition from emerging African historiography and the new cohort of constructivist anthropologists that were critical of the origins of their discipline. Nevertheless, this way of looking at African history continues to be popular not only in the public sphere but also within academia itself (and is sometimes oddly combined with constructivism). It is most prominent in the field of development studies, a field founded on the assumption that its targets are not yet "modern" (enough). Let me illustrate this with a "poverty monitoring" recently conducted in Niassa under the auspices of the Swedish Embassy by the consulting firm ORGUT. This monitoring was intended as an "informed" qualitative amplification and correction of the "traditional" poverty monitoring based on quantitative data.[102] The Swedish embassy intended to assess the impact of development and poverty reduction policies "from the bottom."[103] In what was to become known as the "Niassa Reality Checks," three administrative posts of Niassa Province were to be visited annually. One of these administrative posts was Meluluca, the post to which Nkholongue belongs. ORGUT highlighted the importance of taking into account the history of the places under investigation.[104] Following Bourdieu, the "reality checkers" argued that "[h]istory and structural conditions are lived experiences that matter for peoples'

---

101 Thus, J. Clyde Mitchell hinted at the changes brought about by colonization in his *Yao Village* but stressed that these had "not yet affected the pattern of social relationships appreciably" and that "the social structure remained little altered." His chapter *The Village through Time* was primarily about the "typical life history" of a village, characterized by repetitive cycles of events. Similarly, Poly Hill concluded in her *Rural Hausa* that "despite some measure of 'modernization', there are many ways in which economic life remains basically unchanged […]." It should be noted that this static representation differed significantly from her much more dynamic findings about the rural cocoa farmers of southern Ghana. See: J. Clyde Mitchell, *The Yao Village: A Study in the Social Structure of a Malawian People* (1956; repr., Manchester: Manchester University Press, 1971), 213–214; Hill, *Rural Hausa*, 31; Polly Hill, *The Migrant Cocoa-Farmers of Southern Ghana: A Study in Rural Capitalism* (1963; repr., Hamburg: Lit-Verlag, 1997).
102 "Poverty Monitoring – Niassa Reality Check," Sweden Abroad, accessed November 21, 2018, https://www.swedenabroad.se/en/about-sweden-non-swedish-citizens/mozambique/development-and-aid-mozambique/poverty-monitoring—niassa-reality-check/.
103 "Poverty Monitoring – Niassa Reality Check."
104 See for example: ORGUT, "Inception Report," Reality Checks in Mozambique: Building Better Understanding of the Dynamics of Poverty and Well-Being (ORGUT Consulting, 2011), 12–13, accessed October 10, 2014, http://www.cmi.no/publications/file/4508-reality-checks-in-mozambique.pdf.

perceptions of themselves and their strategies for improving their lives."[105] This, then, is how Meluluca's history was described by ORGUT's research team:

> Meluluca was traditionally an isolated and poor community, heavily affected by the war up till 1992. Fishing and agricultural production were primarily for subsistence, and being "refugees" in Malawi was the main experience most people had with the world outside. The community was also very "traditionalist", with strong influence of traditional authorities (*regulos* and *rainhas*), dominance of the Muslim faith, a matrilineal kinship-system, and prevalence of polygamy. Only a very few had the resources and possibilities to relate to other population centres such as Metangula and Lichinga. This changed dramatically in 2008, when the new road to Metangula was constructed with the help of an NGO and the community suddenly 'opened up' to the world outside.[106]

ORGUT's outline of history resonates perfectly with the five stereotypes which Jean Pierre Olivier de Sardan singled to out to appear "in varying degrees, in the conversation and writings of rural development professionals" and to, "divergent as they may appear, enter into combination with each other in variable proportions."[107] They are 1) "the consensual village community," which is represented in the outline as the unquestioned and very vague unit of analysis; 2) "the peasant as an individual petty entrepreneur," who in the example appears implicitly after the construction of the road in 2008; 3) "the peasantry and its traditionalism," characterized in the excerpt by the influence of "traditional authorities," the dominance of the Muslim faith, the matrilineal kinship-system and the prevalence of polygamy; 4) "the submissive and passive peasantry," identified in the outline through its poverty and status as refugees; and 5) "the uncaptured, restive, rebellious peasantry," in the excerpt described as isolated and producing primarily for subsistence.

No doubt, scholars with closer affinity to history working in less practical settings are generally more careful with such stereotypes. But the boundaries are fluid. ORGUT's monitoring in Niassa was led by Inge Tvedten, an anthropologist who has also used his findings from the monitoring in publications in scholarly

---

105 ORGUT, "Sub-Report, District of Lago: Year One, 2011," Reality Checks in Mozambique: Building Better Understanding of the Dynamics of Poverty and Well-Being (ORGUT Consulting, 2011), 9. See also the methodological considerations in another article on the research conducted within the framework of the "reality checks": Sam Jones and Inge Tvedten, "What Does It Mean to Be Poor? Investigating the Qualitative-Quantitative Divide in Mozambique," *World Development* 117 (2019): 158.
106 ORGUT, "Sub-Report, District of Lago: Year Four, 2014," Reality Checks in Mozambique: Building Better Understanding of the Dynamics of Poverty and Well-Being (ORGUT Consulting, 2014), 17.
107 Jean-Pierre Olivier de Sardan, *Anthropology and Development: Understanding Contemporary Social Change* (London: Zed Books, 2005), 81.

journals.[108] Moreover, we will see throughout this book that even historians are often presuming a previously existing "traditional way of life," when, for example, describing disruptions brought to a locality by external forces. In Chapter 4, I will discuss how analyses of colonization tend to ignore the impact of the slave trade. In Chapter 7, I will point out the fact that life before resettlement was not as stable and unchanging as it is often portrayed. And in Chapter 11, I will reflect on the widespread practice of describing societies as "traditionally matrilineal." Among historians, the Aboriginal Delusion also survives in the way ethnic categories are still used comparatively uncritically to explain pre-colonial history. Often, concrete histories tend to become ever more essentialized existences the further we look back.[109]

Arguably, modes of the Aboriginal Delusion have even become stronger in recent times, as for example socially constructed terms like "indigenous" or "native" have (again) become widely acceptable categories in both leftist[110] politics and academia.[111] This is in my eyes also due to the rise and popularization of postcolonial

---

[108] Inge Tvedten and Rachi Picardo, "'Goats Eat Where They Are Tied Up': Illicit and Habitual Corruption in Mozambique," *Review of African Political Economy* 45, no. 158 (2018): 552; Jones and Tvedten, "What Does It Mean to Be Poor?"

[109] Certainly, this also has to do with the lack of sources, as argued for example by: Kate A. Crehan, *The Fractured Community: Landscapes of Power and Gender in Rural Zambia* (Berkeley: University of California Press, 1997), 54.

[110] The stress is on leftist politics, as rightists never ceased to value such categories, even if for other aims.

[111] On the questionability of the return of such categories, see especially the criticism by Adam Kuper. Others such as Barnard or Guenther have taken somewhat more moderate stands, while agreeing with Kuper on the ahistoricity of "indigenous claims," highlighting the usefulness of the employment of "indigeneity" for political reasons. I am, however, convinced that the political fight for social justice can and should rely on more appropriate categories (class, equality etc.). Well-intentioned approaches based on timeless culturalisms may be able to contest certain inequalities, but are bound, in my view, to produce new ones. Many of the critical responses to Kuper are in fact symptomatic of the problematic analyzed by him, such as for example Sidsel Saugestad who believes that there is a possibility "to salvage what is now left of resources, including culture, language, and treasured aspects of social organization [...]" (Asch et al. 2004, 264). Such a perspective not only ignores that history as a social fact is not reversible, but also suggests a nonhistorical moment for the world outside Europe. See: Adam Kuper, "The Return of the Native," *Current Anthropology* 44, no. 3 (2003): 389–402; Michael Asch et al., "On the Return of the Native," *Current Anthropology* 45, no. 2 (2004): 261–267; Michael Asch et al., "More on the Return of the Native," *Current Anthropology* 47, no. 1 (2006): 145–149; Mathias Guenther et al., "The Concept of Indigeneity," *Social Anthropology* 14, no. 1 (2006): 17–32; Alan Barnard, "Kalahari Revisionism, Vienna and the 'Indigenous Peoples' Debate," *Social Anthropology* 14, no. 1 (2007): 1–16; Karl-Heinz Kohl, "Der 'Ureinwohner' kehrt zurück," Welt-Sichten, May 19, 2017, accessed April 9, 2020, https://www.welt-sichten.org/artikel/32756/der-ureinwohner-kehrt-zurueck.

theory. Critics of postcolonial studies have argued that much of the field with its focus on the difference between "Europe" and "non-Europe" ("colonizer"/"colonized," "west"/"east," "core"/"periphery" and "north"/ "south") has done the opposite of overcoming the construction of orientalisms, and even contributed to revitalizing them.[112] Despite the field's ritual deference to difference, hybridity, and multiplicity, the louder voices of postcolonial studies have a strong tendency to lump people along the old binaries.[113] The culturalist focus of the field has tended to obscure differences and inequalities (including political, economic, gender, and generational) within the societies of both "Europe" and "non-Europe."[114] "Indigeneity" has also been revived as part of the environmental turn. While this turn has produced many valuable historical analyses,[115] it has also led to a problematic populist quest and celebration of "indigenous knowledge" that pre-existed (capitalist) colonization, and that has allegedly survived it.[116]

This book hopes to raise awareness of the historicity of life in rural Africa. It hopes to show that there was almost always a disruption before the disruption. As far as the sources allow us to look back, Nkholongue was never an isolated or static place outside history. The village's formation in the slave trade highlights the problematic of such concepts such as "first-comers." And even for earlier periods, oral traditions reveal the crucial importance of migration in pre-colonial reality, complicating narratives of the legitimate owners of land and highlighting the need to consider the constant re-working of what was local and what not.[117]

---

112 Vivek Chibber, *Postcolonial Theory and the Specter of Capital* (London: Verso, 2013); Vasant Kaiwar, *The Postcolonial Orient: The Politics of Difference and the Project of Provincialising Europe* (Leiden: Brill, 2014).
113 On this point, see: Paul Tiyambe Zeleza, "The Troubled Encounter between Postcolonialism and African History," *Journal of the Canadian Historical Association* 17, no. 2 (2007): 93–94. Furthermore, it has been argued that even the concepts of "hybridity," "ambivalence," and the like still tend to rely on fixed categories as a starting point. See: Bart Moore-Gilbert, "Spivak and Bhabha," in *A Companion to Postcolonial Studies*, ed. Henry Schwarz and Sangeeta Ray (Malden: Blackwell, 2007), 463.
114 For the culturalist focus and the homogenization of both "Europe" and "non-Europe," see for example: Neil Lazarus, "'Third Worldism' and the Political Imaginary of Postcolonial Studies," in *The Oxford Handbook of Postcolonial Studies*, ed. Graham Huggan (Oxford: Oxford University Press, 2013), 332–333.
115 See for example: David Anderson, *Eroding the Commons: The Politics of Ecology in Baringo, Kenya, 1890–1963* (Oxford: James Currey, 2002).
116 For such a problematic approach, see: Leigh Brownhill and Terisa E. Turner, "Ecofeminism at the Heart of Ecosocialism," *Capitalism Nature Socialism* 30, no. 1 (2019): 1–10.
117 On this point, see as well the important comments by Carola Lentz on pre-colonial land rights saying that they were always "ambiguous, negotiable and politically embedded": Carola Lentz, "First-Comers and Late-Comers: Indigenous Theories of Landownership in West Africa," in *Land*

The Legacy Mode

The Legacy Mode is the way of explaining the concrete characteristics of the present—usually problems—as a consequence of abstract structures of the past, seemingly obliterating the need for empirical analysis of how things came to be as they are. Frederick Cooper has called this way of doing history "leapfrogging legacies," highlighting the jumping over of a lot of history that misses how a specific factor "is affected over time by the never-ending flow of historical experience."[118] Thereby, in the context of the African continent, the most common legacy factor is colonialism.[119] The "post" in postcolonial, for example, presupposes that everything can and must be explained in terms of reference to the colonial past.

This tendency to attribute to colonialism ever more explanatory power is problematic for three reasons. First, it assumes, as Cooper puts it, that there was "an essence of being colonized independent of what anybody did [or experienced] in a colony."[120] But just as rural Africa was not an entity outside history, neither was colonialism a system outside history, and its *modi operandi* differed greatly both in temporal and geographical perspective. Second, this tendency returns the focus to European agency and non-European victimhood. This is particularly palpable within a certain strand of postcolonial studies. Concerned with Eurocentric constructions of the Other, this strand has offered "endless occasion for speaking about EuroAmerica, perpetuating the Eurocentrism it would formally re-

---

and the Politics of Belonging in West Africa, ed. Richard Kuba and Carola Lentz (Leiden: Brill, 2006), 35.
118 Frederick Cooper, "Mahmood Mamdani, Citizen and Subject: Contemporary Africa and the Legacy of Late Colonialism. Princeton: Princeton University Press, 1996. xii. + 353 pp.," *International Labor and Working-Class History* 52 (1997): 157. See as well: Frederick Cooper, *Colonialism in Question: Theory, Knowledge, History* (Berkeley: University of California Press, 2005), 17–18. For another comprehensive critique of this way of writing history, see: Martin J. Wiener, "The Idea of 'Colonial Legacy' and the Historiography of Empire," *Journal of The Historical Society* 13, no. 1 (2013): 1–32.
119 Another is the slave trade. For examples of legacy explanations in this regard, see: Walter Rodney, *How Europe Underdeveloped Africa* (London: Bogle-L'Ouverture, 1972); Joseph Inikori and Stanley Engerman, eds., *The Atlantic Slave Trade: Effects on Economies, Societies, and Peoples in Africa, the Americas, and Europe* (Durham: Duke University Press, 1992); Nathan Nunn, "The Long-Term Effects of Africa's Slave Trades," *Quarterly Journal of Economics* 123, no. 1 (2008): 139–176; Nathan Nunn and Leonard Wantchekon, "The Slave Trade and the Origins of Mistrust in Africa," *American Economic Review* 101, no. 7 (2011): 3221–3252; Warren Whatley and Rob Gillezeau, "The Impact of the Transatlantic Slave Trade on Ethnic Stratification in Africa," *American Economic Review* 101, no. 3 (2011): 571–76; Graziella Bertocchi, "The Legacies of Slavery in and Out of Africa," *IZA Journal of Migration* 5, no. 1 (2016): 24.
120 Cooper, *Colonialism in Question*, 17.

pudiate," as Arif Dirlik has put it so aptly.[121] In the words of Cooper, it has thus "tended to obscure the very history whose importance it has highlighted."[122] Last but not least, the focus on colonial omnipotence exaggerates the significance of the colonial moment at the expense of other factors. In this regard, Richard Reid has for example pointed to the neglect of research into pre-colonial history, stating that "political scientists and historians alike have been much more excited by what colonialism 'imagined' and 'invented' than by what already existed."[123]

This book demonstrates the importance of valuing real experiences of real people for historical explanation. Emphasizing how greatly colonial presence and policies varied at the local level over time (Chapters 4, 5, 7), the book shows that people did not necessarily experience this period as coherent and that differing encounters and associations with colonialism also depended on people's age. In the case of Nkholongue, the colonial state was notable by its absence rather than its presence for much of its existence (Chapter 5). The book also makes clear that the opinions and reactions of people from a small village could be very different when confronted with the same colonial policies. This was the case, for example, at the beginning of colonization, when people's position in the regional slave trade strongly informed their response to the arrival of Europeans. Analysts certainly do well to study the European origins of the unprecedented growth and transformation of the slave trade. After all, this book argues for the crucial importance of the Winds of History, of historical developments beyond the reach of Nkholongue's inhabitants. But this book also underscores that the knowledge of these structures alone adds little to understanding the reasoning on which people in Nkholongue based their decisions. They read the slave trade primarily in terms of their own local divisions. For them, the slave traders were other Africans, not the Europeans (see Chapters 2, 3, 4), and this continues to be a "memory" employed in local politics even nowadays (Chapter 10).

Neither the legacy of the slave trade nor the legacy of colonialism are by themselves satisfying approaches to explain history from the viewpoint of Nkholon-

---

121 See: Arif Dirlik, "Is There History after Eurocentrism? Globalism, Postcolonialism, and the Disavowal of History," *Cultural Critique*, no. 42 (1999): 10–11. On this point, see as well: Dirlik, 28; Arif Dirlik, "How the Grinch Hijacked Radicalism: Further Thoughts on the Postcolonial," *Postcolonial Studies* 2, no. 2 (1999): 154; Chibber, *Postcolonial Theory and the Specter of Capital*, 291; Zeleza, "The Troubled Encounter between Postcolonialism and African History," 125.
122 Frederick Cooper, "Postcolonial Studies and the Study of History," in *Postcolonial Studies and Beyond*, ed. Ania Loomba et al. (Durham: Duke University Press, 2005), 401.
123 Reid, "Past and Presentism," 149. On this point, see as well: Alexander Keese, *Ethnicity and the Colonial State: Finding and Representing Group Identifications in a Coastal West African and Global Perspective (1850–1960)* (Leiden: Brill, 2016); Thomas Spear, "Neo-Traditionalism and the Limits of Invention in British Colonial Africa," *The Journal of African History* 44, no. 1 (2003): 3–27.

gueans. The current revival of the memory of the "liberation war" by the Mozambican government is prone to produce local (and regional) contradictions. For while most people from the region supported Frelimo at the beginning of the war, many ended up on the side of the colonial state towards the end of it (Chapter 7). Furthermore, many people experienced independence not primarily as their political liberation, but foremost as a deterioration of their economic conditions (Chapter 8). Microhistorical analysis makes these experiences and perspectives visible and also understandable; leapfrogging over them does little to explain complicated histories.

Such perspectives are in the end not only formative for scholarly theory but also necessary to make these theories broadly acceptable beyond academia. Legacy explanations are often not easily translatable to local contexts. Ignoring the historical viewpoints of Nkholongue's inhabitants on these issues will make it difficult to convince them of the important role of structures and European actors behind the scene. This book shows that, to this end, scholars need to lay open the complexities of connections and chains from macro to micro (and back again), and to bring their abstract models such as the construction of the Other into relation with local outcomes and real experiences.

The One-Way-Analysis

The One-Way-Analysis is the way to see history as a linear and mostly irreversible process, often along a model of "continuity and change." Historians have repeatedly criticized such models, for example with regard to "globalization." Against the presentist focus on globalizing processes, they have highlighted that the great period of global expansion was the time before 1914, followed by a nationalist drawback in the years after.[124] Despite these criticisms, the One-Way-Analysis continues to enjoy considerable popularity and to be applied to many processes. In general, it still seems more interesting to explore growing connections than past and ongoing disconnections.[125]

This book intends to reveal that a more dynamic perspective considering processes of reversal and disconnection is absolutely crucial to understanding the complexities of history. In his inspiring *Remotely Global*, Charles Piot has argued that

---

[124] For an example, see: Jeffry A. Frieden, *Global Capitalism: Its Fall and Rise in the Twentieth Century* (New York: W.W. Norton, 2006).
[125] The importance of also examining disconnections has however recently been highlighted by Roland Wenzlhuemer. See: Roland Wenzlhuemer, "Connections in Global History," *Comparativ: Zeitschrift für Globalgeschichte und vergleichende Gesellschaftsforschung* 29, no. 2 (2019): 106–121.

many seemingly "traditional" features of Kabre society in northern Togo are in fact modernities forged by the long encounter with Europe over the last three centuries.[126] While a very similar argument could be made about Nkholongue, this book will show that Nkholongue was not equally "remotely global" throughout its history. Its role, place and connections to the world changed. There were also processes of increasing isolation, localization, and nationalization.

In many ways, for example, Nkholongueans moved much more widely ("globally") in earlier times than nowadays (see Chapter 2 on the slave trade or Chapter 6 on labor migration). If ORGUT identified the Civil War as a moment of connections to the "world outside," they ignored that the war was in reality a time when most people certainly moved, but many in very circumscribed contexts that were everything but global (Chapter 9). Similarly, the colonial state influenced life in Nkholongue more strongly in the first quarter of the 20th century than in the second (Chapter 5). And in the economic sphere, there were not only phases of growing market connections (Chapters 2, 7, 10), but also moments of reversal to subsistence production (Chapters 6 and 8). The analysis proposed in this book also allows for a consideration that connections were growing in one sphere of life while declining in another. Furthermore, new connections to new entities often went hand in hand with disconnections to older ones. Thus, while Nkholongue started to become integrated into the Portuguese Empire in the wake of colonization, older ties to the Wayao of Unango and the Swahili Empire began to lose importance.

This book hopes to heighten awareness of the dynamism of history beyond processes of globalization, connectedness or isolation. Thus, Chapter 10 explores the legal return of the "traditional authorities," while Chapter 11 considers that matrilineal norms and practices could not only vanish or survive but also gain importance at certain points in time. Chapter 6 not only examines the dynamics between subsistence and market production but reflects on the history of social stratification within the village in the long run, highlighting that stratification was greatest in the 19th century, when many villagers were even owned by a tiny minority (Chapter 2). At the level of the village, the end of the slave trade and the beginning of colonization in many ways resulted in a process of social homogenization (Chapters 3 and 4). To assume that only now social differentiation is endangering a previously more or less egalitarian village community is to ignore such dynamics.

The book reveals similar kinds of dynamics in relation to settlement patterns. Both colonial and post-colonial modernization schemes were built on the premise

---

[126] Charles Piot, *Remotely Global: Village Modernity in West Africa* (Chicago: University of Chicago Press, 1999), 1.

that people have to live closer together (Chapters 7, 8, 10). Urbanity has always been associated with modernity and thus the present. While undoubtedly a general global trend towards urbanization is undeniable, this book questions the one-way-imagery from village to town or cities. This is done not only with regard to the experiences of individuals who lived temporarily in urban environments and then again returned to rural lifeworlds, but also with regard to Nkholongue as a settlement itself. This book shows that agriculture has not always determined the daily lives of Nkholongue's inhabitants as fully as one might assume at first glance. Rather, the settlement was at times marked by attributes normally associated with urban areas. These include the importance of trade and transport, the significance of manufacturing, but also a comparatively high population density (Chapters 2 and 6). In the time of the slave trade, Nkholongue was a very compact settlement surrounded by a stockade (Chapter 2). It was only in the wake of colonization that people began to leave the settlement in order to live in more rural settings (Chapter 4). Nkholongue, however, remained (or returned to be) a comparatively densely populated village because of its role as a "firewood station" of the Anglican steamships. Only after the Anglican church sold its last steamship did agriculture regain importance at the expense of trade, and people began to live in more dispersed ways again (Chapter 6). During the War of Independence, most inhabitants were forced to live in a town setting (Chapter 7), only to be pushed back again into rurality in the years that followed (Chapter 8). The Civil War, then, led to people living closer together once more (Chapter 9).

Overall, this book shows that many things in Nkholongue have obviously come a different and longer way than they seem to have at first glance. Many apparent continuities are in fact not real continuities, but rather revived practices and patterns. In Nkholongue, the Winds of History left little room for linear or gradual development.

1.5 Topics and Key Findings of the Chapters

Each of the chapters has a specific analytical focus and is guided by specific research questions. The literature related to these research questions is discussed at the beginning of each chapter. Each chapter examines the extent to which the experience of Nkholongue is able to shed new light on old questions, to support earlier generalizations, or to generate new questions on topics or events whose significance historians have not yet really noticed.[127] As a rule, most chapters have a

---

[127] This terminology has been taken from: Sandwell, "History as Experiment," 125.

chronological focus and pick up where the previous chapter ends. However, references to developments in other periods of the village's history are not uncommon, and Chapters 6 and 11 in particular follow a more longitudinal and diachronic approach. What are the topics and key findings of the chapters?

Chapter 2 focuses on the time between the 1850s and 1890s, and analyzes Nkholongue's formation. The chapter demonstrates Nkholongue's "global origins" by showing how the growth of the slave trade led to the village's foundation. It tells how the village came into being when the ancestors of the present chief settled here around 1880 to use the place as a trading point on the eastern shores of the lake for slaves and ivory coming from across the lake on their way to the Indian Ocean. In the process, slaves were also settled in the village itself. It is their descendants who today make up the majority of Nkholongue's population. The chapter discusses these developments in Nkholongue in relation to the existing historiography on the slave trade and slavery on the African continent, complicating the still dominant notion of the "slavery-to-kinship continuum." For example, it will be highlighted that the "internal" and "external" slave trade cannot be separated as neatly as is sometimes thought. Moreover, it will be emphasized that cultural assimilation was no one-way-street in the case of Nkholongue, at least not in the long run. Thus, it was the descendants of the slaveholders who began to speak the language of their (former) slaves, and not the other way round.

Chapter 3 analyzes the beginning of the spread of Islam in Nkholongue in the 1890s. Existing explanations on the early Islamization in the Lake Malawi region have usually claimed that the "chiefs" were key players in Islam's early spread. The experience of Nkholongue, however, points to the fact that factors of an "Islamization from below" must be taken into consideration. Thus, my research supports the findings of a strand of newer research on Islamization in other parts of rural Africa, and extends the scope of their argument geographically. These findings are especially interesting, because, by pure coincidence, evidence referring to the spread of Islam in Nkholongue featured in previous literature to serve as evidence for the theory of Islamization having been driven by the chiefs. The chapter shows how the very same evidence supports a completely new understanding if read through the microhistorical lens.

Chapter 4 focuses on the village's colonization around the turn of the century. Asking the question "One Village, One People?" it points to the fact that the villagers' perceptions of and reactions towards colonization were not necessarily uniform. It, thus, counters narratives of colonization that tend to ignore such pre-colonial heterogeneity. Consequently, the chapter will analyze colonization from two distinct perspectives, that of Nkholongue's chief and that of the majority of Nkholongue's population. It will be shown how Nkholongue's chief skillfully adapted to ever new situations, and, thus, succeeded to stay in power despite his previous slave trading activities. Eventually, he even supported the colonizing forces in their fight against other rebellious chiefs of the region. The old power relations were thus in many ways perpetuated. But, based on the evidence of changing settlement patterns, this chapter will also show that colonization nonetheless allowed many people to gain more autonomy from their former masters. The chapter thus argues that, on the local level, colonization surprisingly resulted in a process of social homogenization.

Chapter 5 analyzes the changes of the local penetration of colonialism from the time of initial colonization until the early 1960s. In doing this, the chapter addresses the widespread lack of periodization in previous works on (Portuguese) colonialism and counters the assumption that the experience of colonial domination was static over time. The chapter highlights the changing levels of colonial exploitation and also of resistance against this exploitation. Against the claims of previous literature, it shows that the history of colonialism around Nkholongue was precisely not one of increasing integration and exploitation. On the contrary, it will be demonstrated that, in Nkholongue, the "mother of poverty" (Isaacman) was not the famous cotton regime of the *Estado Novo* of the 1940s, but rather the cotton planted on plantations in the early 1920s. These plantations have so far been largely ignored by historiography.

Chapter 6 examines the interplay of subsistence, migration, and the market in the long run. Its rationale is based on the observation that both popular and scholarly narratives of the history of rural Africa are still widely framed by ideas of tradition and stagnation in spite of the continent's century-long integration into the global economy and repeated counterclaims by scholars who have proposed more dynamic narratives. The chapter endorses these counterclaims by highlighting Nkholongue's changeful economic past. Among other things, it demonstrates the varying significance of subsistence production over time. The central argument of the chapter is that the inhabitants of Nkholongue have not remained but have become the subsistence-oriented peasants that they are nowadays. Special attention is given to the early 1950s when Nkholongue's pottery manufacture broke down as a consequence of the end of Lake Malawi's "steamer era." This breakdown led to a growing dependence on subsistence production and labor migration, and, in combination with local soil erosion, resulted in the emigration of the majority of Nkholongue's population to a new location some miles north of the previous settlement.

Chapter 7 analyzes the regional history of the Mozambican War of Independence (1964–1974). It has two central objectives. The first is to address the lack of research on the (social) history of the war. Most historical narratives are still following the simplistic nationalist focus on liberation. As a second objective, the chapter contributes to the research on the global phenomenon of strategic resettlement in guerrilla conflicts. Thereby, it joins the calls of recent scholarship to take the investigation of the experience and the agency of the resettled seriously. As for the first objective, the chapter suggests a more dynamic picture and demonstrates how many inhabitants of Nkholongue, being initially supporters of the nationalists, came to work for the Portuguese war effort in the course of the war. As for the second objective, it shows that the wartime experiences of Nkholongue's population urge us to consider that the Portuguese strategy to "win people's hearts and minds" was not just about (international) propaganda but had in fact noticeable effects on the ground, and also resulted in considerable support for the Portuguese forces.

Chapter 8 focuses on the subsequent period of the first years after Mozambican Independence in 1975. It addresses the previous lack of research into the social history of decolonization both on a Mozambican and a continental scale. It demonstrates that the moment of independence—usually associated with joy as far as it concerns the former colonized—could also evoke quite different feelings. This was due to the fact that many of Nkholongue's inhabitants had ended up on the "wrong" side of the war. Some even fled to Malawi out of fear of reprisals. The chapter highlights that the more optimistic inhabitants were also alienated quickly from Frelimo's nation-building project, partly because of the party's (violent) top-down-behavior but mainly because of the deterioration of the economic situation, which resulted in a loss of purchasing power and forced people again to revert to subsistence production, which had lost part of its importance during the previous years of the war.

Chapter 9 examines the local history of the Mozambican Civil War, and, thus, constitutes one of the first historical studies of the course of the war in Mozambique's far north. It takes up the debate on Renamo's social base within Mozambique during the war. Building on the findings from Chapter 8, the chapter starts with the observation that Nkholongue might have constituted a fertile recruiting ground for Renamo. Possible support for Renamo is further suggested by the party's local successes in the post-war elections of 1994 and 1999. However, the chapter will demonstrate that most villagers did not side with Renamo during the conflict. On the contrary, Nkholongue's population suffered badly from the repeated attacks by the South-African-backed rebels. It will be argued that it was only after the war and in spite of these attacks that Renamo was able to win considerable political support in Nkholongue. The chapter, thus, shows that the revisionists' claim of Renamo acquiring a social base during the war cannot be transferred to every setting in (northern) Mozambique where the party celebrated political successes after the conflict. Instead, it confirms the findings of older research that highlighted Renamo's brutal recruiting methods and war tactics. As for military tactics, the chapter also offers an innovative comparison of the strategies used in the War of Independence and the Civil War by the respective governments and guerrilla/rebel forces.

Chapter 10 analyzes the effects of the resurgence of "traditional authorities" and customary laws in governance and development policy since the 1990s. As part of this resurgence, institutions like chiefs have regained prominence as legitimate representatives of "their communities" across sub-Saharan Africa. The chapter joins other researchers in criticizing the widespread mantra that the official recognition of "traditional authorities" by the Mozambican state in 2000 was just a formalization of what already existed on the local level. The chapter will also highlight the role of the numerous (eco)tourism projects that have either been planned or realized in or around Nkholongue since the 2000s. It will show how both the state and private companies arrived with ideas of a community with common values, authorities and institutions and discovered a much more complex and heterogeneous reality on the ground. Thereby, the chapter also outlines the roles of the state and tourism projects in producing new local realities including new conflicts. Thus, the chapter suggests that the legal changes and the ecotourism projects, while aiming at empowering the "community," also reconfigured the "community" and could even weaken the sense for and of communality in certain ways.

Chapter 11 addresses the dearth of research on the history of matriliny in the long run. The chapter provides an analysis of the current status of matrilineal principles in Nkholongue and also attempts to trace the local history of matriliny from the time of the slave trade to the present. The lack of reliable sources will be mitigated by combining qualitative information from interviews and written sources with quantitative and genealogical data from the village surveys. In this way, it will be possible to show that matriliny has proven surprisingly resilient against all Winds of History in some areas of village life (chiefly succession and inheritance for example), but not in others. Thus, it will be demonstrated that, beginning in the 1960s, the earlier norm of uxorilocal marriage lost ground to a more virilocal pattern. This trend had its roots in the Christian areas of the region and was most likely reinforced by the decline in long-distance labor migration.

1.6 Notes on Spelling and Terminology

Most of the names of places and dynasties of the region do not have a coherent standardized form of how they are spelled. Nkholongue, for example, appears in various forms in different sources, and even nowadays there is no uniformity in spelling. Variants include "Colongue," "Nkholongwe," "Nkolongwe," "Kalongwe" and even "Garongo." Similarily, Chingomanje is also spelled "Chingomanji," "Chingomanja," or "Chingomange." For this book, I have decided to stick to Nkholongue and Chingomanje. Quotations where the original differs from these variants have also been changed, whereby the original form is given in the footnote. The same applies for other names and place names such as Metangula (with variants such as "M'tengula"), Messumba (with variants such as "Msumba" or "M'sumba"), Kalanje (with variants such as "Kalanji"), or Meluluca (with variants such as "Mluluka" or "Meluluka").

While the name Nkholongue appears already in the first written sources,[128] early sources by Anglican missionaries referred to the village preferentially as Chikole. The name of Chikole is still known to older villagers but is no longer in use in everyday conversations. The name Chikole will not be used in this book. My research into the origins and meanings of these two names did not yield a conclusive picture and will not be discussed in this book.

If I speak of Nkholongue outside of a discussion of Malango, this usually includes the residents of both Malango and Nkholongue proper. Whenever it is necessary to make an explicit distinction, and that distinction is not obvious from the context, I will speak of Nkholongue proper to emphasize the difference.

I have chosen to use the modern-day-terminology for administrative units whenever appropriate. This is especially true for the period after 1929. Consequently, what in colonial times was called the *Concelho de Lago* and, then, the *Circunscrição de Lago* will be referred to as the Lago District. Only for the period before 1929 will I speak of the *Concelho de Lago*, since this was hierarchically a different kind of administrative unit. Correspondingly, what in colonial times was called the *Distrito do Niassa*[129] will be referred to as Niassa Province.

Unless otherwise indicated, all translations are mine. In some cases, where it appeared necessary or appropriate, the quotations are reproduced in the original language in the footnotes.

---

128 George H. Swinny, "With Chingomanje," *Central Africa* (CA) 5, no. 56 (1887): 112–118; V., "A Golden Deed," *African Tidings*, no. 107 (September 1898): 99–100.
129 The name of this administrative unit was changed back and forth numerous times, but *Distrito do Niassa* was the most endurable of all names. For an overview of these changes, see: Nuno Santos, *O desconhecido Niassa* (Lisboa: Junta de Investigações do Ultramar, 1964), Quadro IV.

2 Linking the Global with the Local: A Village Crafted by the Slave Trade

2.1 "When our parents came here, it was not themselves who wanted to come here"

It has already been stated in the introduction that Nkholongue's formation was strongly linked to the slave trade. The village came into existence when the ancestors of the present chief settled here around 1880. They originally came from a place called Unango in the highlands east of the lake. Nkholongue's elite not only used the village as a transit point for slaves, but also bought slaves for their own needs and settled them in Nkholongue. It is their descendants who today make up the majority of the village's population. Two older sisters described this process as follows in one of my first interviews in 2010:

> When our parents came here, it was not themselves who wanted to come here. Nor did they flee from a war in Nkhotakota. No, at that time, [...] it was something else that happened that we cannot know ourselves.[1]

Nkholongue's origins in the slave trade are not only still visible in the current social structure of the village, but also still "audible." The Chinyanja dialect of the villagers, especially of the older ones, still differs markedly from that spoken in other villages of the region. While people in Metangula pronounce the Chinyanja word for fish as *nchomba*, those from Nkholongue say *nsomba*.[2] Older people in Nkholongue do not speak the actual Chinyanja of the lakeshore. They speak what they call Chimarimba, a dialect named after the region of Marimba, the ancient name of the Nkhotakota area on the other side of the lake in what is now Malawi.

This chapter attempts to uncover the local ongoings of the slave trade, something most people were reluctant to talk about. Looking at Nkholongue's origins in the slave trade, this chapter examines a part of the "internal" dimension of Africa's

---

1 PA, I004: interview with *P0147* (♀, ~1928), *P0129* (♀, *1930*) (Nkholongue, August 25, 2010), min 00:30:36–00:31:00.

2 *Nsomba* is also used in the area south of Nkholongue. However, this is the result of a more recent development due to the fact that many of the people living there were refugees in Malawi during the War of Independence and the Civil War. Other features of the dialect of Nkholongue, such as intonation, differ from those of other villages in the south. On this point, see also: PA, I150: interview with *P1483* (♀, *1950*), *P1481* (♂, *1954*) (Lussefa, June 15, 2016), min 00:32:16–00:33:12.

∂ Open Access. © 2023 the author(s), published by De Gruyter. [CC BY-NC-ND] This work is licensed under the Creative Commons Attribution-NonCommercial-NoDerivatives 4.0 International License.
https://doi.org/10.1515/9783110765007-005

slavery. In doing so, the chapter has four objectives. The first is to complicate the "slavery-to-kinship continuum," which is still considered by many to be a characteristic feature of African slavery. Second, this chapter aims to bring the study of slavery to a region for which the topic has been little explored so far. Third, by focusing on a concrete and illustrative example, this chapter hopes to contribute to the popularization of the knowledge about the complicated effects of the slave trade inside the African continent, which remains limited and has arguably even trended downward in recent years. Last but not least, this chapter intends to show how the local realities of Nkholongue have been shaped by global processes from the very beginning.

As for the first objective, the chapter connects to a long-standing discussion on African slavery going back to the 1970s and the work of Suzanne Miers and Igor Kopytoff. Focusing on the differences between slavery systems in Africa and those in the Americas, Miers and Kopytoff interpreted slavery in Africa as a much milder form than its American counterpart. Amongst other things, they highlighted the ease with which a slave could be integrated into kinship groups, describing this process as the "slavery-to-kinship continuum."[3] Their analysis contrasted with concurrent studies by other scholars such as Claude Meillassoux, who emphasized the exploitative and coercive character of slave labor, or Antony Hopkins who highlighted the economic motivations for its use.[4] At the end of the 1970s, the "slavery-to-kinship continuum" was critically discussed in two important review articles by Martin Klein and Frederick Cooper. They both argued for the need to continue the analysis of economic exploitation and not to forget the coercive mechanisms inherent in the process of slavery. Cooper, in particular, argued for avoiding the dangers of ahistoricity and essentialization that he saw in previous approaches, and especially in that of Miers and Kopytoff.[5] In his own work, he showed how a plantation system based on slavery developed in parts of Africa during the 19th century that was not so dissimilar to its counterparts in the Americas.[6]

---

3 Suzanne Miers and Igor Kopytoff, eds., *Slavery in Africa: Historical and Anthropological Perspectives* (Madison: University of Wisconsin Press, 1977).
4 Claude Meillassoux, ed., *L'esclavage en Afrique précoloniale* (Paris: François Maspero, 1975); Antony G. Hopkins, *An Economic History of West Africa* (Harlow: Longman, 1973), 23–27.
5 Cooper's piece was generally more critical, that of Klein more appreciative. See: Frederick Cooper, "The Problem of Slavery in African Studies," *The Journal of African History* 20, no. 1 (1979): 103–125; Martin A. Klein, "The Study of Slavery in Africa," *The Journal of African History* 19, no. 4 (1978): 599–609.
6 Frederick Cooper, *Plantation Slavery on the East Coast of Africa* (New Haven: Yale University Press, 1977). Such studies were also made for West Africa, a recent and comprehensive example being: Mohammed Bashir Salau, *The West African Slave Plantation: A Case Study* (New York: Palgrave Macmillan, 2011).

In the early 1980s, Paul Lovejoy reinforced the need for historical analyses in his synthesis with his "transformation thesis," arguing that the previously existing forms of slavery and the whole course of African history were transformed by the expansion of the Atlantic slave trade.[7]

In spite of these criticisms, the idea of a "slavery-to-kinship continuum" has continued to be seen as a distinctive feature of slavery in Africa, as Gareth Austin has recently noted.[8] The experience from Nkholongue seems to confirm the view that slaves (or at least their descendants) assimilated into the slave-owning communities at first glance. However, this chapter will highlight important reservations and also some modifications to what Cooper has called the "absorptionist analysis."[9] First, the proximity to the experiences of concrete individuals will hopefully sharpen the view that any integration into one kinship unit was only possible through the violent separation from another. Second, this chapter points to the danger of a teleological analysis: social homogenization did occur in Nkholongue at some time, but we have too little information to say whether it would have occurred to the same degree without abolition. Several sources indicate the contempt with which Nkholongue's slave trading chief looked upon his slaves. Furthermore, internal and external slave trade cannot be separated as neatly as is sometimes assumed. The evidence relating to Nkholongue shows that they not only resulted from the same process and occurred in the same location but could also involve the same individuals. The dividing line between slaves in transit and permanently settled slaves was most probably quite fluid. Last but not least, cultural assimilation in Nkholongue was not a one-way-street. In the long run, it was the descendants of the slaveholders who began to speak the language and, following my findings in Chapter 3, also the religion of their (former) slaves. This may have been primarily a result of abolition, but it still gives us reason to doubt the uni-linearity of such processes in general.[10]

With regard to the second objective of the chapter, other scholars have highlighted the lack of studies on the history of slavery in the region, even if I would not go so far as Liazzat Bonate to say that "[t]he internal, local social history of slavery in northern Mozambique is yet to be written[.]"[11] In fact, there are some

---

7 Paul E. Lovejoy, *Transformations in Slavery: A History of Slavery in Africa* (Cambridge: Cambridge University Press, 1983).
8 Gareth Austin, "Slavery in Africa, 1804–1936," in *The Cambridge World History of Slavery*, ed. David Eltis et al., vol. 4 (Cambridge: Cambridge University Press, 2017), 180.
9 Cooper, "The Problem of Slavery in African Studies," 104.
10 Austin, "Slavery in Africa," 180.
11 Liazzat Bonate, "Traditions and Transitions: Islam and Chiefship in Northern Mozambique ca. 1850–1974" (PhD thesis, University of Cape Town, 2007), 53. Malyn Newitt has formulated this

existing studies such as Nancy Hafkin's on the coastal areas and those by Edward Alpers and Benigna Zimba on the interior.[12] In particular, Alpers' work on the trade among the Wayao is of interest and value. He has pointed to important questions concerning the effects of the trade on local society, arguing that the growing importance of the slave trade facilitated the rise of large territorial chiefdoms.[13] His work, however, can be criticized for focusing too much on the two Yao chiefdoms of Mataka and Makanjira. This limitation, it must be conceded, was a consequence of the limited sources available to him. With the Wayao of Unango, this chapter aims to draw attention to actors in the slave trade who have so far largely escaped the attention of historians. Another new aspect is that this and the following two chapters also address the history of the abolition of the slave trade and slavery in northern Mozambique, a topic that has received scant attention in relation to this region.

Concerning the third objective of the chapter, it can be noted that the popularization of the knowledge of the history of slavery within the African continent has lagged behind that of the Atlantic slave trade and slavery in the Americas, even within academia outside the circumscribed field of the specialists. An edited volume on slavery in Africa from 2013 highlighted this fact, saying that "[u]nbeknownst to most, more slaves were probably kept within Africa than were ever exported."[14] This lack of popularization can be explained, at least in part, by the

---

argument less radically and, in my opinion, more correctly: Malyn Newitt, "Michel Cahen's Review of a Short History of Mozambique: Some Thoughts," *Lusotopie* 17, no. 1 (2018): 170.

12 Nancy Hafkin, "Trade, Society, and Politics in Northern Mozambique, c.1753–1913" (PhD thesis, Boston, Boston University, 1973); Edward A. Alpers, *Ivory & Slaves in East Central Africa* (Berkeley: University of California Press, 1975); Edward A. Alpers, "Trade, State, and Society among the Yao in the Nineteenth Century," *The Journal of African History* 10, no. 3 (1969): 405–420; Benigna Zimba, "Slave Trade and Slavery in Southeastern Africa: Interviews and Images," in *Slave Routes and Oral Tradition in Southeastern Africa*, ed. Benigna Zimba, Edward Alpers, and Allen Isaacman (Maputo: Filsom, 2005), 295–335. See as well the overview by Eduardo Medeiros and the recent publication by Palmer and Newitt on the manuscripts of the British Consul Henry O'Neill: Eduardo Medeiros, *As etapas da escravatura no norte de Moçambique* (Maputo: AHM, 1988); Hilary C. Palmer and Malyn Newitt, *Northern Mozambique in the Nineteenth Century: The Travels and Explorations of H.E. O'Neill* (Leiden: Brill, 2016).

13 Alpers, "Trade, State, and Society."

14 Alice Bellagamba, Sandra E. Greene, and Martin A. Klein, "Introduction. When the Past Shadows the Present: The Legacy in Africa of Slavery and the Slave Trade," in *The Bitter Legacy: African Slavery Past and Present*, ed. Alice Bellagamba, Sandra E. Greene, and Martin A. Klein (Princeton: Markus Wiener, 2013), 2. This has also led some historians to conclude that the study of Africa's internal slave trade and slavery has always been neglected. See: Benjamin W. Kankpeyeng, "The Slave Trade in Northern Ghana: Landmarks, Legacies and Connections," *Slavery & Abolition* 30, no. 2 (2009): 209–221.

ambivalent relationship of historiography to this politically charged topic.[15] The resurgent national historiography of the 1960s was not eager to highlight "internal" divisions,[16] while the impetus to find African slavery as a milder form of unfree labor was certainly also driven in order to challenge the old claims of the European civilizing mission. The neglect of knowledge popularization about slavery in Africa has arguably even been reinforced in recent years by the popularity of postcolonial theory at Western universities, in that it has reconsolidated the old emphasis on European agency and African victimhood (see also my comments on this in the introduction of the book),[17] even if certain authors considered part of the postcolonial canon have at times emphasized the problems and dangers of such a perspective. Achille Mbembe has for example criticized how deviations from the paradigm of African victimization in the Atlantic slave trade are "immediately denounced as 'non-authentic' and 'non-African.'"[18]

This chapter hopes to demonstrate the importance of discussing the complicated effects of the slave trade inside the African continent. While there is no doubt about the importance of examining and naming the key actors at the top end of this global trade network, it is also necessary to lay open the ongoings at its bottom end. Recent research in European countries has done much to challenge the alleged innocence of individuals and institutions in the slave trade. But, as this chapter hopes to show, the supposedly innocent village also has its slave trade legacies to deal with. As will be demonstrated at various other points in this book, an understanding of these is crucial for a thorough analysis of Nkholongue's history.

Exploring these local entanglements does not mean ignoring their global background. Rather, connected to the fourth objective of this chapter and consistent with the argument of this book as a whole, it will be shown that the arrival of

---

15 On this point, see: Alice Bellagamba, Sandra E. Greene, and Martin A. Klein, *African Slaves, African Masters: Politics, Memories, Social Life* (Trenton: Africa World Press, 2017), 2; Joseph C. Miller, "Breaking the Historiographical Chains: Martin Klein and Slavery," *Canadian Journal of African Studies/Revue Canadienne des Études Africaines* 34, no. 3 (2000): 513; Kristin Mann, *Slavery and the Birth of an African City: Lagos, 1760–1900* (Bloomington: Indiana University Press, 2007), 10.
16 Miller, "Breaking the Historiographical Chains," 513–514.
17 In Switzerland, for example, most scholars working on slavery and slave trade are almost exclusively concerned with pointing out "Swiss" involvement in the slave trade and colonialism. For examples, see: Patricia Purtschert, Barbara Lüthi, and Francesca Falk, eds., *Postkoloniale Schweiz: Formen und Folgen eines Kolonialismus ohne Kolonien* (Bielefeld: transcript, 2012); Bernhard C. Schär, "Rösti und Revolutionen: Zur postkolonialen Re-Lektüre der Schweizer Geschichte," *Widerspruch*, no. 72 (2018): 9–19.
18 Achille Mbembe, "The Subject of the World," in *Facing up to the Past: Perspectives on the Commemoration of Slavery from Africa, the Americas and Europe*, ed. Gert Oostindie (Kingston, Jamaica: Ian Randle Publishers, 2001), 21.

the globalized slave trade was the first major blow in the biographies of Nkholongue's future inhabitants that we can reconstruct with a fair degree of certainty. The expansion of the slave trade to the shores of the lake in the 19th century would define the everyday realities of the region's inhabitants in profound ways and for decades. Regional developments mirror those described by Andrew Hubbell for the Niger Bend, which in his words "had become a vast, roiling theater of conflict and competition, with quarrels, skirmishes and warfare occurring between and within villages."[19] Reading this process from a global perspective will undoubtedly blur the lines between perpetrators and victims. Still, this chapter hopes to show that, from a local perspective, such differences were not only discernible, but also crucial for the making of history. It was these differences that led to the formation of Nkholongue.

Many questions that will be explored in connection with the topic of slave trade and slavery in Nkholongue cannot be answered conclusively. While Nkholongue's origins in the slave trade are well documented, the available sources severely limit the possibilities of reconstructing the lives of slaves in the village. They also do not allow for a thorough analysis of the changing social relations within the village from the time of the slave trade to the present. Nevertheless, the comparatively dense contextual knowledge, owing to the micro-perspective of this study, will doubtlessly help narrow down possible developments.

In what follows, I will first outline the developments at the macro level that set the stage for Nkholongue's formation, a formation which will be examined in a second step. In the third and final part, we will look at the slave trade in Nkholongue and reflect on what it might have meant to be a slave there.

2.2 The Lake Malawi Region in the 19th Century

Today, in Nkholongue, everybody speaks the same mother tongue: Chinyanja. But when the village was formed in the second half of the 19th century, its population came from two "ethnic groups": the Wayao (Sg. Yao, people who speak Chiyao) and people belonging to the Maravi cluster (people who speak Chinyanja/Chichewa). We have to use the term "ethnic groups" in this regard cautiously, as it might evoke too fixed ideas of something like common identity, loyalty, or even unity.[20]

---

19 Andrew Hubbell, "A View of the Slave Trade from the Margin: Suroudougou in the Late Nineteenth-Century Slave Trade of the Niger Bend," *The Journal of African History* 42, no. 1 (2001): 38.
20 Historical inquiries into ethnicity as "identity marker" in the long-term perspective are rare. An exception is Alexander Keese's study on ethnicity in coastal West Africa and various articles in the book *Ethnicity and the Long-Term Perspective* which he edited. See: Keese, *Ethnicity and the Colo-*

In the 19th century, neither the Wayao nor the people from the Maravi cluster disposed of any larger centralized political unit.[21] Even the political and social alliances of the time were by far not congruent with a common ethnicity.[22] Furthermore, people were able to change their identity between Yao and Maravi rather easily.[23] This was, certainly, facilitated by the cultural similarities of the two groups.[24]

The Wayao are considered the "traditional" inhabitants of the highlands east of the southern part of Lake Malawi. They trace their origin to the mystical mountain of Yao, a treeless mountain covered only by grass, from where they slowly scattered into different sub-groups.[25] Up into the 19th century, the area of their dispersal was more or less limited to what is today the Niassa Province of Mozambique. They had, however, a long history of long-distance trade to the Indian Ocean. In the 18th century, the Wayao were recognized by the Portuguese to be the principal traders at both Kilwa and *Ilha de Moçambique*.[26]

Different regional names such as Anyanja, Mang'anja or Achewa have been used to identify people belonging to the Maravi cluster. In the 19th century, Europeans often referred to them as Anyasa, which is the Chiyao variant of Anyanja and translates as "people of the lake." Historically, Maravi settlement was concentrated on the areas to the west and south-west of Lake Malawi. In the 19th century, however, many villages on the eastern shores of Lake Malawi were equally populated by people belonging to the Maravi. These called themselves Anyanja. It is uncertain, when these Anyanja reached the region. Huhn thinks an arrival between

---

nial State; Alexander Keese, ed., *Ethnicity and the Long-Term Perspective: The African Experience* (New York: Peter Lang, 2010).
21 John McCracken, *A History of Malawi 1859–1966* (Woodbridge: James Currey, 2012), 28.
22 See for example: Gerhard Liesegang, "Guerras, terras e tipos de povoaçoes: Sobre uma 'tradiçao urbanística' do norte de Moçambique no século XIX," *Revista Internacional de Estudos Africanos*, no. 1 (1984): 171; McCracken, *A History of Malawi 1859–1966*, 19–20.
23 J.B. Webster, "From Yao Hill to Mulanje Mountain: Ivory and Slaves and the Southwestern Expansion of the Yao (CC/H/142/77)," in *History Seminar Papers 1977/78* (Chancellor College, Zomba, 1977), 5; Alpers, *Ivory & Slaves*, 7; Mitchell, *The Yao Village*, 14. A prominent example in this respect is Makanjira, a powerful Yao chief who is said to have been of Anyanja origin. See: J. Clyde Mitchell, "The Yao of Southern Nyasaland," in *Seven Tribes of British Central Africa*, ed. Elizabeth Colson and Max Gluckman (1951; repr., Manchester: Manchester University Press, 1959), 307.
24 On the cultural similarities, see: Brian Morris, *The Power of Animals: An Ethnography* (Oxford: Berg, 1998), 6–9.
25 The first attempt to codify this scattering literally was done by Yohanna B. Abdallah, the first Yao priest of the UMCA: Yohanna B. Abdallah, *The Yaos: Chiikala Cha Wayao*, ed. Meredith Sanderson, 2nd ed. (1919; London: Frank Cass, 1973).
26 Alpers, *Ivory & Slaves*, 58–66.

1830 and 1840 is likely.[27] But the late Gerhard Liesegang believed that a Maravi presence on the eastern lakeshore can be dated back to the 17th century or even earlier.[28]

In any case, around 1840, the situation around what was to become Nkholongue was more or less one whereby the relatively narrow stretch of lowlands was primarily inhabited by Anyanja, and the land east of this stretch, the highlands, by people belonging to the Wayao. From the 1840s onward, this setting—whether stable or not—was disrupted by two almost simultaneous and externally driven processes.[29] These were the dramatic expansion of the trade in slaves and ivory to the Indian Ocean and the immigration of Ngoni-speaking people from the south.

The so-called Arab slave trade across the Indian Ocean has a much longer history than the more famous Atlantic slave trade. Up to the end of the 18th century, the annual number of slaves being traded on the East African Coast was, however, relatively small. Furthermore, slaves came from regions relatively close to the coast. The long-distance trade revolved mainly around ivory. This changed from the end of the 18th century onward. The rising demand for slaves on the East African coast was fueled by such factors as the development of the French plantation colonies on the Mascarene Islands, the British attempt to contain the slave trade in West Africa after 1807, and last but not least the growing importance of the plantation economy within East Africa itself.[30] Clove production in Zanzibar experienced a considerable boom, attracting ever more Omani investors and prompting the sultan of Oman to move his capital from Muscat to the archipelago.[31] The growing demand for slaves drove their places of origin further and further inland. Over the course of the 19th century, the importance of slaves from the Lake Malawi re-

---

27 Arianna Huhn, "Sustenance and Sociability: Foodways in a Mozambican Town" (PhD thesis, Boston, Boston University, 2013), 40.
28 Liesegang shared his version with me in an email sent on September 18, 2015. In his view, lineages tend to be highly "telescoped" in oral traditions. His detailed reflections on telescoping in the oral tradition of the Anyanja of the eastern lakeshore have not been published, but he hinted at them in an online paper available at academia.edu: Gerhard Liesegang, "Sobre telescopação e de-telescopação: Como a tradição dinâstica dos Tembe e Khosa," September 2014, accessed January 18, 2018, https://www.academia.edu/8441504/Sobre_Telescopa%C3%A7%C3%A3o_e_De-Telescopa%C3%A7%C3%A3o_Como_a_tradi%C3%A7%C3%A3o_din%C3%A2stica_dos_Tembe_e_Khosa. See also: Liesegang, "Guerras, terras e tipos de povoaçoes," 170.
29 A good overview of these processes is given in: McCracken, *A History of Malawi 1859–1966*, 25–31.
30 Alpers, *Ivory & Slaves*, 150–238; Leroy Vail and Landeg White, *Capitalism and Colonialism in Mozambique* (London: Heinemann, 1980), 16–41; Abdul Sheriff, *Slaves, Spices, & Ivory in Zanzibar: Integration of an East African Commercial Empire into the World Economy, 1770–1873* (London: James Currey, 1987), 33–76; Cooper, *Plantation Slavery on the East Coast of Africa*, 38–46.
31 Cooper, *Plantation Slavery on the East Coast of Africa*, 62.

gion rose to such a level that, according to Frederick Cooper, "Wanyasa" (people from Lake Malawi/Nyasa) became a generic term for people of slave origin in Zanzibar.[32]

It needs to be emphasized that both slave traders and slaves came from the same region. Around 1860, the Wayao had become among the most important slave traders of the region but at the same time they also made up a significant proportion of the slaves.[33] Warfare seems to have been the most common means to acquire slaves. Different groups were fighting each other in order to sell the captives.[34] In this constellation, the victims of yesterday could be the perpetrators of tomorrow.[35]

The political instability of the region was further exacerbated by the immigration of the Angoni. This patrilineal people had migrated from far away, namely from what is now South Africa as a result of what is commonly referred to as the *Mfecane*, a wave of extraordinary violence in the early 19th century in not yet colonized areas. Its causes were the subject of controversy in the late 1980s and early 1990s, after Julian Cobbing had denounced the previously accepted explanation of purely self-inflicted black-on-black destruction as a fabrication to justify colonization and apartheid. Instead of internal factors, Cobbing highlighted the growing imperialistic pressures, such as the growing demand for slaves in Portuguese-controlled Delagoa Bay and for laborers in the Cape Colony.[36] Regardless of the causes, the violence led to a surge of migrations and displacements. Some migrated as far north as Lake Malawi. They became known as the Angoni. After

---

32 Cooper, 120, 240–241. For the importance of slaves from the Lake Malawi region, see also: Alpers, *Ivory & Slaves*, 239; Abdul Sheriff, "Localisation and Social Composition of the East African Slave Trade, 1858–1873," *Slavery & Abolition* 9, no. 3 (1988): 141.
33 Alpers, *Ivory & Slaves*, 239–241.
34 Alpers, 230, 240–41. Examples of "intra-ethnic" warfare are given by: Abdallah, *The Yaos*, 40–43; Webster, "From Yao Hill to Mulanje Mountain."
35 Edward Alpers, for example, has argued that the Wayao were able to transform their situation of being victims of the Makua-Lomwe people to their east into another in which they were invading the Maravis to the west of them. See: Alpers, *Ivory & Slaves*, 251. See also: W.H.J. Rangeley, "The Ayao," *The Nyasaland Journal* 16, no. 1 (1963): 10; Abdallah, *The Yaos*, 34–36.
36 Julian Cobbing, "The Mfecane as Alibi: Thoughts on Dithakong and Mbolompo," *The Journal of African History* 29, no. 3 (1988): 487–519; Christopher Saunders, "Conference Report: Mfecane Afterthoughts," *Social Dynamics* 17, no. 2 (1991): 171–177; Norman Etherington, "A Tempest in a Teapot? Nineteenth-Century Contests for Land in South Africa's Caledon Valley and the Invention of the Mfecane," *The Journal of African History* 45, no. 2 (2004): 203–219.

reaching the lake around the 1840s, they quickly emerged as a major player in the struggle for the region's resources.[37]

The fight for slaves and other resources, probably further worsened by periods of drought, had destructive effects on life in the affected areas. The first Europeans who visited the region in the second half of the 19th century painted a devastating picture of the situation that they encountered. Albrecht Roscher, the first European to make a verifiable journey through this area, reported in a letter home in 1859 that "[t]here is a terrible famine in the country of the Wayao. Here at the lake it's better, but there are still shortages, as whole stretches are ravaged by the slave wars."[38]

When David Livingstone visited the region six years later, he had to pass through large tracts that were uninhabited, but still bore "all the marks of having once supported a prodigious iron-smelting and grain-growing population."[39] In his journal, Livingstone related the following reasons for this desertion:

> Some say slave wars, and assert that the Makua from the vicinity of Mozambique played an important part in them; others say famine; others that the people have moved to and beyond Nyassa.[40]

Certainly, we must be careful not to accept these observations too uncritically, since the picture that was painted resonated with the European propaganda for the need of a civilizing mission. Nevertheless, the accounts of European travelers are backed by oral traditions of the migratory movements that began as a result of the crisis. The most massive of these movements was that of a large number of Wayao who migrated to what is now southern Malawi.[41]

While many people were enslaved or forced to migrate as a consequence of these developments, others came to considerable power. Previous scholars have

---

[37] Patrick M. Redmond, "A Political History of the Songea Ngoni from the Mid-Nineteenth Century to the Rise of the Tanganyika African National Union" (PhD thesis, University of London, 1972), accessed July 12, 2019, https://eprints.soas.ac.uk/29676/1/10752648.pdf.

[38] "Nachrichten von Dr. Roscher in Inner-Afrika," *Mittheilungen aus Justus Perthes' Geographischer Anstalt über wichtige neue Erforschungen auf dem Gesamtgebiete der Geographie* 6 (1860): 281.

[39] David Livingstone, *The Last Journals of David Livingstone in Central Africa*, ed. Horace Waller (New York, 1875), 76. See also: Livingstone, 72, 83.

[40] It is "Makoa" in the original. See: Livingstone, *Last Journals*, 83.

[41] Edward A. Alpers, "The Yao in Malawi: The Importance of Local Research," in *The Early History of Malawi*, ed. Bridglal Pachai (London: Longman, 1972), 168–178; Webster, "From Yao Hill to Mulanje Mountain"; Nancy Northrup, "The Migrations of Yao and Kololo into Southern Malawi: Aspects of Migrations in Nineteenth Century Africa," *The International Journal of African Historical Studies* 19, no. 1 (1986): 59–75.

singled out the Yao chiefdoms of Mataka and Makanjira, and the Swahili-ruled town of Nkhotakota as prime hubs of the slave trade in the region.[42] Nkhotakota was founded around 1860 by Salim bin Abdullah, who was to become known as the first Jumbe of Nkhotakota. Abdullah had initially come to the region as a mere trader, but he then subjected local Chewa chiefs on the western shore of the lake to his political power and took residence there.[43]

Interestingly, previous research has largely ignored the question of how these important slave traders interacted with each other. Little is known about the trade routes east of Lake Malawi.[44] Some maps and descriptions from that time and also some later reconstructions by scholars suggest a certain collaboration between these three important hubs of the slave trade. Slaves have been portrayed as having been transported from Nkhotakota on the western shore of the lake to Lussefa on its eastern shore and from there to Muembe, Mataka's town, somewhat inland and, then, finally to the Indian Ocean. Makanjira's town on the south-eastern shores has equally often been depicted as lying on the supply route for Muembe.[45]

Such accounts ignore the fact that there is ample evidence that the dynasties of Mataka, Makanjira, and Jumbe were in reality mostly bitter rivals. The rivalry

---

[42] Alpers, "Trade, State, and Society."

[43] George Shepperson, "The Jumbe of Kota Kota and Some Aspects of the History of Islam in British Central Africa," in *Islam in Tropical Africa*, ed. I. M. Lewis (London: Oxford University Press, 1966), 193–207; Harry W. Langworthy, "Swahili Influence in the Area between Lake Malawi and the Luangwa River," *African Historical Studies* 4, no. 3 (1971): 575–602.

[44] The UNESCO Research Program "Slave Routes and Oral Tradition in Southeastern Africa" aimed at reconstructing these routes. Its findings have, though, been very limited. See: Zimba, "Slave Trade and Slavery in Southeastern Africa."

[45] Henry O'Neill, "Document No. 131: Consul O'Neill to the Marquis of Salisburgy, Mozambique, 13 December 1879," in *Slave Trade No. 1 (1881): Correspondence with British Representatives and Agents Abroad, and Reports from Naval Officers and the Treasury, Relative to the Slave Trade* (London: Houses of Parliament, 1881), 166; Good, *The Steamer Parish*, 52, 67–69; Medeiros, *As etapas da escravatura no norte de Moçambique*, 42. McCracken just mentions the importance of the Nkhotakota-Lussefa crossing without giving any further details on the geography of that route after Lussefa. See: McCracken, *A History of Malawi 1859–1966*, 26–27. For Nkhotakota having been portrayed as the principal assembly point of slaves on the western shore, see as well: Stuart, "Christianity and the Chewa," 23. For Lussefa being depicted as the prime entrepôt of slaves on the eastern shores of the lake, see as well: Edward D. Young, *Nyassa, a Journal of Adventures: Whilst Exploring Lake Nyassa, Central Africa, and Establishing the Settlement of "Livingstonia"* (London: John Murray, 1877), 98; Edward D. Young, "On a Recent Sojourn at Lake Nyassa, Central Africa," *Proceedings of the Royal Society of London* 21, no. 4 (1877): 229; James Frederick Elton, *Travels and Researches among the Lakes and Mountains of Eastern & Central Africa*, ed. H.B. Cotterill (London: John Murray, 1879), 298–99; James Stewart, "The Second Circumnavigation of Lake Nyassa," *Proceedings of the Royal Geographical Society and Monthly Record of Geography*, New Monthly Series 1, no. 5 (1879): 292.

was especially pronounced between the Jumbes on the one side, and the Matakas and Makanjiras on the other, and can be traced back to at least the 1860s.

The limited nature of cooperation between these different slave traders becomes visible if we look at the way the first European visitors of the region tried to reach Lussefa from Muembe. For, when those Europeans arrived at Muembe in 1866 and 1875, Mataka both times made his visitors to believe that he was the ruler of Lussefa. However, both times realities proved to be more complex. So, when Livingstone wanted to travel to Lussefa in 1866, Mataka did not let him because the place had just been looted and burned, apparently as a result of conflict with the Jumbe.[46] When the Anglican missionaries then visited Muembe in 1875, Mataka, while posing as the ruler of Lussefa, was in fact anxious that they not go to the lakeshore, fearing that the missionaries might ally with his rival Makanjira.[47] At almost the same time, affiliates of the Church of Scotland approached Lussefa on the lake from the south. Like the Anglican missionaries, they too intended to open a mission station in Lussefa. They first stopped at Makanjira's, believing him to be the ruler of the town,[48] mistakenly as it turned out.[49] When they finally arrived in Lussefa, they described it as an Arab settlement.[50]

There are many reasons to believe that Lussefa was, in fact, indirectly controlled by the Jumbes of Nkhotakota. The main allies of the Jumbes on the eastern side of the lake were most probably neither Mataka nor Makanjira, but the Wayao of Unango, the group to which Chingomanje, Nkholongue's founder, belonged.

The Wayao of Unango have received considerable scholarly attention, but less for their deeds in the 19th century than for the role they played in post-colonial Mozambique when Unango was President Samora Machel's "city of the future," a city to be built in the middle of nowhere.[51] But although their focus of research was on more recent times, the anthropologist José Raimundo and others also studied the early history of the area through oral traditions. What is interesting for this chapter is that they came to the conclusion that the Wayao of Unango did not live

---

[46] Livingstone, *Last Journals*, 79. Livingstone's comments on the question of the dispute over Lussefa are rather obscure in his published diary, they are however much clearer in his unpublished field diary, but still remain somewhat enigmatic. See: Livingstone, 72, 85; David Livingstone, "Field Diary IV, 1 July – 5 September 1866," Livingstone Online, 31–32, 68–69, 71–72, accessed October 29, 2021, http://livingstoneonline.org/in-his-own-words/catalogue?query=liv_000004&view_pid=liv%3A000004. See also: Stuart, "Os Nyanja, o U.M.C.A. e a Companhia do Niassa, 1880–1930," 14.
[47] Edward Steere, *A Walk to the Nyassa Country* (Zanzibar: UMCA, 1876), 26. See also: Julius Richter, *Evangelische Mission im Nyassa-Lande* (Berlin: Evangel. Missionsgesellschaft, 1892), 149.
[48] Young, *Nyassa, a Journal of Adventures*, 93.
[49] Young, 96.
[50] Young, 98.
[51] Tomás Vieira Mário, "Unango: Nasce uma cidade," *Tempo*, no. 506 (June 22, 1980): 7.

in Unango prior to 1870.[52] Rather, they had lived near Mbemba mountain. Raimundo was able to identify three different motives for the migration from Mbemba to Unango around 1870: 1) attacks by the Angoni, 2) warfare between different Wayao groups, and 3) lack of water around Mbemba.[53] The migration and the motives behind it are also corroborated by the interviews conducted by the research group of the AHM in the early 1980s.[54]

Something that has been neglected in the literature on Unango and the history of the regional slave trade is the role the Wayao of Unango played in the trade. Their alliance with the Jumbes is well documented for the 1880s and 1890s when Unango's caravans were said to be "among the very largest and most important of those that pass from the lake districts to the coast."[55] We can assume that the relationship between the Jumbe and the Wayao of Unango went back to at least 1859. This is suggested by the evidence that can be gathered about the journey of Albrecht Roscher. Roscher was the first European to make a documented crossing of the region. He reached the lake at Lussefa on November 19, 1859, only two months after Livingstone had arrived at the lake's south end.[56] He then stayed in Lussefa for about four months, after which he was killed in uncertain circumstances on his return to the Indian Ocean. His journals and notes have all been lost. We only have some of his letters at our disposal and the record of the testi-

---

[52] José A. Raimundo, "La place et le rôle des villageois dans le processus de mise en oeuvre de la politique agraire au Mozambique: le cas des communautés Ajaua de la Province de Nyassa (1975 à 2005)" (PhD thesis, Vincennes, Université de Paris VIII, 2008), 58. Rosemary Galli, who conducted research in Unango on Mozambique's post-colonial land policies, dates this migration somewhat earlier, namely between 1850 and 1860, but without giving any explanation for her conclusion: Rosemary E. Galli, *Peoples' Spaces and State Spaces: Land and Governance in Mozambique* (Lanham: Lexington, 2003), 24.
[53] Raimundo, "La place et le rôle des villageois," 62–64.
[54] AHM, Secção Oral, Transcrito NI 12: N.° 139–142, Entrevista com um grupo de velhos em Lumbiza (Unango, Niassa), interview by Gerhard Liesegang, Teresa Oliveira, and Mueojuane Mainga Vicente, July 17, 1981, 1, 3; AHM, Secção Oral, Transcrito NI 13: N.° 142–143, Entrevista com o ex-régulo Nampanda em Mapudje (Unango, Niassa), July 17, 1981, 8.
[55] The quotation is from: Chauncy Maples, "Unangu," *The Nyassa News* (*TNN*), no. 2 (November 1893): 49. See as well: William Percival Johnson, "Inclosure 2 in No. 2: Mr. Johnson to Commissioner Johnston," in *Africa. No. 5 (1893). Papers Relative to the Suppression of Slave-Raiding in British Central Africa* (London, 1893), 7–8.
[56] Roscher's servant Rashid and one of Roscher's letters gave the name of the place as "Nussewa." It is, however, quite certain that this must be Lussefa, as Roscher stated in a letter that "Nussewa" is just opposite of "Marimba" (Nkhotakota). There is no other place opposite Nkhotakota that bears any similar phonetic resemblance to "Nussewa" except Lussefa. See: "Nachrichten von Dr. Roscher in Inner-Afrika," 281.

mony that his servant Rashid gave before the British Consul Rigby at Zanzibar.[57] As scant as this evidence seems at first glance, it is still surprising that historians have largely ignored it for other purposes than describing Roscher's own journey, as a close examination of it allows us to draw some interesting conclusions.

First, this evidence confirms that power in Lussefa was already contested in 1860. Roscher's servant Rashid reported of an attack on Lussefa by the Angoni while they stayed there. Second, the evidence from Roscher's journey allows us to substantiate the early importance of the relationship between the Wayao of Unango and the Jumbes of Nkhotakota. According to the sources, Roscher was traveling to the lake in a caravan led by a certain "Salim bin Abdullah." Because of the identical names, and the destination of the caravan on the lake, we can be quite sure that this must have been the first Jumbe of Nkhotakota.[58] On the way to the lake, the caravan came to the town of a Yao chief whose name is given as "Sultan Kingomanga." This "Kingomanga" took over Roscher from Abdullah and escorted him to Lussefa.

There are at least three indications supporting the assumption that "Kingomanga" was an ancestor of the Chingomanjes' of Nkholongue. First, we have the phonetic similarity of the names. This is how one would pronounce the name in Kiswahili, maybe apart from the ending -a, but the first missionaries of the UMCA also pronounced/wrote Chingomanje similarly, i. e. "Chingomanja" or "Chigomaga."[59] Second, this would make sense as the alliance between the Jumbes and the Chingomanjes is well-documented for later periods. Third, Rashid reported that "Kingomanga" resided at a place called "Mamemba," an approximate three and a half day journey from the lake. Most interpretations have, so far, identified

---

57 Extracts from these letters were published in a contemporary German geographical journal: "Nachrichten von Dr. Roscher in Inner-Afrika." For Rashid's testimony, see: C.P. Rigby, "Proceedings No. 43 of 1860," *Transactions of the Bombay Geographical Society* 16 (1863): xlvi–lii.

58 Rigby, "Proceedings No. 43 of 1860," xlix. This interpretation is also shared by: Eduardo Medeiros, *História de Cabo Delgado e do Niassa (c. 1836–1929)* (Maputo: Central Impressora, 1997), 114; François Bontinck, "Un explorateur infortuné: Albrecht Roscher (1836–1860)," *Africa: Rivista Trimestrale di Studi e Documentazione dell'Istituto Italiano per l'Africa e l'Oriente* 44, no. 3 (1989): 404–405. In some accounts, Abdullah is said to have reached the Nkhotakota area as early as the 1840s. But he is usually said to have established his political power there only between 1861 and 1863. See: MNA, NCK/3/9/5: Kota-Kota (Marimba) District Book, Vol. I, 1st April 1907–30th June 1930, 34–35; Langworthy, "Swahili Influence," 583–584; Shepperson, "The Jumbe of Kota Kota," 196.

59 Swinny, "With Chingomanje," *CA* 5, no. 56 (1887): 114; William Bellingham, *The Diary of a Working Man (William Bellingham) in Central Africa, December, 1884, to October, 1887*, ed. J. Cooke Yarborough (London: Society for Promoting Christian Knowledge, 1888), 120; AUMCA, TC/G: George H. Swinny, "Nyasaland Diaries (1884–1887), Vol. I-III"; AUMCA, A1(VI)A, f. 950–952: Letter from William Bellingham to W.H. Penney ([Likoma], October 17, 1885), f. 951.

"Mamemba" with Muembe, the capital of the famous already-mentioned Yao chief Mataka.[60] However, I am convinced that "Mamemba" was a corruption not of Muembe but Mbemba, which fits Rashid's indication of the time needed to travel there much better than Muembe.[61] This interpretation is also in line with the fact that Raimundo's interviewees explicitly mentioned the importance of Chingomanje in connection with their stay at Mbemba.[62] The Mbemba version would also explain why, in the aftermath of Roscher's assassination, David Livingstone was unsuccessful in trying to locate "Kingomanga" in Muembe.[63] It also makes more sense as the ruler of Muembe was undoubtedly Mataka, a name that can be barely confused with "Kingomanga."[64]

The same connection between "Kingomanga" and Chingomanje was apparently made by George Swinny, the first Anglican missionary to settle in Nkholongue in 1886. Apparently, he asked about Roscher in Nkholongue.[65] According to Swinny's

---

[60] Livingstone, *Last Journals*, 93; Karl Wand, *Albrecht Roscher: Eine Afrika-Expedition in den Tod* (Darmstadt: Roether, 1986), 121; Liesegang, "A história do Niassa, ca. 1600–1920. Cap. VI."

[61] This is certainly the case if we consider that Roscher was ill and had to be carried often. Livingstone gave the distance from Muembe to Lussefa at five days (without having made the journey himself). The Anglican missionary Glossop made the journey from Nkholongue to Unango, which is a little bit longer than that from Lussefa to Mbemba, in approximately three and a half days in 1895: Livingstone, *Last Journals*, 72; A. Glossop, "From Likoma to Unangu," *CA* 13, no. 154 (October 1895): 149–153.

[62] Raimundo, "La place et le rôle des villageois," 59.

[63] David Livingstone, "Unyanyembe Journal, 28 January 1866–5 March 1872," Livingstone Online, 156, accessed January 10, 2018, https://livingstoneonline.org/in-his-own-words/catalogue?view_pid=liv%3A000019. The contents of Livingstone's journal are completely distorted in the published version, and namely in a way that implies that Livingstone met "Kingomango." See: Livingstone, *Last Journals*, 93.

[64] Even back then, not everyone was convinced with the identification of "Mamemba" as Muembe. See: "Livingstone's Reisen in Inner-Afrika, 1866–1873," *Mittheilungen aus Justus Perthes' Geographischer Anstalt über wichtige neue Erforschungen auf dem Gesamtgebiete der Geographie* 21 (1875): 89.

[65] He did not write this explicitly in his diary, but a small note in the margins on the last page of his second diary tells us that Swinny had information from Rigby's report and that he was most probably looking for clues to solve the geographical puzzle as he had put all the names in scare quotes. The wording of the note indicates that Swinny had not read the original report, but the entry of Livingstone's diary on the Zambezi expedition in which Livingstone had quoted from Rigby's report: David Livingstone and Charles Livingstone, *Narrative of an Expedition to the Zambesi and Its Tributaries* (New York: Harper, 1866), 420. Swinny was not the only member of the UMCA looking for Roscher. Bishop Smythies who had visited the lake in July/August 1886 (and thus while Swinny was writing the second volume of his diary) was also looking for his traces: AUMCA, A1(V)A Printed Matters, f. 13: Charles Alan Smythies, *A Journey to Lake Nyassa and Visit to the Magwangwara and the Source of the Rovuma in the Year 1886* (Kiungani, n.d.).

diary, a villager named Saidi told him that Roscher was killed "in a village beyond another Lussefa" by Mataka's people and that "his friend Chingomanja was with him but escaped to M'ponda's the other side of the lake where is now living."[66] While at first glance this piece of evidence seems to contradict the interpretation that the Chingomanjes of Nkholongue had any relation to the "Kingomanga" from Rigby's report, it seems more plausible to read Saidi's statement as an indication that he knew something about Roscher but preferred to be vague so as to not implicate his chief's predecessor in the murder of a white man.[67] It could also be that problems of translation were at play. For, while the statement as it stands suggests that the Chingomanje who went to M'ponda's and the other side of the lake had nothing to do with Nkholongue's Chingomanje, it is noteworthy that the founding myth of Nkholongue says that the first place Nkholongue's Chingomanje went after leaving Mbemba and Unango was M'ponda.[68] With regard to "the other side of the lake," it also noteworthy that the first Chingomanje is said to have died on the other side of the lake in Nkhotakhota, from where the remains of his grave were later taken to Nkholongue.[69]

---

[66] It is "Losewa" and "Mponda" in the original. Underlining as in the original. See: AUMCA, TC/G: George H. Swinny, "Nyasaland Diaries (1884–1887), Vol. III," 31. Saidi named the place of killing as "Chikala kwa Kawinga [as much as Chikala of Kawinga], where salt is manufactured." The only place I could find with this name is on the western shore of Lake Chilwa, located some 170 miles south of Nkholongue. While Lake Chilwa was indeed known for its salt extraction, it is unlikely that Roscher had reached Lake Chilwa instead of Lake Malawi, let alone on its western shore. In a letter, Roscher clearly stated that Lussefa was opposite Marimba (Nkhotakota). For the location of Chikala of Kawinga, see: A. Hetherwick, "Notes of a Journey from Domasi Mission Station, Mount Zomba, to Lake Namaramba, August 1887," *Proceedings of the Royal Geographical Society and Monthly Record of Geography* 10, no. 1 (January 1888): 25. For salt extraction at Lake Chilwa, see: Alpers, *Ivory & Slaves*, 25–26. For the letter, see: "Nachrichten von Dr. Roscher in Inner-Afrika," 281.
[67] It is also noteworthy in this regard that Saide placed the responsibility for the murder of Roscher on Mataka, who was an enemy of Chingomanje at the time.
[68] There are several places around the lake that have been called M'ponda, and my informant was referring to what is nowadays the Mozambican town of Meponda, about 50 miles south Nkholongue, rather than one of the M'pondas on the other side of the lake. Various distortions may have been at work to explain the difference. However, it seems implausible that there were two different Chingomanjes, staying near two different places both called Lussefa and going to two different places both called M'ponda. See: PA, I003: interview with *P0792* (♂, 1917) (Nkholongue, August 20, 2010), min 00:09:25–00:10:19.
[69] PA, I003: interview with *P0792* (♂, 1917) (Nkholongue, August 20, 2010), min 00:43:16–00:46:12; PA, I007: interview with *P0298* (♀, ~1922) (Nkholongue, September 1, 2010), min 00:49:06–00:51:25; PA, I107: interview with *P1074* (♀, ~1940) (Malango, April 5, 2016), min 01:36:35–01:37:08; PA, Chadreque Umali, *História de Nyanjas* (Metangula, 1996), 22.

In any case, it seems plausible that the Chingomanjes were already involved in the slave trade and had already known Jumbe before they came to settle at the lake.

2.3 The Formation of Nkholongue

Only those from Nkholongue arrived at the end, as a result of the slave war.[70]

This quote from one of my older interlocutors refers to the fact that when Chingomanje settled at the lake with his followers around 1880, most of the neighboring (Anyanja) chiefdoms were already in existence. But the quote also refers to the fact that it is within the just described context of slave trade, forced migration, and political instability that one needs to understand the formation of Nkholongue. Little of this context was, though, presented to me by the 93-year-old Chief Chingomanje VII when he told me about how his ancestors came to Nkholongue in our first interview in 2010. Rather, he pictured it as a quite peaceful arrival.

"We, ourselves, were moving like grasshoppers. Moving this side, that side. Wayao, Achewa, Anyanja," he began his story and, then, told me how Chingomanje traveled with a group of five brothers and sisters. While the five women remained nameless,[71] the men had names: the first born was Nampanda, the second born Kalanje, the third born Chingomanje, the fourth born Chiwoza, and the fifth born Chipango. Coming from the mountain of Yao, they came to the mountain of Unango. There, Nampanda, Kalanje, and Chiwoza found a place to live. But Chingomanje did not find a place. He continued his journey to M'ponda at the lake and, from there, he traveled north:

> When they left M'ponda, they came to Lussefa. The chief Chitepete welcomed them. When they left Chitepete, they came to Meluluca. There, Chingomanje asked the Chief Nanja: "This side, is there any people or is there no people?" Nanja said that there is only one person there, Chief Maniamba. So, they went to Chief Maniamba. They asked him the same question as they had Nanja. Maniamba answered: "From this side, I am the last one. From here going there, there is nobody. Only, very far, you will find people. But, in all of this part, there is no one." When Chingomanje surveyed the place, he saw that it was good. So, he wanted to stay here. Before he stayed, he went up to Metangula to Chief Chilombe. When he met Chilombe,

---

[70] PA, I128: interview with *P1426* (♂, *1929*) (Malindi (Mangochi District, Malawi), May 28, 2016), min 01:54:12 – 01:54:49.

[71] In a later interview, he tried to remember the names of the sisters as well. See: PA, I017: interview with *P0792* (♂, *1917*), *P0793* (♀, *1939*) (Nkholongue, October 14, 2011), min 00:09:00 – 00:15:00.

they made friendship and Chingomanje told him: "I myself, I will stay now between Maniamba and you. I am here in the middle."⁷²

While there is no question that Chingomanje VII accurately depicted the late coming of his ancestors, the details of this settlement and the peacefulness in which it is said to have occurred must be scrutinized very critically. For, there is little doubt that his ancestors' relationship with their prospective neighbors was not one of equal terms. The Anglican missionary William Percival Johnson, who came to the lake in 1882, described Chingomanje's arrival as follows in 1900:

> This village was occupied by Chingomanje, who came from the hills twenty years ago (shortly before I came up to the Lake), as there was a good shelter for dhows there. Previous to that the whole country had been in [Anyanja] hands.⁷³

The version that the land around Nkholongue had previously been uninhabited was also disputed by some of my interviewees. They claimed that the place had been populated before and stated that the ancestors of the family of Blokhuta and not the Chingomanjes were the first-comers.⁷⁴ One villager⁷⁵ put it like this:

> Up to this day, they don't want to reveal the secret that the first family living here was the Blokhuta family.⁷⁶

The validity of such statements is difficult to verify due to their political nature, as they are directly linked to the question of the legitimate leadership of the village. We will return to this discussion in Chapter 10. In any case, the Anglican missionaries' accounts show that, in these days, the Wayao of Unango dominated the whole lakeshore area from Lussefa up to Metangula. While Nkholongue was under direct Yao rule, the other villages like Metangula, Meluluca, or Lussefa re-

---

72 PA, I003: interview with *P0792* (♂, *1917*) (Nkholongue, August 20, 2010), min 00:03:58–00:18:59.
73 William P. Johnson, "Mohammedanism on Lake Nyasa (1st Part)," *CA* 18, no. 208 (1900): 53.
74 PA, I100: interview with *P0025* (♀, *1948*) (Nkholongue, February 22, 2016), min 00:37:46–00:37:55; PA, I144: interview with *P0411* (♂, *1965*) (Nkholongue, June 8, 2016), min 00:29:52–00:31:27; PA, I120: interview with *P1102* (♂, *1932*) (Malango, April 21, 2016), min 01:47:16–01:47:36.
75 He was a member of the Blokhuta family on his maternal side, but one of the Chingomanje family on his paternal. He passed away in 2012. He lived with his wife virilocally next to his father. In the village survey he identified himself as part of the Blokhuta family. His wife, however, said that he belonged to the Chingomanjes.
76 PA, I033: interview with *P0643* (♂, *1981*) (Nkholongue, June 9, 2012), min 00:44:02–00:44:22.

mained under nominal Nyanja rule, but became dependent on Unango.[77] In the words of missionary Johnson, Chingomanje was Unango's "outpost" on the lake.[78]

The origins of this dependency are not entirely clear. If one follows my theory about Roscher, it can be asserted that the dealings of the Wayao of Unango in Lussefa went back to at least 1859. It seems possible that Chingomanje settled at the lake in order to secure the trade route to Nkhotakota. This is at least suggested by the information that Chief Nampanda gave me when I interviewed him in 2011. He stated that Chingomanje was sent to the lake to gain better control of the area as it had become insecure as a consequence of the wars with the Angoni.[79] In Meluluca, however, people told me that it was their ancestors that went to Unango to ask the Wayao for help in their fight against the Angoni and Yao chiefs from the southern end of the lake.[80]

We can assume that Nkholongue was not the first base of the Chingomanjes on the lake after they left Unango. First, this is, of course, suggested by the above-quoted account of Chingomanje VII who presented his ancestor's journey as one from the south to Nkholongue. Second, when the British engineer James Stewart visited Lussefa on the steamer of the Free Church of Scotland in 1878, he observed that the place's chief "was called Kitepete, or sometimes, indifferently, Kungumanje."[81] Now, "Kitepete" or "Chitepete" is the name of Lussefa's current dynasty of chiefs. "Kungumanje" points to the possibility that the Chingomanjes might have then been present in Lussefa. Third, one of my interviewees told me that his ancestors did not cross the lake from Nkhotakota to Nkholongue directly, but first were brought by Jumbe to Lussefa and only migrated to Nkholongue from there.[82]

---

[77] "Notes," *TNN*, no. 4 (May 1894): 138; William Percival Johnson, *My African Reminiscences 1875–1895* (Westminster: UMCA, 1924), 183; Johnson, "Inclosure 2 in No. 2: Mr. Johnson to Commissioner Johnston," 8. The missionaries frequently called Meluluca "Kalanje's town" on the lake. See: AUMCA, E2, f. 277–278: Letter from J. A. Williams to Mr. Travers (Unangu, April 13, 1894); Glossop, "From Likoma to Unangu," *CA* 13, no. 154 (October 1895): 149; "Postbag: Opening of the Church at Unangu," *CA* 12, no. 137 (1894): 75. See also: William Percival Johnson, "News from the Stations: III. The Chauncy Maples," *Nyasaland Diocesan Chronicle* (*NDC*), no. 55 (April 1917): 16.
[78] Johnson, *African Reminiscences*, 145.
[79] PA, I019: interview with *Chief Nampanda* (Unango, October 15, 2011), min 00:10:41–00:13:43. For a very similar statement, see: PA, I087: interview with *P1452* (♂, 1927) (Lichinga, September 10, 2013), min 00:00:00–00:04:02.
[80] PA, I123: interview with *P1460* (♀), *P1461* (♂, ~1935), *P1462* (♂, ~1935) (Meluluca, April 25, 2016).
[81] Stewart, "Second Circumnavigation," 292. Stewart's companion Frederick Elton only mentioned "Kitepete": Elton, *Travels and Researches*, 299.
[82] PA, I008: interview with *P0299* (♂, 1938) (Nkholongue, September 1, 2010), min 0:02:29–00:04:11. Similarly, another interviewee stated that his ancestors had first lived in Meluluca but came here because of problems with lions. However, this one explicitly denied that his ancestors had been

And, fourth, we can observe that the timing of Chingomanje's arrival in Nkholongue correlates with the decline of Lussefa's importance as the major *entrepôt* opposite Nkhotakota. While up to 1880s, Lussefa was always referred to as the central crossing point on the east side of the lake, later accounts highlight the role of Nkholongue and Meluluca.[83]

Presumably, this move northward was not voluntary, but was caused by the growing pressure by Makanjira from the south.[84] Makanjira had settled at the south-eastern end of Lake Malawi in the early 1870s.[85] His rivalry with Jumbe and Chingomanje is well documented and can be dated back to his arrival at the lake or even earlier.[86] The conflicts with Makanjira seem to have made Lussefa a rather unsafe landing-place for dhows coming from Nkhotakota. At any rate, the trade between Nkhotakota and Lussefa seems to have suffered in those years. The Scottish missionary Robert Laws, who visited both Lussefa and Nkhotakota twice within three years, wrote after his second visit that "[n]othing struck me more forcibly, both at Nkhotakota and Lussefa, than the blight that had apparently fallen on both places since our former visit in 1875."[87] His fellow missionary James Stewart similarly reported after the 1878 visit that Lussefa's "glories and prosperity seem to belong to the past; desolation, dirt, and decay now hold possession of the place."[88]

While the theory that Jumbe and Chingomanje were driven out of Lussefa by Makanjira and other Yao chiefs cannot be supported by any explicit evidence, it also makes much sense if we look at what happened when Chingomanje was al-

---

slaves. See: PA, I096: interview with *P1216 (♂, 1957)* (Malango, February 1, 2016), min 01:28:52–01:33:10.

83 "Notes," *TNN*, no. 2 (November 1893): 62; AUMCA, A1(VI)A, f. 946–949: Letter from William Bellingham to W.H. Penney ([Likoma], October 1, 1885); AUMCA, TC/G: George H. Swinny, "Nyasaland Diaries (1884–1887), Vol. I," 110, 121; AUMCA, TC/G: George H. Swinny, "Nyasaland Diaries (1884–1887), Vol. II," 53; AUMCA, TC/G: George H. Swinny, "Nyasaland Diaries (1884–1887), Vol. III," 34, 37.
84 For this pressure, see as well: Harry W. Langworthy, "Central Malawi in the 19th Century," in *From Nyasaland to Malawi: Studies in Colonial History*, ed. Roderick J. Macdonald (Nairobi: East African Publishing House, 1975), 15–17.
85 Young, *Nyassa, a Journal of Adventures*, 73. See also: Alpers, "Trade, State, and Society," 414.
86 See for example: Langworthy, "Swahili Influence," 590; Henry O'Neill, "Paper No. 38: Consul O'Neill to Earl Granville, Mozambique, 30 April 1883," in *Slave Trade No. 1 (1884). Correspondence with British Representatives and Agents Abroad, and Reports from Naval Officers and the Treasury, Relative to the Slave Trade: 1883–1884* (London: Houses of Parliament, 1884), 1; Langworthy, "Central Malawi in the 19th Century," 16–17.
87 It is "Kotakota" and "Losewa" in the original. See: Robert Laws, "Voyage on Lake N'yassa," *The Free Church of Scotland Monthly Record*, no. 189 (April 1, 1878): 84.
88 Stewart, "Second Circumnavigation," 292. However, his companion Frederick Elton, who visited the village for the first time, still called it "a respectable one." See: Elton, *Travels and Researches*, 299. For the situation in 1875, see as well: Young, *Nyassa, a Journal of Adventures*, 98.

ready settled at Nkholongue in the 1880s. Nkholongue, being a perennial river north of Lussefa, was more secure but not secure enough: in June 1886, Nkholongue was destroyed, according to missionary George Swinny by Makanjira's people.[89] Then, in July 1887, the village was again burnt down, this time apparently by an alliance of Mkalawiri[90] and Mataka.[91] The Anglican missionary Charles Smythies, who had witnessed the village lying in ruins, noted in his diary that "[t]here are often quarrels between Jumbe and the great chiefs on this side, & then they seem to visit it on his weaker friend Chingomanje, whom they are all to attack."[92]

Obviously, Nkholongue's formation did not fall into a period in which the domination of the Wayao of Unango over the lakeshore was uncontested, but rather into a period when this "domination"—if it had ever existed in some pure form—was increasingly put into question.

2.4 The Slave Trade and Slavery in Nkholongue

While there is some uncertainty about the exact dealings of the Wayao of Unango with Jumbe and the slave trade in the years prior to the 1880s, the situation becomes much clearer after the settlement of the Chingomanjes in Nkholongue and the almost simultaneous arrival of the missionaries of the UMCA in the region. Both oral testimony and the missionaries' accounts clearly show that Kalanje, the main chief of Unango, was Chingomanje's senior and Jumbe their common ally.[93]

---

89 It is "Makanjila" and "Losewa" in the original. See: AUMCA, TC/G: George H. Swinny, "Nyasaland Diaries (1884–1887), Vol. I," 111.
90 This Yao chief resided south of Lussefa.
91 AUMCA, A1(V)B, f. 368–404: Charles Alan Smythies, [Diary/Report of Bishop Smythies' Third Visit to Nyasa (July to Sept.)] (Likoma, 1887); AUMCA, A1(V)A Printed Matters, f. 19: Charles Alan Smythies, *A Journey from Zanzibar to Lake Nyassa and Back, in the Year 1887* (Westminster: UMCA, n.d.). See as well: AUMCA, A1(V)A Printed Matters, f. 19: Charles Alan Smythies, *A Journey from Zanzibar to Lake Nyassa and Back, in the Year 1887* (Westminster: UMCA, n.d.), 13.
92 AUMCA, A1(V)B, f. 368–404: Charles Alan Smythies, [Diary/Report of Bishop Smythies' Third Visit to Nyasa (July to Sept.)] (Likoma, 1887), f. 398A.
93 For Kalanje being Chingomanje's superior, see: PA, I154: interview with P0367 (♂, 1936), P0373 (♀, 1940) (Nkholongue, June 18, 2016), min 01:08:22–01:10:08; PA, I113: interview with P0367 (♂, 1936) (Nkholongue, April 13, 2016), 01:49:50–01:49:59; Johnson, "Inclosure 2 in No. 2: Mr. Johnson to Commissioner Johnston," 7–8. For Kalanje being Jumbe's ally, see: J.E. Hine, *Days Gone by: Being Some Account of Past Years Chiefly in Central Africa* (London: John Murray, 1924), 137; "Notes," *TNN*, no. 2 (November 1893): 62. For Chingomanje being Jumbe's ally, see: AUMCA, A1(V)B, f. 368–404: Charles Alan Smythies, [Diary/Report of Bishop Smythies' Third Visit to Nyasa (July to Sept.)] (Likoma, 1887); AUMCA, TC/G: George H. Swinny, "Nyasaland Diaries (1884–1887),

These sources also substantiate Kalanje's and Chingomanje's involvement in the slave trade. The situation in Nkholongue was such that "slave caravans continually passed and repassed."[94] Swinny described the way from Nkholongue to Unango to be "well trodden by slave caravans and Yao traders bound for the coast."[95] The missionaries frequently reported of dhows plying between Nkhotakota and Nkholongue.[96] Some of them belonged to Jumbe, but Chingomanje and Kalanje also had their own boats.[97] One villager described the use of Chingomanje's dhow as follows:

> With this boat, they traveled from here to Nkhotakhota, caught people there, and took them here. Then, they went again to the other side, grabbed people there and took them here. This is the way, how [Chingomanje] was moving with this boat.[98]

Chingomanje VII put it like this in one of our later interviews:

Vol. II," 55; PA, I008: interview with *P0299* (♂, *1938*) (Nkholongue, September 1, 2010), min 00:03:35 – 00:04:11; PA, I014: interview with *P0147* (♀, *~1928*), *P0129* (♀, *1930*) (Nkholongue, September 8, 2010), min 00:27:00 – 00:27:24; AUMCA, A1(V)A Printed Matters, f. 19: Charles Alan Smythies, *A Journey from Zanzibar to Lake Nyassa and Back, in the Year 1887* (Westminster: UMCA, n.d.), 13.
94 Johnson, "Mohammedanism on Lake Nyasa (1st Part)," *CA* 18, no. 208 (1900): 53. For "sightings" of caravans in Nkholongue by missionaries, see: AUMCA, A1(VI)D, f. 44 – 47: Letter from William P. Johnson to W.H. Penney (February 21, 1888), f. 44; AUMCA, A1(V)B, f. 368 – 404: Charles Alan Smythies, [Diary/Report of Bishop Smythies' Third Visit to Nyasa (July to Sept.)] (Likoma, 1887), f. 398 – 399; AUMCA, TC/G: George H. Swinny, "Nyasaland Diaries (1884 – 1887), Vol. III," 37; AUMCA, TC/G: George H. Swinny, "Nyasaland Diaries (1884 – 1887), Vol. II," 54. See as well: Johnson, *African Reminiscences*, 145.
95 AUMCA, A1(VI)A, f. 1270 – 1293: Letter from George Swinny to W.H. Penney (Isle of Likoma, May 15, 1886), f. 1273. Part of this letter, including the quotation, were later printed in *Central Africa*: "The Charles Janson," *CA* 4, no. 45 (1886): 135. See also: AUMCA, TC/G: George H. Swinny, "Nyasaland Diaries (1884 – 1887), Vol. II," 59.
96 For evidence, see: AUMCA, A1(VI)A, f. 946 – 949: Letter from William Bellingham to W.H. Penney ([Likoma], October 1, 1885); AUMCA, TC/G: George H. Swinny, "Nyasaland Diaries (1884 – 1887), Vol. I," 110, 121; AUMCA, TC/G: George H. Swinny, "Nyasaland Diaries (1884 – 1887), Vol. II," 53; AUMCA, TC/G: George H. Swinny, "Nyasaland Diaries (1884 – 1887), Vol. III," 34, 37.
97 PA, I001: interview with *P0050* (♂, *~1922*) (Nkholongue, August 17, 2010), min 00:25:26 – 00:26:39; PA, I003: interview with *P0792* (♂, *1917*) (Nkholongue, August 20, 2010), min 00:15:19 – 00:16:22; PA, I002: interview with *P0128* (♂, *1928*) (Nkholongue, August 18, 2010), min 00:58:27 – 00:59:00; PA, I005: interview with *P0641* (♂, *1952*) (Nkholongue, August 27, 2010), min 01:11:29 – 01:12:03; PA, I012: interview with *P0367* (♂, *1936*) (Nkholongue, September 3, 2010), min 00:43:13 – 00:45:38. Smythies noted that "Chingomanje & his people have one or two dhows." See: AUMCA, A1(V)B, f. 368 – 404: Charles Alan Smythies, [Diary/Report of Bishop Smythies' Third Visit to Nyasa (July to Sept.)] (Likoma, 1887), f. 398A.
98 PA, I005: interview with *P0641* (♂, *1952*) (Nkholongue, August 27, 2010), min 01:12:03 – 01:12:22.

> We, the Chingomanjes, listen, those Chingomanjes, they went to other side of the lake to buy people. With those people, they went to Tanzania to sell them.[99]

The presence of the slave trade in Nkholongue is thus well documented. But we know very little about how it worked in detail. It seems that the local chiefs demanded a toll for passing caravans.[100] But the quotations above clearly suggest that Chingomanje, apart from providing the infrastructure for the trade, was also actively involved in it. He might thereby have participated in Kalanje's caravan, which went to the coast of the Indian Ocean on an annual basis.[101] Other caravans were organized by Swahili traders, who were frequently present in Nkholongue.[102]

Nkholongue was not only a reloading point, but also a destination for slaves. The situation in Nkholongue was such that the majority of the village's population had not come with Chingomanje from Unango but was brought here from the other side of the lake. The Anglican missionary William P. Johnson described the social structure of Nkholongue like this:

> Chingomanje's village was like most of these Yao places. He himself and his kindred (by the mother) you could count on the fingers of a hand; then he had one or two sons and some trusty overseers [...]; the rest were slaves [...].[103]

Though the exact ratio between slave owners and slaves might be exaggerated in this statement, the tendency is, as will be discussed below, clearly confirmed by other sources and by the data from my interviews and surveys.

What were the reasons for the settlement of these slaves? Various factors may have interacted here, including questions of political power, social status, lineage and gender, and economics. As in other parts of Africa, social and political significance among the Wayao was defined very much by what has been called the

---

99 PA, I017: interview with *P0792* (♂, *1917*), *P0793* (♀, *1939*) (Nkholongue, October 14, 2011), min 01:12:47–01:13:01.
100 "Nyasaland and the Slave Traffic," *The Anti-Slavery Reporter* 14, no. 5 (September 1894): 282. Evidence that Kalanje levied taxes on caravans is found in: Arthur Fraser Sim, *The Life and Letters of Arthur Fraser Sim* (Westminster: UMCA, 1897), 116.
101 AUMCA, A1(XI), f. 457–462: Letter from Bishop Hine to Travers (Unangu, May 22, 1901), f. 461.
102 Johnson, *African Reminiscences*, 145, 183; "Notes," *TNN*, no. 8 (May 1895): 272; AUMCA, TC/G: George H. Swinny, "Nyasaland Diaries (1884–1887), Vol. II," 54. See as well: "Nyasaland and the Slave Traffic," 282.
103 It is "Chingomanji" in the original. See: Johnson, *African Reminiscences*, 145.

"wealth-in-people paradigm,"[104] regionally epitomized by the negative maxim that "a chief without people is nothing."[105] However, the purchase of slaves did not just allow a chief to enlarge his following but also rearranged his position within the kinship unit. The Wayao and Maravi are "traditionally" matrilineal people (this ascription will be analyzed critically in Chapter 11). Under normal circumstances, a chief's children would not belong to his own lineage, but to that of his wife. By marrying a slave wife, a chief could avoid this, and thus increase the reproductive capacity of his kinship group considerably as the slave wife's children would belong to his matriliny.[106] Kalanje was said to have 20 slave wives according to one source and 42 according to another.[107] For Nkholongue, such (possibly inflated) numbers are not available, but the occurrence of slave marriages was reported in the oral histories collected by the late Chadreque Umali, a local historian from the lakeshore area. In his history of the chiefdoms of the region, he wrote about Nkholongue:

> Chingomanje made boats in which he took ebony to Marimba in order to exchange it for women. While the pretty women resulting from this trade stayed with him, he offered the rest to his relatives and his slaves.[108]

The possible effects of the slave trade on matrilineal principles have repeatedly been highlighted. In line with this, Jonna Katto has recently argued that the slave trade went hand in hand with a masculinization of (political) authority in Niassa.[109] As I have pointed out in the introduction of this book, the problem is

---

104 For a discussion of the concept, see: Jane I. Guyer, "Wealth in People and Self-Realization in Equatorial Africa," *Man (New Series)* 28, no. 2 (1993): 243–65; Jane I. Guyer and Samuel M. Eno Belinga, "Wealth in People as Wealth in Knowledge: Accumulation and Composition in Equatorial Africa," *The Journal of African History* 36, no. 1 (1995): 91–120.
105 Mitchell, *The Yao Village*, 37. This maxim is valid for most groups living around the lake. For similar descriptions in the case of the Achewa and the Lakeside Tonga, see: Fabiano Kwaule, "Kanyenda, the Mwale Expansion into Nkhota-Kota and the Swahili Challenge, 1750–1890," in *History Seminar Papers 1978/79* (Chancellor College, Zomba, 1979), 20. This maxim also surfaced in my interviews. See: PA, I001: interview with *P0050* (♂, ~1922) (Nkholongue, August 17, 2010), min 00:06:00–00:07:18; PA, I128: interview with *P1426* (♂, 1929) (Malindi (Mangochi District, Malawi), May 28, 2016), min 00:46:53–00:47:59. See as well: MLM, 018: interview with *L. M.*, transcript Chinyanja (Malango, June 27, 2007).
106 Alpers, "Trade, State, and Society," 412.
107 Yohanna B. Abdallah, "A Letter From Unangu," *African Tidings*, no. 68 (June 1895): 58; Robert Howard, "The Hearer's Service at Nyasa," *CA* 19, no. 221 (May 1901): 79.
108 PA, Chadreque Umali, *História de Nyanjas* (Metangula, 1996), 22.
109 Jonna Katto, "'The *Rainha* Is the Boss!': On Masculinities, Time and Precolonial Women of Authority in Northern Mozambique," *Gender & History*, January 7, 2022, 12.

that we largely lack the sources to answer this question conclusively. Almost all we have are either observations made by outside male observers from patriarchal societies at a time when the slave trade had been raging for decades, or retrospective memories influenced by the norms of the time of their recollection. Above, I highlighted the namelessness of Chingomanje's sisters in this regard. Still, there is some evidence that European visitors misunderstood female (political) authority if they found it and thus contributed from the outset to who was eligible to be considered a political authority and who not. For example, when the Anglican bishop Smythies visited Unango in 1887, Chief Kalanje, his "ideal" conversation partner, was absent. Instead, it was a woman who welcomed the bishop in Kalanje's place. Smythies perceived this woman, who remained nameless in his account, to be such "a very superior woman for this country," and to be able to speak so "well" that he felt the need to "congratulate" her on being able to do so.[110]

We can be quite certain that this woman Smythies met was part of Unango's chiefly matrilineage. Symthies' statement can be read as clear evidence of the authority female members of this lineage enjoyed at the time. However, since the encounter took place in the midst of the slave trade, we can also note that the trade may have weakened this authority at this point, but evidently had not yet broken it. It can also be asserted that the slave trade obviously did not break the matrilineal system of succession, even if this does not mean that some slave traders did not attempt to do so.[111]

In any case, the acquisition of slaves might have allowed Chingomanje not only to rearrange his position in the matriliny but also to increase his following to secure his position against his external rivals such as Makanjira and Mataka. Moreover, we can assume that the slaves also had economic functions to fulfill, namely to help provide provisions and infrastructure for the slave trade.[112] The importance of mobilizing labor in this regard is suggested by the fact that the supply of labor in Nkholongue was obviously not as abundant and cheap as one might be-

---

110 AUMCA, A1(V)A Printed Matters, f. 19: Charles Alan Smythies, *A Journey from Zanzibar to Lake Nyassa and Back, in the Year 1887* (Westminster: UMCA, n.d.), 12. For the description of the same meeting in his diary/report of the journey, see: AUMCA, A1(V)B, f. 368–404: Charles Alan Smythies, [Diary/Report of Bishop Smythies' Third Visit to Nyasa (July to Sept.)] (Likoma, 1887), f. 397.
111 It must be noted in this regard that powerful women were obviously also involved in the slave trade and tried to use this to their benefit. See: Benigna Zimba, "Memories of Slave Trade and Slavery Achivanjila I and the Making of the Niassa Slave Routes," in *Slave Routes and Oral Tradition in Southeastern Africa*, ed. Benigna Zimba, Edward Alpers, and Allen Isaacman (Maputo, 2005).
112 It should also be noted in this context that Abdallah did not describe the enlargement of the lineage as a motive for the purchase of slaves in his history of the Wayao. Rather, he wrote that the Wayao took some of the slaves "to the coast to buy trade-goods with them, others they kept at home to hoe the gardens, build houses, and do other village work." See: Abdallah, *The Yaos*, 31.

lieve. Thus, while the missionaries of UMCA were easily able to get the permission to settle in Nkholongue for free, they had much more trouble in getting workers, at least at the price the missionaries were willing to pay for them.[113]

Caravans heavily depended on the ability to refit with sufficient food provisions. This might even have constituted a central reason that important slave routes crossed the lake at all (apart from the fact that the journey across the lake marked a clear watershed between the slave's point of origin and their new destiny). The availability of food was at that time much better at the lake than elsewhere, as Albrecht Roscher had also noted in the letter quoted earlier (see p. 63). The Zanzibar-based missionary Horace Waller explained the importance of the lake in this regard by saying, "if [the slave dealers] do not refit at Lake Nyassa, where food is always to be procured, the slaves will starve on their way to the coast."[114] In his reminiscences, W.P. Johnson explicitly mentioned that the organization of caravans in Nkholongue included not only the collection of slaves but also the procurement of provisions for the journey.[115] With year-round water and abundant fishing grounds, the lake offered natural advantages in this regard, but still required the necessary human labor to make effective use of them.

Given these different functions for slaves, we can assume that the status of different slaves in the village also varied significantly. Furthermore, people's unfree status was not necessarily definite and not necessarily hereditary. Rather, there seem to have existed significant possibilities for social mobility. Writing about the region in general, W.P. Johnson stated that slave men who married women of the chief's family were already regarded as "free people," and so were children born to men of the chief's kindred by slave wives.[116]

However, the prospects for such mobility may often not have been so certain. The evidence suggests that the boundaries between slaves in transit and slaves settled permanently were fairly fluid. Thus, in an encounter that George Swinny had in a neighboring village of Nkholongue in 1886, a slave begged Swinny to convey

---

113 AUMCA, TC/G: George H. Swinny, "Nyasaland Diaries (1884–1887), Vol. II," 54. My own observations in this regard confirm those of Michelle Liebst, who has highlighted the importance that the procuring of labor had in the everyday life of missionaries of the UMCA at Zanzibar. See: Michelle Liebst, "African Workers and the Universities' Mission to Central Africa in Zanzibar, 1864–1900," *Journal of Eastern African Studies* 8, no. 3 (2014): 366–381.
114 Royal Commission on Fugitive Slaves, *Report of the Commissioners, Minutes of the Evidence, and Appendix, with General Index of Minutes of Evidence and Appendix: Presented to Both Houses of Parliament by Command of Her Majesty* (London, 1876), 39.
115 Johnson, *African Reminiscences*, 145.
116 William Percival Johnson, *Nyasa. The Great Water* (1922; repr., New York: Negro Universities Press, 1969), 22. See also: "Marriages," *Likoma Diocesan Quarterly Paper* (*LDQP*), no. 12 (July 1906): 306.

him to Nkhotakota. Swinny noted in his diary that he "could only tell him to be a good servant to his master then he w[ould] not be so likely to be sold."[117] The missionary Duff MacDonald similarly pointed to this possibility of sale at any time when he described the use of slaves in the lake region:

> The male slaves [the chief or headman] employs in farming, building, making baskets, sewing garments, and such masculine pursuits. He keeps all these persons strictly at their duties, and at the same time welcomes an opportunity of selling them at a profit. The gain thus realised he lays out in purchasing more people.[118]

Most caravans did not resemble a sealed truckload that was packed at the point of departure and only opened at the destination. Rather, their composition changed on the way. W.P. Johnson stated that slaves who were transported across the lake "might be sold anywhere on the long way down to the coast, where there was a demand for them and means to buy them."[119] Similarly, published freed-slave accounts suggest that many slaves "passed through a number of hands, several changing owners three or four times before reaching the coast."[120]

As for their daily duties, many slaves seem to have had roles best described by the term "serfs." For, while we have no reliable information in this respect for the specific situation in Nkholongue, in Nkhotakota, "slaves" were said to be able to cultivate their own fields, but had to pay 25 percent of their harvest to their owner.[121] Similarly, for the lake area in general, Johnson stated that slaves were expected to grow their own food, but that their masters were able to claim as much of their harvest as they wanted to.[122] He further noted that they could also be obliged to work in their master's field.[123]

Against the image of the "slavery-to-kinship continuum," social stratification in Nkholongue seems to have been significant in general. While some slaves might have been integrated into the free kinship units rather quickly, others were undoubtedly a different "class" of people. Thus, Johnson once heard Chingomanje bargain with a Swahili trader about "hides with two legs (i.e. slaves), and

---

117 AUMCA, TC/G: George H. Swinny, "Nyasaland Diaries (1884–1887), Vol. II," 73; AUMCA, A1(VI)A, f. 1270–1293: Letter from George Swinny to W.H. Penney (Isle of Likoma, May 15, 1886), f. 1281.
118 Duff MacDonald, *Africana; or the Heart of Heathen Africa: Vol. I—Native Customs and Beliefs* (London: Simpkin Marshall, 1882), 147.
119 Johnson, *African Reminiscences*, 90.
120 Alpers, *Ivory & Slaves*, 241.
121 Sim, Arthur Fraser, "A Letter from Kota-Kota," *CA* 13 (1895): 35. See as well: Sim, *Life and Letters*, 136.
122 Johnson, *The Great Water*, 54.
123 Johnson, 36.

hides with four legs (i.e. goats)."¹²⁴ Nkholongue's social stratification is also evident from the way Johnson described the procedure of his regular visits to Nkholongue in 1888:

> Chingomanje's is the next village after Messumba. There we have now preaching at [Chingomanje's] verandah or wherever the King's court follows him. The audience is not numerous things [sic]. They are on a small scale except the heap of stones where I have another preaching for the Anyanja part of the village.¹²⁵

While Johnson portrayed the social structure of Nkholongue largely in binary terms, we can assume that this was in reality somewhat more complex. As for the region in general, Johnson stated that each village was constituted by people from "four classes." The first class consisted of the chief's kindred, the second were other "weaker free people" who had taken shelter with him, the third were temporary inhabitants like traders, and the fourth slaves.¹²⁶ We can assume that "free people" beyond the chiefly lineage were present in Nkholongue. Thus, some of my interviewees emphasized that their ancestors had not been slaves even though they came from Nkhotakota. As people were generally reluctant to tell me about the slave status of their ancestors, we have to be very cautious with such claims.¹²⁷ But, some of the indications from the interviews in this regard fit surprisingly well with documentary evidence. One interviewee, for example, portrayed his ancestor as an independent skipper of a dhow. According to his statement, Nkholongue belonged to his ancestor and Chingomanje was just taking care of the place for him.¹²⁸ While there is little reason to doubt Chingomanje's political authority over Nkholongue, the independence of the captains of the dhows is clearly supported by other evidence. Thus, Johnson recounted in his memoirs that the skipper of one of the dhows coming to Nkholongue had once gone "on strike with his crew, because the Chief at Unango had paid them too little money!"¹²⁹

---

124 William P. Johnson, "More about the Yaos," *TNN*, no. 3 (February 1894): 78. For other description of the same scene, see: Johnson, *African Reminiscences*, 145; Johnson, "Mohammedanism on Lake Nyasa (1st Part)," *CA* 18, no. 208 (1900), 54.
125 It is "Sumba" and "Nyasa" (instead of "Anyanja") in the original. See: AUMCA, A1(VI)B, f. 233–240: Letter from William P. Johnson to W.H. Penney (1888), f. 233–234.
126 Johnson, *The Great Water*, 21–22.
127 See for example: PA, I093: interview with *P0050* (♂, ~1922) (Nkholongue, January 19, 2016), min 00:08:00–00:09:19.
128 PA, I128: interview with *P1426* (♂, 1929) (Malindi (Mangochi District, Malawi), May 28, 2016), min 00:02:11–00:05:24, 00:27:00–00:31:32, 01:42:07–01:50:59.
129 It is "Unangu" in the original. See: Johnson, *African Reminiscences*, 141.

As for the proportions of the four classes, Johnson stated that they varied from village to village, but that in the villages of the Wayao the non-slaves were usually very few. Johnson noted that the social structure of the Yao villages resembled that of Nkhotakota in this regard.[130] For there, the missionary Arthur Fraser Sim estimated that about three quarters of the population were serfs.[131] This also seems to be a figure that approximately matches the genealogical data from the village surveys.[132]

In light of this ratio, we have to ask how the slaves were made to stay with their owners? Certainly, we must consider direct force. Nkholongue's elite possessed guns, and the village was surrounded by a stockade. We can suspect that the stockade around Nkholongue was not only built to keep possible enemies out, but also to keep possible fugitives in. Johnson explicitly mentioned that Chingomanje had "trusty overseers."[133] But there were yet other factors that prevented slaves from running away. Slaves often had nowhere to go. Many lost their "free home" when they were enslaved or never had one as they were already born as slaves. Furthermore, being transported across the lake had more or less cut the cord to their former homes.

In addition, it is important in this regard to recall that the boundaries between slaves in transit and permanently settled slaves seem to have been fluid. Staying with a reasonably good master might have been the best option they had, as this offered them at least some sort of protection and prevented them from the alternative of being sold to the coast. There is no doubt that, as in other regions of Africa, the threat of sale "had operated as an important mechanism of social control over slaves."[134] As will be argued in Chapter 4, the end of this threat greatly loosened the control of masters over their slaves.

2.5 Conclusion

This chapter has shown how the advance of the slave trade led to the formation of Nkholongue. I have thereby attempted to draw attention to understudied processes

---

130 Johnson, *The Great Water*, 21–22.
131 Sim, Arthur Fraser, "A Letter from Kota-Kota," *CA* 13 (1895): 35.
132 For an approximate idea, see Table 15 on p. 410.
133 Johnson, *African Reminiscences*, 145.
134 Robin Law refers here to the threat of "overseas sales." However, he also suggests that this can be said for sales in general. See: Robin Law, ed., *From Slave Trade to "Legitimate" Commerce: The Commercial Transition in Nineteenth-Century West Africa* (Cambridge: Cambridge University Press, 1995), 16.

that were triggered by this global trade at the micro-level inside the African continent. The first inhabitants of what was to become the village of Nkholongue certainly did not know anything about India's taste for clove or about sugar production in Brazil, but it was essentially such realities at such distant places that across a good many chain links set the stage for the formation of their little village. And what happened in this little village also contributed—even though in this case it is barely measurable—to the realities far away.

The chapter has further contributed to deepening our knowledge of the slave trade in the Lake Malawi region by shedding light on the cooperation and rivalries of different rulers involved in the slave trade and in particular by highlighting the previously ignored role of the Wayao of Unango as allies of Nkhotakota on the eastern side of the lake. Several findings in this chapter also contribute to the history of the slave trade and slavery in Africa as a whole. Let me highlight four of them:

First, this chapter has shown that the purchase of slaves indeed seems to have worked as a means of enlarging one's kinship unit and rearranging one's position in the unit, confirming basic assumptions of the "slavery-to-kinship continuum." However, I have also emphasized the violent nature of the process. In particular, I have stressed that the idea of straightforward integration should beware of the danger of *ex post facto* reconstruction, by underlining that the path of integration was apparently often uncertain in light of the continuing possibility of being sold. The formation of Nkholongue clearly illustrates that the processes that triggered the demand for slavery inside and outside the continent cannot be neatly separated.

Second, this chapter has also provided evidence to challenge ideas of the absoluteness and unilinearity of kinship integration. As has been stated, the descendants of both slave traders and slaves were generally reluctant to talk about this history in detail. This largely corresponds with the experiences of other scholars in other areas of Africa.[135] However, like Cooper's informant on the Kenyan coast,[136] all my interviews informed me openly about their ancestor's origin on the other side of the lake. Following Cooper, the very recollection of these places of origin can be read as an element of the slaves' cultural resistance to being absorbed and assimilated.[137] In this sense, Orlando Patterson's "social death" was ob-

---

135 Examples include that of Jaap van Velsen among the Lakeside Tonga and that of Kristin Mann in Lagos. See: Velsen, *The Politics of Kinship*, 256–257; Mann, *Slavery and the Birth of an African City*, 18. See as well: Martin A. Klein, "Studying the History of Those Who Would Rather Forget: Oral History and the Experience of Slavery," *History in Africa* 16 (1989): 209–217.
136 Cooper, *Plantation Slavery on the East Coast of Africa*, 240–241.
137 Cooper, "The Problem of Slavery in African Studies," 124–125.

viously never complete in the case of Nkholongue.[138] This becomes even more evident if one considers the processes of cultural assimilation of Nkholongue's chiefly lineage to the village's majority slave population in the long run (see especially Chapter 3 in this regard).

Third, this chapter has demonstrated that Nkholongue was not only a location of the slave trade, but that the slave trade engraved itself into the very fabric of Nkholongue's "villageness." This points to the general need to reflect more about the short- and long-term effects of the slave trade on such micro-levels of society usually associated with intimacy. As a reloading point in the slave trade, Nkholongue was certainly a particular setting in this regard. However, the usual focus on the slave trade tends to disguise the large number of slaves kept inside the African continent.[139]

Finally, I hope that this chapter has provided a reasonable basis for understanding that many of the more recent twists and turns of Nkholongue's history lose weight when analyzed without considering the implications of the village's emergence as a result of the slave trade. At various points in this book, we will see how incorporating this knowledge can both complicate and enhance our analysis of various processes. In the next chapter, for example, we will discuss the ways in which Islamization may have facilitated the changes in Nkholongue's social structure that were necessitated by the approaching end of the slave trade. In Chapter 4, we will use Nkholongue's origins in the slave trade as a starting point to reflect that colonization may have been perceived differently by different people in the village. While in Chapter 10, we will see that the knowledge of the village's formation not only challenges the idea of "traditional authorities" as a legitimate grassroots institution, but is also still used by villagers to question the legitimacy of Nkholongue's elite.

---

[138] This insight of course also connects to works of various scholars who have shown how cultural resistance survived the passage across the Atlantic. For an overview, see: Lisa A. Lindsay, "Slavery, Absorption, and Gender: Frederick Cooper and the Power of Comparison," *History in Africa* 47 (2020): 65–74.

[139] In relation to the Lake Malawi region, the British "lay" ethnologist Hugh Stannus guessed that most slaves were kept in the region and only a minority sold. See: Hugh Stannus, "The Wayao of Nyasaland," in *Varia Africana III*, ed. E. A. Hooton and Natica I. Bates (Cambridge: The African Department of the Peabody Museum of Harvard University, 1922), 280.

3 Christianity's Double: Islamization as Slave Emancipation

3.1 Chiefs as Key Players?

Today, Nkholongue's population is almost exclusively Muslim. However, the spread of Islam in Nkholongue only began after the first attempts by Anglican missionaries to gain a foothold in the village. Or, as one interviewee put it:

> Here, there was no Islam. Islam arrived belatedly. Here, there was the religion of Christianity.[1]

The focus of this chapter is on the analysis of Islam's initial spread in the village during the 1890s. Most scholars who have conducted research on Islamization in the Lake Malawi region have claimed that the chiefs were key players in the initial spread of Islam. In this chapter, this argument will be examined critically.

The case of Nkholongue is particularly interesting with regard to this question since contemporary witness accounts of the situation in Nkholongue and some neighboring villages served as central evidence for the argument that Islamization had been driven by the chiefs. This chapter shows that our microhistorical lens challenges the previous reading of these sources. It will thus be argued that far from being a simple top-down process, the spread of Islam in Nkholongue should be interpreted as an Islamization that was at least partly driven from below. With this observation, my study joins recent scholarship in other rural "out-of-the-way" areas of Africa that have equally questioned the elite bias of the previous research on Islamization in these regions.[2] My study, thus, also aims at overcoming the previous focus on Christianity as the central religion of former and freed slaves. It, however, also suggests that, for the region as a whole, we can observe that Christianity and Islam in many ways spread hand in hand and shared a very similar timeline and causality.

Few in-depth studies of the regional history of Islam have been carried out. Most of the publications are articles that draw their arguments mainly from pub-

---

[1] PA, I013: interview with *P0367* (♂, *1936*) (Nkholongue, September 8, 2010), min 00:04:26 – 00:04:47.
[2] Brian Peterson, *Islamization from Below: The Making of Muslim Communities in Rural French Sudan, 1880–1960* (New Haven: Yale University Press, 2011); Felicitas Becker, *Becoming Muslim in Mainland Tanzania 1890–2000* (Oxford: Oxford University Press, 2008); Philip Gooding, "Islam in the Interior of Precolonial East Africa: Evidence from Lake Tanganyika," *The Journal of African History* 60, no. 2 (2019): 191–208.

lished sources.³ Exceptions include the works of Robert Greenstein and Alan Thorold who have both undertaken extensive fieldwork in Malawi. However, their PhD theses remain unpublished.⁴ While globally there is an increasing interest in the study of Islam, this does not yet seem to have reached the region. Most inquiries into the topic have been carried out between 1970 and 2000. Liazzat Bonate's more recent work on Islam in northern Mozambique focuses on the coastline of the Indian Ocean and does not really take developments in Niassa into consideration.⁵

Scholars have typically explained the spread of Islam around the shores of Lake Malawi as having had multiple phases with distinct agents, motives, and target groups. There is more or less an agreement on the course of events in the initial phase, during which Islam's presence was felt above all in Swahili trading centers like Nkhotakota. During this phase, local chiefs began to adapt cultural signs of Swahili coast life. Later, the first slave-trading chiefs of the Wayao converted to Islam, probably under the influence of Swahili scribes they had employed. Edward Alpers has explained these conversions citing the chiefs' "need for political and ritual legitimisation and [their] desire for the regularisation of their economic ties with Zanzibar and the advantages offered to this end by the attainment of literacy in Arabic script."⁶ Makanjira III is said to have become a Muslim around 1870, Mataka II in the 1880s.⁷

These chiefs seem to have adapted Islam only as court religion. It was only after 1890 that Islam's spread began to "take off," as Edward Alpers has put it.⁸ From then onward, however, Islam spread rapidly first and foremost among the Wayao and on such a scale that being a Muslim was soon the identity mark of being a Yao. The moment of Islamization among the Wayao is surprising: though

---

3 Edward A. Alpers, "Towards a History of the Expansion of Islam in East Africa: The Matrilineal Peoples of the Southern Interior," in *The Historical Study of African Religion*, ed. Terence O. Ranger and Isaria N. Kimambo (London: Heinemann, 1972), 172–201; Edward A. Alpers, "East Central Africa," in *The History of Islam in Africa*, ed. Nehemia Levtzion and Randall L. Pouwels (Athens: Ohio University Press, 2000), 303–325; David S. Bone, "An Outline History of Islam in Malawi," in *Malawi's Muslims: Historical Perspectives*, ed. David S. Bone (Blantyre: CLAIM, 2000), 13–26; Augustine W.C. Msiska, "The Spread of Islam in Malawi and Its Impact on Yao Rites of Passage, 1870–1960," *The Society of Malawi Journal* 48, no. 1 (1995): 1995–1995; David S. Bone, "Islam in Malawi," *Journal of Religion in Africa* 13 (1982): 126–138.
4 Thorold's thesis is available. In Greenstein's case it is not even certain whether he finished it. For Thorold's thesis, see: Alan Thorold, "The Yao Muslims: Religion and Social Change in Southern Malawi" (PhD thesis, Cambridge, Churchill College, 1995).
5 Liazzat Bonate, "Islam in Northern Mozambique: A Historical Overview," *History Compass* 8, no. 7 (2010): 573–593.
6 Alpers, "Towards a History of the Expansion of Islam in East Africa," 192.
7 Alpers, 182–185; Bone, "An Outline History of Islam in Malawi," 15.
8 Alpers, "East Central Africa," 309.

they had had trade contacts with Muslim societies for centuries, it was only in the very last decade of the 19th century that Islam began to take a foothold among them. Even more surprising is that it seems that Islam's "take off" began almost concurrently with the military efforts of the British troops to stop the slave trade. Scholars have, thus, highlighted the seemingly paradoxical "fact that the popular spread of Islam took place at a time when the secular advantages of becoming a Muslim were fast disappearing."[9] This late spread of Islam is all the more surprising given that there were already numerous Christian missionaries active in the region who had responded to Livingstone's call for "Christianity and Commerce."[10]

The overriding question is why so many people of the region converted to Islam at precisely that seemingly disadvantageous moment of time when they could have done so before. Answers to this question differ on the basis of what place and time one focuses on. While, for example, David Bone, Alan Thorold, and Edward Alpers have set the beginning of the popular spread in the years before the slavers' defeat around 1895, Robert Greenstein has placed this clearly after it.[11] Furthermore, while Bone and Thorold have had rather clear-cut opinions on the course of it, Edward Alpers has been much more ambiguous on the importance of different factors.[12] What most of them have in common is that they have described Islam as spreading downwards from the chiefs to their subjects, at least in an initial phase.[13] It is only Greenstein who has placed the emphasis on different actors. But let us have a closer look at the different explanations.

---

9 McCracken, *A History of Malawi 1859–1966*, 101.
10 Few colonies in Africa witnessed such a density of different Christian actors of different denominations as Nyasaland has. One has to imagine that "[o]n the eve of the First World War, missionaries in Nyasaland numbered around 200, compared with only 107 planters and 100 government officials." See: McCracken, 108.
11 Bone, "Islam in Malawi," 128; Thorold, "The Yao Muslims," 123–28; Alpers, "East Central Africa," 307–8; Robert Greenstein, "The Nyasaland Government's Policy Towards African Muslims, 1900–25," in *From Nyasaland to Malawi: Studies in Colonial History*, ed. Roderick J. Macdonald (Nairobi: East African Publishing House, 1975), 145.
12 Alpers, "Towards a History of the Expansion of Islam in East Africa," 188–189.
13 Bone, "Islam in Malawi," 128; Bone, "An Outline History of Islam in Malawi," 16; Thorold, "The Yao Muslims," 123–128; Alan Thorold, "Yao Conversion to Islam," *Cambridge Anthropology* 12, no. 2 (1987): 24; Alpers, "Towards a History of the Expansion of Islam in East Africa," 188; Msiska, "The Spread of Islam in Malawi," 79; McCracken, *A History of Malawi 1859–1966*, 105; Liazzat Bonate, "Islam and the Yao," Oxford Islamic Studies Online, accessed May 22, 2018, http://www.oxfordisla micstudies.com/article/opr/t343/e0055?_hi=0&_pos=1; Lena Eile, *Jando: The Rite of Circumcision and Initiation in East African Islam* (Lund: Plus Ultra, 1990), 81–83; Manuel Gomes da Gama Amaral, *O povo Yao = Mtundu Wayao: Subsídios para o estudo de um povo do noroeste de Moçambique* (Lisboa: IICT, 1990), 378. For recent reproductions of this argument, see: Signe Arnfred, "Implications of

Bone and Thorold have highlighted the reasoning of the old political elite who saw their economic position endangered by the activities of the British. They have argued that the old elite saw Islamization as a political and moral means to counteract the imposition of colonial rule.[14] According to this interpretation, Islamization was thought to strengthen the bonds between the local slave-trading chiefs and their Swahili trading partners. They have further argued that the military defeat of the chiefs did not stop the spread of Islam, but instead further strengthened its hold on the Wayao, as "[l]ed by their chiefs many Yao communities embraced Islam the more firmly as a way of asserting their tribal and cultural identity in the face of European domination."[15]

Alpers and Msiska have remained somewhat less specific about the motives behind the popular spread of Islam by highlighting the different opinions of contemporary observers.[16] Based on remarks by Ian Linden, Alpers has, for example, supposed that the immediate threat of European dominance exacerbated social tensions and led to a rapid proliferation of (Islamic) magical charms and talismans which might have given the people a semblance of security.[17] But, while Alpers has highlighted very different factors for and agents of Islamization, he has ultimately come to the same conclusion that the internal agents of change "were first and foremost the great Yao and Makua chiefs."[18]

Greenstein is the only one where chiefs play a rather minor role. He divided the expansion of Islam in present day Malawi into two phases: the first phase was pre-colonial and concentrated on the chiefs of the Wayao, and the second was colonial. In Greenstein's argumentation, it was only after colonization that the popular spread of Islam effectively began. Greenstein argued that the major cause for this popular spread "was the charisma and initiative" of itinerant Muslim preachers. It is noteworthy that Greenstein classified the origins of these preachers as "insiders" of newly Islamized societies on the one hand and non-elites on the other, saying that "[t]hough the agents of change would have to be regarded as elites, they

---

Matriliny: Gender and Islam in Northern Mozambique," *International Feminist Journal of Politics* 23, no. 2 (2021): 224–225; Katto, *Women's Lived Landscapes of War and Liberation in Mozambique*, 23–24.

14 Bone, "Islam in Malawi," 128; Thorold, "The Yao Muslims," 123–128.
15 Bone, "Islam in Malawi," 128–129.
16 Alpers, "Towards a History of the Expansion of Islam in East Africa," 188–189.
17 Alpers, 189.
18 Alpers, 193.

were also local men of peasant origin which was significant in that their effort were directed entirely at the peasant village level."[19]

Thorold has criticized Greenstein for his argumentation rather strongly, stating that Greenstein's view was an inevitable result of his dependence on oral history interviews with Muslim clergymen, which led Greenstein to portray Islam's history in the region as "a sort of hagiography."[20] Thorold did not deny the growing influence of this individual figures for later periods, but remained convinced that "it was the strategies of the chiefs rather than the proselytising efforts of the sheikhs that was responsible for the major Yao conversions to Islam."[21] But, as we will now see, events in Nkholongue seem to have resembled Greenstein's model rather than Thorold's. It thereby needs to be highlighted that this conclusion draws only partially on oral history evidence. It is based mainly on the same evidence Thorold has used himself, but this time read and interpreted differently, namely using our microhistorical lens.

In what follows, we will first look at the early history of the Anglican Mission in Nkholongue, as understanding this history will facilitate the subsequent analysis of early Islamization in Nkholongue.

3.2 The Anglican Mission in Nkholongue

As pointed out in the introduction of this book, Nkholongue was one of the first targets of the UMCA in its second attempt to gain a foothold in the Lake Malawi region. In contrast to their initial unsuccessful attempt in Magomero in the 1860s, the missionaries could now rely on a growing presence of Europeans on the western and southern sides of the lake. Furthermore, they were also better prepared. To counter the problems of the earlier attempt, the UMCA's missionaries now relied on a more mobile and secure base for their evangelism: the steamboat.[22] This combination of technology and Christianization has been aptly analyzed by Charles Good in his *The Steamer Parish*.[23]

---

19 Robert Greenstein, "Shayks and Tariqas: The Early Muslim 'Ulama' and Tariqa Development in Malawi, c.1885–1949 (CC/H/429/76)," in *History Seminar Papers 1976/77* (Chancellor College, Zomba, 1976), 1.
20 Thorold, "The Yao Muslims," 133.
21 Thorold, 133.
22 "The Bishop's Departure for Africa: Farewell Meeting and Services," *CA* 2, no. 14 (February 1884): 24–25; "Steamer for Lake Nyassa," *CA* 2, no. 14 (February 1884): 21; William Percival Johnson, "A Letter from the Rev. W. P. Johnson," *CA* 2, no. 16 (April 1884): 56–59.
23 Good, *The Steamer Parish*.

Nkholongue was to become a prime visiting place for the mission's steamers. The fact that Nkholongue was a hub for the slave trade did not deter the missionaries. Rather, it more than appealed to their ideas of working in the midst of the slave trade. Already then, "poverty" and "moral injustices" were as much a marketing instrument as they are in today's development industry.[24] Even if being ideologically on opposite corners, the slave traders and the missionaries were looking for the same thing in many ways: anchorage was something the mission's steamers needed as much as the slaver's dhows. Consequently, the missionaries praised the "excellent harbour" in Nkholongue.[25] Both the slave traders and the missionaries were dependent on a sufficient supply of food and workers. Here, again, the slave trading centers seemed to be equally promising to the missionaries.[26] The latter also highlighted the house-building capacities in Nkholongue, which had apparently been influenced by Swahili techniques.[27] Another factor concerned language. The missionaries, having their headquarters at Zanzibar, were delighted to find a good many Kiswahili speakers in the village.[28] Last but not least, the concentration of the houses, which was a direct result of the slave trade, must have been a great attraction for the missionaries as it facilitated missionary work immensely. In many respects, the UMCA's missionaries were thus looking for exactly that which the slave trade had itself equally either sought or brought there.

One of the leading missionaries on the lake, George Swinny, was especially taken with Nkholongue's chief. In May 1886, after several short visits to the place, he wrote back home stating he was on "excellent terms" with him.[29] In November 1886, Swinny and his wife decided to rent two houses in the village and to settle there for the coming months.[30] The station at Nkholongue should have paved the way to opening communications with Unango.[31] But Swinny's stay in Nkholongue turned out to be much too short for such an aim. Hardly begun, it ended

---

[24] Note for example that the missionaries' settling at Nkholongue was described by W.P. Johnson as "one of the most chivalrous efforts" of the mission: Johnson, *African Reminiscences*, 141. See also: Chauncy Maples, "Two Sonnets," *CA* 5, no. 56 (1887): 119.
[25] AUMCA, TC/G: George H. Swinny, "Nyasaland Diaries (1884–1887), Vol. I," 110.
[26] AUMCA, TC/G: George H. Swinny, "Nyasaland Diaries (1884–1887), Vol. II," 54.
[27] Bellingham, *Diary of a Working Man*, 81.
[28] AUMCA, A1(VI)A, f. 946–949: Letter from William Bellingham to W.H. Penney ([Likoma], October 1, 1885), 80. For the knowledge of Swahili, see also: AUMCA, TC/G: George H. Swinny, "Nyasaland Diaries (1884–1887), Vol. I," 111.
[29] AUMCA, A1(VI)A, f. 1270–1293: Letter from George Swinny to W.H. Penney (Isle of Likoma, May 15, 1886).
[30] AUMCA, A1(VI)A, f. 1374: [George H. Swinny], "Postscript," November 29, 1886; AUMCA, TC/G: George H. Swinny, "Nyasaland Diaries (1884–1887), Vol. III," 22–23.
[31] "The Charles Janson," *CA* 4, no. 45 (1886): 134.

abruptly. By the end of January 1887, Swinny suffered a severe attack of fever and had to be evacuated to the Scottish Mission at Bandawe on the other side of the lake. There, he died on February 13, 1887.[32]

We know little about the religious impact of Swinny's work in Nkholongue, but we can assume that it was limited.[33] During his stay in Nkholongue, he had started a small school for boys and began to preach regularly to the people of the village. His school was attended by approximately ten pupils.[34] After Swinny's death, the school was temporarily carried on by W.P. Johnson.[35] The mission's steamer continued to visit the place on a regular basis for about three years.[36] In 1888, Johnson described his visits in Nkholongue as follows:

> [D]o not let any false ideas of Christian affection be imputed to this very heathen village. [...] I generally speak at the chief's verandah, and again on a heap of stones, to an Anyanja class. The most hopeful man is one who is sorely afflicted.[37]

After Swinny's death, the missionaries' relationship with Chingomanje began to quickly deteriorate. Johnson was much less favorable toward Chingomanje than Swinny, and Chingomanje had clearly preferred Swinny. This was apparently owing to Swinny's liberality in giving presents to facilitate evangelism.[38] This also comes out in Johnson's description of Chingomanje's reaction to the news of Swinny's death. Johnson reported that Chingomanje remained silent for a moment and then only asked:

> Well, has the musical-box which he promised me arrived?[39]

---

32 R. M. H., "In Memoriam – George Hervey Swinny," *CA* 5, no. 55 (July 1887): 97–99; Bellingham, *Diary of a Working Man*, 123.
33 Oral history did not reveal anything in this respect. Today's villagers seem to have never heard of Swinny.
34 AUMCA, TC/G: George H. Swinny, "Nyasaland Diaries (1884–1887), Vol. III."
35 Johnson, *African Reminiscences*, 143–44; Bellingham, *Diary of a Working Man*, 124. It is not clear for how long the school was exactly continued. Johnson writes of a "native teacher" that was put there, but this most probably does not refer to the 1880s, but to the late 1890s and thus the mission's second attempt to gain a foothold in Nkholongue. See: Johnson, *African Reminiscences*, 146; Johnson, "Mohammedanism on Lake Nyasa (1st Part)," *CA* 18, no. 208 (1900): 56; AUMCA, A1(V)B, f. 368–404: Charles Alan Smythies, [Diary/Report of Bishop Smythies' Third Visit to Nyasa (July to Sept.)] (Likoma, 1887).
36 "News from Lake Nyassa," *CA* 5, no. 53 (May 1887): 67; "Letters from From Rev. W. P. Johnson," *CA* 7, no. 78 (June 1889): 95.
37 It is "Nyassa" (instead of "Anyanja") in the original. See: William P. Johnson, "A Bird's-Eye View of Our Nyassa Work," *CA* 6, no. 68 (August 1888): 111.
38 AUMCA, A1(IX), f. 215–216: Letter from Chauncy Maples to W.H. Penney (October 14, [1886]).
39 Johnson, *African Reminiscences*, 146.

Chingomanje's expectation of material gains was most probably not only linked to economic considerations, but also to questions of social status. For one needs to know that Chingomanje had begged Swinny for a musical-box on the foundation that Jumbe had one.[40]

The reason for the deterioration of the relations between the missionaries and Chingomanje must also be understood in the context of the general political developments in the region. As will be discussed in detail in the next chapter, Chingomanje's initial favorable attitude towards the missionaries had also been the result of political considerations: it seems quite certain that he thought that the presence of the Europeans in his village might protect him against attacks from his enemies. In those years, the political situation in the region, however, changed significantly. This had to do, on the one hand, with the arrival of a Portuguese expedition at the south end of the lake, and, on the other, with the developments on the other side of the lake. There, the British secular forces had begun to fight the slave trade actively and militarily. In their policy of *divide et impera*, the British forces started to pay the Jumbe of Nkhotakota an annual "pension" for his allegiance and his promise to stop the slave trade.[41] The reaction of Chingomanje and other Yao chiefs on the east side of the lake was not long in coming: the missionaries were seen as part of the British forces and, thus, not welcomed any more. Various chiefs told the missionaries that they needed to give them "big presents like Jumbe got, or not come here again."[42] Concerning Chingomanje, one missionary wrote in a letter in October 1890:

> Chingomanje has had absurd ideas of his right and importance instilled into him by coast men. He hears all about Jumbe's pension (£300 a year), and not altogether unnaturally thinks he is slighted, for religious prospect he has none. I shall be deeply grieved if all these Yaos have to be added to the impassable land south [...].[43]

---

[40] AUMCA, TC/G: George H. Swinny, "Nyasaland Diaries (1884–1887), Vol. II," 56. It is noteworthy that musical boxes seem to have been a prime desire among the slave traders of the lake area. See: Ian Linden, "Mponda Mission Diary, 1889–1891. Part III: A Portuguese Mission in British Central Africa," *The International Journal of African Historical Studies* 7, no. 4 (1974): 726; Ian Linden, *Catholics, Peasants, and Chewa Resistance in Nyasaland: 1889–1939* (Berkeley: University of California Press, 1974), 23.

[41] The subsidy was first paid by the African Lakes Company, but then overtaken by the British Government. See: McCracken, *A History of Malawi 1859–1966*, 58.

[42] "Our Post Bag: Extracts from Dr. Hine's Letter," *CA* 8, no. 90 (June 1890): 96.

[43] It is "Chingomanji" in the original. See: George Sheriff, "A Letter from Mr. Sheriff, Captain of the 'Charles Janson.,'" *CA* 9, no. 99 (March 1891): 38.

Again, we can observe the importance Chingomanje assigned to questions of status. Jumbe was clearly his central point of reference. But Jumbe's agreement with the British forces endangered Chingomanje's income from the slave trade without giving him anything in return.[44] When the missionaries later made another effort to find an agreement with Chingomanje, they found Nkholongue "thronged with coast people."[45] Nkholongue now made such a hostile impression on the missionaries that one of their companions went back to the steamer to get his revolver. No agreement was reached with Chingomanje, and when the missionaries returned to the steamer the Swahili traders present are said to have audibly asked: "Are they letting the Europeans off?"[46]

For the next years, the missionaries were excluded from Nkholongue. Chingomanje's annoyance about the British threatening his trading activities was certainly a reason for his exclusion of the missionaries. There is no doubt that he felt highly discriminated against in comparison to Jumbe. But we can also note that, with the shifting power balance on the lake, Chingomanje may have put his faith increasingly into other groups. In relation to this, we will discuss the role of the Portuguese expedition in the next chapter. Furthermore, we can assume that Swahili traders ("coast men") gained influence over Chingomanje's political reasoning. A further factor in this regard may have been the reaction to colonization by Makanjira, Chingomanje's long-standing enemy.

Makanjira had been hostile towards the Europeans from the outset. Although we have little explicit evidence, it seems likely that the former rival and enemy Makanjira gained, at least temporarily, some political appeal for Chingomanje and other petty slave traders as someone who fought for the old order. After the British forces had been defeated in a first battle at Makanjira's in December 1891, missionary Johnson wrote that "[t]he Yaos are elated, building two new dhows south of Messumba."[47] According to him, the heads of the dead Europeans had been brought as far as Lussefa in order to show them to the people.[48] But such methods doubtlessly did not just attract the chiefs towards Makanjira, but also put pressure on them to not deal with the Europeans. Mkalawili, a Yao chief south of Lussefa, was explicitly summoned by Makanjira to "turn out the *Mzungu* ['white

---

44 According to Bishop Maples, Kalanje stated: "Since all the ivory is getting finished up, pray tell us what we are to do if we don't sell slaves, in order to get cloth and other necessaries from the coast." See: Maples, "Unangu," *TNN*, no. 2 (November 1893): 49.
45 Johnson, *African Reminiscences*, 183.
46 Johnson, 184.
47 It is "M'sumba" in the original. See: William P. Johnson, "The Disaster at Makanjila's," *CA* 10, no. 114 (June 1892): 78.
48 Johnson, *African Reminiscences*, 205.

man']."[49] In November 1890, Johnson wrote that Makanjira was "master of Mkalawili's, Lussefa, Meluluca and almost Chingomanje's," as he had seen him "smash them all" in the previous years.[50] While in another letter he wrote that Makanjira was "eating up" the whole lakeshore including Chingomanje.[51]

But we have to be careful not to overstress Makanjira's influence on Nkholongue and the neighboring villages in terms of both quality and duration. For, as we shall see in the next chapter, Chingomanje, Kalanje, and Mkalawili clearly distanced themselves from his influence before his assassination by one of his own relatives and before the final defeat of his successor against the British in 1894, by sending messengers to the British in early 1893 with the intention of accepting British rule (for details see Chapter 4).[52] It seems that by this time Makanjira had already lost his persuasiveness as an alternative to the British.

The whole episode of the Anglican exclusion is important for the question of Islamization, as it was exactly during that time that Islam began to spread in Nkholongue and the neighboring villages.

3.3 The Spread of Islam

At first glance, some clues seem to support the argument of Islamization having been a conservative means for Chingomanje and other chiefs to counteract the end of the slave-trading era. First and foremost, these come from a two-piece article published in 1900 by W.P. Johnson in the UMCA's monthly magazine *Central Africa* in which he analyzed the spread of Islam in Nkholongue and the neighboring villages.[53] This article was used by various scholars as a central foundation for this "conservative" argument.[54] In the article, Johnson wrote that Islam had not established any foothold in Nkholongue when they started their work there in the

---

49 Herbert Barnes, *Johnson of Nyasaland: A Study of the Life and Work of William Percival Johnson* (Westminster: UMCA, 1933), 124.
50 It is "Mluluka" and "Losefa" in the original. See: Barnes, 89.
51 TNA, FO 84/2021, f. 402: W.P. Johnson to Mr. Buchanan, enclosed in Buchanan (Acting-Consul Central Africa) to Foreign Office (Blantyre, October 18, 1890).
52 For the murder of Makanjira, see: Chauncy Maples, "The Death of Makanjila," *CA* 11, no. 132 (December 1893): 180–181.
53 Johnson, "Mohammedanism on Lake Nyasa (1st Part)," *CA* 18, no. 208 (1900); William P. Johnson, "Mohammedanism on Lake Nyasa (2nd Part)," *CA* 18, no. 209 (1900): 79–82.
54 Thorold, "The Yao Muslims," 122–28; Bone, "Islam in Malawi," 128; S.V. Sicard, "The Arrival of Islam in Malawi and the Muslim Contribution to Development," *Journal of Muslim Minority Affairs* 20, no. 2 (2000): 294; David S. Bone, "Towards a History of Islam in Malawi," in *History Seminar Papers 1982/83* (Chancellor College, Zomba, 1983), 3.

1880s. He stated that the Muslim traders passing through Nkholongue did not proselytize, as "they regarded the ordinary native, not as an object of teaching, but as a two-legged goat wanted as a slave."[55] According to Johnson, it was only during the troubles with Makanjira and the missionaries' exclusion from Nkholongue and the neighboring villages that Islam began to spread like "wild-fire."[56] Johnson stated that the Islamization of the Yao initiation rites was the main means for the spread of Islam, a statement which was taken as an evidence for the key role of the chiefs as they were said to be in control of these rites. In his memoirs, Johnson described the events of that period as follows:

> It was very noticeable how in these years there was a recrudescence of the craze for Mohammedanism. It seemed as if the slavers, checked by the government, were determined to extend their moral force. As always, they used the native attachment to the old Yao initiation dances [...] in order to introduce gradually another dance which was regarded as an initiation into Mohammedanism [...].[57]

Johnson's claims also seem to be supported by the religious geography of the Lago District in the 21st century: while the old slave trading centers south of Metangula, from where the missionaries where excluded during "the troubles,"[58] are today all predominantly Muslim, the villages north of Metangula, and thus the villages which were less involved in the slave trade and to which the missionaries could always go, are all predominantly Christian. The picture becomes even more solidified in light of Johnson's remarks concerning Makanjira's influence over the region. After all, Makanjira was one of the first Yao chiefs to convert to Islam.

However, such a reading of Johnson's writings overlooks the fact that his two-part article is in reality quite ambiguous on the questions of the chiefs' role. It also ignores the fact that precisely in the case of Nkholongue and the neighboring villages there is ample evidence contradicting this interpretation.

We have already seen that Jumbe was a role model for Chingomanje. But this was interestingly not the case with regard to religion. While Jumbe was a Muslim, there is no evidence that Islam had any appeal to Chingomanje. We know that he had welcomed the Anglican missionaries and, in a letter back home, Swinny even wrote that he understood that Chingomanje "had refused some time ago to become a Mussulman."[59] Apparently, there was no mosque or any other outward sign of

---

55 Johnson, "Mohammedanism on Lake Nyasa (1st Part)," *CA* 18, no. 208 (1900): 54.
56 Johnson, "Mohammedanism on Lake Nyasa (1st Part)," *CA* 18, no. 208 (1900): 54.
57 Johnson, *African Reminiscences*, 202.
58 Johnson, "Mohammedanism on Lake Nyasa (1st Part)," *CA* 18, no. 208 (1900): 54.
59 AUMCA, A1(VI)A, f. 1270–1293: Letter from George Swinny to W.H. Penney (Isle of Likoma, May 15, 1886), f. 1291.

Islam in Nkholongue apart from the Muslim traders passing in the caravans when Swinny settled there in the 1880s.

Certainly, there is no doubt that Islam began to gain a foothold in Nkholongue in the 1890s.[60] In his article of 1900, Johnson wrote that there was already a mosque in the village. This is confirmed by a report of the *Companhia do Nyassa*, the Portuguese chartered company that came to occupy "its territory" in the same year.[61] But Johnson's article gives us no explicit evidence that Chingomanje converted to Islam, nor do we learn from it whether it was him who was really responsible for the spread of Islam among his villagers. Rather the opposite was the case, as can be seen from what Johnson wrote about Chingomanje's attachment to Islam:

> [N]ot one of Chingomanje's family really go in for this worship. Those who do are all Amalimba[62] slaves from the other side of the Lake, with a sprinkling of men who have lived at the coast, but of much the same extraction originally, the dhow-builders, &c.[63]

It might have been possible for a scholar interested in Islamization to overlook this section. But it certainly catches the eye of the microhistorian concerned with the village of Nkholongue. Here, the knowledge of Nkholongue's social composition clearly helps us understand what Johnson was actually saying: in the case of Nkholongue, the main practitioners of Islam came precisely from the same people who had constituted Johnson's heap-of-stones-class. They were not only former and current slaves, but also from the village's Chinyanja-speaking majority population. While this observation alone does not yet allow any conclusions to be drawn about the questions of the driving force behind Islamization, it opens up new possible perspectives, at least if one considers that the end of the slave-trading era also endangered Nkholongue's (forced) social cohesion. We can assume that, if Chingomanje had indeed used Islamization as a means to preserve his legitimacy as leader, he would have participated in the worship in order to demonstrate his ritual

---

60 Most reports about this spread were written in retrospective after the missionaries' return to the place. Among the earliest ones is: J.E. Hine, "Work in Nyasaland: Its Prospects and Needs," *CA* 15, no. 180 (1897): 197.
61 AHM, Códice 11–2485: Documento N.° XXXVII: Extractos dos apontamentos particulares do Capitão Trindade dos Santos, relativos estabelecimentos das missões na região do Lago, in *Documentos sobre as Missões Inglesas das Universidades na parte portuguesa da região do Lago Niassa depois da occupação pela Companhia em 1901, Vol. 1*, 58.
62 This refers to the name Marimba, the name of the Nkhotakota area. "Amarimba" translates as people from Marimba. Note that "l" and "r" are interchangeable in Chinyanja/Chichewa.
63 Johnson, "Mohammedanism on Lake Nyasa (1st Part)," *CA* 18, no. 208 (1900): 56–57.

authority. Thus, his absence casts doubt on his assumed key role as an agent of Islamization.

This becomes even more evident when one looks at what Chadreque Umali had to say about Islamization in Nkholongue in his manuscript on the history of the Anyanja in Lago District. Umali's account goes as follows: in the beginning, there were some Anglicans in Nkholongue. But then Salimo, a son of the chief, and his younger brother traveled to Tanzania, where they converted to Islam. Upon their return, they wanted to proselytize in Nkholongue, but Chingomanje firmly refused. However, the two sons took advantage of a moment when their father Chingomanje was absent from the village to recruit boys and initiate them into Islam with the *jando* dance (dance of an initiation rite for boys). When their father came back, there was a fierce quarrel between him and his sons. Eventually, his sons left Nkholongue and settled a little north of the village, on the creek of Malango. Umali's account concludes that from that moment on there were more Muslims than Christians in Nkholongue.[64]

In his introduction, Umali wrote that he received the information about the history of Nkholongue from a person that was originally from Nkholongue but lived around Messumba at the time when Umali spoke to him.[65] We could be skeptical about the factuality of Umali's account, but the story makes a great deal of sense if we cross-check it with other reports: there is no reference to a settlement in Malango in the early reports of the Anglican missionaries.[66] It was in 1900 that Johnson wrote of the spread of Islam in Nkholongue and the villages south of it. It is also shortly afterwards (1901) that Malango makes its first appearance in a written document, namely in the already mentioned report of the *Companhia do Nyassa*. It reads as follows:

> In [Chingomanje's] fields there is yet the settlement of his son, Salimo Chingomanje, on the banks of the river Malango [...].[67]

Obviously, the timing and explicit mentioning of Salimo Chingomanje in this description clearly allows one to back up Umali's story. Chingomanje II bin Mponda

---

64 PA, Chadreque Umali, *História de Nyanjas* (Metangula, 1996), 57–58.
65 PA, Chadreque Umali, *História de Nyanjas* (Metangula, 1996), 2.
66 The 1896 to 1904 logbook of the mission's steamer S.S. CJ makes no reference to Malango for the time before April 1897. Unfortunately, it is empty for the period from April 1897 to November 1902. But from November 1902 onward, it stopped in Malango frequently. See: AUMCA, UX 144: Log Book of S.S. 'Charles Janson', 1896–1904, 35, 37–39, 41–42.
67 AHM, Códice 11–2485: Documento N.° XXXVII: Extractos dos apontamentos particulares do Capitão Trindade dos Santos, relativos estabelecimentos das missões na região do Lago, in *Documentos sobre as Missões Inglesas das Universidades*, 58.

was apparently not only no driving force behind the spread of Islam, but he even seems to have been against it, at least in the beginning.[68] While we cannot know the reasons for this refusal, it needs to be emphasized that Chingomanje was not the only Yao chief of the region who initially refused to become a Muslim. Kalanje did not convert either.[69] He was even said to have "hated" this religion.[70] It was only in the 1910s that his successor became a Muslim.[71]

So if Chingomanje was no key agent of Islamization, who was? Evidently, Salimo Chingomanje played his part in it. But we know very little about him apart from his having gone to the coast and being a son of a Chingomanje. However, in a matrilineal society, being the son of a chief does not necessarily mean anything. Rather the opposite, we can even guess that Salimo might have seen in Islamization an appropriate means to strengthen his status against the matrilineal limitations placed on his position within the village community. Furthermore, we do not know anything about Salimo's mother. In the light of what has been said in the previous chapter, it is very probable that Chingomanje had several wives and that many of them were of slave origin. This, again, would fit Johnson's remark that the main practitioners of Islam in Nkholongue were "Amarimba slaves from the other side of the Lake."[72]

There are many reasons to believe that, in the case of Nkholongue, the people of slave origin were not only the main practitioners of Islam but also important agents of Islamization. In the second, and less noticed part of his 1900 article Johnson stated the following:

> Men who formerly lived here, have been slaves, and in these days have found their way back —old soldiers, indeed—are the moving spirits in the spread of this Mohammedanism. They get young men to "go in" for this new religion; women and family life have no part in the system, nor have chiefs, or indeed any authority.[73]

---

[68] One interviewee explicitly said that the Chingomanje of the time of the Angoni wars—this is Chingomanje II bin M'ponda—had no religion. But he equally asserted that Islam only arrived under the reign of Chingomanje IV Saide Amisse, which in the light of the written documentation is implausible. Therefore, the value of his statement in this respect is questionable. See: PA, I113: interview with *P0367 (♂, 1936)* (Nkholongue, April 13, 2016), min 01:29:56–01:31:01.
[69] Yohanna B. Abdallah, "Letter to the Editor: Unangu, April 9th 1907," *LDQP*, no. 15 (April 1907): 388.
[70] Yohanna B. Abdallah, "News from the Stations: VI. Unangu," *NDC*, no. 42 (January 1914): 13.
[71] Yohanna B. Abdallah, "News from the Stations: VI. Unangu," *NDC*, no. 43 (April 1914): 39; Yohanna B. Abdallah, "News from the Stations: VI. Unangu," *NDC*, no. 45 (October 1914): 98.
[72] Johnson, "Mohammedanism on Lake Nyasa (1st Part)," *CA* 18, no. 208 (1900): 56–57.
[73] Johnson, "Mohammedanism on Lake Nyasa (2nd Part)," *CA* 18, no. 209 (1900): 80.

Note that Johnson mentions not only the importance of former slaves, but also of young men. A very similar depiction of events can be found in a letter that Herbert Barnes, another missionary, sent to his mother in 1899. In it he wrote about Nkholongue and some neighboring villages:

> These villages [...] have fallen under the spell of Islam more or less—that is a good many younger people from here go to the coast where Mohammedans prevail, they come back with just a tincture of Mohammedanism & they call themselves Wa-Islam[74], despise their native & heathen chiefs who are behind the time & play off Islam with its easy creed against the white man [...][75]

Taking Barnes', Johnson's, and Umali's accounts together, we can conclude that the villagers of Nkholongue were not mere receivers of Islam, but it was young men from among their midst who, having been on the coast of the Indian Ocean, brought it back from there. Furthermore, we can observe that these youngsters had a clear motivation to go against the authority of their "traditional" chiefs who according to all these accounts had no part in the spread of Islam, but were instead challenged by it.[76] Furthermore, we can note that at least some of these young men were of a lower social background.

All these characteristics are to some extent personified by Isa Chikoka. According to Greenstein, Chikoka was one of the most important propagators of Islam on the east side of the lake.[77] This is also confirmed by my own interviewees, who remembered him as the most important Muslim figure of the region.[78] Chikoka was originally from Lussefa and, according to Johnson, he was taken prisoner in a raid in 1887 by Makanjira's men when he was still a boy. He was then sold to the coast and came to Zanzibar, where he learned to read Arabic and converted to Islam.

---

74 This means "people of Islam."
75 AUMCA, A1(XII), f. 424–435b: Letter from Herbert Barnes to His Mother (Losefa, December 4, 1899), f. 424.
76 Fabiano Kwaule observed somewhat similar developments with regard to Islamization in Nkhotakota. According to Kwaule, Jumbe recruited sons of Chewa chiefs to convert them to Islam. These young men then "formed the spearhead in the spreading of Islam among the Chewa in Nkhota-kota" and "would very quickly come to look down upon traditional Chewa leadership." See: Fabiano Kwaule, "Kanyenda and the Swahili Challenge," in *Malawi's Muslims: Historical Perspectives*, ed. David S. Bone (Blantyre, 2000), 66.
77 Greenstein, "Shayks and Tariqas," 17.
78 PA, I155: interview with *P0713 (♂, 1944)* (Nkholongue, June 18, 2016), min 00:18:58–00:19:22; PA, I068: interview with *P0367 (♂, 1936)* (Nkholongue, September 2, 2013), min 01:38:26–01:40:42; PA, I016: interview with *P1483 (♀, 1950), P1481 (♂, 1954), P1482 (♂, 1937)* (Lussefa, October 9, 2011), min 00:28:33–00:39:29; PA, I057: interview with *P0262 (♀, ~1940)* (Malango, August 28, 2013), min 01.07:16–01:11:23; PA, I152: interview with *P1476 (♂, ~1935)* (Milombe, June 16, 2016).

Upon his manumission, he returned to the eastern shores of the lake and began to proselytize. It is unclear when exactly Chikoka returned to the region as Johnson mentions his presence only in 1914 for the first time. It is, thus, uncertain whether he had already played a role in the early spread of Islam.[79]

But while Chingomanje quite certainly played no key role in Islam's early spread, it would be wrong to totally ignore the role of the old elites in (consolidating) Islamization. Not all the agents of Islamization were newly converted lower-class men. In the case of Nkholongue, this is best indicated by the fact that Sheik Bwana bin Jafali lived in the village for a while after the initial spread of Islam. Sheik Bwana had been the leading Muslim teacher in Nkhotakota. When Jumbe IV was deposed by the British in 1895, he came to Nkholongue and stayed here for one or two years before he finally went on to live on the coast of the Indian Ocean.[80] The Anglican missionaries did not explicitly accredit him with any greater role in the popular spread of Islam. However, Johnson mentioned that Sheik Bwana had a disciple in Nkholongue named Thubiri who acquired such an impressive knowledge of Arabic and the Koran during the short time of Bwana's stay in Nkholongue that he was himself referred to as a "Mohammedan teacher" after Sheik Bwana's departure.[81] However, neither Thubiri nor Sheik Bwana are still remembered by the present-day inhabitants of Nkholongue.

Another person from the old elite that needs to be considered is Abdallah Mkwanda (c. 1860–1930). According to Greenstein, Mkwanda was born at Makanjira's into a wealthy trading family. Mkwanda studied Islam in Kilwa at the Indian Ocean and when he returned to the lake region in the 1890s, he apparently became what Greenstein has called "the individual most responsible for Muslim expansion in Malaŵi."[82] Mkwanda combined itinerant preaching of Islam and trading activities. Because of his language abilities, he was also esteemed by the early European traders who came to region.[83] It now appears that, in the early 1900s, he was working as a local middleman of the Swiss trader Ludwig Deuss in Metangula. Different sources suggest that Mkwanda, while living in Metangula, was on good terms with

---

[79] Johnson, *African Reminiscences*, 146; AUMCA, A1(XXIV), f. 199–201: Letter from William Percival Johnson to Mr. Travers ([Chia], December 13, 1914); Alpers, "East Central Africa," 310.
[80] Johnson, "Mohammedanism on Lake Nyasa (1st Part)," *CA* 18, no. 208 (1900): 56; J. S. Wimbush, "A Survey of the Work of the 'Charles Janson,'" *CA* 16, no. 183 (March 1898): 44; "S.S. C. M.," *LDQP*, no. 20 (July 1908): 487–490.
[81] William Percival Johnson, "Coast Influence," *CA* 26, no. 312 (December 1908): 318; "S.S. C. M.," *LDQP*, no. 20 (July 1908): 489–490.
[82] Greenstein, "Shayks and Tariqas," 14.
[83] Greenstein, 14–15.

Thubiri and Bwana Azizi Chingomanje, one of the most important sons of the Chingomanje of that time.[84]

But, again, Mkwanda is equally not remembered by my interviewees, and the Anglican missionaries have also not attributed to him any explicit role in Islam's local spread. Certainly, they called him a "fanatical Mohammedan," but, in general, their accounts suggest that Mkwanda was interested more in his local economic enterprises than in his religious ones.[85] Nevertheless, this points to the fact that, from a local and pragmatic standpoint, colonization had not just simply erased all the previous secular benefits of becoming a Muslim. The Swiss trader Deuss, for example, was said to have been particularly fond of Muslims.[86] Furthermore, the local soldiers and policemen of the *Companhia do Nyassa* were initially almost all Muslim Makuas from the coast of the Indian Ocean.[87] Obviously, Islam worked just as well with commerce as Christianity did.

3.4 Conclusion

This chapter has scrutinized the claim by different scholars that the old slave-trading chiefs had a key role in the early spread of Islam in the Lake Malawi region. Taking the case of Nkholongue, this chapter has shown that the village's chief barely had such a pivotal role. My findings are especially interesting as previous scholars have used evidence referring to Nkholongue and the surrounding villages to substantiate the alleged key role of the chiefs in the regional spread of Islam. My study suggests that in Nkholongue initial Islamization took place from below rather than from above. It thus supports the findings of recent works by other scholars like Felicitas Becker or Brian Peterson who have emphasized the role of commoners and slaves in the process of Islamization, and thus challenged the previous standard chronology of Islam coming to a region in three stages, first

---

84 See especially Section 4.2.
85 AUMCA, A1(XI), f. 457–462: Letter from Bishop Hine to Travers (Unangu, May 22, 1901), f. 461; "News from the Stations: S.S. 'C.M.,'" *LDQP*, no. 4 (July 1904): 78–79; AUMCA, C4, f. 50–51: Letter from [Bishop Hine] to Mr. Travers (Mponda's, December 31, 1900), 3; C.B. Eyre, "Travelling to Unangu," *CA* 25, no. 289 (January 1907): 6; James Sutherland, *The Adventures of an Elephant Hunter* (London: Macmillan, 1912), 177–179.
86 Greenstein, "Shayks and Tariqas," n. 64.
87 AUMCA, C4, f. 112–119: Herbert Barnes, "The Portuguese on the East Side of Lake Nyasa," December 1900, 7.

by trade, then gaining a foothold as court religion of local chiefs and finally spreading downwards to the common people.[88]

The chapter has shown that the spread of Islam followed a very similar timeline as the spread of Christianity, resulting in a general Abrahamization of the regional religious landscape. Obviously, the conversion to Islam could serve (former) slaves as a means of social advancement just as conversion to Christianity could. The case of Islamization in Nkholongue points to the fact that Christianity was the religion of abolition disseminated from above at the centers of the new (European) elites, Islam the religion of abolition negotiated across social hierarchies at the centers of the old (slave trading) elites.

Other motives for the success of Islam are difficult to pin down. The evidence from Nkholongue suggests that its spread might also have been connected to an inter-generational conflict. In this reading, young men were attracted by the experience of what was in their eyes probably a more modern way of life. Furthermore, it has also been suggested that especially (former) slaves saw conversion as a comparatively easy way to improve their social status. Moreover, members of the old established Muslim clergy like Sheik Bwana might have seen fewer impediments for spreading their religion, as the end of the slave trade made the conversion of previously potential slaves less problematic.

We can assume that Nkholongue's chief had little power to oppose these developments, as his own position was clearly weakened by the course of events. The motives for his initial opposition remain in the dark. In any case, it seems that, after some initial resistance, Nkholongue's old elite accepted Islamization rather quickly, probably also because the spread of Islam facilitated the changes to Nkholongue's social structure that were made necessary by the approaching end of the slave trade.

The question in what way Islamization was also driven by a gender conflict is difficult to answer. As will, however, be shown in Chapter 11, Islam was not necessarily incompatible with the continued existence of matrilineal principles. Similarly, it is difficult to assess in what way Islamization was also driven by anti-European feelings. There are clear indications that such feelings were present among the leading Muslims even if, in general, these feelings seem to have been directed more against the Christian missionaries than against Europeans in general.[89] It has been argued by Alpers in this respect that the resistance of Yao chiefs against

---

88 Becker, *Becoming Muslim*; Peterson, *Islamization from Below*. For the previous standard chronology, see: David Robinson, *Muslim Societies in African History* (Cambridge: Cambridge University Press, 2004), 28, 41.
89 See for example: "S.S. C. M.," *LDQP*, no. 18 (January 1908): 438. This question will still be discussed on pp. 174–181.

Portuguese colonization "surely reinforced the emerging Yao sense of cultural distinctiveness as an increasingly Muslim people."[90] However, such a perspective totally ignores the fact that neither in the late pre-colonial nor in the early colonial period was there anything even close to a Yao unity. Rather, as we will see in the following chapters, different groups of the Wayao continued to fight each other as European colonization progressed.[91]

---

90 Alpers, "East Central Africa," 310.
91 See especially pp. 172–174.

4 One Village, One People? The Colonization of Masters and Slaves

4.1 "They let them enter": Looking Beyond Resistance in Mozambique

"They let them enter,"[1] Paulo Litumbe, the first Anglican bishop of the Diocese of Niassa, answered when asked about the resistance of the Anyanja against the Portuguese occupation as part of AHM's oral history project in the early 1980s. In Maúa, a group of elders told the interviewers that it was their own people who went to the Portuguese and begged them to come to put an end to the (slave) wars.[2] Doubtlessly, the historians of newly independent Mozambique were looking for different narratives of colonization: "resistance" was the key plot of the era, and explanations going beyond the simple binary of colonizer and colonized were not very popular. Since then, research on colonialism in Africa has certainly transcended the dualism of collaboration and resistance. Talking about colonialism today also means talking about its "complexities, tensions, ambiguities, and contradictions."[3] Nevertheless, the resistance paradigm still looms large in the historiography of Africa in general and that of Mozambique in particular.[4] This chapter at-

---

[1] Certainly, statements about the colonial period of an Anglican bishop in socialist Mozambique have to be assessed critically. But one must also know that Litumbe was a prisoner of the PIDE/DGS during the Mozambican War of Independence. For his statement, see: AHM, Secção Oral, Transcrito MPC 011: N.° 88–89, Entrevista com Paulo Litumbe, October 15, 1980, 26. See also: Paulo Litumbe, "Appendix 4: Bishop Paulo Litumbe's Memoirs," in *Dancing Their Dreams: The Lakeshore Nyanja Women of the Anglican Diocese of Niassa*, by Helen E.P. van Koevering (Malawi, 2005), 145–70.
[2] AHM, Secção Oral, Transcrito NI 6: N.° 398–399 Entrevista com um grupo de velhos de Maúa (Niassa), interview by Gerhard Liesegang, António Sopa, and Mueojuane Mainga Vicente, September 16, 1982, 26–27.
[3] Harvey Amani Whitfield and Bonny Ibhawoh, "Problems, Perspectives, and Paradigms: Colonial Africanist Historiography and the Question of Audience," *Canadian Journal of African Studies/Revue Canadienne des Études Africaines* 39, no. 3 (2005): 583. See also: Dennis Laumann, *Colonial Africa, 1884–1994* (New York: Oxford University Press, 2012).
[4] David Robinson's observation from 2000 that, despite the criticisms of oversimplifications, "the dichotomization still affects research subjects, judgements, and basic interpretative texts" is in many ways still true today. See: David Robinson, *Paths of Accommodation: Muslim Societies and French Colonial Authorities in Senegal and Mauritania, 1880–1920* (Athens: Ohio University Press, 2000), 58. See as well the recent edited volume by Nuno Domingos, Miguel Bandeira Jerónimo and Ricardo Roque, which sets out to question "simplistic dualisms underlying the opposition between resistance and domination": Nuno Domingos, Miguel Bandeira Jerónimo, and Ricardo

∂ Open Access. © 2023 the author(s), published by De Gruyter. This work is licensed under the Creative Commons Attribution-NonCommercial-NoDerivatives 4.0 International License.
https://doi.org/10.1515/9783110765007-007

tempts to explain why some people of the region "let" the colonialists "enter." By doing so, the chapter hopes to resolve blind spots in the historiography of the colonization of northern Mozambique.

Northern Mozambique was colonized not by the Portuguese state itself, but by a private chartered company, the *Companhia do Nyassa*. The historiographical assessment of the *Companhia*'s reign is unequivocal: weak, but brutal to the utmost. Leroy Vail referred to it as "the rule of the feeble." His quotation of the British vice-consul based in Porto Amélia (today's Pemba), who described the *Companhia*'s territories as "a land of blood and tears, where the most brutal ill-treatment is no crime and murder merely a slight indiscretion," has found numerous recitations.[5] The *Companhia*'s rule has been compared to the systems of rubber extraction in King Leopold's Congo and cocoa cultivation on São Tomé.[6] If there were a list of the worst examples of colonialisms in history, the *Companhia do Nyassa* would certainly rank among the top. William G. Clarence-Smith called it "a prime example of all that was worst in the system of colonial chartered companies,"[7] and René Pélissier named it the "quintessence of the most egoist European domination,"[8] stating that its methods "seem to have been taken from a catalog of the worst abuses of Portuguese colonization."[9] In light of such a verdict, the matter of what colonization meant for the population of Nkholongue seems fairly straightforward. One is tempted to already know the perspective of the colonized.

Roque, eds., *Resistance and Colonialism: Insurgent Peoples in World History* (Cham: Palgrave Macmillan, 2019), 24.
5 See: Leroy Vail, "Mozambique's Chartered Companies: The Rule of the Feeble," *The Journal of African History* 17, no. 3 (1976): 401; Barry Munslow, *Mozambique: The Revolution and Its Origins* (London: Longman, 1983), 30; Allen Isaacman and Barbara Isaacman, *Mozambique: From Colonialism to Revolution* (Boulder: Westview, 1983), 37; Barry Munslow, "State Intervention in Agriculture: The Mozambican Experience," *The Journal of Modern African Studies* 22, no. 2 (1984): 201; Stuart, "Os Nyanja, o U.M.C.A. e a Companhia do Niassa, 1880–1930," 23, 44; René Pélissier, *História de Moçambique: Formação e oposição 1854–1918*, vol. 1 (Lisboa: Estampa, 2000), 393; Galli, *Peoples' Spaces and State Spaces*, 29; Harry G. West, *Kupilikula: Governance and the Invisible Realm in Mozambique* (Chicago: University of Chicago Press, 2005), 101. For an earlier use of the same quotation in connection with immigration from Mozambique to Nyasaland, see: Thomas Galligan, "The Nguru Penetration into Nyasaland," in *From Nyasaland to Malawi: Studies in Colonial History*, ed. Roderick J. Macdonald (Nairobi: East African Publishing House, 1975), note 39.
6 Malyn Newitt, *Portugal in Africa: The Last Hundred Years* (London: Longman, 1981), 85; Pélissier, *História de Moçambique: Formação e oposição 1854–1918*, 2000, 1:393.
7 William G. Clarence-Smith, *The Third Portuguese Empire, 1825–1975: A Study in Economic Imperialism*, (Manchester 1985), 133.
8 Pélissier, *História de Moçambique: Formação e oposição 1854–1918*, 2000, 1:396.
9 Pélissier, 1:391.

But previous research on the *Companhia* and its territories has its blind spots, and these become most visible when one looks at history through the micro-lens. The central blind spot is a consequence of the fact that pre-colonial "African societies" (not to speak of pre-colonial "African villages") have been regarded as too homogeneous units living in a well-established equilibrium. This flaw is not a unique feature of research on the *Companhia do Nyassa* but rather a widespread problem of scholarship on colonial conquest and colonization in general. With the exception of the field of the study of slavery and its "abolition" in Africa (see below), many historians tend to neglect the heterogeneity and rivalries within Africa when discussing colonization.[10] Derek Peterson has similarly argued that many accounts of modern Africa "treat colonialism as an encounter between two sides, measuring the inventions of colonial history against a pre-colonial baseline."[11] The problem is that this idea of a baseline distorts history, falling prey to what I have called the Aboriginal Delusion in the introduction of this book. Take, for example, this remark by Malyn Newitt on the relative absence of the *Companhia*'s administration in much of its territories from his otherwise very thoughtful standard work on Mozambican history:

> The first fifteen years of the Nyassa Company's life were, in so far as economic development or the establishment of a modern state were concerned, a farcical failure. [...] But seen from another point of view, these fifteen years saw the chiefs of northern Mozambique mostly retaining their independence and the majority of the African population able to continue their traditional pattern of life without incorporation into the colonial state.[12]

Newitt is certainly right to point out that the *Companhia* had a very limited reach in transforming society in many ways and areas. But he ignores here what he himself so aptly described a few chapters earlier, namely that in reality there was no such thing as a "traditional pattern of life" (anymore) and that the long-distance

---

[10] My criticism in this regard is certainly not new. For example, as early as 1977, Allen and Barbara Isaacman criticized "[t]he failure of most scholars, including ourselves, to consider carefully the process of class formation during the nineteenth century" with regard to the analysis of colonization. However, I am not entirely convinced that most later works, including their own, have really attempted, let alone managed, to lay open the complexities and implications of political and economic divisions with African societies at the time of colonization. See: Allen Isaacman and Barbara Isaacman, "Resistance and Collaboration in Southern and Central Africa, c. 1850–1920," *The International Journal of African Historical Studies* 10, no. 1 (1977): 41.
[11] Derek R. Peterson, "Culture and Chronology in African History," *The Historical Journal* 50, no. 2 (2007): 496.
[12] Malyn Newitt, *A History of Mozambique* (Bloomington: Indiana University Press, 1995), 373.

trade of the 19th century had brought about a very strong stratification of society.¹³ The blow of colonization had been preceded by other storms.

While previous storms are often mentioned, their implications are not always fully taken into consideration for the analysis of future ones. Thus, Rosemary Galli mentioned the impact of the slave trade on local society in her outline of the history of Unango, but then spoke only of the "Unango people" when analyzing colonization, implying that all people in Unango had the same perspective.¹⁴ Similarly, in his work on the Makonde Plateau, Harry West wrote how "powerful settlement heads" swallowed "local counterparts into their own settlements, making political subordinates of them and their people" in a pre-colonial region "wracked by drought, famine, interethnic conflict, and slave raiding," only to state somewhat later in the book how colonization "produced tensions between ordinary Muedans and elders [...] used as native intermediaries" and "alienated plateau youths from the heads of their settlements."¹⁵

The point here is not to deny the brutality of colonization nor to understate that colonialism created tensions but to emphasize that ignoring earlier tensions distorts the analysis of colonization and also of the moment when Africans had "moved from being the Enslavable Other to the Enslaving Other."¹⁶ With regard to northern Mozambique, no scholar has yet examined how colonization affected the social hierarchies produced by the slave trade of the 19th century, let alone how these hierarchies affected colonization. We know very little about what colonization meant for the former numerous slaves and serfs, and how they themselves approached this political change. With the lakeshore's "early history" in mind, it becomes clear that different actors had different viewpoints on this new blow of history.

Of course, we can expect that life was different at some point in the past, but I hope it has been adequately shown that the formation of Nkholongue was anything but idyllic. Here, things had fallen apart long before actual colonization.¹⁷ Undoubtedly, it is easy (and correct) for the analyst to conclude that already Nkho-

---

13 See: Newitt, 267–297.
14 Galli, *Peoples' Spaces and State Spaces*, 22–32.
15 West, *Kupilikula*, 20, 83.
16 Cooper, *Colonialism in Question*, 104.
17 In contrast to Chinua Achebe's fictional but influential Igbo village where things began to fall apart with the arrival of the white man. See: Chinua Achebe, *Things Fall Apart* (1958; repr., London: Penguin, 2006). For examples of the questionable influence of Achebe's fictional account on historiography, see: Laumann, *African World Histories*, 14; Philip Curtin, "The European Conquest," in *African History: From Earliest Times to Independence*, by Philip Curtin et al., 2nd ed. (Harlow: Longman, 1995), 417.

longue's formation was conditioned by a global colonial regime (as has been shown in Chapter 2), and that consequently the village's social hierarchies were shaped by the activities of Europeans long before their actual arrival. But in order to understand the perspectives of the people living along the shores of Lake Malawi at the time of "effective occupation," we have to put this analysis aside. It is their perspectives that determined how they reacted to and assessed colonization, and it is their perspectives that I will try to reconstruct in this chapter and the next.

While such issues are new for northern Mozambique, they have been increasingly studied for other regions of Africa. This is especially true of the fate of slavery and slaves during the process of colonization.[18] In addition, this chapter connects to works that have started to explore the role of "intermediaries, interpreters, and clerks" in the making of colonial Africa.[19] However, rather than being a study of colonialism with African agency, it aims at analyzing people's lives at the time of colonization, showing how people saw their circumstances and made their decisions.[20]

This is no easy task, as source-wise this is a difficult period in the history of Nkholongue. The archives of the *Companhia do Nyassa* have apparently been de-

---

18 Frederick Cooper, *From Slaves to Squatters: Plantation Labor and Agriculture in Zanzibar and Coastal Kenya, 1890–1925* (New Haven: Yale University Press, 1980); Ahmad Sikainga, *Slaves into Workers: Emancipation and Labor in Colonial Sudan* (Austin: University of Texas Press, 1996); Martin A. Klein, *Slavery and Colonial Rule in French West Africa* (Cambridge: Cambridge University Press, 1998); Suzanne Miers and Martin A. Klein, eds., *Slavery and Colonial Rule in Africa* (Portland: Frank Cass, 1999); Mann, *Slavery and the Birth of an African City*; Jan-Georg Deutsch, *Emancipation without Abolition in German East Africa, c. 1884–1914* (Oxford: James Currey, 2006) ; Felicitas Becker et al., "Researching the Aftermath of Slavery in Mainland East Africa: Methodological, Ethical, and Practical Challenges," in *Slavery & Abolition* 44, no. 1 (2023).
19 Lawrance, Osborn, and Roberts, *Intermediaries, Interpreters, and Clerks*. For the increasing interest in the agency of "Africans" in the making and working of colonialism, see also: Joël Glasman, "Penser les intermédiaires coloniaux: Note sur les dossiers de carrière de la police du Togo," *History in Africa* 37 (2010): 51–81; John Parker and Richard J. Reid, "Introduction. African Histories: Past, Present, and Future," in *The Oxford Handbook of Modern African History*, ed. John Parker and Richard J. Reid (Oxford: Oxford University Press, 2013), 9; Heather J. Sharkey, "African Colonial States," in *The Oxford Handbook of Modern African History*, ed. John Parker and Richard J. Reid (Oxford: Oxford University Press, 2013), 151–152, 162–163; John Parker and Richard Rathbone, *African History: A Very Short Introduction* (Oxford: Oxford University Press, 2007), 109.
20 I take inspiration from Cooper, who has argued for not overly foregrounding colonialism in people's lives but focusing primarily on their viewpoints. See: Cooper, "Conflict and Connection," 1534; Frederick Cooper, *Decolonization and African Society: The Labor Question in French and British Africa* (Cambridge: Cambridge University Press, 1996), 8–9.

stroyed,[21] and the amount of material in the archives of the UMCA in Oxford drops off rapidly for the time after colonization. The interviews are not much help either: this period corresponds exactly to what Jan Vansina called the "floating gap," the blurred interval between the plenty information of recent and the formalized traditions of origin of earlier times.[22]

Still, I trust to be able to present certain insights. The analysis is divided into two parts. In the first part, we will look at colonization through the lens of Chingomanje bin M'ponda, the chief who ruled Nkholongue at the time. Due to source limitations, this part will focus on the years between the arrival of the first Europeans in the region in the 1880s to about 1902. It will discuss how Chingomanje bin M'ponda skillfully adapted to the challenges of colonization and succeeded in avoiding direct confrontations with European powers despite his slave-trading activities. In the end, he even supported the forces of the *Companhia* in their fight against less compliant chiefs of the region.

The second part of this chapter will reflect on how colonization affected people's everyday lives. The focus will thereby not be on colonial exploitation, which will still be discussed in the next chapter, but on the changing relationships between (former) slaves and slave holders. It will be argued that colonization indeed opened up the space for (former) slaves to shake off their dependence from their masters. To demonstrate this, we will have a look at the changing settlement patterns. It will be shown that most settlements were highly concentrated in the decades before colonization. This changed with the end of the slave trade and the end of the wars connected to it. The end of these wars made it much more feasible for people to settle wherever they wanted. As a result, the previously compact settlements began to spread out all across the region.

4.2 Chief Chingomanje bin M'ponda: One Who Knows How to Speak and Act with Strangers

It is a common claim that many African chiefdoms were colonial inventions, and that many chiefs were appointed by the European powers only following coloniza-

---

21 Liesegang, "The Arquivo Histórico de Moçambique and Historical Research in Maputo," 5. In 1938, a Portuguese inspector, however, wrote that the *Companhia*'s officials had taken with them all the documents: AHU, N° 1665–1 1B MU ISAU: Armando Pinto Corrêa, "Relatório duma Inspecção às Circunscrições do Distrito de Moçambique (1936–37)" (Lourenço Marques, 1938), 126–127.
22 Jan Vansina, *Oral Tradition as History* (Madison: University of Wisconsin Press, 1985), 23.

tion,[23] even though the "nature and extent of 'invention' has been called into doubt."[24] This assertion also appeared in some of my interviews in varying guises. One version says that the land around Nkholongue belonged to Nsossa. Chingomanje had no power here. He was a mere visitor from Unango who came to Nkholongue to buy fish. But when he came here, he made friends with Nsossa. And later when Nsossa had to go to the other side of the lake to care for his sick brother, he asked Chingomanje to look after the village in his absence. Now it so happened that the white man arrived at that very moment and thus appointed Chingomanje as the chief of Nkholongue—wrongfully.[25]

However attractive such a story might be in portraying the appointment of Chingomanje as the result of a cultural misunderstanding in which neither party understood what the other was talking about, or in which Chingomanje cleverly deceived the naive colonizers with long-lasting consequences, it has little to do with what happened in Nkholongue. Chingomanje was in power when the Anglican missionaries first came there in the 1880s, he was in power when a Portuguese military mission visited the place in 1889, and he was in power when the place was finally colonized by the *Companhia do Nyassa* in 1901.

In a way, Chingomanje was no exception. Most chiefs of the region were able to keep their power after colonization. Of course, their influence, rights, and duties changed. But there were fewer replacements than might be expected.[26] In another way, however, Chingomanje was an exception. For many of the other slave trading chiefs of some significance were drawn into wars with the European colonizers, and many of them were deposed in the course of colonization. Not so Chingomanje and his relative Kalanje. One might attribute this "accomplishment" to their advantage of being residents in what would become Portuguese territory, as this

---

[23] Kate Baldwin, *The Paradox of Traditional Chiefs in Democratic Africa* (New York: Cambridge University Press, 2016), 35–37; Justin Willis, "Chieftaincy," in *The Oxford Handbook of Modern African History*, ed. John Parker and Richard Reid (Oxford: Oxford University Press, 2013), 213–217; Kristin Phillips, *An Ethnography of Hunger: Politics, Subsistence, and the Unpredictable Grace of the Sun* (Bloomington: Indiana University Press, 2018), 54–55.

[24] Richard Reid, "States of Anxiety: History and Nation in Modern Africa," *Past & Present* 229, no. 1 (2015): 262. See as well: Spear, "Neo-Traditionalism and the Limits of Invention in British Colonial Africa."

[25] PA, I100: interview with *P0025 (♀, 1948)* (Nkholongue, February 22, 2016), min 00:37:59–00:42:22. For similar and other versions, see: PA, I144: interview with *P0411 (♂, 1965)* (Nkholongue, June 8, 2016), min 00:31:27–00:33:17; PA, I096: interview with *P1216 (♂, 1957)* (Malango, February 1, 2016), min 01:19:27–01:25:03.

[26] For an exception, see: PA, Chadreque Umali, *História de Nyanjas* (Metangula, 1996), 19; Chauncy Maples, "Letter from Archdeacon Maples," *CA* 12, no. 134 (February 1894): 26–29; PA, I030: interview with *Chief Namtima (♀) and Councellors* (Maniamba, April 6, 2012).

gave them more time to adjust to the new situation. However, other chiefs who were based in the future territories of the *Companhia*, such as Mataka or Malinganile, acted differently. They sought confrontation and were both defeated in the end.

For the British territories, John McCracken has argued that the colonial government's determination to impose its "rule by force ensured that there was little chance that even the most diplomatically astute of Yao chiefs could have avoided being sucked into the war."[27] The economic interests of the British clashed too much with those of the Yao chiefs. But Chingomanje managed to escape war and remain in power, even if weakened. And it must be emphasized that it was not only the dynasty of the Chingomanjes that survived the end of the slave trade era, but it was one and the same person who remained in power.

Flags and Diplomacy on the Eve of Colonization

Chingomanje bin M'ponda was born around 1850.[28] Oral history is very vague about the first Chingomanjes, and it is no easy task to reconcile the information from the interviews with the information from the written sources, since the holders of the title were usually depersonalized in both types of sources and thus just called "Chingomanje" after the name of the dynasty. However, we can assume that Chingomanje bin M'ponda was the second Chingomanje in oral history terms. He received the title in "the year of the comet" (1882) after the death of his predecessor and was probably the first Chingomanje to settle permanently in Nkholongue.[29] From all the information we can gather, it seems most plausible that he died in 1921.[30]

---

27 McCracken, *A History of Malawi 1859–1966*, 67.
28 One Anglican missionary estimated Chingomanje's age at 35 to 40 in 1886. See: Chauncy Maples, "Nyassa News," *CA* 4, no. 48 (1886): 186.
29 According to the missionaries, his predecessor died in the "year of the comet," which the missionaries gave as 1882, probably referring to comet C/1882 R1. See: Bellingham, *Diary of a Working Man*; Augustine Ambali, *Thirty Years in Nyasaland* (Westminster: UMCA, 1931), 34–35.
30 The death of Chingomanje in 1921 is reported by the Anglican priest Yohanna Abdallah. However, since the missionaries' reports about Nkholongue become sparser over time, it is uncertain whether this was really Chingomanje II or already his successor. But we can be fairly certain that Chingomanje bin M'ponda was still in power in 1912, because at that time another missionary wrote that "the old chief Chingomanje has consented to receive a teacher again after the lapse of many years," obviously referring to the same Chingomanje who had sent the missionaries away in 1900. See: Yohanna B. Abdallah, "News from the Stations: VII. Unangu," *NDC*, no. 73 (Octo-

As we have already seen in Chapter 2, Chingomanje II bin M'ponda was a slave trader and slave owner. His village served as a transshipment point for other traders and as an outpost of the Wayao of Unango. Furthermore, he was an ally of the Jumbe of Nkhotakota. We can note that the dynasty of the Chingomanjes was a relatively important player in regional politics, certainly when compared to today. However, if one follows the interpretation laid out in Chapter 2, it can also be noted that the Chingomanjes had already lost political and economic ground on the eve of European colonization. Attacks by various opponents such as the Angoni, Makanjira, or Mataka had disputed their position and driven them from their previous bases in Mbemba and Lussefa. Their ally Jumbe showed little willingness to come to their assistance, as he was obviously in trouble himself. The Chingomanjes' loss of status becomes even more apparent if Roscher's "Kingomanga" is considered as part of this dynasty (see pp. 67–69). According to the testimony of Roscher's servant, Kingomanga was a territorial chief capable of mobilizing a considerable number of men. He put the strength of Kingomanga's force that arrested the murderers of Roscher at 50 men.[31]

Chingomanje II bin M'ponda still breathed some of this glory, but reality had made him a rather minor player in the slave traders' power struggle. "He had a few guns," is how missionary William Percival Johnson described him.[32] The Anglican missionaries could observe his decline in real time. While William Bellingham described Nkholongue as a large village in 1885, Chingomanje was said to have only very few people in 1887.[33] Bishop Smythies wrote that Chingomanje had lost many of his people in attacks by other Yao chiefs.[34] Johnson went so far as to pity "the wretched slaver, who has lost so many of his family," saying that he always appeared "to be very lonely in his house with the stockade round."[35] In 1894, Johnson estimated the population of Nkholongue to be a mere 300.[36]

Yet despite his insecure position, Chingomanje could still speak with a considerable amount of self-confidence. Johnson credited him with "plenty courage of a sort," and stated that Chingomanje would just laugh when he, Johnson, spoke about

---

ber 1921): 12–13; Frank Winspear and William Percival Johnson, "News from the Stations: II. The Chauncy Maples," *NDC*, no. 37 (October 1912): 935.
31 Rigby, "Proceedings No. 43 of 1860," lii.
32 Johnson, *The Great Water*, 101.
33 AUMCA, A1(VI)A, f. 946–949: Letter from William Bellingham to W.H. Penney ([Likoma], October 1, 1885), f. 947; AUMCA, A1(V)A Printed Matters, f. 19: Charles Alan Smythies, *A Journey from Zanzibar to Lake Nyassa and Back, in the Year 1887* (Westminster: UMCA, n.d.), 13.
34 AUMCA, A1(V)B, f. 368–404: Charles Alan Smythies, [Diary/Report of Bishop Smythies' Third Visit to Nyasa (July to Sept.)] (Likoma, 1887).
35 Johnson, *African Reminiscences*, 146.
36 Johnson, "More about the Yaos," *TNN*, no. 3 (February 1894): 78.

the Angoni.³⁷ On one occasion, Chingomanje explained to Johnson that he "would willingly fight the Angoni in the day time," but since they "came at any time in the night, it was worth while to throw them a truss of cloth (as you might throw something to the wolves) for they always went off with it."³⁸ And another time Johnson heard him bargaining with a Swahili trader over "hides with two legs (i.e. slaves), and hides with four legs (i.e. goats)."³⁹

Chingomanje's self-confidence was not entirely without foundation. Although weakened by the course of events, Chingomanje II was no political nobody: when a group of Angoni threatened the region in 1887, many inhabitants of Metangula, including their chief Chilombe, sought refuge in his stockade.⁴⁰ In an interesting inversion of what happened exactly 100 years later during the Mozambican Civil War (see Chapter 9, pp. 345–346), Chilombe was said to always sleep in Nkholongue and only go to his village during daytime.⁴¹ The story of Chilombe's flight to Nkholongue during the Angoni wars was even related in two of my interviews.⁴² After all, Chingomanje still had armed men and he had powerful allies.⁴³

But Chingomanje's readiness to pay a ransom to the Angoni in order to prevent an attack on his village was certainly not a strong man's answer in everyone's eyes.⁴⁴ For Johnson, there was no doubt that Chingomanje's self-confident talk was above all a sign of his self-overestimation, and he emphasized Chingomanje's political insignificance whenever possible, and sometimes even in quite derogatory terms, describing his village, for example, as "completely pagan with a veneer of cosmopolitan brigandage."⁴⁵ But precisely such formulations suggest that Johnson's repeated emphasis on Chingomanje's unimportance also resulted from his

---

37 Johnson, *African Reminiscences*, 143.
38 Johnson, *The Great Water*, 19, 101.
39 Johnson, "More about the Yaos," *TNN*, no. 3 (February 1894): 78. For other description of the same scene, see: Johnson, *African Reminiscences*, 145; Johnson, "Mohammedanism on Lake Nyasa (1st Part)," *CA* 18, no. 208 (1900): 54.
40 Johnson, *African Reminiscences*, 142.
41 AUMCA, TC/G: George H. Swinny, "Nyasaland Diaries (1884–1887), Vol. III," 37.
42 PA, I113: interview with *P0367* (♂, *1936*) (Nkholongue, April 13, 2016), min 01:27:51–01:29:20; PA, I017: interview with *P0792* (♂, *1917*), *P0793* (♀, *1939*) (Nkholongue, October 14, 2011), min 00:33:40–00:39:00.
43 On the existence of guns in Nkholongue, see: Johnson, *The Great Water*, 101; AUMCA, TC/G: George H. Swinny, "Nyasaland Diaries (1884–1887), Vol. III," 34–35.
44 AUMCA, TC/G: George H. Swinny, "Nyasaland Diaries (1884–1887), Vol. III," 41.
45 Johnson, *African Reminiscences*, 141. See also: AUMCA, A1(XXIV), f. 202–207: Letter from William Percival Johnson to Bishop (Monkey Bay, [1890]); Johnson, "More about the Yaos," *TNN*, no. 3 (February 1894): 78; Johnson, "Inclosure 2 in No. 2: Mr. Johnson to Commissioner Johnston," 7–8. Johnson's view was also shared by Sheriff: Sheriff, "A Letter from Mr. Sheriff, Captain of the 'Charles Janson,'" *CA* 9, no. 99 (March 1891): 38.

unease with other fellow missionaries who, in his eyes, had been successfully lulled by Chingomanje, the "wretched slaver." Not without reason did Johnson attest to him being "a clever man [who] knew how to speak and act with strangers."[46]

Chingomanje played his cards quite successfully, at least if one considers his rather insecure position. It is obvious that he saw the appearance of a new player, the Anglican missionaries, as a chance to regain some of his standing or at least to protect himself from further losses. So it was probably not only the prospect of material gains or status symbols, which I have referred to in Chapter 3, but also political considerations that prompted him to let the missionaries come to his village. A very similar argument has been made by Ian Linden for the chief Mponda II at the south end of the lake, who accepted the Catholic missionaries of the White Fathers in his town. Linden wrote: "By being housed inside the town stockade the Catholics would [...] be a guarantee of intervention by at least one of the European powers if the town was again in danger of being overrun."[47]

According to William Bellingham, Chingomanje had even been anxious to have the missionaries in his village.[48] In any case, their presence seems to have helped prevent an attack by the Angoni in 1887. It was the missionaries who went ahead to the Angoni's camp to negotiate. According to Swinny, the leaders of the Angoni "hid themselves, being afraid of the Europeans," at the approach of the missionaries.[49] After the incident, Swinny claimed:

> I may add that the [Angoni] appear to have lost none of their dread of a white face [...] Also the fact of our being resident just outside Chingomanje's village may have had something to do with their temperate behaviour towards that chief.[50]

Chingomanje's attitude toward the missionaries was situational and calculated, depending on what they would provide him in changing circumstances. We have already seen that the relations between the mission and Chingomanje began to cool down considerably after Swinny's death and froze up completely in 1890. The rea-

---

46 Johnson, *African Reminiscences*, 141.
47 Linden, *Catholics, Peasants, and Chewa Resistance in Nyasaland*, 23.
48 AUMCA, A1(VI)A, f. 946–949: Letter from William Bellingham to W.H. Penney ([Likoma], October 1, 1885); Bellingham, *Diary of a Working Man*, 81.
49 AUMCA, TC/G: George H. Swinny, "Nyasaland Diaries (1884–1887), Vol. III," 39. These Angoni belonged to the chiefdom of the Angoni chief Mhalule. See: TNA, FO/84/1883, f. 250–256: Acting Consul Buchanan to Consul Hawes (Mudi, April 12, 1888), 2. Mhalule was the paramount chief of the Njelu chiefdom c. 1874–89. See: P.H. Gulliver, "Political Evolution in the Songea Ngoni Chiefdoms, 1850–1905," *Bulletin of the School of Oriental and African Studies* 37, no. 1 (1974): 82–97.
50 Swinny, "With Chingomanje," *CA* 5, no. 56 (1887): 115. See also: Swinny, "With Chingomanje," *CA* 5, no. 56 (1887): 118.

sons for his decision to expel the missionaries were certainly varied, but two main causes can be discerned: first, it had become obvious that the British presence could do more harm than good to his political and economic position. And second, there is reason to believe that the missionaries' place as gift-giver and European shield was to be filled by someone else, for, in the meantime, a new player had appeared on the scene.

The Portuguese military expedition under António Maria Cardoso reached the lake at its southern end on December 12, 1888. It was 1,200 men and 2,000 carriers strong. The original objective of Cardoso's expedition had been to establish a permanent Portuguese base in the town of Chief Cuirassia, who had already accepted Portuguese vassalage during an earlier mission in 1886. But Cardoso found out that Cuirassia had been driven from the lake by Makanjira in the meantime. He wrote back home that it would be impossible to comply with the original instructions since Makanjira was opposed to their aims. However, while waiting for new instructions, Cardoso began a rather successful series of treaty-making with chiefs along the eastern shores of Lake Malawi.[51]

Interestingly, most of these treaties were not made with chiefs living at the southern end of the lake, where the Portuguese mission was based, but with chiefs living in the area extending north from Makanjira's to present-day Cobué.[52] The first of these chiefs to accept Portuguese vassalage on January 17, 1889, was none other than Kalanje. Other chiefs of the region followed him in March 1889, including Maniamba (Ngolocolo), Masanje (Messumba), Maendaenda (Chia), Mapunda (Ngofi), Chitesi (Chigoma) and Chingomanje bin M'ponda. Of all these chiefs, Kalanje was the only one who signed the treaty personally in his town.[53] All other chiefs, including Chingomanje bin M'ponda, sent an envoy to Cuirassia to sign the respective document. Three months later, Kalanje, Masanje, Maniamba, and Chingomanje sent emissaries to Quelimane on the Indian Ocean to confirm their vassalage in front of the Portuguese governor of the district.[54]

In the treaties, the chiefs agreed to provide protection to all Portuguese travelers passing through their territory, to obey all orders of the Portuguese king, and

---

51 Eric Axelson, *Portugal and the Scramble for Africa: 1875–1891* (Johannesburg: Witwatersrand University Press, 1967), 183–185.
52 Antonio M. Cardoso, "Documento N.° 38: O Sr. Antonio Maria Cardoso ao Ministro da Marinha, telegramma, transmitido por Lourenço Marques, 10 de Abril de 1889," in *Negocios externos: Documentos apresentados ás cortes na sessão legislativa de 1890* (Lisboa: Imprensa Nacional, 1890), 19.
53 According to the treaty, the signing took place in his capital on the eastern shores of the lake. This probably refers to Meluluca, as this was frequently called Kalanje's town on the lake.
54 *Termos de Vassallagem nos Territorios de Machona, Zambezia e Nyassa 1858 a 1889* (Lisboa: Imprensa Nacional, 1890), 4, 55–59.

to defend and honor the Portuguese flag they had received. The British—missionaries and civil servants alike—were furious over these treaties. They complained that the chiefs had been enticed into signing the documents by the offer of gifts and by the expectation of receiving guns and gunpowder.[55] To demonstrate the political worthlessness of these treaties, Johnson later recounted a moment when he was in Njiri (near Unango) looking for his list of his local parishioners, which he had misplaced. On that occasion, the people of Njiri allegedly handed him a piece of paper that turned out to be precisely such a treaty.[56] Johnson explained:

> [I]t was supposed that it might be the piece of paper I was looking for, as one piece of paper was considered as good as another. This will show how little the natives understood the meaning of the agreements.[57]

Writing in a similar vein, the British vice-consul of Quelimane, who had attended the ratification ceremony involving Chingomanje's envoy in June 1889, said that it had been a farce.[58] In his words:

> Some five or 6 "sovas" (chiefs) were supposed to be represented, each by two ambassadors, who on being questioned did not seem to know in the least whom they represented; and so manifest was the muddle that the Governor postponed the ceremony for a couple of days to afford time for the proper schooling of the ambassadors.[59]

---

55 William Percival Johnson, "The Portuguese Flag in Nyassaland," *CA* 7, no. 80 (August 1889): 123–124; Axelson, *Portugal and the Scramble for Africa*, 184–185; "Letters from From Rev. W. P. Johnson," *CA* 7, no. 78 (June 1889): 95–96.
56 The chief of Njiri is Licole. A treaty with a "Licole Massussa," based "east of Lake Nyassa," was made on 19 August 1889. See: *Termos de Vassallagem nos Territorios de Machona, Zambezia e Nyassa 1858 a 1889*, 71–72.
57 Johnson, *African Reminiscences*, 195.
58 Vice-Consul Ross did not provide any information on the date of the ceremony or the chiefs involved. However, it is clear from the available documents that his account referred to the ratification ceremony that involved Chingomanje. According to Portuguese sources, four ratification ceremonies took place in Quelimane in the first half of 1889. One on April 6 involving two chiefs; one on April 11 again involving two chiefs; one on May 27 involving just one; and one on June 15 involving five chiefs including Chingomanje. The final clue pointing to this interpretation comes from the wording of Ross' message, which reads: "Since writing on [June] the 19th. no more 'termos de vassalagem' have been made by the natives from the Nyassa before the local authorities. The last one which I was invited to attend showed plainly what a farce these 'termos' have been." See: *Termos de Vassallagem nos Territorios de Machona, Zambezia e Nyassa 1858 a 1889*; TNA, FO/84/1969, f. 200–205: Vice-Consul Ross to Acting Consul Smith, July 11, 1889.
59 TNA, FO/84/1969, f. 200–205: Vice-Consul Ross to Acting Consul Smith, July 11, 1889.

It is of course tempting to follow the cynicism inherent in these two statements. At first glance, one is invited to question the general authenticity of these contracts: if there were no other circumstantial evidence it would seem highly justified to doubt whether these encounters took place at all. The treaties instead seem to constitute an arbitrary compilation of names of alleged chiefs and their entourage. The spelling of the names is totally different from that used by the Anglicans, Kalanje given as "Carange" and Chingomanje as "Quingomage bin Maponda." References to the locations of the respective chiefdoms are almost non-existent, usually indicating just "East of Nyassa." Without historical and geographical knowledge of the region it is impossible to get anything out of these contracts. From a legal perspective, they appear to be as improvised and worthless as the British vice-consul depicted them.

However, the cynicism masks the fact that this treaty-making was not just about buying off "ignorant natives" with dubious presents. There is no doubt that both the British vice-consul and missionary Johnson themselves either misinterpreted or misrepresented the political and cultural codes of the whole business.

The central clue to this can be found by a close reading of the proper contracts through our microhistorical lens: among Chingomanje's envoys in Quelimane was one of his sons, named as Mussélimo Chingomanje in the contract.[60] The point is that this Mussélimo Chingomanje also appears as a witness to Kalanje's ratification, but this time he is identified as Kalanje's nephew. This is a detail which perfectly reflects the brotherly relationship between the two rulers, and a detail that would hardly have found its way into the treaties had these encounters taken place with the sort of randomness as pictured by the British vice-consul.

It is likely that the Portuguese were indeed somewhat ignorant of the specific state of affairs of their new "vassals" and may have even missed the fact that Kalanje and Chingomanje were related, since they even spelled Mussélimo's name differently in the two treaties. But the fact that the initial agreement with the most important of these five chiefs was signed in his country, while the other lesser chiefs had sent envoys to the Portuguese camp, suggests that the Portuguese were well aware of the local power hierarchies. These hierarchies are also reflected from the perspective of the "vassals": while the other chiefs all sent family members as "ambassadors," Kalanje's group included his scribe. The fact that Kalanje indeed had his own clerk is supported by other sources from the Anglican missionaries.[61]

---

[60] One wonders if this "Mussélimo Chingomanje" might be identical with "Salimo Chingomanje" (see Chapter 3, p. 97).
[61] "Notes," *TNN*, no. 6 (November 1894): 207; J.E. Hine, "Opening of a New Station at the Yao Country," *CA* 12, no. 134 (February 1894): 25.

Kalanje, Chingomanje, and the other chiefs would barely have sent emissaries to Quelimane, which is more than 350 miles away from their homes, if they had not considered these treaties important. There is no doubt that Kalanje, Chingomanje and some other chiefs did indeed recognize the treaties as some form of political allegiance. They knew perfectly well that the hoisting of the Portuguese flag had a political meaning, and those who had not yet grasped that meaning would now quickly learn it. This becomes clear when one looks at what happened on the ground after the signing of the treaties.

Shortly after Chief Chitesi, who was based opposite Likoma Island, had received and hoisted the flag, missionary Johnson rushed to him to persuade him to give it back.[62] In May 1889, Bishop Maples wrote with satisfaction that none of the chiefs on the shores who had received the flag still retained it. He also attributed this development to the fact that Makanjira had sent an envoy as far as Chitesi's to "make quite certain that Chitesi was not flying the flag, and to tell him that Makanjira had utterly rejected all Portuguese overtures, and begged all his friends, *i.e.* those Nyanja chiefs, Chitesi, Maendaenda, Masanje &c., to do the same, and to persist in so doing."[63] While this allayed the missionaries' fear of a Portuguese "invasion," it clearly shows that, by May 1889 at the latest, even the most "out-of-the-way" chiefs must have been aware of the political nature of the whole affair.

Interestingly, some chiefs did neither what Makanjira demanded nor what the missionaries thought they did. Instead, they kept the flag and when the *Companhia* arrived to colonize the territory more than ten years later, they were still in possession of it and now could try to utilize their asset if they so wanted. In the case of Chingomanje, an officer of the *Companhia* reported in 1901:

> This chief has the Portuguese flag given to him by Mr. A. M. Cardoso on 6 May 1889, and he ratified his vassalage in the middle of June of the same year in front of the ex-district of Quelimane. He is a friend of the Portuguese and obsequious.[64]

Even more revealing is a look at what had happened in the meantime. By 1893, the Portuguese forces had long since disappeared from the lake, and there was no sign of them returning any time soon. The British, however, were becoming firmly es-

---

62 Johnson, "The Portuguese Flag in Nyassaland," *CA* 7, no. 80 (August 1889).
63 It is "Chitezi," "Makanjila," and "Nyassa" in the original. See: Chauncy Maples, "The Portuguese on the Nyassa," *CA* 7, no. 82 (October 1889): 147.
64 AHM, Códice 11–2485: Documento N.º XXXVII: Extractos dos apontamentos particulares do Capitão Trindade dos Santos, relativos estabelecimentos das missões na região do Lago, in *Documentos sobre as Missões Inglesas das Universidades*, 58.

tablished on the other side of the lake. Moreover, they were fighting the slave trade with full force, controlling traffic on the lake and confiscating dhows if necessary. At this point of time, Chingomanje sent a message to the Anglican mission of Messumba. The incident was reported in *Mtenga Watu*, the mission's Chinyanja "newspaper," as follows:

> In the month of January, the children of Chingomanje, by the name of Bwana Azizi and Abdallah, came here. They were together with the children of Achibwana, Kachapuchapu Kazanje and Medi. All of them brought a letter [saying] that Bwana Chingomanje wishes to reconcile with the whites and that Mdachi (Kalanje) wanted the English to give him the flag for his dhow.[65]

Missionary Johnson later reported the case to the British commissioner of the British Central Africa Protectorate (later Nyasaland) with the following words:

> I HAVE [sic] had the pleasure of conveying to you wishes for peace and for the Flag from Kalanje of Unango, and Mkalawili—this in the substantial form of messengers of some rank, amongst them Kalanje has sent his heir. Chingomanje, who sends his heir, is Kalanje's younger relative, only important from his dhows. Kalanje and Mkalawili own the country from Messumba to Makanjira's boundary. Kalanje is most afraid of his dhows, and Mkalawili most afraid of his neighbour Makanjira. I have told them a Flag means "kushika mguu," ["to become subject to someone"] and that I, as a teacher, have nothing to do with it, but hope for peace. Kalanje sends the largest caravans to the coast, and promises (as far as that goes) to stop slaves going. Mr. Nicoll [the British Resident in Nkhotakota] last time received these people civilly, and said he would refer the matter to you. This trip they come down again, and wish to go on in our boat to wait on you in person. I can but recommend their suit to your kind attention, rejoicing meanwhile that their country is reopened to Europeans.[66]

I was unable to find any explicit evidence regarding a possible response from the British commissioner. Certainly, one can expect that the British government did not really consider this an opportunity to colonize the area around Nkholongue, since this territory had been granted to Portugal in the Anglo-Portuguese Treaty of 1891

---

[65] It is "Chingomanji" in the original. See: Richard Philipo Mzinda, "Nkani Za Msumba," *Mtenga Watu* 2, no. 12 (April 1893). The sentence about Kalanje's desire for a flag is somewhat corrupted in the Chinyanja original, which makes an accurate translation difficult. There is however little doubt that the meaning has been correctly reflected, since the same request was described unambiguously by another member of the Anglican church in another article. See: William Y., "Nkani Za Kumuka Kuunangu," *Mtenga Watu* 2, no. 19 (August 1894): 282–285.
[66] It is "Unengo," "Msumbu," and "Makanjila" in the original. See: Johnson, "Inclosure 2 in No. 2: Mr. Johnson to Commissioner Johnston."

in spite of Portugal's total absence from the region.[67] However, a little over a year after these diplomatic endeavors, the British vice-consul Sharpe observed how Kalanje was flying the British flag on his dhows.[68] At the same time, Bishop Maples reported that Kalanje was still "sporting" the Portuguese flag on his Unango hill.[69] Obviously, Kalanje and Chingomanje were serving two masters, but primarily their own ends. It is also noteworthy in this context that Kalanje—who hoisted the Portuguese flag and the Union Jack simultaneously—was calling himself *mdachi*, the Kiswahili expression for "a German," ostensibly because in this way Kalanje, whose caravans also crossed into German territory, wanted to express his status, since the "Germans" were said to be such a powerful nation.[70]

Kalanje and Chingomanje had adapted to the new situation fairly quickly. These were not the seducible chiefs of imperial imaginations, but experienced diplomats. And it seems that Chingomanje himself thought that he was coping well with the new challenges. For it was around this time that missionary Johnson heard a Swahili trader flatter Chingomanje by expressing admiration at "his having the flags of all nations in his village."[71] Johnson, who should have known better, refuted this flattery and rather triumphantly assured his readers that Chingomanje's village "had no flag of any kind."[72]

Johnson missed the punchline. Chingomanje, together with his relative Kalanje, not only had "the flags of all nations," but also successfully hosted the representatives of different "nations" in his village: the missionaries reopened their school in Nkholongue in 1895 or 1896, this time run by what they called a "native teacher."[73] And at the same time, Nkholongue was also the place of residence of some Swahili traders and the aforementioned Sheik Bwana, Jumbe's former

---

67 Newitt, *A History of Mozambique*, 352–355.
68 TNA, FO/2/66, f. 179–191: Alfred Sharpe (Vice-Consul) to the Commissioner, March 14, 1894. For another identical observation at around the same time, see: AUMCA, E1, f. 1001–1002: Letter from William Percival Johnson to Bishop ([1894]). It needs to be emphasized that this observation was made before the British took direct political control of Nkhotakota and officially began to hand out British flags to all dhows going there. For this development, see: Sim, *Life and Letters*, 111.
69 Maples, "Unangu," *TNN*, no. 2 (November 1893): 49.
70 Abdallah, "A Letter From Unangu," *African Tidings*, no. 68 (June 1895). For Kalanje being called *mdachi*, see also: Mzinda, "Nkani Za Msumba," *Mtenga Watu* 2, no. 12 (April 1893). For Kalanje's caravans going to German territory, see: AUMCA, A1(XI), f. 457–462: Letter from Bishop Hine to Travers (Unangu, May 22, 1901). According to the Anglican priest Abdallah, Kalanje had received a black *joho*—a sort of a cloak—as a present from the "Germans" and was gladly wearing it whenever possible. See: Abdallah, "A Letter From Unangu," *African Tidings*, no. 68 (June 1895).
71 Johnson, "More about the Yaos," *TNN*, no. 3 (February 1894): 78.
72 Johnson, "More about the Yaos," *TNN*, no. 3 (February 1894): 78.
73 AUMCA, E2, f. 142: R. Webb, "African Tour May 1896 – Nov. 1896," 161; Robert Webb, *A Visit to Africa 1896* (Westminster: UMCA, 1897), 24.

head teacher in Nkhotakota, who had come here into exile after the last Jumbe had been deposed by the British administration.[74]

Chingomanje and Kalanje cast their nets wide and did not cease their trading activities either. They, however, adapted to the new situation and seem to have avoided trading in slaves, concentrating instead on the "legitimate" ivory trade. Certainly, the missionaries always suspected that Kalanje had not given up the "illegitimate" trade,[75] but Kalanje and Chingomanje were clever or lucky enough to not get caught in slave trading on the lake. There is little concrete evidence about the continuation of trading activities in Nkholongue in the 1890s, but in 1895 Nkholongue was still described as "a favourite port for the dhows."[76] Furthermore, in 1899, shortly before Nkholongue's colonization by the *Companhia*, a new dhow was built in the village.[77] This can be taken as a clear sign that Chingomanje was not willing to leave the trade to the British, who were about to oust the local traders from the lake transport.[78]

By the time the *Companhia*'s troops arrived in late 1900, Kalanje and Chingomanje had certainly already lost some of their former power, but in some ways their hold also seemed less threatened than it had been some 20 years before. Their arch enemy Makanjira had been deposed by the British, and the Angoni subjugated by German forces. Mataka, another of their enemies, had already been challenged by a joint British-Portuguese military expedition, which was reportedly actively welcomed by the Yao chiefs of Unango.[79] For Kalanje and Chingomanje, the future did not look so bleak on the eve of colonization.

The Arrival of the *Companhia* in Late 1900

The way they were colonized must therefore have come as a surprise to them, if not a blow to their ideas. We have to be critical of the reports about the *Compan-*

---

74 For the traders, see: "Notes," *TNN*, no. 8 (May 1895): 8. For Sheik Bwana, see Chapter 3, p. 100.
75 Glossop, "From Likoma to Unangu," *CA* 13, no. 154 (October 1895): 149; Sim, *Life and Letters*, 116, 144. This suspicion was certainly also fueled by the fact that Kalanje repeatedly expressed his opposition to the policy of abolition in front of the missionaries. See for example: Maples, "Unangu," *TNN*, no. 2 (November 1893): 49.
76 Glossop, "From Likoma to Unangu," *CA* 13, no. 154 (October 1895): 1895.
77 AUMCA, A1(XII), f. 414–423: Letter from Herbert Barnes to His Mother (Losefa, November 26, 1899).
78 For the ousting of local traders, see: TNA, FO/2/68, f. 79–80: John L. Nicoll to C. A. Edwards (Kajulu, August 28, 1894); Glossop, "From Likoma to Unangu," *CA* 13, no. 154 (October 1895): 149.
79 AUMCA, A1(X-XI), f. 275–279: Letter from Bishop Hine to Mr. Travers (S.S. Charles Janson, March 9, 1898).

hia's arrival in the region, because they mainly represent the views of the missionaries of the UMCA on the events. They were certainly not neutral observers of these events. However, that the *Companhia*'s initial appearance was accompanied by a particularly high level of violence and injustices is beyond question. Still, there is also reason to believe that the British missionaries and their supposed "subjects" were disproportionately intimidated compared to other residents of the region as the Portuguese officers were obviously anxious to demonstrate who the new masters of the territory were.

It was certainly no coincidence that Messumba, which had become the center of the Anglican church on the "Portuguese" mainland, was chosen as location for the *Companhia*'s first headquarters. On December 23, 1900, the Portuguese commander José Nolasco selected a site for the construction of the Portuguese fort, "a spot close to the Mission and between it and the main part of the village—a spot also crowded with houses."[80] According to missionary Herbert Barnes, Nolasco ordered the immediate demolition of these 30 to 40 houses. If one follows Barnes, the situation escalated on Christmas Day. In the morning, a "foraging excursion" of the *Companhia*'s *askaris* ("native" soldiers) in the village had startled the inhabitants of Messumba, causing many to flee into the hills. Then, in the afternoon, the remaining people were herded to work at the fort's construction site, and even required to continue working after sunset. According to Barnes, Christmas Day culminated with the Portuguese forces surrounding the church during the evening service and pointing their rifles through the building's "open" windows. When people left the church after worship, many of them were beaten up.[81]

Most probably, the *Companhia*'s construction plans in Messumba at a moment so central to the Christian liturgical year were little more than a show of force as the building site in Messumba was abandoned before anything substantial had been built, and the headquarters was moved to Metangula, which had actually been designated as the location for the *Companhia*'s headquarters before the *Companhia*'s troops arrived at the lake.[82] But while much of the "preliminary bluster"[83]

---

[80] AUMCA, C4, f. 112–119: Herbert Barnes, "The Portuguese on the East Side of Lake Nyasa," December 1900, 2.

[81] AUMCA, C4, f. 112–119: Herbert Barnes, "The Portuguese on the East Side of Lake Nyasa," December 1900. For a description of the same events by another member of the UMCA, see: Ambali, *Thirty Years in Nyasaland*, 54–57.

[82] AUMCA, A1(X-XI), f. 275–279: Letter from Bishop Hine to Mr. Travers (S.S. Charles Janson, March 9, 1898). Metangula had even been inspected by Portuguese officers in 1898 with a view to future occupation. See: MNA, 2/KOM/1/1: "Kota Kota Mission Diary, 1894 August 17–1911 January 2," entry dated February 26, 1898.

[83] AUMCA, C4, f. 50–51: Letter from [Bishop Hine] to Mr. Travers (Mponda's, December 31, 1900), 4.

was directed against the mission and its "subjects,"[84] abuses were reported from everywhere, seemingly arbitrarily directed against everyone. At the construction site of the *Companhia*'s headquarters in Metangula, "multitudes of men and women" were reportedly forced "to work at building and getting materials without any pay whatever."[85] The *Companhia*'s *askaris*, it was stated, had "free license to insult, outrage, rob and ill-use in any way the native population in all the places they enter"[86] and "to seize for immoral purposes any women they come across."[87] The missionaries mainly attributed this "abominable ill-treatment" of the "natives" to the fact that the *Companhia*'s *askaris*—mostly Makua soldiers from the coast—were not provided with food, but had to procure it themselves by looting in the villages.[88]

Even though Chingomanje was called a "friend" by one of the *Companhia*'s officials, his village does not seem to have been spared such mistreatment. According to missionary Eyre, in December 1901, Chingomanje was ordered to send a woman to the Portuguese fort or else his village would be punished—a woman was sent. And at an unspecified date of the same year, Chingomanje told the missionaries that a woman of his village had been forcibly taken to Metangula by the *askaris*, but that he had managed to get her back by going to the Portuguese commander.[89]

Chingomanje was not the only chief to face such demands. In October, the Unango chiefs Kalanje and Nampanda were also forced to send a woman each to the *Companhia*'s headquarters. Bishop Hine explained this practice by saying that the Portuguese officers wanted concubines for themselves and their *askaris*.[90] However, the fact that each chief was required to send one woman clearly shows that this

---

84 Other examples come from Meluluca where the Companhia's officers were said to have threatened to tie up the Anglican teacher unless he closed the school. While, in Mtonya, the teacher Petro was said to have been flogged for no reason "except that he was one of 'the English'." See: AUMCA, C4: Letter from [Bishop Hine] to Mr. Travers (Likoma, December 9, 1900).
85 "The Nyasa Disturbances," *CA* 19, no. 221 (May 1901): 80.
86 AUMCA, C4, f. 50–51: Letter from [Bishop Hine] to Mr. Travers (Mponda's, December 31, 1900), 1.
87 AUMCA, C4, f. 50–51: Letter from [Bishop Hine] to Mr. Travers (Mponda's, December 31, 1900), 2.
88 AUMCA, C4, f. 112–119: Herbert Barnes, "The Portuguese on the East Side of Lake Nyasa," December 1900, 7; MNA, UMCA 1/2/17/1: Letter from C.B. Eyre to the Chairman and Directors of the Companhia do Nyassa, Lisbon (Westminster, April 23, 1902), 4.
89 MNA, UMCA 1/2/17/1: C.B. Eyre, "Appendix to a Letter from C.B. Eyre to the Chairman and Directors of the Companhia do Nyassa, Lisbon" (April 23, 1902), 3–4. A copy of the same letter can also be found in: AUMCA, TC/G2: Letter from C.B. Eyre (Westminster, April 23, 1902); AHM, Códice 11–2485: Documento N.° LXXVII: Relatório, de 23 de Abril de 1902, de Reverendo Eyre ao Presidente das Secções Estrangeiras, in *Documentos sobre as Missões Inglesas das Universidades*, 115–134.
90 AUMCA, A1(XIII), f. 5–8: Letter from Bishop Hine to Mr. Travers (Msumba, October 6, 1901). See as well: MNA, UMCA 1/2/17/1: Letter from C.B. Eyre to the Chairman and Directors of the Companhia do Nyassa, Lisbon (Westminster, April 23, 1902), 6.

sexual abuse was certainly also intended as a show of force not only against the abused women but also against the newly colonized chiefdoms as a whole.

Still, we can doubt whether this was really perceived as a humiliation by the (former) slave-trading chiefs like Chingomanje or Kalanje, as long as they could choose which woman was to be sent. It is telling that Chingomanje sent a woman when summoned to do so but reclaimed another who had been taken by the *askaris* without his consent. It must also be considered that other chiefs acted differently: in Chilowelo (south of Lussefa), for example, many women were said to have gone into hiding because their chief had refused the *Companhia*'s demand stating that no woman was available for such a purpose.[91]

But the task of reconstructing Chingomanje's perspective and of analyzing his actions in this matter is even more complicated. For around the time of the arrival of the *Companhia*, Nkholongue's Anglican "native" teacher—who, by the way, lived with his wife in the village[92]—had eloped into British territory with one of Chingomanje's wives.[93] While this was possibly—provided she left voluntarily—not so bad for the woman concerned, it seems evident that for Chingomanje this must have come as a great personal humiliation, for which he held the missionaries responsible. As consequence of the incident, Chingomanje barred the missionaries from having a teacher in his village for more than ten years.[94]

The most interesting part of this story is, however, related to the fact that Chingomanje filed a complaint about this case at the *Companhia*'s headquarters. The *Companhia*'s officials then turned to the authorities of British Central Africa in order to get the woman back—without success.[95] Chingomanje thus complained to the missionaries about the *Companhia*'s misconduct, and to the *Companhia*'s

---

91 MNA, UMCA 1/2/17/1: C.B. Eyre, "Appendix to a Letter from C.B. Eyre to the Chairman and Directors of the Companhia do Nyassa, Lisbon" (April 23, 1902), 3.
92 Wimbush, "A Survey of the Work of the 'Charles Janson,'" *CA* 16, no. 183 (March 1898): 44.
93 The missionaries remained rather vague about this incident in their publications, only referring to the misconduct of their teacher in articles published many years later: Winspear and Johnson, "News from the Stations: II. The Chauncy Maples," *NDC*, no. 37 (October 1912): 935; William Percival Johnson and H.A. Machell Cox, "News from the Stations: Station III," *NDC*, no. 65 (October 1919): 17–22. More detailed information on the case can only be found in unpublished material of the mission. See: AUMCA, AI(VI)B, f. 1802: Notes for a Biog. of W. P. Johnson, pt. Natives, N. 4.
94 Winspear and Johnson, "News from the Stations: II. The Chauncy Maples," *NDC*, no. 37 (October 1912): 935.
95 AHM, Códice 11–2485: Documento N.º XXXIX: Extracto do relatório do Sargento Mario Viegas, Chefe do Concelho do Lago, escripto no Ibo, em 20 de Dezembro de 1901, in *Documentos sobre as Missões Inglesas das Universidades*, 68. See also: AHM, Códice 11–2485: Documento N.º XXXVII: Extractos dos apontamentos particulares do Capitão Trindade dos Santos, relativos estabelecimentos das missões na região do Lago, in *Documentos sobre as Missões Inglesas das Universidades*, 58.

men about the missionaries' misconduct, demonstrating once more his diplomatic flexibility.

But Chingomanje's personal business aside, the arrival of the *Companhia* made the chiefs' previous diplomacy appear to be of little value. This is at least the impression one gets when following the descriptions of the missionaries. In April 1901, the first Yao priest of the UMCA, Yohanna B. Abdallah, wrote that the Unango chiefs were "afraid of these Portuguese officials," and that they did "not know what to do."[96] And in mid-1901, Bishop Hine said that Kalanje was in a "state of fright" because the village of a neighboring chief had been sacked by the Portuguese *askaris* in what Hine called a "clear sweep."[97] It must be added that the chief whose village had been destroyed had been an opponent rather than an ally of Kalanje. This shows all the more how uncertain the situation had become in just a couple of months.

Yet it probably escaped the missionaries' notice that some chiefs were quicker to come to terms with the new situation than the missionaries themselves. Kalanje, for example, in his alleged "state of fright," asked Hine to write a letter in French on his behalf to the Portuguese commander to inquire of the country's new authorities whether his annual caravan would still be allowed to enter German territory or would now have to head for a port on the Portuguese coast.[98] Obviously, diplomacy, anticipation, and accommodation still seemed to be better weapons to Kalanje than resistance or flight.

Chingomanje's Role in the Making of the Colonial State

Chingomanje was also ready to accept the new authorities. This is shown by a case related to orders given to the chiefs after the arrival of the new Portuguese commander Mario Viegas in Metangula in 1901. Viegas had informed all the chiefs that the missionaries were no longer allowed to buy firewood for the engines of their steamers without his permission. The first place the missionaries were denied the purchase of firewood as a result of this order was Malango. Proud of his success, Viegas wrote to his superiors that the chief in question—obviously Chingomanje or his representative in Malango—had notified the missionaries about the new regulation. The missionaries were not allowed to buy firewood in Malango until they had obtained a license for "wooding" at the *Companhia*'s head-

---

96 AUMCA, A6, f. 189: Letter from Y.B. Abdallah to a Friend (Unangu, April 18, 1901).
97 J.E. Hine, "News from Nyasa," *CA* 19, no. 225 (September 1901): 154.
98 AUMCA, A1(XI), f. 457–462: Letter from Bishop Hine to Travers (Unangu, May 22, 1901).

quarters. Viegas concluded his report by saying: "That's the way how I made [the chiefs] understand that the real authorities were the Portuguese."[99]

But while Chingomanje apparently accepted the new rulers and their rules rather quickly, other chiefs were less compliant.[100] By the end of 1901, the villages around Ngofi, near Cobué, were said to be in open rebellion because local officials of the *Companhia* had acted in a "cruel and rapacious manner [toward the inhabitants of the area], tying up and flogging numbers of them, and exacting from them fines of Ivory, cattle etc."[101] Four chiefdoms of the area—including that of Mataka of Cobué (not to be confounded with Mataka of Muembe) and that of Chitesi—were among the rebels. Following a few minor skirmishes, the Portuguese forces evacuated their local military base to Metangula on January 8, 1902. After they had left, the insurgents burnt the base.[102]

It is necessary to highlight this episode, first, to show that other chiefs opted differently, and second, because of the role that Chingomanje II was to play in it. Chingomanje II had not only reluctantly accepted Portuguese authority, but rather began to actively support the *Companhia*'s colonizing endeavors, carrying their goods and troops. Chingomanje's dhow, formerly used to transport slaves, was now used to colonize the eastern shores of Lake Malawi. The evidence is as follows:

On January 7, 1902, the commander of the relief forces dispatched to Ngofi wrote to the headquarters in Metangula asking his superiors to urgently send him Chingomanje's dhow, first to bring food and then to evacuate himself as he was sick.[103] Later, when the Portuguese forces were fearing an attack on Metangula as a consequence of the events around Ngofi, they began to reinforce their contin-

---

99 AHM, Códice 11–2485: Documento N.º XXXIX: Extracto do relatório do Sargento Mario Viegas, Chefe do Concelho do Lago, escripto no Ibo, em 20 de Dezembro de 1901, in *Documentos sobre as Missões Inglesas das Universidades*, 65–66.
100 Already in the first half of 1901, the chief Mataka of Cobué reportedly refused to accept Portuguese authority. See: "The Nyasa Disturbances," *CA* 19, no. 221 (May 1901).
101 MNA, UMCA 1/2/17/1: Letter from C.B. Eyre to the Chairman and Directors of the Companhia do Nyassa, Lisbon (Westminster, April 23, 1902), 7.
102 MNA, UMCA 1/2/17/1: Letter from C.B. Eyre to the Chairman and Directors of the Companhia do Nyassa, Lisbon (Westminster, April 23, 1902), 7–13; TNA, FO/2/605, f. 177–186: C.B. Eyre, "Re Portuguese Nyassaland Co.," enclosed in C.B. Eyre to Mr. Sharpe (Blantyre, February 9, 1902), f. 178. For the perspective of the *Companhia*'s officers on the matter, see: AHM, Códice 11–2485: Documento N.º LXVIII: Informação, de 16 de Janeiro de 1902, do 1.º Cabo João Rosa Junior, in *Documentos sobre as Missões Inglesas das Universidades*, 99–101; AHM, Códice 11–2485: Documento N.º LXIX: Declaração do soldado José Guerreiro, in *Documentos sobre as Missões Inglesas das Universidades*, 101–103.
103 AHM, Códice 11–2485: Documento N.º LXVII: Carta, de 7 Janeiro de 1902, do 1.º Cabo João Rosa Junior, mandado em soccorro a N'gofi ao Sargento Lopes Branco, Chefe do Concelho do Lago, in *Documentos sobre as Missões Inglesas das Universidades*, 98–99.

gent there with troops from Luwangwa, again using Chingomanje's dhow according to missionary Eyre.[104] In early February 1902, when there were still rumors of war, Eyre reported that the Portuguese forces were "keeping close to the [fort]," and once more it was "Chingomanje's Dhow" that was "in attendance."[105] And when in April 1902 the commander of the *Companhia*'s headquarters in Metangula traveled with his troops to Ngofi to clarify the situation, he again explicitly referred to using Chingomanje's dhow for transportation.[106]

Of course, we can suspect that Chingomanje was forced to provide his dhow to the *Companhia*. However, there is more to suggest that he retained full control over it, probably making it available in exchange for payment and/or privileged status: first, a dhow is of little use without a skipper and a crew. It must have been safer for the *Companhia*'s officials to provide incentives in this case than to risk having a dhow without the necessary navigational skills. And second, this is also indicated by the fact that both the *Companhia*'s officials and missionary Eyre explicitly referred to the dhow as that of Chingomanje. The *Companhia*'s commander even gave the dhow a name, writing that he traveled "on board of the dhow 'Patria'[107] of chief Chingomanje" ("a bordo da lancha 'Patria' do régulo Chingomange").[108] We can assume that he would hardly have used such a wording if he had considered the dhow to be under his sole command.

Further evidence that the *Companhia* was actively supported by people from Nkholongue can be found in the documents relating to the controversy between the Anglican mission and the representatives of the *Companhia*. After the arrival of the *Companhia* on the lakeshore, the missionaries lodged several complaints against officials of the *Companhia*.[109] Probably the most severe complaint was

---

[104] TNA, FO/2/605, f. 177–186: C.B. Eyre, "Re Portuguese Nyassaland Co.," enclosed in C.B. Eyre to Mr. Sharpe (Blantyre, February 9, 1902), f. 184–185. On the *Companhia*'s fear of an attack, see: AHM, Códice 11–2485: Documento N.° LXV: Nota n.° 7, de 11 de Janeiro de 1902, do Sargento Lopes Branco, Chefe do Concelho do Lago, ao Governador Intérino M. Pereira, in *Documentos sobre as Missões Inglesas das Universidades*, 97.
[105] TNA, FO/2/605, f. 177–186: C.B. Eyre, "Re Portuguese Nyassaland Co.," enclosed in C.B. Eyre to Mr. Sharpe (Blantyre, February 9, 1902), f. 186.
[106] AHM, Códice 11–2485: Documento N.° CV: Nota, de 13 de Abril de 1902, do Sargento Lopes Branco, Chefe Interino do Concelho do Lago, ao Commandante da Força Policial (Ibo), in *Documentos sobre as Missões Inglesas das Universidades*, 184.
[107] "Pátria" is the Portuguese word for "fatherland/motherland." We can of course doubt that this was the actual name of the dhow, although it could have been a translation.
[108] AHM, Códice 11–2485: Documento N.° CV: Nota, de 13 de Abril de 1902, do Sargento Lopes Branco, Chefe Interino do Concelho do Lago, ao Commandante da Força Policial (Ibo), in *Documentos sobre as Missões Inglesas das Universidades*, 184.
[109] "Troubles at Nyasa," *CA* 19, no. 220 (April 1901): 57. See as well: AUMCA, TC/G2.

made by missionary Eyre in February 1902 after the incidents around Ngofi. In his letter to the *Companhia*'s headquarters in Lisbon, he described and listed a wide range of mistreatment and abuse, including the two cases of sexual exploitation of women from Nkholongue. The *Companhia*'s officials, for their part, actively documented evidence of the missionaries' misconduct, listing the case of the Anglican teacher who had "abducted" one of Chingomanje's wives. After Eyre's official complaint, the *Companhia*'s commissioner in Metangula, Lopes Branco, began to support certain allegations against the mission with testimonies from "natives."

One claim was that the mission had facilitated the escape of Chief Manhica, a chief wanted by the *Companhia* for an alleged attempt at rebellion. To support his claim, Branco presented three "native" witnesses, all of whom have already made appearances in Chapter 3.[110] The first was Abdallah Mkwanda,[111] identified as the local shopkeeper of the Swiss trader Ludwig Deuss in Metangula and said to be from M'ponda at the south end of the lake. We can be fairly certain that this is the same Abdallah Mkwanda who was characterized by Greenstein as the most influential Muslim teacher of the Lake Malawi region.[112] The second witness was Azize b. Chingomanje, identified as son of Chingomanje b. M'ponda and said to live in Nkholongue. The third witness was a certain "Tubair," identified as a teacher and said to live in Nkholongue. There is little doubt that "Tubair" is identical with Thubiri, the Muslim disciple of Sheik Bwana.

It is important to know that around this time Abdallah Mkwanda was somewhat like the chief interpreter of the *Companhia* in Metangula. However, he had not only supported the *Companhia*'s activities with his language skills, but, according to the missionaries' reports, also used the *Companhia*'s authority for his own aims. Missionary Hine described Mkwanda as a "fanatical Mohamedan'" and char-

---

110 AHM, Códice 11–2485: Documento N.° CXV: Auto de investigação levantado contra o Reverendo Bispo de Likoma, pelo Chefe Interino do Concelho do Lago, sargento Lopes Branco, in *Documentos sobre as Missões Inglesas das Universidades*, 198–200.

111 In Branco's report, the name appears as "Abdalla Mekuanda."

112 Greenstein's Mkwanda was born at Makanjira's and not at M'ponda's. However, there is ample evidence that it must have been the same person. See: Greenstein, "Shayks and Tariqas," 14–16; AHM, Códice 11–2485: Documento N.° CIII: Auto de investigação levantado em 13 de Abril de 1902, em M'tangula, pélo Chefe Interino do Concelho do Lago, Lopes Branco, contra um padre da Missão, in *Documentos sobre as Missões Inglesas das Universidades*, 178–180; AHM, Códice 11–2485: Documento N.° CIV: Auto de investigação levantado em 15 de Abril de 1902, em M'tangula, pélo Chefe Interino do Concelho do Lago, Lopes Branco, contra padres da Missão, in *Documentos sobre as Missões Inglesas das Universidades*, 180–183; William Percival Johnson, "The Yaos: A Defence, and a Suggestion," *TNN*, no. 2 (1893): 57; "Letters from From Rev. W. P. Johnson," *CA* 7, no. 78 (June 1889): 92.

acterized him as a fierce opponent of Christianity.[113] He was already present at the above-mentioned confrontations in Messumba during Christmas and reportedly played a central role in coordinating the "assaults" against the mission.[114] He was further said to have used the *Companhia*'s power to resolve economic feuds with the local population to his advantage.[115]

Azizi b. Chingomanje was not just any son of Chingomanje II, he was the most prominent son of Chingomanje. He has already appeared above as the leader of the envoy sent by Chingomanje II to the missionaries in 1893 to ask for the British flag. He is comparatively well remembered in oral tradition and was called "Bwana Azizi" as a sign of respect.[116] We do not know anything about Azize b. Chingomanje's religious convictions at the time of the incident with certainty, but many years later he was said to be a "prominent and sincere Mohammedan."[117]

Branco's coalition of anti-mission witnesses is at any rate an interesting one, since at least two of them were Muslims and two of them were residents of a village whose chief had just expelled the mission school. It is likely that Branco had also chosen his witnesses because of their common anti-mission disposition, and that the three witnesses also had their motives for testifying against the mission. In any case, we have another indication that Chingomanje and his entourage were not among the early opponents of the *Companhia*, but rather supported it in the early making of the colonial state.

This making was, however, not a linear process. While it seemed to make sense for Chingomanje II, his son Bwana Azizi and Thubiri to side with the *Companhia* in early 1902, they may have regretted their support later. This is because the decision-makers of the *Companhia* preferred not to further antagonize the British residents of the lakeshore area. In June 1902, the interim governor of the *Companhia*'s territories wrote that it was clear that the *Companhia*'s officials bore the brunt of the blame for the whole affair. He called Lopes Branco's attempts to prove alleged misconduct on the part of the missionaries "a further blatant foolery" that only

---

113 AUMCA, A1(XI), f. 457–462: Letter from Bishop Hine to Travers (Unangu, May 22, 1901).
114 AUMCA, A1(XI), f. 457–462: Letter from Bishop Hine to Travers (Unangu, May 22, 1901); Ambali, *Thirty Years in Nyasaland*, 56.
115 "News from the Stations: S.S. 'C.M.,'" *LDQP*, no. 4 (July 1904): 78–79; AUMCA, C4, f. 50–51: Letter from [Bishop Hine] to Mr. Travers (Mponda's, December 31, 1900), 3; C.B. Eyre, "Travelling to Unangu," *CA* 25, no. 289 (January 1907): 6; Sutherland, *Adventures*, 177–179.
116 "Bwana" translates as much as "master" in Kiswahili.
117 See: "News from the Stations: V. Msumba," *NDC*, no. 130 (January 1936): 7–9.

added to the bad image of the *Companhia*'s authorities in the eyes of the missionaries.[118] Consequently, the *Companhia*'s local officials were recalled.

After the arrival of the *Companhia*'s new "men on the spot," relations between the *Companhia* and both the mission and the rebellious villages improved considerably.[119] In April 1903, the missionaries reported that peace had been made with the "natives,"[120] and five months later the missionaries and 1,500 "natives" gathered in Metangula to celebrate the birthday of the king of Portugal. On that occasion, the Anglican bishop thanked Metangula's new commissioner "and congratulated him in his successful efforts to bring order out of chaos."[121]

One may wonder whether the change of administration resulted in reprisals against men like Abdallah Mkwanda or Chingomanje II, who had sided with the very people who had fallen from grace. Unfortunately, the sources do not allow us to examine this question as virtually nothing can be gleaned from the documentary evidence about the relations between Chingomanje II and the *Companhia* with regard to the period after mid-1902.

4.3 Changing Settlement Patterns as a Sign of Emancipation

While the reaction of Chingomanje to colonization can be reconstructed at least until 1902, the possibilities of doing so for the majority of Nkholongue's inhabitants are much more limited. Observations by Europeans about changing social relations must be treated with caution. Their talk of "social revolution" fits all too well with the propaganda of the European civilizing mission.[122] In any case, European accounts of the fate of slavery in the area around Nkholongue are not only potential-

---

118 AHM, Códice 11–2485: Documento N.º XCII: Extracto do officio confidencial extra de 20 de Junho de 1902, do Governador Intérino Martins Pereira, ao Presidente do Concelho d'Administração, in *Documentos sobre as Missões Inglesas das Universidades*, 165–166.
119 AUMCA, A1(XV), f. 45–46: Letter from Bishop Trower to Mr. Travers (Likoma, October 8, 1902); AUMCA, A1(XV), f. 35–38: Letter from Bishop Trower to Mr. Travers (Malindi, August 9, 1902); Herbert Barnes, "Portuguese Troubles in Nyasaland," *CA* 22, no. 264 (1904): 241–246.
120 H., "News of Portuguese East Africa," *CA* 21, no. 244 (April 1903): 65.
121 P. Y., "Notes: King of Portugal's Birthday," *LDQP*, no. 1 (October 1903): 15–16.
122 The British resident of Nkhotakota, for example, reported in 1896 that "[t]he natives of this district are becoming much more independent of their chiefs than they were formerly and slaves are shaking off the yoke of slavery. [...] a social revolution is being rapidly accomplished[.]" See: Alfred J. Swann, "Summary of 1895 Report on the Marimba District," *British Central Africa Gazette*, April 15, 1896.

ly biased, but also superficial.[123] Nevertheless, it can be stated that colonization did indeed reduce the dependence of slaves on their masters regionally. This becomes clearest if we look at the changing settlement patterns.

Chapter 2 revealed that the lakeshore area was anything but a peaceful place in the second half of the 19th century. Nkholongue was attacked and even burnt to the ground at least twice. As a result of the political instability, most people lived in very compact villages, which were usually surrounded by some sort of barrier. In the case of Unango, people lived on the escarpments of a mountain.[124] In the case of Nkhlongue, the village was protected by a stockade. The ruins of this fortification are still visible today on a peninsula called *linga*, after the Chinyanja word for "stockade" (see Map 3 on p. 216).

I have already explained that the political situation at that time facilitated the control of slaves and serfs. Even if slaves could have escaped their masters, they simply had nowhere to go. Rather than risk being captured by other groups, many may have preferred to stay under the "protection" of their present master. Others who were nominally free may have even sought the shelter of powerful chiefs, placing themselves in a state of servitude to avoid a worse fate.

These conditions changed significantly with European colonization. The arrival of the European powers not only brought an end to the slave trade, but also to the wars tied to the trade. Even oral tradition clearly attributes the end of these wars to the arrival of the Europeans.[125] In this context, the special situation of the area around Nkholongue must be highlighted. This area had been conceded

---

123 For examples, see: AHM, Códice 11–2485: Documento N.° CLVI: Extractos do relatório, de 26 de Setembro de 1908, do Chefe do Concelho do Lago, Dr. Guerra Lage, intitulado: "Concelho do Lago – Informações relativas aos anos de 1905, 1906 e 1907," in *Documentos sobre as Missões Inglesas das Universidades*, 248–260; Augusto Neuparth, "A Fronteira Luso-Allemã de Moçambique VI," *Revista Portugueza Colonial e Maritima* XIX, No. 138 (1908), 13; AHM, SNI, Secção B, cx. 1097: Jaime Asdrubal Casqueiro: "Inquerito sobre escravidão ou servidão indigena" (Maniamba: Administração da Circunscrição Civil de Lago, February 15, 1937); AHM, SNI, Secção B, cx. 1097: Gastão Porto de Moraes: "Inquerito sobre escravidão ou servidão indigena" (Unango: Secretaria do Posto Administrativo, February 6, 1937).
124 For this process of agglomeration in the region, see: Liesegang, "Guerras, terras e tipos de povoaçoes."
125 PA, I001: interview with *P0050* (♂, ~1922) (Nkholongue, August 17, 2010), min 01:17:05–01:17:37; PA, I009: interview with *P0128* (♂, 1928) (Nkholongue, September 1, 2010), min 01:15:51–01:17:09; AHM, Secção Oral, Transcrito NI 12: N.° 139–142, Entrevista com um grupo de velhos em Lumbiza (Unango, Niassa), interview by Gerhard Liesegang, Teresa Oliveira, and Mueojuane Mainga Vicente, July 17, 1981, 5; AHM, Secção Oral, Transcrito NI 13: N.° 142–143, Entrevista com o ex-régulo Nampanda em Mapudje (Unango, Niassa), July 17, 1981, 7; AHM, Secção Oral, Transcrito NI 15: N.° 145–147, Entrevista com Ali Bonomali e um grupo de velhos em Nazinhendje (Unango, Niassa), July 18, 1981, 7.

to Portugal in treaties with Germany (1886) and the United Kingdom (1891). The fact that the British and German forces began colonizing the adjacent territories years before the arrival of the *Companhia* in 1900 had the effect that important slave traders of the region were brought down before the "Portuguese" lakeshore area was "effectively occupied." By 1895, both the Jumbe and Makanjira had been deposed by the British, and by 1898 the Angoni living in the north had been subdued by German forces.[126] Consequently, the threat of slave raids had already declined around Nkholongue before 1901.

The inhabitants of the region seem to have quickly grasped the new opportunities and started to leave the previously compact settlements. The process of disaggregation could be observed everywhere as early as 1899. People began to "spread out thin all along the lakeshore,"[127] and in places like Unango they started to come down from the mountain.[128] By 1904, only a few houses were reportedly still located on the mountain, and the former town of up to 5,000 inhabitants was now scattered within 10 to 20 miles of Mount Unango.[129] In retrospect, missionary Barnes described this process as follows:

> The scattering referred to was a result of the peace from raiding enjoyed by the lakeside people after the establishment of British power on the Lake. Formerly every village was a crowded collection of huts inside a stockade, the *linga*. In 1899 these were beginning to disappear and by now nothing is left in most villages but the name *linga*, referring to the line of the vanished stockade. The crowded village or town became a widely separated group of tiny hamlets planted in every suitable bay.[130]

Not only did the houses begin to spread out, but also, and most importantly, people's fields, which had formerly been located as close as possible to the villages.[131] Undoubtedly, the more dispersed way of life facilitated people's daily lives, mainly

---

126 McCracken, *A History of Malawi 1859–1966*, 57–65; Redmond, "A Political History of the Songea Ngoni from the Mid-Nineteenth Century to the Rise of the Tanganyika African National Union," 179–181.
127 Herbert Barnes, "Work in the Nyasa Villages," *CA* 17, no. 203 (November 1899): 199–203. See as well: Robert Howard, *Five Years Medical Work on Lake Nyasa: A Report to the Medical Board of the Universities' Mission on the Health of the European Missionaries in the Likoma Diocese* (London: UMCA, 1904), 37.
128 AUMCA, A1(XII), f. 352–355: Letter from Herbert Barnes to His Mother, July 10, 1899, f. 355; AHM, Secção Oral, Transcrito NI 12: N.° 139–142, Entrevista com um grupo de velhos em Lumbiza (Unango, Niassa), interview by Gerhard Liesegang, Teresa Oliveira, and Mueojuane Mainga Vicente, July 17, 1981, 5; Howard, *Five Years Medical Work*, 67.
129 Howard, *Five Years Medical Work*, 67.
130 Barnes, *Johnson of Nyasaland*, 134.
131 Herbert Barnes, "A Year's Changes at the Lake," *CA* 20, no. 229 (1902): 7–8.

because it met their economic needs much better than a life in compact settlements. This concerned not only the easier access to and control over agricultural land, but also the potentially closer proximity to resources such as (drinking) water, building materials and firewood. While the missionaries acknowledged that this development was "probably a good thing for the people," they themselves were far less happy about it, as it complicated evangelism substantially.[132]

After the arrival of the *Companhia*, the dispersal was likely even accelerated, as this way of life perfectly facilitated evading the dangers of the new era, especially taxation and forced labor. In 1919, the Anglican missionary Cox summed up the motives as follows:

> Year by year the villages have been getting more and more split up mainly I think in search of better fields, and also partly that each little group of houses wanted to be quite on their own, and partly in the hope that they might evade taxation.[133]

We can expect that the increasing freedom of movement made possible by the end of the slave wars also benefited the (former) slaves and serfs, because it reduced the hold their masters had over them.[134] Therefore, social stratification within villages like Nkholongue presumably decreased with colonization.

The increasing freedom of the (former) slaves is also reflected in the fact that some of them returned to their places of origin. Thus, the British Resident in Nkhotakota wrote in his annual report of 1910/1911 about the people who had immigrated to the district:

> Some of these have been sold in the old days of the slave trade and are now returning home again. A certain number of such native[s] have thus been gradually repatriating themselves for many years past.[135]

---

132 The quotation is from: Frank Winspear, "News from the Stations: III. The Chauncy Maples," *NDC*, no. 44 (July 1914): 63. See as well: Barnes, "A Year's Changes at the Lake," *CA* 20, no. 229 (1902); "Notes on the Mtonya and Yao Plateau," *LDQP*, no. 6 (January 1905): 159–161; Yohanna B. Abdallah, "News from the Stations: VI. Unangu," *NDC*, no. 46 (January 1915): 15; H.A. Machell Cox and Lawrence Chisui, "News from the Stations: V. Msumba," *NDC*, no. 62 (January 1919): 14–16; Augustine Ambali, "News from the Stations: IV. Ngoo," *NDC*, no. 65 (October 1919): 22.
133 Johnson and Cox, "News from the Stations: Station III," *NDC*, no. 65 (October 1919): 21. Note that the *Companhia* tried to counteract this development, albeit with limited success. See: Johnson and Cox, "News from the Stations: Station III," *NDC*, no. 65 (October 1919); Yohanna B. Abdallah, "News from the Stations: VII. Unangu," *NDC*, no. 65 (October 1919): 25–26.
134 The same point has been made for other regions of Africa. See: Law, *From Slave Trade to "Legitimate" Commerce*, 16.
135 It is "Kota Kota" in the original. See: MNA, NCK/5/1/1: G. F. Manning, "Annual Report: Marimba District, 1910–11" (Kota-Kota, April 12, 1911), 23.

Seven years later, this return of former slaves was still evident:

> The Nkhotakota population is still in many ways more unsettled than other Districts owing to the terrible extent to which it was devastated by slave raids as a result of which there is still a steady return of natives to their old homes.[136]

Although there is little evidence of the course of these developments in the specific case of Nkholongue, the village was at least partly affected by them. The formation of Malango coincides exactly with the first phase of dispersion in the 1890s. And those who had moved to Malango did not stay there for long, but left the lakeshore under the leadership of Salimo Chingomanje's son Saide Salimo to live in a more fertile region.[137] We can assume that this happened in the 1910s, when many people left the lakeshore area for the hills after the final subjugation of Mataka and Malinganile, the last resistant chiefs from the slave trade era.[138] However, it must also be said that, in comparison to other villages, Nkholongue remained a comparatively compact settlement until the 1950s. But this was mainly owed to the village's role as a "wooding station" of the Anglican steamships, which made the village's population less dependent on agriculture (see Chapter 6).

An impression of possible changes in Nkholongue's social structure is also provided by the "ethnographic census" of 1940, according to which the population of Nkholongue was 287, of whom 85 (29.6%) were identified as Wayao and 202 (70.4%) as Anyanja.[139] This ratio suggests that the proportion of slave descendants in 1940 was somewhat lower than the proportion of slaves at the end of the 19th century. However, such a calculation ignores considerations of marriage practices, the reliability of the data of this census, and the instability of ethnic ascriptions. Today, for example, almost all villagers of Nkholongue refer to themselves as Anyanja. This indicates, however, that identities based on one's "origin" were still more salient in 1940 than they are today.

---

136 MNA, NCK/5/1/2: Annual Report: Kota-Kota District, 1917–18 (Kota-Kota, n.d.), 4.
137 PA, Chadreque Umali, *História de Nyanjas* (Metangula, 1996), 58; PA, I099: interview with *P1420* (♂, ~1922) (Ngongo, February 16, 2016), min 00:04:14–00:04:51; PA, I114: interview with *P1074* (♀, ~1940), *P1141* (♂, 1932) (Malango, April 15, 2016), min 00:06:25–00:10:30.
138 Winspear and Johnson, "News from the Stations: II. The Chauncy Maples," *NDC*, no. 37 (October 1912). According to the logbook, the Anglican steamship CM "wooded" in Malango in April 1918. This is an indication that people may still have lived there at that time. However, this was the last documented occurrence of "wooding" at Malango. See: Archives of the Society of Malawi (ASM), Chauncy Maples Log 1914–1924.
139 AHM, Biblioteca, 1282j: Manuel Simões Alberto, *Os negros de Moçambique: Censo etnográfico* (Lourenço Marques, 1942), 59.

4.4 Conclusion

This chapter started by noting that previous research on colonization has often ignored the pre-colonial political and social heterogeneity of societies in northern Mozambique. Accordingly, I have sought to challenge historical portrayals that tend to homogenize people's experiences of and reaction to colonization. To achieve this goal, I have tried to analyze the experience of colonization from two distinct perspectives, that of Nkholongue's slave-trading chief Chingomanje II bin M'ponda and that of the village's majority population.

The first part has shown that Chingomanje II bin M'ponda was an able diplomat who skillfully adapted to ever new situations and thus succeeded in holding on to power despite his previous involvement in the slave trade. While he doubtlessly acted in an independent manner vis-à-vis the Europeans, he was ultimately no opponent of colonial rule. Rather, he ended up supporting the colonizing forces in their fight against other rebellious chiefs of the region.

The second part has highlighted that while the old power relations of the village thus remained intact on the surface, many people may have indeed benefited from improved economic and social opportunities as a result of colonization. This was less because the European powers were fighting for their emancipation[140] than because they had fought the slave-trading chiefs, and thus put an end to the wars that had so severely curtailed people's freedom in the decades before. It has been argued that this development can be measured best by the dispersal of the earlier compact settlements. Previous research has often analyzed this dispersal as the result of colonial violence and the state's attempt to integrate people into the colonial economy.[141] My findings, however, clearly show that while this (forced) integration of people into the colonial economy may have catalyzed the process, the change in settlement patterns preceded these attempts and first and foremost reflected people's need for adequate farming possibilities. It thus supports other research on other parts of Africa that has described similar processes

---

[140] As other researchers have shown, the colonial powers were generally reluctant in fighting slavery as an institution. See: Deutsch, *Emancipation without Abolition*, 2; Christine Whyte, "'Freedom but Nothing Else': The Legacies of Slavery and Abolition in Post-Slavery Sierra Leone, 1928–1956," *The International Journal of African Historical Studies* 48, no. 2 (2015): 231–250; Emily Lynn Osborn, "Work and Migration," in *The Oxford Handbook of Modern African History*, ed. John Parker and Richard J. Reid (Oxford: Oxford University Press, 2013), 197.

[141] McCracken, *A History of Malawi 1859–1966*, 67–68; Barry Neil-Tomlinson, "The Nyassa Chartered Company: 1891–1929," *The Journal of African History* 18, no. 1 (1977): 118; William Finnegan, *A Complicated War: The Harrowing of Mozambique* (Berkeley: University of California Press, 1992), 114.

of settlement dispersal during colonization.¹⁴² However, this way of emancipation only existed in regions of the continent where there was abundant land for settlement.¹⁴³

There is no doubt that the end of the slave trade and wars reduced the hold of chiefs over their subjects and made ordinary people less dependent on the protection of powerful players. This is not to say that colonization did not bring significant new hardships into people's daily lives, as has already been hinted at in this chapter and will be further elaborated on in the next.¹⁴⁴ This is only to echo the findings of Jan-Georg Deutsch who has argued that "it is sometimes overlooked that after the conquest some of the socially marginalised groups, such as slaves, encountered a new range of economic and social opportunities, notably a greater freedom of movement, that were previously unavailable to them."¹⁴⁵ In this context, one could also add what was discussed in the previous chapter regarding the opportunities that Islamization offered people to improve their social status. In the end, "enslaved men and women had their own expectations about the colonial conquest and readily grasped the change of power and the opportunities it offered."¹⁴⁶

Overall, this chapter hopes to have succeeded in contributing to the reconstruction of "the lived experience of African peoples under colonial rule in all

---

142 See for example: Michael B. Gleave, "Hill Settlements and Their Abandonment in Western Yorubaland," *Africa: Journal of the International African Institute* 33, no. 4 (1963): 343–52; Marilyn Silberfein, "Cyclical Change in African Settlement and Modern Resettlement Programs," in *Rural Settlement Structure and African Development*, ed. Marylin Silberfein (New York: Routledge, 1998), 48–49; Sara Berry, *No Condition Is Permanent: The Social Dynamics of Agrarian Change in Sub-Saharan Africa* (Madison: University of Wisconsin Press, 1993), 37. The importance of accurately analyzing chronology and causality in this context is shown by the fact that some researchers have presented the situation of settlement patterns at the time of colonization in contradictory ways. Iva Peša, for example, described the pre-colonial settlements of Zambia as defensive and concentrated on one page only to portray them as dispersed and scattered on the next without providing any explanation for this difference. See: Peša, *Roads through Mwinilunga*, 3–4.
143 On this point, see as well: Martin Chanock, "A Peculiar Sharpness: An Essay on Property in the History of Customary Law in Colonial Africa," *The Journal of African History* 32, no. 1 (1991): 71.
144 In this regard, there is good reason why Eric Allina has called his study of the colonial system of forced labor in Central Mozambique *Slavery by Any Other Name*. However, as Allina himself points out, it is also important to reflect on the different characteristics of different types of unfree labor and status and the implications of these different characteristics for people's lives. Furthermore, around Nkholongue, forced labor never took on the lasting significance it did in the areas Allina has analyzed. See: Eric Allina, *Slavery by Any Other Name: African Life under Company Rule in Colonial Mozambique* (Charlottesville: University of Virginia Press, 2012).
145 Deutsch, *Emancipation without Abolition*, 209.
146 Bellagamba, Greene, and Klein, "When the Past Shadows the Present," 6.

its complexities and contradictions."[147] The following three chapters will delve further into this diversity of experiences of colonial rule, highlighting in particular their stark variations in temporal perspective.

---

[147] Parker and Rathbone, *African History*, 93.

5 The Grandmother of Poverty: A (Local) Periodization of Colonialism

5.1 The Colonial State on the Periphery: A History of Absence?

When I started with my first interviews, I was expecting to hear much more about colonial exploitation than I ended up doing. To my surprise, colonial violence and abuses were relatively absent from many narratives, and when I raised issues such as taxation, people confirmed the problems, but their accounts often remained impersonal and superficial. Arianna Huhn made a similar observation during her fieldwork in the neighboring town of Metangula, even noting that "[n]ever did any of my informants mention forced participation in cotton cultivation, or subjugation to the notorious [*palmatória*] (paddle) and *chicote* (whip) beatings of the PIDE[.]"[1] Huhn explained the absence of such statements by the minimal presence of the colonial state in the area.[2]

There are certainly methodological problems here. My background as a white European may have played a role, as well as the fact that many people do not like to talk about personal suffering at length. My later research revealed that the colonial state was not as absent, peaceful, and non-exploitative as my initial experience and Huhn's observation would suggest. Still, there is no doubt that the relative absence of complaints about colonial violence in Huhn's and my interviews is also rooted in the fact that Portuguese rule was locally indeed rather tenuous during most of the 1930s, 1940s, and 1950s—the years that could be meaningfully reached by the interviews of our projects. Portuguese presence only increased significantly in the early 1960s in the face of the coming war.

There has been a tendency to essentialize colonialism, and Portuguese colonialism in particular.[3] I have already addressed this question in the previous chapter by highlighting that people viewed colonization from different perspectives. In this chapter, the focus is on the fact that many works portray colonialism as a timeless and unchanging system. They have neglected to analyze the temporal variations of colonialism. This is especially palpable in the case of Portuguese colonialism. With respect to Mozambique, the most prominent example of this static vision of colonialism is doubtlessly Allen Isaacman's analysis of the Mozambican cotton regime

---

1 Huhn, "Sustenance and Sociability," 61.
2 Huhn, 61.
3 Cooper, *Colonialism in Question*, 17.

("Cotton is the Mother of Poverty").[4] With his standard work, Isaacman perpetuated the belief that little changed within the Portuguese colonial system apart from some rhetorical concessions. As Alexander Keese has recently put it pointedly, "stagnation and absence of change are often taken for granted" in the cases of territories under authoritarian Spanish and Portuguese rule.[5]

There is little doubt that the rhetoric often did not materialize, or materialized differently. There was no such thing as a lusotropical multiracial harmony beyond the propaganda. However, the problem is that the idea of stagnation often seems to be a premise rather than an outcome of research on Portuguese colonialism. This can be gleaned not only from the lack of rigor in dealing with chronology and context in many studies, but also from the findings of a number of works that emphasize that there were indeed important changes that materialized. William Gervase Clarence-Smith was certainly one of the first to seriously point to the "profound mutations which Portuguese imperialism underwent during the swan song of empire."[6] Later, Anne Pitcher argued convincingly that the Portuguese cotton regime was not as static as Isaacman and others had claimed, but in fact moved from "co-

---

[4] Isaacman, *Cotton Is the Mother of Poverty*. See as well the overview of Mozambican history he wrote together with his wife: Isaacman and Isaacman, *Mozambique: From Colonialism to Revolution*. For an analogous critique of Isaacman's work, see: M. Anne Pitcher, "Review of Cotton Is the Mother of Poverty: Peasants, Work, and Rural Struggle in Colonial Mozambique, 1938–1961 by Allen Isaacman," *Journal of Southern African Studies* 22, no. 4 (1996): 689–691. See also Michel Cahen's reviews of the studies of Jeanne Penvenne and Eric Allina on forced labor, both of which Cahen criticized for their lack of periodization. However, it must be noted that in the case of Allina's work Cahen's specific criticism that Allina ignored the impact of Circular 818/D-7 (1942) (more on this on pp. 161–162) seems misplaced, as Allina's work dealt with forced labor under the *Companhia de Moçambique*, whose charter expired in 1942. Cahen may be correct in highlighting that, at the colony-wide level, the worst period of forced labor only began then. But this (unsubstantiated) argument fails to recognize the importance of local context and chronologies, which I intend to highlight in this chapter. For Cahen's reviews, see: Michel Cahen, "Notes de lecture: Les Africains et la ville," *Le Mouvement social*, no. 204 (2003): 153–154; Michel Cahen, "Slavery, Enslaved Labour and Forced Labour in Mozambique," *Portuguese Studies Review* 21, no. 1 (2013): 253–265. For the works of Penvenne and Allina, see: Jeanne Penvenne, *African Workers and Colonial Racism: Mozambican Strategies and Struggles in Lourenço Marques, 1877–1962* (Portsmouth: Heinemann, 1995); Allina, *Slavery by Any Other Name*.
[5] Alexander Keese, "Forced Labour in the 'Gorgulho Years': Understanding Reform and Repression in Rural São Tomé e Príncipe, 1945–1953," *Itinerario* 38, no. 1 (2014): 103. See as well: Alexander Keese, *Living with Ambiguity: Integrating an African Elite in French and Portuguese Africa, 1930–61* (Stuttgart: Franz Steiner, 2007), 31.
[6] Clarence-Smith, *The Third Portuguese Empire*, 192.

ercion to incentives."[7] Since the 2000s, Alexander Keese has highlighted the scale and effects of pre-1961 reforms in various works. Among other things, he has shown that working conditions of plantation workers in the colony of São Tomé e Príncipe showed signs of improvement during the term of governor Carlos da Sousa Gorgulho (1945–1953), countering teleological interpretations informed by the knowledge of the brutal endpoint of his reign, the massacre of Batepá.[8] Most recently, the case for the importance of considering the situatedness and shifting character of Portuguese colonial discourse and practice on the ground has been made by Samuel Coghë in his work on population politics in Angola.[9]

With regard to other colonial powers, various scholars have followed Frederick Cooper's example and see the post-1945 period as a time of fundamental change that would also have allowed for outcomes other than decolonization.[10] In line with this, Miguel Bandeira Jerónimo and António Costa Pinto have successfully established the debate on "late colonialism" within the study of the Portuguese Empire.[11] However, authoritarian Portugal is still generally considered to have been less capable of reform than the "liberal" empires of Great Britain or France. In Cooper's words, Portugal "tried to join the development bandwagon without making political concessions."[12] Cosmetics and rhetoric remain the key terms to de-

---

7 M. Anne Pitcher, "From Coercion to Incentives: The Portuguese Colonial Cotton Regime in Angola and Mozambique, 1946–1974," in *Cotton, Colonialism, and Social History in Sub-Saharan Africa*, ed. Allen Isaacman and Richard Roberts (Portsmouth: Heinemann, 1995), 119–146.
8 Keese, "Forced Labour in the 'Gorgulho Years.'" See as well: Alexander Keese, "'Proteger os pretos': Havia uma mentalidade reformista na administração portuguesa na África Tropical (1926–1961)?," *Africana Studia*, no. 6 (2003): 97–125; Keese, *Living with Ambiguity*.
9 Samuël Coghe, *Population Politics in the Tropics: Demography, Health and Transimperialism in Colonial Angola* (Cambridge: Cambridge University Press, 2022), 12.
10 Cooper, *Decolonization and African Society*; Cooper, *Colonialism in Question*, 204–230; Martin Thomas, Bob Moore, and L.J. Butler, *Crises of Empire: Decolonization and Europe's Imperial States, 1918–1975* (London: Bloomsbury, 2008); Martin Thomas and Andrew S. Thompson, "Rethinking Decolonization: A New Research Agenda for the Twenty-First Century," in *The Oxford Handbook of the Ends of Empire*, ed. Martin Thomas and Andrew S. Thompson (Oxford: Oxford University Press, 2018), 1–26.
11 Miguel Bandeira Jerónimo and António Costa Pinto, "The International and the Portuguese Imperial Endgame: Problems and Perspectives," *Portuguese Studies* 29, no. 2 (2013): 137–141; Miguel Bandeira Jerónimo and António Costa Pinto, "A Modernizing Empire? Politics, Culture, and Economy in Portuguese Late Colonialism," in *The Ends of European Colonial Empires*, ed. Miguel Bandeira Jerónimo and António Costa Pinto (Basingstoke: Palgrave Macmillan, 2015), 51–80.
12 Frederick Cooper, "Decolonization in Tropical Africa," in *The Oxford Handbook of the Ends of Empire*, ed. Martin Thomas and Andrew S. Thompson (Oxford: Oxford University Press, 2018), 319. See as well: Andreas Stucki, *Violence and Gender in Africa's Iberian Colonies: Feminizing the Portuguese and Spanish Empire, 1950s–1970s* (Cham: Palgrave Macmillan, 2019), 96; Martin Thomas, "Contrasting Patterns of Decolonization: Belgian and Portuguese Africa," in *Crises of Empire: De-*

scribe developments in the Portuguese Empire during the last decades of colonialism, as if everything was only "for the Englishmen to see." This perspective may have its justification; after all, Portugal was doubtlessly an authoritarian regime. None of the other major colonial powers officially allowed the use of forced labor for as long and systematically as Portugal, and none was ready to fight a protracted war in a colony without settlers and economic significance like Guinea-Bissau.

Nevertheless, the premise of cosmetic change might also prevent us from discovering important similarities among all empires, both in terms of tentative reform and violent oppression. Keese, for example, has repeatedly pointed out how a comparative view can unearth unexpected similarities as well as unexpected differences.[13] The premise of mere rhetoric might also deter us from thinking about the possibility that Portugal may have acted even more cautiously at certain times than its more "liberal" counterparts, who were under far less scrutiny from international opinion. In the end, civilizing propaganda was no monopoly of Portuguese imperialism.

This book addresses the issue of changes over time in the experience of (Portuguese) colonialism on the ground. It does so in two ways. First, it argues that the Portuguese colonial state had to take account of local responses and that it indeed proved more capable of reform than is commonly assumed, and especially so in the period after 1960. The latter will be primarily an argument covered in Chapter 7. Second, and this is the main thrust of this chapter, it underlines the crucial importance of local context and chronology for understanding people's experiences of colonialism and their responses to it. Focusing on the period between initial colonization in 1900 and the beginning of decolonization around 1960, this chapter will show that, from the perspective of Nkholongue, the level of colonial exploitation varied greatly over time. This had less to do with changes in colonial legislation than with 1) reforms of the administrative structure of the region, 2) the comings and goings of different colonial "men on the spot," and 3) changes in the supra-regional economic and political situation.

The analysis of the presence and character of colonialism around Nkholongue will reveal a timeline that deviates markedly from the two standard chronologies of colonialism in northern Mozambique, one of which postulates a steadily increasing economic exploitation after the dissolution of the *Companhia do Nyassa*

---

colonization and Europe's Imperial States, 1918–1975, ed. Martin Thomas, Bob Moore, and L.J. Butler (London: Bloomsbury, 2008), 394.
13 Keese, "Forced Labour in the 'Gorgulho Years,'" 110; Keese, *Living with Ambiguity*. On this point, see as well: Allina, *Slavery by Any Other Name*, 12–13; Coghe, *Population Politics in the Tropics*, 10–12.

and the region's full integration into the colony of Mozambique,[14] and the other which depicts very limited state presence until the outbreak of the war in the 1960s.[15] This chapter will show that the history of colonialism around Nkholongue was no one-way-street. The colonial presence in terms of economic activity and exploitation was larger during the time of the *Companhia* (1901–1929) than during the subsequent years of the *Estado Novo*. From the perspective of Nkholongue, it was the *Estado Novo* and not, as usually claimed, the *Companhia* that failed to establish an effective presence in its territories.[16] This will be exemplified by looking at local cotton extraction. Around Nkholongue, the "mother of poverty"[17] was not the cotton cultivated during the cotton regime of the *Estado Novo*, but the cotton grown on plantations in the early 1920s, at a time when both the administration and economy of the region were largely controlled by British capital.

This analysis not only allows us to bring local variety and complexity into the bigger picture, but also to challenge important foundations of the bigger picture. It allows us to question the often-made but inadequately researched claim that there was a direct connection between the extremely harsh conditions of Portuguese colonialism and the awakening of a national consciousness that led to the armed struggle of the 1960s.[18] Isaacman et al. have, for example, asserted a direct link between the cotton regime and Frelimo's success in garnering support in northern Mozambique.[19] Focusing on a region that became a prime recruiting ground for Frelimo, this chapter demonstrates that this assertion rests on shaky foundations and chronologies. This becomes all the more evident when one considers that cotton cultivation was much more important in southern Niassa, where Frelimo proved to be far less successful.

The availability of sources for this analysis is similarly limited as in the case of the previous chapter. Furthermore, it is uneven for different periods. Written accounts of the time of the *Companhia* come mainly from the pens of Anglican missionaries. For later years, the number of available sources from the missionaries becomes smaller, but we do have governmental inspection reports for certain

---

14 For an example, see: Funada-Classen, *The Origins of War in Mozambique*, 116.
15 For examples, see: Thomas H. Henriksen, *Revolution and Counterrevolution: Mozambique's War of Independence, 1964–1974* (Westport: Greenwood, 1983), 159; Huhn, "Sustenance and Sociability," 61; Cláudia Castelo, "Colonatos e aldeamentos no Niassa, Moçambique: Processos e impactos sociais em tempo de guerra (1964–1974)," *Tempo* 27, no. 3 (2021): 483.
16 Newitt, *A History of Mozambique*, 373; Vail, "Mozambique's Chartered Companies."
17 Isaacman, *Cotton Is the Mother of Poverty*.
18 For more on this point and a comprehensive survey of the literature, see: Keese, *Living with Ambiguity*, 27–36. See as well: Keese, "Proteger os pretos," 98.
19 Allen Isaacman et al., "'Cotton Is the Mother of Poverty': Peasant Resistance to Forced Cotton Production in Mozambique, 1938–1961," *African Studies* 13, no. 4 (1980): 614–615.

years. In addition, these later years can also be reached through oral history accounts. However, it needs to be considered that these accounts are not only "memories" filtered through more than 50 years of life experiences, but also "memories" of a topic that has been intensively discussed by "official" anti-colonial discourse. All these factors complicate the reconstruction of a clear periodization. Still, I am convinced that the basic trends can be identified on an empirically sound basis.

The chapter is divided into three major parts. In the first part, we will look at the changing local presence of the colonial administration and economy. Knowledge of this changing presence is crucial to understand the changing levels of colonial exploitation, which will be analyzed in the second part. In the final part, we will examine people's reactions to Portuguese colonialism.

5.2 The Ruins of the *Companhia* in Metangula

It is commonly claimed that the *Companhia do Nyassa* did nothing to "develop" its territories administratively and economically. This is true insofar as the "development" of the colonial administration and economy remained very rudimentary in most areas. But, from the perspective of the lakeshore area, this claim must be revised. Until the 1960s, the region would never again experience such a strong presence of the colonial state and economy as it did under *Companhia* rule. From the perspective of the lakeshore, Sayaka Funada-Classen's assertion that the end of the *Companhia* was a turning point on which "Niassa would undergo a sudden change and [lose] its 'remoteness'"[20] is misleading.

Metangula's Administrative Decline

To understand this, we have to have a closer look at the history of the colonial administration in the area. As already mentioned in the previous chapter, the *Companhia* made Metangula its headquarters on the lake. At the beginning, Metangula was the seat of a relatively large administrative unit called *Concelho do Lago*, which included the entire territory of the modern districts of Lago and Sanga, as well as parts of the territory of the modern districts of Lichinga, Ngauma and, in the end, even Mandimba.[21] But in 1922, Metangula lost some of its impor-

---

20 Funada-Classen, *The Origins of War in Mozambique*, 116.
21 Companhia do Nyassa, "Relatório e Contas apresentados à Assembleia Geral Ordinária em 9 de Dezembro de 1912" (Lisboa, 1912), 6, 31; Companhia do Nyassa, "Relatório e Contas apresentados à

tance within the framework of an administrative reform. It remained the seat of an administrative unit called *Concelho do Lago*, which was, however, strongly reduced in size and subordinated to the "Western Inspection Zone," with its headquarters in faraway Mandimba.[22] Metangula underwent another downgrade when the territories of the *Companhia* were incorporated into the Portuguese colony of Mozambique in 1929: the headquarters of what was now called the *Circunscrição do Lago* (hereafter usually referred to as the "Lago District") were moved from the lake to Maniamba on Niassa's *planalto*. In the new hierarchy, Metangula was no more than a simple administrative post.[23] Almost overnight, the town ceased to be an administrative and political center, and Nkholongue lost its proximity to the central representation of the colonial state in the region.

In 1938, a Portuguese inspector described the entire area of the former "Western Inspection Zone" as a "paralyzed territory."[24] The region's administration was totally understaffed. It was also largely preoccupied with itself. The various inspection and government reports leave little doubt about the self-perpetuating nature of Portuguese bureaucracy in northern Mozambique. What later became the postcolonial Niassa Province underwent more than ten reorganizations of its adminis-

---

Assembleia Geral Ordinária em 4 de Dezembro de 1916" (Lisboa, 1916), 27–28; Companhia do Nyassa, "Relatório e Contas apresentados à Assembleia Geral Ordinária em 3 de Dezembro de 1918" (Lisboa, 1918), 28.

22 For the reform in general, see: Companhia do Nyassa, "Relatório e Contas apresentados à Assembleia Geral Ordinária em 2 de Dezembro de 1919" (Lisboa, 1919), 8; Companhia do Nyassa, "Relatório e Contas apresentados à Assembleia Geral Ordinária em 2 de Dezembro de 1920" (Lisboa, 1920), 5–6; Companhia do Nyassa, "Report of the Council of Administration to Be Presented to the Ordinary General Meeting of Shareholders to Be Held in Lisbon, on Monday, December 3, 1912" (Lisbon, 1923). For the procedure of the reform on the ground, see: H.A. Machell Cox, "News from the Stations: V. Msumba," *NDC*, no. 77 (October 1922): 13; AIMC, VIII-7, 1, N. 113: Giovanni Chimio, "Appunti sulla Zona Ovest del territorio della Compagnia del Nyassa," 1926, 3; H.A. Machell Cox, "News from the Stations: IV. Msumba," *NDC*, no. 94 (January 1927): 8; Companhia do Nyassa, *A Companhia do Nyassa: Factos e documentos* (Lisboa, 1928), 9. Previous research has not documented these changes adequately: Medeiros, *História de Cabo Delgado e do Niassa (c. 1836–1929)*, 157–164; Santos, *O desconhecido Niassa*, fig. IV.

23 Legally, the relocation was first decided in 1929, then apparently reversed in 1932, and finally confirmed in 1934. In practice, the relocation was apparently carried out only once, probably in 1931 or 1932. See: Santos, *O desconhecido Niassa*, fig. IV; "Notices, Notes and News," *NDC*, no. 110 (January 1931): 3; H.A. Machell Cox, "News from the Stations: V. Msumba," *NDC*, no. 117 (October 1932): 9–10; "News from the Stations: V. Msumba," *NDC*, no. 120 (July 1933): 7–8; "News from the Stations: V. Msumba," *NDC*, no. 123 (April 1934): 9–11.

24 AHU, N° 1665–1 1B MU ISAU: Armando Pinto Corrêa, "Relatório duma Inspecção às Circunscrições do Distrito de Moçambique (1936–37)" (Lourenço Marques, 1938), 126.

trative subdivisions between 1929 and 1975.[25] Some of the administrative posts that existed on paper all along, such as Macaloge, were not "opened" until the 1960s. Or, as one inspector wrote in 1944, "Macaloge is a myth."[26]

Certainly, the administrative post of Metangula was no myth, but it is evident that the administrative changes left their mark. Under *Companhia* rule, the town had witnessed the continuous presence of a European administration. With the incorporation of the territory into the colony of Mozambique, these times became a thing of the past. By 1933, there was not a single Portuguese official in Metangula. A visitor described a "native" male nurse as the apparent "master" of the peninsula.[27] The post was then re-occupied in 1934, but only for about two years.[28] In 1937, only two of the five administrative posts of Lago District were fully staffed: Metangula, Cobué, and Macaloge were all without a *chefe de posto* (head of an administrative post).[29] And during the 1944 inspection, Metangula was again "unoccupied," staffed only by "the native teacher, the interpreter, and 4 *cipaios* [native guards]."[30] The Portuguese inspector lamented that the former buildings of the *Companhia* had fallen into ruins, terming the lakeshore "moribund lands."[31]

It was not until the second half of the 1940s that the presence of the colonial state began to increase again somewhat. Metangula was once more continuously

---

25 Santos, *O desconhecido Niassa*, fig. 4; AHU, Biblioteca, L9560: José Guardado Moreira, "Governo do Distrito do Niassa: Relatório do ano de 1972" (Vila Cabral, May 31, 1973), 2–5.
26 AHU, N° 1662–2 1B MU ISAU: Carlos Silveira, "Inspecção Administrativa Ordinária na Circunscrição do Lago: Relatório Sumário" (Cuamba, June 12, 1944), attached as Doc. I to "Inspecção Administrativa Ordinária na Província de Niassa, Segunda Parte: Relatório do Inspector" (Moçambique, February 28, 1945), 3.
27 Pedroso de Lima, "8.000 quilómetros através de Moçambique," *Boletim Geral das Colónias* 11, no. 118 (Abril de 1935): 62.
28 "News from the Stations: V. Msumba," *NDC*, no. 123 (April 1934); "News from the Stations: V. Msumba," *NDC*, no. 130 (January 1936): 9.
29 AHM, SNI, Secção B, cx. 1097: Jaime Asdrubal Casqueiro, "Inquerito sobre escravidão ou servidão indigena" (Maniamba: Administração da Circunscrição Civil de Lago, February 15, 1937).
30 AHU, N° 1662–2 1B MU ISAU: Carlos Silveira, "Inspecção Administrativa Ordinária na Circunscrição do Lago: Relatório Sumário" (Cuamba, June 12, 1944), attached as Doc. I to "Inspecção Administrativa Ordinária na Província de Niassa, Segunda Parte: Relatório do Inspector" (Moçambique, February 28, 1945), 7. See as well: AHM, ISANI, cx. 97: Carlos Silveira, "Relatório e documentos referentes à Inspecção Ordinária feita na Província do Niassa. 2.A Parte, 1944," February 28, 1945, 12.
31 AHU, N° 1662–2 1B MU ISAU: Carlos Silveira, "Inspecção Administrativa Ordinária na Circunscrição do Lago: Relatório Sumário" (Cuamba, June 12, 1944), attached as Doc. I to "Inspecção Administrativa Ordinária na Província de Niassa, Segunda Parte: Relatório do Inspector" (Moçambique, February 28, 1945), 5.

"occupied" by a *chefe de posto*.³² Furthermore, "scientific" missions such as the *Missão Antropólogica de Moçambique* ("Anthropological Mission of Mozambique") in 1946 and the Hydrographic Mission in the second half the 1950s came to the region to gather knowledge about it.³³ The strongest temporary reinforcement of the colonial presence in the region was caused by the "Mission for the Combat of the Trypanosomiasis" (MCT), which was delegated to Metangula after an outbreak of sleeping sickness in the vicinity of Nkholongue in 1946 (more on it below on pp. 186–189). But in spite of these developments, the presence of the colonial state along the lakeshore remained limited until the early 1960s. As late as 1961, almost 80 years after the Berlin Conference, a Portuguese inspector still spoke of the need to achieve the "effective occupation" of the area.³⁴ It was only the coming war that was to change this situation drastically (see Chapter 7).

From "Free Trade" to "Autarky," From Steamboat to Railway

The history of the colonial economy in the region paralleled the history of the administrative presence. The region that was to become the modern-day Lago District was never a thriving center of the colonial economy. However, if there was a time when the colonial economy gained a foothold in the region, it was under *Companhia* rule. The reason for this lies in the fact that the period of the *Companhia* and that of the *Estado Novo* were characterized by two completely different economic

---

32 Unfortunately, the data are incomplete to provide a comprehensive list of Metangula's *chefes de posto*. However, it seems fairly certain that Metangula did not have a permanent *chefe de posto* again until 1947. Two others seem to have served only as interim *chefes* or to have stayed in Metangula only very briefly in 1942 and 1946 respectively. See: Instituto Nacional de Estatística (Portugal), *Anuário Estatístico do Ultramar* (Lisboa, 1942), 218; *Anuário de Lourenço Marques* (Lourenço Marques: A. W. Bayly, 1946), 888; *Anuário de Lourenço Marques* (Lourenço Marques: A. W. Bayly, 1947), 1140; AHM, ISANI, cx. 99: Manuel M. R. de L. Texeira, "Relatório da Inspecção Ordinária ao Distrito do Lago da Província do Niassa, 1950/51," 18–19.
33 The Anthropological Mission was a pseudo-scientist and racist mission to measure the physical constitution and intelligence of the local "natives." It visited Metangula for two days in September 1946. Nkholongue's chief Chingomanje was one of the "targets" of these measurements. See: AHU, MAM 5, 46/2, pt. 4: Metangula, n.d. More information about this "mission" can be found here: António Augusto, "Medições de inteligência de algumas tribos indígenas das Zambézia e do Niassa, Moçambique," *Anais da Junta das Missões Geográficas e de Investigações Coloniais* 3, no. 5 (1948). For the Hydrographic Mission, see: Instituto Hidrográfico, *Roteiro da costa portuguesa do Lago Niassa* (Lisboa, 1963); AHU, IPAD/MU/DGOPC/DSH/1749/13221: José A. B. Fernandes, "Reconhecimento hidrográfico da costa portuguesa do Lago Niassa" (Lourenço Marques, April 25, 1959).
34 AHD, MU/GM/GNP/RNP/0064/01681: Mário Costa (Inspector Superior) ao Chefe Inspecção Superior da Administração Ultramarina (Lourenço Marques, May 30, 1961), 1.

ideologies, a change that was fully in line with global trends: while the *Companhia* was in many ways a child of the "free trade era" of the 19th century, the *Estado Novo* pursued a policy of economic protection and autarky.

This change of economic policy and global economic realities had far-reaching consequences for such a marginal border region as the lakeshore area. The Metangula of the early 20th century was barely connected to the *Companhia*'s headquarters on the Indian Ocean. But it was intimately linked to the neighboring colony of Nyasaland. This connection was facilitated by the many British steamships plying on the lake at that time. It was through Nyasaland that most investors and traders came to the region, and it was to Nyasaland that most exports went. The region's incorporation into the colony of Mozambique, possibly reinforced by the effects of the Great Depression, put an end to this "officially sanctioned" inflow of capital and outflow of commodities. The emphasis here is on "officially sanctioned," as the economic ties of the region to Nyasaland continued to be of great importance to the inhabitants of the region. As we will see in the next chapter, labor migration to Nyasaland, for example, continued to play a crucial role in this regard. The difference, however, is that labor migration under the *Companhia* was encouraged (if not enforced) from above, while under the *Estado Novo* it was in many ways sustained from below.

From the end of the 1920s, the proximity to Nyasaland no longer facilitated the exploitation of the region by European capital as before. Now it was only the connection to the Mozambican ports on the ocean that counted. In this respect, the northern parts of Niassa were clearly left out. Only the southern parts of Niassa around Nova Freixo (Cuamba) lost their "remoteness" at this moment of history. Even Vila Cabral, Niassa's new capital built in the 1930s, remained an economic backwater of colonialism. This uneven "integration" is also evident when looking at the history of the transport infrastructure: while the southern parts of Niassa were connected to the railroad network starting in the 1940s, the extension of the line to Vila Cabral was not completed until 1969.[35] The long-planned connection to the lake and to Metangula was never realized. In short, what happened with the appearance of the *Estado Novo* was a peripheralization of the lake region.

---

35 The railway reached Niassa's border in 1942. In 1951, Nova Freixo (Cuamba) was connected to the network and, in 1963, Catur. See: Santos, *O desconhecido Niassa*, 195; AHU, Biblioteca, L9467: Nuno Egídio, "Governo do Distrito do Niassa: Relatório do ano de 1971," Confidencial (Vila Cabral, March 2, 1972), 116–117.

Traders and Planters During the Time of the *Companhia*

Largely ignored by previous literature, a surprising number of European businessmen settled in the region around Metangula during the time of the *Companhia*. The first of them came here before the *Companhia* occupied the area. One of them was the German trader Salomon Kahn, who had settled in Nkhotakota in 1895 and whose dhows also operated around Metangula.[36] In 1898, Kahn merged his business with another European trader, Ludwig Deuss, the employer of the already mentioned Abdallah Mkwanda (see Chapters 3 and 4). Deuss was a naturalized Swiss of "German" descent and one of the most important businessmen in the Lake Malawi region prior to World War One. He had his base at Fort Johnston at the south end of the Lake. In 1901 or earlier, Deuss' company opened a permanent trading branch in Metangula, headed, at least initially, by another European, a certain Martin Gundlach.[37]

A further European, Leonhard Botmann, had lived in Metangula with his "Austrian" wife since about 1906. Botmann had various occupations in Metangula: he worked as a labor agent for South African mines, owned extensive concessions for wild rubber extraction, cultivated cassava, cotton and tobacco, and owned the steamboat S.S. *Adventure*.[38] He also ran processing machinery for cotton, tobacco, and rubber. In 1913, he sold his Metangulan property to the M'tengula Plantations & Transport Company LTD, a company set up by an investor from New Zealand for that very purpose. Botmann then became the local manager of this company.[39]

---

36 Greenstein, "Shayks and Tariqas," 15.
37 AHM, Códice 11–2485: Documento N.° CVIII: Extracto da carta, de 28 de Maio de 1902, de L. W. Deuss, ao Governador dos Territórios, in *Documentos sobre as Missões Inglesas das Universidades*, 190–192. Adolphe Linder, *Os Suíços em Moçambique* (Maputo: AHM, 2001), 99; McCracken, *A History of Malawi 1859–1966*, 178; Greenstein, "Shayks and Tariqas," 15 & n. 64. Deuss took full control of the company after Kahn had been evacuated to Europe due to "mental illness." See: MNA, 2/KOM/1/1: "Kota Kota Mission Diary, 1894 August 17–1911 January 2," entry dated September 4 and 5, 1899.
38 "S.S. 'C.M.,'" *LDQP*, no. 10 (January 1906): 259; William Percival Johnson, "S.S. C.M.," *Nyasaland Diocesan Quarterly Paper (NDQP)*, no. 26 (January 1910): 664–65; Medeiros, *História de Cabo Delgado e do Niassa (c. 1836–1929)*, 246; John MacKenzie, "The Naval Campaigns on Lakes Victoria and Nyasa, 1914–18," *The Mariner's Mirror* 71, no. 2 (1985): 176; AHM, Secção Oral, Cassettes N.° 157–159: Entrevista com um grupo de velhos de Seli (Metangula), interview by Gerhard Liesegang, Teresa Oliveira, and Mujuane Mainga Vicente, July 22, 1981, N.° 159B: 235–294.
39 TNA, BT 31/21645/130505: I. W. Raymond Esqre. and Mtengula Plantations & Transport Company Limited: Agreement, November 10, 1913; Companhia do Nyassa, "Boletim N.° 190," 1913; "A New Zealander's Investments," *The Press (Christchurch)*, March 7, 1914.

Other European businessmen operating in the region prior to World War One included an Italian named Louis Ferri, who came to the area in 1903 to recruit labor for South African mines,[40] a group of Europeans who ran a tobacco plantation in Njiri near Unango,[41] and the Swiss Karl Schenk, whose business interests included cotton farming and elephant hunting.[42]

Evidence of the scale of production or trade of these various actors is very sparse. However, some further idea of this can be gleaned from the applications for land concessions, at least some of which were published in the *Boletim* of the *Companhia*. Deuss, for example, applied for 1,000 m^2 in "Mecueoe"[43] and 1,000 m^2 in Metangula in 1912 for the construction of "trading houses."[44] Schenk, for his part, applied in 1913 for 1,000 m^2 each in Metangula and Unango for the construction of houses.[45] And the M'tengula Plantations & Transport Company LTD was granted 4,000 ha for agricultural purposes in 1914.[46] A newspaper article from the same year claimed that the company owned around 8,000 ha of land and had the concessionary lease for wild rubber extraction over an area covering 400,000 ha.[47]

---

40 AUSPG, Philip Young, "Diary of Philip Young, Engineer on the 'Chauncy Maples', 1901–1903," transcribed by Catherine Wakeling, 169.

41 It was run by a certain Albert Matthaei and his agents Mr. Bets and Walter Storpp until 1913, when it was overtaken by a South African named G.H. Nourse. Yohanna Abdallah gave Matthaei's name as "Matthais." Matthaei had been a business partner of Botmann. See: TNA, BT 31/21645/130505: I. W. Raymond Esqre. and Mtengula Plantations & Transport Company Limited: Agreement, November 10, 1913; Abdallah, "News from the Stations: VI. Unangu," *NDC*, no. 42 (January 1914): 13; Medeiros, *História de Cabo Delgado e do Niassa (c. 1836–1929)*, 183.

42 Schenk had initially come to the region as a missionary of the White Fathers in Nyasaland. But in 1907 he left the mission and settled in northern Mozambique. Schenk is the grandfather of Filipe José Couto, former rector of Eduardo Mondlane University (2007–2011), and Pedro Couto, former Mozambican Deputy Minister of Finance (2005–2015) and Minister of Mineral Resources and Energy (2015–2016). See: Companhia do Nyassa, "Boletim N.° 189," 1913, 1754–55; Linder, *Os Suíços em Moçambique*, 171; Augusto Massari, *Gli italiani nel Mozambico portoghese: 1830–1975* (Torino: L'Harmattan Italia, 2005), 118, 141; AGMAfr. Rome, Dossiers personnels: L. Kaufmann, "Charles Schenk" (Rome, September 23, 1992); Swiss Federal Archives (SFA), E2200.167–03#1000/254#21*: Consulat de Suisse to Eidg. Justiz- & Polizeidepartement, Polizeiabteilung (Bern), (November 27, 1926). For his activity as a cotton farmer, see: MNA, LC 1/6/7: Custodian of Enemy Property, "Report by the Custodian of Enemy Property, Nyasaland, on the Liquidation of the Business of Mr. L. W. J. Deuss" (Zomba, September 7, 1919), 1–2.

43 Maybe, this is Micuio south of Metangula.

44 Linder, *Os Suíços em Moçambique*, 99; Companhia do Nyassa, "Boletim N.° 169," 1912, 1520.

45 Companhia do Nyassa, "Boletim N.° 189," 1754–55.

46 Companhia do Nyassa, "Relatório e Contas apresentados à Assembleia Geral Ordinária em 30 de Dezembro de 1915" (Lisboa, 1915).

47 "A New Zealander's Investments."

These economic activities of European settlers in the region were disrupted by the outbreak of World War One. Northern Mozambique became a battleground when German troops led by General Lettow-Vorbeck invaded the area in 1917. Furthermore, the outbreak of the war led to the severance of trade relations between different colonies and to the interment of "alien subjects." Deuss, for example, was interned by the British and his property confiscated under the Trading with the Enemy Act of 1914, partly because he was not considered a "true" Swiss, aned partly because most of his capital came from a German lender.[48] Botmann and his wife also got into trouble with the Portuguese and British authorities and were also arrested.[49]

Although the war interrupted the economic developments that had taken place before the war, it did not put a definitive end to the activities of European businessmen in the region. A new wave of settlers reached the region in the early 1920s. This time it was above all British planters from Nyasaland who came to the area and opened numerous cotton plantations, many of them right on the doorsteps of Nkholongue. This post-war cotton boom was short-lived but had far-reaching consequences for the people of the region, as we will see in the next section.

The presence of European settlers in the region ended in the 1920s. The incorporation of the territories of the *Companhia* into the colony of Mozambique marked the end of this international phase of colonialism. Never again was the colonial state regionally capable of extracting as much agricultural produce as under *Companhia* rule. This fact was expressed in the many subsequent lamentations by Portuguese government officials about the lost "prosperity," which was still visible in the form of the ruins of the old trading houses in Metangula until at least the 1950s.[50] "It is Metangula that was once the flourishing and bustling seat of the *Circunscrição*,"[51] wrote one inspector in 1944. While another noted in 1937:

---

48 For more information on Deuss, see various documents in MNA LC/1/6/3 – 7 and: Linder, *Os Suíços em Moçambique*, 99.
49 ASM, Private Diary of A.M.D. Turnbull 1917–1918. It seems that they were able to return to Metangula after their release and remained there for at least a few years, as they were still listed as subscribing members of the British Overseas Club residing in Metangula for the years 1918–20. See: Overseas Club and Patriotic League: List of Subscribing Members 1918–19, London, 370; Overseas Club and Patriotic League: List of Subscribing Members 1919–20, London, 275.
50 António Gomes e Sousa, "Elementos para uma monografia agrícola do Distrito do Niassa (conclusão)," *Portugal Colonial: Revista de Propaganda e Expansão Colonial* 4, no. 51 (1935): 10; Alice Gomes e Sousa, "O Lago Niassa (excerptos dum diário)," *Portugal Colonial: Revista de Propaganda e Expansão Colonial* 4, no. 50 (1935): 13; AHU, N° 1662 – 2 1B MU ISAU: Carlos Silveira, "Inspecção Administrativa Ordinária na Circunscrição do Lago: Relatório Sumário" (Cuamba, June 12, 1944), attached as Doc. I to "Inspecção Administrativa Ordinária na Província de Niassa, Segunda Parte: Relatório do Inspector" (Moçambique, February 28, 1945), 5 – 6; AHM, ISANI, cx. 99: Manuel

[T]here is, at the moment, not one European that dedicates himself to [agriculture] in the whole former district of Niassa. [...] Earlier, in the times of the *Companhia*, there was [at least] a handful of white farmers in Metangula and Amaramba. But, we have to confess that, in this respect, we have regressed.[52]

5.3 Colonial Exploitation along the Lakeshore

It is essential to have an idea of the administrative and economic changes just described in order to understand the experiences of the people of Nkholongue with colonialism. For as we shall now see, the extent of colonial exploitation and the number of abuses were significantly higher during *Companhia* rule than afterwards. This was not necessarily the result of a general change in the mindset of the state and its representatives, but primarily a consequence of the fact that, from a local point of view, the colonial state lost much of its former capacity to enforce its policies of economic exploitation. Furthermore, the region's geographic remoteness and the lack of transportation infrastructure made such an enforcement far less reasonable from the state's perspective.

In the following, we will look at the local history of three different ways the state used to force people into the colonial economy: 1) taxation, 2) forced labor, and 3) the cotton regime.

Taxing the "Natives"

In Nkholongue, taxation was the colonial state's longest lasting instrument for forcing people into the colonial economy. Taxes were introduced in 1903. In the beginning, they were levied as a "hut tax" and could also be paid in kind, or as W.P. Johnson put it, "1 goat per hut, or so much flour or 100 fish, or 30 days work at Metangula."[53] The missionaries' accounts leave little doubt that tax collection

---

M. R. de L. Texeira, "Relatório da Inspecção Ordinária ao Distrito do Lago da Província do Niassa, 1950/51," 17.
51 AHU, N° 1662–2 1B MU ISAU: Carlos Silveira, "Inspecção Administrativa Ordinária na Circunscrição do Lago: Relatório Sumário" (Cuamba, June 12, 1944), attached as Doc. I to "Inspecção Administrativa Ordinária na Província de Niassa, Segunda Parte: Relatório do Inspector" (Moçambique, February 28, 1945), 5.
52 AHU, N° 1665–1 1B MU ISAU: Armando Pinto Corrêa, "Relatório duma Inspecção às Circunscrições do Distrito de Moçambique (1936–37)" (Lourenço Marques, 1938), 127.
53 In the original it is "Mtengula." See: AUMCA, A1(XXIV), f. 183–186: Letter from William Percival Johnson to Mr. Travers, [1903].

under *Companhia* rule involved extremely violent practices and led to widespread unrest. The editor of the Nyasaland Diocesan Chronicle described the meaning of *nkhondo*, the Chinyanja word for war, in 1917 as "war of any kind from a village row upwards; also at times the forcible collection of taxes."[54] The *Companhia*'s policemen were said to raid villages at night to look for tax evaders. Different sources confirm that the wives of tax evaders were sometimes held for ransom until their husbands paid the taxes.[55] As a consequence, the women were said to hide in the forest at night during the times of tax collection.[56]

But while some missionaries criticized these practices, others played down the state's responsibility and blamed the troubles on people's negligence in providing the "modest sum."[57] An unnamed missionary, probably W.P. Johnson, objected to complaints by Muslims living in Lussefa that they were "up to their mouths in the water" because of white oppression. He stated:

> What prejudice! [T]he people at Lussefa live in a fertile country, and only pay 4 shillings hut tax, and hardly any, or no, forced labour or sudden calls, and yet the reference to approximate drowning was explained to refer to white oppression. The truth is, in such places the white man has upset vested interests. Selling the weaker brethren was such a much more gentlemanly thing to do, and so much more beer and women in it than in regular work.[58]

Of course, it would be wrong to attach too much importance to these statements for understanding the perspective of the colonized. Above all, they show that the Anglican mission and the *Companhia* were in reality part of the same grand European colonization project. And yet, it is essential to acknowledge the obvious differences in the missionaries' assessment of different episodes of Portuguese rule on the lakeshore. It is noticeable that, with a few exceptions, most of the *Companhia*'s "men on the spot" fared relatively well in the accounts of the missionar-

---

54 See: William Percival Johnson, "News from the Stations: III. The Chauncy Maples," *NDC*, no. 54 (January 1917): 16. See also: B.W. Randolph, *Arthur Douglas: The Story of His Life* (Westminster: UMCA, 1912), 242. The same polysemy was to be found in Northern Rhodesia: Fergus Macpherson, *Anatomy of a Conquest: The British Occupation of Zambia, 1884–1924* (Harlow: Longman, 1981), 112.
55 Randolph, *Arthur Douglas*, 215; AHM, Secção Oral, Transcrito NI 04: N.° 154–155, Entrevista com um grupo de velhos em Chiwanga, interview by Gerhard Liesegang, Teresa Oliveira, and Mujuane Mainga Vicente, July 9, 1981, 8. This practice was also reported from other parts of the *Companhia*'s territories. See: Harry G. West, "'Who Rules Us Now?' Identity Tokens, Sorcery, and Other Metaphors in the 1994 Mozambican Elections," in *Transparency and Conspiracy: Ethnographies of Suspicion in the New World Order*, ed. Harry G. West and Todd Sanders (Durham: Duke University Press, 2003), 99; Vail, "Mozambique's Chartered Companies," 400.
56 Randolph, *Arthur Douglas*, 214.
57 "Notes," *NDQP*, no. 24 (July 1909): 588. See as well: Randolph, *Arthur Douglas*, 215.
58 "S.S. C. M.," *LDQP*, no. 18 (January 1908), 438.

ies. While the missionaries made official complaints about the *Companhia*'s policies in 1901/2 and, as we shall see, in the early 1920s, there are none for most other years. In 1907, missionary Eyre, who had previously been at the forefront of the missionaries' complaints against the *Companhia*, was pleased to observe that the Portuguese commissioner in Metangula had "done much to allay the feeling which was formerly excited amongst the natives, by injudicious and crude methods of administration."[59]

The writings of the missionaries show that not every year of *Companhia* rule was characterized by the same level of exploitation and abuse, and also that the collection of taxes was not every year as violent as described above. While, for example, missionary Arthur Douglas called taxation a "beast" that caused serious trouble in 1909, he reported a completely different situation in 1910:

> [The tax collector] has accomplished in fifteen days, without running in a single person, the entire taxation of his district, whereas the people last year had three months bad time, with continual night raids by the police, and during that time our girls' schools were practically closed, as the women and girls hide away, the policy of the government official being to run-in the females whilst their husbands and fathers look for their tax money. But, as I say, this year the whole business round here has been achieved in a wonderfully short time with really no discomfort. One chief reason was that a very large number of men have lately returned from their work at Johannesburg, so there has been a good supply of money in the country.[60]

This last sentence suggests that the "smoothness" of tax collection probably depended less on the attitude of the tax collector than on the local availability of money. The evidence shows that the people of the lakeshore pursued very different paths to obtain the tax money in different places and at different times. Some interviewees, for example, indicated that they sold agricultural products or fish.[61] In 1911 and 1912, missionaries reported that people were collecting rubber and taking it to the store in Metangula (probably Botmann's).[62] Compared to other villages, the people of Nkholongue had some advantage in earning money. For, as will be explained in more detail in the next chapter, the village served as a "wooding station" for the steamships of the Anglican mission during long periods of colonial rule. The

---

59 C.B. Eyre, "The Portuguese in Central Africa," *CA* 25, no. 293 (1907): 133.
60 Randolph, *Arthur Douglas*, 242.
61 PA, I012: interview with *P0367* (♂, *1936*) (Nkholongue, September 3, 2010), min 00:19:58–00:20:51; PA, I063: interview with *P1488* (♂, *~1930*) (M'chepa, August 31, 2013), min 00:04:45–00:07:01.
62 Augustine Ambali, "News from the Stations: IV. Msumba," *NDC*, no. 32 (July 1911): 884; "News from the Stations: VI. Unangu," *NDC*, no. 33 (October 1911): 834–835; Yohanna B. Abdallah, "News from the Stations: VI. Unangu," *NDC*, no. 36 (July 1912): 910–911.

sale of firewood and other items such as pots allowed Nkholongue's population to gain tax money with relative ease.⁶³

But in many other lakeside villages, much of the tax money was earned not locally, but through labor migration to Tanganyika, Nyasaland, Southern Rhodesia and especially to the gold mines of South Africa. The *Companhia* had actively contributed to the coupling of taxation and labor migration, as already in 1904, the *Companhia*'s tax collector had reportedly strolled through the villages together with the labor agent from South Africa. Or, in the words of missionary Herbert Barnes:

> Picture the pair working the Lakeside together—the Portuguese sergeant asking for four silver shillings or the equivalent in work at Metangula, and side by side with him a smooth-tongued agent of the Rand offering the four shillings on the spot plus a small sum in cloth to console the wife or mother. All perfectly fair and straightforward, and I suppose any man would prefer to have his tax paid for the year even at the cost of exile for an uncertain period rather than stay at home and see the hut burnt as a penalty.⁶⁴

Nominally, the tax level fluctuated widely over time. Table 1 gives an approximate overview of these variations. But if we want to measure the tax burden over time, we must first and foremost consider the amount of work that was required to earn the tax money. We have already learned that the state regarded 30 days of work as the equivalent of the tax of four shillings in 1903. My interviews indicate that until the early 1960s, tax defaulters usually had to work for the government, primarily building and maintaining roads.⁶⁵ The work equivalent of the tax seems to have remained more or less at one month throughout the period.⁶⁶ However, the information from the interviews is not entirely consistent in this regard. One interviewee, for example, stated that people had to work for only one week.⁶⁷ Also, the only

---

63 PA, I129: interview with *P1426* (♂, *1929*) (Malindi (Mangochi District, Malawi), May 29, 2016), min 02:06:05–02:06:14; PA, I014: interview with *P0147* (♀, *~1928*), *P0129* (♀, *1930*) (Nkholongue, September 8, 2010), min 00:04:58–00:05:33.
64 It is "Mtengula" in the original. See: Barnes, "Portuguese Troubles in Nyasaland," *CA* 22, no. 264 (1904): 245.
65 PA, I010: interview with *P0792* (♂, *1917*) (Nkholongue, September 3, 2010), min 00:24:18–00:25:12; PA, I011: interview with *P0050* (♂, *~1922*) (Nkholongue, September 3, 2010), min 00:07:49–00:09:49; PA, I012: interview with *P0367* (♂, *1936*) (Nkholongue, September 3, 2010), min 00:22:02–00:23:45.
66 PA, I120: interview with *P1102* (♂, *1932*) (Malango, April 21, 2016), min 01:50:20–01:50:53; PA, I123: interview with *P1460* (♀), *P1461* (♂, *~1935*), *P1462* (♂, *~1935*) (Meluluca, April 25, 2016), min 01:12:01–01:12:08.
67 PA, I114: interview with *P1074* (♀, *~1940*), *P1141* (♂, *1932*) (Malango, April 15, 2016), min 02:52:50–02:52:53.

interviewee who admitted having once been unable to pay the tax himself stated that he worked at the construction site of the naval base in Metangula in 1962 for one month and still received a salary after the tax had been deducted.[68]

1903	4 shillings (levied as hut tax)
1909	4 shillings (levied as poll tax)
1915	5 shillings
1921	5 shillings (extended to unmarried women)
1922	18 shillings
1923	6 shillings, 5 shillings
1945	10 shillings for men, 5 shillings for unmarried women
1947	women exempted from taxation

Table 1: Tax levels, 1903–1961.[69]

Different works at different times in history generated different incomes. It is impossible to give a comprehensive overview. Only a few examples can be given: one interviewee stated that they received six pence for a cubic meter of firewood.[70] At a tax rate of 10 shillings in 1945, this would have meant that someone would have had to sell 20 cubic meters of firewood to meet the tax burden. In the early 1920s, the monthly wages of men on local plantations were said to be equal to the tax burden. However, women, who were equally liable for taxes at the time, earned

---

[68] PA, I094: interview with P0727 (♂, ~1940) (M'chepa, January 27, 2016), min 00:15:16–00:17:58.
[69] The sources for the data in the table are for the year 1903: Barnes, "Portuguese Troubles in Nyasaland," *CA* 22, no. 264 (1904): 245. For 1909: William Percival Johnson, "S. S. C. M.," *NDQP*, no. 25 (October 1909): 628. For 1915: Yohanna B. Abdallah, "News from the Stations: VI. Unangu," *NDC*, no. 48 (July 1915): 22. For 1921: "News from the Stations: V. Msumba," *NDC*, no. 74 (January 1922): 11–12. For 1922: Yohanna B. Abdallah, "News from the Stations: VIII. Unangu," *NDC*, no. 75 (April 1922): 14–15. For 1923: Yohanna B. Abdallah, "News from the Stations: VII. Unangu," *NDC*, no. 78 (January 1923): 11–12; H.A. Machell Cox, "News from the Stations: V. Msumba," *NDC*, no. 80 (July 1923): 10–11. For 1945: "News from the Stations: Msumba," *NDC*, no. 151 (March 1945): 30–32. For 1947: "Novo Regime do Imposto Indígena," *Moçambique: Documentário Trimestral*, no. 45 (1946): 172–176. On the fact that the change of 1947 was indeed implemented in Nkholongue, see: PA, I012: interview with P0367 (♂, 1936) (Nkholongue, September 3, 2010), min 00:21:34–00:21:52.
[70] PA, I093: interview with P0050 (♂, ~1922) (Nkholongue, January 19, 2016), min 00:19:22–00:20:04.

only half the men's salary, but had to pay the same tax.[71] During World War One, salaries were said to be "very high wages out here," namely between 9/6[72] and 12 shillings. This means that the 800 men who were reportedly employed as road builders had to work less than half a month to earn their tax money.[73] If we consider only the days of work required to earn the tax money, the ratio was even "better" in the case of labor migration: between 1902 and 1912, migrant workers in South Africa had a minimum wage of £20 per year, without having to pay for room and board.[74] This means that they would have had to work less than four days to meet the tax burden.

Various works that people were forced to do to pay the tax could cause significant burdens. Labor migration, for example, affected the whole family and especially potential wives, who were left alone to care for family and their fields and were also left alone at the mercy of the tax collector.[75] Furthermore, especially in the early years, mortality rates among mine workers from the region were considerable.[76] Exact figures are not available, but the high death rates were cited as a reason for banning labor recruitment for the South African mines in the area north of the Savé river in 1913. From then on, there was no more official recruitment along the lakeshore, even though the ban was lifted in 1933.[77] However, the ban did not stop people from going there. As we will see in Section 6.2, men later simply went to Nyasaland to join the South African labor agency Wenela there.

From my interviews it appears that the more violent methods of tax collection disappeared over time and came to an end before the mid-1950s. Several interviewees reported that they still saw tax evaders being captured, tied up, and taken to Metangula. Some interviewees also mentioned beatings in connection with this

---

[71] MNA, UMCA 1/2/17/1: A Letter to the Bishop of Nyasaland re Forced Labour on Lake Nyasa in Portuguese East Africa (Msumba, January 15, 1921), 5.

[72] Nine shillings and six pence.

[73] Yohanna B. Abdallah, "News from the Stations: VI. Unangu," *NDC*, no. 51 (April 1916): 22–23; Augustine Ambali, "News from the Stations: IV. Msumba," *NDC*, no. 51 (April 1916): 20–21.

[74] Simon E. Katzenellenbogen, *South Africa and Southern Mozambique: Labour, Railways, and Trade in the Making of a Relationship* (Manchester: Manchester University Press, 1982), 60; "S.S. 'C.M.,'" *LDQP*, no. 10 (January 1906), 259; AHM, SNI, cx. 745, Anno de 1912, Processo 3: [Labour contract], July 16, 1912.

[75] Johnson, "News from the Stations: III. The Chauncy Maples," *NDC*, no. 54 (January 1917); "News from the Stations: Msumba," *NDC*, no. 151 (March 1945); MLM, 027: interview with *D. N.*, Portuguese translation of the Chinyanja transcript (M'chepa, June 28, 2007).

[76] On deaths in mines among labor migrants from the lakeshore, see: Johnson, "S. S. C. M.," *NDQP*, no. 25 (October 1909): 628; Winspear and Johnson, "News from the Stations: II. The Chauncy Maples," *NDC*, no. 37 (October 1912): 934–35.

[77] Katzenellenbogen, *South Africa and Southern Mozambique*, 60–62.

brutal form of tax collection. But since these accounts were as a rule impersonal and superficial, it is very difficult to place them chronologically.[78] The evidence indicates that, under the *Estado Novo*, these violent methods were used arbitrarily rather than systematically, and occurred at a time when most of my interviewees were still children. This is shown, for example, by the fact that two approximately 80-year-old sisters, when asked if they could tell us the name of a tax defaulter who had been carried away in the manner they had described, said we should ask two other villagers who, as the oldest inhabitants of the village, might know.[79] One interviewee, who was born in 1936, explicitly confirmed that these methods were used when he was a child but had disappeared by the time he had grown up.[80] The only one of my interviewees who confirmed that he had once been unable to pay the tax in 1962 was not rounded up as described above. Rather, he recounted that the chief of his village (M'chepa) went to the government and asked them to give him a job so that he could pay the tax.[81]

The last Portuguese *chefe de posto* explicitly associated with such methods by my interviewees was called Liwala, a Chiyao nickname referring to his bald

---

[78] PA, I010: interview with *P0792* (♂, *1917*) (Nkholongue, September 3, 2010), min 00:24:18–00:25:12; PA, I012: interview with *P0367* (♂, *1936*) (Nkholongue, September 3, 2010), min 00:21:52–00:23:45; PA, I123: interview with *P1460* (♀), *P1461* (♂, *~1935*), *P1462* (♂, *~1935*) (Meluluca, April 25, 2016), min 01:11:57–01:13:30; PA, I154: interview with *P0367* (♂, *1936*), *P0373* (♀, *1940*) (Nkholongue, June 18, 2016), min 00:37:38–00:40:46; PA, I087: interview with *P1452* (♂, *1927*) (Lichinga, September 10, 2013), min 01:17:16–01:20:16; PA, I114: interview with *P1074* (♀, *~1940*), *P1141* (♂, *1932*) (Malango, April 15, 2016), min 02:47:13–02:47:38; PA, I014: interview with *P0147* (♀, *~1928*), *P0129* (♀, *1930*) (Nkholongue, September 8, 2010), min 00:06:28–00:07:40. For those who mentioned beatings in connection with tax collection, see: PA, I135: interview with *P1494* (♂, *1942*) (Nkhotakota, June 2, 2016), min 01:20:29–01:22:51; PA, I038: interview with *P1439* (♂, *~1940*) (Malango, August 15, 2013), min 00:49:56–00:50:18; PA, I052: interview with (♀, *1940*) (Nkholongue, August 26, 2013), min 00:35:52–00:36:56.
[79] PA, I035: interview with *P0743* (♀, *~1930*), *P0765* (♀, *~1932*) (Nkholongue, July 28, 2012), min 01:07:12–01:11:34. Similarly: PA, I120: interview with *P1102* (♂, *1932*) (Malango, April 21, 2016), min 01:50:20–01:51:44.
[80] PA, I154: interview with *P0367* (♂, *1936*), *P0373* (♀, *1940*) (Nkholongue, June 18, 2016), min 00:42:25–00:44:47. This also coincides with the testimony of a woman from Mepochi who was interviewed by Jonna Katto for her research on female veterans of the War of Independence. The woman, born in 1939, described a violent act of tax collection that had occurred when she was still a child. See: Jonna Katto, *"Grandma Was a Guerrilla Fighter": Life Memories of the Women Who Fought for Mozambique's Independence in Northern Niassa* (Tallinna: Tallinna Raamatutrükikoda, 2018), 32.
[81] PA, I094: interview with *P0727* (♂, *~1940*) (M'chepa, January 27, 2016), min 00:15:16–00:17:50. For a similar description, see: PA, I011: interview with *P0050* (♂, *~1922*) (Nkholongue, September 3, 2010), min 00:07:49–00:09:49.

head.⁸² This was probably Gastão Porto de Morais, who was head of the administration of Metangula from about 1946 to the early 1950s. Before coming to Metangula, Morais had been head of the administration of Unango for up to 20 years.⁸³ Liwala's successors in Metangula were described as comparatively reasonable characters by the Anglican missionary John Paul. The *chefe* Reis, for example, was said to occasionally seize people for work, but Paul also stated that people liked him because "he was easygoing and [...] hardly ever left Metangula to tour his vast area."⁸⁴ According to Paul, the situation definitely improved with the arrival of the new district administrator, António Borges de Brito. Paul described him as a "benign paternalist" who "came to love Maniamba and the people in his area almost as much as I came to love Messumba and the people in my area."⁸⁵ If one follows Paul, the behavior of Borges de Brito and his new head in Metangula, Ferreira de Silva, contrasted sharply with that of their predecessors:

> [Ferreira de Silva] and the Administrator, Borges de Brito, were determined to develop the area [...] They were determined to get to know the area well and to listen to all complaints; in complete contrast to most of their predecessors, who had been posted to northern Mozambique as a punishment, and were content, as had been Reis, simply to stay put and do little, apart from, every so often, seizing people and forcing them to work on the road, or sending them away to places like Beira for work in the docks.⁸⁶

---

82 PA, I133: interview with *P1473* (♂ ~1938), *P1504* (♀) (Limbi, June 1, 2016), min 01:00:18–01:00:54; PA, I120: interview with *P1102* (♂, 1932) (Malango, April 21, 2016), min 01:50:20–01:51:29; PA, I142: interview with *P0743* (♀, ~1930) (Nkholongue, June 8, 2016), min 01:15:42–01:16:35; PA, I135: interview with *P1494* (♂, 1942) (Nkhotakota, June 2, 2016), min 01:25:04–01:28:32.

83 See: AHM, Secção Oral, Transcrito NI 14: N.° 143–144, Entrevista com um grupo de velhos em Ngongote (Unango, Niassa), July 18, 1981, 4. For Morais' time in Unango, see: de Lima, "8.000 quilómetros," 63; AHU, N° 1662–2 1B MU ISAU: Carlos Silveira, "Inspecção Administrativa Ordinária na Circunscrição do Lago: Relatório Sumário" (Cuamba, June 12, 1944), attached as Doc. I to "Inspecção Administrativa Ordinária na Província de Niassa, Segunda Parte: Relatório do Inspector" (Moçambique, February 28, 1945), 4; "News from the Stations: Unangu," *NDC*, no. 152 (July 1945): 30–31. For Morais' time in Metangula, see: AHM, ISANI, cx. 99: Manuel M. R. de L. Teixeira, "Relatório da Inspecção Ordinária ao Distrito do Lago da Província do Niassa, 1950/51," 18–19.

84 John Paul, *Mozambique: Memoirs of a Revolution* (Harmondsworth: Penguin, 1975), 27. In contrast, Liwala was said to have visited Nkholongue twice a year according to one of my interviewees: PA, I112: interview with *P0129* (♀, 1930), *P0128* (♂, 1928) (Nkholongue, April 12, 2016), min 02:08:38–02:09:47.

85 Paul, *Memoirs of a Revolution*, 52.

86 Paul, 64. None of my interviewees ever reported that anyone was sent to Beira. Mateus Kida, a Frelimo veteran, stated that people were forcibly recruited in the region for the construction of the road from Cobué to Nova Olivença in 1960. However, the way he described this incident suggests that this was a rather isolated occurrence from a regional perspective. See: Mateus Kida, "A abertura das frentes de combate em Niassa," in *Simpósio 50 anos da Frelimo (1962–2012): Fontes para*

5.3 Colonial Exploitation along the Lakeshore — 159

It is important to note that the behavior of the Portuguese "men on the spot" was probably more relevant for the improvement of the situation regarding tax collection than changes in the system. Paul contrasted Borges de Brito's behavior to that of the administrator of the *Concelho de Vila Cabral*, who, according to Paul, "tyrannized over the blacks" and always carried "a *palmatório* [sic] (a perforated flat piece of wood used for beating the palms of the hands) and a *chicote* (a whip made out of a strip of hippopotamus hide) in his car."[87] Also, around Unango, more violent methods of tax collection appear to have been still used in the 1950s, as one of Katto's interviewees, who was born in 1951, stated that she had witnessed a round-up there as a child.[88]

The dynamics of the tax burden depended not only on the Portuguese "men on the spot," the tax rate, and the available opportunities to earn the tax money, but also on the changing presence of the colonial state around Nkholongue. The administrative downgrading of Metangula made tax evasion easier and less dangerous. This becomes obvious if one looks at the strength of the state's police forces in the region. In 1944, there were only three *cipaios* stationed in Metangula for the collection of the hut tax. In 1961, the number was five for Metangula and 36 for the Lago District as a whole.[89] The next army contingent was stationed in Vila Cabral. It was responsible for a territory as large as the state of Pennsylvania or Switzerland and Austria combined.[90] From the perspective of Nkholongue, the *Companhia* possessed quite different capacities. According to the *Companhia*'s annual report for 1906, 70 *cipaios* were stationed in Metangula.[91] And, in 1908, the entire *Concelho* had a standing force of 100 *cipaios* and 26 "native" soldiers.[92] Since most of them were stationed close to Nkholongue, the state's capacity to en-

---

a nossa história, ed. Carlos Jorge Siliya, Benigna Zimba, and Páscoa Themba, Colecção Memórias do Combatente (Maputo: Centro de Pesquisa da História da Luta de Libertação Nacional, 2012), 113.
87 Paul, *Memoirs of a Revolution*, 71. Isaacman et al. have quoted Paul's characterization of the administrator of the *Concelho de Vila Cabral* to illustrate the standard version of a Portuguese administrator but failed to mention that Paul had used him to paint the negative counterpart of Borges de Brito. See: Isaacman et al., "'Cotton Is the Mother of Poverty': Peasant Resistance to Forced Cotton Production in Mozambique, 1938–1961," 589.
88 Katto, "Grandma Was a Guerrilla Fighter," 221.
89 AHD, MU/GM/GNP/RNP/0064/01681: Mário Costa, "Ocupação administrativa do Distrito do Niassa," May 22, 1961, 2.
90 This contingent was joined in 1961 by another contingent stationed in Nova Freixo (Cuamba). See: AHD, MU/GM/GNP/RNP/0064/01681: Mário Costa, "Ocupação administrativa do Distrito do Niassa," May 22, 1961, 2.
91 Companhia do Nyassa, "Relatório e Contas apresentados a Assembleia Geral Ordinária em 30 de Julho de 1906" (Lisboa, 1906), 20–21.
92 *Annuário de Moçambique 1908* (Lourenço Marques: Imprensa Nacional, 1908), 656.

force its laws locally was undoubtedly far greater in the time of the *Companhia* than later.

P.A. Metangula		1940 11,525	1964 11,336	- 1.6%
Road villages		**7,396**	**5,916**	**- 20.0%**
Reg. Massumba	Mechuma	2,029	1,720	-15.2%
Reg. Massanje	Messumba	3,293	2,216	- 32.7%
Reg. Machequene	Chiuanga	714	690	- 3.4%
Reg. Chilombe	Metangula	1,360	1,290	- 5.1%
Non-road villages		**4,129**	**5,420**	**+ 31.3%**
Northern non-road villages		1,167	1,780	+ 52.5%
Reg. Tandamula	Mbamba	489	835	+ 70.8%
Reg. Maendaenda	Chia	678	945	+ 39.4%
Southern non-road villages		2,962	3,640	+ 22.9%
Reg. Chingomanje	Nkholongue	287	550	+ 91.6%
Reg. Angorocoro	Ngolocolo	626	600	- 4.2%
Reg. Menhanja	Meluluca	779	780	+ 0.1%
Reg. Chitepete	Lussefa	62	760	+ 1125.8%
Reg. Paja	Ucungu	732	-	- 100%
Reg. Amelane	Chinuni	476	950	+ 99.6%

Table 2: Number of inhabitants by chiefdoms of the P.A. Metangula, 1940 and 1964.[93]

The fact that tax evasion became easier is also suggested by the available population statistics of 1940 and 1964 (see Table 2). The comparison of the figures of 1940 and 1964 shows wide fluctuations for several villages. Oral history indicates that the 1940s and 1950s were characterized by considerable emigration of people

---

[93] Sources of the figures: AHM, Biblioteca, 1282j: Manuel Simões Alberto, *Os negros de Moçambique: Censo etnográfico* (Lourenço Marques, 1942), 59; ANTT, SCCIM N.° 24 (folhas 247–253): Mapa comparativo da população do Distrito distribuída por regedorias e relacionada aos anos de antes da eclosão da subversão (1964/1965), e depois da subversão, para controle dos elementos refugiados (Vila Cabral, June 1972).

from the region to Nyasaland.⁹⁴ This probably explains the overall stagnant numbers and also the decline in population in the villages with road access. The fact that the population in villages without road access nevertheless increased, and by more than 90 percent in the case of Nkholongue, can therefore best be read as a sign of the state's limited knowledge of the number of its subjects in 1940.⁹⁵

Forced Labor

Taxation was an "indirect" mechanism to force people into the colonial economy. The colonial state also knew more "direct" mechanisms to achieve this. The Labor Code of 1899 included a "legal obligation to work."⁹⁶ Under this law, employers could submit requisitions for laborers to the administration, which then recruited these workers, by force if necessary.⁹⁷ This recruitment of forced laborers for private purposes was legally abolished in 1926, and the subsequent Labor Code of 1930 stipulated "only" a "moral obligation to work." Forced labor recruitment was still possible under the new law, but now limited to public purposes.⁹⁸ This form of work included the *contribuição braçal* ("manual contribution"), an annual unpaid short-term labor obligation on public works.⁹⁹ But the application of the new labor law remained ambiguous. Furthermore, the Governor-General's redefinition of African labor obligations, communicated by the Circular 818/D-4 of October 1942, officially provided for the return to a system of forced recruitment for private pur-

---

94 For examples of people who left Nkholongue for Nyasaland before the Mozambican War of Independence and did not return to Mozambique, see: PA, I128: interview with *P1426 (♂, 1929)* (Malindi (Mangochi District, Malawi), May 28, 2016); PA, I131: interview with *P1434 (♂, 1942)* (Lifuwu (Salima District, Malawi), May 31, 2016); PA, I134: interview with *P1490 (♀, 1944)* (Nkhotakota, June 2, 2016); PA, I135: interview with *P1494 (♂, 1942)* (Nkhotakota, June 2, 2016); PA, I138: interview with *P1498 (♂, 1940)* (Nkhotakota, June 2, 2016); PA, I137: interview with *P1496 (♀, 1950), P1497 (♂, 1964)* (Nkhotakota, June 2, 2016).
95 Certainly, one can also suspect a movement from the road to the non-road villages. But the most plausible motive for this migration would just again support the argument that this was an easy way to escape the state's burdens. Furthermore, there is no evidence of such a migration in oral history accounts.
96 Vail and White, *Capitalism and Colonialism in Mozambique*, 134–135. For the history of forced labor in Mozambique, see as well: Allina, *Slavery by Any Other Name*.
97 MNA, UMCA 1/2/17/1: Provisional Regulations for the Recruiting and Supply of Native Labour in the Territories of the Co. da Nyasa, July 1921.
98 Vail and White, *Capitalism and Colonialism in Mozambique*, 249–53.
99 David Hedges et al., *História de Moçambique Vol. 3: Moçambique no auge do colonialismo, 1930–1961* (Maputo: UEM, 1993), 95, 143.

poses.[100] It was not until the reforms of 1961 that these practices were finally abolished from a legal perspective.[101]

In the case of Nkholongue, these more "direct" methods of forcing people into the colonial economy were only used at certain times in the village's history. This was not so much because of the legislative changes but mainly because the local presence of both the colonial state and economy was tenuous for many years, and thus the local demand for workers limited. It was primarily under *Companhia* rule that such methods were used. At two points in time, they were used most extensively: during World War One and in the early 1920s.

The availability of sources for analyzing local developments during World War One is limited. However, there is no doubt that the outbreak of the war increased the local demand for labor substantially. Initially, the rising demand for labor was caused by the state's sudden efforts to improve the local infrastructure. In 1915, it was reported that the *Companhia* was making roads everywhere[102] and had "commanded that everybody must hoe the road."[103] Later, after the invasion by German troops, people were recruited as carriers and *askaris* for the troops of the Entente. Recruitment was regionally so extensive that in early 1918 the missionaries in Unango were unable to find anyone to repair the roof of their church.[104] If one follows the reports of the Anglican missionaries, the adult male population was almost completely absent as most of the men had been commandeered by the government.[105]

Undoubtedly, this development also affected the population of Nkholongue even though there is no explicit evidence to support this. The local suffering caused by the war was considerable. This was not only due to the high death toll among the carriers and *askaris*,[106] but also because the situation disturbed the local availability of food, as food production was largely left to the women. Furthermore, all surplus food was requisitioned for military purposes.[107] The situation was further

---

100 Zachary Kagan Guthrie, "Labor, Mobility and Coercion in Central Mozambique, 1942–1961" (PhD thesis, Princeton University, 2014), 45–67; Vail and White, *Capitalism and Colonialism in Mozambique*, 280–82.
101 Vail and White, *Capitalism and Colonialism in Mozambique*, 383.
102 Abdallah, "News from the Stations: VI. Unangu," *NDC*, no. 46 (January 1915).
103 Augustine Ambali, "News from the Stations: IV. Msumba," *NDC*, no. 46 (January 1915): 14–15.
104 Yohanna B. Abdallah, "News from the Stations: VII. Unangu," *NDC*, no. 59 (April 1918): 21.
105 Ambali, "News from the Stations: IV. Msumba," *NDC*, no. 46 (January 1915); Cox and Chisui, "News from the Stations: V. Msumba," *NDC*, no. 62 (January 1919).
106 For the deaths of carriers and *askaris* along the lakeshore, see: Cox and Chisui, "News from the Stations: V. Msumba," *NDC*, no. 62 (January 1919).
107 For the lack of food during this period, see: Augustine Ambali, "News from the Stations: IV. Msumba," *NDC*, no. 57 (October 1917): 19–20; Augustine Ambali, "News from the Stations: IV.

exacerbated by the looting by German troops when they invaded northern Mozambique (see pp. 178–180) and by the spread of Spanish flu after the war, which claimed many lives along the lakeshore.[108]

Precise figures on the death toll of the local population are not available for the lakeshore area; the Anglican missionaries merely reported that there was a "sad number of gaps from death" among the men recruited for war purposes, "but not so many as in some [other] districts."[109] For the territory of the *Companhia* as a whole, the available estimates should be taken with caution; a real investigation seems not to have taken place. One source speaks of 50,000 deaths from carrier services, lack of food, and killings in battle,[110] another of tens of thousands of deaths from the war and especially the influenza pandemic that followed.[111] This can be contrasted with a probably also not very reliable count of the territory's population of 521,135 in 1923.[112] Notwithstanding these uncertainties, qualitative sources confirm that the death toll from war and pandemic for the territory of the *Companhia* as a whole was enormous.

The second time that forced recruitment was used extensively in the area was in the early 1920s, when world cotton prices soared.[113] It was quite certainly these high prices that prompted various companies to set up cotton plantations along the

---

Ngoo Bay," *NDC*, no. 58 (January 1918): 15–16; H.A. Machell Cox, "News from the Stations: III. S.S. Chauncy Maples," *NDC*, no. 58 (January 1918): 15; Yohanna B. Abdallah, "News from the Stations: VII. Unangu," *NDC*, no. 63 (April 1919): 27–28. Missionary Eyre reported, for example, from Metonia that "[m]any fields are not hoed, or partly neglected, in consequence of the number of men who had to go as carriers; [...]" See: C.B. Eyre, "News from the Stations: VIII. Mtonya," *NDC*, no. 63 (April 1919): 29. For a very similar analysis, see: AHM, GGM XX, cx. 182: José Mendes dos Reis, "Relatório do Delegado do Governo aos Territorios da Companhia do Nyassa, de Setembro de 1924 a Março de 1925" (Lisboa, May 20, 1925), 41. For the requisition of all surplus foodstuffs for military purposes, see: Yohanna B. Abdallah, "News from the Stations: VI. Unangu," *NDC*, no. 53 (October 1916): 25–26; Cathrew Fisher, "The Bishop's Letter," *NDC*, no. 53 (October 1916): 1–2; MNA, S1/576/19: Letter from E.F. Colvile (Resident) to the Chief Secretary (March 7, 1919).

108 For the spread of the Spanish flu in the region, see: "Spanish Influenza," *NDC*, no. 62 (January 1919): 7–8; Abdallah, "News from the Stations: VII. Unangu," *NDC*, no. 63 (April 1919); Augustine Ambali, "News from the Stations: IV. Ngoo Bay," *NDC*, no. 63 (April 1919): 23–24; Lawrence Chisui, "News from the Stations: V. Msumba," *NDC*, no. 63 (April 1919): 24–26; Johnson and Cox, "News from the Stations: Station III," *NDC*, no. 65 (October 1919), 20. See as well: A.G. Blood, *The History of the Universities' Mission to Central Africa*, vol. 2: 1907–1932 (London: UMCA, 1957), 177.
109 Cox and Chisui, "News from the Stations: V. Msumba," *NDC*, no. 62 (January 1919): 14–15.
110 TNA, FO/371/11932, f. 91–94: Translation of Report by the Intendente of the Government at Ibo (Lisbon, March 20, 1925), f. 91.
111 AHM, GGM XX, cx. 182: José Mendes dos Reis, "Relatório do Delegado do Governo aos Territorios da Companhia do Nyassa, de Setembro de 1924 a Março de 1925" (Lisboa, May 20, 1925), 42.
112 AHM, SNI, Secção D, cx. 1248: Censo da População (Ano de 1923, Processo No. 22).
113 On the high price of cotton at this time, see: Isaacman, *Cotton Is the Mother of Poverty*, 26.

lakeshore.¹¹⁴ In 1920, one British company alone planned to open ten plantations, each to be headed by a European manager. The Anglican missionaries welcomed this development initially. Missionary Cox wrote in July 1920:

> This may possibly affect school attendances adversely. But on the whole it should be a great benefit to the natives, as it will enable them to get work to pay their tax and buy clothing without going out of their own country. I was especially glad to hear that the Company wishes to make some kind of social centre for their white employees at Metangula, and that Mrs. Easterbrook and other ladies will probably be coming out next year.¹¹⁵

In the course of the rainy season 1920/21, the effects of the "boom" were felt everywhere. Throughout the region, Anglican missionaries reported that the people were busy working on the plantations. Augustine Ambali, who was responsible for the area between Metangula and Cobué, wrote that he had no more schoolboys in his stations because they had all gone to work.¹¹⁶ Even in places as far away as Unango or Metonia, people were recruited for work on the lakeshore plantations.¹¹⁷ Yohanna Abdallah wrote from Unango that one "can see villages full of women and little children—not a single man to be found."¹¹⁸

The plantations were located in different areas of the lakeshore, but the central area was just next to Nkholongue. In April 1921, missionary Cox described the dramatic change there as follows:

> Any old hand revisiting the district would be astonished to see cotton plantations stretching along almost continuously from the [sic] Ngolocolo to Lussefa. It has revolutionised the whole life of those villages.¹¹⁹

For the inhabitants of the region, the "revolution" proved disastrous. The main problem was that the demand for labor was so high that it could barely be satis-

---

114 These plantations have been largely ignored by scholars. Statistics published by Anne Pitcher imply that there was no cotton production in the territories of the *Companhia* prior to 1924. See: M. Anne Pitcher, "Sowing the Seeds of Failure: Early Portuguese Cotton Cultivation in Angola and Mozambique," *Journal of Southern African Studies* 17, no. 1 (1991): 70.
115 It is "Mtengula" in the original. See: H.A. Machell Cox, "News from the Stations: V. Msumba," *NDC*, no. 68 (July 1920): 8–10.
116 Augustine Ambali, "News from the Stations: IV. Ngoo Bay," *NDC*, no. 70 (January 1921): 8–9.
117 C.B. Eyre, "News from the Stations: VIII. Mtonya," *NDC*, no. 71 (April 1921): 14–15; Yohanna B. Abdallah, "News from the Stations: VII. Unangu," *NDC*, no. 71 (April 1921): 13–14.
118 Yohanna B. Abdallah, "News from the Stations: VII. Unangu," *NDC*, no. 70 (January 1921): 10–11.
119 It is "Ngolokolo" and "Losefa" in the original. See: H.A. Machell Cox, "News from the Stations: Station III," *NDC*, no. 71 (April 1921): 9–10. See as well: Ambali, "News from the Stations: IV. Ngoo Bay," *NDC*, no. 70 (January 1921).

fied. This problem was exacerbated by the fact that the *Companhia*'s employees, including the *Concelho*'s administrator, began to run their own plantations. As a result, the administration began to force people to work on the plantations most extensively. According to Cox, the government either ordered chiefs to send a certain number of men or simply sent the *cipaios* to seize men indiscriminately. Chiefs who failed to send the requested number were imprisoned and subjected to corporal punishment. The same happened to men who failed to show up for work. When the demand for labor climbed further, women were also targeted as laborers. In January 1921, it was said that even children as young as nine were "recruited" in regions as far as 20 to 30 miles from the plantations.[120]

The work was paid for. But money alone was of little use when there was no food on the market.[121] The demand for laborers for the cotton plantations was so high that people had to neglect their own fields. Such a constellation could not last long. In April 1922, missionary Austin Matthew reported from Messumba:

> The fact that so many men last year had to work on the cotton plantations instead of in their fields reduced the area under cultivation, with the result that after a satisfactory rainfall last year, there is now a scarcity of food. There is less cultivation still this year, as the men are at work on the plantations again, and the women have to spend a good deal of time travelling the country in search of food. The policy which brings about such a state of things can only end in disaster, and as is usually the case, it is the innocent who are suffering now and will suffer worse later on.[122]

As in 1902, the missionaries sent complaints to the *Companhia*'s headquarters in Europe about the abuses occurring along the lakeshore.[123] It is unclear to what extent these complaints were taken as grounds for change. But in 1922, the *Concelho*'s administrator was replaced by another under whose methods the *Concelho* was "settling down more happily."[124] At the same time, the cotton boom was already

---

120 MNA, UMCA 1/2/17/1: A Letter to the Bishop of Nyasaland re Forced Labour on Lake Nyasa in Portuguese East Africa (Msumba, January 15, 1921).
121 The market for food, which had been almost non-existent even before, was further decimated by plantation work. Or, as Missionary Cox put it, "[w]e used to look upon Meluluca as one the best centres for getting food for our carriers as we went round. But that is wholly reversed now, owing to the various plantations that have been started there." ("Mluluka" in the original) See: H.A. Machell Cox, "News from the Stations: Station III," *NDC*, no. 70 (January 1921): 8.
122 "News from the Stations: V. Msumba," *NDC*, no. 75 (April 1922): 13.
123 MNA, UMCA 1/2/17/1: Letter from H.A. Machell Cox to Cathrew Fisher ([London], June 23, 1921), MNA, UMCA 1/2/17/1: Letter from H.A. Machell Cox to Leys, (Westminster, July 12, 1921).
124 The quotation is from: Cox, "News from the Stations: V. Msumba," *NDC*, no. 77 (October 1922). For other similar evidence, see: "The Bishop's Letter," *NDC*, no. 77 (October 1922): 1–2; "News from the Stations: IV. Msumba," *NDC*, no. 91 (April 1926): 9.

coming to an end again. In July 1922, one of the largest companies, the British East Nyasa Estates, was closing down, "partly because of labour troubles, but mainly because of the home market," as missionary Matthew put it. Matthew welcomed this development, saying there would be "less trouble about forced labour," but simultaneously explained that now one source of money to pay the tax was gone.[125]

Some plantations continued to operate after 1922, although it is not entirely clear for how long.[126] In any case, it seems that the problems with forced labor indeed disappeared, at least from the missionaries' point of view. Also, the tax level, which had seen a steep rise to 18 shillings in the previous months, was again lowered significantly. In addition, the new commissioner of Metangula allowed people to pay the tax in kind if necessary.[127] Despite these improvements, it took more than five years for the food situation to return to normal.[128] It was not until 1927 that missionary Cox could finally report the following:

> It should be recorded with thankfulness that there has been very little hunger this year in this district. Since the war a state of semi-famine between November and March had become almost chronic. It had been caused not so much by bad seasons as by the excessive calls on labour first by the war and then by the forced labour demanded by various companies. Now in more settled conditions the position has worked round to the normal.[129]

Again, there is no explicit evidence that Nkholongue's population was indeed affected by these developments. While the statements of many interviewees clearly suggest that their parents had suffered more under Portuguese colonialism than

---

[125] Both quotations are from: Austin F. Matthew, "News from the Stations: V. Msumba," *NDC*, no. 76 (July 1922): 13–14.

[126] According to her logbook, the S.S. Chauncy Maples loaded 101 bales of cotton and 175 bales of tobacco on December 23, 1923, implying there was still some production in the area in 1923. See: ASM, Chauncy Maples Log 1914–1924.

[127] Matthew, "News from the Stations: V. Msumba," *NDC*, no. 76 (July 1922).

[128] For some examples of reports of hunger or famine during these years, see: Augustine Ambali, "News from the Stations: IV. Ngoo Bay," *NDC*, no. 75 (April 1922): 12–13; Augustine Ambali, "News from the Stations: IV. Ngoo Bay," *NDC*, no. 76 (July 1922): 13; Augustine Ambali, "News from the Stations: IV. Ngoo Bay," *NDC*, no. 77 (October 1922): 13; Abdallah, "News from the Stations: VII. Unangu," *NDC*, no. 78 (January 1923); Augustine Ambali, "News from the Stations: IV. Ngoo Bay," *NDC*, no. 78 (January 1923): 9; Yohanna B. Abdallah, "News from the Stations: VII. Unangu," *NDC*, no. 79 (April 1923): 13; H.A. Machell Cox, "News from the Stations: V. Msumba," *NDC*, no. 79 (April 1923): 12–13; C.B. Eyre, "News from the Stations: VI. Mtonya," *NDC*, no. 79 (April 1923): 13; Augustine Ambali, "News from the Stations: IV. Ngoo Bay," *NDC*, no. 80 (July 1923): 9–10; Augustine Ambali, "News from the Stations: IV. Ngoo Bay," *NDC*, no. 83 (April 1924): 6; Augustine Ambali, "News from the Stations: VI. Ngoo Bay," *NDC*, no. 88 (July 1925): 16–17.

[129] H.A. Machell Cox, "News from the Stations: IV. Msumba," *NDC*, no. 95 (April 1927): 7.

they did,[130] no one was really able to tell me anything about the cotton plantations of the 1920s. Only some interviewees from the villages around Ngolocolo and Lussefa had some but still very vague knowledge about these plantations.[131] However, given what the missionaries wrote about the impact of these plantations on everyday life in the region, there is little doubt that people from Nkholongue were equally affected by both the recruitment of forced labor during this period and the "state of semi-famine" that followed.

There is also little doubt that the population of the region would never again suffer such systematic violence and exploitation as in the early 1920s. Never again would the colonial state engage in forced recruitment as it had then. None of my interviewees described such recruitment practices for later times. The reason for this is not to be found in the legal changes of the system, but primarily in the developments discussed in the second section of this chapter. One interviewee from Unango explained this change in AHM's oral history project of the early 1980s as follows:

> The forced labor was in the time of the *Companhia*! In the time of the government [refers to the time of the *Estado Novo*], there was not much work.[132]

---

130 PA, I041: interview with *P0951* (♀, *1948*), *P0242* (♂, *1945*) (Malango, August 16, 2013), min 00:10:03–00:11:41; PA, I154: interview with *P0367* (♂, *1936*), *P0373* (♀, *1940*) (Nkholongue, June 18, 2016), min 00:36:21–00:43:13; PA, I047: interview with *P0596* (♂, *~1950*) (Metangula, August 21, 2013), min 00:09:21–00:10:18; PA, I087: interview with *P1452* (♂, *1927*) (Lichinga, September 10, 2013), min 00:26:52–00:29:02; PA, I058: interview with *P1074* (♀, *~1940*) (Malango, August 28, 2013), min 01:49:24–01:50:40.

131 In my interviews, these plantations were usually associated with a British planter (nick-)named "Chambika" who was said to have lived in Lussefa. See: PA, I063: interview with *P1488* (♂, *~1930*) (M'chepa, August 31, 2013), min 0011:43–00:15:37; PA, I152: interview with *P1476* (♂, *~1935*) (Milombe, June 16, 2016), min 00:29:30–00:35:16; PA, I016: interview with *P1483* (♀, *1950*), *P1481* (♂, *1954*), *P1482* (♂, *1937*) (Lussefa, October 9, 2011), min 00:00:03–00:07:35; PA, I123: interview with *P1460* (♀), *P1461* (♂, *~1935*), *P1462* (♂, *~1935*) (Meluluca, April 25, 2016), min 00:32:01–00:38:39. For "Chambika," see as well: AHM, Secção Oral, Transcrito NI 04: N.° 154–155, Entrevista com um grupo de velhos em Chiwanga, interview by Gerhard Liesegang, Teresa Oliveira, and Mujuane Mainga Vicente, July 9, 1981, 84; AHM, Secção Oral, Transcrito MPC 011: N.° 88–89, Entrevista com Paulo Litumbe, October 15, 1980, 36–37.

132 AHM, Secção Oral, Transcrito NI 16: N.° 149–150, Entrevista com um grupo de velhos em Nsainga (Unango, Niassa), July 19, 1981, 35.

The Mozambican Cotton Regime

The later limited capacity of the state to integrate the people living in the lakeshore area into the colonial economy is also evident in the way the Mozambican cotton regime (1938–1961) was implemented on the ground. Under the cotton regime, peasants all across Mozambique were first urged and later forced to grow cotton for the Portuguese textile industry. Cotton was not to be grown on plantations with wage labor but on the private lands of the peasants. The Mozambican cotton regime has attracted a great deal of scholarly attention and spawned such famous books as Allen Isaacman's *Cotton is the Mother of Poverty*.[133] Forced cotton cultivation was particularly widespread in the northern parts of Mozambique, where cotton growing became "the distinctive feature of colonial life" in the two decades after 1938.[134] However, while Isaacman has rightly argued that the Portuguese cotton regime went hand in hand with the integration of Niassa into the colonial economy,[135] it must be emphasized that this integration did not affect all parts of Niassa. Of the 132,849 tons of cotton produced there between 1940 and 1961, 60.6 percent came from the *Circunscrição de Amaramba*, 30.8 percent from the *Circunscrição de Marrupa*, 8.1 percent from the *Concelho de Vila Cabral*, and only 0.4 percent from the *Circunscrição de Lago/Maniamba*.[136] In Nkholongue, cotton was not grown for two decades, but only for two years, most likely in the first part of the 1940s.

On the question to what extent cotton cultivation was forced, the information from my interviews diverges. For example, while one interviewee emphasized that the cotton company had its own troops,[137] others described cotton more as a vol-

---

[133] Isaacman, *Cotton Is the Mother of Poverty*. See as well: Isaacman et al., "'Cotton Is the Mother of Poverty': Peasant Resistance to Forced Cotton Production in Mozambique, 1938–1961"; Pitcher, "From Coercion to Incentives"; Allen Isaacman and Arlindo Chilundo, "Peasants at Work: Forced Cotton Cultivation in Northern Mozambique, 1938–1961," in *The Rise and Fall of Modern Empires*, ed. Owen White, vol. 1: Social Organization, 4 vols. (Farnham: Ashgate, 2013), 69–102.
[134] Newitt, *A History of Mozambique*, 455.
[135] Allen Isaacman, *Cotton Is the Mother of Poverty: Peasants, Work, and Rural Struggle in Colonial Mozambique, 1938–1961* (Portsmouth: Heinemann, 1996), 74–77. Similarly: Funada-Classen, *The Origins of War in Mozambique*, 83–85.
[136] These numbers are taken from: Nelson Saraiva Bravo, *A cultura algodeira na economia do norte de Moçambique* (Lisboa: Junta de Investigações do Ultramar, 1963). See also Bravo's own analysis regarding the difference between the different administrative subunits of Niassa: Bravo, 227–228.
[137] PA, I107: interview with *P1074* (♀, ~1940) (Malango, April 5, 2016), min 00:47:18–00:47:22. This could refer to the police-like overseers that could be employed by the cotton concession companies from 1941 onward. See: Hedges et al., *História de Moçambique Vol. 3*, 92. For others who said or implied that it was forced: PA, I035: interview with *P0743* (♀, ~1930), *P0765* (♀, ~1932) (Nkholongue,

untary cash crop that yielded almost nothing and was therefore abandoned very quickly.[138] One interviewee who claimed that her mother had planted cotton put it this way:

> They took the harvest to Metangula, where they had built a house where cotton could be sold. Now when the people saw the price, they thought that it is better to grow only our food, otherwise there will be hunger. And so the people gave up growing cotton.[139]

However, it is fairly certain that there was considerable fear that the state would enforce the cultivation of cotton. Some interviewees recounted that people boiled the seedlings before planting them to prevent the plants from growing.[140] Furthermore, based on documents I was unable to consult, Isaacman et al. found that protests against cotton cultivation took place in the administrative posts of Unango and Metangula in 1945 and 1946.[141] The resistance to cotton could have been not only a response to the government's demands of that time, but above all a consequence of the devastating experience with cotton cultivation in the early 1920s. There are several indications for such a reading. One interviewee who reported the cooking of the seedlings described this as a preventive measure, as the chief and the elders knew that the village would face hunger.[142] Missionary Cox, who had witnessed the disaster of the 1920s, wrote about the cotton regime in Messumba in 1943:

July 28, 2012), min 00:59:30–01:05:41; PA, I048: interview with *P1446 (♂, ~1945)* (Metangula, August 21, 2013), min 00:29:45–00:30:34; PA, I004: interview with *P0147 (♀, ~1928), P0129 (♀, 1930)* (Nkholongue, August 25, 2010), min 01:20:53–01:23:14; PA, I008: interview with *P0299 (♂, 1938)* (Nkholongue, September 1, 2010), min 00:36:19–00:38:12.

138 PA, I153: interview with *P1477 (♂, ~1940)* (Micucue, June 17, 2016), min 00:24:35–00:27:09; PA, I075: interview with *P1218 (♀, 1930)* (Metangula, September 6, 2013), min 00:38:53–00:39:58; PA, I118: interview with *P1218 (♀, 1930)* (Malango, April 21, 2016), min 01:54:03–01:55:24; PA, I120: interview with *P1102 (♂, 1932)* (Malango, April 21, 2016), min 01:30:10–01:30:50; PA, I002: interview with *P0128 (♂, 1928)* (Nkholongue, August 18, 2010), min 00:43:16–00:46:29.

139 PA, I118: interview with *P1218 (♀, 1930)* (Malango, April 21, 2016), min 01:54:53–01:55:11.

140 PA, I013: interview with *P0367 (♂, 1936)* (Nkholongue, September 8, 2010), min 01:13:40–01:15:54; PA, I106: interview with *P0262 (♀, ~1940)* (Malango, April 4, 2016), min 02:13:45–02:15:05; PA, I008: interview with *P0299 (♂, 1938)* (Nkholongue, September 1, 2010), min 00:35:31–00:35:56; PA, I014: interview with *P0147 (♀, ~1928), P0129 (♀, 1930)* (Nkholongue, September 8, 2010), min 00:02:03–00:03:10.

141 Isaacman et al., "'Cotton Is the Mother of Poverty': Peasant Resistance to Forced Cotton Production in Mozambique, 1938–1961," 596, 602. At the time of my research, these documents were in the storage rooms of the AHM on *Av. Samuel Filipe Magaia*.

142 PA, I013: interview with *P0367 (♂, 1936)* (Nkholongue, September 8, 2010), min 01:13:55–01:15:43.

> The Boma ['government'] are trying to establish [cotton] as a cash crop in the village. It is immensely unpopular, at any rate just around here, and our boys have inherited the attitude of their elders towards it.[143]

It is also noteworthy that one interviewee began to describe the cotton regime of the 1940s when asked what he knew of the *Companhia*. When questioned whether this was really the *Companhia*, he replied:

> Yes, the *Companhia*. But now not exactly as powerful as [before] because the government, the *governo*, had entered.[144]

We cannot know how and why this historical analogy has "entered" into his memory. We can suspect possible commonalities between the two cotton schemes, such as identical staff, similar recruitment practices, resembling consequences, or—and I think this is the most plausible reading—that cotton was simply very strongly identified with the *Companhia*.[145]

In any case, all the evidence points to the fact that the state did little to enforce cotton cultivation after the initial unsuccessful attempts.[146] Obviously, state officials had to take local responses into account. This is also shown by the statement of one interviewee born around 1930. She stated that the Portuguese officials did accept people's unwillingness to grow cotton but wanted to send them tobacco instead. However, according to her testimony, people also rejected tobacco because it would cause hunger too. Therefore, they asked the Portuguese for rice since this obviously had the advantage of being wanted as a cash crop and edible at the same time. If one follows her statement, rice was then sent.[147]

---

[143] "Notes and Jottings: Escola Central," *CA* 61, no. 724 (April 1943): 47.
[144] "Ehee a companhia. Koma tsopano not exactly as powerful as older chifukwa yalowa government, governo.", PA, I128: interview with *P1426 (♂, 1929)* (Malindi (Mangochi District, Malawi), May 28, 2016), min 02:05:21–02:05:37.
[145] For the association of the *Companhia* with cotton, see as well: PA, I123: interview with *P1460 (♀), P1461 (♂, ~1935), P1462 (♂, ~1935)* (Meluluca, April 25, 2016), min 00:32:05–00:32:20; PA, I010: interview with *P0792 (♂, 1917)* (Nkholongue, September 3, 2010), min 00:11:35–00:12:16.
[146] PA, I107: interview with *P1074 (♀, ~1940)* (Malango, April 5, 2016), min 00:43:01–00:48:39; PA, I013: interview with *P0367 (♂, 1936)* (Nkholongue, September 8, 2010), min 01:15:54–01:16:25. See as well Footnote 138.
[147] PA, I142: interview with *P0743 (♀, ~1930)* (Nkholongue, June 8, 2016), min 00:22:46–00:24:43. The greater appeal of growing surplus food crops compared to other non-edible export cash crops has long been highlighted by researchers for others region of Africa. See: Monica van Beusekom, *Negotiating Development: African Farmers and Colonial Experts at the Office Du Niger, 1920–1960* (Portsmouth: Heinemann, 2002); John Tosh, "The Cash-Crop Revolution in Tropical Africa: An Agricultural Reappraisal," *African Affairs* 79, no. 314 (1980): 89.

Her reference to rice must be understood in the context of the rice cultivation scheme launched by the colonial government in 1942.[148] The evidence shows that this scheme, modeled along the lines of the cotton scheme, also reached the region. But as in the case of cotton, the government seems to have done little to enforce it locally against the will of the people, and rice never seems to have attained any importance as a cash crop in Nkholongue. Rather, the statements of two interviewees suggest that the scheme was seen as a welcome opportunity to appropriate the rice grains distributed as seedlings for one's own food production.[149]

The colonial state had regionally not only limited capacities to enforce its policies but also limited economic reasons to do so in such a marginal area.[150] This is also apparent from the following dialogue between António Rola, a researcher of AHM's oral history project, and the aforementioned bishop Paulo Litumbe (*1914, †1994):

A.R.: But people could just quit it? There were no reprisals from the Portuguese colonial administration if people, for example, refused to do the planting?
P.L.: There was no such exaction. I know very well that there was no such exaction because there was no transport for this. It would have been necessary to transport it to Malawi on Malawian boats. Therefore, they just quit it.[151]

Here, again, we see the reference to the 1920s, when cotton had been directly exported to the other side of the lake. In the 1940s, the rationale of the cotton regime would have required export via Portuguese roads and railways, an infrastructure that was however still far too rudimentary in this remote area.

---

148 Hedges et al., *História de Moçambique Vol. 3*, 93; Newitt, *A History of Mozambique*, 456–57.
149 AHM, Secção Oral, Transcrito MPC 011: N.º 88–89, Entrevista com Paulo Litumbe, October 15, 1980, 37–38; PA, I152: interview with *P1476* (♂, ~*1935*) (Milombe, June 16, 2016), min 00:31:20–00:32:17; PA, I107: interview with *P1074* (♀, ~*1940*) (Malango, April 5, 2016), min 00:43:52–00:43:57; PA, I142: interview with *P0743* (♀, ~*1930*) (Nkholongue, June 8, 2016), min 00:22:46–00:24:43.
150 Due to poor results, cotton cultivation was officially discontinued in the entire Lago District in 1950. See: Bravo, *A cultura algodeira*, 141, 228.
151 A.R.: "Mas as pessoas podiam deixar e não havia da parte da Administração do regime colonial português represálias ou, quando as pessoas, por exemplo, recusavam-se a fazer a plantação?" / P.L.: "Não havia exigência. Sei muito bem que não havia exigência porque também não havia bom transporte para isso. Porque era preciso transportar por barcos de Malawi, até Malawi. Portanto deixaram.", AHM, Secção Oral, Transcrito MPC 011: N.º 88–89, Entrevista com Paulo Litumbe, October 15, 1980, 38.

5.4 Reactions: Resistance, Accommodation, and Intermediaries

We have already touched on the question of the reactions of the people of Nkholongue to colonialism at several points in this book. The response of Chingomanje II to initial colonization was discussed at length in the previous chapter, and people's reactions to the cotton regime have been addressed in the preceding pages. In this section, we will attempt to analyze these reactions more systematically. The analysis is divided into three parts. First, I will outline the ways people from the region challenged colonial rule and discuss how people from Nkholongue participated in these struggles. The second part will look at the role of colonial intermediaries from the village. The third and final part will then use the example of the Mission for the Combat of the Trypanosomiasis (MCT) to illustrate the complexities of the relationship between the colonial state and the people living in the region.

Resistance Against Colonialism

The history of regional resistance to Portuguese colonialism between 1901 and 1962 (the year Frelimo was founded) can be divided into three phases. The first phase (1901–1912) was that of colonial conquest, when various chiefs of the region attempted to oppose colonial occupation. The second was that of World War One, when local Muslims cooperated or sympathized with the cause of the Central Powers. The third phase was the period that followed characterized by passive resistance such as tax evasion and emigration.

It has already been discussed in the previous chapter that Nkholongue's chief and his entourage supported the forces of the *Companhia* in their fight against the insurgents around Ngofi. The same observation can be made for the *Companhia*'s subsequent clashes with the two Yao chiefs Malinganile and Mataka. Malinganile and Mataka, who both resided on Niassa's *planalto*, were the two chiefs of the region who offered prolonged resistance to the *Companhia*. It was only in 1912 that they were finally subjugated. After the *Companhia*'s occupation of the lakeshore, Malinganile had even gone on the attack, committing several raids on lakeshore villages in 1904 and in 1911.[152] He even raided the village that was right next to the *Companhia*'s headquarters.[153] Malinganile and Mataka were both long-time op-

---

[152] Barnes, "Portuguese Troubles in Nyasaland," *CA* 22, no. 264 (1904): 242–243; "Notes and News," *NDC*, no. 33 (October 1911): 820.
[153] Ernesto Jardim de Vilhena, *Companhia de Nyassa: Relatorios e memorias sobre os territorios pelo governador* (Lisboa: Typographia da "A Editora," 1905), 289–290.

ponents of Chingomanje and his Unango relatives. Malinganile even reportedly attributed the 1904 attacks to a feud he had with a person from Nkholongue, or in the words of the missionaries:

> Malinganile has written to say he had no quarrel with the villages he raided, still less with Capt. Galhardo [local head of the *Companhia*], but the conduct of one of Chingomanje's people had compelled him to be disagreeable in self-defence.[154]

I could not find out more about this, and there is no explicit evidence that Nkholongue was attacked by Malinganile in 1904. Other missionary reports indicate that the conflict between the *Companhia* and Malinganile involved the aforementioned Abdallah Mkwanda.[155] Since Mkwanda apparently maintained close relations with people from Chingomanje's entourage, it is conceivable that Malinganile referred to the same conflict in his letter quoted by the missionaries.

In any case, we can be fairly certain that men from Nkholongue were among the 200 to 300 fighters recruited by the *Companhia* along the lakeshore to take action against Malinganile in 1904.[156] In 1907, it was with the support of troops from Unango that the *Companhia* succeeded in temporarily driving Malinganile from his hometown.[157] Then, when the *Companhia* made its final move against Mataka in 1912, their force included 3,000 "natives" from the lakeshore, Unango, and the entire region.[158]

The *Companhia* could count on this broad support in its wars with Mataka and Malinganile, partly because the two chiefs continued to attack "innocent" villages, and partly because of long-standing rivalries dating back to pre-colonial times. In

---

[154] It is "Chingomanji" in the original. See: "News from the Stations: S.S. 'C.M.,'" *LDQP*, no. 3 (April 1904): 52.

[155] Yohanna B. Abdallah, "News from the Stations: Unangu," *LDQP*, no. 4 (July 1904): 78–79; AUMCA, C4, f. 50–51: Letter from [Bishop Hine] to Mr. Travers (Mponda's, December 31, 1900), 3; Eyre, "Travelling to Unangu," *CA* 25, no. 289 (January 1907): 6; Sutherland, *Adventures*, 177–179.

[156] Barnes, "Portuguese Troubles in Nyasaland," *CA* 22, no. 264 (1904): 243. On the recruitment of locals at this time, see also: Vilhena, *Companhia de Nyassa: Relatorios e memorias*, 289–290.

[157] Eyre, "The Portuguese in Central Africa," *CA* 25, no. 293 (1907). This attack had been preceded by fights between Kalanje's and Malinganile's men, in which some of Kalanje's fighters (including one of his nephews) had been killed. See: Eyre, "Travelling to Unangu," *CA* 25, no. 289 (January 1907): 6.

[158] Yohanna B. Abdallah, "News from the Stations: VI. Unangu," *NDC*, no. 38 (January 1913): 963–964; Augustine Ambali, "News from the Stations: IV. Msumba," *NDC*, no. 38 (January 1913): 961–962. Again, we have no definite evidence of recruitment in Nkholongue, but the sub-chief of Malo, a neighboring village, was said to have participated in the war against Mataka. See: António de Melo Serrano, "Um reconhecimento no Distrito do Lago," *Anais do Instituto de Medicina Tropical* 8, no. 4 (1951): 675.

AHM's oral history project, Bishop Litumbe explained the support of the Anyanja people for the *Companhia* as follows:

> [The Wayao] were their enemies as they had been attacked by the Wayao before. Now when the Portuguese came, they saw that now we have liberty. Therefore, they allied with the Portuguese to fight against Mataka.[159]

In an interview in Unango, the AHM's research group even explicitly asked whether the introduction of the colonial tax had not led the people of Unango to join forces with Mataka against the Portuguese. If one follows their answer, this was obviously not the case.[160] Considering the historical background, it is not so surprising that as late as 1912 many people still considered the elimination of rivals from pre-colonial times as more urgent than a common front against their new colonial masters.

Muslim Resistance during World War One

The case seems to have been different for the second phase. There is evidence that people from Nkholongue were actively involved in a plot against the Entente (and thus Portugal) during World War One. However, it must be emphasized that previous literature has significantly exaggerated the extent of support German troops received when they invaded northern Mozambique. Claims that German troops were widely welcomed by the population as "liberators" are based on a superficial and misleading reading of the available sources.[161] There is little doubt that the experience of the majority of the locals was one of being looted rather than liberated. To understand this, it is important to distinguish between the German pre-invasion propaganda among the people of Mozambique and the actual interaction of German troops with the local populations after the invasion.

German propaganda began to circulate in 1915, two years before the German invasion. This propaganda was directed mainly at the Muslim population of the re-

---

159 AHM, Secção Oral, Transcrito MPC 011: N.° 88–89, Entrevista com Paulo Litumbe, October 15, 1980, 26.
160 AHM, Secção Oral, Transcrito NI 15: N.° 145–147, Entrevista com Ali Bonomali e um grupo de velhos em Nazinhendje (Unango, Niassa), July 18, 1981, 6–7.
161 This narrative of liberation has become widely accepted. See: Stuart, "Os Nyanja, o U.M.C.A. e a Companhia do Niassa, 1880–1930," 32–34; René Pélissier, *História de Moçambique: Formação e oposição 1854–1918*, vol. 2 (Lisboa: Estampa, 2000), 405–6; Newitt, *A History of Mozambique*, 419; Medeiros, *História de Cabo Delgado e do Niassa (c. 1836–1929)*, 148; Neil-Tomlinson, "The Nyassa Chartered Company," 120.

gion. The most prominent case in this regard is that of the so-called "dynamite man." In this case, Ndelemani, a man from Lussefa, was handed over to the Anglican missionaries on Likoma Island by people from the Portuguese mainland. They accused him of having planned an attack on the Anglican mission. Ndelemani was carrying not only "three packages of nitroglycerine explosives,"[162] but also a green flag with the red crescent, considerable sums of money, several letters written in Arabic characters, and a proclamation by the German government in East Africa reporting that the Ottoman sultan had declared the "holy war" against the British. Ndelemani stated that he had received these objects in Mwaya in German East Africa in order to bring them to none other than Isa Chikoka, the Muslim missionary from Lussefa, whom we have already met in Chapter 3.[163] One of the letters was even addressed to Chikoka. In it, the German *Schutztruppe* (lit. "protection force") commander Walter von Falkenstein informed Chikoka about the worldwide successes of the alliance of Muslims, Germans and Austrians in their fight against the Entente. According to the translation of the letter, he advised Chikoka to "[d]ispose clever men well for the hiding of our secret and you will be happy in the Government together with your people."[164]

The British investigation of the case concluded that the dynamite was to be used against the British steamers on the lake.[165] Missionary Barnes explained that Ndelemani was equipped not only with dynamite but also with a device for drilling wood ("auger"). Apparently, the idea had been to send Ndelemani "down to the wooding-stations of the Lake steamers, all of which were in British hands, to bore holes in a few stacked-up logs and insert the dynamite well in. The steamers, it was hoped, would stoke up with this firewood and explosions would follow."[166] If this was indeed the plan, it seems likely that the target was not just any "wooding station" on the lakeshore, but precisely that of Nkholongue, which was the principal port of the steamers in the Muslim area on the Portuguese shore of the lake (and the one closest to Lussefa). "Wooding" was occasionally

---

162 MNA, UMCA 1/2/15/1: Frank Winspear, "Copy of a Letter to the District Resident Chinteche" (Likoma, July 15, 1915).
163 MNA, UMCA 1/2/15/1: Frank Winspear, "Copy of a Letter to the District Resident Chinteche" (Likoma, July 15, 1915); MNA, UMCA 1/2/15/1: Frank Winspear, "Copy of a Letter to the Chefe do Concelho, Mtengula" (Likoma, July 15, 1915); TNA, CO/525/63, f. 194–203: G. Smith (Governor) to C.O. (Zomba, November 15, 1915).
164 TNA, CO/525/63, f. 200–201: Captain Falkenstein to Mwalima [sic] Isa (June 18, 1915), Enclosure No. 1 in G. Smith (Governor) to C.O. (Zomba, November 15, 1915). Falkenstein's letter to Chikoka was later also printed in a British newspaper. See: "War News for Darkest Africa: German Message to a Nyasa Notable," *The Times*, January 14, 1916.
165 TNA, CO/525/63, f. 194–203: G. Smith (Governor) to C.O. (Zomba, November 15, 1915), 2.
166 Barnes, *Johnson of Nyasaland*, 179.

done in other places, but nowhere as regularly as in Nkholongue. Furthermore, there is some indication that at least one person from Nkholongue was involved in the affair, namely the Muslim teacher Thubiri (see as well Chapter 3). This at least emerges from a note by the Anglican missionary W.P. Johnson from 1917, which states that Thubiri "was in deep water over the Germans but has been refloated all right."[167]

Unfortunately, the origin of this note is somewhat obscure and the note itself was taken out of context.[168] Furthermore, I could find out little about the legal investigations of the case other than that Chikoka and three others (two of them Muslims) were arrested and sent to the *Companhia*'s headquarters in Porto Amélia.[169] All that I could determine is that while the British authorities tried and shot Ndelemani in the presence of prominent Muslims, Chikoka was able to return to the lake, where he died in the 1950s.[170]

It is difficult to unravel the exact role and motivations of Chikoka and even more so of Thubiri in this matter, but it does not seem entirely unlikely that they were indeed thinking about joining the "holy war." The information from Falkenstein's letter implies that he and Chikoka had discussed the plan in some form beforehand.[171] Evidence suggests that Muslims around Nkholongue and Lussefa saw an opportunity to suppress Christian colonization and to accelerate the spread of their own religion after the outbreak of the war. The missionaries had faced

---

[167] AUMCA, AI(VI)B, f. 1802: Notes for a Biog. of W. P. Johnson, pt. Natives, N. 5.
[168] I found the note in a collection of handwritten notes by and about W.P. Johnson. This collection was compiled by Herbert Barnes in preparation for his biography of Johnson. The source of the note seems to be a letter Johnson wrote to missionary Cox in 1917.
[169] Bishop Fisher was unsure whether Chikoka had been sent to Porto Amélia "as a witness or as a criminal." Governor Smith, however, wrote unambiguously that Chikoka had been "arrested," and W.P. Johnson stated that the four had been sent there "in chains." See: MNA, UMCA 1/2/15/1: Letter from Cathrew Fisher (Bishop of Nyasaland) to Hector Duff (Chief Secretary, Zomba) (Likoma, August 18, 1915); TNA, CO/525/63, f. 194–203: G. Smith (Governor) to C.O. (Zomba, November 15, 1915), 2; MNA, UMCA 1/2/17/1: Letter from W.P. Johnson to the Bishop (Njafua, [1915]). See as well: MNA, UMCA 1/2/17/1: Letter from A. F. Matthew to the Bishop, August 13, 1915; William Percival Johnson, "News from the Stations: III. The Chauncy Maples," *NDC*, no. 53 (October 1916): 22.
[170] On Ndelemani's fate, see: TNA, CO/525/63, f. 194–203: G. Smith (Governor) to C.O. (Zomba, November 15, 1915), 2; Greenstein, "The Nyasaland Government's Policy," 161. For Chikoka's date of death, see: Greenstein, "Shayks and Tariqas," 17. I was unable to find any information on the question of when Chikoka returned to the lake. However, another of his fellow prisoners was already back on the lakeshore by early 1916. See: MNA, UMCA 1/2/17/1: Letter from W.P. Johnson to the Bishop (Njafua, [1915]); MNA, UMCA 1/2/17/1: Letter from A.F. Matthew to the Bishop, August 13, 1915; "Saved by His Daughter," *CA* 34, no. 404 (1916): 233.
[171] Falkenstein confirmed the reception of a letter from Chikoka.

Muslim hostility in the region before.[172] In 1908, an unnamed missionary wrote that Lussefa was "full of much anti-mission, anti-white men prejudice."[173] While in 1905, a Muslim teacher was reported to be preaching "Africa for the Africans" in Nkhotakota.[174]

The outbreak of the war helped promote ideas that challenged the existing order, particularly through the spread of millennialist ideas. In one account from the war period, W.P. Johnson wrote that "[n]ot a few of the Mohammedans argue, 'the Mzungu [white man] has a good time in this life, how then can he have one in the next?[']"[175] And in another he recorded that "the idea of a Mohammedan revival ha[d] been very strong these two years and the expectation of one Mselimu ha[d] held the field."[176]

Mselimu in this context refers to the *Mahdi*, the eschatological redeemer of Islam.[177] Chikoka's proximity to eschatological traditions is underpinned by his own name, Isa, the Arabic/Muslim version of Jesus. Most eschatological traditions of Islam either equate the second coming of Isa with the arrival of the *Mahdi* or see Isa as the companion of the *Mahdi* with whom he will jointly defeat the *Al-Masih ad-Dajjal*, the Muslim version of the Antichrist.[178] It seems probable that Isa Chikoka predicted a radical transformation of society in the near future. Such a reading is also supported by the fact that the way two of my interviewees spoke about Chikoka clearly carried a whiff of millenarianism. Both interviewees stated that Chikoka not only preached the word of god, but also predicted the War of Independence, and, according to one of them, the Mozambican Civil War (1976–1992).[179]

We can assume that ideological resistance to the existing colonial order indeed increased in Nkholongue and neighboring Muslim villages with the onset of the

---

172 "An Ordination at Nyasa," *CA* 21, no. 243 (March 1903): 42; AUSPG, Philip Young, "Diary of Philip Young, Engineer on the 'Chauncy Maples', 1901–1903," 131–132.
173 "S.S. C. M.," *LDQP*, no. 18 (January 1908), 438.
174 MNA, 2/KOM/1/1: "Kota Kota Mission Diary, 1894 August 17–1911 January 2," entry dated October 5, 1904.
175 Johnson, "News from the Stations: III. The Chauncy Maples," *NDC*, no. 54 (January 1917).
176 Johnson, "News from the Stations: III. The Chauncy Maples," *NDC*, no. 53 (October 1916): 21.
177 *Mselimu* or *Msilimu* can also mean as much as just "Muslim" in Kiswahili. There is though no doubt that the word in this context referred to the *Mahdi*. See: "News from the Stations: III. The Chauncy Maples," *NDC*, no. 48 (July 1915): 18; Richard Reusch, *Der Islam in Ost-Afrika mit besonderer Berücksichtigung der muhammedanischen Geheim-Orden* (Leipzig: Adolf Klein, 1931), 235; *Anlagen zum Jahresbericht über die Entwicklung der deutschen Schutzgebiete in Afrika und der Südsee im Jahre 1905/1906* (Berlin: Mittler, 1907), 33.
178 Many thanks to Ricarda Stegmann for helping me with this question.
179 PA, I152: interview with *P1476* (♂, ~1935) (Milombe, June 16, 2016), min 00:03:00–00:04:43; PA, I120: interview with *P1102* (♂, 1932) (Malango, April 21, 2016), min 00:12:36–00:13:56.

war. As elsewhere, it was apparently Mahdism that served as an important ideological means of resistance to colonial rule.[180] The case of Ndelemani shows that some people from the region were willing to take action.[181] The mood, however, was geared as much against the British as against the Portuguese. Falkenstein's letter did not refer to Portugal at all. This is not really surprising, considering that Portugal was still neutral at that time, but it is more than noteworthy, since the previous literature and many British sources usually explained the support for German troops as having been based on hostility to Portuguese colonialism.[182]

In my opinion, the commonly accepted narrative of the course of the war in northern Mozambique has misinterpreted not only people's motives, but also the extent of support when the German troops actually entered the territory. It is important to know in this context that German troops never occupied any part of Mozambique for long but moved around quickly. Metangula, for example, was occupied by a small unit of two German soldiers and 15 *askaris* in May 1917. They only stayed for four days during which they, according to the Anglican priest Yohanna Abdallah, went round the villages and collected all the cattle that they could find.[183] In Unango, they stayed longer, namely for about three weeks.[184]

Certainly, there are reports that the German forces indeed received some support after their invasion. Thus, Abdallah, who had escaped from Unango during the German advance, stated in a letter to the Anglican bishop of Nyasaland that all Muslims and Muslim chiefs of Unango were siding with the Germans.[185] Already

---

180 For the importance of Mahdism in challenging colonial rule elsewhere, see: Sebastian Gottschalk, *Kolonialismus und Islam: Deutsche und britische Herrschaft in Westafrika (1900–1914)* (Frankfurt: Campus Verlag, 2017), 153–204; Paul E. Lovejoy and J. S. Hogendorn, "Revolutionary Mahdism and Resistance to Colonial Rule in the Sokoto Caliphate, 1905–6," *The Journal of African History* 31, no. 2 (July 1990): 217–244.
181 But of course, we can also assume that not everyone from Nkholongue approved of an attack on the steamers, considering that it was the steamers that provided an important income opportunity for the villagers.
182 TNA, WO 95/5329/3: Paraphrase Telegram N.F. 2906 from General Northey to Secretary of State for the Colonies, May 15, 1917; Stuart, "Os Nyanja, o U.M.C.A. e a Companhia do Niassa, 1880–1930," 32–33; Pélissier, *História de Moçambique: Formação e oposição 1854–1918*, 2000, 2:406–409; Medeiros, *História de Cabo Delgado e do Niassa (c. 1836–1929)*, 148; Milton Correia, "Os Yao e o contexto da luta armada de independência nacional em Moçambique (1964–1974)" (PhD thesis, Universidade de São Paulo, 2017), 107–109.
183 MNA, UMCA 1/2/15/1: Letter from Yohannah Abdallah to Cathrew Fisher (Mcwela (Chisindo), May 25, 1917).
184 MNA, UMCA 1/2/15/1: Letter from Yohannah Abdallah to Cathrew Fisher (Mcwela (Chisindo), May 25, 1917); MNA, UMCA 1/2/15/1: Letter from Yohannah Abdallah to Cathrew Fisher (Mcwela, June 5, 1917).
185 MNA, UMCA 1/2/15/1: Letter from Yohannah Abdallah to Cathrew Fisher (Mcwela, June 5, 1917).

in 1915, shortly after Ndelemani's capture, Abdallah had reported that he believed the chiefs of Unango were receiving letters from the Germans and that their sympathies were all with them.[186] He now explained the chiefs' support for the Germans with these same letters.[187] The support of the Unango chiefs for the Germans is also indicated by the fact that two of them, Kalanje and Chipango, even went with the German forces when they left Unango.[188]

Still, we have to be careful not to overstate the extent of free and willing support that the population provided to the German forces. Various sources show that the procurement of supplies was the main concern of the German military. They had been driven out of German East Africa by the advancing British forces and now had to constantly scramble for food and ammunition. Even in the case of Unango, the support was not as clear-cut as one might assume on the basis of the above. Abdallah's statements are in fact rather contradictory in this respect. His description of the viewpoint of Kalanje and Chipango, for example, does not really suggest enthusiastic partisanship for the Germans, since he wrote that they had been "carried off."[189] Furthermore, he reported that the Germans apparently only needed "goods & food & c." and that the German forces left Unango "with loads of food and cattle & lot of property which they [had] looted at Metangula, Metonia and Unango."[190]

The significance of looting for the German forces also becomes evident when one looks at what happened in Muembe, the temporary headquarters of the Germans in the region. Here the Germans are said to have reinstated the son of the old Mataka, who had been deposed by the *Companhia* in 1912.[191] If one follows the description of the German commander Lettow-Vorbeck on the conditions in

---

[186] Stuart, "Os Nyanja, o U.M.C.A. e a Companhia do Niassa, 1880–1930," 32; MNA, UMCA 1/2/15/1: Cathrew Fisher, "Letter from Cathrew Fisher (Bishop of Nyasaland) to Hector Duff (Chief Secretary, Zomba)" (Likoma, October 14, 1915), 32.
[187] MNA, UMCA 1/2/15/1: Letter from Yohannah Abdallah to Cathrew Fisher (Mcwela (Chisindo), May 25, 1917).
[188] Yohanna B. Abdallah, "News from the Stations: VI. Unangu," *NDC*, no. 57 (October 1917): 20.
[189] Abdallah, "News from the Stations: VI. Unangu," *NDC*, no. 57 (October 1917). They returned to Unango after little more than six months. See: Abdallah, "News from the Stations: VII. Unangu," *NDC*, no. 59 (April 1918).
[190] It is "Mtengula," "Mtonya," and "Unangu" in the original. See: MNA, UMCA 1/2/15/1: Letter from Yohannah Abdallah to Cathrew Fisher (Mcwela, June 5, 1917). The looting of German forces in Unango is also supported by statements from an interview of AHM's oral history project. See: AHM, Secção Oral, Transcrito NI 14: N.° 143–144, Entrevista com um grupo de velhos em Ngongote (Unango, Niassa), July 18, 1981, 1.
[191] TNA, WO 95/5329/3: Paraphrase Telegram N.F. 2906 from General Northey to Secretary of State for the Colonies, May 15, 1917.

Muembe, one must be very cautious about claiming that the German forces could indeed count on broad support. Lettow-Vorbeck indeed stated that the people from Muembe were friendly to them. But he also reported that despite their friendliness the people hid their food and were not really willing to give any of it to them. According to Lettow-Vorbeck, the German *askaris* thus had to locate the hiding places and steal the food.[192]

Most people of northern Mozambique did not take sides in the war and certainly did not help the German forces "in every way," as a British military report put it.[193] Rather, most people tried to protect their lives and belongings. Furthermore, we can also surmise that while there was some sympathy for the German forces at the beginning of the invasion, this quickly faded as the war progressed. This becomes evident when we look at what happened in Unango toward the end of the war. For when there was a danger that the German troops might return there in the second half of 1918, Abdallah reported that "[a]ll Unango people had left their houses by night and cleared out."[194] According to him, they still did not return to Unango even after the German forces had moved back into former German East Africa, "as they were much afraid that perhaps the Germans [would] make [a] detour, and invade Unango as they did before."[195]

The alleged siding with the German troops is further called into question by the fact that there is no evidence that the inhabitants of the region resisted the troops of the Entente after they had landed in Metangula in early 1918.[196] Rather, the Entente troops were able to mobilize a large portion of the region's male population as carriers.[197] So it seems fair to say that most people were involved on the

---

[192] Paul von Lettow-Vorbeck, *Meine Erinnerungen aus Ostafrika* (Leipzig: Koehler, 1920), 221. Similarly, those interviewed by Sayaka Funada-Classen who were still able to recount stories from World War One did not portray their support as very enthusiastic. See: Funada-Classen, *The Origins of War in Mozambique*, 114–115. For another vivid account of the plundering nature of German troops in northern Mozambique, see: C.B. Eyre, "News from the Stations: VII. Mtonya," *NDC*, no. 57 (October 1917): 21–23.
[193] TNA, WO 95/5329/3: Paraphrase Telegram N.F. 2943 from General Northey to Secretary of State for the Colonies, May 22, 1917.
[194] It is "Unangu" in the original. See: Yohanna B. Abdallah, "News from the Stations: VII. Unangu," *NDC*, no. 62 (January 1919): 17.
[195] It is "Unangu" in the original. See: Abdallah, "News from the Stations: VII. Unangu," *NDC*, no. 62 (January 1919).
[196] Abe J.B. Desmore, *With the 2nd Cape Corps Thro' Central Africa* (Cape Town: Citadel, 1920), 52–53; Timothy J. Stapleton, *No Insignificant Part: The Rhodesia Native Regiment and the East Africa Campaign of the First World War* (Waterloo, Canada: Wilfrid Laurier University Press, 2006), 122.
[197] Abdallah, "News from the Stations: VII. Unangu," *NDC*, no. 59 (April 1918); Cox and Chisui, "News from the Stations: V. Msumba," *NDC*, no. 62 (January 1919); Lawrence Chisui, "News from

side of the Entente troops rather than that of the Germans, even though this involvement was most certainly similarly unenthusiastic as that for the Germans.

Between Accommodation and Emigration

For the time after the war until the advent of national resistance in the early 1960s (see Chapter 7), there is no evidence that people from the region actively challenged the tenuous Portuguese rule. The modest number of policemen clearly indicates that the colonial state had little to fear in this regard.[198] It is noteworthy that in 1950, a Portuguese inspector saw no danger in granting people's request for rifles and gunpowder to defend their fields against animals, stating that "given the pacifist nature of the native and low efficiency of his arms, there is nothing to fear."[199]

However, this does not mean that all people were comfortable with the situation. Most interviewees emphasized the problems people had with taxation.[200] Another frequently voiced complaint concerned the system of carrying the Portuguese on *machilas* ("palanquins"), which was reportedly used occasionally until the early 1950s but was mainly associated with the period of the *Companhia*. The statements clearly show that this work was not only poorly paid, but also perceived as a racist humiliation. However, none of my interviewees seem to have personally carried a *machila*.[201] Some interviewees mentioned other more isolated ex-

---

the Stations: V. Msumba," *NDC*, no. 59 (April 1918): 19–20; "News from the Stations: IV. Ngoo Bay," *NDC*, no. 59 (April 1918): 18–19; Yohanna B. Abdallah, "News from the Stations: VII. Unangu," *NDC*, no. 60 (July 1918): 16–17.
198 The same point has been made for Nyasaland. See: John McCracken, "Coercion and Control in Nyasaland: Aspects of the History of a Colonial Police Force," *The Journal of African History* 27, no. 1 (1986): 130.
199 AHM, ISANI, cx. 99: Manuel M. R. de L. Texeira, "Relatório da Inspecção Ordinária ao Distrito do Lago da Província do Niassa, 1950/51," 22.
200 For examples, see: PA, I135: interview with *P1494 (♂, 1942)* (Nkhotakota, June 2, 2016), min 01:20:29–01:22:51; PA, I038: interview with *P1439 (♂, ~1940)* (Malango, August 15, 2013), min 00:49:56–00:50:18; PA, I052: interview with *(♀, 1940)* (Nkholongue, August 26, 2013), min 00:35:52–00:36:56.
201 PA, I117: interview with *P1458 (♂, ~1945)* (Micundi, April 20, 2016), min 00:36:56–00:38:43, 01:39:56–01:40:51; PA, I118: interview with *P1218 (♀, 1930)* (Malango, April 21, 2016), min 00:15:18–00:19:00; PA, I125: interview with *P1463 (♂, 1951)* (Ngala, April 27, 2016), min 00:00:24–00:06:55; PA, I131: interview with *P1434 (♂, 1942)* (Lifuwu (Salima District, Malawi), May 31, 2016), min 02:05:03–02:07:27; PA, I121: interview with *P0527 (♂, ~1918)* (Maniamba, April 22, 2016), min 00:42:03–00:46:55; PA, I142: interview with *P0743 (♀, ~1930)* (Nkholongue, June 8, 2016), min 00:00:01–00:08:00; PA, I119: interview with *P0855 (♂, 1954)* (Malango, April 21, 2016),

periences of colonial injustices. This included one who described how he was once beaten by *cipaios* because he had left his identity card at home.²⁰² Another recounted how labor migrants sometimes had trouble bringing their savings home because those were taken away by state agents upon their return.²⁰³ And still another stated that people were sometimes beaten when they passed in front of the administration building in Metangula without greeting it.²⁰⁴

People's dissatisfaction with the situation resulted in flight rather than rebellion. The entire period of Portuguese rule was marked by the emigration of people to the neighboring colonies of Tanganyika and Nyasaland.²⁰⁵ Emigration from the Portuguese lakeshore peaked in the early 1920s, due to the sudden increase in taxes and the high demand for forced labor.²⁰⁶ While the exodus of that time was mainly caused by push factors, the trickling out of many other (later) years seems to have been caused by a combination of push and pull factors. Many interviewees lamented that the Portuguese side of the lake had been a land of poverty. Living conditions in Nyasaland were described as much better than in Mozambique. This was not only due to a better wage-tax ratio, but mainly because there were more jobs in Nyasaland to earn the money to pay the taxes and to buy consumer goods.²⁰⁷ While most migrants were labor migrants who used the proximity

---

min 01:31:57–01:32:43; PA, I111: interview with *P0266* (♂, ~1932) (Metangula, April 11, 2016), min 00:39:09–00:40:05.

202 PA, I117: interview with *P1458* (♂, ~1945) (Micundi, April 20, 2016), min 00:41:55–00:44:57.
203 PA, I094: interview with *P0727* (♂, ~1940) (M'chepa, January 27, 2016), min 00:11:03–00:13:21.
204 PA, I118: interview with *P1218* (♀, 1930) (Malango, April 21, 2016), min 01:40:12–01:42:53.
205 The Archdeacon of Messumba wrote in 1951 of the "constant exodus" of people to Nyasaland and Tanganyika that made the missionaries' work "extremely difficult." See: MNA, 145/DOM/2/4/10: Letter from Stanley Pickard (Archdeacon of Msumba) to the Bishop, September 24, 1951. See as well: Camilo Silveira de Costa, "O Niassa visto por dentro," *Boletim Geral do Ultramar* 35, no. 411–412 (1959): 176–177; Maciel Santos, "The Peasant Tax in Northern Mozambique (1929–1939): Forced Cultivation, a Growth Factor?," in *Administration and Taxation in Former Portuguese Africa*, by Philip Havik, Alexander Keese, and Maciel Santos (Newcastle upon Tyne: Cambridge Scholars, 2015), 146.
206 For the emigration in the early 1920s, see: MNA, NCK/5/1/2: Annual Report: Kota-Kota District, 1921–22 (Kota-Kota, April 14, 1922), 2; MNA, NSF 4/1/1: C. T. Verry, "Annual Report on the South Nyasa District for the Year Ended the 31st, March, 1923," March 31, 1923, 1; MNA, NSF 4/1/1: C. T. Verry, "Annual Report on the South Nyasa District for the Year Ended the 31st, March, 1924" (April 12, 1924), 1; MNA, NSF 4/1/1: Annual Report, S. Nyasa 1924/25 (April 16, 1925), 4; "News from the Stations: I. Likoma," *NDC*, no. 76 (July 1922): 8–11; "News from the Stations: IX. Malindi," *NDC*, no. 78 (January 1923): 13; AHM, GGM XX, cx. 182: José Mendes dos Reis, "Relatório do Delegado do Governo aos Territorios da Companhia do Nyassa, de Setembro de 1924 a Março de 1925" (Lisboa, May 20, 1925), 27–30.
207 PA, I154: interview with *P0367* (♂, 1936), *P0373* (♀, 1940) (Nkholongue, June 18, 2016), min 00:36:21–00:40:46; PA, I048: interview with *P1446* (♂, ~1945) (Metangula, August 21, 2013), min 00:47:34–00:48:08; PA, I094: interview with *P0727* (♂, ~1940) (M'chepa, January 27, 2016), min

to the border as a means of socio-economic arbitrage,[208] others never returned, either because they had planned to do so from the beginning or because they had discovered new, more feasible livelihoods while on labor migration.[209]

But while some fled from the colonial state, others accommodated themselves to the situation, or even tried to use it to their advantage. The evidence shows that the colonial state could count on the support of local intermediaries throughout its existence. The role of Chingomanje II in the making of the early colonial state has already been highlighted in the previous chapter. While in this section, it has been demonstrated that many people from the region supported the *Companhia* in its battles against Malinganile and Mataka. Also, the process of tax collection depended primarily on local actors, namely the chiefs and local policemen, the *cipaios*. Alexander Keese has aptly observed that it was the *cipaios* who "made up much of the face of colonialism that African subjects encountered locally."[210] In Nkholongue, as elsewhere, it was the *cipaios* who went to the villages to enforce tax collection if necessary and to take tax defaulters to the administration. Or, as this episode of an interview with a woman from Nkholongue illustrates:

She: Those who had no tax receipt were tied up. But they were not arrested by the white people like Liwala [nickname of a *chefe de posto*]. This one only sent them.
Q: And the people who arrested the people?
She: The soldiers. It was the soldiers who arrested them.
Q: Where did they come from, these soldiers?
She: They came from here.
Q: Who was it?
She: Here there was the father of B.. Do you know him?[211]

00:08:12–00:08:34, 00:22:44–00:24:13; PA, I038: interview with *P1439* (♂, ~1940) (Malango, August 15, 2013), min 00:01:16–00:02:12; PA, I087: interview with *P1452* (♂, 1927) (Lichinga, September 10, 2013), min 01:17:16–01:20:16. See as well: AHM, GGM XX, cx. 182: José Mendes dos Reis, "Relatório do Delegado do Governo aos Territorios da Companhia do Nyassa, de Setembro de 1924 a Março de 1925" (Lisboa, May 20, 1925), 31; AHU, N° 1665–1 1B MU ISAU: Armando Pinto Corrêa, "Relatório duma Inspecção às Circunscrições do Distrito de Moçambique (1936–37)" (Lourenço Marques, 1938), 167; MLM, 018: interview with *L. M.*, transcript Chinyanja (Malango, June 27, 2007), 1.

208 On the concept of borderland arbitrage, see: Helena Pérez-Niño, "Post-Conflict Agrarian Change in Angónia: Land, Labour and the Organization of Production in the Mozambique-Malawi Borderland" (PhD thesis, SOAS, University of London, 2014), 71–72.

209 For people who left Nkholongue for Nyasaland before the Mozambican War of Independence and did not return to Mozambique, see Footnote 94 in this chapter.

210 Alexander Keese, "Tax in Practice: Colonial Impact and Renegotiation on the Ground," in *Administration and Taxation in Former Portuguese Africa, 1900–1945*, by Philip Havik, Alexander Keese, and Maciel Santos (Newcastle upon Tyne: Cambridge Scholars, 2015), 90.

211 PA, I142: interview with *P0743* (♀, ~1930) (Nkholongue, June 8, 2016), min 01:15:52–01:16:52.

In the beginning, the *cipaios* of the *Companhia* were composed mainly of Makua soldiers from the coast of the Indian Ocean. However, the *Companhia* began to supplement and then replace them with locally recruited men in the first years after its arrival.[212] It is impossible to determine the involvement of people from Nkholongue in this early phase. However, Chingomanje's participation in the making of the colonial state and the proximity of Nkholongue to Metangula allow us to assume that recruitment also took place here. Furthermore, in 1919, an inhabitant of Nkholongue was said to be the "head captain" of the government in Metangula.[213]

For later periods, the participation of inhabitants of Nkholongue in the ranks of the *cipaios* is confirmed by oral history.[214] According to my interviewees, future *cipaios* first had to serve in the military for two or three years. After that they were sent to an administrative post in their district of origin to work as *cipaios*.[215] This means that the *cipaios* who policed Nkholongue were mostly from the region, and, as the dialogue above indicates, apparently sometimes even came from the village itself.[216] Statements from my interviews were, however, inconsistent regarding the extent to which being a *cipaio* was a voluntary choice or not.[217]

---

212 TNA, FO/2/605, f. 177–186: C.B. Eyre, "Re Portuguese Nyassaland Co.," enclosed in C.B. Eyre to Mr. Sharpe (Blantyre, February 9, 1902), f. 177; Vilhena, *Companhia de Nyassa: Relatorios e memorias*, 268.
213 Johnson and Cox, "News from the Stations: Station III," *NDC*, no. 65 (October 1919).
214 PA, I114: interview with P1074 (♀, ~1940), P1141 (♂, 1932) (Malango, April 15, 2016), min 02:43:34–02:50:58; PA, I120: interview with P1102 (♂, 1932) (Malango, April 21, 2016), min 01:52:01–01:52:34; PA, I107: interview with P1074 (♀, ~1940) (Malango, April 5, 2016), min 02:05:22–02:06:46; PA, I129: interview with P1426 (♂, 1929) (Malindi (Mangochi District, Malawi), May 29, 2016), min 01:42:33–01:44:28; PA, I135: interview with P1494 (♂, 1942) (Nkhotakota, June 2, 2016), min 01:28:32–01:28:59. For *cipaios* who came from neighboring villages, see: Serrano, "Um reconhecimento no Distrito do Lago," 675.
215 PA, I123: interview with P1460 (♀), P1461 (♂, ~1935), P1462 (♂, ~1935) (Meluluca, April 25, 2016), min 01:19:25–01:20:56; PA, I114: interview with P1074 (♀, ~1940), P1141 (♂, 1932) (Malango, April 15, 2016), min 01:25:37–01:28:07, 02:43:34–02:50:50; PA, I107: interview with P1074 (♀, ~1940) (Malango, April 5, 2016), min 02:05:38–02:06:46. There is virtually no research on the recruitment of *cipaios*. However, Maria Neto, in her study of the social history of the city of Huambo in Angola, also found out that former soldiers were favored as *cipaios*. See: Maria da Conceição Neto, "In Town and Out of Town: A Social History of Huambo (Angola), 1902–1961" (PhD thesis, SOAS, University of London, 2012), 266, accessed August 28, 2017, http://eprints.soas.ac.uk/13822/1/Neto_3375.pdf.
216 PA, I135: interview with P1494 (♂, 1942) (Nkhotakota, June 2, 2016), min 01:28:45–01:29:17. Anglican missionary John Paul noted that some of the *cipaios* in Metangula were locals and others came from Maniamba. See: Paul, *Memoirs of a Revolution*, 27. 23 of Lago's 28 *cipaios* who continued to be employed by the post-colonial government after independence were originally from the Lago District. See: APGGN, QJ: Administração do Distrito de Metangula, "Relação dos elementos de iden-

5.4 Reactions: Resistance, Accommodation, and Intermediaries — 185

The chiefs played an equally important role in the process of tax collection. Already the instruction for the collection of the hut tax published by the *Companhia* in 1903 provided for the central role of the chiefs. Article 4 explicitly stated that the tax was to be collected by the chiefs without direct interference by the administration whenever possible and convenient. For this service, the chiefs were entitled to five percent of the tax collected.[218]

The role of the chiefs in this process was less clearly defined under the *Estado Novo*.[219] In theory, the Portuguese Empire was not designed to rely on the means of indirect rule for colonial domination, as the British Empire did, for example. In practice, chiefs seem to have played a crucial role in such processes in many places of the Portuguese Empire as well.[220] At the time of the *Estado Novo*, however, their share of the tax collected was not as clearly defined as under the *Companhia*. The inspection report of 1937 shows that the transition from the *Companhia* to the *Estado Novo* had led precisely to the problem that the local chiefs still expected their old shares. The local administration was not sure how to deal with this demand and had therefore asked the Department of Native Affairs in Lourenço Marques in 1931 to determine the amount to be paid to the chiefs for their cooperation. But obviously the matter had not been settled by 1937 and thus continued to depend on local arrangements.[221] It is unclear whether the problem was ever resolved. During the 1944 inspection, the inspector noted that the chiefs were receiving a share of taxes collected but continued to call for an explicit regulation.[222]

However, the chiefs were not only agents of the colonial state. There is no doubt that they also tried to defend at least certain interests and needs of their communities, if only to avoid stirring up too much resentment among them. Certainly, the power relations within the communities and the possible resistance to

---

tificação completa, dos Guardas Administrativos em serviço nesta área administrativa, conforme Cir. Conf. 29/MI/75, de 13 de Dezembro de 1975," March 10, 1976.
217 PA, I114: interview with *P1074* (♀, ~1940), *P1141* (♂, 1932) (Malango, April 15, 2016), min 01:27:47–01:28:07; PA, I120: interview with *P1102* (♂, 1932) (Malango, April 21, 2016), min 01:52:34–01:52:48; PA, I123: interview with *P1460* (♀), *P1461* (♂, ~1935), *P1462* (♂, ~1935) (Meluluca, April 25, 2016), min 01:19:14–01:20:56.
218 Companhia do Nyassa, "Boletim N.° 60," 1903, 417.
219 Keese, "Tax in Practice," 89–90.
220 Alexander Keese, "Taxation, Evasion, and Compulsory Measures in Angola," in *Administration and Taxation in Former Portuguese Africa, 1900–1945*, by Philip Havik, Alexander Keese, and Maciel Santos (Newcastle upon Tyne: Cambridge Scholars, 2015), 120–122.
221 AHU, N° 1665–1 1B MU ISAU: Armando Pinto Corrêa, "Relatório duma Inspecção às Circunscrições do Distrito de Moçambique (1936–37)" (Lourenço Marques, 1938), 161.
222 AHM, ISANI, cx. 97: Carlos Silveira, "Relatório e documentos referentes à Inspecção Ordinária feita na Província do Niassa. 2.A Parte, 1944," February 28, 1945, 35–36.

certain state policies set clear limits to their capacity to simply carry out the state's orders. It is also evident that the state itself considered them to be representatives of their communities as much as representatives of the state. In April 1912, for example, five chiefs from around Messumba were taken into custody by the police because the taxes of their chiefdoms had not yet been paid.²²³ While in 1915, when the tax was raised to five shillings to the disapproval of the people, the chiefs of Unango "were kept at the [government] for certain days, till the money fixed was accepted."²²⁴

In the case of Nkholongue, the history of the behavior of the chiefs cannot be assessed in detail due to the lack of sources. At least for later periods, their cooperation with the government in collecting taxes is well documented. Many interviewees told me that they paid the tax to the chief, who then passed it on to the government.²²⁵ On the other hand, we have seen in the previous chapter that the chief is also said to have supported the boiling of cotton seedlings to save the village from the cotton regime. For 1950, it is furthermore documented that the chiefs of the region (including Chingomanje) approached the Portuguese inspector with the demand to increase the salaries of the workers and to reduce the taxes.²²⁶

Mission for the Combat of the Trypanosomiasis (MCT)

The complexity of the relationship between the colonial state and the people living in Nkholongue can be illustrated in part for the case of the Mission for the Combat of the Trypanosomiasis (MCT). It was in the second half of the 1940s that the region around Nkholongue was severely affected by an outbreak of the sleeping sickness. The disease caused the death of many people and almost all cattle and goats. The

---

223 Augustine Ambali, "News from the Stations: IV. Msumba," *NDC*, no. 36 (July 1912): 910–911.
224 Abdallah, "News from the Stations: VI. Unangu," *NDC*, no. 48 (July 1915): 22.
225 PA, I120: interview with *P1102 (♂, 1932)* (Malango, April 21, 2016), min 01:53:11–01:53:52; PA, I058: interview with *P1074 (♀, ~1940)* (Malango, August 28, 2013), min 00:15:30–00:18:35; PA, I075: interview with *P1218 (♀, 1930)* (Metangula, September 6, 2013), min 00:37:01–00:38:53; PA, I016: interview with *P1483 (♀, 1950), P1481 (♂, 1954), P1482 (♂, 1937)* (Lussefa, October 9, 2011), min 00:39:29–00:48:07; PA, I062: interview with *P0713 (♂, 1944)* (Nkholongue, August 30, 2013), min 00:11:54–00:15:10; PA, I112: interview with *P0129 (♀, 1930), P0128 (♂, 1928)* (Nkholongue, April 12, 2016), min 02:09:55–02:10:11.
226 AHM, ISANI, cx. 99: Manuel M. R. de L. Texeira, "Relatório da Inspecção Ordinária ao Distrito do Lago da Província do Niassa, 1950/51," 21.

epicenter of the disease was in the neighboring chiefdom of Ngolocolo, where 54 people were said to have died as a consequence of it in just six months in 1946.[227]

The way in which the colonial state responded to this outbreak should be seen in the context of what Philip Havik has called the *Estado Novo*'s post-war effort to modernize its colonies. In 1945, just one year before the outbreak, the Portuguese government had established the empire-wide "commission for the study of and combat against sleeping sickness." The fight against the sleeping sickness became one of the cornerstones of Portugal's ambition to be a "modern" colonial power and civilizing producer of scientific knowledge. As in the case of other colonial powers, the colonies thereby served as a "living laboratory" for testing both new drugs and programs of population control.[228] From the perspective of the colonial state, the outbreak of the sleeping sickness around Nkholongue came at an opportune time.

Between 1946 and the mid-1950s, the MCT carried out extensive operations in the region. These included medical treatment for those infected and prophylaxis for the rest, the organization of hunting brigades to eliminate elephants (which had apparently introduced the disease into the region), and even the resettlement of about 500 inhabitants of Malo, the village most affected by the disease.[229] This

---

[227] Jaime Neves, "A tripanossomíase rodesiense na região do Meluluca," *Moçambique: Documentário Trimestral*, no. 76 (1953): 39. Fourteen people are said to have still died after the beginning of the treatments by the MCT. See: Neves, 44. For a person from Nkholongue who is said to have died of the disease, see: PA, I118: interview with *P1218* (♀, 1930) (Malango, April 21, 2016), min 01:51:30–01:52:15. For people who are said to have had the disease: PA, I063: interview with *P1488* (♂, ~1930) (M'chepa, August 31, 2013), min 00:20:09–00:22:00; PA, I112: interview with *P0129* (♀, 1930), *P0128* (♂, 1928) (Nkholongue, April 12, 2016), min 02:06:17–02:06:48; PA, I106: interview with *P0262* (♀, ~1940) (Malango, April 4, 2016), min 00:38:04–00:38:59; PA, I129: interview with *P1426* (♂, 1929) (Malindi (Mangochi District, Malawi), May 29, 2016), min 02:03:38–02:05:14.
[228] Philip Havik, "Public Health and Tropical Modernity: The Combat against Sleeping Sickness in Portuguese Guinea," *História, Ciências, Saúde-Manguinhos* 21, no. 2 (2014): 641–66. For other colonial powers, see: Helen Tilley, *Africa as a Living Laboratory: Empire, Development, and the Problem of Scientific Knowledge, 1870–1950* (Chicago: University of Chicago Press, 2011).
[229] For information on the local delegation of the MCT, see: Serrano, "Um reconhecimento no Distrito do Lago"; Neves, "A tripanossomíase rodesiense na região do Meluluca"; AHM, ISANI, cx. 99: Manuel M. R. de L. Texeira, "Relatório da Inspecção Ordinária ao Distrito do Lago da Província do Niassa, 1950/51," 18. The houses of the resettled were burned down. The resettled were reportedly compensated for their loss. Furthermore, those who survived the disease were exempted from taxation. See: PA, I123: interview with *P1460* (♀), *P1461* (♂, ~1935), *P1462* (♂, ~1935) (Meluluca, April 25, 2016), min 00:49:29–00:49:35; Neves, "A tripanossomíase rodesiense na região do Meluluca," 41; PA, I127: interview with *P1468* (♂), *P1469* (♂), *P1470* (♂), *P1471* (♀) (Malo, May 2, 2016), min 00:18:12–00:20:39.

resettlement also involved several families from Nkholongue who had previously emigrated to Malo.[230]

For this analysis, the MCT's arrival in the region is interesting because it shows how little trust people had in the colonial state. The MCT's attempt to prophylactically treat the people of the region with antripol injections met with widespread (passive) resistance. People were initially reluctant to receive the injection and ran away when the MCT's team approached.[231] This reluctance was apparently also fueled by the belief that it was the MCT's staff who were spreading the disease with these injections.[232]

But while some people from the region ran away from the MCT, others worked for it. One of my interviewees worked as a medical assistant for the MCT and was responsible for the injections.[233] He was originally from Maniamba but married in Nkholongue while working for the MCT.[234] He described their methods as follows:

> We had to have a good relationship with the local people. Because when they learned about our work with the injections, they just ran away as soon as they saw us. So the only way [to success] was to be patient.[235]

Another interviewee was employed as a houseboy by Jaime Neves, the Portuguese head of the MCT. According to this interviewee, Neves had hired 11 young men like him just to take care of his house in Metangula:

> We were 11. He paid 50, 50, 50 to all 11 of us. At the end of the day, one was tempted to ask if this was a gathering or what. But it was just the house of Jaime Neves.[236]

While this can be read as a blatant sign of colonial inequality, the interviewee made it clear that he was very satisfied with the work and that, for him, 50 escudos was a lot of money.[237] Neves' stay on the lakeshore generates similar tensions of interpretation in another respect. For during his stay at the lake, he had an inti-

---

230 PA, I113: interview with *P0367* (♂, *1936*) (Nkholongue, April 13, 2016), min 02:34:20–02:34:39; Neves, "A tripanossomíase rodesiense na região do Meluluca," 41.
231 Neves, "A tripanossomíase rodesiense na região do Meluluca," 40; PA, I035: interview with *P0743* (♀, *~1930*), *P0765* (♀, *~1932*) (Nkholongue, July 28, 2012), min 00:20:15–00:28:32; PA, I121: interview with *P0527* (♂, *~1918*) (Maniamba, April 22, 2016), min 00:48:09–00:48:28; PA, I106: interview with *P0262* (♀, *~1940*) (Malango, April 4, 2016), min 00:38:59–00:40:12.
232 PA, I106: interview with *P0262* (♀, *~1940*) (Malango, April 4, 2016), min 00:35:19–00:38:04.
233 PA, I121: interview with *P0527* (♂, *~1918*) (Maniamba, April 22, 2016), min 00:48:09–00:48:28.
234 PA, I121: interview with *P0527* (♂, *~1918*) (Maniamba, April 22, 2016), min 01:13:54–01:14:23.
235 PA, I121: interview with *P0527* (♂, *~1918*) (Maniamba, April 22, 2016), min 00:48:09–00:48:28.
236 PA, I111: interview with *P0266* (♂, *~1932*) (Metangula, April 11, 2016), min 00:51:33–00:53:27.
237 PA, I111: interview with *P0266* (♂, *~1932*) (Metangula, April 11, 2016), min 01:04:00–01:05:17.

mate relationship with one of Nkholongue's young women, namely the older sister of his assistant's wife. We cannot know the exact circumstances of what everybody called a "marriage" ("ukwati"), but the woman in question herself did not appear to look back on it with bad memories, recalling rather proudly that Neves even sent goats to ask for her hand.[238] The case is interesting in that Neves was simultaneously one of the last Portuguese reported to have been carried in a *machila*.[239] This suggests that even if people from Nkholongue rejected a system, others from the village were willing to support it for economic or other reasons.

5.5 Conclusion

This chapter has attempted to analyze the experiences of Nkholongue's inhabitants with Portuguese colonialism from the time of initial colonization in 1900 until the early 1960s. Thereby, it sought to highlight how these experiences changed in the same place over time. In doing so, it aimed at addressing the lack of periodization in many works on Portuguese colonialism. Although the analysis has been somewhat constrained by a fragmentary and uneven set of sources, several results can still be obtained:

First, it can be noted that the level of colonial exploitation varied greatly over time. The toll of forced labor was horrendous during World War One and during the early 1920s, but not during most other periods of the village's history. Taxation was an issue throughout the era, and above all in the earlier periods included highly violent practices. Still, the tax burden was not the same throughout, but depended on factors such as changing tax levels, changing income possibilities, and changing attitudes of tax collectors, as well as the changing ability of the state to enforce its policies locally. In this context, it has also been shown that, in the case of Nkholongue, the "mother of poverty" was not the famous cotton regime of the *Estado*

---

238 PA, I142: interview with *P0743* (♀, ~1930) (Nkholongue, June 8, 2016), min 00:55:38 – 00:57:51. See as well: PA, I035: interview with *P0743* (♀, ~1930), *P0765* (♀, ~1932) (Nkholongue, July 28, 2012), min 00:32:40 – 00:37:25. For other interviewees calling it a "marriage," see: PA, I113: interview with *P0367* (♂, 1936) (Nkholongue, April 13, 2016), min 02:30:12 – 02:30:31; PA, I121: interview with *P0527* (♂, ~1918) (Maniamba, April 22, 2016), min 01:13:54 – 01:14:23.
239 PA, I117: interview with *P1458* (♂, ~1945) (Micundi, April 20, 2016), min 00:38:05 – 00:38:34; PA, I121: interview with *P0527* (♂, ~1918) (Maniamba, April 22, 2016), min 00:46:10 – 00:46:55; PA, I142: interview with *P0743* (♀, ~1930) (Nkholongue, June 8, 2016), min 00:56:13 – 00:56:34.

Novo, but the cotton planted on plantations in the early 1920s, when the heavy use of forced labor led to widespread hunger.[240]

Second, the evidence shows that these changing levels of colonial exploitation were not primarily the result of reforms in the colonial legal system, but rather of changes in the administrative and economic structures. Nkholongue was much more affected by the colonial state and economy until the mid-1920s than in later years. This was not only because Metangula ceased to be an administrative center of the state, but also because the economic policies of the *Estado Novo* prevented the inflow of European capital and settlers from the neighboring colony of Nyasaland. Along the lakeshore, it was the *Estado Novo* rather than the *Companhia* that failed to exploit the area.

Third, we have seen that the colonial state could count on the support of villagers throughout its existence. People from the village not only acted as intermediaries, but also supported the colonial state in suppressing the resistance to colonial conquest. In the long run, the people from Nkholongue did little to directly challenge the colonial state. Rather, those who were dissatisfied with the situation emigrated to Nyasaland.

Fourth, the study of the regional course of World War One has shown that there are indeed indications that Muslims from Nkholongue and the surrounding villages were involved in a plot against the British steamers on the lake. It has, however, also been demonstrated that previous research on the war has exaggerated the support people provided to German troops when they invaded northern Mozambique.

Jane Burbank and Frederick Cooper have argued that empires in world history have typically produced neither consistent loyalty nor constant resistance, but what they called "contingent accommodation."[241] The lessons from Nkholongue may confirm this, but "contingency" loses parts of its randomness when we look at history through the microhistorical lens. The behavior of the population of Nkholongue was guided by the available possibilities and its historical experiences. Chapter 7 will show that the opportunities for resistance changed significantly with Frelimo's appearance in the 1960s. As a result, many initially joined the nationalists. However, the concrete war experiences again prompted most people

---

240 Previous research has ignored these plantations. Galli and Medeiros, for example, both stated that cotton was not grown at the time of the *Companhia*. See: Galli, *Peoples' Spaces and State Spaces*, 32; Medeiros, *História de Cabo Delgado e do Niassa (c. 1836–1929)*, 186. Pitcher's statistics on early cotton production in Angola and Mozambique do not list cotton exports from the territories of the Companhia do Nyassa until 1924. See: Pitcher, "Sowing the Seeds of Failure," 70.
241 Jane Burbank and Frederick Cooper, *Empires in World History: Power and the Politics of Difference* (Princeton: Princeton University Press, 2010), 14.

to abandon their support for the nationalists and to come to terms with Portuguese colonialism once more.

6 Uncaptured Again: History and the Subsistence Mantra of Development Studies

6.1 A Déjà-Vu of Economic Transformation

> Lago/Meluluca has traditionally been a relatively isolated community depending on subsistence agriculture and fishing. The community is currently in a process of considerable change, primarily as a result of the improved road built from the district capital Metangula in 2008. This has not only set in motion enhanced economic activities particularly in fishing, but also processes of increasing inequalities between the poor and the better-off.[1]

In the introduction to this book, I raised the issue of the misleading portrayal of the history of the area around Nkholongue by the development consultants of the Swedish embassy (see pp. 40–42). The quotation above—focusing on the local economy—is an alternative version to that presented in the introduction. It is recited here to highlight the topos of the subsistence cultivator now being suddenly modernized. This is a topos that remains popular in development studies and is frequently used in descriptions of the current situation in Niassa.[2]

But for the historian of social change in Africa, this topos also causes a striking sense of déjà-vu. Since the beginning of colonization, scholars and observers have repeatedly described the ongoing social transformation of "traditional" African society. Consider the anthropological studies of the Rhodes-Livingstone Institute or, with respect to Nkholongue, the revolution of village life that missionary Cox thought he saw during the plantation boom of the early 1920s (see p. 164). Scholarly labels and priorities have changed over time, but processes described as "peasantization," "proletarianization," "modernization," "deagrarization," "livelihood diversification," or "globalization" have all tended to postulate an inescapable and linear path of economic transformation from past to future.

---

[1] ORGUT, "1st Reality Check in Mozambique: Brief," accessed December 4, 2020, https://www.sida.se/globalassets/global/countries-and-regions/africa/mozambique/brief-1st-reality-checks-final.pdf.
[2] For examples, see: Jennifer Landry and Praxie Chirwa, "Analysis of the Potential Socio-Economic Impact of Establishing Plantation Forestry on Rural Communities in Sanga District, Niassa Province, Mozambique," *Land Use Policy* 28, no. 3 (2011): 542–51; Anne Kristine Thorsen, "Reducing Social Vulnerabilities through Foreign Investments: A Case-Study of Niassa Green Resources in Northern Mozambique" (Master thesis, Universitetet i Stavanger, 2017); Winfridus Overbeek, *O avanço das monoculturas de árvores em Moçambique: Impactos sobre as comunidades camponesas na Província de Niassa. Um relatório de viagem* (Montevideo: World Rainforest Movement, 2010).

Given the recurrent affirmations of the radical transformation of "traditional" African society, it is surprising that notions of the "uncaptured" subsistence cultivators keep popping up in political and scholarly discussions about the need for development in Africa. Time and again, the goal has been "to break through the barriers of subsistence agriculture into more commercialised medium-scale stature,"[3] as the OECD-FAO Agricultural Outlook for 2016–2025 put it. Words such as "continue," "persistence," "remain," and "still" are omnipresent in descriptions of the current state of rural Africans.[4] In the words of Jeffrey Sachs, "a large part of the African population continues to eke out an existence as subsistence farmers working tiny land plots."[5]

The central goal of this chapter is to demonstrate that a village seemingly dependent on subsistence since time immemorial possesses a surprisingly dynamic and globally connected economic past. It will be shown that Nkholongue's inhabitants have not stayed but have become the subsistence-oriented "peasants" who they are nowadays. The importance of subsistence production[6] has not just stagnat-

---

[3] OECD and FAO, eds., *OECD-FAO Agricultural Outlook 2016–2025. Special Focus: Sub-Saharan Africa* (Paris: OECD Publishing, 2016), 91. On this point, see as well: Tania Murray Li, "Indigeneity, Capitalism, and the Management of Dispossession," *Current Anthropology* 51, no. 3 (2010): 396.
[4] Evelyn Dietsche and Ana Maria Esteves, "Local Content and the Prospect for Economic Diversification in Mozambique," in *Mining for Change: Natural Resources and Industry in Africa*, ed. John Page and Finn Tarp (Oxford: Oxford University Press, 2020), 209–10; Wilma A Dunaway, "Nonwaged Peasants in the Modern World-System: African Households as Dialectical Units of Capitalist Exploitation and Indigenous Resistance, 1890–1930," *Journal of Philosophical Economics* 4, no. 1 (2010): 19; James Ernest Murton, Dean Bavington, and Carly A Dokis, "Introduction: Why Subsistence?," in *Subsistence under Capitalism: Historical and Contemporary Perspectives*, ed. James Ernest Murton, Dean Bavington, and Carly A Dokis (Montreal: McGill-Quenn's University Press, 2016), 3–36; John W McArthur and Jeffrey D. Sachs, "A General Equilibrium Model for Analyzing African Rural Subsistence Economies and an African Green Revolution," *Africa Growth Initiative Working Paper*, no. 12 (June 2013): 4; Ousmane Badiane and Tsitsi Makombe, "Agriculture, Growth, and Development in Africa," in *The Oxford Handbook of Africa and Economics. Volume II: Policies and Practices*, ed. Célestin Monga and Justin Yifu Lin (Oxford: Oxford University Press, 2015), 307; Sarah Alobo Loison, "Rural Livelihood Diversification in Sub-Saharan Africa: A Literature Review," *The Journal of Development Studies* 51, no. 9 (2015): 1127; Megumi Muto and Takashi Yamano, "The Impact of Mobile Phone Coverage Expansion on Market Participation: Panel Data Evidence from Uganda," *World Development* 37, no. 12 (2009): 1887; Holger Kirscht, *Ein Dorf in Nordost-Nigeria: Politische und wirtschaftliche Transformation der bäuerlichen Kanuri-Gesellschaft* (Münster: LIT Verlag, 2001), 310.
[5] Jeffrey Sachs, "Africa's Demographic Transition and Economic Prospects," in *The Oxford Handbook of Africa and Economics*, ed. Célestin Monga and Justin Yifu Lin, vol. 2: Policies and Practices (Oxford: Oxford University Press, 2015), 877.
[6] Note that I do not use the term "subsistence economy," which is sometimes confused with that of "subsistence production." In my view, the term "subsistence economy" is not only too vague to

ed or decreased over time, rather there have been phases in which the significance of subsistence production also increased. Furthermore, systems of subsistence—this includes types of products planted and locations of fields—have equally changed. It will also be seen that many individuals have had very different main means of income during their lifetimes such as wage labor or market production even if their main occupation today might be subsistence production.[7] The chapter shows that, in the case of Nkholongue, livelihood diversification is no new phenomenon.[8] Last but not least, the chapter will highlight that, despite its traditional appearance, the local fishing sector has a long history of capitalist-like relations of production.

With this goal, the chapter tries to challenge the notions of rural inertia in Africa which are connected to the longstanding and profound impact of the arguments of substantivists in academia and public debate alike.[9] Going back to Karl Polanyi's characterization of non-capitalist and pre-industrialist societies, substantivists have argued that cultural forces—the moral economy—rather than market forces continue to dominate resource allocation in rural Africa. In the words of Göran Hydén, one of the substantivists' more prominent representatives, the Afri-

---

allow for reasonable analysis, but also evokes rigid notions of "uncapturedness." Following Elwert and Wong, my notion of "subsistence production" is also not limited to agricultural or food production but includes other sectors such as handicraft, household work and house construction. On a conceptual level, my notion of subsistence also includes the care sector (including the care of children and elderly). See: Georg Elwert and Diana Wong, "Subsistence Production and Commodity Production in the Third World," *Review (Fernand Braudel Center)* 3, no. 3 (1980): 503.

[7] This is consistent with recent findings of Zachary Guthrie, who argued that his migrant workers engaged in many different occupations over the course of their lives. See: Zachary Kagan Guthrie, *Bound for Work: Labor, Mobility, and Colonial Rule in Central Mozambique, 1940–1965* (Charlottesville: University of Virginia Press, 2018). See also Frederick Cooper's recent call for an analysis of social relations of production in relation to the worker over the life course: Frederick Cooper, "The 'Labour Question' in Africa and the World," in *General Labour History of Africa*, ed. Stefano Bellucci and Andreas Eckert (Woodbridge: James Currey, 2019), 627–628.

[8] Livelihood diversification is usually considered a phenomenon that began to appear in the 1980s. See: Deborah F. Bryceson, "Domestic Work," in *General Labour History of Africa*, ed. Stefano Bellucci and Andreas Eckert (Woodbridge: James Currey, 2019), 301–332.

[9] For the potency of these arguments, see: Henry Bernstein, "Considering Africa's Agrarian Questions," *Historical Materialism* 12, no. 4 (2004): 117–118; Bernd E.T. Mueller, "The Agrarian Question in Tanzania: Using New Evidence to Reconcile an Old Debate," *Review of African Political Economy* 38, no. 127 (2011): 24; Peter Geschiere, "Witchcraft: The Dangers of Intimacy and the Struggle over Trust," in *Trusting and Its Tribulations: Interdisciplinary Engagements with Intimacy, Sociality and Trust*, ed. Vigdis Broch-Due and Margit Ystanes (New York: Berghahn, 2016), 69; Elizabeth Harrison, "'People Are Willing to Fight to the End': Romanticising the 'Moral' in Moral Economies of Irrigation," *Critique of Anthropology* 40, no. 2 (2020): 194–217; Johanna Siméant, "Three Bodies of Moral Economy: The Diffusion of a Concept," *Journal of Global Ethics* 11, no. 2 (2015): 163–175.

can peasantry remains "uncaptured" as a consequence of its "economy of affection."[10]

The arguments of substantivists have fed very different currents of intellectual thinking, some of which celebrate successful (egalitarian) peasant resistance à la James Scott and others of which are essentially Afro-pessimistic.[11] Arguments by substantivists have also found much resonance in the development industry. This is not surprising, as the development discourse is generally based on the premise that its target is "aboriginal, not yet incorporated into the modern world."[12] It is, however, noteworthy that development discourse has increasingly used substantivist arguments not only to describe the status quo of its targets, but also to propose a particular path of modernization. Such approaches can be linked to the Chayanovian tradition of the "agrarian question," which has viewed peasants as a central actor in rural development.[13] They include what has been defined by its critics as "neo-classical neo-populism" or "dynamic versions of agrarian populism."[14] These approaches are informed by substantivism insofar

---

10 Göran Hydén, *Beyond Ujamaa in Tanzania: Underdevelopment and an Uncaptured Peasantry* (Berkeley: University of California Press, 1980). For a newer publication, in which Hydén argued that his claim still holds validity in 2007, see: Göran Hydén, "Governance and Poverty Reduction in Africa," *Proceedings of the National Academy of Sciences* 104, no. 43 (2007): 16754. For his newest version of "economy of affection," see: Göran Hydén, Kazuhiko Sugimura, and Tadasu Tsuruta, eds., *Rethinking African Agriculture: How Non-Agrarian Factors Shape Peasant Livelihoods* (London: Routledge, 2020).
11 For Scott, see: James C. Scott, *The Moral Economy of the Peasant: Rebellion and Subsistence in Southeast Asia* (New Haven: Yale University Press, 1976); James C. Scott, *Weapons of the Weak: Everyday Forms of Peasant Resistance* (New Haven: Yale University Press, 1985); James C. Scott, *The Art of Not Being Governed: An Anarchist History of Upland Southeast Asia* (New Haven: Yale University Press, 2009).
12 James Ferguson, *The Anti-Politics Machine: "Development," Depoliticization, and Bureaucratic Power in Lesotho* (Cambridge: Cambridge University Press, 1990), 71.
13 Paul Hebinck, "Post-Apartheid Land and Agrarian Reform Policy and Practices in South Africa: Themes, Processes and Issues," in *In the Shadow of Policy: Everyday Practices in South Africa's Land and Agrarian Reform*, ed. Paul Hebinck and Ben Cousins (Johannesburg: Wits University Press, 2013), 6.
14 For the resonance of such ideas in the development industry, see: Mueller, "The Agrarian Question in Tanzania"; Geschiere, "Witchcraft: The Dangers of Intimacy and the Struggle over Trust," 69. For the definition of "neo-classical neo-populism," see: Terence J. Byres, "Neo-Classical Neo-Populism 25 Years On: Déjà Vu and Déjà Passé. Towards a Critique," *Journal of Agrarian Change* 4, no. 1–2 (2004): 17–44. For the definition of the dynamic version of "agrarian populism," see: Gareth Austin, *Labour, Land, and Capital in Ghana: From Slavery to Free Labour in Asante* (Rochester: University of Rochester Press, 2005), 25–26. The most vocal critic of all modes of "agrarian populism" remains Tom Brass. See: Tom Brass, *Peasants, Populism and Postmodernism: The Return of the Agrarian Myth* (London: Frank Cass, 2000); Tom Brass, "Weapons of the Week, Weakness of

as they assume that rural Africa continues to consist of a largely homogeneous and non-capitalist peasantry shaped by communitarian values. Combining neo-populist enthusiasm for smallholder agriculture with neo-classical market fundamentalism, they believe that these "traditional" values can be used to deliver a more egalitarian modernization that avoids the usual pains of capitalist transformation. Ideas and notions of such agrarian populism are popular among a wide range of actors, including NGOs, social movements such as Vía Campesina, and even UN institutions. They can be found, for example, in the current United Nations' decade of family farming (2019–2028). Thus, family farmers are equated with "traditional communities," described as "caretakers of the environment," and said to promote "social inclusion and equity" and "preservation/transmission of knowledge and culture."[15]

The criticism of substantivism expressed in this chapter is not new.[16] Historians have long warned against the danger of characterizing African economies as "subsistence economies."[17] The essentialist notion of the "uncaptured" peasant is at odds with the findings of several distinguished scholars, including Polly Hill, Colin Bundy, Sara Berry, Antony Hopkins, and Martin Klein. All of them have made compelling cases for the historical extent of market involvement of African agriculturalists.[18] The term seems particularly inappropriate given what we know about the history of the slave trade and especially the history of colonialism. Just think of the history of forced labor, the history of labor migration and the history

---

the Weapons: Shifts and Stasis in Development Theory," *Journal of Peasant Studies* 34, no. 1 (2007): 111–153; Tom Brass, *Class, Culture and the Agrarian Myth* (Leiden: Brill, 2014).
15 FAO and IFAD, "United Nations Decade of Family Farming 2019–2028 – Global Action Plan" (Rome: FAO, 2019), 12. On the popularity of agrarian populism among social movements, see as well: Hebinck, "Post-Apartheid Land and Agrarian Reform Policy and Practices in South Africa," 7; Mueller, "The Agrarian Question in Tanzania."
16 Poly Hill called it a dead duck in relation to West Africa in 1978 already. See: Polly Hill, "Problems with A. G. Hopkins' Economic History of West Africa," *African Economic History*, no. 6 (1978): 127. See as well: Rosemary E. Galli and Jocelyn Jones, *Guinea-Bissau: Politics, Economics and Society* (London: Pinter, 1987), 6.
17 Paul Tiyambe Zeleza, *A Modern Economic History Africa*, vol. 1: The Nineteenth Century (Dakar: Codesria, 1993), 6; Masao Yoshida, "African Economic History: Approaches to Research," in *Writing African History*, ed. John Edward Philips (Rochester: University of Rochester Press, 2005), 308.
18 Hill, *The Migrant Cocoa-Farmers of Southern Ghana*; Berry, *No Condition Is Permanent*; Colin Bundy, *The Rise and Fall of the South African Peasantry* (London: Heinemann, 1979); Hopkins, *An Economic History of West Africa*; Martin A. Klein, ed., *Peasants in Africa: Historical and Contemporary Perspectives* (Beverly Hills: Sage, 1980).

of colonial intermediaries. It also seems difficult to reconcile it with the arguments of dependency theory and its idea of the development of underdevelopment.[19]

Despite this considerable opposition, substantivists' stereotypes have remained important and influential in academia. Achille Mbembe, for example, has repeatedly referred to Africa as the "last frontier of capitalism" in recent years.[20] Even historians continue to nurture such ahistorical notions of uncapturedness.[21] Thus, Eric Hobsbawm claimed in his standard work *The Age of Extremes* that "[m]ost of [black Africa's] inhabitants did not need their states, which were usually too weak to do much harm, and, if they grew too troublesome, could probably be by-passed by a retreat into village self-sufficiency."[22] Iva Peša's recent history of social change in northwestern Zambia represents a somewhat contradictory combination of neo-liberal and substantivist arguments,[23] in which people responded "astutely and eagerly" to market incentives and, at the same time, possessed a seemingly infinite power and autonomy in evading state demands and

---

19 The incompatibility of dependency theory and agrarian populism was already highlighted in the 1980s by Kenneth Good and Gaving Kitching. See: Kenneth Good, "The Reproduction of Weakness in the State and Agriculture: Zambian Experience," *African Affairs* 85, no. 339 (1986): 264–265; Gavin Kitching, *Development and Underdevelopment in Historical Perspective: Populism, Nationalism, and Industrialization* (London: Routledge, 1982), 176.
20 For a critique of this representation, see: Horman Chitonge, "Capitalism in Africa: Mutating Capitalist Relations and Social Formations," *Review of African Political Economy* 45, no. 155 (2018): 158–167. Mbembe can certainly not be called a full-fledged substantivist. But even more so his repeated use of the phrase is questionable: António Guerreiro, "Achille Mbembe: 'África é a última fronteira do capitalismo,'" *Público*, December 9, 2018, accessed December 10, 2018, https://www.publico.pt/2018/12/09/mundo/entrevista/africa-ultima-fronteira-capitalismo-1853532;
Thomas Blaser, "Africa and the Future: An Interview with Achille Mbembe," Africa is a Country, accessed January 27, 2021, https://africasacountry.com/2013/11/africa-and-the-future-an-interview-with-achille-mbembe/; Achille Mbembe, *Out of the Dark Night: Essays on Decolonization* (New York: Columbia University Press, 2021), 36.
21 This is also argued by: Harrison, "'People Are Willing to Fight to the End'"; Siméant, "Three Bodies of Moral Economy"; Joseph Morgan Hodge, "Writing the History of Development (Part 1: The First Wave)," *Humanity: An International Journal of Human Rights, Humanitarianism, and Development* 6, no. 3 (2015): 437. Hyden's "economy of affection" has remained a catchphrase within political science and development studies. It was one already in the 1990s. See: Edward A. Alpers, "Africa Reconfigured: Presidential Address to the 1994 African Studies Association Annual Meeting," *African Studies Review* 38, no. 2 (1995): 6.
22 Eric J. Hobsbawm, *The Age of Extremes: The Short Twentieth Century, 1914–1991* (1994; repr., London: Abacus, 1995), 352. The narrative of rural inertia is also prominent in the work of Catherine Coquerie-Vidrovitch. See: Catherine Coquery-Vidrovitch, *Afrique noire: permanences et ruptures*, 2. éd. rév (Paris: L'Harmattan, 1992), 145–47.
23 This combination resonates with "neo-classical neo-populism."

maintaining their communitarian traditions.[24] It is telling that James Brennan has only recently called Hopkins' seminal 1973 book still "vaguely radical [...] in the confident way that it dismisses substantivists and modernization theorists alike for positing a traditional Africa characterized by anti-capitalist values."[25]

The field of literature about development and social change in Africa is vast and diverse. It crosses into many different scholarly disciplines. The subfield of studies that comes closest to this chapter are the more empirical (regional) case studies that focus on rural change in the long run. They include the work of Gareth Austin, Chima Korieh, Elias Mandala, Susan Martin, Iva Peša, Leroy Vail, Landeg White, Megan Vaughan and Henrietta Moore.[26] While following different foci and arguments, the work of these scholars have all contributed to counter images of rural inertia in Africa. However, this chapter stands out from most of these studies in four areas:

First, most studies on rural change in Africa have tended to analyze history in a linear model of "continuity and change."[27] In line with the considerations presented in the introduction to this book (see Section 1.4), this chapter proposes a more dynamic model, highlighting for example moments of discontinuity in processes that might at first glance appear to be continuous. The chapter thus hopes to contribute to what James Ferguson calls "the dismantling of linear teleologies of emergence and development."[28] This chapter emphasizes that the history of eco-

---

24 Peša, *Roads through Mwinilunga*, 126.
25 James R. Brennan, "Book Review of Africa, Empire and Globalization: Essays in Honor of A.G. Hopkins," *Britain and the World* 8, no. 2 (2015): 254–55.
26 Elias C. Mandala, *Work and Control in a Peasant Economy: A History of the Lower Tchiri Valley in Malawi, 1859–1960* (Madison: University of Wisconsin Press, 1990); Elias C. Mandala, *The End of Chidyerano: A History of Food and Everyday Life in Malawi, 1860–2004* (Portsmouth: Heinemann, 2005); Henrietta L. Moore and Megan Vaughan, *Cutting Down Trees: Gender, Nutrition, and Agricultural Change in the Northern Province of Zambia, 1890–1990* (Portsmouth: Heinemann, 1994); Austin, *Labour, Land, and Capital in Ghana*; Chima J. Korieh, *The Land Has Changed: History, Society and Gender in Colonial Eastern Nigeria* (Calgary: University of Calgary Press, 2010); Susan M. Martin, *Palm Oil and Protest: An Economic History of the Ngwa Region, South-Eastern Nigeria, 1800–1980* (Cambridge: Cambridge University Press, 1988); Peša, *Roads through Mwinilunga*; Vail and White, *Capitalism and Colonialism in Mozambique*.
27 Thus, Megan Vaughan and Henrietta Moore have described the transition from slash-and-burn agriculture to semi-permanent fields as well as the growing dependence of people on the market as linear processes. See: Moore and Vaughan, *Cutting Down Trees*, 23, 46. The same applies for the work of Iva Peša even though she pretends to question narratives of linear change. Her model of "gradual and incremental" change, while overcoming older ideas of transformative change, remains a very linear model. See: Peša, *Roads through Mwinilunga*.
28 James Ferguson, *Expectations of Modernity: Myths and Meanings of Urban Life on the Zambian Copperbelt* (Berkeley: University of California Press, 1999), 17.

nomic life of Nkholongue's population is not one of ever-increasing interdependence with the world economy. It is not a history of a gradual integration into world markets. Nor is it necessarily a history of growing dependence, at least not in every aspect of daily life. Looking at economic history from Nkholongue's vantage point, one will also notice phases of decreasing interdependence in the village's economy.

Second, the state usually plays a central role in works of historians on rural change in Africa. While the (economic) policies of the state and their local implications play a role in other chapters of this book (see Chapters 5, 7, 8, and 10), the state is absent in a significant part of the processes analyzed in this chapter. This is in line with the argument here that while Nkholongue was on the margins of state control and influence for many periods of its existence, the village's economy was nevertheless connected to (global) capitalism. The chapter thus intends to highlight that even remote and seemingly isolated areas could experience significant economic change. Nkholongue's population never experienced the kind of peasant-led cash-crop revolution that happened in South Africa or many colonies of West Africa, and was also only marginally affected by colonial forced labor schemes such as the Portuguese cotton regime, as highlighted in Section 5.3. Still, the nature of Nkholongue's economy has changed considerably during the last 140 years.

Third, some studies on rural change have been surprisingly monosyllabic when it comes to the local impact of the slave trade.[29] While the reach of the slave trade into the region of study is frequently mentioned, its effects on local developments are often either downplayed or then described vaguely in very general or abstract terms. Rarely is its presence truly considered for the analysis of the history of rural change.[30] This chapter is not concerned with the period of the slave trade. However, together with the findings of the previous chapters (see especially Chapter 2), this chapter argues for the importance of reflecting the impact of the

---

29 Exceptions are: Austin, *Labour, Land, and Capital in Ghana*; Vail and White, *Capitalism and Colonialism in Mozambique*.
30 Moore and Vaughan, *Cutting Down Trees*, chaps. 1, 3; Korieh, *The Land Has Changed*. Elias Mandala describes the slave trade as a dramatic and disruptive process, but with no or only limited long-term effects. See: Mandala, *Work and Control in a Peasant Economy*, 67–79, 270. Similarly, Peša writes that the slave raids "caused disruption and propelled profound, but not permanent change." See: Peša, *Roads through Mwinilunga*, 62. In her work on the Ruvuma Region, Doris Schmied claimed that "long-distance trade existed as an independent entity parallel to the subsistence economy." See: Doris Schmied, *Subsistence Cultivation, Market Production and Agricultural Development in Ruvuma Region, Southern Tanzania* (Bayreuth: Eckhard Breitinger, 1989), 60.

slave trade on local communities and their economies, even though the availability of sources may often limit detailed analysis.

Fourth, most studies by historians on rural change are regional studies. Henrietta Moore and Megan Vaughan have even explicitly explained why they did not make a village study, highlighting residential mobility and the smallness and instability of villages.[31] This chapter argues that the focus on the economic history of a single village can not only be justified but also valuable. Justified, first, because Nkholongue proved to be a comparatively stable settlement, and second, because mobility can be accounted for by including the life histories of emigrants, as has been done in this study. Valuable, first, because a local study can reveal dynamics that might be flattened by a more regional approach, and second, because the focus on one village can best serve the goal of refuting ahistorical notions of rural inertia. After all, the "traditional African village" has always been the reference point for those who argue that African societies are not part of the capitalist world.[32] Moreover, it is hoped that the focus on one village will contribute to make tangible the experiences of the people who ought to be developed.[33]

"History matters" has long been a commonplace in discussions of poverty and development in Africa.[34] Sweden's reality checkers also highlighted the importance of considering the history of their research sites.[35] Even Jeffrey Sachs argued for first "taking a 'history'" of his Millennium Villages.[36] However, contrary to this advocacy for micro-level analyses, explanations for the persistence of poverty in Africa usually take place on a much larger scale.[37] The same is true of a number of

---

31 Moore and Vaughan, *Cutting Down Trees*, xvii.
32 Chitonge, "Capitalism in Africa," 163.
33 The need for concrete case studies is also emphasized by Mueller, who argues that the mostly theoretical and abstract nature of the discussion on the "agrarian question" has contributed to the fact that scientific findings have found so little resonance in the development community. See: Mueller, "The Agrarian Question in Tanzania," 25.
34 Morten Jerven, *Africa: Why Economists Get It Wrong* (London: Zed Books, 2015), 72.
35 ORGUT, "Inception Report," 9, 12–13; Jones and Tvedten, "What Does It Mean to Be Poor?," 158.
36 Jeffrey Sachs, "The End of Poverty: Economic Possibilities for Our Time," *European Journal of Dental Education* 12, Special Issue: Global Congress on Dental Education III (2008): 20. In his book, he put it this way: "Providing economic advice to others requires a profound commitment to search for the right answers, not to settle for superficial approaches. It requires a commitment to be thoroughly steeped in the history, ethnography, politics, and economics of any place where the professional adviser is working." See: Jeffrey Sachs, *The End of Poverty: Economic Possibilities for Our Time* (New York: Penguin, 2005), 80–81. For a critical assessment of the Millennium villages project, see: Japhy Wilson, "Paradoxical Utopia: The Millennium Villages Project in Theory and Practice," *Journal of Agrarian Change* 17, no. 1 (2017): 122–143.
37 See for example Sachs' own "analysis" for the reasons of poverty in Africa: Sachs, *The End of Poverty*, 2005, chap. 3. It is also worth repeating in this context that the Millennium Villages are

historians who, over the past 15 years, have underscored the importance of introducing historical rigor to the debates of development led by scholars from other disciplines:[38] they have as a rule focused on quantifiable macro-processes.[39] This also applies to the activists in the global peasant movement, who, with their focus on transnational agrofood companies have ignored examining what Tania Murray Li has called "capitalism from below" or the "microprocesses of dispossession among small-scale farmers."[40]

This chapter hopes to rectify the discrepancy between the widespread development credo of "small is beautiful"[41] and the ignorance of local history and trajectories. It is divided into three parts. The first part is concerned with a specific period of subsistence reversal in Nkholongue's history. Focusing on the 1940s and 1950s, it will highlight the importance that the manufacture of pots had acquired as a result of Nkholongue's role as a firewood station of the Anglican steamships. Pots were not only sold to passengers but also bartered for food in neighboring villages. As will be shown, the end of the steamer era in 1953 meant that this pottery livelihood became much less feasible. The result was profound changes in village life, including the migration of most of the village population to the Malango river and the increasing importance of food subsistence production. Parts 2 and

---

rarely what most people would consider a "village," but in fact constitute much larger units (see Section 1.2). See also in this regard the allegedly well-informed analysis of Lago's history by Sweden's reality checkers, which in reality remains very superficial and schematic. See: ORGUT, "Sub-Report, District of Lago: Year One, 2011," 8–9.

38 Examples are: Antony G. Hopkins, "Making Poverty History," *The International Journal of African Historical Studies* 38, no. 3 (2005): 513–531; Antony G. Hopkins, "The New Economic History of Africa," *The Journal of African History* 50, no. 2 (2009): 155–177; Gareth Austin, "The 'Reversal of Fortune' Thesis and the Compression of History: Perspectives from African and Comparative Economic History," *Journal of International Development* 20, no. 8 (2008): 996–1027; Gareth Austin and Stephen Broadberry, "Introduction: The Renaissance of African Economic History," *The Economic History Review* 67, no. 4 (2014): 893–906; Morten Jerven, "A Clash of Disciplines? Economists and Historians Approaching the African Past," *Economic History of Developing Regions* 26, no. 2 (2011): 111–124; Jerven, *Africa: Why Economists Get It Wrong*; Morten Jerven et al., "Moving Forward in African Economic History: Bridging the Gap between Methods and Sources," African Economic History Working Paper Series, no. 1 (Lund: Lund University, 2012).
39 This is also argued by: Andreas Eckert, "Scenes from a Marriage: African History and Global History," *Comparativ: Zeitschrift für Globalgeschichte und vergleichende Gesellschaftsforschung* 29, no. 2 (2019): 41.
40 Li, "Indigeneity, Capitalism, and the Management of Dispossession," 396. See as well: Tania Murray Li, *Land's End: Capitalist Relations on an Indigenous Frontier* (Durham: Duke University Press, 2014). Mike Davis speaks of "petty exploitation" and "relentless micro-capitalism" in his *Planet of Slums*. See: Mike Davis, *Planet of Slums* (London: Verso, 2006), 181.
41 E.F. Schumacher, *Small Is Beautiful: Economics as If People Mattered* (London: Blond & Briggs, 1973).

3 take a more diachronic perspective. Part 2 will analyze the nature of agricultural production in Nkholongue in the long run, highlighting that while farming was primarily for subsistence at most points in time, crops and techniques nevertheless changed significantly and not infrequently as a result of changes in the overall economy. The final part will deal with processes of commercialization and social differentiation within local fisheries, showing that they had been going on since colonial times.

6.2 The Rise and Fall of Nkholongue's Pottery Manufacture in the 1940s and 1950s

It is tempting to read the first two decades of the 21st century as the moment when Nkholongue's economy started to change and finally started to "open up to the world outside."[42] Similar to the development advisors at the Swedish Embassy, I was also initially seduced by this image of ongoing first-time transformation. The village surveys conducted in 2012 and 2016 seemed to provide further evidence of this fact. They showed that households produced a significant part of the food they consumed in subsistence. This concerned above all the cassava used for the polenta-like stiff porridge called *nsima*, eaten as a standard meal twice per day. In the 2012 survey, 80 percent of households reported having a *machamba* or farm.[43] The exceptions were some "external" employees of the newly arrived tourism enterprise Mbuna Bay, some younger people, and migratory fishermen, locally called *makuli*.[44] A majority of the households indicated that they were self-sufficient when it came to cassava production. But the surveys also showed that all households depended to varying degrees on money and market when it came to other needs. This concerned consumer goods such as clothes and shoes, but also ingredients for the side dishes eaten with *nsima* such as cooking oil, salt, and

---

[42] See the quotation from the report by ORGUT in Section 1.4 ("The Aboriginal Delusion") on p. 41.

[43] *Machamba* is a Swahili loanword for agricultural fields used in Mozambican Portuguese. Literature on agriculture in Malawi or Zambia often refers to "gardens" instead. Paul Zeleza has criticized the use of the word "garden" as an uncritical adoption of the colonial nomenclature that drew a distinction between the "primitive" gardens of the "natives" and the progressive farms of the settlers. From an analytical viewpoint, a similar criticism could be raised against *machamba* which was the "native" counterpart of the settlers' *fazenda*. See: Paul Tiyambe Zeleza, "Review of Cutting Down Trees: Gender, Nutrition, and Agricultural Change in the Northern Province of Zambia, 1890–1990," *The International Journal of African Historical Studies* 28, no. 2 (1995): 404–6.

[44] The word *makuli* is most likely derived from the English "coolie worker." See: R.H. Gower, "Swahili Borrowings from English," *Africa: Journal of the International African Institute* 22, no. 2 (1952): 155.

fish. Most households indicated that they generated their income either through working for Mbuna Bay or fishing.

Considering the recent arrival of Mbuna Bay and the boom of fisheries at the time, these all seemed to indicate the ongoing "process of considerable change" described by the development consultants of the Swedish embassy and quoted at the beginning of this chapter. In this section, the factuality of this development shall not be questioned. But it will be demonstrated that this process of considerable transformation had been preceded by other processes of considerable transformation. Thereby, changing economic relationships to the "world outside" had often deeply impacted local economic processes and not rarely been accompanied by significant migration and changes in the settlement structure.

We have already come across such moments in the preceding parts of the book. Thus, in the previous chapter we have seen how the extensive use of forced labor on cotton plantations disturbed local food production in the early 1920s and thus resulted in widespread famine. While in Section 4.3, we have seen how the end of the slave trade triggered migration and changing settlement patterns. Though the evidence is scarce, there is reason to claim that the end of the slave trade also involved changes in local food production and consumption. Thus, the emigration of Saide Salimo's group to the lake's hinterland in the 1910s (see p. 134) can be read as a sign of retreat into food subsistence. According to the local historian Chadreque Umali, Mtucula, the name they gave to their new location, translates to "he who does not eat is not a person" and was meant to say "that people had to work in order to have food."[45] In what follows, we will focus on another past process of considerable economic change that allows for a better and more systematic analysis: the rise and fall of Nkholongue's pottery manufacture in the 1940s and 1950s.

At first glance, the 1940s and 1950s seem to constitute a period offering plenty of evidence to substantiate Nkholongue's historical economic "uncapturedness." For, as we have already seen in the previous chapter, Nkholongue was definitely on the margins of Portuguese colonialism during this period. The Portuguese cotton regime of 1938 was only rudimentarily implemented, and the state's capacity to tax its subjects was limited. We might expect, then, that the village's economy during this period was indeed relatively isolated and static, and that subsistence production was the main occupation of the people. A closer look, however, reveals a period of profound local economic change that occurred largely outside the influence and scrutiny of the Portuguese colonial state. Still, the transformation of that time cannot be understood without considering global developments.

---

45 PA, Chadreque Umali, *História de Nyanjas* (Metangula, 1996), 58.

Next stop "Nkholongue Station": "Wooding" in the "Steamer Parish"

A prime cause of the transformation was the end of what Charles Good called the "steamer parish."[46] We have already come across the importance of steamboats for the Anglican mission UMCA for their evangelism. Steamboats had generally played an important role in the early colonization of the region and had also been used by the governments of Germany and Great Britain.[47] The steamboats frequently anchored in Nkholongue because the village served them as a "wooding station," as a place to buy the firewood needed for the engines. The most frequent guest in Nkholongue was the S.S. Chauncy Maples, known locally primarily by her acronym CM (see Figure 2). CM was the flagship of the Anglican mission. She had initially been designed and used as a floating combination of church, classroom, and hospital. From 1921 onward, however, she was used for transportation and communication work between the different stations of the mission around the lake. Timetables changed over time, but CM was a regular guest in Nkholongue from her maiden voyage in 1901 until her end of service in 1953. Table 3 provides an approximate overview of the frequency of stops in Nkholongue at various points in history.

Geography certainly contributed to the fact that Nkholongue served CM as a "wooding station." The village was ideally situated between two important centers of the Anglican mission, Messumba and Nkhotakota. Both Messumba and Metangula, with their adjacent steep mountains and relatively dense population were not suitable as "wooding stations." But Nkholongue, with its comparatively flat backcountry and limited population offered perfect conditions. Furthermore, the bay of Nkholongue protected the anchorage against the frequent southerly winds.[48] It is noteworthy that the mission's steamers used Nkholongue as a "wooding station" even between 1901 and 1912, when the mission was not allowed to have a school in Nkholongue because of the conflict it had with Chingomanje II (see Section 4.2). This further speaks to Nkholongue's suitability as a "wooding station," although it can also be assumed that the mission was interested in maintaining a foothold in this predominantly Muslim village.

---

46 Good, *The Steamer Parish*.
47 The Portuguese colonial state was the only one that never had any steamboat on the lake.
48 See as well: PA, I107: interview with *P1074* (♀, ~1940) (Malango, April 5, 2016), min 00:06:04–00:08:47; PA, I128: interview with *P1426* (♂, 1929) (Malindi (Mangochi District, Malawi), May 28, 2016), min 03:40:23–03:40:42.

6.2 The Rise and Fall of Nkholongue's Pottery Manufacture in the 1940s and 1950s

	Frequency of stops
before 1901	two stops per month by S.S. Charles Janson (CJ)[49]
1901–1914	two stops per month by S.S. CM,[50] plus occasional stops by S.S. CJ[51]
1914–1921	only occasional stops by S.S. CM and S.S. CJ[52] (CM commandeered by the British Government because of the war)
1921–1922	one stop per month by S.S. CM[53]
1922–c. 1930	no official stops[54] ("Wooding" at Metangula, because of orders by the *Companhia*[55])
c. 1930–1951	two stops per month by S.S. CM[56]
1952	one stop per month by S.S. CM[57]

Table 3: Stops of the Anglican steamboats in Nkholongue.

---

49 Regular stops are documented for 1896 and 1897 (despite its title, the logbook contains no entries for the years 1898–1901): AUMCA, UX 144: Log Book of S.S. "Charles Janson", 1896–1904.
50 Regular stops are documented for 1903–1906: AUMCA, A4(VI)1: Log of the S.S. "Chauncy Maples", 1903–1906.
51 AUMCA, UX 144: Log Book of S.S. "Charles Janson", 1896–1904.
52 CM's logbook lists only one stop by S.S. CM in Malango in 1918. For S.S. CJ, one stop is documented for April 1915. We can though assume that there were several undocumented stops: ASM, Chauncy Maples Log 1914–1924; Abdallah, "News from the Stations: VI. Unangu," *NDC*, no. 48 (July 1915): 22.
53 ASM, Chauncy Maples Log 1914–1924.
54 This is documented for 1922 to 1924 by the entries of CM's logbook and for 1928 by the official timetable. See: ASM, Chauncy Maples Log 1914–1924; MNA, UMCA 1/2/21: Order of Sailing S.S. Chauncy Maples, 1928 (Diocese of Nyasaland).
55 MNA, UMCA 1/2/17/1: Letter from A.F. Matthew to the Bishop, May 30, 1922.
56 Regular stops are documented for 1939 and 1949. We can assume that this timetable was in use from about 1931 when the government allowed the captain of S.S. CM to "make his own arrangements [regarding firewood] at as many places as he likes." We also have a documented occurrence of "wooding" at Nkholongue already for late 1930. See: H.A. Machell Cox, "News from the Stations: IV. Msumba," *NDC*, no. 110 (January 1931): 8–9; MNA, UMCA 1/2/20/13/1: Letter from H.A. Machell Cox to the Bishop (Luchimanje, July 29, 1931); Harry P. Liponde, "My Job: IV. Life on the 'Chauncy Maples,'" *CA* 57, no. 676 (1939): 65–68; MNA, 145/DOM/2/4/11: Order of Sailing S.S. Chauncy Maples, 1949 (Diocese of Nyasaland).
57 MNA, UMCA 1/2/22/3: Order of Sailing S.S. Chauncy Maples, 1952 (Diocese of Nyasaland).

		April	May	June	July	Aug.	Sept.	Oct.	Nov.	Dec.
M	Dep. Malindi	T 19	M 16	M 13	M 1	M 15	M 12	M 10	M 28	W 21
M	Bar Mponda's	19	16	13	18	15	12	10	28	
T	Mkope Nkudzi Malopa	20 W	17	14	19	16	13	11	29	
W	Nkhotakota	21 Th	18	15	20	17	14	12	30	
Th	**Chingomanje** Messumba	22 F	19	16	21	18	15	13	Dec. 1	
F	Ngoo Likoma	23 S	20	17	22	19	16	14	2	24
M	Mbamba Bay Liuli	25	23	20	25	22	19	17	5	27
T	Njambe Mkiri Mbaha Manda	26	24	21	26	23	20	18	6	28
Th	Njambe Liuli Mbamba Bay	28	26	23	28	25	22	20	8	29
F	Likoma	29	27	24	29	26	23	21	9	30
S	Ngoo Messumba	30	28	25	30	27	24	22	10	31
M	**Chingomanje** Nkhotakota	May 2	30	27	Aug. 1	29	26	24	12	Jan. 2
T	Chilowelo Malopa Pilidzinja	3	31	28	2	30	27	25	13	3
W	Mkope Bar Mponda's	4	June 1	29	3	31	28	26	14	4
Th	Malindi	5	2	30	4	Sept. 1	29	27	15	5

Table 4: Order of Sailing S.S. Chauncy Maples, 1949.

The importance attached to the steamboats in the daily lives of Nkholongue can be gathered from oral history. While the information from the interviews about the time before 1960 was as a rule rather sketchy, it proved to be surprisingly detailed as far as the steamboats were concerned. I still vividly remember how my third interview partner began to enumerate the ships he had seen navigating on the lake. He always emphasized whether the particular ship was powered by diesel or by firewood, a piece of information the importance of which I began to realize only later.[58] Also, people still remembered that CM always came from Nkhotakota on Thursday, which fits perfectly with CM's timetables of 1939, 1949, and 1952 (see the example of the 1949 timetable in Table 4).[59] One interviewee even stated that CM stopped in Nkholongue on its northbound trips on Thursday and southbound on Monday, an impressive accuracy for something that dates back more than 60 years, especially in a place where time and numbers usually led to numerous misunderstandings in the process of interviewing.[60] Undoubtedly, CM's timetables gave a rhythm to life in Nkholongue.

CM's regular stops in Nkholongue enabled the villagers to earn money by selling firewood they had cut, collected and dried. We have already seen in the previous chapter that the money people earned through CM could be used to pay taxes. The money was also used to buy products such as salt or clothes. In the early days, the missionaries even used salt and clothes as direct payment for firewood. This is noteworthy because salt and clothes competed with locally produced alternatives. In the case of clothing, this was the "traditional" bark cloth, locally called *chiwondo*. Some interviewees said they still wore *chiwondo* as children, but the basic tenor of my interviewees suggests that by the 1940s *chiwondo* had already largely disappeared around Nkholongue.[61] In the case of salt, the subsis-

---

[58] PA, I003: interview with *P0792 (♂, 1917)* (Nkholongue, August 20, 2010), min 01:45:32–01:50:56.
[59] This timetable is based on: MNA, 145/DOM/2/4/11: Order of Sailing S.S. Chauncy Maples, 1949 (Diocese of Nyasaland).
[60] PA, I001: interview with *P0050 (♂, ~1922)* (Nkholongue, August 17, 2010), min 01:06:47–01:07:00; PA, I007: interview with *P0298 (♀, ~1922)* (Nkholongue, September 1, 2010), min 00:30:12–00:32:10; PA, I004: interview with *P0147 (♀, ~1928), P0129 (♀, 1930)* (Nkholongue, August 25, 2010), min 00:27:37–00:27:52.
[61] PA, I008: interview with *P0299 (♂, 1938)* (Nkholongue, September 1, 2010), min 00:13:02–00:11:38; PA, I045: interview with *P0242 (♂, 1945)* (Malango, August 17, 2013), min 00:18:17–00:20:10; PA, I046: interview with *P1045 (♀, 1932)* (Malango, August 20, 2013), min 00:46:20–00:50:46; PA, I087: interview with *P1452 (♂, 1927)* (Lichinga, September 10, 2013), min 01:20:16–01:21:23; PA, I011: interview with *P0050 (♂, ~1922)* (Nkholongue, September 3, 2010), min 00:49:54–00:51:23; PA, I082: interview with *P1141 (♂, 1932)* (Malango, September 8, 2013), min 00:03:34–00:04:48; PA, I123: interview with *P1460 (♀), P1461 (♂, ~1935), P1462 (♂, ~1935)* (Meluluca, April 25, 2016), min 01:05:24–01:06:44. Around Metonia, some of the Wayao apparently still

Figure 2: CM during its "Golden Jubilee Voyage" in 1951. Source: "MV Chauncy Maples," Wikipedia, accessed April 20, 2019, https://en.wikipedia.org/w/index.php?title=MV_Chauncy_Maples&oldid= 881783935.

tence equivalent was a salt derived from plant ashes (potash), locally called *chidulo*. Evidence explicitly referring to Nkholongue documents how the salt brought by the steamer began to replace its locally produced alternative. In 1896, a missionary described the purchase of wood in Nkholongue as follows:

---

wore garments made of bark cloth in the 1940s. This fits with the testimony of an interviewee who claimed to have seen *chiwondo* only when Wayao from the *planalto* came to the lakeside to buy fish. See: "Mtonya," *CA* 61, no. 724 (1943): 46; PA, I058: interview with *P1074 (♀, ~1940)* (Malango, August 28, 2013), min 00:32:57–00:34:04. See as well the observations by Gerhard Liesegang, who stated that in some areas of northern Mozambique bark cloth was still in general use until the 1940s: Gerhard Liesegang, "A First Look at the Import and Export Trade of Mozambique, 1800–1914," in *Figuring African Trade: Proceedings of the Symposium on the Quantification and Structure of the Import and Export and Long Distance Trade in Africa 1800–1913*, ed. Gerhard Liesegang, Helma Pasch, and Adam Jones (Berlin: Dietrich Reimer, 1986), 493–494.

6.2 The Rise and Fall of Nkholongue's Pottery Manufacture in the 1940s and 1950s — 209

> In the afternoon I again went ashore to take a photo of the purchase of wood, a pinch of salt being given for each log brought. Native salt thus used, coarse dark stuff, which is made from the ashes of the burnt root of a water plant "mchele."[62]

CM's stops were more than just an opportunity to sell firewood. "Wooding" was time consuming. Since there was no pier, all the wood had to be first loaded on small tender boats and then transported by them to the steamer anchored off the beach. CM's "wooding" provided a platform for exchange for the residents of Nkholongue as well as the steamer's crew and passengers. The villagers of Nkholongue were able to purchase different goods.[63] These included salt, which by the 1940s was no longer used as payment for firewood but was traded by crew members.[64] Beside trades, there were also other forms of exchange. CM's captain, for example, offered the village a trap for catching lions after the villagers told him about problems with these animals.[65] One interviewee, who was still a child at the time, recounted how he and his friends would drive their canoes to the steamer, board it, and play with the children of the whites while the steamer was anchored at Nkholongue. Sometimes, he said, they received "little things."[66] In addition to this exchange of goods and ideas, CM's stops also facilitated people's mobility. Several of my interviewees used CM for their journeys.[67]

One of the most important functions of CM's stops in Nkholongue was that they provided the women of Nkholongue with an opportunity to sell their clay pots. Those became a most wanted and famous good. Or, as one interviewee put it: "Passengers coming [to Nkholongue], the first thing they wanted to get [was]

---

62 AUMCA, E2, f. 142: R. Webb, "African Tour May 1896 – Nov. 1896," 126–127.
63 PA, I093: interview with *P0050 (♂, ~1922)* (Nkholongue, January 19, 2016), min 00:21:27–00:22:17; MLM, 018: interview with *L. M.*, transcript Chinyanja (Malango, June 27, 2007).
64 PA, I128: interview with *P1426 (♂, 1929)* (Malindi (Mangochi District, Malawi), May 28, 2016), min 03:40:42–03:40:56; PA, I002: interview with *P0128 (♂, 1928)* (Nkholongue, August 18, 2010), min 00:37:04–00:37:24; PA, I007: interview with *P0298 (♀, ~1922)* (Nkholongue, September 1, 2010), min 00:30:12–00:31:05.
65 PA, I014: interview with *P0147 (♀, ~1928), P0129 (♀, 1930)* (Nkholongue, September 8, 2010), min 00:12:07–00:13:01; PA, I015: interview with *P0367 (♂, 1936)* (Nkholongue, September 9, 2010), min 00:38:17–00:39:52. The trap was still in the village at the time of fieldwork and was in the possession of Chief Chingomanje VIII.
66 PA, I105: interview with *P0242 (♂, 1945)* (Malango, April 4, 2016), min 00:06:42–00:09:27.
67 PA, I053: interview with *P0189 (♀, 1940)* (Nkholongue, August 27, 2013), min 00:09:08–00:10:18; PA, I113: interview with *P0367 (♂, 1936)* (Nkholongue, April 13, 2016), min 02:52:30–02:59:05; PA, I093: interview with *P0050 (♂, ~1922)* (Nkholongue, January 19, 2016), min 00:11:11–00:12:39; PA, I004: interview with *P0147 (♀, ~1928), P0129 (♀, 1930)* (Nkholongue, August 25, 2010), min 00:28:14–00:29:11; PA, I111: interview with *P0266 (♂, ~1932)* (Metangula, April 11, 2016), min 01:24:46–01:25:18.

pots."⁶⁸ Little is known about the origins of the fame of Nkholongue's pottery.⁶⁹ However, CM's stops at Nkholongue were certainly an important factor, if not in the creation, at least in the rise of the pottery market. Already in 1921, the Anglican missionary William Percival Johnson wrote that the pots "of Nkholongue village are so good that they are coveted by the women as far off as Monkey Bay,"⁷⁰ an impressive 90 miles from Nkholongue as the crow flies. Many years later, the pots of Nkholongue were even worth a comment to Henry Masauko Chipembere, the most important political opponent of Malawi's first president Hastings Kamuzu Banda. Chipembere praised the pottery of Nkholongue, saying that the people of Nkholongue "make pots and other cooking or water keeping utensils of a quality that has not been seen anywhere else in central and East Africa."⁷¹

While pottery was the main attraction for passengers traveling on CM, the people of Nkholongue also sold other handicraft. Interviewees particularly emphasized the role of ivory carving. In 1949, one British visitor traveling on CM described how "Africans came on board selling beautifully-made waterpots of brown earth with polished blacklead necks, which looked like silver" when the steamer was "wooding" at Nkholongue.⁷² And in 1951, another passenger of CM reported that a "boat-load [of pots] was put aboard for some Church Dignitary further up the lake" when they were at Nkholongue, and further: "The Natives also do Silver Work, carve in Ivory and make Palm Mats."⁷³

---

68 PA, I128: interview with *P1426* (♂, 1929) (Malindi (Mangochi District, Malawi), May 28, 2016), min 03:41:06 – 03:41:25.

69 One interviewee claimed that her ancestors had already brought the skill with them from Nkhotakota. See: PA, I128: interview with *P1426* (♂, 1929) (Malindi (Mangochi District, Malawi), May 28, 2016), min 03:41:28 – 03:41:33.

70 It is "Chikole" in the original. See: Johnson, *The Great Water*, 62. Johnson mentioned the pots of Nkholongue in the same breath as the pots at the north end of the lake, most probably referring to the pots of Ikombe, which have remained famous to this day and have also received considerable scholarly attention. On Ikombe pottery, see: Sac Waane, "Pottery-Making Traditions of the Ikombe Kisi, Mbeya Region, Tanzania," *Baessler-Archiv* 25 (1977): 251–317; Eginald Mihanjo, "Transformation of the Kisi Pottery Enterprise in Southwest Tanzania," in *Negotiating Social Space: East African Microenterprises*, ed. Patrick O. Alila and Poul O. Pedersen (Trenton: Africa World Press, 2001), 273–290; Shakila Halifan Mteti, "Engendering Pottery Production and Distribution Processes among the Kisi and Pare of Tanzania," *International Journal of Gender and Women's Studies* 4, no. 2 (2016): 127–141.

71 It is "Nkholongwe" in the original. See: Henry B.M. Chipembere, *My Malawian Ancestors*, 1969, 11.

72 Sybil Baber, "Journey up Lake Nyasa," *CA* 68, no. 807 (1950): 43–45.

73 The capital letters are as in the original. See: Ralph J. Whiteman, "A Traveller's Letter Home: Jubilee Voyage of the 'SS Chauncy Maples' (Written in October 1951)," June 2011, 6, accessed August 9, 2011, http://www.chauncymaples.org/newsletter/chauncy_maples_jubilee_voyage.pdf.

6.2 The Rise and Fall of Nkholongue's Pottery Manufacture in the 1940s and 1950s

The production of goods for CM was clearly gendered. Pottery was women's work. Ivory carving and cutting firewood was done by men.[74] The latter is noteworthy because cutting firewood for domestic use was and remained a female task.[75] One interviewee explained this difference by the different type of wood needed for CM.[76] However, nowadays, fuelwood-cutting (for cooking) is also done by men if it is for sale. It can therefore be assumed that the male domain in firewood cutting for CM was also due to a more general idea of women's work belonging to the domestic sphere. It is all the more interesting that pottery remained women's work.

This becomes even more evident when one considers that the importance of Nkholongue's pottery went beyond that of a supplementary income. For the pots were not only sold for money to the passengers of CM, but also bartered for food, especially cassava, in other villages along the lakeshore.[77] An 86-year-old woman recounted:

> In our culture, since our ancestors, our mothers who gave birth to us, and even our grandmothers, agriculture was not so important. In their custom, they placed much faith in pots. These pots, we carried them on our heads to Metangula and sold[78] them there for food.[79]

The importance of the pot production for food procurement was also emphasized by James Amanze, professor of theology at the University of Botswana and a descendant from Nkholongue on his father's side. He described the significance of Nkholongue's pottery as follows:

---

[74] PA, I093: interview with *P0050* (♂, *~1922*) (Nkholongue, January 19, 2016), min 00:23:32–00:29:27; PA, I106: interview with *P0262* (♀, *~1940*) (Malango, April 4, 2016), min 00:20:02–00:24:13; PA, I035: interview with *P0743* (♀, *~1930*), *P0765* (♀, *~1932*) (Nkholongue, July 28, 2012), min 00:39:41–00:43:24.
[75] My findings put into question the claim by Charles Good that the cutting of firewood for the steamer was women's work. See: Good, *The Steamer Parish*, 178.
[76] PA, I108: interview with *P1074* (♀, *~1940*) (Malango, April 6, 2016), min 00:13:36–00:19:26.
[77] PA, I112: interview with *P0129* (♀, *1930*), *P0128* (♂, *1928*) (Nkholongue, April 12, 2016), min 00:03:13–00:03:38; PA, I138: interview with *P1498* (♂, *1940*) (Nkhotakota, June 2, 2016), min 00:15:08–00:15:22; PA, I105: interview with *P0242* (♂, *1945*) (Malango, April 4, 2016), min 00:55:49–01:06:40; PA, I106: interview with *P0262* (♀, *~1940*) (Malango, April 4, 2016), min 01:58:37–02:05:20.
[78] The word used in the Chinyanja original is *kugulitsa*, which corresponds to the English "to sell," and differs from the Chinyanja expression for "to barter," which is *kusinthanitsa*. However, the description of process shows that, as a rule, this was a direct exchange of different goods not including the exchange of money.
[79] PA, I112: interview with *P0129* (♀, *1930*), *P0128* (♂, *1928*) (Nkholongue, April 12, 2016), min 00:01:59–00:02:29.

> The women were extremely skilled in making pots from clay. They were very skilled indeed the best in the entire region. Because Nkholongue was not good for agriculture women used to carry lots and lots of pots on their backs and heads and go to sell them at Micuio, Metangula, Chuanga, Chia and sometimes all the way to Ngoo. They used to exchange their pots for food. This became their lifetime work and there was a lot of competition on making these pots.[80]

The information from the interviews differed slightly as to the origins of this bartering of pots for food. Some interviewees, like the 86-year-old woman quoted above, described it as a conscious way of life, as a part of their ancestors' customs.[81] Others, however, emphasized the necessity, and pointed out that the reason for the barter was a lack of food.[82] It is plausible that these different perceptions relate to different times, for making a living by pottery became increasingly impractical in the 1950s.[83] This change was caused, at least in part, by the end of CM.

The End of CM and the Refounding of Malango

There were several reasons for the end of the steamer era in Nkholongue. For one of my interviewees, born in 1936, the main reason was however obvious:

> By the time, when CM, it was moving here continuously, I was young like this one (pointing to a boy). Then, when it changed, not coming here, it's now, ourselves we are grown up and by then it was using fuel. And at first, they were using firewood. So, they changed now to be using fuel. So here, they stopped it, not coming here.[84]

What this interviewee reflected on here was the change in technology that was happening at the time. M.V. *Ilala*, for example, the lake's new "flagship," commis-

---

[80] It is "Nkholongwe," "Mikuyu," "Mtengula," and "Chiwanga" in the original. See: PA, James Amanze, "Nkholongue Village, Niassa," email, May 5, 2018.
[81] For other examples, see: PA, I138: interview with P1498 (♂, 1940) (Nkhotakota, June 2, 2016), min 00:15:08 – 00:15:22, 00:19:34 – 00:19:46; PA, I105: interview with P0242 (♂, 1945) (Malango, April 4, 2016), min 00:58:36 – 00:59:23, 01:04:52 – 01:05:45.
[82] PA, I057: interview with P0262 (♀, ~1940) (Malango, August 28, 2013), min 01:11:23 – 01:13:12; PA, I105: interview with P0242 (♂, 1945) (Malango, April 4, 2016), min 00:55:49 – 00:57:20.
[83] Locally produced pots were (still) in high demand among the population in the 1940s, especially during World War Two. Monica Wilson pointed out that the trade in pots at the north end of the lake increased during the war because imported goods were scarce. See: Monica Wilson, *For Men and Elders: Change in the Relations of Generations and of Men and Women among the Nyakyusa-Ngonde People, 1875 – 1971* (New York: Africana, 1977), 11.
[84] PA, I013: interview with P0367 (♂, 1936) (Nkholongue, September 8, 2010), min 00:25:14 – 00:25:47.

6.2 The Rise and Fall of Nkholongue's Pottery Manufacture in the 1940s and 1950s — 213

sioned in 1951 for the transport company Nyasaland Railways was not a steamship running on firewood like most previous vessels, but a motor ship powered by a diesel engine.[85]

The immediate reason for the end of CM, however, was not this change in technology, but the fact that it had become too expensive for the mission to operate the steamer. Compared to the heydays of missionary work at the end of the 19th century, it had become increasingly difficult to raise money in Europe for such projects.[86] Furthermore, the institutionalization of the church and the growing infrastructure such as roads, telegraphs etc. had reduced the need for the mission to have its own CM-sized steamer.[87]

CM made its last trip for the mission in 1953. After that, some transport was taken over by a small schooner, the M.V. Paul. But this boat, which had been converted to diesel propulsion in 1953, no longer had a need to go to Nkholongue.[88] CM was sold in 1956 to a Rhodesian company which used her for fishing in the British waters of the lake. It was only after the government of Malawi had bought CM to use her as a passenger ship that her steam engine was finally replaced by a diesel engine in 1965. So, although somewhat inaccurate in the specific case of CM, my interviewee had a very correct perception of the general trend: global technical progress, combined with economic and cultural developments at other places around the world cut Nkholongue off from the most technically advanced transport infrastructure it ever had.

The end of the steamer era had a significant impact on life in Nkholongue. Even if direct causalities are difficult to substantiate, there is no doubt that it fueled a change in settlement patterns that was connected to a growing importance of subsistence food production. We have already discussed the point that Nkholongue was also affected by the dispersal of settlements after colonization (see Section 4.3). Between the 1890s and 1950, several people had left the village and moved to other places such as Malango or Malo. Nevertheless, it must be emphasized that Nkholongue remained or returned to being a comparatively compact settlement in the 1940s.[89] According to my interviewees, most houses were located on the plain around the small peninsula of Linga between the two intermittent creeks

---

85 P.A. Cole-King, *Lake Malawi Steamers* (Limbe: Department of Antiquities, 1987).
86 The UMCA was struck by a financial crisis after World War Two: Good, *The Steamer Parish*, 206.
87 Good, 205–213.
88 Good, 212.
89 The sources do not allow us to say how Nkholongue's spatial organization changed from 1900 to the 1940s. We must therefore keep in mind the possibility that there were processes of disaggregation, which were then again followed by processes of aggregation.

of Nkholongue and Cabendula (see Figure 3 and Map 3).[90] In 1951, António Serrano, a member of the MCT (Mission for the Combat of the Trypanosomiasis, see Section 5.4), described Nkholongue as a large village situated on a small plain cultivated with cassava.[91] "Large village" here does not refer to the large number of inhabitants of the community, but precisely to the comparatively large settlement. The statistics clearly show that Chingomanje's chiefdom had few inhabitants compared to other neighboring communities.[92] However, while other chiefdoms of the region were spread over various hamlets, Nkholongue's population was concentrated in one relatively compact village.

We can assume that Nkholongue remained so compact because the regular stops of CM had made the village's inhabitants less dependent on agriculture than other people in the region. In any case, the end of CM set in motion what was probably the most massive change in Nkholongue's spatial organization since the village had been first founded in the 19th century. During the 1950s, most of Nkholongue's population left the previous location of the village. Some migrated south to neighboring village of M'chepa, but the majority migrated north to the creek of Malango. When the Portuguese forces resettled the population of Nkholongue in 1966 during the Mozambican War of Independence, the majority of Nkholongue's population, including the village's chief, did not live at the previous location of the village but precisely around the bay of Malango.[93]

We have already dealt with another "emigration wave" to Malango, that of Salimo Chingomanje in the 1890s (see Sections 3.3 and 4.3). Salimo is said to have lived in Malango until his death. But as already mentioned, his son Saide Salimo left Malango with his family to live in Matawale and later in Mtucula. Information from my interviews indicates that no one resided in Malango after Saide Salimo's departure.[94] António Serrano's article on the local outbreak of the sleeping sickness con-

---

[90] PA, I107: interview with *P1074* (♀, *~1940*) (Malango, April 5, 2016), min 00:51:21–01:36:01, 02:08:12–02:53:11; PA, I111: interview with *P0266* (♂, *~1932*) (Metangula, April 11, 2016), min 00:08:56–00:15:08; PA, I112: interview with *P0129* (♀, *1930*), *P0128* (♂, *1928*) (Nkholongue, April 12, 2016), min 01:18:12–01:21:27; PA, I113: interview with *P0367* (♂, *1936*) (Nkholongue, April 13, 2016), min 00:46:43–00:57:15.
[91] Serrano, "Um reconhecimento no Distrito do Lago," 673.
[92] See Table 2 on p. 160.
[93] PA, I153: interview with *P1477* (♂, *~1940*) (Micucue, June 17, 2016), min 00:35:38–00:36:12; PA, I113: interview with *P0367* (♂, *1936*) (Nkholongue, April 13, 2016), min 00:39:34–00:40:21; PA, I115: interview with *P0160* (♂, *1952*) (Metangula, April 18, 2016), min 01:35:31–01:35:55.
[94] PA, I111: interview with *P0266* (♂, *~1932*) (Metangula, April 11, 2016), min 00:05:55–00:08:34; PA, I107: interview with *P1074* (♀, *~1940*) (Malango, April 5, 2016), min 01:41:22–01:41:51.

firms that no one lived there in 1950.[95] The emigration to Malango and M'chepa was not a sudden event but a gradual move. Interviewees indicated that they initially only tilled fields and had temporary houses (*chisani*) here. Only after some time did they move to Malango permanently.[96] The first migrants seem to have left Nkholongue around 1953. Towards the end of the 1950s, people living in Malango began to outnumber people living in Nkholongue.[97]

Figure 3: Aerial view of Nkholongue showing the plain between the creeks of Nkholongue and Cabendula. The bay of Malango can be seen in the top left of the photograph. Photograph taken by Robert Layng in 2010.

Most of my interviewees did not make a causal connection between the cessation of CM and their emigration to Malango or M'chepa. Rather, they stated that they went to Malango to look for new fields because they suffered from hunger in

---

[95] Serrano's detailed maps do not show a settlement on the Malango. Likewise, he did not mention one. The omission would be odd, since it is precisely the creek of Malango that is mentioned in his article as a "frontier" of the sleeping sickness. His article is dated January 24, 1951. See: Serrano, "Um reconhecimento no Distrito do Lago."
[96] PA, I135: interview with *P1494* (♂, *1942*) (Nkhotakota, June 2, 2016), min 00:40:14–00:41:27; PA, I058: interview with *P1074* (♀, *~1940*) (Malango, August 28, 2013), min 01:07:47–01:10:55.
[97] PA, I113: interview with *P0367* (♂, *1936*) (Nkholongue, April 13, 2016), min 00:33:40–00:35:24; PA, I120: interview with *P1102* (♂, *1932*) (Malango, April 21, 2016), min 00:03:50–00:04:38; PA, I135: interview with *P1494* (♂, *1942*) (Nkhotakota, June 2, 2016), min 00:40:14–00:41:27.

Map 3: Modern-day Nkholongue and the previous location of the village around Linga. Please note that the creeks/rivers on the map are all intermittent ones that flow only during rainy season. Map by the author using Map data©2019 from Google Maps.

Nkholongue.⁹⁸ The reasons given for the origins of this food scarcity vary slightly. Many cited some sort of soil degradation.⁹⁹ Others pointed to the fact that the people simply were not growing enough crops,¹⁰⁰ while some linked it to the rising lake level that had destroyed homes and fields.¹⁰¹

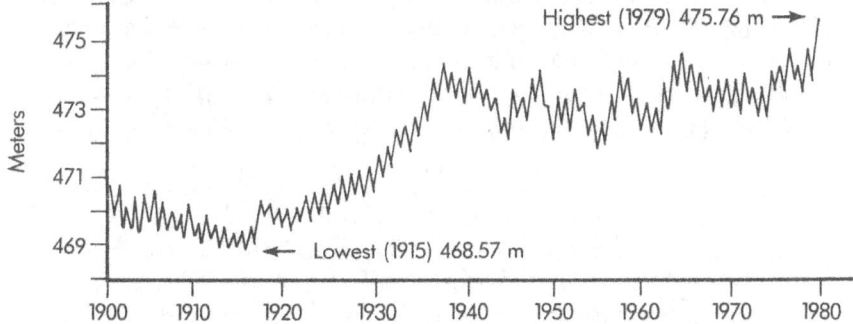

Figure 4: Level of Lake Malawi, 1900–1980. Source: Elias C. Mandala, Work and Control in a Peasant Economy: A History of the Lower Tchiri Valley in Malawi, 1859–1960 (Madison: University of Wisconsin Press, 1990), 6. Reprinted by permission of the University of Wisconsin Press. © 1990 by the Board of Regents of the University of Wisconsin System. All rights reserved.

It is difficult to determine a definite causal chain, but we can be fairly certain that different factors fueled each other and that the cessation of CM exacerbated an already critical situation. The rise of the lake level by up to five meters is well documented by many different sources. It destroyed houses and fields alike and forced people to retreat inland.¹⁰² It thus also reduced the size of Nkholongue's already

---

98 PA, I109: interview with *P1081* (♀, *1945*) (Malango, April 6, 2016), min 00:30:15–00:30:55; PA, I118: interview with *P1218* (♀, *1930*) (Malango, April 21, 2016), min 01:20:22–01:21:06.
99 PA, I116: interview with *P1457* (♀) (Metangula, April 18, 2016), min 00:44:44–00:44:55; PA, I057: interview with *P0262* (♀, *~1940*) (Malango, August 28, 2013), min 01:11:23–01:13:12; PA, I118: interview with *P1218* (♀, *1930*) (Malango, April 21, 2016), min 01:20:22–01:21:06; PA, I109: interview with *P1081* (♀, *1945*) (Malango, April 6, 2016), min 00:11:40–00:12:07.
100 PA, I112: interview with *P0129* (♀, *1930*), *P0128* (♂, *1928*) (Nkholongue, April 12, 2016), min 01:14:18–01:15:35; PA, I106: interview with *P0262* (♀, *~1940*) (Malango, April 4, 2016), min 02:03:04–02:04:09; PA, I100: interview with *P0025* (♀, *1948*) (Nkholongue, February 22, 2016), min 00:04:52–00:05:13, 00:08:38–00:09:18.
101 PA, I048: interview with *P1446* (♂, *~1945*) (Metangula, August 21, 2013), min 00:01:44–00:02:40; PA, I058: interview with *P1074* (♀, *~1940*) (Malango, August 28, 2013), min 01:07:47–01:10:55.
102 For evidence from the interviews, see: PA, I004: interview with *P0147* (♀, *~1928*), *P0129* (♀, *1930*) (Nkholongue, August 25, 2010), min 00:10:13–00:11:33; PA, I002: interview with *P0128* (♂, *1928*) (Nkholongue, August 18, 2010), min 01:04.30–01:06:57; PA, I001: interview with *P0050* (♂,

small plain. But it was certainly not a direct cause for the emigration. For, as Figure 4 shows, the rise of the lake level took place before 1940.[103] It is evident that the rise added pressure on the land. The fact that there was a significant degree of soil degradation in Nkholongue is confirmed not only by oral history but also by the statement of a European passenger on CM who wrote in 1951 that there was "a tremendous amount of erosion."[104] It is obvious that the ongoing degradation of the soil in Nkholongue increased people's dependence on trade and barter to obtain food. With the cessation of CM, one important part of the income disappeared and all the pressure shifted to bartering with neighboring villages.[105] It seems that the pressure became too intense, not only because people no longer felt safe but also because their increasing need to barter pots for food was not welcome in other places. One interviewee stated that it was Chilombe, the chief of Metangula, who forbade them to come to Metangula and sell their pots. According to her, this was why people started going to Malango to grow cassava.[106]

Emigration to Malango and M'chepa went hand in hand with an increase in the importance of agriculture and thus a decrease in the importance of pottery. One interviewee explicitly referred to the fact that in Malango they did farm and no longer go to other places to exchange pots for food.[107] Thus, the 1950s saw a growing emphasis on subsistence food production.

However, the increasing importance of subsistence food production did not lead to a general decoupling of Nkholongue's population from the market. Money was still needed to pay the taxes, and the appetite of Nkholongue's population for goods such as clothes had not disappeared. On the contrary, the region around Nkholongue does not seem to have been exempt from the worldwide emer-

---

~1922) (Nkholongue, August 17, 2010), min 01:23:00–01:23:54; PA, I104: interview with *P0298* (♀, ~1922) (Nkholongue, March 1, 2016), min 00:42:54–00:44:18.
103 The chronology of the rise is also documented by reports of the Anglican missionaries based in Messumba: "News from the Stations: V. Msumba," *NDC*, no. 116 (July 1932): 16–17; "News from the Stations: V. Msumba," *NDC*, no. 119 (April 1933): 9; "News from the Stations: V. Msumba," *NDC*, no. 127 (April 1935): 7–8; "News from the Stations: V. Msumba," *NDC*, no. 134 (June 1937): 8–10.
104 Whiteman, "Traveller's Letter Home," 26.
105 One interview partner was quite explicit about this causality: PA, I120: interview with *P1102* (♂, *1932*) (Malango, April 21, 2016), min 01:25:25–01:25:50.
106 PA, I072: interview with *P0262* (♀, *~1940*) (Malango, September 5, 2013), min 00:26:35–00:29:56; PA, I106: interview with *P0262* (♀, *~1940*) (Malango, April 4, 2016), min 01:58:50–02:00:35.
107 PA, I105: interview with *P0242* (♂, *1945*) (Malango, April 4, 2016), min 01:07:25–01:07:29. For others who mainly highlighted the increasing importance of agriculture in Malango in general, see: PA, I100: interview with *P0025* (♀, *1948*) (Nkholongue, February 22, 2016), min 00:04:52–00:05:13; PA, I112: interview with *P0129* (♀, *1930*), *P0128* (♂, *1928*) (Nkholongue, April 12, 2016), min 01:14:15–01:17:34.

gence of a consumer society at that time.[108] New desires and lifestyles were the result. Tailoring, for example, had become a most popular apprenticeship around that time.[109] Two of my interviewees had traveled to Nkhotakota with CM in the 1940s, learnt tailoring there, and brought home a sewing machine.[110] In Metangula, an "Indian" trader named Osman had opened a store around the same time, selling clothes, sugar, and salt, among other things.[111] For most of those born before the 1950s, Osman's store was a prominent and positive reference point in the interviews, which can be clearly taken as a sign of the centrality of growing consumer aspirations in the population.[112]

What people lost with the end of CM was an important place to generate income. The demand for firewood had evaporated and the sale of handicraft lost its main market. People had to find new ways to generate income to pay taxes and buy consumer goods. And they did. Compared to their fellow craftswomen, the village's ivory carvers seem to have been more successful in taking their business to

---

108 On the fact that these developments also occurred elsewhere in rural Africa, see: Korieh, *The Land Has Changed*, 193–194.
109 Around Nkholongue, tailoring was and is a male profession. One interviewee stated that, for a woman, it was only possible in Messumba to be a tailor. It is therefore possible that, around Messumba, Christian missionaries promoted this as a female profession. This would, however, require further investigation. See: PA, I114: interview with *P1074* (♀, ~1940), *P1141* (♂, 1932) (Malango, April 15, 2016), min 02:30:53–02:32:10. For interviewees who learned to tailor, see: PA, I005: interview with *P0641* (♂, 1952) (Nkholongue, August 27, 2010), 00:13:40–00:16:55; PA, I066: interview with *P0085* (♂, 1960) (Nkholongue, September 1, 2013), min 00:05:20–00:12:18; PA, I141: interview with *P0375* (♂, 1962) (Nkholongue, June 6, 2016), min 00:29:45–00:31:18; PA, I099: interview with *P1420* (♂, ~1922) (Ngongo, February 16, 2016), min 00:58:24–00:58:57. For another villager who learned to tailor, see: MLM, 018: interview with *L. M.*, transcript Chinyanja (Malango, June 27, 2007).
110 PA, I011: interview with *P0050* (♂, ~1922) (Nkholongue, September 3, 2010), min 00:00:00–00:07:49; PA, I002: interview with *P0128* (♂, 1928) (Nkholongue, August 18, 2010), min 00:13:33–00:16:00, 00:41:50–00:42:17.
111 According to the information provided by an interviewee, it can be assumed that this was a branch of Osman Adam LTD, a trading company based in Blantyre (Malawi), as he explicitly named the store "Osman Adam" and not just "Osman." However, since this interviewee spent a long time of his life in Nyasaland, and Osman Adam LTD was a prominent company there, it is also possible that he simply got something mixed up. The fact that the same interviewee also reported that Osman of Metangula obtained his goods in Tanganyika rather contradicts the version that Osman of Metangula was a branch of a Nyasaland-based company. See: PA, I010: interview with *P0792* (♂, 1917) (Nkholongue, September 3, 2010), min 00:28:42–00:37:23.
112 PA, I038: interview with *P1439* (♂, ~1940) (Malango, August 15, 2013), min 01:21:07–01:22:46; PA, I046: interview with *P1045* (♀, 1932) (Malango, August 20, 2013), min 00:46:20–00:50:46; PA, I004: interview with *P0147* (♀, ~1928), *P0129* (♀, 1930) (Nkholongue, August 25, 2010), min 00:53:32–00:57:42; PA, I007: interview with *P0298* (♀, ~1922) (Nkholongue, September 1, 2010), min 00:13:11–00:16:18.

other places. Since ivory carvers were more mobile than their fellow craftswomen, they were able to travel around and offer their skills elsewhere.¹¹³ While little is known about the mobility of carvers prior to the cessation of CM, it can be observed that after 1953 at least two important ivory carvers from Nkholongue moved to work outside the village. One of them went to Mandimba to work at the house of a Portuguese cotton functionary and the other went to live near Lupilichi at the camp of some Portuguese hunters.¹¹⁴

Male labor migration seems to have generally increased after the end of CM. One interviewee born in 1936 stated:

> I have already told you about the job of our ancestors, the job of the steamer, this one of CM, right? [I told you t]hat our ancestors received from that job. Well, when we began to mature, that job no longer existed. We could only go to Nyasaland and do the job there [...].¹¹⁵

While there are no data on the changing importance of labor migration in the long run,¹¹⁶ the growing importance of labor migration in the 1950s appears to have been a development that was not limited just to Nkholongue but affected the wider region. As mentioned in the previous chapter, labor migration to Nyasaland and South Africa had begun to play a role after the introduction of the hut tax in 1903. By the 1950s and early 1960s, labor migration had become so widespread that it was considered part of the standard curriculum of a young man. Of my interviewees who were adults at the time of the outbreak of the War of Independence, almost all had gone abroad at least once on labor migration. Some of them migrated permanently and never returned to Nkholongue or returned very late in their

---

113 The mobility of potters was limited, as the quality of the pots depended not only on their skill but also on the quality of the clay that could be used. Cultural reasons may have also contributed to the fact that men were able to move around more easily than women.

114 For the one who went to Mandimba, see: PA, I113: interview with *P0367 (♂, 1936)* (Nkholongue, April 13, 2016), min 00:04:20–00:09:17, 00:17:27–00:18:58. For the one who went to Lupilichi, see: PA, I040: interview with *P1030 (♀, 1965), P1009 (♀, 1958), P1029 (♂, ~1959)* (Malango, August 16, 2013), min 00:07:11–00:27:27; AHD, MU/GM/GNP/RNP/0032/00342: PIDE Moçambique, "Informação N.° 996 – SC/CI(2)," September 30, 1969, 1. See as well: PA, James Amanze, "Nkholongue Village, Niassa," email, May 5, 2018.

115 PA, I154: interview with *P0367 (♂, 1936), P0373 (♀, 1940)* (Nkholongue, June 18, 2016), min 00:37:38–00:40:46.

116 An isolated collective recruitment contract from 1912 that I found in the holdings of the AHM lists workers from Lussefa, Ngolocolo, and Metangula, but none from Nkholongue. See: AHM, SNI, cx. 745, Anno de 1912, Processo 3: [Labour contract], July 16, 1912.

lives.[117] The same is true for the same age cohort of interviewees from other villages of the region.[118]

An idea of the extent of labor migration at that time can also be gained from population statistics (see Table 5). The 1957 tax census for the administrative post of Metangula includes only 66 adult men for every 100 adult women. While part of this striking ratio can certainly be explained by tax evasion,[119] we can assume that, in the 1950s, the difference was mainly due to labor migration. Presuming an equal ratio of the sexes in society, more than 1,000 men are missing from the 1958 tax census. In other words, 20 percent of the male population were absent. Considering that not all labor migrants were permanently absent (and thus may have been included in the tax census), the level of absenteeism could even have been considerably higher at certain times of the year. In line with this, the Portuguese geographer Raquel Soeiro de Brito, who visited the region in the early 1960s, noted that "almost all Anyanja emigrate temporarily."[120]

---

117 For those who went to South Africa, see: PA, I038: interview with P1439 (♂, ~1940) (Malango, August 15, 2013), min 00:13:18–00:13:55; PA, I056: interview with P1102 (♂, 1932) (Malango, August 28, 2013), min 00:00:16–00:01:52; PA, I013: interview with P0367 (♂, 1936) (Nkholongue, September 8, 2010), min 00:13:41–00:23:04; PA, I087: interview with P1452 (♂, 1927) (Lichinga, September 10, 2013), min 00:22:13–00:26:52. For labor migrants with other destinations (including Nyasaland, Tanganyika, Southern and Northern Rhodesia), see: PA, I093: interview with P0050 (♂, ~1922) (Nkholongue, January 19, 2016), min 01:59:59–02:01:33; PA, I002: interview with P0128 (♂, 1928) (Nkholongue, August 18, 2010), min 00:13:33–00:16:00; PA, I003: interview with P0792 (♂, 1917) (Nkholongue, August 20, 2010), min 01:07:59–01:14:53, 01:20:22–01:33:01; PA, I048: interview with P1446 (♂, ~1945) (Metangula, August 21, 2013), min 00:28:35–00:29:45. For an exception who did not go abroad, see: PA, I111: interview with P0266 (♂, ~1932) (Metangula, April 11, 2016), min 01:20:03–01:20:56.
118 PA, I123: interview with P1460 (♀), P1461 (♂, ~1935), P1462 (♂, ~1935) (Meluluca, April 25, 2016), min 01:01:48–01:05:24; PA, I149: interview with P1501 (♂, 1949), P1513 (♂, 1943) (Chinuni, June 11, 2016), min 00:16:49–00:18:12; PA, I152: interview with P1476 (♂, ~1935) (Milombe, June 16, 2016), 00:28:25–00:39:45; PA, I094: interview with P0727 (♂, ~1940) (M'chepa, January 27, 2016), min 00:24:46–00:26:13; PA, I099: interview with P1420 (♂, ~1922) (Ngongo, February 16, 2016), min 00:48:27–00:48:51. One could also add the labor migrants interviewed by the oral history projects of Arianna Huhn and the AHM. For examples, see: MLM, 018: interview with L. M., transcript Chinyanja (Malango, June 27, 2007); AHM, Secção Oral, Cassettes N.° 157–159: Entrevista com um grupo de velhos de Seli (Metangula), interview by Gerhard Liesegang, Teresa Oliveira, and Mujuane Mainga Vicente, July 22, 1981, N.° 159B: 308–399. For an exception, see: PA, I063: interview with P1488 (♂, ~1930) (M'chepa, August 31, 2013), min 00:07:10–00:07:40.
119 One indication of this is the higher number of underage men compared with the number of underage women. But the large differences between the 1957 and 1958 census in the number of minors also point to the fact that non-taxpayers may have been generally underrepresented in these censuses. This is also suggested by the low number of children in general.
120 Raquel Soeiro de Brito, *No trilho dos descobrimentos: Estudos geográficos* (Lisboa: Comissão Nacional para as Comemorações dos Descobrimentos Portugueses, 1997), 199. Such a picture was

	1957		1958	
Total	9,686		10,682	
Men	4,305	80 men per 100 women	4,893	85 men per 100 women
Women	5,381		5,789	
Adults	6,137		6,247	
Men >18	2,434	66 adult men per 100 adult women	2,561	69 adult men per 100 adult women
Women >18	3,678		3,686	
Children	3,597		4,435	
Men <18	1,871	110 boys per 100 girls	2,332	111 boys per 100 girls
Women <18	1,703		2,103	

Table 5: Tax censuses of the administrative post of Metangula, 1957–1958.[121]

One of the most popular destinations for labor migration was South Africa.[122] This is surprising because, as has already been discussed in the previous chapter, there was actually no more official recruitment for the Rand mines along the lakeshore after 1912. Such recruitment had even been prohibited for about two decades. However, this did not stop people from going there on their own. They now simply went to Nyasaland and joined Wenela,[123] the South African labor agency there.[124]

This shows the importance of people's agency in upholding labor migration to the mines. In line with this and what has been said above about the growing consumer aspirations, most labor migrants explained their migration less in terms of the need to get the tax money than in terms of their desire to get clothes and con-

---

not uncommon in the larger region. In Zambia's Eastern Province, the percentage of adult males who were absent from home was reportedly 60 percent in 1958. See: Jim Pletcher, "Ecological Deterioration and Agricultural Stagnation in Eastern Province, Zambia," *The Centennial Review* 35, no. 2 (1991): 375.

121 AHM, SNI, cx. 66, A/23/4/10 1959–1962: Mapa comparativo dos recenseamentos dos anos de 1957 e de 1958: Circunscrição de Maniamba (Maniamba, December 31, 1958).
122 See Footnotes 117 and 118.
123 Wenela was the popular name of the Witwatersrand Native Labour Association.
124 Alexopoulou and Juif have shown that the prohibition "did not prevent residents of the northern districts from travelling to the recruitment stations [in the southern districts.]" However, the fact that people also went to recruitment stations abroad does not seem to have been taken into account in their reflections. See: Kleoniki Alexopoulou and Dácil Juif, "Colonial State Formation without Integration: Tax Capacity and Labour Regimes in Portuguese Mozambique (1890s–1970s)," *International Review of Social History* 62, no. 2 (August 2017): 215–252.

sumer goods.¹²⁵ Or, as one person from Malango interviewed by Arianna Huhn, put it:

> We went to Nyasaland because we wanted to dress well. For, that time, there was no job here.¹²⁶

There is no doubt that this kind of labor migration had its attractive sides for young men. Labor migrants were comparatively rich people who brought with them not only money and clothes but also such attractions as phonographs.¹²⁷ One interviewee responded to my question as to whether young men had no choice but to go abroad in this way:

> That was not an obligation. It was like this: you stay here and you have a friend who was there. The day that he returns, you see him well dressed with a coat and even shoes. Sometimes he comes with a bicycle. [...] Then you start to see it like this: I will also go, I will also have it.¹²⁸

As this quotation however already suggests, push factors continued to play an important role, even if in the 1950s the pressures came less from the state than from local society. After all, work in the mines was not without danger. According to the statements of two interviewees, accidents occurred regularly.¹²⁹ The pressure was not only to get nice clothes, but also to find the money to pay for marriage. One labor migrant from Chinuni for example stated that "you didn't get married, if you didn't go."¹³⁰ In the same vein, the Portuguese forestry engineer Camilo

---

125 One exception was: PA, I063: interview with *P1488 (♂, ~1930)* (M'chepa, August 31, 2013), min 00:08:28–00:08:54.
126 "[P]ofuna tivale vabwino wanthu amayenda kupita kunyasaland (Malawi) kuti nyengoyo muno muli ata ntchito.", MLM, 018: interview with *L. M.*, transcript Chinyanja (Malango, June 27, 2007). For other similar statements, see: PA, I135: interview with *P1494 (♂, 1942)* (Nkhotakota, June 2, 2016), min 01:08:06–01:08:15; PA, I094: interview with *P0727 (♂, ~1940)* (M'chepa, January 27, 2016), min 00:23:10–00:24:13; MLM, 025: Song by Various Women (Nkholongue, June 27, 2007); PA, I154: interview with *P0367 (♂, 1936), P0373 (♀, 1940)* (Nkholongue, June 18, 2016), min 00:36:21–00:44:47. See as well: Katto, *"Grandma Was a Guerrilla Fighter,"* 85.
127 PA, I105: interview with *P0242 (♂, 1945)* (Malango, April 4, 2016), min 00:46:54–00:49:21. See as well: Katto, *"Grandma Was a Guerrilla Fighter,"* 226.
128 PA, I111: interview with *P0266 (♂, ~1932)* (Metangula, April 11, 2016), min 01:20:23–01:20:56.
129 PA, I013: interview with *P0367 (♂, 1936)* (Nkholongue, September 8, 2010), min 00:35:06–00:35:42; PA, I056: interview with *P1102 (♂, 1932)* (Malango, August 28, 2013), min 00:12:40–00:32:14.
130 PA, I149: interview with *P1501 (♂, 1949), P1513 (♂, 1943)* (Chinuni, June 11, 2016), min 00:18:02–00:18:06. For similar statements, see: PA, I094: interview with *P0727 (♂, ~1940)* (M'chepa, January 27, 2016), min 00:08:52–00:09:41.

Costa wrote in a 1959 article on Niassa that "many do not consider themselves 'men' unless they have been abroad."[131]

As labor migration was overwhelmingly male, it becomes clear that the revival of food subsistence production of the 1950s depended mainly on female labor. With the absence of male labor, it was the women who did the work at homes and farms and also supported the less productive forces of the community.[132] In light of the decreasing importance of pottery manufacture, the 1950s in Nkholongue can thus be read as a history of female retreat into subsistence production and of growing male labor mobility.

Subsistence, Migration, and the Market: Economic Dynamics in the Long Run

As stated above, the fall and rise of Nkholongue's pottery manufacture was not the only example of the dynamic and multidirectional nature of the interplay of subsistence, migration, and the market in Nkholongue's history. Another example are the economic processes in the late colonial and early post-colonial period, which will be discussed in the two following chapters. Reflecting on the patterns of subsistence reversal in Nkholongue's history in the long run, we can gather at least five insights.

First, we can assert that processes of subsistence reversal generally do not appear as a conscious "exit option" by the people. Rather, the major movements (back) to subsistence in Nkholongue's history all seem to have been triggered by externally induced market disruptions. Thus the "exit option" was in reality

---

131 Costa, "O Niassa visto por dentro," 177.
132 Going back to arguments by Harold Wolpe, the contribution of the (female) subsistence economy to "cheap" migrant labor has been repeatedly highlighted. As Cooper and Austin have pointed out, however, it may be shortsighted to view this process only in terms of the exploitation of subsistence labor. Rather, they have argued that the system could also be used by Africans to meet their needs in various ways. See: Harold Wolpe, "Capitalism and Cheap Labour-Power in South Africa: From Segregation to Apartheid," *Economy and Society* 1, no. 4 (1972): 425–456; Gareth Austin, "The Return of Capitalism as a Concept," in *Capitalism: The Reemergence of a Historical Concept*, ed. Jürgen Kocka and Marcel van der Linden (London: Bloomsbury, 2016), 217–18; Frederick Cooper, "Africa in a Capitalist World," in *Crossing Boundaries: Comparative History of Black People in Diaspora*, ed. Darlene Clark Hine and Jacqueline McLeod, Blacks in the Diaspora (Bloomington: Indiana University Press, 1999), 401. See as well the comments by Clarence-Smith, who emphasized that migrant labor was not necessarily "cheap" when productivity levels are considered: William G. Clarence-Smith, "'Thou Shalt Not Articulate Modes of Production,'" *Canadian Journal of African Studies/Revue Canadienne des Études Africaines* 19, no. 1 (1985): 21–22.

more necessity than preference.¹³³ We have seen this in the previous pages with regard to the end of CM. A similar process could be observed in the time after independence. As will be discussed in detail in the next chapter, the majority of Nkholongue's population was resettled to Metangula as part of the Portuguese counter-insurgency strategy. Resettlement went hand in hand with the increasing importance of wage labor.¹³⁴ People were still able to farm in Metangula, but the evidence clearly shows that agriculture lost its previous importance due to the fact that many men found employment with the growing Portuguese military apparatus. This reduced people's dependence on subsistence production, or as one interviewee put it:

> Now, as for food, even if someone couldn't farm, he had a job. We earned money and could buy food with it.¹³⁵

But, for most villagers, this was only a temporary change. After the war, many jobs disappeared again and most of the resettled returned to Nkholongue or Malango, a return that was accompanied by a renewed focus on (subsistence) agriculture. This retreat into subsistence was re-inforced by the fact that the years that followed independence were characterized by widespread shortages of consumer goods such as salt, sugar and clothes. These shortages drove people (back) into subsistence production, even in areas where it had hitherto not existed for a considerable time span.

An example for this is the case of salt. We have already discussed in the previous pages how the locally produced *chidulo* salt had been replaced by "imported" salt with the arrival of the mission steamers. With salt barely available on the market in the years after independence, people resorted to making *chidulo*. They "were using the same method that their parents had used before,"¹³⁶ as one interviewee

---

133 This evidence supports an older similar argument made in relation to the socialist period in Mozambique by Peter Meyns. See: Peter Meyns, "Zur Praxis ländlicher Entwicklungspolitik in Afrika – Anmerkungen zu Mozambique und Tanzania," in *Agrargesellschaften im portugiesisch-sprachigen Afrika*, ed. Peter Meyns (Saarbrücken: Breitenbach, 1988), 52.
134 Some authors such as Carlos Bozzoli, Tilman Brück and Paul Collier have singled out processes of reversal to subsistence as wartime coping strategies. This cannot be confirmed for the case of Nkholongue. Rather, here, the two wars went hand in hand with growing dependence on the market and wage labor. See: Carlos Bozzoli and Tilman Brück, "Agriculture, Poverty, and Postwar Reconstruction: Micro-Level Evidence from Northern Mozambique," *Journal of Peace Research* 46, no. 3 (2009): 377–397; Paul Collier, "On the Economic Consequences of Civil War," *Oxford Economic Papers* 51, no. 1 (1999): 168–183.
135 PA, I037: interview with *P0855* (♂, 1954) (Malango, August 14, 2013), min 00:48:29–00:48:51.
136 PA, I005: interview with *P0641* (♂, 1952) (Nkholongue, August 27, 2010), min 00:51:15–00:51:44. For a similar statement, see: PA, I078: interview with *P0258* (♂, 1953) (Nkholongue, September 7,

put it. Similarly, people began to use extracts from the roots of the *njujo* tree as a substitute for "imported" soap to wash clothes.¹³⁷

It needs to be highlighted, however, that processes of reversal to subsistence could have their limits. Thus, while salt and soap were replaced by local substitutes after independence, the same was not the case with clothes. Despite the lack of clothes in the years after independence, there was no return to the formerly locally produced *chiwondo* bark cloth. This is all the more interesting because 60 years earlier a similar shortage of clothes, which had been caused by the disruptions of World War One, had still led to a regional revival in the use and production of bark clothes. Thus, in October 1916, missionary Eyre reported from Metonia that cloth was unobtainable and that, therefore, many people were resorting to bark cloth.¹³⁸ While in October 1920, Augustine Ambali wrote from Ngoo that "every man and woman and child wears bark-clothes" as in "antiquity times," since clothes were almost unavailable.¹³⁹ Obviously, wearing *chiwondo* was no longer viable in the 1970s. We can assume that it had become unimaginable to wear *chiwondo* in everyday life. Also, even heavily worn clothes were probably still valued as the more attractive option over the less practical bark cloth. Furthermore, the knowledge of making *chiwondo* had largely vanished.

Second, reverting to subsistence in one area could go hand in hand with increasing market integration in another. This has been demonstrated in the previous pages, when the importance of subsistence food production based on female labor grew simultaneously with the significance of male labor migration. Similar processes could be observed in the years after independence. At the same time as labor migration had lost its importance and market shortages led to an increase in the importance of subsistence production in some sectors (*nsima* flour, salt and soap production), attempts at stronger market integration could be observed in others. Thus, the government of newly independent Mozambique promoted agri-

---

2013), min 00:32:37–00:32:57. See as well: PA, I042: interview with *P1193 (♀, 1953)* (Malango, August 17, 2013), min 00:42:10–00:45:46.

137 The Latin name of the tree is *Ekebergia benguelensis*. PA, I115: interview with *P0160 (♂, 1952)* (Metangula, April 18, 2016), min 02:14:12–02:15:34; PA, I162: interview with *P0512 (♀, 1967)* (Nkholongue, June 22, 2016), min 00:18:31–00:19:08; PA, I042: interview with *P1193 (♀, 1953)* (Malango, August 17, 2013), min 00.45:46–00:47:43; PA, I046: interview with *P1045 (♀, 1932)* (Malango, August 20, 2013), min 00:42:50–00:46:20.

138 "News from the Stations: VII. Mtonya," *NDC*, no. 53 (October 1916): 26–28.

139 Augustine Ambali, "News from the Stations: IV. Ngoo Bay," *NDC*, no. 69 (October 1920): 9–10. Similar processes of reversal have been observed for northwestern Zambia for the same time by Peša: Peša, *Roads through Mwinilunga*, 291.

6.2 The Rise and Fall of Nkholongue's Pottery Manufacture in the 1940s and 1950s — 227

cultural intensification and especially surplus production of maize.[140] Furthermore, fishing cooperatives were to improve the marketing of fish (see Section 6.4). In both cases, the successes were very limited, and still, the policies had tangible effects on the ground.

The period after independence also saw the beginning of a professionalization of the construction of houses. After independence, the walls of houses began to be built of sun-dried mud bricks instead of the plastered skeletons of trunks and beams.[141] The point is that the old way of building walls was done "in subsistence" by the senior male member of the household. Bricklaying, by contrast, was and is a professionalized activity. Household members often dry their own bricks, but they will usually pay someone to lay them.[142] Since both types of construction relied on local building materials, market shortages did not directly stand in the way of the increasing use of extra-household labor.

Third, the economic history of Nkholongue shows that people have long been active in diversifying their livelihoods and adapting their activities according to new realities. Rather than becoming life-long subsistence farmers, men in particular pursued a great many different occupations over the course of their lives. We have however also seen that it would be wrong to assume that it was simply so that the men provided for the extra-income while the women stayed at home and se-

---

[140] PA, I119: interview with *P0855* (♂, *1954*) (Malango, April 21, 2016), min 01:23:25–01:24:06; PA, I108: interview with *P1074* (♀, *~1940*) (Malango, April 6, 2016), min 01:03:32–01:03:35; PA, I118: interview with *P1218* (♀, *1930*) (Malango, April 21, 2016), min 02:01:21–02:03:18; PA, I106: interview with *P0262* (♀, *~1940*) (Malango, April 4, 2016), min 01:45:32–01:46:03; APGGN, QJ: Alfredo Filimone Lituri, "Relatório da Administração do Distrito de Metangula, Julho 1975" (Metangula, August 4, 1975), 2; APGGN, 1 A: Júlio Reis and Alfredo Filimone Lituri, "Relatório do Distrito de Metangula," Primeira Reunião de Administradores, Comissários Políticos e Grupos Dinamizadores dos Distritos da Província do Niassa (Metangula, May 16, 1976), 2; APGGN, 1 A: Frelimo, "Relatório do Distrito de Metangula, por ocasião do Conselho Provincial" (Metangula, January 1, 1977), 4; "Niassa: Libertar a riqueza de uma terra fértil," *Tempo*, Número especial: Dedicado à viagem presidencial à Província do Niassa (December 26, 1979): 56–80; Joan Antcliff, "After Ten Years ...... and Now Peace," *Lebombo Leaves* 63, no. 12 (1975): 10. See as well: Olaf Tataryn Juergensen, "Peasants on the Periphery: A Geohistory of Rural Change in Mozambique, c.1960–1992" (PhD thesis, Kingston (Canada), Queen's University, 1996), 215–16.
[141] PA, I062: interview with *P0713* (♂, *1944*) (Nkholongue, August 30, 2013), min 00:23:11–00:24:12; PA, I093: interview with *P0050* (♂, *~1922*) (Nkholongue, January 19, 2016), min 00:41:44–00:45:46; PA, I100: interview with *P0025* (♀, *1948*) (Nkholongue, February 22, 2016), min 00:24:30–00:25:42; PA, I117: interview with *P1458* (♂, *~1945*) (Micundi, April 20, 2016), min 02:05:26–02:06:45.
[142] PA, I096: interview with *P1216* (♂, *1957*) (Malango, February 1, 2016), min 00:41:42–00:44:07; PA, I117: interview with *P1458* (♂, *~1945*) (Micundi, April 20, 2016), min 02:06:45–02:07:41; PA, I097: interview with *P1454* (♂, *~1951*) (Malango, February 5, 2016), min 01:32:15–01:32:43.

cured the subsistence as agricultural workers. The rise and fall of Nkholongue's pottery manufacture demonstrates that this relationship was far more complicated. Also, in the long run, women's role in diversifying livelihoods was not only in agriculture. Although it was again mainly men who took up wage labor in the *aldeamento*[143] of Metangula during the Mozambican War of Independence, women also generated extra-income, for example, by selling firewood. Moreover, pottery never lost its significance completely, as the *ndiwo* side dish has continued to be cooked in locally made pots to this day. And while the production of pots suffered further due to competition from imported pots and containers during the time in Metangula,[144] pottery also regained importance at other times or under other circumstances. Thus, two women who fled to Malawi during the war claimed that it was precisely during the war that their pottery skills became more important again, allowing them to eke out a living as refugees in Malawi until the moment they could harvest from their own new fields.[145] In recent years, the production of pots has seen a surprising revival in the village since the Mbuna Bay lodge set up two handicraft shops for tourists, one at the lodge in Nkholongue and the other at the Girassol Hotel in Lichinga. This has allowed the women of the village to sell their pots to tourists and visitors, much as their mothers had done to the passengers of the S.S. Chauncy Maples more than 60 years ago.

Last but not least, it is important to highlight that subsistence did not simply linger on perpetually throughout Nkholongue's history.[146] It was not that there was just such a thing as extra-subsistence work or extra-subsistence production that was simply activated or deactivated depending on the market situation. Rather, the examples from Nkholongue's history show that people re-oriented their economic lives several times profoundly. The major movements back to subsistence were even all connected to processes of migration. Furthermore, subsistence production itself changed considerably since the 19th century. Subsistence production was not an isolated sector of economic life outside history. Rather, subsistence techniques were repeatedly modified, and not uncommonly as a consequence of ex-

---

143 The *aldeamentos* were strategic villages to which the Portuguese forces resettled the rural populations during the Mozambican War of Independence. For more on this, see Chapter 7.
144 PA, I112: interview with *P0129* (♀, *1930*), *P0128* (♂, *1928*) (Nkholongue, April 12, 2016), min 00:03:50–00:04:53; PA, I108: interview with *P1074* (♀, *~1940*) (Malango, April 6, 2016), min 00:25:49–00:26:49; PA, I157: interview with *P1455* (♂, *1952*) (Tulo, June 18, 2016), min 00:26:32–00:26:54.
145 PA, I100: interview with *P0025* (♀, *1948*) (Nkholongue, February 22, 2016), min 00:17:38–00:18:54; PA, I007: interview with *P0298* (♀, *~1922*) (Nkholongue, September 1, 2010), min 00:55:40–00:59:05, 01:09:28–01:12:12.
146 As for example suggested by: Deborah F. Bryceson, "The Scramble in Africa: Reorienting Rural Livelihoods," *World Development* 30, no. 5 (2002): 727; Bryceson, "Domestic Work," 316.

changes with the outside world. This shall be demonstrated in more detail by looking at the history of cassava cultivation in Nkholongue.

6.3 From Sorghum to Cassava to Maize to Cassava: Complicating the History of Subsistence Food Production

We have already seen at the beginning of the previous section that subsistence food production played an important role in the village at the time of research. In 2012, 80 percent of the households had a farm.[147] Most of these farms were cassava farms, located in the vicinity of the village on the rather flat stretch between the shores of the lake and the first hills of the hinterland. According to the village survey of 2016, only nine out of 127 registered households had a farm (usually an additional one) outside these lowland areas. Five of them were located near the neighboring village of Ngolocolo along the banks of the Luina river and used mainly for rice production. Four were highland farms, locally called *mpanje*,[148] located about a 60-minute walk from the lake in hilly forest land. They were used for maize cultivation.[149]

While the previous section focused on showing that the significance of subsistence production changed over time, this section intends to demonstrate that agricultural subsistence production itself changed considerably. Cassava, while today doubtlessly the central subsistence crop of Nkholongue, was not always the most important crop people cultivated to meet their subsistence needs. The adoption of cassava as the main staple crop only occurred in the 20th century. Being no "indigenous" food of Africa, it was originally brought to the continent from South America by Portuguese traders in the 16th century. When Nkholongue was established in the second half of the 19th century, it was already known along the lakeshore.[150] But it was not yet cultivated as widely as nowadays. My older interviewees all indicated that their parents had still relied primarily on sorghum.[151]

---

147 According to the Swedish "Reality Checks" this number was even higher in neighboring villages, as they observed that all households "have access to at least one agricultural field." See: ORGUT, "Sub-Report, District of Lago: Year One, 2011," 16.
148 *Mpanje* or *mphanje* translates as "uncultivated land."
149 Maize is also planted through inter-cropping in the lowland areas. However, this maize is not used to produce flour, but is consumed as corncob. In Nkholongue's Chinyanja, this is called *chimanga chotafuna* (sg.) or *vimanga votafuna* (pl.), as much as "maize to chew." Sometimes *maçaroca* (the Portuguese expression for corncob) is also used for maize cultivated for this purpose.
150 AUMCA, A1(VI)A, f. 1270–1293: Letter from George Swinny to W.H. Penney (Isle of Likoma, May 15, 1886); William P. Johnson, "A Visit to the Magwangwara in July, 1882," *CA* 1, no. 3 (1883): 38.

Oral accounts differ as to the local origins of cassava. The majority stated that cassava spread from the north to the south.[152] Some of my interviewees claimed that cassava came from Nkhotakota,[153] while others associated the rise of cassava with missionary activity.[154] As for explanations for the rise of cassava, several interviewees emphasized cassava's role as a food security crop.[155] Two placed it in the context of the Portuguese cotton regime. While one of them implied that it was indeed the Portuguese who pushed them to grow cassava around the time of the cotton campaign, the other merely stated that they used the former cotton

---

151 PA, I001: interview with *P0050* (♂, ~1922) (Nkholongue, August 17, 2010), min 00:45:36–00:46:15; PA, I112: interview with *P0129* (♀, 1930), *P0128* (♂, 1928) (Nkholongue, April 12, 2016), min 00:37:57–00:42:15; PA, I113: interview with *P0367* (♂, 1936) (Nkholongue, April 13, 2016), min 00:21:10–00:21:41; PA, I046: interview with *P1045* (♀, 1932) (Malango, August 20, 2013), min 00:05:42–00:07:41; PA, I052: interview with (♀, 1940) (Nkholongue, August 26, 2013), min 00:02:19–00:05:00; PA, I111: interview with *P0266* (♂, ~1932) (Metangula, April 11, 2016), min 00:57:53–00:58:28; PA, I106: interview with *P0262* (♀, ~1940) (Malango, April 4, 2016), min 01:56:35–01:57:22.
152 PA, I132: interview with *P1439* (♂, ~1940), *P1507* (♀, ~1930), *P1508* (♀) (Ndegue (Salima), June 1, 2016), min 02:29:07–02:29:24; PA, I123: interview with *P1460* (♀), *P1461* (♂, ~1935), *P1462* (♂, ~1935) (Meluluca, April 25, 2016), min 00:42:49–00:47:42; PA, I112: interview with *P0129* (♀, 1930), *P0128* (♂, 1928) (Nkholongue, April 12, 2016), min 00:41:19–00:41:38; MLM, 037: interview with *S. M.*, Portuguese translation of the Chinyanja transcript (Meluluca, June 29, 2007); PA, I002: interview with *P0128* (♂, 1928) (Nkholongue, August 18, 2010), min 00:47:00–00:47:39; PA, I120: interview with *P1102* (♂, 1932) (Malango, April 21, 2016), min 01:27:56–01:28:56.
153 PA, I118: interview with *P1218* (♀, 1930) (Malango, April 21, 2016), min 00:43:14–00:44:53; PA, I106: interview with *P0262* (♀, ~1940) (Malango, April 4, 2016), min 01:56:35–01:57:22; PA, I112: interview with *P0129* (♀, 1930), *P0128* (♂, 1928) (Nkholongue, April 12, 2016), min 00:41:23–00:41:28.
154 AHM, Secção Oral, Transcrito NI 04: N.° 154–155, Entrevista com um grupo de velhos em Chiwanga, interview by Gerhard Liesegang, Teresa Oliveira, and Mujuane Mainga Vicente, July 9, 1981, 60; MLM, 043: interview with *C. J. C.* (Chia, July 4, 2007), 18; PA, I120: interview with *P1102* (♂, 1932) (Malango, April 21, 2016), min 01:27:56–01:28:54. Beyond doubt, cassava was already present along the lakeshore when the missionaries arrived there (see Footnote 150). However, it might be that they promoted its cultivation or introduced new varieties.
155 PA, I002: interview with *P0128* (♂, 1928) (Nkholongue, August 18, 2010), min 00:48:47–00:52:16; PA, I043: interview with *P1148* (♂, 1960) (Malango, August 17, 2013), min 00:46:44–00:50:12; PA, I057: interview with *P0262* (♀, ~1940) (Malango, August 28, 2013), min 00:26:35–00:29:56; PA, I120: interview with *P1102* (♂, 1932) (Malango, April 21, 2016), min 01:28:54–01:30:10. It is possible that cassava spread during years of famine. Apart from the famine conditions during World War One and the early 1920s, which we have already discussed on pp. 162–167, we have evidence of droughts around Metangula for the years of 1935 and 1949. See: H.A. Machell Cox, "News from the Stations: V. Msumba," *NDC*, no. 128 (July 1935): 7–9; "The Bishop's Letter," *NDC*, no. 161 (June 1949): 1–9.

fields to subsequently plant cassava on them.[156] In fact, the cultivation of cassava was actively promoted by the colonial government in other regions of Mozambique precisely because it freed up labor and the better soils for the cotton regime.[157] But since the cotton regime was short-lived in the case of Nkholongue and the importance of agriculture was rather low at the time, the impact of colonial promotion of cassava cultivation may have been limited here.

It is also likely that cassava's rise went hand in hand with the growing importance of labor migration. While other crops like sorghum or maize were grown in a relatively labor-intensive system of slash-and-burn agriculture on highland farms, cassava could be grown in a much less labor-intensive process on marginal soils along the shores of the lake that requires much less shifting than highland farms.[158] Especially because clearing highland farms was and is men's work, it seems evident that the prolonged periods of men's absence made cassava cultivation more attractive. In other contexts, cassava has therefore also been referred to as a "women's crop." But the introduction of cassava did not simply reduce the necessary labor input in general; while cassava cultivation is not overly labor-intensive, the processing of cassava into flour is all the more time-consuming. Cassava thus did not just replace another crop; its adoption also "entailed a significant shift in the gender division of labor."[159]

The information on exactly when cassava superseded sorghum as the staple crop of the region is inconclusive. Certainly, the transition did not occur all at once. Different communities and different families were still relying on other crops, while some had already switched to cassava.[160] Seedlings needed their time to spread.[161] In 1928, missionary Cox wrote of the impossibility of settling

---

156 PA, I001: interview with *P0050* (♂, ~1922) (Nkholongue, August 17, 2010), min 01:45:47–01:48:54; PA, I112: interview with *P0129* (♀, 1930), *P0128* (♂, 1928) (Nkholongue, April 12, 2016), min 00:41:54–00:42:51.
157 Isaacman, *Cotton Is the Mother of Poverty*, 164–65. See as well: Merle L. Bowen, *The State Against the Peasantry: Rural Struggles in Colonial and Postcolonial Mozambique* (Charlottesville: University Press of Virginia, 2000), 36.
158 The connection between the rise of cassava and the increasing importance of labor migration was made by: PA, I111: interview with *P0266* (♂, ~1932) (Metangula, April 11, 2016), min 01:00:30–01:00:51.
159 Moore and Vaughan, *Cutting Down Trees*, 87.
160 MLM, 037: interview with *S. M.*, Portuguese translation of the Chinyanja transcript (Meluluca, June 29, 2007).
161 However, unlike other crops, cassava has the advantage of being propagated by cuttings. Its propagation, therefore, does not require the direct curtailment of others' harvest. Nevertheless, as with other crops, future cassava growers depended on others to provide them with the cuttings.

on a common Thanksgiving date because the crops of the region varied so much from one place to another. He reported:

> So this year the villages where the maize was the main crop observed their day on June 17th. whilst the millet folk kept theirs on July 15th. At Messumba itself we are still waiting, as *our main crop is cassava*.[162]

In the case of Nkholongue, we can assume that sorghum had more or less lost its former importance by 1950 at the latest. In 1951, a European visitor traveling aboard the CM observed cassava to be the chief food of Nkholongue. This observation was apparently based on his sighting of the cassava fields around the village.[163] However, oral history accounts show that some villagers focused on growing rice in Ngolocolo around this time.[164] Furthermore, there is reason to believe that people's emigration to Malango was related not only to a growing importance of agriculture in general, but also to that of cassava in particular. One interviewee stated that it was the chief of Metangula who gave them cassava cuttings, which they used to plant the new fields in Malango.[165] Cassava was undoubtedly the most important food of the village when the population was resettled to Metangula by Portuguese troops in 1966.[166]

---

[162] It is "Msumba" in the original. Emphasis as in the original. See: H.A. Machell Cox, "News from the Stations: IV. Msumba," *NDC*, no. 101 (October 1928): 16.
[163] Whiteman, "Traveller's Letter Home," 26.
[164] PA, I105: interview with *P0242* (♂, *1945*) (Malango, April 4, 2016), min 00:55:49–00:57:20; PA, I107: interview with *P1074* (♀, *~1940*) (Malango, April 5, 2016), min 01:34:15–01:34:39; PA, I108: interview with *P1074* (♀, *~1940*) (Malango, April 6, 2016), min 01:16:15–01:23:18; PA, I109: interview with *P1081* (♀, *1945*) (Malango, April 6, 2016), min 00:12:07–00:16:11; PA, I118: interview with *P1218* (♀, *1930*) (Malango, April 21, 2016), min 00:39:51–00:40:40; PA, I129: interview with *P1426* (♂, *1929*) (Malindi (Mangochi District, Malawi), May 29, 2016), min 02:15:04–02:16:19; PA, I131: interview with *P1434* (♂, *1942*) (Lifuwu (Salima District, Malawi), May 31, 2016), min 00:18:05–00:18:54; PA, I166: interview with *P1479* (♀, *~1922*), *P1505* (♂, *1957*) (Nampula, June 28, 2016), min 00:00:52–00:03:30; PA, I112: interview with *P0129* (♀, *1930*), *P0128* (♂, *1928*) (Nkholongue, April 12, 2016), min 00:25:41–00:27:43; PA, James Amanze, "Nkholongue Village, Niassa," email, May 5, 2018.
[165] PA, I072: interview with *P0262* (♀, *~1940*) (Malango, September 5, 2013), min 00:26:35–00:29:56.
[166] This is evident from the reports of the Portuguese navy units that helped the population to transport the harvest of their fields to Metangula during the War of Independence. See: ADN, FO/F002/SC002/117: Anexo "A" (Dispositivo e Actividade das F. Navais na ZIN) ao SITREP Circunstanciado N° 23/66 (Nampula, June 6, 1966), 7; AHMar, Coloredo, Pasta 058/MO: Relatório da Companhia N° 6 de Fuzileiros, referente à comissão em Moçambique desde 19 de Março de 1965 a 18 de Maio de 1967, n.d., chap. III, 3–5; AHMar, Coloredo, Pasta 156/MO: Anexo "A" (Dispositivo e Actividade das F. Navais na ZIN) ao SITREP Circunstanciado N° 35/66 (Nampula, August 29, 1966), 4; AHMar, Coloredo, Pasta 156/MO: Anexo "A" (Dispositivo e Actividade das F. Navais na ZIN) ao SITREP Circunstan-

After independence, the newly independent government of Mozambique tried to make people plant maize as a way out of the "monoculture of cassava,"[167] as a local government report put it in 1975 (see also Chapter 8). As elsewhere, post-colonial officials viewed cassava as a backward subsistence crop to be replaced by the more progressive maize. People were urged to produce surpluses for the markets in order to substitute the income formerly generated by labor migration.

As a consequence, the people of Nkholongue and Malango indeed began to increasingly grow maize after independence in the *mpanje* farms in the hilly hinterland. *Mpanje* translates as "uncultivated land" and refers to the fact that this was previous forest land that was slashed and burned in order to cultivate maize. *Mpanje* fields are normally used for a couple of years, after which new tracks of forest are cleared. While the location and system seem to have resonated with the form sorghum had been cultivated in earlier years,[168] younger people perceived *mpanje* as something new at the time. One interviewee said:

> *Mpanje* is something new. In the past, there was no *mpanje*. There was only cassava.[169]

And another stated:

> Maybe, it existed before I grew up. But, my father never told me that "let's go to *mpanje*" or "we are making *mpanje*," no.[170]

---

ciado N° 36/66 (Nampula, September 5, 1966), 2, 4; AHMar, Coloredo, Pasta 156/MO: Anexo "A" (Dispositivo e Actividade das F. Navais na ZIN) ao SITREP Circunstanciado N° 50/66 (Nampula, December 12, 1966).
167 APGGN, QJ: Alfredo Filimone Lituri, "Relatório da Administração do Distrito de Metangula, Julho 1975" (Metangula, August 4, 1975), 2. See as well: APGGN, 1 A: Júlio Reis and Alfredo Filimone Lituri, "Relatório do Distrito de Metangula," Primeira Reunião de Administradores, Comissários Políticos e Grupos Dinamizadores dos Distritos da Província do Niassa (Metangula, May 16, 1976), 2. For the local promotion of maize, see: PA, I118: interview with *P1218 (♀, 1930)* (Malango, April 21, 2016), min 00:42:39–00:42:57; APGGN, 1 A: Relatório resumido da situação sócioeconómica e cultural do Distrito do Lago, 1983, July 20, 1983, 3–4; PA, I119: interview with *P0855 (♂, 1954)* (Malango, April 21, 2016), min 01:23:25–01:24:06; PA, I127: interview with *P1468 (♂), P1469 (♂), P1470 (♂), P1471 (♀)* (Malo, May 2, 2016), min 00:40:44–00:41:15.
168 PA, I106: interview with *P0262 (♀, ~1940)* (Malango, April 4, 2016), min 01:56:35–01:57:22; PA, I120: interview with *P1102 (♂, 1932)* (Malango, April 21, 2016), 01:26:40–01:27:10; PA, I112: interview with *P0129 (♀, 1930), P0128 (♂, 1928)* (Nkholongue, April 12, 2016), 00:37:57–00:39:18; PA, I093: interview with *P0050 (♂, ~1922)* (Nkholongue, January 19, 2016), min 00:48:21–00:51:20.
169 PA, I117: interview with *P1458 (♂, ~1945)* (Micundi, April 20, 2016), min 01:28:52–01:28:56.
170 PA, I115: interview with *P0160 (♂, 1952)* (Metangula, April 18, 2016), min 02:30:48–02:30:58.

This post-independence revival of slash-and-burn agriculture is noteworthy, since the post-colonial policy of maize promotion was actually intended to enhance agricultural intensification. In this view, slash-and-burn shifting cultivation was considered a backward technology. Such situations have been described for other regions. In their book *Cutting Down Trees*, Henrietta Moore and Megan Vaughan have for example shown that slash-and-burn agriculture in northern Zambia (there called *citemene*) survived despite post-colonial efforts to promote agricultural intensification.[171] In Nkholongue, the effects on the ground were even more at odds with official government policy. Here, slash-and-burn agriculture was evidently not continued against all odds, but only (re-)introduced as a result of the government's demands for modernization.

The significance of maize production since independence has been unsteady and locally uneven along the lakeshore. In the case of Nkholongue, marketing of maize beyond subsistence production remained limited in the long run despite the government's efforts to the opposite. The growing importance of maize cultivation after independence was disrupted by the coming of the Mozambican Civil War as this made agriculture in the forests unsafe.[172] After the war, however, many people again returned to open maize fields. The number of maize fields declined again in the 21st century. As mentioned earlier, only four households had a *mpanje* farm in the 2016 survey. This decline was probably due to the fact that the boom in fisheries and tourism was more compatible with the focus on cassava, which, as described above, is less labor-intensive in terms of male labor.[173] One interviewee described this shift of labor from agriculture to fishing by saying that the young men nowadays are only busy spreading out the sardine-like *ussipa* to dry it in the sun before it is "exported" to Metangula or to Niassa's capital Lichinga. In his words:

> There was a lot of food here in Malango. I'm not kidding. The boys of today don't want to weed. The weeding of theirs is just to spread what? – *Ussipa*.[174]

But *mpanje* farming has remained an option. It was during my fieldwork in 2016 that some people in Malango made the decision to reopen their fallow *mpanje* fields, as market prices of maize had been very high in the preceding years.

---

171 Moore and Vaughan, *Cutting Down Trees*, 234–235.
172 As we will see in Chapter 9, Nkholongue's chief was abducted by Renamo while he was staying at his maize field at Mang'ombo.
173 In other places the *mpanje* boom continued, as could easily be recognized by the many cultivated fields in the forests at the time of research.
174 PA, I119: interview with *P0855 (♂, 1954)* (Malango, April 21, 2016), min 01:27:24–01:27:41.

Their main objective was thereby not to produce surplus maize, but to substitute the maize they had purchased to supplement or vary their cassava staple.[175]

Local Channels of Labor Mobilization in Agriculture: A History of Family Labor

While the period since independence has seen some attempts to increase the marketing of maize, farming in Nkholongue's history has mainly been aimed to meet subsistence needs.[176] In the 2016 survey, only three households reported earning money by selling agricultural produce or laboring in the fields of others. This reflects the fact that labor mobilization in agriculture has mainly taken place within the (nuclear) family. The principal productive unit seems to have always been the family-household consisting usually of a woman, her husband, and her children.[177] Even in the period of the slave trade, agricultural labor seems to have mainly been organized at this level, even if each family had to give up part of its harvest to the chief or work some time on their master's fields.[178] A certain kind of obligation to work for the chief existed into the colonial period. Information from the interviews is, however, imprecise as to the details and extent of this duty and the timing of its disappearance. In later periods, the obligation seems to have been primarily in the form of working in the chief's fields on certain days of the year, the yield of these fields being directed rather toward meeting the chief's subsistence needs ("reproduction") than toward marketing ("production").

The larger kinship has not formed a regular channel for mobilizing agricultural labor in recent times. This is in line with the observation that land has long been held individually.[179] There is, however, a kind of neighborhood cooperation that people call *Chidao*. It has been used to mobilize labor on certain days for plastering the houses or for communal work in the individually held fields. *Chidao* is the local variation of the beer-work-parties that have existed in similar forms in many parts of sub-Saharan Africa. The one whose field was worked that day had to provide the

---

175 It also needs to be emphasized in this regard that Mozambique's government continues to promote the cultivation of maize. I could myself witness this in 2016 when during a conversation with the village's chief a state official arrived on his motorbike with ten hoes to be freely distributed among maize cultivators.
176 For the period of the slave trade, however, there is some uncertainty on this issue.
177 The same has been argued for the Achewa in Malawi: Mandala, *Work and Control in a Peasant Economy*, 50–51; Brian Morris, *An Environmental History of Southern Malawi: Land and People of the Shire Highlands* (Cham: Palgrave Macmillan, 2016), 88; Harri Englund, "The Self in Self-Interest: Land, Labour and Temporalities in Malawi's Agrarian Change," *Africa* 69, no. 1 (1999): 149.
178 See Section 2.4.
179 H.A. Machell Cox, "Communal Cultivation," *CA* 27, no. 316 (April 1909): 100–101.

others with food and a kind of beer made from millet or sorghum. *Chidao* is hardly practiced nowadays. It seems to have been still common in the first half of the 20th century, primarily at the time of the preparation of a new field. In 1909, missionary Cox wrote that, especially around Nkhotakota, this kind of communal work was used for all the heavier steps of cultivation.[180] Cox's observation runs somewhat counter to the usual argument by Elias Mandala and others that voluntary collaboration between different households was never common in the larger region.[181] The historical relevance of this type of work is, however, difficult to assess in the specific case of Nkholongue. It is also difficult to determine the exact chronology of its decline; some say that it began with the War of Independence but others claim that it was still practiced occasionally after the Civil War. In addition, there are also some very old interviewees who stated that they themselves never or only very rarely engaged in *Chidao* and usually just saw others doing it.[182] There is some reason to believe that its decline in agriculture was linked to the rise of the less-labor intensive cassava as a staple crop.[183]

The rise of maize cultivation after independence seems to have not led to a revival of *Chidao*. Rather, this seems to have been linked to a growing importance of wage labor. For at least in recent years, labor peaks in *mpanje* fields have largely been satisfied by hiring temporary workers. In cassava fields, the recruitment of temporary workers is very rarely seen but is not non-existent. As cassava "remains" the chief produce of Nkholongue it can be said that wage labor has current-

---

[180] Cox, "Communal Cultivation," *CA* 27, no. 316 (April 1909).
[181] Mandala, *Work and Control in a Peasant Economy*; Englund, "The Self in Self-Interest," 149.
[182] PA, I116: interview with *P1457* (♀) (Metangula, April 18, 2016), min 00:24:17–00:28:42; PA, I070: interview with *P1448* (♀, ~1935) (Metangula, September 3, 2013), min 00:06:08–00:10:33; PA, I051: interview with *P0481* (♀, 1942) (Nkholongue, August 26, 2013), min 01:35:58–01:40:41; PA, I059: interview with *P0090* (♀, ~1932) (Metangula, August 29, 2013), min 01:15:36–01:17:01; PA, I049: interview with *P0267* (♀, 1949) (Nkholongue, August 23, 2013), min 00:51:47–00:54:11; PA, I062: interview with *P0713* (♂, 1944) (Nkholongue, August 30, 2013), min 00:39:13–00:40:37; PA, I057: interview with *P0262* (♀, ~1940) (Malango, August 28, 2013), min 01:29:58–01:32:44; PA, I054: interview with *P0554* (♀, 1949) (Nkholongue, August 27, 2013), min 01:03:52–01:06:10; PA, I053: interview with *P0189* (♀, 1940) (Nkholongue, August 27, 2013), min 00:35:44–00:37:02; PA, I166: interview with *P1479* (♀, ~1922), *P1505* (♂, 1957) (Nampula, June 28, 2016), min 00:26:00–00:27:18. For an old person who claimed to have never taken part in *Chidao*, see: PA, I104: interview with *P0298* (♀, ~1922) (Nkholongue, March 1, 2016), min 00:47:31–00:48:04.
[183] The Anglican missionary D.J. Hitchman wrote, for example, about the situation in Northern Rhodesia in 1942: "Harvesting is also a communal job where the crop is sorghum or maize; but where it is the root-crop, cassava, the women take their hoes and dig it up as it is needed, there being no special time of harvest." See: D.J. Hitchman, "Men, Manners and Modes in Northern Rhodesia: VI. To Each His Task," *CA* 60, no. 714 (June 1942): 52.

ly little importance in local agricultural production. The case is, however, different in other lakeside villages, where maize production is more widespread.

Some Qualifications on Cassava's Role in Nkholongue's History

In the long run, the history of agricultural production in Nkholongue shows that while farming was mostly for subsistence, it has by no means been static and outside of market relations. Types and volumes of cultivated crops changed over time precisely because of the interconnectedness of people's (economic) lives with the world outside.

Furthermore, it has to be stated that cultivation practices have not necessarily remained the same. This is shown by the way cassava has been harvested in Nkholongue. It is commonly considered an advantage of cassava that the crop can be preserved in the soil itself until it is needed for consumption.[184] This is also the technique used by the villagers of Nkholongue today. However, until the 2000s, it was still standard practice to harvest the whole field, slice the roots, dry them, and store them in bags.[185] Interestingly, both harvesting techniques had long been in use along the eastern lakeshore. Already in 1922, missionary Johnson noted that people north of Cobué left the ripe cassava in the ground until it was needed, while people down south dug up and stored the year's crop all at once.[186] I have not been able to determine with certainty why people in Nkholongue originally stored cassava in bags and why they changed the system at precisely that time.[187] But the advantages and disadvantages of the both systems seem clear: bag-stored cassava tends to develop a bad taste over time. In turn, it is much easier

---

[184] Emmanuel Akyeampong and Hippolyte Fofack, "The Contribution of African Women to Economic Growth and Development in the Pre-Colonial and Colonial Periods: Historical Perspectives and Policy Implications," *Economic History of Developing Regions* 29, no. 1 (2014): 48.

[185] PA, I124: interview with P0376 (♂, 1968) (Nkholongue, April 26, 2016), min 00:22:44–00:23:58; PA, I112: interview with P0129 (♀, 1930), P0128 (♂, 1928) (Nkholongue, April 12, 2016), min 01:39:03–01:40:35; PA, I094: interview with P0727 (♂, ~1940) (M'chepa, January 27, 2016), min 01:49:23–01:50:47.

[186] Johnson, *The Great Water*, 39. Leaving the ripe cassava in the ground was also the standard practice on the other side of the lake already in the 1940s. See: Veronica Berry and Celia Petty, eds., *The Nyasaland Survey Papers 1938–1943: Agriculture, Food, and Health* (London: Academy Books, 1992), 50. See as well: Velsen, *The Politics of Kinship*, 16.

[187] It noteworthy in this respect that around Messumba the old system of storing cassava in bags is still in use: PA, I097: interview with P1454 (♂, ~1951) (Malango, February 5, 2016), min 02:09:02–02:11:56.

to defend against human and animal thieves, and the method of harvesting everything at once was what people were used to from the crops they had grown before.

The history of agricultural production in Nkholongue allows us to also make some qualifications with regard to cassava's "reputation." Cassava has long been a controversial crop. While being at times valued as a drought-resistant famine crop, it has been often regarded as the crop of the "lazy" and the poor, and one with limited nutritional value and marketing potential. As mentioned above, post-colonial officials, in particular, viewed it as a backward subsistence crop to be replaced by the more progressive maize. In recent years, however, the tide seems to have turned. A group of agricultural economists called it "Africa's best-kept secret," and a development assistant named it the "root" of community development. Iva Peša speaks of a "rebellious crop" that allowed people to evade state demands and simultaneously "freed up labour" to diversify income strategies.[188] Peša has also emphasized that cassava has in reality been marketed to a considerable degree.[189] Many of her arguments are similar to those of Achim von Oppen who had already designated cassava as a "safeguard for autonomy" and as "way to the market"[190] 20 years earlier.

While the history of cassava in Nkholongue confirms some of these newer findings with regard to food security and livelihood diversification, there are three reasons why the role of cassava as an expression of people's autonomy and economic strength should not be overemphasized in the case of Nkholongue.[191] First, we have seen that the adoption of cassava affected the gender division of labor. From this perspective, cassava above all strengthened men's autonomy but less that of women. Second, the stance of the colonial government toward cas-

---

188 Felix I. Nweke, John K. Lynam, and Dunstan S.C. Spencer, *The Cassava Transformation: Africa's Best-Kept Secret* (East Lansing: Michigan State University Press, 2002); Rodah Namwalizi Lester, *Cassava Is the Root: Community Development with Women. Recipes for Africa* (Toronto: lulu.com, 2010); Iva Peša, "'Cassava Is Our Chief': Negotiating Identity, Markets and the State through Cassava in Mwinilunga, Zambia," in *Transforming Innovations in Africa: Explorative Studies on Appropriation in African Societies*, ed. Jan-Bart Gewald, André Leliveld, and Iva Peša (Leiden: Brill, 2012), 178; Peša, *Roads through Mwinilunga*, 128.
189 Peša, *Roads through Mwinilunga*, 81, 125–126. Korieh offers evidence for the importance of marketed cassava flour (*gari*) in Nigeria. See: Korieh, *The Land Has Changed*. In northern Mozambique considerable amounts of cassava were equally marketed in colonial times. See: Bravo, *A cultura algodeira*, 222.
190 Achim von Oppen, "Cassava, 'The Lazy Man's Food'? Indigenous Agricultural Innovation and Dietary Change in northwestern Zambia (ca. 1650–1970)," in *Changing Food Habits: Case Studies from Africa, South America and Europe*, ed. Carola Lentz (Amsterdam: Harwood, 1999), 43–71.
191 This interpretation of the functions of cassava is central to Peša's argument. See: Peša, *Roads through Mwinilunga*, 8–9, 120–121.

sava was decidedly more positive in the Portuguese case than in the British. Unlike in colonial Zambia, cassava cultivation was clearly in line with state interests in colonial Niassa.[192] Third, the identity of being "cassava-eaters" is not as decidedly positive in Nkholongue as it is in northwestern Zambia and elsewhere.[193] At least nowadays, most people in Nkholongue seem to prefer to eat maize or rice if they can get them. Cassava in this regard indeed appears as the food of the poor.

6.4 Fishing *Ussipa*: A History of Capitalism from Below

The previous sections have shown how the livelihoods of Nkholongue's inhabitants have changed considerably over time. They have also highlighted that there were numerous economic connections with the world outside. However, they may have also given the impression that all villagers were affected by these changes and connections in more or less the same manner. This section attempts to highlight the importance of recognizing processes of social differentiation between the inhabitants of Nkholongue. It thus intends to challenge views that tend to ignore the existence of social inequality in villages and the class character of rural development.

While the lack of (historical) statistics on income and property restricts the analysis of the extent of social stratification in the long run, the village's history offers plenty of evidence to substantiate social stratification. The village's roots in the slave trade already speak volumes in challenging the notion of the homogeneous village community. In fact, the first years of the village's existence constitute doubtlessly the purest example of intra-village social stratification given the fact

---

192 For evidence from Niassa, see: APGGN, 1 A: Luciano Rebelo, "Relatório da Reunião de Administradores realizada em Vila Cabral nos dias 15 e 16 de Agosto de 1969" (Vila Cabral, August 30, 1969), 8. See as well: Bravo, *A cultura algodeira*, 210–211. But even in Northern Rhodesia, the government's attitude toward cassava was more ambiguous than Peša suggests. Several scholars have shown that the British officials at times promoted and even enforced the cultivation of cassava in Zambia (including in the region of her study) and elsewhere. See: Moore and Vaughan, *Cutting Down Trees*, 43; Obi Iwuagwu, "The Spread of Cassava (Manioc) in Igboland, South-East Nigeria: A Reappraisal of the Evidence," *Agricultural History Review* 60, no. 1 (2012): 74–75; Chewe M. Chabatama, "Peasant, Farming, the State, and Food Security in the North-Western Province of Zambia, 1902–1964" (PhD thesis, Toronto, Unversity of Toronto, 1999); Donald H. Bwalya, "Agricultural Change in the Northern Province of Zambia, 1948–1978: A Case Study of Maize Production in Kasama District" (Master thesis, Lusaka, University of Zambia, 1989), 18–22, accessed April 20, 2020, http://dspace.unza.zm/bitstream/handle/123456789/1950/BwalyaDHJ0001.PDF?sequence=2&isAllowed=y. Peša, herself, presents examples in her book that the attitude of the government toward cassava was historically much more ambiguous. See: Peša, *Roads through Mwinilunga*, 117.
193 For the positive identification with cassava in these regions, see: Oppen, "Cassava, 'The Lazy Man's Food'?," 45, 47, 67; Peša, *Roads through Mwinilunga*, 9.

that villagers were bought and owned by other villagers (see Chapter 2). As I argued in Section 4.3, social inequalities at the level of the community appear to have diminished with colonization, as the end of the slave trade reduced the power of masters over their slaves. For later periods, the extent of social stratification is difficult to assess in detail. From the interviews, it is however clear that people have perceived inequalities between each other throughout the village's existence. One female informant, for example, denied my question of whether she had also cut fuelwood for the steamers not with reference to her sex but with reference to her social standing, saying "[n]o, back then I was rich."[194] For colonial times, the wealthy of the village were identified as comprising three main groups: the ivory carvers, those who had traveled extensively (as for example labor migrants), and those who had kinship ties to the colonial elite.[195] The latter was also the case for the woman just quoted, whose father was a black customs officer from Maputo who had several relationships with local women while working in Metangula.[196] Another interviewee had a half-brother who was the offspring of his mother's relationship with an "Indian" trader from Vila Cabral.[197] His half-brother not only enabled him to attend a Catholic boarding school, but also paid him a sewing machine and provided him with a place for his tailoring business

---

[194] PA, I118: interview with *P1218* (♀, *1930*) (Malango, April 21, 2016), min 00:46:56–00:47:17. Similarly, another interviewee explained that her father did not sell firewood on the basis that he was a Muslim preacher always traveling around. See: PA, I106: interview with *P0262* (♀, *~1940*) (Malango, April 4, 2016), min 00:18:59–00:20:02.

[195] PA, I105: interview with *P0242* (♂, *1945*) (Malango, April 4, 2016), min 00:46:13–00:47:46; PA, I118: interview with *P1218* (♀, *1930*) (Malango, April 21, 2016), min 01:45:06–01:45:30; PA, I120: interview with *P1102* (♂, *1932*) (Malango, April 21, 2016), min 01:38:59–01:40:33; PA, I111: interview with *P0266* (♂, *~1932*) (Metangula, April 11, 2016), min 00:28:28–00:30:31; PA, I131: interview with *P1434* (♂, *1942*) (Lifuwu (Salima District, Malawi), May 31, 2016), min 02:01:19–02:01:58; PA, I112: interview with *P0129* (♀, *1930*), *P0128* (♂, *1928*) (Nkholongue, April 12, 2016), min 00:31:20–00:33:05; PA, I132: interview with *P1439* (♂, *~1940*), *P1507* (♀, *~1930*), *P1508* (♀) (Ndegue (Salima), June 1, 2016), min 02:31:58–02:33:35; PA, I108: interview with *P1074* (♀, *~1940*) (Malango, April 6, 2016), min 01:30:18–01:32:00.

[196] PA, I118: interview with *P1218* (♀, *1930*) (Malango, April 21, 2016), min 00:03:02–00:15:06. Her father's origin is also "visible" in her second name (patronym), which is a Portuguese name, something that is most uncommon for people of her age.

[197] PA, I135: interview with *P1494* (♂, *1942*) (Nkhotakota, June 2, 2016), min 00:29:36–00:30:28; PA, I129: interview with *P1426* (♂, *1929*) (Malindi (Mangochi District, Malawi), May 29, 2016), min 02:11:41–02:13:41; PA, I112: interview with *P0129* (♀, *1930*), *P0128* (♂, *1928*) (Nkholongue, April 12, 2016), min 00:31:20–00:33:53.

in Vila Cabral.[198] He also supported another sibling, taking him to Vila Cabral and giving him work as a shop assistant. This second half-brother, who also worked as an ivory carver, was able to earn enough money to send his children to a private school in Nampula.[199] My interviewees characterized wealthy people of the past above all in terms of their access to goods and commodities and their ownership of durable assets. Thus, rich people were said to eat well, to have big houses with glass windows, and to own such attractions like phonographs.[200]

The question here is when and in what ways such social inequalities also influenced labor relations inside the village. As Helena Pérez-Niño has recently argued in her study of tobacco farmers in Tete, it is not wealth in the first place but "the relational aspects of the social division of labour and the ownership of the means of production"[201] that define social differentiation. As we have seen in the previous section, agriculture was barely affected in this regard. However, the case is quite different with regard to fisheries, a sector that, as we will now see, has a long history of separation of labor from the means of production.

For observers from outside, fishing as practiced in Nkholongue nowadays might appear as a traditional activity destined to meet subsistence needs. The development consultants of the Swedish embassy are not the only ones to think so. In his recent work on land tenure in Cobué, the anthropologist Elísio Jossias has claimed that fishing is done first and foremost to satisfy the "needs of redistributive consumption" of the households involved.[202] This is certainly not the case in the lakeside villages south of Metangula nowadays. While the situation around Cobué may be less pronounced, around Nkholongue the market is today undoubtedly the first priority. Fish gets exported as far as Lichinga and Malawi. In particular, catching the sardine-like *ussipa* requires comparatively high investments. Since the early 2000s, *ussipa* catching is done at night with large nets made of in-

---

198 PA, I002: interview with *P0128 (♂, 1928)* (Nkholongue, August 18, 2010), min 00:24:21–00:26:35; PA, I009: interview with *P0128 (♂, 1928)* (Nkholongue, September 1, 2010), min 00:02:21–00:04:03, 00:21:18–00:35:06.
199 PA, I166: interview with *P1479 (♀, ~1922), P1505 (♂, 1957)* (Nampula, June 28, 2016), min 00:06:52–00:11:05, 01:09:38–01:14:21.
200 PA, I105: interview with *P0242 (♂, 1945)* (Malango, April 4, 2016), min 00:47:46–00:55:02; PA, I131: interview with *P1434 (♂, 1942)* (Lifuwu (Salima District, Malawi), May 31, 2016), min 02:02:00–02:02:31; PA, I132: interview with *P1439 (♂, ~1940), P1507 (♀, ~1930), P1508 (♀)* (Ndegue (Salima), June 1, 2016), min 02:31:58–02:33:35.
201 Pérez-Niño, "Post-Conflict Agrarian Change in Angónia," 277.
202 Elísio Jossias, "'O primeiro a chegar é o dono da terra': Pertença e posse da terra na região do Lago Niassa" (PhD thesis, Universidade de Lisboa, 2016), 148.

dustrial fibers.[203] *Ussipa* swarms are attracted with light and then driven into the nets by beating paddles against the sides of boats and canoes or on the water surface. Until about 2012, oil lamps were used as light sources. Today, LED bulbs, powered by car batteries, are used. In the daytime, the car batteries are either recharged by solar panels or sent to Metangula where they can be connected to *Cahora Bassa*, the common term for the national grid in Mozambique. Five to six men are needed to work one net.

Figure 5: Fishing *ussipa*: dugout canoe with car battery and LED light bulbs. Photograph taken by the author in April 2016.

In spite of the "traditional" appearance, *ussipa* fishing also involves a clear separation of labor from the means of production. The owners of the means of production (including the boats, dugout canoes, net, battery and light bulbs) often do not participate in proper fishing, but let others do the work for them. As a rule, the owner receives half of the night's haul. The other half is divided equally among the workers. Even though fishing is still a widespread activity in Nkholongue, there is a significant degree of professionalization. The best sign of this is the already mentioned *makuli* households. The *makuli* are fishermen from outside the village who have settled in simple makeshift houses made out of straw on Malan-

---

203 According to my interviewees, the system was introduced from Malawi: PA, I163: interview with *P0028* (♂, *1969*) (Nkholongue, June 22, 2016), min 00:24:02–00:24:44; PA, I097: interview with *P1454* (♂, *~1951*) (Malango, February 5, 2016), min 01:21:39–01:22:10; PA, I086: interview with *P0375* (♂, *1962*) (Nkholongue, September 9, 2013), min 00:09:48–00:11:26.

go's main beach. But the professionalization is even evident on the level of the original village population. In the 2016 survey (which did not include the *makuli* households), about 45 percent of the households reported buying fish within the village. Sixteen percent said that they would receive their fish from relatives, friends, or neighbors. Only 34 percent of households (43 households) had members who were directly involved in fishing. Of these, about half were owners of fishing nets, and the other half worked for the owners of such nets.

Fishing *ussipa* nowadays has little to do with an alleged subsistence mode of production. Rather, this is nothing other than capitalism in the sense that private owners of fishing nets and boats exploit the labor of others, extracting surpluses through wage-labor-like relations. The boom in fisheries, fueled by Mozambique's overall economic growth and facilitated by improved transportation infrastructure, has certainly strengthened this evolution of capitalism from below in recent years. However, the roots of this constellation go back much further.

Market integration of the local fisheries is old. In colonial times, and most probably even in pre-colonial times, there was a significant amount of bartering between the lakeshore population and the Wayao population from Niassa's *planalto*. Fish was exchanged for other food like maize, millet or beans.[204] While it is difficult to quantify the extent of this bartering, the information from the interviews suggest that, for Nkholongue, fish-for-grain exchange never reached the importance of the pottery-for-food bartering. However, unlike pottery, fish was exported from all lakeshore villages. Fish was also already sold in colonial times, even though the quantity of the bartering was more significant. The German agronomist Hermann Pössinger gave the example of a household in Cobué that in 1962/63 earned 600 Escudos from the sale of fish.[205] This amount corresponded to the salary of a village chief at that time and was slightly more than five times the annual tax.[206] The means of production were also bought on the market in colonial times.[207] While the oldest fishing nets were produced locally by professional crafts-

---

[204] PA, I058: interview with *P1074* (♀, ~1940) (Malango, August 28, 2013), min 00:34:04–00:38:17; PA, I120: interview with *P1102* (♂, 1932) (Malango, April 21, 2016), min 01:33:56–01:35:21. This barter was also observed by: Brito, *No trilho dos descobrimentos*, 181; Hermann Pössinger, *Landwirtschaftliche Entwicklung in Angola und Moçambique* (München: IFO, 1968), 201–4; Hermann Pössinger, *Bericht über eine Reise nach Angola und Moçambique* (München: IFO, 1964), 34. Before the appearance of "imported" (European) hoes, fish might also have been used to be bartered for hoes that were produced on the *planalto*. For, according to William Percival Johnson, hoes were rarely made along the lake but mostly came "from the people in the hills." See: Johnson, *The Great Water*, 43.

[205] My thanks go to Andreas Stucki for drawing my attention to Pössinger's report: Pössinger, *Landwirtschaftliche Entwicklung in Angola und Moçambique*, 203–204.

[206] Pössinger, 200, 204.

[207] Pössinger, 204.

men from a plant of the nettle family locally called *thingo*,²⁰⁸ nets made of industrial nylon fibers had already appeared then. Simultaneously, people also began to use mosquito nets for fishing.²⁰⁹

The most important observation for our analysis of the local development of capitalism is however that the system of distribution of the catch between the owner of the means of production and the workers already existed in colonial times. It was also already applied to *thingo* nets.²¹⁰ According to the Portuguese geographer Raquel Soeiro de Brito, who carried out research in the region in the early 1960s, the distribution was two thirds for the owner of the net and one third for the net's workers at that time.²¹¹ Later, when AHM's oral history team visited the region in 1981, the distribution was 50–50 and thus equivalent to the present formula.²¹²

The historical division of labor and ownership of the means of production is also confirmed by a survey that the Mozambican *Instituto de Investigação Pesqueira* (IIP) conducted in the region in June 1983. It provided detailed numbers of owners and workers for each village of the lakeshore. In the case of Nkholongue and Malango, there were 76 fishermen, of whom 26 (34 %) were labeled as "proprietors" and 50 (66 %) as "assistants."²¹³ The survey also highlighted the importance of market production, stating that more than 50 percent of the lakeshore's production was illegally exported to Malawi and Tanzania. The IIP's investigators explained this by the "inability of [local] society to absorb fishermen's capital."²¹⁴

---

208 The plant belongs to the genus of *Pouzolzia*.
209 Pössinger, *Landwirtschaftliche Entwicklung in Angola und Moçambique*, 203; Brito, *No trilho dos descobrimentos*, 206; PA, I083: interview with *P1102 (♂, 1932), P1074 (♀, ~1940), P1141 (♂, 1932)* (Malango, September 8, 2013), min 00:02:21–00:13:42.
210 PA, I117: interview with *P1458 (♂, ~1945)* (Micundi, April 20, 2016), min 00:48:11–00:50:03; PA, I123: interview with *P1460 (♀), P1461 (♂, ~1935), P1462 (♂, ~1935)* (Meluluca, April 25, 2016), min 00:57:21–01:01:48; PA, I119: interview with *P0855 (♂, 1954)* (Malango, April 21, 2016), min 00:15:38–00:17:40.
211 Brito, *No trilho dos descobrimentos*, 206. See as well: PA, I113: interview with *P0367 (♂, 1936)* (Nkholongue, April 13, 2016), min 02:41:25–02:42:05; PA, I117: interview with *P1458 (♂, ~1945)* (Micundi, April 20, 2016), min 00:48:42–00:49:41; PA, I123: interview with *P1460 (♀), P1461 (♂, ~1935), P1462 (♂, ~1935)* (Meluluca, April 25, 2016), min 00:59:01–01:00:50; PA, I129: interview with *P1426 (♂, 1929)* (Malindi (Mangochi District, Malawi), May 29, 2016), min 02:17:36–02:20:02.
212 AHM, Secção Oral, Cassettes N.° 157–159: Entrevista com um grupo de velhos de Seli (Metangula), interview by Gerhard Liesegang, Teresa Oliveira, and Mujuane Mainga Vicente, July 22, 1981, N.° 158A: 000–046.
213 Alfredo V. R. Massinga and Patricio Contreras, "The Fishing Centres of Lake Niassa (Mozambique)," *Revista de Investigação Pesqueira (Maputo)*, no. 17 (1988): 40.
214 Massinga and Contreras, 14. On this point, see as well: APGGN, 1 A: Carta N.° 286/DPIEN/F-1/985 ao Director Provincial do Comércio Interno do Niassa, October 24, 1985.

This inability was most probably a consequence of the general market disruptions in Mozambique after independence. Accordingly, an FAO report from 1992 stated that the commercialization of fish had suffered in the region after Mozambican Independence "due to the breakdown of the Portuguese colonial commercialization network which used to play a very important role in the supply of fishing equipment, materials and consumer goods, and also commercialize the surplus production of the local fishermen."[215]

Mozambique's post-independence government made efforts to steer local fisheries in a direction compatible with socialism. It encouraged people to form fishing cooperatives, obviously with little success as the IIP survey showed. It also established the *Combinado Pesqueiro* in Metangula in 1980. The *Combinado Pesqueiro* was to distribute/sell fishing equipment to the people and to advise them on fishing methods and fish processing technologies.[216] According to my interviewees, it also bought up surplus fish and employed several fishermen from Nkholongue directly as wage laborers.[217] One of the *Combinado*'s two *Posto de Apoio e Compras* ('post of support and purchases') was installed in Nkholongue.[218] The importance of the *Combinado* for Nkholongue's fishery was short-lived as its activities were first hampered by internal problems and misuse of resources[219] and then more or less paralyzed by the Mozambican Civil War from 1985 onward.[220]

---

215 G.W. Ssentongo and Nfamara J. Dampha, "Report of the Technical Consultation between Malawi and Mozambique on the Development and Management of the Fisheries of Lakes Malawi, Chilwa and Chiuta," UNDP/FAO IFIP Project (Bujumbura, March 1992), 68–69, accessed September 2, 2015, http://www.fao.org/docrep/014/am851e/am851e.pdf.
216 For the date of the *Combinado*'s establishment, see: APGGN, 1 A: Relatório resumido da situação sócioeconómica e cultural do Distrito do Lago, 1983, July 20, 1983, 5. For a rather impressionist article on the *Combinado*, see: Peter Sketchley, "Fishing Co-operatives on Lake Niassa: Seeds of a New Socialist Society or New Roots for an Old Exploiting Class?," *Review of African Political Economy* 9, no. 24 (1982): 85–95.
217 PA, I141: interview with *P0375* (♂, *1962*) (Nkholongue, June 6, 2016), min 00:59:41–01:01:50; PA, I145: interview with *P0284* (♂, *1966*), *P0273* (♀, *1950*) (Metangula, June 9, 2016), min 00:52:47–00:53:23; PA, I122: interview with *P1459* (♀, *1942*), *P1464* (♀, *~1974*) (Capi, April 22, 2016), min 00:39:37–00:40:01; PA, I124: interview with *P0376* (♂, *1968*) (Nkholongue, April 26, 2016), min 01:15:21–01:34:50; PA, I115: interview with *P0160* (♂, *1952*) (Metangula, April 18, 2016), min 03:21:02–03:22:39; PA, I105: interview with *P0242* (♂, *1945*) (Malango, April 4, 2016), min 02:27:54–02:48:05; PA, I094: interview with *P0727* (♂, *~1940*) (M'chepa, January 27, 2016), min 01:36:11–01:37:38.
218 Helena Motta, "Processamento artesanal de pescado em Moçambique," Instituto de Investigação Pesqueira, Boletim de Divulgação, no. 30 (Maputo, 1990), 4.
219 APGGN, QJ: Carta N.° 282/D/86 de Manuel Luis Gonçalves (Director da Unidade de Direcção da Pesca de Pequena Escala) à Direcção Provincial da Industria e Energia de Niassa (Maputo, April 30, 1986); APGGN, 1 A: Carta de Salomão Cossa (Chefe do Serviço Provincial de Pescas do Niassa) ao

While the boom in the 21st century was certainly unprecedented both in terms of quantity and quality,[221] the local fisheries had long known processes of market integration, social differentiation and accumulation. As nowadays, these processes were however not always recognized as such or were discussed somewhat contradictorily. Thus, the FAO report quoted above could tell of the breakdown of commercialization after independence, but simultaneously record that fishing in colonial times was "mainly fishing for subsistence by individual fishermen."[222] In a similar vein, a British observer who visited in Metangula in the early 1980s witnessed "virtually no signs of accumulation or differentiation between the fishermen and the subsistence peasants alongside them."[223]

Nkholongue's history, however, shows that there was more than meets the eye. While differentiation might have been indeed limited, there was at least one who was expanding his business rather quickly and against all turnings of the tide. This was Salimo Chiboa. According to my interviewees, he had made his money initially as an ivory carver and, then, as a trader and owner of fishing nets. During the War of Independence, he was resettled to Metangula. There he opened a store,[224] and, later, also one of Metangula's first guest houses.[225] His activities were also not cur-

---

Secretário das Pescas (Maputo) (Ref. 194/DPIEN/F-1/86), (July 14, 1986); APGGN, QJ: Telegrama N.° 467/GAB/58, Dirigente da Província do Niassa ao Secretário de Estado das Pescas (Maputo) (Lichinga, November 12, 1985); PA, I105: interview with *P0242* (♂, *1945*) (Malango, April 4, 2016), min 02:42:26–02:43:01; APGGN, 1 A: Encontro havido entre sua Excelência o Governador da Província e a Senhora Maria Teresa Sousa, esposa do Senhor Jorge, Director do Pescado de Metangula (Metangula, February 16, 1983); PA, I141: interview with *P0375* (♂, *1962*) (Nkholongue, June 6, 2016), min 00:53:39–00:56:23, 00:57:18–00:57:29.

220 Ssentongo and Dampha, "Report of the Technical Consultation between Malawi and Mozambique on the Development and Management of the Fisheries of Lakes Malawi, Chilwa and Chiuta," 70. According to one of my interviewees, the *Combinado*'s *Posto de Apoio e Compras* at Ngoo was destroyed by Renamo: PA, I105: interview with *P0242* (♂, *1945*) (Malango, April 4, 2016), min 02:38:15–02:44:23.

221 This was also perceived as such by my interviewees, several of whom also claimed that the availability of fish inside the village had declined because of commercialisation.

222 Ssentongo and Dampha, "Report of the Technical Consultation between Malawi and Mozambique on the Development and Management of the Fisheries of Lakes Malawi, Chilwa and Chiuta," 68.

223 Sketchley, "Fishing Co-operatives on Lake Niassa," 86.

224 PA, I117: interview with *P1458* (♂, *~1945*) (Micundi, April 20, 2016), min 01:35:13–01:37:17; PA, I120: interview with *P1102* (♂, *1932*) (Malango, April 21, 2016), min 01:39:14–01:40:33; PA, I079: interview with *P0510* (♂, *1963*) (Nkholongue, September 7, 2013), min 00:06:11–00:07:18; PA, I141: interview with *P0375* (♂, *1962*) (Nkholongue, June 6, 2016), min 00:17:13–00:17:36, 00:22:15–00:24:33.

225 PA, I117: interview with *P1458* (♂, *~1945*) (Micundi, April 20, 2016), min 01:36:09–01:36:17; PA, I162: interview with *P0512* (♀, *1967*) (Nkholongue, June 22, 2016), min 00:26:50–00:26:59.

tailed by socialism after independence. Instead, he was able to turn his shop into a consumer cooperative.[226] One interviewee described his role as follows:

> He was the leader, because this shop belonged to him. Now those of Frelimo wanted to smash the shop and said, "we don't want everyone to have their own shop, we only want cooperatives with each shop having 60 members." Well, he used his money to just gather 60 people. *Pronto*, registration, *pronto*.[227]

Chiboa might have been an exception, but his history also exemplifies the characteristics of the development of capitalism in Nkholongue. On the one hand it is certainly inherent in the logics of capitalism that one will not find too many capitalists on the level of an African village, where many invest, but most fail on the way to becoming capitalists. Those who are successful emigrate to town. On the other hand, several specific circumstances may have limited this development, including the racist legislation in colonial times, the market disruptions after independence and the two wars which interrupted or redirected processes of differentiation.[228] Also, the fact that nobody has really been landless in Nkholongue has limited the leverage potential capitalists have on (cheap) laborers.[229]

6.5 Conclusion

For almost 150 years, Africa has been time and again "the object of a transformative project, of turning 'tradition' into 'modernity'."[230] This chapter has set out to challenge notions of inertia and isolation that continue to dominate development discourse and to influence academic writing about rural Africa. It has done so by

---

226 PA, I162: interview with *P0512* (♀, *1967*) (Nkholongue, June 22, 2016), min 00:23:39–00:25:00; PA, I141: interview with *P0375* (♂, *1962*) (Nkholongue, June 6, 2016), min 00:14:19–00:21:53; PA, I163: interview with *P0028* (♂, *1969*) (Nkholongue, June 22, 2016), min 00:17:15–00:18:33; PA, I066: interview with *P0085* (♂, *1960*) (Nkholongue, September 1, 2013), min 00:13:22–00:14:52; PA, I117: interview with *P1458* (♂, *~1945*) (Micundi, April 20, 2016), min 01:35:13–01:36:17.
227 PA, I141: interview with *P0375* (♂, *1962*) (Nkholongue, June 6, 2016), min 00:16:46–00:17:13.
228 It is however important to note in this regard that the wars often went hand in hand with processes of (temporary) proletarianization as is shown by the experiences of both people resettled to Metangula during the War of Independence and wartime refugees in Malawi (see Chapter 7). See also: Pérez-Niño, "Post-Conflict Agrarian Change in Angónia," 196.
229 The *makuli* households could however be considered as a further step towards proletarianization in this regard.
230 Cooper, "Africa in a Capitalist World," 391. See as well: Pauline Peters, "Land Appropriation, Surplus People and a Battle over Visions of Agrarian Futures in Africa," *Journal of Peasant Studies* 40, no. 3 (2013): 551–552.

directly addressing the economic history of a specific place, highlighting the incompatibility of this history with existing essentialist explanations.

This chapter has shown that Nkholongue, although exhibiting all the trappings of a subsistence-oriented village in transformation, has a much more dynamic economic history than one might expect. Far from having just recently been "connected to the world outside," the population of Nkholongue has in reality been connected to (global) markets throughout the village's history. It has also been demonstrated that the village's economy changed significantly as a consequence of these connections. We have also seen that the level of dependence on subsistence production for different products varied highly over time.

Nkholongue's unique position in this respect certainly needs to be highlighted. Not every village's history was so intrinsically connected to the slave trade, and not every village visited regularly by a steamship over a period of more than 50 years. However, many other changes that have been discussed affected the other villages as much as they did Nkholongue. This concerns among others the history of fishing, the history of labor migration, the history of salt and clothing, and many aspects of the history of agriculture. Furthermore, even if Nkholongue's women stood alone with their skills in making pots, those who bought the pots with food were equally part of this market exchange.

There is no doubt that the inhabitants of Nkholongue have not remained but rather become the peasants and fishermen that they are today. The awareness of these dynamics on the micro-scale alone does, of course, little to explain the "big" questions of the development industry. However, the reflection of these dynamics, certainly, contributes to refute certain popular claims, to clear up the historical contradictions that are inherent to many of those explanations, and to improve our knowledge of capitalism's history at its (African) periphery. Let me just single out five aspects in this respect:

First, the term "uncapturedness" seems to be quite inappropriate to describe the economic experience of Nkholongue's inhabitants. Rather, the people of Nkholongue have long interacted with (global) capitalism, and their lives have been marked and constrained by it at many turns.[231] This chapter has also highlighted how this interaction has influenced production within the village in manifold ways.

---

231 This terminology has been taken from John Saul and Colin Leys who have argued that "Africa south of the Sahara exists in a capitalist world, which marks and constrains the lives of its inhabitants at every turn, but is not of it." I, however, doubt whether it is appropriate to say that sub-Saharan Africa is indeed not of this capitalist world. See: John S. Saul and Colin Leys, "Sub-Saharan Africa in Global Capitalism," *Monthly Review: An Independent Socialist Magazine* 51, no. 3 (1999).

Second, the experience of Nkholongue's contradicts globalization teleologies. From the perspective of Nkholongue, the claim that, in the 21st century, "Africans are more likely to travel longer distances in search of employment"[232] than they have before is misleading. Here, it was the opposite. The inhabitants of Nkholongue were much more likely to travel longer distances in search of employment in the 20th than in the 21st century. The importance of labor migration to South Africa illustrates that many people indeed had far more intense experiences with the "world outside" than being refugees in Malawi, as claimed by the development consultants of the Swedish embassy. One has to consider that some labor migrants were even flown to South Africa by plane.[233] The teleology of increasing mobility seems even more strongly misplaced if we add to this analysis of the forced long-distance transportation of slaves to their labor destinations in the 19th century.

Third, my research confirms the assumptions and findings of others who have claimed that "livelihood diversification" is in a fact not as new a phenomenon as is commonly claimed.[234] Most people in Nkholongue did not grow up to become lifelong cassava farmers. Rather, above all the men pursued very diverse types of work in the course of their lives.[235] However, the fall and rise of Nkholongue's pottery manufacture demonstrates that, among women too, economic life was historically not as monotonous as one might expect at first glance. There is no doubt that, in the case of Nkholongue, "livelihood diversification" existed *avant la lettre.*

---

[232] Osborn, "Work and Migration," 203.
[233] PA, I087: interview with *P1452 (♂, 1927)* (Lichinga, September 10, 2013), min 00:22:13–00:26:52; PA, I013: interview with *P0367 (♂, 1936)* (Nkholongue, September 8, 2010), min 00:20:55–00:22:03.
[234] The term "livelihood diversification" has been popularized by Deborah Bryceson: Deborah F. Bryceson, "Deagrarianization and Rural Employment in Sub-Saharan Africa: A Sectoral Perspective," *World Development* 24, no. 1 (1996): 97–111; Deborah F. Bryceson, "Multiplex Livelihoods in Rural Africa: Recasting the Terms and Conditions of Gainful Employment," *The Journal of Modern African Studies* 40, no. 1 (2002): 1–28. See as well: Alobo Loison, "Rural Livelihood Diversification in Sub-Saharan Africa." For those who have claimed that this phenomenon might have, in fact, not increased in importance, but just been increasingly recognized, see: Grace Carswell, "Livelihood Diversification: Increasing in Importance or Increasingly Recognised? Evidence from Southern Ethiopia," *Journal of International Development* 14, no. 6 (2002): 789–804; Erik Green, "Diversification or De-Agrarianization? Income Diversification, Labor, and Processes of Agrarian Change in Southern and Northern Malawi, Mid-1930s to Mid-1950s," *Agricultural History* 82, no. 2 (2008): 164–192; Frank Ellis, "Household Strategies and Rural Livelihood Diversification," *Journal of Development Studies* 35, no. 1 (1998): 5.
[235] This confirms the findings of Zachary Kagan Guthrie, who in his work on labor migrants from Central Mozambique argued that most of his interviewees did not engage in just one type of labor during their lifetimes, but rather in many different ones. See: Guthrie, *Bound for Work*. On this point, see as well: Moore and Vaughan, *Cutting Down Trees*, 143–147.

Fourth, this chapter has highlighted the repeated profound reorganization of economic life in Nkholongue. With regard to Nkholongue, this chapter has thus not only disproved ideas of rural stasis but also invalidated linear one-way models of transition from subsistence to market production.[236] In Nkholongue, subsistence production did not just continue to exist. It disappeared and reappeared in different areas at different times. It remained an important option throughout Nkholongue's history especially with regard to flour production, though as the evidence shows it was not necessarily the first option. Rather, subsistence production in Nkholongue's history appears to have been more necessity than choice. The most pronounced reversals to subsistence were all a consequence of (external) market disruptions. The chapter has thus also shown that Nkholongue's inhabitants should not be essentialized as "risk-averse" peasants driven by an unchanging "subsistence ethic,"[237] even though they were certainly not unaware of the dangers that a reduction or abandonment of subsistence production could mean for their fate (as shown in their resistance against cotton cultivation, see Section 5.3).

Fifth, this chapter has shown that Nkholongue has not only been part of the capitalist world for a long time, but that capitalist relations of production also began to develop inside the village economy. While the development of capitalism has certainly still been limited, this chapter has, with regard to the fishing sector, underlined the importance of examining production practices closely. Social differentiation can be greater than it appears at first glance. My study underlines the danger of approaching so-called smallholders as a homogeneous group with common interests and concerns. Those considered "subalterns" can also be capitalists.[238] This, of course, connects to the much older study on cocoa farmers in Southern Ghana by Poly Hill, who called them capitalists rather than peasants.[239]

It has been more than 40 years since Sherilyn Young wrote that "faith in a static Africa can evidently not be eliminated by a single submission to the ordeal of

---

236 Sociologist Tony Waters has for example claimed that this transition constitutes a "socio-ecological divide" that, once crossed, allows no turning back. See: Tony Waters, *The Persistence of Subsistence Agriculture: Life beneath the Level of the Marketplace* (Lanham: Lexington, 2006), 2. For similar arguments, see: Bridget O'Laughlin, "Proletarianisation, Agency and Changing Rural Livelihoods: Forced Labour and Resistance in Colonial Mozambique," *Journal of Southern African Studies* 28, no. 3 (2002): 527; Pérez-Niño, "Post-Conflict Agrarian Change in Angónia," 119, 195; Giovanni Arrighi, "Labour Supplies in Historical Perspective: A Study of the Proletarianization of the African Peasantry in Rhodesia," *The Journal of Development Studies* 6, no. 3 (1970): 197–234.
237 These terms are taken from: Scott, *The Moral Economy of the Peasant*, 2–5.
238 On this point, see also Holger Droessler who even uses the term "subaltern capitalists": Holger Droessler, "Copra World: Coconuts, Plantations and Cooperatives in German Samoa," *The Journal of Pacific History* 53, no. 4 (2018): 417–435.
239 Hill, *The Migrant Cocoa-Farmers of Southern Ghana*.

academic inquiry."[240] This chapter represents another attempt to help overcome this persistent faith. As has hopefully been shown, Nkholongue's economic past has been shaped by more than "The Unpredictable Grace of the Sun."[241]

---

240 Sherilynn Young, "Fertility and Famine: Women's Agricultural History in Southern Mozambique," in *The Roots of Rural Poverty in Central and Southern Africa*, ed. Robin Palmer and Neil Parsons (London: Heinemann, 1977), 66.
241 "The Unpredictable Grace of the Sun" is a quote from Kristin Phillips' *Ethnography of Hunger* (2018), a book on the Singida region of Tanzania. Phillips' concept of "subsistence citizenship" falls within the tradition of substantivism. Livelihood diversification is portrayed as a recent process; agricultural and pastoral subsistence work is said to still trump all other work. Phillips' emphasis on the annual cycle of life runs through the book. According to Phillips, deviations from the regular cycle are almost entirely due to environmental factors such as drought or disease. Accordingly, Phillips' chapter on the past is titled *The Unpredictable Grace of the Sun*. See: Phillips, *An Ethnography of Hunger*.

7 Being Resettled: A Social History of the Mozambican War of Independence

7.1 How "Loyalty" Became a Viable Option

This chapter focuses on a process that affected the majority of people living in the war zones of the Mozambican War of Independence (1964–1974): their resettlement by Portuguese forces. As part of the Portuguese resettlement program in Mozambique, nearly one million people were relocated or "regrouped"[1] into strategic villages, the *aldeamentos*.[2] The Portuguese *aldeamentos* scheme did not limit itself to resettlement, however, but went hand in hand with a promise of modernization for those resettled.

The combination of forced resettlement and propagation of social advancement for the resettled has been a paradigmatic counter-insurgency approach since World War Two.[3] It has been applied in conflicts such as the Mau-Mau-Insurgency in Kenya, the Algerian War of Independence or the Vietnam War.[4] The Portuguese forces also used the same strategy in their other decolonization wars in Angola and Guinea-Bissau. The combination of resettlement and development certainly suited the zeitgeist of modernization theory, but it was also a response to the war strategies that the insurgents had adopted in these conflicts. They all followed the Maoist credo that the guerrilla must move among the population like a fish moves in water. In other words, the insurgents sought to do everything possible to maintain good relations with the population of the war zones in order to obtain their support in form of recruits, food, and information. The counterstrategy to this tactic was to deprive the fish of its water. While resettlement aimed to distance

---

[1] It is often ignored that not all those living in *aldeamentos* had been relocated there. Rather, most *aldeamentos* were built around pre-existing villages.

[2] Higher numbers circulating in part of the literature have no foundation in the sources. Given what has been said in the previous footnote, we must even assume that the number of those who had been effectively resettled was lower. For a reliable figure of the population of the *aldeamentos* in August 1973 (based on documents of the Portuguese Ministry of Defence), see: Amélia Neves de Souto, *Caetano e o ocaso do "Império": Administração e guerra colonial em Moçambique durante o Marcelismo (1968–1974)* (Porto: Afrontamento, 2007), 231.

[3] Moritz Feichtinger, "'A Great Reformatory': Social Planning and Strategic Resettlement in Late Colonial Kenya and Algeria, 1952–63," *Journal of Contemporary History* 52, no. 1 (2017): 5; Andreas Stucki, *Aufstand und Zwangsumsiedlung: Die kubanischen Unabhängigkeitskriege 1868–1898* (Hamburg: Hamburger Edition, 2012), 371–372.

[4] For an overview, see: Christian Gerlach, *Extremely Violent Societies: Mass Violence in the Twentieth-Century World* (Cambridge: Cambridge University Press, 2010), 177–234.

people from the enemy physically, modernization aimed to do so emotionally. Promising social and economic progress in the form of the creation of income opportunities and the construction of schools, hospitals, and wells, governments sought to "win people's hearts and minds." The Portuguese Governor of Niassa Province described this government policy in 1970 as follows:

> There is no doubt that a war of the kind we have it in Niassa can only be won if we consider a well-directed promotion of rural progress for the population to be more important than the actual actions of the armed or militarized forces. This war is not about the conquest of territories, but essentially about the conquest of people.[5]

Despite its considerable dimensions, the Portuguese *aldeamentos* program has been examined only superficially. The existing literature is critical of it, with some scholars using Frelimo's terminology of calling the *aldeamentos* "concentration camps."[6] There are two different lines of argumentation: the first considers the Portuguese propagation of social progress as a mere propaganda tool, directed more at the Western public than at the resettled themselves. It regards the program primarily as an instrument of military control that caused a tremendous amount of suffering to the resettled.[7] The other line argues that the colonial government has not or only partially achieved its own goal of offering people the promised modernization. It claims that, as a result of this failure, the program even boomeranged for the state, as it alienated the population even further from it.[8] Both lines of argumentation have in common that they come to their con-

---

5 AHM, GGM XX, cx. 2097: Nuno Egídio, "O Niassa: Relatório Anual de 1970" (Vila Cabral, February 28, 1971), 30.
6 For examples, see: Galli, *Peoples' Spaces and State Spaces*, 36; Andreas Stucki, "Frequent Deaths: The Colonial Development of Concentration Camps Reconsidered, 1868–1974," *Journal of Genocide Research* 20, no. 3 (2018): 322–323.
7 Isaacman and Isaacman, *Mozambique: From Colonialism to Revolution*, 100–102; Galli, *Peoples' Spaces and State Spaces*, 36–37; Stucki, *Violence and Gender in Africa's Iberian Colonies*, 88–91.
8 Brendan F. Jundanian, "Resettlement Programs: Counterinsurgency in Mozambique," *Comparative Politics* 6, no. 4 (1974): 519–540; Henriksen, *Revolution and Counterrevolution*, 143–170; João Paulo Borges Coelho, "Protected Villages and Communal Villages in the Mozambican Province of Tete (1968–1982): A History of State Resettlement Policies, Development and War" (PhD thesis, University of Bradford, 1993), 160–282; John P. Cann, *Counterinsurgency in Africa: The Portuguese Way of War, 1961–1974* (Westport: Greenwood, 1997), 143–168; Stephen Lubkemann, *Culture in Chaos: An Anthropology of the Social Condition in War* (Chicago: University of Chicago Press, 2008), 115–116; Ian F.W. Beckett, "The Portuguese Army: The Campaign in Mozambique, 1964–1974," in *Armed Forces and Mordern Counterinsurgency*, ed. Ian F.W. Beckett and John Pimlott (London: Croom Helm, 1985), 146–148; Castelo, "Colonatos e aldeamentos no Niassa."

clusions using a surprisingly thin line of evidence.[9] They have as a rule also neglected to listen to the voices of those resettled.[10]

The patterns that characterize research on the Portuguese resettlement program in Mozambique are consistent with the state of research on other cases of such programs. As in Mozambique, the resettled have usually been perceived either "as an object of government atrocities or as [a] problem of government control,"[11] but rarely as actors in their own right. Similarly, research on strategic resettlement in other conflicts has been highly critical of the success or even attempt of (colonial) governments to "win people's hearts and minds." Instead, many scholars have stressed the centrality of repression and coercion in spite of the propaganda to the contrary.[12]

In contrast to this, and to my initial surprise, my interviewee's descriptions of their resettlement hardly revolved around elements of repression and coercion. Rather, most interviewees even showed understanding for their relocation and described the *aldeamento* as place where they found peace and about which they had little to complain. Symptomatic of this benign portrayal of resettlement is the testimony of one villager interviewed by MLM's oral history project in 2007. Not even using the word resettlement, he said: "I fled from here to go to the government, and the government protected me and took care of me."[13]

This chapter explains why people perceived their resettlement the way they did, and how "loyalty" to the colonial state became a viable option for many Nkholongueans during the war. The chapter will also reflect on the generalizability of the experiences of Nkholongueans and consider how the processes at work in

---

9 An exception is Borges Coelho, whose work was at the times however still marked by a slight partisan bias: Borges Coelho, "Protected Villages and Communal Villages."
10 An important exception is the already mentioned work on the war in the Maúa district by Funada-Classen. However, she does not reflect her research in the context of the previous research on *aldeamentos* or resettlement. See: Funada-Classen, *The Origins of War in Mozambique*. Another exception is the book of the Isaacmans on the Cahora Bassa dam, which is, though, still markedly influenced by the nationalist liberation narrative and tends to interpret people's experiences mainly through the prism of victimhood. See: Allen Isaacman and Barbara Isaacman, *Dams, Displacement, and the Delusion of Development: Cahora Bassa and Its Legacies in Mozambique, 1965–2007* (Athens: Ohio University Press, 2013), chap. 4.
11 Gerlach, *Extremly Violent Societies*, 179.
12 David French, *The British Way in Counter-Insurgency, 1945–1967* (Oxford: Oxford University Press, 2011), 174–99; Stacey Hynd, "Small Warriors? Children and Youth in Colonial Insurgencies and Counterinsurgency, ca. 1945–1960," *Comparative Studies in Society and History* 62, no. 4 (2020): 685. For an overview of this type of literature, see: Karl Hack, "'Devils That Suck the Blood of the Malayan People': The Case for Post-Revisionist Analysis of Counter-Insurgency Violence," *War in History* 25, no. 2 (2018): n. 6.
13 MLM, 026: interview with S.F., transcript Chinyanja (Nkholongue, June 27, 2007), 5.

Nkholongue can connect to observations and findings by scholars from other settings. Recent studies by Daniel Branch and François-Xavier Hautreux have emphasized the importance of including the analysis of loyalism as part of the explanation of the wars in Kenya and Algeria.[14] This importance is also evident in most other cases of counter-insurgency wars if one considers that the number of armed locals on the government side usually clearly exceeded the number of guerrillas.[15] But, in general, we still know very little about this group, their attitudes and motives.

Against the convention of dividing groups of people into either nationalists or loyalists, this chapter will underline the critical importance of shifting political attitudes during the war, showing how Nkholongue's inhabitants actively supported Frelimo at the beginning of the conflict, but ended up mostly helping the Portuguese war effort. Part of this change can be explained by the regional development of the war. Initially, the momentum was doubtlessly on Frelimo's side. Rapid decolonization seemed within reach. However, these prospects turned upside down when the colonial state strengthened its (military) forces after the outbreak of the war and succeeded in significantly destabilizing and decimating Frelimo's regional presence. Part of people's shifting alliances can thus be explained by what has been referred to as "attentisme," "fence-sitting," or "free-riding" in relation to other conflicts.[16] As Neil MacMaster put with regard to Algeria, "[w]hich side you ended up fighting on or supporting might have had little to do with the global po-

---

[14] Daniel Branch, *Defeating Mau Mau, Creating Kenya: Counterinsurgency, Civil War, and Decolonization* (Cambridge: Cambridge University Press, 2009); David Anderson and Daniel Branch, "Allies at the End of Empire—Loyalists, Nationalists and the Cold War, 1945–76," *The International History Review* 39, no. 1 (2017): 1–13. In relation to the lusophone cases, see the recent publications by Pedro Aires Oliveira and Fatima Rodrigues: Pedro Aires Oliveira, "Saved by the Civil War: African 'Loyalists' in the Portuguese Armed Forces and Angola's Transition to Independence," *The International History Review* 39, no. 1 (2017): 126–142; Fatima da Cruz Rodrigues, "Vidas deslocadas pelo colonialismo e pela guerra," *Estudos Ibero-Americanos* 45, no. 2 (2019): 49–63.
[15] Gerlach, *Extremly Violent Societies*, 194–95. Borges Coelho offers a statistic of "locally" recruited troops for the Portuguese wars in Mozambique, Angola, and Guinea-Bissau. He also points to the role of militias but does not include them in his count. See: João Paulo Borges Coelho, "African Troops in the Portuguese Colonial Army, 1961–1974: Angola, Guinea-Bissau and Mozambique," *Portuguese Studies Review* 10, no. 1 (2002): 129–150.
[16] Neil MacMaster, "The 'Silent Native': Attentisme, Being Compromised, and Banal Terror during the Algerian War of Independence, 1954–1962," in *The French Colonial Mind, Vol. 2: Violence, Military Encounters, and Colonialism*, ed. Martin Thomas (Lincoln: University of Nebraska Press, 2011), 283–303; Stathis N. Kalyvas and Matthew Adam Kocher, "How 'Free' Is Free Riding in Civil Wars? Violence, Insurgency, and the Collective Action Problem," *World Politics* 59, no. 2 (2007): 177–216; Stathis N. Kalyvas, *The Logic of Violence in Civil War* (Cambridge: Cambridge University Press, 2006), 40, 226–234.

litical or ideological divisions (nationalism versus French colonialism), but more to do with accidents of time and place, what Hamoumou calls 'local contingencies.'"[17] Local developments around Nkholongue mirrored those observed by Daniel Branch for Kenya, where "[t]he loss of insurgent control triggered a move towards loyalism."[18]

However, this chapter will argue that the shifting ideological alliances were to a certain degree also genuine. As Frelimo was able to win people for their political project at the beginning the war, Portuguese forces equally succeeded in convincing people that staying with the Portuguese Empire might be the better alternative. This chapter will show that the Portuguese state indeed made an effort to "win people's hearts and minds" that locally materialized. Similar to what Stephan Malinowski and Moritz Feichtinger have done for the French war in Algeria, this chapter will highlight that the war against Mozambican Independence cannot be explained simply by the brutal actions of a reactionary and racist colonial state using the language of modernization and change as a mere propaganda tool.[19] Taking up the discussion from Chapter 5, the following pages will highlight that, at least in the case examined here, the Portuguese colonial system proved more capable of reform than is commonly assumed. Thus, Portuguese forces were indeed eager to provide the resettled with acceptable living conditions. Schooling rates, for example, rose rapidly during the war. Furthermore, there was a marked change in the use of repression and violence in those years. While Portuguese forces systematically destroyed fields and food outside the *aldeamentos* throughout the war, they indeed started to avoid direct killings of people outside their control. In this regard, my findings connect to the observations of Karl Hack, who has called for the examination of the "lifecycles of particular types of violence" in relation to the British counter-insurgency campaign in Malaya.[20]

In general, this chapter will emphasize the importance of chronology and context. In his research on resettlement in Kenya and Algeria, Moritz Feichtinger has shown that people's differing assessments and interpretations of strategic resettlement "can be explained by the simple fact that they often refer to distinct phases"

---

[17] MacMaster, "The 'Silent Native,'" 295. Similar observations have been made by Stathis Kalyvas: Kalyvas, *The Logic of Violence in Civil War*, 38–48.
[18] Branch, *Defeating Mau Mau*, 116.
[19] Moritz Feichtinger and Stephan Malinowski, "'Eine Million Algerier lernen im 20. Jahrhundert zu leben': Umsiedlungslager und Zwangsmodernisierung im Algerienkrieg 1954–1962," *Journal of Modern European History* 8, no. 1 (2010): 107–135.
[20] Hack, "'Devils That Suck the Blood of the Malayan People.'"

of resettlement.[21] My research points out that such divergent opinions also depend crucially on what people had experienced before their resettlement. Like other chapters before it, this one equally underscores the importance of not falling prey to what I call the Aboriginal Delusion (see Section 1.4) and to consider the disruptions that preceded the disruption. Crucial in this case is that the disruption of the resettlement was preceded by the disruption of the war experience.

With the analysis of the wartime experiences of the inhabitants of Nkholongue, this chapter also seeks to complicate our knowledge of the history of the war in Mozambique. Despite some more critical accounts, this remains largely framed by Frelimo's liberation script. Frelimo is still seen widely as "the ideal movement of 'people's war' and national liberation"[22] and said to have enjoyed massive support among the peasants of northern Mozambique.[23] Recent research on the war has again largely focused on liberation fighters,[24] or then perpetuated the notion of Portugal as an imminently brutal and unreformable colonial power.[25] An important exception is Sayaka Funada-Classen's study of the war events in the district of Maúa, in which she has argued how the war not only created unity but also disunity among the inhabitants of the war zones.[26] This chapter will show that

---

21 Moritz Feichtinger, "'Villagization': A People's History of Strategic Resettlement and Violent Transformation. Kenya & Algeria, 1952–1962" (PhD thesis, Bern, Universität Bern, 2016), 137.
22 Terence O. Ranger, *Peasant Consciousness and Guerilla War in Zimbabwe: A Comparative Study* (London: James Currey, 1985), 6.
23 Bowen, *The State Against the Peasantry*, 213–14; Kajsa Johansson, "Peasant Collective Action against Disembedding Land: The Case of Niassa Province, Mozambique," in *Social Movements Contesting Natural Resource Development*, ed. John F. Devlin (London: Routledge, 2019), 35. The narrative that Frelimo won the war because it was able to gain the support of the "local people" is still very popular. See for example: Joseph Hanlon, ed., "Mozambique News Reports & Clippings," no. 492 (June 28, 2020), 1.
24 Katto, *Women's Lived Landscapes of War and Liberation in Mozambique*; Liazzat Bonate, "Muslim Memories of the Liberation War in Cabo Delgado," *Kronos* 39, no. 1 (2013): 230–56; Joel das Neves Tembe, ed., *História da Luta de Libertação Nacional*, vol. 1 (Maputo: Ministério dos Combatentes, 2014); Benigna Zimba, ed., *A mulher moçambicana na Luta de Libertação Nacional: Memórias do Destacamento Feminino* (Maputo: Centro de Pesquisa da História da Luta de Libertação Nacional, 2012).
25 Mustafah Dhada, *The Portuguese Massacre of Wiriyamu in Colonial Mozambique, 1964–2013* (London: Bloomsbury, 2016); Castelo, "Colonatos e aldeamentos no Niassa."
26 Funada-Classen, *The Origins of War in Mozambique*. A similar argument has been made by Ana Margarida Santos for Cabo Delgado. See: Ana Margarida Santos, "The Past in the Present: Memories of the Liberation Struggle in Northern Mozambique," 7° Congresso Ibérico de Estudos Africanos (Lisboa, 2010), accessed October 30, 2019, http://www.observatori.org/paises/pais_70/documentos/_Mozambbique_The%20past%20in%20the%20present.pdf; Ana Margarida Santos, "Resistance and Collaboration: Conflicting Memories of the Liberation Struggle (1964–1974) in Northern Mozambique," *Social Evolution & History* 13, no. 2 (2014): 151–175.

in regard to Niassa, the number of people living under the control of Frelimo in the so-called liberated areas was in fact tiny at the end of the war. This is a dynamic that has so far been barely recognized in any systematic manner, but which has very important implications for the history of Mozambican nationalism.

The chapter is divided into three parts. First, we will have a short look at Frelimo's memory politics. An understanding of these is important for a critical interpretation of any analysis of the war that draws on oral history. The main focus will be on the *dinheiro dos antigos combatentes* ('money of the former combatants'), a war pension that has been granted to former fighters. In a second part, we will look at the course of the war from the perspective of the inhabitants of Nkholongue, analyze their resettlement to Metangula, and examine people's life in the *aldeamento*. In the last part, we will zoom out and reflect on how the wartime experiences of Nkholongue's population can improve our analysis of similar wars in general and the Mozambican War of Independence in particular.

7.2 Buying History with Money: Frelimo's Fake Veterans

We have already discussed various challenges that need to be considered when conducting and interpreting interviews (see especially Section 1.3). However, the topic of the Mozambican War of Independence requires special attention. The main reason for this is the *dinheiro dos antigos combatentes*. The sudden increase in the number of recipients of this pension, which began in 1999, has so far been largely ignored by scholars.[27] My fieldwork experience has undoubtedly taught me how important this pension has become in relation to local (memory) politics.

The increase in the number of the recipients of the *dinheiro dos antigos combatentes* must be understood in the context of a major revival of the politics of memory by Frelimo since the late 1990s. In addition to the distribution of money to "veterans," these politics include the frequent holding of commemorative ceremonies, the installation of statues, the promotion of the publication of war memoirs and partisan historiography, and the naming of schools and streets after the struggle's heroes.[28] In 2000, the Mozambican government created a ministry responsible exclusively for the affairs of former combatants. Since its inception, this ministry has supported the dissemination of the history of the armed

---

27 Wiegink has at least touched upon it. See: Nikkie Wiegink, *Former Guerrillas in Mozambique* (Philadelphia: University of Pennsylvania Press, 2020), 171, 183–187.
28 For a selection of such publications, see: Zimba, *A mulher moçambicana na Luta de Libertação Nacional*; Ana Bouene Mussanhane, ed., *Protagonistas da Luta de Libertação Nacional* (Maputo: Marimbique, 2012); Tembe, *História da Luta de Libertação Nacional*.

struggle through talks, lectures, television debates and radio transmissions.[29] The district of Lago, one of the two districts where the first shots of the armed struggle were fired, has played an important role in the government's efforts to use remembrance for political ends. Between 2008 and 2014, it hosted three major commemorations for fallen heroes of the armed struggle, all of which were attended by Mozambique's president. At these ceremonies, the government distributed heroic biographies of the commemorated among the population.[30]

While all these efforts may have had some impact on people's "memory" and the way they think it is proper to talk about the war, there is little doubt that the most important effects have been caused by the *dinheiro dos antigos combatentes*. The first payments of this pension date back to 1986, when the Mozambican government established a law on pensions of the members of the Mozambican armed forces. This law declared all veterans of the armed struggle as members of the armed forces. Thereby, a veteran was not only one who had fought with a weapon in his or her hand, but also one who had provided logistical support.[31] Initially, the number of recipients of pensions was relatively small. It began to rise around 1999, and especially after 2002 when the government passed the *Estatuto do Combatente* ('Statute of the Veteran').[32] With this statute, the government introduced an additional one-time participation bonus for those who were recognized as war veterans. People were invited to hand in their story of war participation, on the basis

---

[29] From 2012 to May 2014 alone the ministry supported the realization of 2,220 talks, 47 TV debates and 94 radio transmissions. See: "Combatentes homenageados," Notícias Online, May 21, 2014, accessed August 3, 2014, http://www.jornalnoticias.co.mz/index.php/politica/16120-combatentes-home nageados.
[30] For the ceremonies in Lago, see: "Moçambique lembrou-se de Kajika," *Faísca: O Jornal do Niassa*, no. 644 (June 14, 2014): 8–10; Assumail Raidone et al., *Vida e obra de Bernabé Adison Kajika (1938–1974)* (Lichinga: ARPAC, 2014); Assumail Raidone, Manuel Vene, and Laurindo Malimusse, *Vida e obra de Francisco Orlando Magumbwa* (Lichinga: ARPAC, 2013). For these ceremonies and booklets in general, see: Amélia Neves de Souto, "Memory and Identity in the History of Frelimo: Some Research Themes," *Kronos* 39, no. 1 (2013): 291–292.
[31] "Decreto n.º 3/86 de 25 de Julho," *Boletim da República (I Série)*, no. 30, 3.º Suplemento (July 26, 1986): 82/14. See as well: Ângelo José Naiene and Arlindo Langa, "Atribuição de pensão aos antigos combatentes desmobilizados: O impacto na reintegração social no centro de produção dos antigos combatentes 25 de Setembro, em Umbeluzi, Distrito de Boane, Província de Maputo, no período 1986–2001" (PhD thesis, Maputo, Universidade Eduardo Mondlane, 2002), accessed August 4, 2014, http://www.saber.ac.mz/bitstream/10857/2172/1/Ap-025.pdf.
[32] "Lei N.º 3/2002, de 17 de Janeiro: Estatuto do Combatente da Luta de Libertação Nacional," *Boletim da República (I Série)*, no. 3, Suplemento (January 17, 2002). See as well: Conselho de Ministros, "Resolução n.º 37/2001: Política sobre os assunto dos antigos combatentes e estratégia de sua implementação," *Boletim da República. Publicação Oficial da República de Moçambique*, no. 20 (May 22, 2001).

of which it was then decided whether or not they qualified for the bonus and pension.³³

I do not have any figures that would allow me to reconstruct the exact increase in the number of pensions. But some data can be used for illustration. In 2006, for example, the government admitted 14,153 new veterans and paid out 1,058 participation bonuses.³⁴ In 2013, almost 40 years after the end of the war, an astonishing 9,472 new participation bonuses were granted to war veterans.³⁵ While from 2014 to 2016, the number of officially registered veterans of the War of Independence rose from 76,160 to 95,743.³⁶

From a methodological perspective, the importance of these pensions cannot be underestimated. Around 2013, the participation bonus corresponded to a one-time payment of about 30,000 to 40,000 MZN (about 1,000 to 1,300 USD at the time), and the monthly pension payments to about 3,000 to 5,000 MZN (100 to 165 USD).³⁷ This was an enormous amount of money in a region where 80 percent of the households spent less than 1,000 MZN (33 USD) in one week, and 37 percent even less than 250 MZN (8 USD) according to figures from 2011.³⁸

In view of these high amounts, it is probably no surprise that the government's new policy raised the hopes of many, especially since some of Nkholongue's former inhabitants had been recognized as war veterans.³⁹ One of my interviewees, who had fought for Frelimo in the 1960s but deserted from the movement during the war and had lived in Malawi ever since, returned to Nkholongue solely to apply for the money.⁴⁰ The sudden appearance of the *dinheiro dos antigos combatentes*

---

33 PA, I087: interview with *P1452* (♂, *1927*) (Lichinga, September 10, 2013), min 01:08:43–01:17:01.
34 República de Moçambique, "Balanço do Plano Económico e Social 2006," 2007, 67, accessed April 20, 2019, http://www.portaldogoverno.gov.mz/por/content/download/1767/14380/version/1/file/pes +2006+balan%25c3%25a7o+anual+2006.pdf.
35 "Mais 33 mil combatentes vão beneficiar de pensões – Jornal Notícias," Notícias Online, January 2, 2014, accessed August 3, 2014, http://www.jornalnoticias.co.mz/index.php/politica/9366-mais-33-mil-combatentes-vao-beneficiar-de-pensoes.
36 "MICO regista perto de 166.800 combatentes," Notícias Online, June 14, 2014, accessed July 16, 2014, http://www.jornalnoticias.co.mz/index.php/politica/17594-mico-regista-perto-de-166-800-com batentes; "PR sobre a fixação de pensões: reduz insatisfação do combatente," Notícias Online, March 14, 2016, accessed July 18, 2019, https://www.jornalnoticias.co.mz/index.php/politica/51279-pr-sobre-a-fixacao-de-pensoes-reduz-insatisfacao-do-combatente.
37 PA, I087: interview with *P1452* (♂, *1927*) (Lichinga, September 10, 2013), min 01:31:06–01:37:33; PA, I051: interview with *P0481* (♀, *1942*) (Nkholongue, August 26, 2013), min 00:48:45–00:49:26. For similar numbers, see as well: Wiegink, *Former Guerrillas in Mozambique*, 184.
38 The numbers on spending are from: ORGUT, "Sub-Report, District of Lago: Year One, 2011," 18.
39 I interviewed three of them and know of one more who has already passed away.
40 In 2013, I met and interviewed him in Malango. But in 2016 he was already back in Malawi where I interviewed him again. PA, I038: interview with *P1439* (♂, *~1940*) (Malango, August 15,

raised not only hopes but also envy. Many of those who began to receive the pension were considered fake veterans who received the money only because they had good relations with certain individuals in the government or because the government considered it important to win their political allegiance.[41]

The result of these politics of memory was that some interviewees clearly tended to exaggerate their support for Frelimo, while others tended to conceal their less "glorious" war roles. The latter group included those who had joined Frelimo at the beginning of the war but deserted from the nationalists later.[42] It also included those who had joined the *Grupos Especiais* (GE), a Portuguese military unit composed of black volunteers.[43] One of them, for example, initially denied most firmly that he had ever fought for the Portuguese. It was only after a while that he angrily confirmed that he had indeed joined the GE. His anger, however, made it clear that he was not prepared to tell us more about it.[44] Another was more talkative. He even complained to me that those who had fought for the whites were not receiving any money, and he expressed his hope that maybe I could do something about it.[45]

2013), min 00:45:29–00:46:36; PA, I132: interview with *P1439 (♂, ~1940), P1507 (♀, ~1930), P1508 (♀)* (Ndegue (Salima), June 1, 2016).

41 For discussions surrounding the selection of true and fake veterans, see for example: PA, I094: interview with *P0727 (♂, ~1940)* (M'chepa, January 27, 2016), min 01:39:37–01:42:03; PA, I096: interview with *P1216 (♂, 1957)* (Malango, February 1, 2016), min 02:31:11–02:32:17; PA, I115: interview with *P0160 (♂, 1952)* (Metangula, April 18, 2016), min 02:53:36–02:55:12; PA, I123: interview with *P1460 (♀), P1461 (♂, ~1935), P1462 (♂, ~1935)* (Meluluca, April 25, 2016), min 02:41:41–02:42:52; PA, I125: interview with *P1463 (♂, 1951)* (Ngala, April 27, 2016), min 01:29:46–01:31:13; PA, I166: interview with *P1479 (♀, ~1922), P1505 (♂, 1957)* (Nampula, June 28, 2016), min 01:15:44–01:19:04; PA, I051: interview with *P0481 (♀, 1942)* (Nkholongue, August 26, 2013), min 00:47:17–00:50:44; PA, I039: interview with *P0898 (♀, 1960)* (Malango, August 15, 2013), min 01:14:02–01:15:38.

42 PA, I056: interview with *P1102 (♂, 1932)* (Malango, August 28, 2013), min 00:40:40–00:47:20; PA, I038: interview with *P1439 (♂, ~1940)* (Malango, August 15, 2013), min 00:21:09–00:25:08; PA, I158: interview with *P0764 (♂, 1962)* (Nkholongue, June 20, 2016), min 00:07:05–00:08:21, 00:37:52–00:38:23; PA, I065: interview with *P0583 (♂, 1972)* (Nkholongue, September 1, 2013), min 00:04:12–00:06:47.

43 For the GE and the "Africanization" of the troops in general, see: Souto, *Caetano e o Ocaso do "Império,"* 283–301; Borges Coelho, "African Troops in the Portuguese Colonial Army."

44 PA, I041: interview with *P0951 (♀, 1948), P0242 (♂, 1945)* (Malango, August 16, 2013). See as well the interview with his ex-wife in which her current husband intervened asking whether it could not cause them troubles with the government when she told us about her ex-husband having fought for the GE: PA, I052: interview with *(♀, 1940)* (Nkholongue, August 26, 2013), min 00:21:35–00:24:24.

45 PA, I037: interview with *P0855 (♂, 1954)* (Malango, August 14, 2013), min 01:17:50–01:21:42.

This clearly shows how people had their own expectations and ideas about what they could gain and/or fear from the interviews they gave me.[46] This also shows how carefully one must interpret oral testimonies on the Mozambican War of Independence. Two factors helped me to address these challenges in the case of my research. First, interviewing a large number of people from the same social setting enabled me to cross-check the information. Second, the longitudinal perspective of my study made it easier to identify biographical inconsistencies.

7.3 From Fighting for the Nationalist to Supporting the Portuguese War Effort

It has already been demonstrated in Chapter 5 that the region around Nkholongue lay at the very periphery of the *Estado Novo*. It was in 1964, the year the war broke out, that the Portuguese Board of the Investigation of the Overseas Territories (*Junta de Investigações do Ultramar*) published a book with the telling title *The Unknown Niassa*.[47] This all changed with the onset of the decolonization wave in Africa. With the independence of neighboring Tanganyika, the Mozambican nationalists had received a suitable base for their goals. The Portuguese government, alarmed not only by the developments across the continent but also by the outbreak of the war in Angola in early 1961, was now quickly realizing that its tenuous presence in northern Mozambique could become a military liability.[48]

Suddenly, the Portuguese government pushed the construction of the colonial infrastructure that had been so long missing. The lakeshore was for the first time professionally surveyed and mapped as part of a hydrographic mission already in the late 1950s.[49] In 1961, Portugal began with the construction of its first navy boat

---

46 Also note in this respect the statement of one interviewee in MLM's oral history project. It shows that he was evidently most afraid that the government could not like what he had said. See: MLM, 026: interview with S.F., transcript Chinyanja (Nkholongue, June 27, 2007).
47 Santos, *O desconhecido Niassa*.
48 AHD, MU/GM/GNP/RNP/0064/01681: Mário Costa, "Ocupação administrativa do Distrito do Niassa," May 22, 1961, 6; AHD, MU/GM/GNP/RNP/0521/01667: Mário Costa, "Relatório da Inspecção ao Distrito do Niassa, de 13 de Abril a 3 de Maio 1960" (Lourenço Marques, June 10, 1961), 15; ANTT, SCCIM N.° 1088 (folhas 37–39): N.° 238/B: Secretário-Adjunto da Defesa Nacional ao Comandante Chefe das Forças Armadas de Moçambique LM, (June 8, 1961).
49 Interestingly, the Hydrographic Mission has retrospectively been identified by some of my interviewees as a sign of the coming war. See: PA, I045: interview with *P0242* (♂, *1945*) (Malango, August 17, 2013), min 00:00:00–00:02:12; PA, I109: interview with *P1081* (♀, *1945*) (Malango, April 6, 2016), min 00:09:40–00:11:10; PA, I052: interview with (♀, *1940*) (Nkholongue, August 26, 2013),

for the lake.⁵⁰ Airstrips were built all across Niassa. And in 1962, the Portuguese government opened the province's first secondary school in Vila Cabral.⁵¹

Due to its strategic location on the lake, Metangula returned to being an important center of the colonial state in the area. It was chosen as the location for the new navy base on the lake. Furthemore, in a reversal of the process of its administrative downgrading in the 1920s (see Section 5.2), it was now restored as the capital of Lago District.⁵² The population of Nkholongue, situated just a stone's throw from the town, all of a sudden found itself again next to the central representation of the colonial state in the region.

The Anglican missionary John Paul, who was present at the inauguration of Metangula's navy base on October 1, 1963,⁵³ wrote in his memoirs that he had never before seen so many Portuguese on the lakeshore as on this occasion.⁵⁴ The first Portuguese commander of the base described the moment when the base's generators were switched on as follows:

> It was shortly after midnight when all of a sudden the whole base was illuminated. Impossible to describe the sensation: it was like being on another planet, like being alone on a shining island surrounded by endless darkness… Despite the late hour, hundreds of people from the village of Chilombe in the bay ran here to see the miracle of the light! The generators were not switched off anymore. A new era had begun.⁵⁵

The new era was one of war. Lago District was one of Frelimo's first recruiting grounds. Shortly after the movement had been founded in Tanganyika in 1962, Frelimo began establishing its clandestine networks, especially in the social environ-

---

min 00:11:43–00:14:31; PA, I054: interview with *P0554 (♀, 1949)* (Nkholongue, August 27, 2013), min 00:05:28–00:08:44. For the Hydrographic Mission in general, see: AHMar, Coloredo, Pasta 066/MO: Alguns elementos relativos às lanchas e infraestruturas da Marinha Portuguesa no Lago Niassa (1957/1975) (Lisboa, 1988), 4–5; Instituto Hidrográfico, *Roteiro da costa portuguesa do Lago Niassa* (Lisboa, 1963); AHU, IPAD/MU/DGOPC/DSH/1749/13221: José A. B. Fernandes, "Reconhecimento hidrográfico da costa portuguesa do Lago Niassa" (Lourenço Marques, April 25, 1959).

50 AHM, SNI, Secção B, cx. 606: Duarte C.P. Pelloso, "Adit.º à Nota-Confidencial nº 570/A/27, de 15/6/961" (Vila Cabral, August 9, 1961).
51 Paul, *Memoirs of a Revolution*, 94–95.
52 AHMar, Coloredo, Pasta 066/MO: Alguns elementos relativos às lanchas e infraestruturas da Marinha Portuguesa no Lago Niassa (1957/1975) (Lisboa, 1988), 14. For the administrative upgrade, see: Portaria n.º 17 320, 21.12.1963, cited by: Alexandre Lobato, "Augusto Cardoso e o Lago Niassa," *Stvdia. Revista Quadrimestral*, no. 19 (1966): 90–91.
53 Lobato, "Augusto Cardoso e o Lago Niassa," 38.
54 Paul, *Memoirs of a Revolution*, 87–88.
55 It is "Chirombe" in the original. See: Sérgio Zilhão, "Depoimento de Comandante de Mar e Guerra Sérgio Zilhão," in *Combater em Moçambique: Guerra e descolonização 1964–1975*, by Manuel A. Bernardo (Lisboa: Préfacio, 2003), 342.

ment of the Anglican mission of Messumba.[56] Lago was also the district where Frelimo fired the first shots of the war on September 24, 1964.[57]

While the remainder of 1964 had seen only sporadic attacks, Frelimo's actions in the region increased in the course of 1965.[58] It was also at this point that Nkholongue's population was visited by Frelimo fighters for the first time. The fighters had established a base near the upper reaches of the Luina river, about five to ten miles from the village. According to my interviewees, the fighters first made contact with Nkholongue's chief in order to win the population's support.[59] This is consistent with the evidence from other places where the chiefs played an important role in winning followers for Frelimo during this phase of the war.[60]

As elsewhere, Frelimo was able to gain considerable support in the form of food and recruits in Nkholongue. Several young men and probably one woman joined Frelimo as fighters, others carried food to the base, and a portion of the population (both women and men) began living near the Luina base.[61] In light

---

56 David F. Ndegue, *A Luta de Libertação na Frente do Niassa*, vol. 1 (Maputo: JV, 2009), 17–42.
57 In Frelimo's liberation narrative, the war began with simultaneous attacks in Niassa and Cabo Delgado on September 25, 1964. Alberto Chipande is credited with having fired the first shot of the war during the attack on the administrative post of Chai (Cabo Delgado). However, according to Portuguese military sources, the attack on the administrative post of Cobué had happened already on September 24, 1964. See: AHMil, FO/63/13/948/3: José R. M. da Matta, "Anexo C (Actividade IN desde 1959 até 10FEV68) ao Relatório Especial de Informações n° 01/68" (Metangula, February 1968), 2; John P. Cann, *Brown Waters of Africa: Portuguese Riverine Warfare 1961–1974* (2007; repr., Solihull: Helion, 2013), 184.
58 For an overview of the initial developments of the war in the area, see: APGGN: António Gonçalves Marques, "Situação política da área do Lago, e evolução dos acontecimentos a partir do dia um do Janeiro de 1965 até à presente data" (Augusto Cardoso, October 23, 1965); AHMar, Coloredo, Pasta 032/MO: Sérgio Zilhão, "Analise dos acontecimentos do Niassa," Confidencial (Metangula, February 10, 1966); AHMil, DIV/2/7/149/6: Batalhão de Caçadores 598. História de Unidade, n.d.; AHMil, FO/63/13/948/3: Matta: Anexo C ao Relatório Especial de Informações n° 01/68.
59 PA, I056: interview with *P1102 (♂, 1932)* (Malango, August 28, 2013), min 00:32:14–00:34:15; PA, I068: interview with *P0367 (♂, 1936)* (Nkholongue, September 2, 2013), min 00:09:37–00:12:30; PA, I038: interview with *P1439 (♂, ~1940)* (Malango, August 15, 2013), min 00:14:20–00:15:05.
60 PA, I095: interview with *P1453 (♂, ~1947), P1506 (♀, ~1950)* (Malango, January 28, 2016), min 00:27:32–00:28:49. This is also confirmed by Frelimo veterans and Portuguese sources. See: João Facitela Pelembe, *Lutei pela pátria: Memórias de um combatente da luta pela libertação nacional* (Maputo, 2012), 73–74; Ndegue, A Luta de Libertação na Frente do Niassa, 134–143; AHMar, Coloredo, Pasta 032/MO: Sérgio Zilhão, "Analise dos acontecimentos do Niassa," Confidencial (Metangula, February 10, 1966).
61 PA, I068: interview with *P0367 (♂, 1936)* (Nkholongue, September 2, 2013), min 00:09:50–00:11:20; PA, I037: interview with *P0855 (♂, 1954)* (Malango, August 14, 2013), min 00:12:16–00:13:35; PA, I040: interview with *P1030 (♀, 1965), P1009 (♀, 1958), P1029 (♂, ~1959)* (Malango, August 16, 2013), min 00:31:50–00:33:05; PA, I041: interview with *P0951 (♀, 1948), P0242 (♂,*

7.3 From Fighting for the Nationalist to Supporting the Portuguese War Effort — 265

of what has been said about Frelimo's memory politics, we must be critical of people's assertion of broad voluntary support.[62] Some testimonies suggest that not everyone was helping Frelimo as willingly and eagerly as many have portrayed it. Several interviewees stated that they had little choice as they were asked to do so by armed men, and others also said that they were afraid of war.[63] Frelimo reinforced these fears by killing several people in the region whom they suspected of being colonial "collaborators."[64]

1945) (Malango, August 16, 2013), min 00:11:41–00:16:38; PA, I058: interview with *P1074* (♀, *~1940*) (Malango, August 28, 2013), min 01:45:28–01:50:40. The men from Nkholongue who joined Frelimo and whose identity I was able to determine with certainty are P1452, P1102, P1439, P1036, P0555, P0581. P0299 also claimed to have joined Frelimo, though his story seems pretty implausible (see Footnote 62). Others were, at times, mentioned as part of the group of those who joined Frelimo, but I was not able to determine their identity beyond any doubt. Among them is one woman. See: PA, I038: interview with *P1439* (♂, *~1940*) (Malango, August 15, 2013), min 00:13–01–00:21:42; PA, I056: interview with *P1102* (♂, *1932*) (Malango, August 28, 2013), min 00:01–02–00:09:35; PA, I087: interview with *P1452* (♂, *1927*) (Lichinga, September 10, 2013), min 00:04–02–00:09:11; PA, I037: interview with *P0855* (♂, *1954*) (Malango, August 14, 2013), min 00:10–02–00:12:16; PA, I058: interview with *P1074* (♀, *~1940*) (Malango, August 28, 2013), min 01:45–08–01:49:12; PA, I158: interview with *P0764* (♂, *1962*) (Nkholongue, June 20, 2016), min 00:06–03–00:08:21; PA, I065: interview with *P0583* (♂, *1972*) (Nkholongue, September 1, 2013), min 00:04–02–00:06:47; PA, I008: interview with *P0299* (♂, *1938*) (Nkholongue, September 1, 2010), min 00:29–08–00:32:57.
62 The are clear indications of cases in which people misrepresented their role. For an example, see: PA, I008: interview with *P0299* (♂, *1938*) (Nkholongue, September 1, 2010), min 00:27:43–00:35:31, 00:46:06–00:52:04. The respective interviewee claimed to have joined Frelimo at the beginning, but also stated that he was later allowed to go to Metangula because of his sick mother. There, according to his statement, he became navigator of a Portuguese fishing boat. In fact, though, he was chief navigator of a Portuguese military boat, and most probably had never joined Frelimo at the beginning. See: AHMar, Colored, Pasta 066/MO: Relação do pessoal civil voluntário para receber instrução nas lanchas, n.d., 1. For another example, see P1453 (originally from Metangula) who claimed to have stayed with Frelimo until the end of the war. His colleague (P1102), though, claimed that they left Frelimo together and went to Malawi. See: PA, I095: interview with *P1453* (♂, *~1947*), *P1506* (♀, *~1950*) (Malango, January 28, 2016), min 00:45:22–00:46:18; PA, I056: interview with *P1102* (♂, *1932*) (Malango, August 28, 2013), min 00:40:40–00:47:20.
63 PA, I094: interview with *P0727* (♂, *~1940*) (M'chepa, January 27, 2016), min 00:38:51–00:38:59; PA, I117: interview with *P1458* (♂, *~1945*) (Micundi, April 20, 2016), min 00:33:52–00:36:56, 00:40:04–00:41:55; PA, I054: interview with *P0554* (♀, *1949*) (Nkholongue, August 27, 2013), min 00:19:41–00:23:04; PA, I059: interview with *P0090* (♀, *~1932*) (Metangula, August 29, 2013), min 00:22:45–00:23:40.
64 For killings by Frelimo of alleged colonial collaborators, see: MLM, 003: interview with *A. S.*, transcript Chinyanja (Micuio, June 18, 2007), 8; APGGN, António Gonçalves Marques, "Situação política da área do Lago, e evolução dos acontecimentos a partir do dia um do Janeiro de 1965 até à presente data" (Augusto Cardoso, October 23, 1965), 2; AHMil, DIV/2/7/149/6: Batalhão de Caçadores 598. História de Unidade, n.d., 4; PA, I094: interview with *P0727* (♂, *~1940*) (M'chepa, January 27,

Nevertheless, I have little doubt that in this phase of the war many of Nkholongue's inhabitants supported Frelimo willingly and readily. The motivations for this support are more difficult to determine in retrospect. It may seem obvious that many were against the racist system of colonialism. However, as has been shown in Chapter 5, previous resistance against colonialism had been limited. Moreover, it is noteworthy that many explained that they themselves had not had bad experiences with Portuguese colonialism, but that it was their parents and elders that told them how they had been exploited by the Portuguese.[65] This fits in with the local developments of colonialism described in Chapter 5, in which the hardships of colonialism were alleviated locally first by the reduced presence of the colonial state from the 1920s onward, and later by more liberal Portuguese "men on the spot." Still, previous experiences and the voices of the elders may have played an important role in people's reasoning to support Frelimo. One interviewee rationalized that even though *machiras* ("palanquins") were no longer in use in the 1960s, they had never forgotten them.[66]

Support for Frelimo was not only a consequence of current and past exploitation, but also a product of expectations for the future. There is little doubt that many backed Frelimo because they hoped for a change for the better, especially in terms of the economic situation. Many blamed the Portuguese for the lack of employment opportunities and for the poverty in the country.[67]

2016), min 00:29:50–00:32:01; ADN, FO/F002/SC002/38: PERINTREP N.° 91 (Lourenço Marques: QG/RMM/2a REP, September 13, 1965), 6. One of Messumba's local teachers was dragged out of his house at midnight and shot by Frelimo fighters on April 2, 1965, because of his sympathies for the Portuguese (he survived). See: Joan Antcliff, *Living in the Spirit* (Herefordshire: Orphans, 2004), 116; Paul, *Memoirs of a Revolution*, 115.

65 PA, I047: interview with *P0596* (♂, ~1950) (Metangula, August 21, 2013), min 00:09:21–00:10:18; PA, I048: interview with *P1446* (♂, ~1945) (Metangula, August 21, 2013), min 00:07:43–00:09:45; PA, I058: interview with *P1074* (♀, ~1940) (Malango, August 28, 2013), min 01:49:24–01:50:40; PA, I087: interview with *P1452* (♂, 1927) (Lichinga, September 10, 2013), min 00:26:52–00:29:02; PA, I125: interview with *P1463* (♂, 1951) (Ngala, April 27, 2016), min 00:54:35–00:55:27.

66 PA, I118: interview with *P1218* (♀, 1930) (Malango, April 21, 2016), min 01:38:48–01:42:53. See as well: PA, I094: interview with *P0727* (♂, ~1940) (M'chepa, January 27, 2016), min 00:33:13–00:33:56; PA, I119: interview with *P0855* (♂, 1954) (Malango, April 21, 2016), min 01:32:07–01:32:43.

67 PA, I076: interview with *P1449* (♂, ~1948) (Metangula, September 6, 2013), min 00:05:08–00:08:34; PA, I054: interview with *P0554* (♀, 1949) (Nkholongue, August 27, 2013), min 00:28:39–00:33:38; PA, I038: interview with *P1439* (♂, ~1940) (Malango, August 15, 2013), min 00:05:21–00:05:29. See as well: Litumbe, "Bishop Paulo Litumbe's Memoirs," 149. Note also the importance that the prominent Frelimo veteran Osvaldo Tazama has attributed to the lack of employment opportunities as a reason for his support for the nationalist cause: Osvaldo Tazama, "Osvaldo Assahel Tazama," in *Protagonistas da Luta de Libertação Nacional*, ed. Ana Bouene Mussanhane (Maputo: Marimbique, 2012), 618–19.

The reasoning to support Frelimo was probably also not only based on experiences made inside Mozambique but also outside. For the people living in Nkholongue, the main reference point had always been Nyasaland. While they regarded the Portuguese side as a place of poverty, the British side of the lake was seen as the place to get employment and goods. One interviewee who joined Frelimo explicitly stated that they wanted to follow the example of Nyasaland, which had gained its independence in 1964.[68] It can also be noted that most of those who entered Frelimo had been to South Africa working in the mines before.[69]

Statements like "we wanted our country" or "we wanted to save our country" were often made in the interviews.[70] This points to the fact that people indeed wanted to overthrow the system of colonialism. However, alternative visions of independence might have locally been as attractive and imaginable as Mozambican nationalism. In other words, one should be cautious in expecting that most people necessarily identified "our country" as Mozambique at that time.[71]

Regardless of the exact motives, it can be said that the example of Nkholongue is hardly consistent with liberation narratives, which assume that the deterioration of the colonial situation and exploitation eventually escalated into armed struggle. Such a revolutionary teleology can hardly be observed in this case.[72] In general, it can be said that the regional followers of Frelimo included many of those who had previously helped sustain the colonial state.[73]

---

68 PA, I038: interview with *P1439* (♂, ~1940) (Malango, August 15, 2013), min 00:01:42–00:08:12.
69 PA, I038: interview with *P1439* (♂, ~1940) (Malango, August 15, 2013), min 00:13:18–00:13:28; PA, I056: interview with *P1102* (♂, 1932) (Malango, August 28, 2013), 00:00:49–00:01:15; PA, I082: interview with *P1141* (♂, 1932) (Malango, September 8, 2013), min 00:12:26–00:18:59; PA, I087: interview with *P1452* (♂, 1927) (Lichinga, September 10, 2013), min 00:22:13–00:26:52.
70 PA, I123: interview with *P1460* (♀), *P1461* (♂, ~1935), *P1462* (♂, ~1935) (Meluluca, April 25, 2016), min 01:28:39–01:29:29; PA, I157: interview with *P1455* (♂, 1952) (Tulo, June 18, 2016), min 00:17:33–00:17:54; PA, I068: interview with *P0367* (♂, 1936) (Nkholongue, September 2, 2013), min 00:09:57–00:10:10; PA, I118: interview with *P1218* (♀, 1930) (Malango, April 21, 2016), min 01:38:48–01:39:29; PA, I049: interview with *P0267* (♀, 1949) (Nkholongue, August 23, 2013), min 00:31:17–00:33:12; PA, I117: interview with *P1458* (♂, ~1945) (Micundi, April 20, 2016), min 00:35:16–00:35:40.
71 On this point, see as well: Milton Correia, "História e textualização: A historiografia da frente do Niassa (Moçambique) 1964–1974," *Revista de História*, no. 178 (2019): 6.
72 Isaacman et al. have for example claimed that there was a direct link between cotton resisters and Frelimo in the Maniamba region. This seems doubtful, especially in light of what has been said in Chapter 5. For the claim, see: Isaacman et al., "'Cotton Is the Mother of Poverty': Peasant Resistance to Forced Cotton Production in Mozambique, 1938–1961," 614–15.
73 They included many chiefs and also family members of *cipaios*. See Footnote 60 and: Katto, "Grandma Was a Guerrilla Fighter," 76, 109, 183.

Portuguese reports from the initial phase of the war reveal plainly that Frelimo had the momentum on its side. The Portuguese forces were rapidly losing control over the region and its population. In mid-1965, entire communities began to "disappear" seeking refuge in the forests.[74] On August 24, 1965, almost all inhabitants of Metangula ran away when the Portuguese forces moved out to pursue a group of five Frelimo fighters who had allegedly tried to "kidnap" some local employees of the navy base.[75] The Portuguese loss of control over the area was so extensive that the Portuguese military reported in October 1965 that "[t]he entire area of the Lago District is infested by subversion. Almost the entire population has taken refuge in the bush and is explicitly helping the terrorists."[76]

This development is confirmed by my interviews, even if in the case of Nkholongue not everyone left the village. Furthermore, the movement patterns were not uniform. While most of those who had left the village claimed to have settled near Frelimo bases,[77] others seem to have tried to avoid both Frelimo and the Portuguese.[78] Both statements from my interviews and written sources show that Frelimo took advantage of people's fear of the Portuguese forces to persuade them to leave their villages.[79] People had every reason to fear the Portuguese forces, as the

---

74 ADN, FO/F002/SC002/38: PERINTREP N.° 77 (Lourenço Marques: QG/RMM/2a REP, June 7, 1965), 1; ADN, FO/F002/SC002/38: Anexo "B" (Contra-Informação) ao PERINTREP N.° 88 (Lourenço Marques: QG/RMM/2a REP, August 23, 1965), 2.
75 ADN, FO/F002/SC002/38: PERINTREP N.° 89 (Lourenço Marques: QG/RMM/2a REP, August 30, 1965), 5; ADN, FO/F002/SC002/38: Anexo "C" (Contra-Informação) ao PERINTREP N.° 89 (Lourenço Marques: QG/RMM/2a REP, August 30, 1965), 1; ADN, FO/F002/SC002/38: Anexo "C" (Contra-Informação) ao PERINTREP N.° 91 (Lourenço Marques: QG/RMM/2a REP, September 13, 1965), 3. Later investigations of the incident pointed to the fact that Frelimo's fighters had incited the population to leave. See: ANTT, PIDE, SC, CI(2), proc. 4276, NT 7336, pt. 1, f. 39–40: PIDE Subdelegação VC, "Auto de Perguntas: Anafi Bonomar" (Vila Cabral, January 28, 1966); ANTT, PIDE, SC, CI(2), proc. 4276, NT 7336, pt. 1, f. 41–43: PIDE Subdelegação VC, "Auto de Perguntas: Saide Adamo" (Vila Cabral, January 28, 1966); ANTT, PIDE, SC, CI(2), proc. 4276, NT 7336, pt. 1, f. 44–47: PIDE Subdelegação VC, "Auto de Perguntas: Momade Lezuani" (Vila Cabral, January 28, 1966).
76 ADN, FO/F002/SC002/38: Anexo "C" (Contra-Informação) ao PERINTREP N.° 94 (Lourenço Marques: QG/RMM/2a REP, October 4, 1965), 2.
77 PA, I042: interview with P1193 (♀, 1953) (Malango, August 17, 2013), min 00:27:35–00:32:14; PA, I054: interview with P0554 (♀, 1949) (Nkholongue, August 27, 2013), min 00:07:47–00:11:47; PA, I062: interview with P0713 (♂, 1944) (Nkholongue, August 30, 2013), min 00:19:56–00:22:24; PA, I052: interview with (♀, 1940) (Nkholongue, August 26, 2013), min 00:19:15–00:20:45.
78 PA, I093: interview with P0050 (♂, ~1922) (Nkholongue, January 19, 2016), min 01:32:08–01:32:49; PA, I039: interview with P0898 (♀, 1960) (Malango, August 15, 2013), min 00:08:00–00:10:38.
79 PA, I055: interview with P0639 (♀, ~1952) (Nkholongue, August 27, 2013), min 00:05:19–00:05:47; PA, I052: interview with (♀, 1940) (Nkholongue, August 26, 2013), min 00:19:15–00:20:45; ANTT, SCCIM N.° 1947: Situação no Distrito do Niassa de 1 a 15 de Setembro de 1965, 22.

latter had reacted to the appearance of Frelimo in a highly repressive manner. In the first months, some villages who had lent support to the nationalists were simply razed to the ground.[80] Around Messumba, the Portuguese secret police PIDE arrested 350 persons on a single morning in July 1965.[81] The same month, the Portuguese forces threatened the population of Metangula during public gatherings with collective reprisals if mines continued to be deployed on the roads. The population was urged to abandon its passivity and take active action against Frelimo.[82] However, Portuguese repression primarily affected the area from Metangula to the north. This included the areas where Frelimo had been most active, but also the areas that were predominantly Christian and more easily accessible by road.[83]

Most people who had left their villages in mid-1965 to live in the forests did not stay there for long, mainly because they had great difficulties finding food.[84] In November 1965, shortly before the beginning of the rainy reason, many people began to return to the Portuguese sphere of influence. Metangula received 500 returnees within a week, and Messumba was crowded with 6,000 refugees, many more than had previously lived there.[85] Also in the case of Nkholongue, many people returned to the village after a short absence. They explained this citing the precarious living

---

[80] ADN, FO/F002/SC002/38: PERINTREP N.° 73 (Lourenço Marques: QG/RMM/2a REP, May 10, 1965); Antcliff, *Living in the Spirit*, 113; Paul, *Memoirs of a Revolution*, 119–20.

[81] Paul, *Memoirs of a Revolution*, 125, 152–54. For the records of the interrogation of some of these, see: ANTT, PIDE, SC, CI(2), proc. 4276, NT 7336, pt. 2, f. 260–389.

[82] ADN, FO/F002/SC002/38: Anexo "B" (Contra-Informação) ao PERINTREP N.° 83 (Lourenço Marques: QG/RMM/2a REP, July 19, 1965), 2.

[83] The latter applies above all to the operations of PIDE, which focused primarily on the social environment of the Anglican mission of Messumba. See the numerous records of interrogation files under: ANTT, PIDE, SC, CI(2), proc. 4276, NT 7336, pt. 1–3; ANTT, PIDE, SC, CI(2), proc. 4276, NT 7337, pt. 4–7.

[84] For the problems that people had in the forests, see especially: ADN, FO/F002/SC002/38: Anexo "B" (Contra-Informação) ao PERINTREP N.° 86 (Lourenço Marques: QG/RMM/2a REP, August 9, 1965), 2; PA, I043: interview with *P1148 (♂, 1960)* (Malango, August 17, 2013), min 00:03:12–00:12:00; PA, I049: interview with *P0267 (♀, 1949)* (Nkholongue, August 23, 2013), min 00:11:00–00:29:42. P1148 lived near Nova Coimbra at the beginning of the war, and P0267 near Bandeze. They both fled into the forests after the outbreak of the war, living there in very difficult conditions. P0267 was pregnant and sick at the time.

[85] ADN, FO/F002/SC002/57: PERINTREP N.° 01 (Nampula: COMZIN/2a REP, November 22, 1965), 14; ADN, FO/F002/SC002/57: PERINTREP N.° 03 (Nampula: COMZIN/2a REP, December 6, 1965), 18–19; Luís S. de Baêna, *Fuzileiros: Factos e feitos na guerra de África. 1961/1974*, vol. 4: Crónica dos feitos de Moçambique (Lisboa: INAPA, 2006), 41.

conditions they had encountered in the forest and the hunger they had suffered there.⁸⁶

The fact that so many sought refuge in Messumba, the center of the Anglican Church, rather than in their former villages or Metangula, shows that their return should not be interpreted as a sign of growing confidence in the Portuguese forces. The latter were aware of their unpopularity and their inquiries into why people had originally fled revealed that most of them—partly instigated by Frelimo— had feared being attacked by the Portuguese forces.⁸⁷ The Portuguese commander of the navy base in Metangula described the situation as follows:

> The fact that the people have returned to the villages does not mean that they are on our side now; they have simply fled from hunger and rain to the side that is stronger at the moment.⁸⁸

To counter the problem of their unpopularity, the Portuguese forces now began to apply their resettlement policy. Already in October 1965, the Portuguese Navy issued an internal guide explaining how people were to be regrouped and resettled in *aldeamentos*.⁸⁹

Nkholongue was to become one of the first villages to be resettled, namely on May 30, 1966. The Portuguese forces had encircled Malango at night (at 4.30 a.m. according to the Portuguese military report describing the mission). It was only when the people woke up and came out of their houses that they saw the soldiers. They were directed to the beach where in the meantime the administrative forces had arrived by boat. At the beach, people were told to pack all their belongings as they would be taken to Metangula to live there. Within one day, the Portuguese

---

86 PA, I062: interview with *P0713 (♂, 1944)* (Nkholongue, August 30, 2013), min 00:19:56–00:23:11; PA, I055: interview with *P0639 (♀, ~1952)* (Nkholongue, August 27, 2013), min 00:05:19–00:05:59; PA, I054: interview with *P0554 (♀, 1949)* (Nkholongue, August 27, 2013), min 00:19:18–00:19:31 and 00:24:41–00:24:54; PA, I039: interview with *P0898 (♀, 1960)* (Malango, August 15, 2013), min 00:08:51–00:10:02. For these problems in the region as a whole, see: ADN, FO/F002/SC002/38: Anexo "B" (Contra-Informação) ao PERINTREP N.º 86 (Lourenço Marques: QG/RMM/2a REP, August 9, 1965), 2; ADN, FO/F002/SC002/57: PERINTREP N.º 03 (Nampula: COMZIN/2a REP, December 6, 1965), 18.
87 ANTT, SCCIM N.º 16 (folhas 142–146): Administração da Circunscrição do Lago, "Resposta ao questionário referido na Nota N° 211/A/13 ao Gabinete de Informações do Governo do Distrito do Niassa" (Maniamba, May 31, 1966), 1.
88 AHMar, Coloredo, Pasta 032/MO: Sérgio Zilhão, "Analise dos acontecimentos do Niassa," Confidencial (Metangula, February 10, 1966), 4.
89 AHMar, Coloredo, Pasta 045/MO: Comando Naval de Moçambique, "IOMOC 16: Instruções Operacionais para protecção, recuperação e internamento de populações," Confidencial (Lourenço Marques, October 28, 1965). See as well: AHMar, Coloredo, Pasta 032/MO: Sérgio Zilhão, "Analise dos acontecimentos do Niassa," Confidencial (Metangula, February 10, 1966), 5.

7.3 From Fighting for the Nationalist to Supporting the Portuguese War Effort — 271

Navy transported the 329 inhabitants of Malango by boat to Metangula.[90] There was little or no resistance against this order. Various interviewees told me explicitly that they were not thinking about an escape on that day, since they had already seen the difficult life of the forests.[91] Moreover, the people who still lived at the old site of Nkholongue were not encircled the same way and later joined the others when they heard about the order to go to Metangula.[92]

But the fact that there was no direct resistance does not mean that everyone was convinced of the plan. Indeed, the Portuguese intelligence report mentions that one woman and one man tried to escape when they surrounded the village.[93] Furthermore, as will be shown below, some people stated that they fled the *aldeamento* after their resettlement. People's reluctance is also apparent in the reaction of other people living further south. Among them was the group of villagers who had migrated from Nkholongue to M'chepa in the 1950s. Most of them fled to Malawi, apparently as a reaction to the resettlement of the people further north:

> We just heard that they had taken the people in Malango and that they had taken the people in Nkholongue. So, we lived there [in M'chepa]. It was when we saw that they took the people in Micundi that we thought: "epa, we can't stay. Let's go." We woke up at night and set out on our journey.[94]

That not all people were willing to go to the *aldeamentos* is also suggested by the significant under-representation of men among the resettled. According to the Portuguese report concerning Nkholongue's resettlement, the number of the resettled

---

90 ADN, FO/F002/SC002/117: Anexo "A" (Dispositivo e Actividade das F. Navais na ZIN) ao SITREP Circunstanciado N° 23/66 (Nampula, June 6, 1966), 6–7; PA, I073: interview with *P1012 (♂, 1955)* (Malango, September 5, 2013), min 00:02:25–00:08:15; PA, I040: interview with *P1030 (♀, 1965), P1009 (♀, 1958), P1029 (♂, ~1959)* (Malango, August 16, 2013), min 00:36:00–00:43:32; PA, I037: interview with *P0855 (♂, 1954)* (Malango, August 14, 2013), min 00:13:35–00:14:37.
91 PA, I062: interview with *P0713 (♂, 1944)* (Nkholongue, August 30, 2013), min 00:22:24–00:23:11; PA, I055: interview with *P0639 (♀, ~1952)* (Nkholongue, August 27, 2013), min 00:09:47–00:10:55; PA, I074: interview with *P0160 (♂, 1952)* (Metangula, September 6, 2013), min 00:07:44–00:08:14.
92 PA, I074: interview with *P0160 (♂, 1952)* (Metangula, September 6, 2013), min 00:07:56–00:08:14.
93 ADN, FO/F002/SC002/117: Anexo "A" (Dispositivo e Actividade das F. Navais na ZIN) ao SITREP Circunstanciado N° 23/66 (Nampula, June 6, 1966), 7.
94 PA, I100: interview with *P0025 (♀, 1948)* (Nkholongue, February 22, 2016), min 00:00:28–00:01:20. Another woman, who was living with her husband in Meluluca at the time, also reported that they fled to Malawi after the population of Malango and Ngolocolo had been brought to Metangula. See: PA, I057: interview with *P0262 (♀, ~1940)* (Malango, August 28, 2013), min 01:17:07–01:21:54.

comprised 122 women, 152 children, and only 55 men.⁹⁵ This means that for every 100 adult women there were only 45 adult men. We have already seen in the previous chapter that the unevenness of the sex ratio had already been the pre-war standard due to the widespread male labor migration to Nyasaland and South Africa. However, if one looks at the pre-war statistics for the P.A. Metangula, there were after all 65 adult men for every 100 adult women in 1958 and 69 adult men for every 100 adult women in 1960. One can think of three explanations for this increased under-representation of men. First, more men than women joined Frelimo as fighters. Second, we can assume that men may have deliberately reduced their age because they were afraid of being recruited by the Portuguese armed forces.⁹⁶ And third, we can assume that more men than women fled the country for the same reason.

Once people arrived in Metangula, they had to stay on the premises of the navy base for the first night. On the second day, those who had relatives or family in Metangula were told to go there, while the others could stay longer at the navy base. In the following days, the resettled began building their own houses. The Portuguese forces supported them by transporting building materials from the forests to the *aldeamento*.⁹⁷ It is noteworthy that the state authorities did not intervene very strongly in the organization of life in the *aldeamento*, at least not at first. Even the land for the fields was not allocated by the government. Rather this

---

95 ADN, FO/F002/SC002/117: Anexo "A" (Dispositivo e Actividade das F. Navais na ZIN) ao SITREP Circunstanciado N° 23/66 (Nampula, June 6, 1966), 7.
96 This is indicated by the changes of the sex ratio in the *aldeamentos* of the administrative post of Metangula in the course of the war. In 1967, there were only 53 adult men for every 100 adult women. In 1971, however, this ratio was 73 to 100 and at the same time the ratio of underage men to underage women had shrunk from 103:100 to 80:100. This may be attributed to the fact that the fear of forced recruitment had vanished and that young men were more likely to (re-)raise their age in order to obtain employment. For the statistical data, see: ANTT, SCCIM N.º 1639 (folha 49): Mapa Geral dos Aldeamentos em 31.7.1967 (Augusto Cardoso, August 12, 1967); AHM, ISANI, cx. 99: Mário Freiria, "Relatório da Inspecção Ordinária à Circunscrição do Lago 1971" (Vila Cabral, July 4, 1971), 3.
97 PA, I037: interview with *P0855 (♂, 1954)* (Malango, August 14, 2013), min 00:15:30–00:16:13; PA, I039: interview with *P0898 (♀, 1960)* (Malango, August 15, 2013), min 00:16:14–00:18:13.; PA, I040: interview with *P1030 (♀, 1965), P1009 (♀, 1958), P1029 (♂, ~1959)* (Malango, August 16, 2013), min 00:42:30–00:46:05; PA, I074: interview with *P0160 (♂, 1952)* (Metangula, September 6, 2013), min 00:08:35–00:10:48; PA, I075: interview with *P1218 (♀, 1930)* (Metangula, September 6, 2013), min 00:21:02–00:26:22; PA, I078: interview with *P0258 (♂, 1953)* (Nkholongue, September 7, 2013), min 00:00:00–00:01:30.

was done "among us," as many interviewees put it. The newcomers had to ask Metangula's original population for land.⁹⁸

The *aldeamento* was surrounded by a barbed wire fence. Both the fields and the forest (as a source of firewood and construction material) were outside this fence. All inhabitants of the *aldeamento* were given an identity card which they had to show when leaving and entering the *aldeamento*. Before sunset, everyone had to return there.⁹⁹ But especially in the beginning, the control was not very strict. In November 1966, for example, a Portuguese navy unit discovered a group of women collecting food at some distance from the *aldeamento* "without escort and protection." The report of the unit stated that "despite the fencing with barbed wire, the population of the *aldeamento* of A. Cardoso continues to leave the *aldeamento* dangerously without escort."¹⁰⁰ Several people were also able to flee from Metangula after their resettlement. One of the more prominent fugitives was Chingomanje V, the chief of Nkholongue. If we follow the statements from the interviews, he had been imprisoned for a short time after the resettlement because the village was suspected of having lent support to Frelimo. After his release, he fled to Malawi.¹⁰¹

---

98 PA, I037: interview with *P0855* (♂, *1954*) (Malango, August 14, 2013), min 00:56:08–00:56:51; PA, I039: interview with *P0898* (♀, *1960*) (Malango, August 15, 2013), min 00:18:32–00:19:17; PA, I042: interview with *P1193* (♀, *1953*) (Malango, August 17, 2013), min 00:18:41–00:19:38; PA, I047: interview with *P0596* (♂, *~1950*) (Metangula, August 21, 2013), min 00:16:39–00:17:44; PA, I058: interview with *P1074* (♀, *~1940*) (Malango, August 28, 2013), min 01:54:23–01:55:05; PA, I078: interview with *P0258* (♂, *1953*) (Nkholongue, September 7, 2013), min 00:11:47–00:12:38; PA, I074: interview with *P0160* (♂, *1952*) (Metangula, September 6, 2013), min 00:11:41–00:11:56.
99 PA, I074: interview with *P0160* (♂, *1952*) (Metangula, September 6, 2013), min 00:10:48–00:14:23; PA, I115: interview with *P0160* (♂, *1952*) (Metangula, April 18, 2016), min 01:52:57–01:54:43; PA, I069: interview with *P0650* (♀, *1939*) (Nkholongue, September 2, 2013), min 00:14:03–00:15:58; PA, I073: interview with *P1012* (♂, *1955*) (Malango, September 5, 2013), min 00:21:29–00:25:08.
100 AHMar, Coloredo, Pasta 303/MO: José Teixeira, "Relatório de Operações N° 32 (Operação 'Chavedouro'), de 210650 a 211700 Novembro de 1966" (Metangula: DFE 5, n.d.). For a similar incident, see: ANTT, SCCIM N.° 1639 (folha 219): Carlos Mesquita, "Relatório N.° 22/67" (Comando Naval de Moçambique. Serviço de Informações Militares, March 10, 1967).
101 The chief was, later, followed by two of his daughters. See: PA, I041: interview with *P0951* (♀, *1948*), *P0242* (♂, *1945*) (Malango, August 16, 2013), min 00:21:07–00:30:18; PA, I068: interview with *P0367* (♂, *1936*) (Nkholongue, September 2, 2013), min 00:29:46–00:32:59; PA, I042: interview with *P1193* (♀, *1953*) (Malango, August 17, 2013), min 00:12:18–00:13:48. For other people who indicated to have fled after the resettlement to Malawi: PA, I133: interview with *P1473* (♂ *~1938*), *P1504* (♀) (Limbi, June 1, 2016), min 00:10:46–00:15:15, 01:03:57–01:07:33; PA, I130: interview with *P1472* (♀, *~1955*) (Mangochi, May 29, 2016), min 00:04:28–00:07:45. For those who indicated to have done so to Tanzania: PA, I041: interview with *P0951* (♀, *1948*), *P0242* (♂, *1945*) (Malango, August 16, 2013), min 00:21:07–00:24:30, 00:25:48–00:30:18. Another interviewee indicated that she fled from Metangula, but later returned to the *aldeamento* because of the difficult life she encountered

But, in general, escapes from the *aldeamento* were not very numerous and seem to have completely stopped in the course of the war. The main reason for this decrease in escapes was not necessarily the enforcement of control, but rather the Portuguese scorched earth policy outside the *aldeamentos* and the comparatively "good" life that people found in the *aldeamento* of Metangula.

The Portuguese Scorched Earth Policy: Starving the Insurgents

It has already been mentioned that the actions of the Portuguese forces against suspected Frelimo supporters were extremely repressive at the beginning of the war. In the course of the conflict, the classification of who was a Frelimo supporter was increasingly determined by his or her dwelling place. All those who lived outside the *aldeamentos* were considered possible enemies. Accordingly, the Portuguese forces began to systematically destroy everything they found outside the *aldeamentos*. Houses and huts were burned down. Food was either destroyed or removed. Crops were harvested or uprooted. This way, life outside the *aldeamentos* was to be made unbearable, the people starved and thus forced to go to the *aldeamentos* themselves.[102] This strategy was described as follows in the operational instructions of an infantry battalion stationed in Metangula from March 1967 to February 1968:

> As a first priority and in coordination with the forces of the navy, continue with the destruction of the enemy camps [...] and create insecurity among the refugee population by gradually depriving them of their means of living.[103]

It is noteworthy that many military and secret service reports specifically recorded the destruction of infrastructure belonging to civilians in contrast to infrastructure belonging to "proper" combatants.[104] The summary of the "positive results" of the navy unit DFE 6, for example, reads as follows:

---

outside: PA, I051: interview with *P0481* (♀, *1942*) (Nkholongue, August 26, 2013), min 00:21:50–00:24:47, 00:26:06–00:32:24.

102 For examples, see: ADN, FO/F002/SC002/57: PERINTREP N.° 16 (Nampula: COMZIN/2a REP, March 7, 1966), 7; ADN, FO/F002/SC002/57: PERINTREP N.° 17 (Nampula: COMZIN/2a REP, March 14, 1966), 4 and 9; ADN, FO/F002/SC002/57: PERINTREP N.° 19 (Nampula: COMZIN/2a REP, March 28, 1966), 9; ADN, FO/F002/SC002/57: PERINTREP N.° 34 (Nampula: COMZIN/2a REP, July 11, 1966), 7.
103 AHMil, DIV/2/7/79/1: Batalhão de Caçadores 1891. História de Unidade (Vila Junqueiro, August 8, 1968), II–85.
104 For an example, see: AHMil, DIV/2/7/150/3: Batalhão de Cavalaria 1879. História de Unidade (Vila Junqueiro, February 1968), II/3-II/5.

g. Destroyed encampments
  (1) TQ [*tipo quartel* ('barracks-like')]   7
  (2) PF [*população fugida* ('refugee population')] 18
  (3) SC [*sem classificação* ('without classification')] 10[105]

Some reports even explicitly mention the killing of civilians, such as the summary of the "positive results" of the navy unit DFE 8 (stationed in Mozambique from 1966 to 1968), which lists not only 35 "guerrillas killed in combat," but also 26 members of the "population killed in combat."[106]

Most of Nkholongue's inhabitants were only indirectly affected by this destruction policy as most of them were resettled comparatively early in the course of the war, at a time when the Portuguese scorched earth policy had not yet been applied as systematically as later. So it was only a minority of Nkholongue's current inhabitants who recounted how they had to hide from the Portuguese aircrafts and cook at night to avoid being discovered. One of them was a woman who had been living on Niassa's *planalto* at the outbreak of the war.[107] Another was one who claimed she had escaped from Metangula to the forests after the resettlement.[108] None of Nkholongue's inhabitants seems to have been captured by Portuguese troops while they were in the forests. Those non-combatants who had not been resettled or not fled in the first place eventually all left the forests and fled either abroad or to one of the *aldeamentos*.[109] The majority of the men from Nkholongue who had joined Frelimo as fighters deserted during the first years of the war.[110] Only in two cases is it credible that they remained with Frelimo until the end of the war.[111]

While most of Nkholongue's inhabitants had only limited direct experience with the Portuguese scorched earth policy, there is little doubt that people's knowledge of it contributed to the fact they did not leave the *aldeamento* once they were

---

[105] AHMar, Coloredo, Pasta 054/MO: Henrique Vasconcelos, "Resumo Histórico da Comissão do DFE 6" (Nampula, August 19, 1970).
[106] AHMar, Coloredo, Pasta 058/MO: João Bastos, "Relatório de Comissão DFE N. 8," n.d., 11.
[107] PA, I049: interview with *P0267* (♀, *1949*) (Nkholongue, August 23, 2013), min 00:12:06–00:15:55, 00:22:20–00:31:17.
[108] PA, I051: interview with *P0481* (♀, *1942*) (Nkholongue, August 26, 2013), min 00:26:06–00:38:27.
[109] This also includes the following interviewee, who lived at Mtucula when the war broke out: PA, I043: interview with *P1148* (♂, *1960*) (Malango, August 17, 2013), min 00:03:12–00:15:12.
[110] PA, I056: interview with *P1102* (♂, *1932*) (Malango, August 28, 2013), min 00:40:40–00:47:20; PA, I038: interview with *P1439* (♂, *~1940*) (Malango, August 15, 2013), min 00:21:09–00:25:08; PA, I158: interview with *P0764* (♂, *1962*) (Nkholongue, June 20, 2016), min 00:07:05–00:08:21, 00:37:52–00:38:23; PA, I065: interview with *P0583* (♂, *1972*) (Nkholongue, September 1, 2013), min 00:04:12–00:06:47.
[111] PA, I087: interview with *P1452* (♂, *1927*) (Lichinga, September 10, 2013), min 00:38:12–00:38:45; PA, I105: interview with *P0242* (♂, *1945*) (Malango, April 4, 2016), min 01:19:45–01:27:48.

there. But, in the case of the *aldeamento* of Metangula, there was an even more important reason that kept people in the *aldeamento*: the good living conditions.

"Finding Peace" in the *Aldeamento* of Metangula

To my own initial surprise, most of those who were resettled to Metangula and stayed there during the war spoke positively about life in the *aldeamento*.[112] Most of my interviewees perceived the barbed wire as a protective rather than a controlling element.[113]

Food security was the prerequisite for the positive assessment of life in the *aldeamento*. Subsistence-oriented peasants (for a critical appraisal of this term, see Chapter 6) like those of Nkholongue have a fundamental problem when they migrate. Either they still have access to their old fields at their new location, or they can take their old harvest with them to it, or they need an alternative source of food until their fields at their new location have yielded something. It was precisely this problem that made life difficult for those who had left the villages at the beginning of the war, and this problem was further exacerbated by the Portuguese forces with their scorched earth policy.

---

[112] PA, I093: interview with *P0050* (♂, ~1922) (Nkholongue, January 19, 2016), min 01:45:44–01:45:58; PA, I156: interview with *P1478* (♀) (Metangula, June 18, 2016), min 00:23:02–00:23:45; PA, I150: interview with *P1483* (♀, 1950), *P1481* (♂, 1954) (Lussefa, June 15, 2016), min 00:20:33–00:21:49; PA, I051: interview with *P0481* (♀, 1942) (Nkholongue, August 26, 2013), min 00:59:25–01:00:53; PA, I080: interview with *P0641* (♂, 1952) (Nkholongue, September 7, 2013), min 00:12:08–00:13:02; PA, I062: interview with *P0713* (♂, 1944) (Nkholongue, August 30, 2013), min 00:36:01–00:37:24; PA, I073: interview with *P1012* (♂, 1955) (Malango, September 5, 2013), min 00:17:21–00:17:48; PA, I069: interview with *P0650* (♀, 1939) (Nkholongue, September 2, 2013), min 00:17:17–00:20:50.

[113] PA, I044: interview with *P1081* (♀, 1945) (Malango, August 17, 2013), min 0:18:13–00:19:20; PA, I047: interview with *P0596* (♂, ~1950) (Metangula, August 21, 2013), min 00:17:44–00:18:08; PA, I049: interview with *P0267* (♀, 1949) (Nkholongue, August 23, 2013), min 00:56:15–00:57:32; PA, I051: interview with *P0481* (♀, 1942) (Nkholongue, August 26, 2013), min 00:58:09–00:59:25; PA, I068: interview with *P0367* (♂, 1936) (Nkholongue, September 2, 2013), min 00:44:53–00:47:00; PA, I069: interview with *P0650* (♀, 1939) (Nkholongue, September 2, 2013), min 00:14:03–00:15:38; PA, I086: interview with *P0375* (♂, 1962) (Nkholongue, September 9, 2013), min 00:04:00–00:04:49; PA, I040: interview with *P1030* (♀, 1965), *P1009* (♀, 1958), *P1029* (♂, ~1959) (Malango, August 16, 2013), min 00:48:14–00:48:36; PA, I062: interview with *P0713* (♂, 1944) (Nkholongue, August 30, 2013), min 00:30:21–00:31:53; PA, I074: interview with *P0160* (♂, 1952) (Metangula, September 6, 2013), min 00:13:53–00:14:23; PA, I066: interview with *P0085* (♂, 1960) (Nkholongue, September 1, 2013), min 00:55:09–00:56:47.

7.3 From Fighting for the Nationalist to Supporting the Portuguese War Effort — 277

In the case of the resettlement of Nkholongue's population, this problem was mitigated in two ways. First, the Portuguese navy brought the people back to the village several times to harvest their fields.[114] Second, the Portuguese administration distributed food at the beginning.[115] In the long run, almost all people were able to receive fairly fertile fields located on the plains around the mouth of the Luchemanje River. Furthermore, dependence on food subsistence production decreased significantly in the *aldeamento*.

In Metangula, the war and the sudden rise of the presence of the colonial state created many income possibilities. In 1958, there had only been two Europeans living in Metangula.[116] This number increased significantly in the years that followed. For the Lago District as a whole, the number of European civilians tripled between 1960 and 1971, from 41 to 129.[117] In addition, the war led to the stationing of about 600 soldiers in the district, most of whom were of metropolitan origin.[118] This

---

114 This was done on June 2, June 26, August 25/26, September 2/3, and December 10, 1966. See: ADN, FO/F002/SC002/117: Anexo "A" (Dispositivo e Actividade das F. Navais na ZIN) ao SITREP Circunstanciado N° 23/66 (Nampula, June 6, 1966), 7; AHMar, Coloredo, Pasta 058/MO: Relatório da Companhia N° 6 de Fuzileiros, referente à comissão em Moçambique desde 19 de Março de 1965 a 18 de Maio de 1967, n.d., chap. III, 3–5; AHMar, Coloredo, Pasta 156/MO: Anexo "A" (Dispositivo e Actividade das F. Navais na ZIN) ao SITREP Circunstanciado N° 35/66 (Nampula, August 29, 1966), 4; AHMar, Coloredo, Pasta 156/MO: Anexo "A" (Dispositivo e Actividade das F. Navais na ZIN) ao SITREP Circunstanciado N° 36/66 (Nampula, September 5, 1966), 2, 4; AHMar, Coloredo, Pasta 156/MO: Anexo "A" (Dispositivo e Actividade das F. Navais na ZIN) ao SITREP Circunstanciado N° 50/66 (Nampula, December 12, 1966), 2; PA, I109: interview with *P1081* (♀, *1945*) (Malango, April 6, 2016), min 00:13:39–00:15:23; PA, I068: interview with *P0367* (♂, *1936*) (Nkholongue, September 2, 2013), min 00:35:35–00:37:13; PA, I001: interview with *P0050* (♂, *~1922*) (Nkholongue, August 17, 2010), min 01:34:08–01:34:28.
115 PA, I001: interview with *P0050* (♂, *~1922*) (Nkholongue, August 17, 2010), min 01:33:43–01:35:12; PA, I037: interview with *P0855* (♂, *1954*) (Malango, August 14, 2013), min 00:15:30–00:16:22; PA, I075: interview with *P1218* (♀, *1930*) (Metangula, September 6, 2013), 00:21:02–00:26:22; PA, I039: interview with *P0898* (♀, *1960*) (Malango, August 15, 2013), min 00:15:28–00:17:00.
116 Paul, *Memoirs of a Revolution*, 27.
117 The boundaries of the district changed during these years. The figure given for 1960 refers to the district in the boundaries of 1971. See: AHM, S.E. a.I p. 5 no. 7i: III Recenseamento Geral da População na Província de Moçambique (1960), Vol. 9: Distrito do Niassa (Lourenço Marques: Direcção Provincial dos Serviços da Estatística, 1969), 20; AHM, ISANI, cx. 99: Mário Freiria, "Relatório da Inspecção Ordinária à Circunscrição do Lago 1971" (Vila Cabral, July 4, 1971), 3.
118 In 1969, for example, there was 1 *Batalhão de Artilharia* (360 men), 2 *Destacementos de Fuzileiros* (80 men each), and 1 *Companhia de Fuzileiros* (120 men) stationed in the area of the district. See: AHMil, FO/63/7/938/3: J. F. Gravito, "Estudo da Situação N° 01 DO SECTOR "A" DA R.M.M." (Vila Cabral, 1969), 95–96; Comissão para o Estudo das Campanhas de África (CECA), *Resenha histórico-militar das campanhas de África, Vol. 4: Dispositivo das nossas forças Moçambique* (Lisboa: Estado-Maior do Exército, 1989), 256 and 260; Baêna, *Factos e feitos na Guerra*, 4: Crónica dos feitos de Mo-

growing European presence produced a lot of jobs as people were needed to cook and to do the laundry, while the military employed men for the maintenance of its infrastructure or as guides for its troops. Others were employed by private businesses such as stores and restaurants.[119] Prostitution and prostitution-like relationships were widespread.[120] In 1969, Metangula's military and administrative apparatus was said to provide permanent employment for about 400 people from the local population.[121] This was a huge number considering the population of the *aldeamento* of approximately 3,400 (half of them children), even if the employees also came from other nearby *aldeamentos*.[122] One interviewee described this development as follows:

> It was when people were brought [to Metangula] that they started to recover, that they started to know the money. For, in Metangula, many, in order to eat, entered the jobs of the whites to make the jobs there. And what we now suddenly saw was the movement of money.[123]

çambique, 150–162. For the standard size of the units, see: Cann, *Counterinsurgency in Africa*, 71–73; Cann, *Brown Waters of Africa*, 94–95.
119 PA, I047: interview with *P0596* (♂, ~1950) (Metangula, August 21, 2013), min 00:20:29–00:23:03; PA, I074: interview with *P0160* (♂, 1952) (Metangula, September 6, 2013), min 00:18:21–00:19:46; PA, I076: interview with *P1449* (♂, ~1948) (Metangula, September 6, 2013), min 00:19:20–00:20:13; PA, I037: interview with *P0855* (♂, 1954) (Malango, August 14, 2013), min 00:21:36–00:22:42; PA, I040: interview with *P1030* (♀, 1965), *P1009* (♀, 1958), *P1029* (♂, ~1959) (Malango, August 16, 2013), min 00:54:02–00:55:19; PA, I068: interview with *P0367* (♂, 1936) (Nkholongue, September 2, 2013), min 00:41:00–00:44:35; PA, I148: interview with *P1500* (♂, ~1946) (Bandeze, June 10, 2016), min 00:06:13–00:06:42.
120 Opinions of interviewees on how to assess relationships between Portuguese soldiers and local women vary widely. Two of my interviewees (a couple), who lived in Lichinga at the beginning of the war, left Lichinga for Metangula, because they were against the relationship that their daughter had a with a Portuguese soldier. Another (female) interviewee regretted, however, that the Portuguese soldiers had not stayed longer, as otherwise all the women today would have children by them. She would have welcomed this, obviously because she saw in it an appropriate path for social advancement. See: PA, I112: interview with *P0129* (♀, 1930), *P0128* (♂, 1928) (Nkholongue, April 12, 2016), min 01:48:24–01:58:13; PA, I039: interview with *P0898* (♀, 1960) (Malango, August 15, 2013), min 01:04:24–01:15:12. For prostitution in the *aldeamento* of Metangula, see as well: APGGN, QJ: Correspondência Confidencial N.° 39/C/GAB: A. Reis Fernandes (Administração de Circunscrição de Lago) ao Comandante do Batalhão de Artilharia 2838 (Augusto Cardoso, January 17, 1969).
121 APGGN, QJ: Correspondência Confidencial N.° 39/C/GAB: A. Reis Fernandes (Administração de Circunscrição de Lago) ao Comandante do Batalhão de Artilharia 2838 (Augusto Cardoso, January 17, 1969).
122 ANTT, SCCIM N.° 1638 (folhas 376–381): Dispositivo das Forças Administrativos em 31 de Março de 1969, n.d.
123 PA, I105: interview with *P0242* (♂, 1945) (Malango, April 4, 2016), min 00:55:49–00:57:20.

This sudden "movement of money" was welcomed by most people, also because it enabled them to buy such products as salt, soap, or clothes in comparatively large quantities. For even though Metangula was located in the middle of the war zone, there were never any supply shortages, and due to the growing European presence, the supply of consumer goods did not decrease in the course of the war but increased. Several interviewees highlighted the low prices, and two of them even recounted that things like soap were just lying around on the beach.[124] One interviewee stated:

> After we had arrived in Metangula, there was no shortage whatsoever anymore.[125]

And one who was still a child at the time commented:

> We had everything, almost to the point of throwing it away.[126]

Such idealizations should be interpreted with caution, since it was precisely goods such as salt, soap, or clothes that disappeared from the market after independence (see Chapter 8). However, the evidence leaves little doubt that a considerable part of Nkholongue's population perceived a significant increase in their material standard of living during the time in the *aldeamento*. It is noteworthy that it is the oral perspective that allows such an assessment, Portuguese sources were often more self-critical about the situation.[127]

The local improvement of the war situation for non-combatants is also apparent in the fact that several people who had fled to Malawi at the beginning of the

---

124 PA, I037: interview with *P0855 (♂, 1954)* (Malango, August 14, 2013), min 01:06:06–01:10:15; PA, I156: interview with *P1478 (♀)* (Metangula, June 18, 2016), min 00:23:02–00:24:13; PA, I099: interview with *P1420 (♂, ~1922)* (Ngongo, February 16, 2016), min 01:01:24–01:01:53; PA, I069: interview with *P0650 (♀, 1939)* (Nkholongue, September 2, 2013), min 00:19:06–00:20:45. For soap lying around on the beach, see: PA, I060: interview with *P0331 (♀, ~1948)*, no audio (Metangula, August 29, 2013); PA, I058: interview with *P1074 (♀, ~1940)* (Malango, August 28, 2013), min 02:00:53–02:01:48.
125 PA, I055: interview with *P0639 (♀, ~1952)* (Nkholongue, August 27, 2013), min 00:13:34–00:13:35.
126 PA, I086: interview with *P0375 (♂, 1962)* (Nkholongue, September 9, 2013), min 00:06:06–00:06:22.
127 For examples, see: AHMil, DIV/2/7/55/4: Batalhão de Caçadores 2906. História de Unidade, n.d., II–52; APGGN, QJ: Correspondência Confidencial N.º 39/C/GAB: A. Reis Fernandes (Administração de Circunscrição de Lago) ao Comandante do Batalhão de Artilharia 2838 (Augusto Cardoso, January 17, 1969); APGGN, QJ: Nuno Egídio ao Administrador da Circunscrição do Lago, "N.º 245/C/GAB: Construções do edifício geminado para funcionários e ampliação da secretaria / reestruturação do aldeamento da Sede," July 28, 1969.

war returned to Metangula while the war was still going on.¹²⁸ Others planned it. In April 1974, shortly before the Carnation Revolution, the Portuguese authorities received a letter from people who had fled from Nkholongue to Malawi after the outbreak of the war. In the letter, the refugees declared their willingness to return to Mozambique if they were allowed to live at the former location of their village.¹²⁹ The Portuguese forces also assessed the situation in the *aldeamento* of Metangula as so relaxed that they saw no reason for imposing restrictions on people to travel to Malawi for visits.¹³⁰ Thus, one interviewee traveled to and from Nkhotakota during the war to visit his second family.¹³¹

Most interviewees described the relationship with the Portuguese as "good."¹³² People as a rule denied that the high military and police presence caused particular problems.¹³³ Similarly, negative changes in their everyday lives were usually either denied or played down, and the *aldeamento* was associated with the place "where they found peace," or "forgot about the war."¹³⁴ While some "forgot

---

128 PA, I006: interview with *P1480* (♂, *1947*) (Nkholongue, August 30, 2010), min 00:25:40–00:28:14; PA, I077: interview with *P1489* (♂) (Metangula, September 6, 2013), min 00:04:31–00:11:34.
129 ANTT, PIDE, SC, CI(2), GU, cx. 10 (NT 7950), f. 30–31: DGS/SUBVC, "Relatório Imediato N.° 2177/74/DI/2/SC" (Vila Cabral, April 17, 1974). Their desire to live at the former location of the village must also be understood in the context of the decentralization of the *aldeamentos* that was taking place at the time. The *aldeamento* of Mondué, for example, had just been opened in early 1974. See: ANTT, SCCIM N.° 1641 (folhas 2–5): Aldeias existentes no Niassa – MAR74 (Vila Cabral, March 23, 1974), 1; APGGN, 1 A: Mapa do Movimento da População da Circunscrição do Lago, Janeiro 1974 (Augusto Cardoso, February 8, 1974); APGGN, 1 A: Mapa do Movimento da População da Circunscrição do Lago, Abril 1974 (Augusto Cardoso, May 5, 1974). Others were still planned: APGGN, QJ: José Guardado Moreira, "IV Plano de Fomento: Ficha Anual de Projecto, 1974" (Vila Cabral, April 22, 1974).
130 APGGN, QJ: Correspondência Confidencial N.° 294/C/GAB: Nuno de Melo Egídio (Governador do Niassa) ao Secretário-Geral da Província de Moçambique (Vila Cabral, September 22, 1969).
131 He even fathered a child while he was in Malawi. See: PA, I139: interview with *P1475* (♀, *1960*), *P1474* (♂, *1972*) (Nkhotakota, June 2, 2016), min 00:06:21–00:07:04.
132 PA, I069: interview with *P0650* (♀, *1939*) (Nkholongue, September 2, 2013), min 00:19:59–00:20:55; PA, I039: interview with *P0898* (♀, *1960*) (Malango, August 15, 2013), min 01:03:48–01:05:33; PA, I045: interview with *P0242* (♂, *1945*) (Malango, August 17, 2013), min 00:15:52–00:16:04; PA, I074: interview with *P0160* (♂, *1952*) (Metangula, September 6, 2013), min 00:16:55–00:17:02; PA, I077: interview with *P1489* (♂) (Metangula, September 6, 2013), min 00:06:37–00:07:16; PA, I086: interview with *P0375* (♂, *1962*) (Nkholongue, September 9, 2013), min 00:13:52–00:14:13.
133 PA, I148: interview with *P1500* (♂, *~1946*) (Bandeze, June 10, 2016), min 00:07:54–00:08:12; PA, I101: interview with *P0316* (♀, *~1952*) (Nkholongue, February 22, 2016), min 00:36:52–00:37:10. One mentioned problems for those who had no ID: PA, I153: interview with *P1477* (♂, *~1940*) (Micucue, June 17, 2016), min 00:40:38–00:41:51.
134 For those who claimed to have found peace, see: PA, I068: interview with *P0367* (♂, *1936*) (Nkholongue, September 2, 2013), min 00:15:08–00:15:15; PA, I055: interview with *P0639* (♀,

about the war" in the *aldeamento*, others began to fight it, but now on the side of the Portuguese forces. Every *aldeamento* was defended by militias who were recruited from the local population.[135] Those who worked for the technical services of the navy base also served the military as guides and porters on its operations.[136] At least three of Nkholongue's population even joined the Special Groups (GE).[137]

Financial incentives seem to have played an important role in motivating people to support the Portuguese war effort. According to the missionary John Paul, a militiaman received the same salary as a teacher.[138] While two former GE claimed that they had been forced to do so,[139] other interviewees highlighted the monetary incentives and stressed that those who joined the GE did so of their own free will.[140] One of the two later himself underscored the amount of his salary by saying:

> At that time things were very cheap. [The Portuguese] had very low prices. So when we got 80, that was a lot of money. We could go and buy us a lot of things and still save a lot at home.[141]

But some statements suggest that money was not the only attraction. The following interviewee, who himself started working for the technical services of the navy base and as guide of the Portuguese troops, explained for example:

> There were those who knew what Frelimo was fighting for, and there were those who did not know what Frelimo was fighting for, so that they even blamed Frelimo. Those lacked political education […] So it happened that many joined the colonial troops, for example the GE or the

---

~1952) (Nkholongue, August 27, 2013), 00:05:47–00:06:17. For those who claimed to have forgotten about the war: PA, I062: interview with *P0713 (♂, 1944)* (Nkholongue, August 30, 2013), min 00:36:01–00:36:47.

135 At least two of Nkholongue's former population served as militias. See: PA, I115: interview with *P0160 (♂, 1952)* (Metangula, April 18, 2016), min 00:18:18–00:19:51.

136 PA, I115: interview with *P0160 (♂, 1952)* (Metangula, April 18, 2016), min 00:29:41–00:35:24; PA, I117: interview with *P1458 (♂, ~1945)* (Micundi, April 20, 2016), min 01:08:04–01:13:57.

137 PA, I115: interview with *P0160 (♂, 1952)* (Metangula, April 18, 2016), min 00:19:28–00:20:25. For a possible fourth, see: PA, I068: interview with *P0367 (♂, 1936)* (Nkholongue, September 2, 2013), min 00:39:36–00:41:00.

138 Paul, *Memoirs of a Revolution*, 183.

139 PA, I041: interview with *P0951 (♀, 1948), P0242 (♂, 1945)* (Malango, August 16, 2013), min 00:35:06–00:35:28; PA, I037: interview with *P0855 (♂, 1954)* (Malango, August 14, 2013), min 00:28:02–00:30:37.

140 PA, I068: interview with *P0367 (♂, 1936)* (Nkholongue, September 2, 2013), min 00:39:36–00:41:00; PA, I073: interview with *P1012 (♂, 1955)* (Malango, September 5, 2013), min 00:14:51–00:16:46; PA, I055: interview with *P0639 (♀, ~1952)* (Nkholongue, August 27, 2013), min 00:13:38–00:16:42; PA, I086: interview with *P0375 (♂, 1962)* (Nkholongue, September 9, 2013), min 00:05:25–00:05:44.

141 PA, I105: interview with *P0242 (♂, 1945)* (Malango, April 4, 2016), min 01:18:54–01:19:02.

GEP.¹⁴² They helped the colonial troops to prevent Frelimo's advance. There were troops consisting only of Africans.¹⁴³

"Modernization" and "Urbanization": Education and Health

In many respects it can be said that the Portuguese modernization propaganda indeed became reality in the case of the *aldeamento* of Metangula, even though the jobs that were created here were certainly not part of some rural extension program, as envisaged by the propaganda, but plainly and simply part of the military apparatus. The modernization did not just affect the economy. Schooling, previously available only at mission schools, was now made possible by the spread of "secularized" schools. Many of Nkholongue's children—especially the boys—now began to go to school.¹⁴⁴

Portuguese sources from this period were self-critical, admitting the rudimentary state of their schools and demanding improvement.¹⁴⁵ However, the quality of these schools was not necessarily poor from a local perspective. This is shown by the development of the teacher-pupil ratio: in 1972, the elementary school of the *aldeamento* of Metangula had seven teachers for 242 male and 116 female pupils. This gives a ratio of about one teacher for every 51 pupils. For the entire district of Lago, the ratio was about one teacher for every 52 pupils.¹⁴⁶ Later, in 1983, there was only one teacher for every 67 pupils, and in 2003 the rate was almost the same again with one teacher

---

142 GEP stands for *Grupos Especiais Paraquedistas*, the paratrooper version of the GE.
143 PA, I074: interview with *P0160* (♂, *1952*) (Metangula, September 6, 2013), min 00:17:06–00:17:44.
144 PA, I073: interview with *P1012* (♂, *1955*) (Malango, September 5, 2013), min 00:10:51–00:13:40; PA, I124: interview with *P0376* (♂, *1968*) (Nkholongue, April 26, 2016), min 00:17:15–00:19:07; PA, I074: interview with *P0160* (♂, *1952*) (Metangula, September 6, 2013), min 00:02:15–00:03:43; PA, I066: interview with *P0085* (♂, *1960*) (Nkholongue, September 1, 2013), min 00:05:20–00:12:18; PA, I071: interview with *P0191* (♂, *1965*) (Nkholongue, September 4, 2013), min 00:07:18–00:10:42; PA, I043: interview with *P1148* (♂, *1960*) (Malango, August 17, 2013), min 00:40:54–00:41:19; PA, I079: interview with *P0510* (♂, *1963*) (Nkholongue, September 7, 2013), min 00:01:34–00:03:13; PA, I086: interview with *P0375* (♂, *1962*) (Nkholongue, September 9, 2013), min 00:02:01–00:03:56. If I am not mistaken, I have not interviewed a single woman from Nkholongue who went to school in the *aldeamento*. Portuguese statistics give a ratio of about two to one. So, in April 1974, there were said to be 381 boys and 197 girls attending school in Metangula. See: APGGN, 1 A: Mapa do Movimento da População da Circunscrição do Lago, Abril 1974 (Augusto Cardoso, May 5, 1974).
145 AHU, Biblioteca, L9560: José Guardado Moreira, "Governo do Distrito do Niassa: Relatório do ano de 1972" (Vila Cabral, May 31, 1973), 30, 36; AHMil, FO/63/13/950/17: José Azevedo, "Relatório Especial de Informações 01/71" (Metangula: Batalhão de Caçadores 2906, July 9, 1971), 14–15.
146 AHU, Biblioteca, L9560: José Guardado Moreira, "Governo do Distrito do Niassa: Relatório do ano de 1972" (Vila Cabral, May 31, 1973), 196–197.

for every 51 pupils.¹⁴⁷ Furthermore, interviewees had largely positive memories of their school days in the *aldeamento*. This was also due to the fact that school attendance was made popular by the distribution of food to the children. Or, as one former pupil put it:

> Even we, who were schoolboys: we always got milk with bread. Yes, always, that was every day.¹⁴⁸

The knowledge of the Portuguese language increased significantly during the time in the *aldeamento*. But we can observe a growing gender gap: while older people hardly speak Portuguese at all, men born in the 1950s and 1960s command a comparatively fair knowledge of it. Among women, the increase in Portuguese language skills has been much less pronounced.

This kind of "social modernization" affected not only the educational but also the health sector. Let me illustrate this with Table 6 which compares the number of people born in a hospital with the number of people born at home, ordered by age cohorts. The figures, taken from the 2016 survey, show that the number of births in hospitals began to rise before independence.

	1926–1955	1956–1965	1966–1975	1976–1985	1986–2000	Total
At home	20 (87%)	9 (56%)	5 (36%)	11 (46%)	8 (50%)	53 (57%)
Hospital	3 (13%)	5 (31%)	9 (64%)	11 (46%)	8 (50%)	36 (39%)
Unknown	0 (0%)	2 (13%)	0 (0%)	2 (8%)	0 (0%)	4 (4%)

Table 6: Number of births at home and at hospital ordered by age cohorts.

Changes in Everyday Life in the *Aldeamento*

There is little doubt that everyday life in the *aldeamento* differed from that in the village beyond the changes already discussed. Other ways had to be taken to fetch

---

147 APGGN, 1 A: Relatório resumido da situação sócioeconómica e cultural do Distrito do Lago, 1983, July 20, 1983, 5; Ministério da Administração Estatal, "Perfil do Distrito de Lago, Província de Niassa" (Maputo, 2005), 34, accessed April 16, 2019, http://www.portaldogoverno.gov.mz/por/content/download/2837/23237/version/1/file/Lago.pdf.
148 PA, I086: interview with *P0375 (♂, 1962)* (Nkholongue, September 9, 2013), min 00:06:55–00:07:38. See as well: PA, I071: interview with *P0191 (♂, 1965)* (Nkholongue, September 4, 2013), min 00:08:21–00:10:42; PA, I074: interview with *P0160 (♂, 1952)* (Metangula, September 6, 2013), min 00:02:43–00:03:43.

water, cut firewood, or go to one's fields. There was less space around the houses and there were other neighbors. Moreover, in the course of the war, the Portuguese administration began to require a grouping of houses that hardly corresponded to the way people had lived before (see Figure 6).¹⁴⁹ Interestingly, my interviewees usually did not highlight these factors by themselves and also tended to play down their importance if asked about them.¹⁵⁰

Nevertheless, we can expect that people's experiences of the *aldeamento* influenced their lives in manifold ways, both in the short and long run. It is important to know that while the population of Nkholongue remained under the jurisdiction of their chief,¹⁵¹ they did not form a spatial unit in the *aldeamento*. People lived all over the *aldeamento*. Many even changed their homes during their stay in Metangula, some more than once.¹⁵² Nkholongue was also not the only village that had been resettled to Metangula. Rather, the town was populated by people from a wide range of other villages.¹⁵³

Living together with people of different origins in a more urban environment doubtlessly impacted people's habits, customs, and ideas in many different ways, even if the individual effects cannot always be reconstructed one-to-one. We

---

149 This more organized grouping was enforced from 1969 onward. See: AHMil, DIV/2/7/55/4: Batalhão de Caçadores 2906. História de Unidade, n.d., II–52; APGGN, QJ: Nuno Egídio ao Administrador da Circunscrição do Lago, "N.° 245/C/GAB: Construções do edifício geminado para funcionários e ampliação da secretaria / reestruturação do aldeamento da sede," July 28, 1969.
150 PA, I109: interview with *P1081 (♀, 1945)* (Malango, April 6, 2016), min 00:43:48–00:44:27; PA, I115: interview with *P0160 (♂, 1952)* (Metangula, April 18, 2016), min 01:57:16–01:58:24; PA, I043: interview with *P1148 (♂, 1960)* (Malango, August 17, 2013), min 00:23:20–00:24:59; PA, I093: interview with *P0050 (♂, ~1922)* (Nkholongue, January 19, 2016), min 01:40:10–01:45:58; PA, I096: interview with *P1216 (♂, 1957)* (Malango, February 1, 2016), min 00:33:15–00:41:42; PA, I101: interview with *P0316 (♀, ~1952)* (Nkholongue, February 22, 2016), min 00:29:27–00:33:08.
151 PA, I051: interview with *P0481 (♀, 1942)* (Nkholongue, August 26, 2013), min 01:10:05–01:11:12; PA, I059: interview with *P0090 (♀, ~1932)* (Metangula, August 29, 2013), min 00:26:53–00:28:55; PA, I068: interview with *P0367 (♂, 1936)* (Nkholongue, September 2, 2013), min 00:39:00–00:39:36; PA, I074: interview with *P0160 (♂, 1952)* (Metangula, September 6, 2013), min 00:08:35–00:09:45; PA, I076: interview with *P1449 (♂, ~1948)* (Metangula, September 6, 2013), min 00:09:35–00:11:10; PA, I078: interview with *P0258 (♂, 1953)* (Nkholongue, September 7, 2013), min 00:11:47–00:12:38.
152 PA, I047: interview with *P0596 (♂, ~1950)* (Metangula, August 21, 2013), min 00:14:59–00:16:39; PA, I049: interview with *P0267 (♀, 1949)* (Nkholongue, August 23, 2013), min 00:54:11–00:54:46; PA, I074: interview with *P0160 (♂, 1952)* (Metangula, September 6, 2013), min 00:09:45–00:10:48; PA, I078: interview with *P0258 (♂, 1953)* (Nkholongue, September 7, 2013), min 00:11:47–00:12:38; PA, I068: interview with *P0367 (♂, 1936)* (Nkholongue, September 2, 2013), min 00:39:00–00:39:36. Still, the majority of those resettled from Nkholongue seem to have lived in the neighborhood of Thungo. See: PA, I115: interview with *P0160 (♂, 1952)* (Metangula, April 18, 2016), min 00:17:43–00:18:06.
153 Including the villages of Micuio, Chipili, M'chepa, Meluluca, Ngolocolo, Lussefa, and Chinuni.

can, for example, expect that different dialects of different people influenced each other. Furthermore, people brought different religions to the *aldeamento*. The majority of those who were resettled to Metangula were Muslims, but the town itself had a significant Christian population. The Muslims, for their part, belonged to two different Sufi "brotherhoods," a majority (including those from Nkholongue) to the *Shadhiliya* and a minority to the *Qadiriya*.[154]

Figure 6: The *aldeamento* of Metangula in 1973. Photograph available at LUGAR DO REAL http://lugardoreal.com, courtesy of Manuel António Lima Torres Ribeiro.

The different communities not only followed different religious practices, but also different cultural codes that could be imitated. As will be further discussed in Chapter 11, there is for example some evidence that the time in the *aldeamento* initiated or accelerated a trend from uxorilocal to virilocal marriage practices. In the Christian areas of the district, virilocality had already replaced uxorilocality

---

[154] A conflict arose between these two brotherhoods during the time in the *aldeamento*, prompting the *Qadiriya* followers to build their own mosque. This mosque was used by people from Nkholongue after the *Qadiriya* followers had been been re-resettled to the newly built *aldeamento* of Meluluca. See: PA, I149: interview with *P1501* (♂, *1949*), *P1513* (♂, *1943*) (Chinuni, June 11, 2016); PA, I115: interview with *P0160* (♂, *1952*) (Metangula, April 18, 2016), min 00:14:50–00:17:43; PA, I118: interview with *P1218* (♀, *1930*) (Malango, April 21, 2016), min 01:26:37–01:27:18.

as the norm long before the war. A similar observation can be made with regard to the housebuilding techniques. I have already pointed out in the previous chapter that before independence the wall of houses had largely been formed by plastering skeletons of trunks and beams (see p. 227). Coincidence or not, the fact is that shortly after their stay in Metangula people from Nkholongue began to build their houses increasingly with sun-dried mud bricks as the Christian populations of the region had already done before the war. People from Nkholongue had known this technique before, but according to statements from my interviewees they had looked at it with a mixture of respect and anxiety until that point.[155]

7.4 Zooming Out: Nkholongue's Experience in the Broader Perspective

In view of the fairly unambiguous verdict of previous literature, one is inclined to read the wartime experiences of Nkholongue's population as a deviation from the standard course of the war.[156] There are indeed many factors that point to the exceptional nature of the perspective of the villagers of Nkholongue. However, some of my findings, combined with sources concerning the wider region, strongly suggest that scholars have so far ignored, neglected or misrepresented certain patterns and processes of the war. In other words, the wartime experiences of Nkholongue's population were unique, but to a certain extent they also reflected more general developments of the war course.

The Particularities of the Wartime Experiences of the Villagers of Nkholongue

Thinking of the particularities of the wartime experiences of the villagers of Nkholongue, six factors need to be highlighted. First, the high military presence prevented the *aldeamento* from ever being attacked by Frelimo. This situation differs from

---

[155] PA, I042: interview with *P1193* (♀, *1953*) (Malango, August 17, 2013), min 00:38:12–00:39:35; PA, I043: interview with *P1148* (♂, *1960*) (Malango, August 17, 2013), min 00:44:07–00:46:44; PA, I046: interview with *P1045* (♀, *1932*) (Malango, August 20, 2013), min 00:07:41–00:09:15, 00:29:23–00:30:04; PA, I048: interview with *P1446* (♂, *~1945*) (Metangula, August 21, 2013), min 00:36:45–00:39:41; PA, I043: interview with *P1148* (♂, *1960*) (Malango, August 17, 2013), min 00:55:39–00:58:43; PA, I094: interview with *P0727* (♂, *~1940*) (M'chepa, January 27, 2016), min 01:43:54–01:44:41.
[156] One colleague once called my findings about the Mozambican War of Independence after a presentation "disconcerting."

that of other *aldeamentos* that were hit by the war—repeatedly at times—and therefore did not offer their inhabitants the security and stability that Metangula did. Second, the presence of various state institutions (civil administration, army, navy, police etc.) may have favored the enforcement of official state policy and prevented arbitrary actions that may have been more common in more remote *aldeamentos*. Third, Metangula's location on the lake guaranteed constant access to drinking and service water, something that was much more difficult to obtain in other *aldeamentos*. Fourth, the location of both the village and the *aldeamento* on the lake also facilitated the transport of people and their belongings. Fifth, Nkholongue's population seems to have benefited from being among the first to be resettled to Metangula. This gave them access to resources such as land at a time when there was still enough available. Evidence from "latecomers" from more distant villages suggests that it was more difficult for these people to secure sufficient farmland.[157] Last but not least, not every *aldeamento* offered so many income opportunities and as good a supply situation as Metangula.[158] The Portuguese forces were well aware of Metangula's special position in this regard. Orlando Cristina, son of a Portuguese trader in Niassa and an important member of the irregular armed forces,[159] wrote for example in May 1968:

> The situation has been like this for four years, and nothing has been done to organize the economic life of the populations [...] Metangula, with its workers in the army and navy, is saving the face of this problem.[160]

While all of these particularities need to be taken into account when thinking about the generalizations that can be drawn from the resettlement experience of Nkholongue, the knowledge of the wartime experiences of Nkholongue's population can undoubtedly help improve our analysis of the general patterns of the war. To this end, seven points can be made.

---

[157] See for example: PA, I149: interview with *P1501 (♂, 1949), P1513 (♂, 1943)* (Chinuni, June 11, 2016), min 00:28:27–00:31:06.
[158] ANTT, PIDE, SC, CI(2), GU, cx. 12, f. 225–237: DGS SUBVC, "Relatório de Situação do Dist do Niassa: Período de 31OUT a 15NOV" (Vila Cabral, November 19, 1972), f. 228–229.
[159] Cristina was an associate of Jorge Jardim, who was an important Portuguese businessman. He repeatedly participated as an irregular member in operations of the Portuguese armed forces in Niassa. After the war he became the first secretary-general of Renamo. See: João M. Cabrita, *Mozambique: The Tortuous Road to Democracy* (Basingstoke: Palgrave, 2000), 133–92; Baêna, *Factos e feitos na Guerra*, 4: Crónica dos feitos de Moçambique, 93–95; AHMar, Coloredo, Pasta 058/MO: Relatório de Comissão DFE N. 8. Anexo Delta: Comissários Políticos, n.d.; AHMar, Coloredo, Pasta 058/MO: João Bastos, "Relatório de Comissão DFE N. 8," n.d., 13–14.
[160] Baêna, *Factos e feitos na Guerra*, 4: Crónica dos feitos de Moçambique, 113.

The Growing Presence of the Colonial State at the Periphery

First, although Metangula occupied a special position, the fact is that the war brought similar developments to other areas that had used to lie at the margins of the colonial state. Portuguese presence in these areas was not necessarily weakened by the outbreak of the war, but rather in many cases rose to higher levels than ever before. It also needs to be emphasized that the people who lived in these areas had had different (pre-war) experiences with the colonial state than the inhabitants of the plantation areas of Zambezia, the cotton zones of southern Niassa, or the racially segregated settler areas of Lourenço Marques.

The Myth of the "Liberated Areas"

Second, my findings allow us to complicate the standard narrative of the course of the Mozambican War of Independence, which is still very much framed by Frelimo's liberation script. While certain elements of this script have recently come under increasing scrutiny,[161] the course of the war is still under-researched and largely marked by ideas of the progressive growth of Frelimo's "liberated areas." According to such ideas, Frelimo received widespread popular support in northern Mozambique and "steadily expanded its 'liberated zones' until they covered the northern fourth of the country."[162] Our knowledge of those "liberated areas" is still very basic and little has been done to challenge Frelimo's propaganda that claimed that they became the cradle of the nation, where Frelimo started to set up a previously missing health and educational infrastructure and where Frelimo began to organize production collectively.[163] A rare exception in this regard are the

---

[161] Paolo Israel, "A Loosening Grip: The Liberation Script in Mozambican History," *Kronos* 39, no. 1 (2013): 10–19; João Paulo Borges Coelho, "Politics and Contemporary History in Mozambique: A Set of Epistemological Notes," *Kronos* 39, no. 1 (2013): 20–31. See as well Michel Cahen's older critical assessment of the Massacre of Mueda: Michel Cahen, "The Mueda Case and Maconde Political Ethnicity: Some Notes on a Work in Progress," *Africana Studia*, no. 2 (1999): 29–46.

[162] Finnegan, *A Complicated War*, 30. For a recent scholarly claim for the importance of Frelimo's successes in Niassa, see: Correia, "História e textualização." How strongly this idea has been popularized is shown by a recent statement by the Portuguese novelist Lídia Jorge, who claimed that at the beginning of 1974 the northern part of Mozambique was "completely taken" by the nationalists. See: Nazaré Torrão, "Entrevista com Lídia Jorge," *Língua-lugar: Literatura, História, Estudos Culturais*, no. 1 (2020): 186.

[163] For examples of this propaganda, see: "Zonas Libertadas: Berço da revolução," *Tempo*, Número especial: Dedicado à viagem presidencial à Província do Niassa (December 26, 1979): 91–95; "O processo eleitoral no Niassa: Entrevista com Aurélio Manave, Primeiro Secretário Pro-

7.4 Zooming Out: Nkholongue's Experience in the Broader Perspective — 289

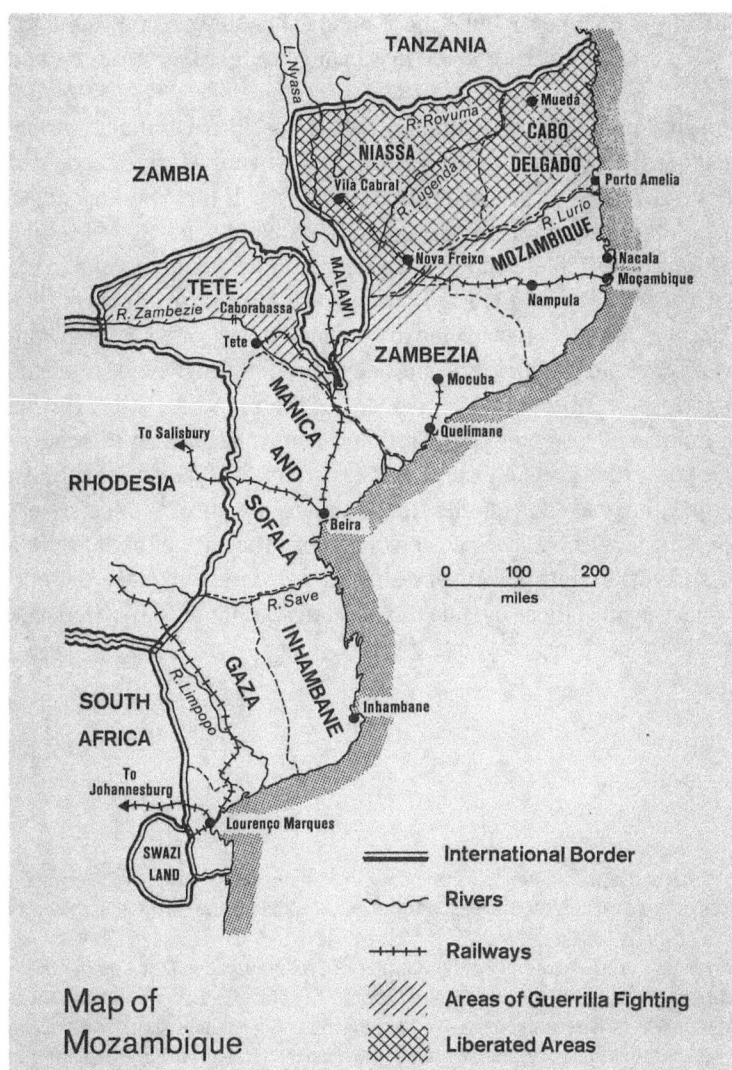

Figure 7: Mozambique and the "liberated areas" in 1969 according to Frelimo's propaganda. Source: Eduardo Mondlane, The Struggle for Mozambique (Harmondsworth: Penguin, 1969).

---

vincial," *Tempo*, no. 376 (December 18, 1977): 36–40; APGGN, 1 A: Síntese do Relatório do Distrito de Maúa, Primeira Reunião de Administradores, Comissários Políticos e Grupos Dinamizadores dos Distritos da Província do Niassa (Lichinga, May 19, 1976), 3.

comments by Yussuf Adam, who set out a more nuanced panorama and stated for example that in Niassa co-operatives were "practically non existent until the end of the war."[164]

My findings substantiate Adam's claim and show that the nationalist propaganda had little to do with realities. As for Niassa, the Portuguese forces succeeded in containing the initial gains of Frelimo rather effectively. If this war was about controlling people, it has to be said that the colonial state did better than Frelimo in the long run of the war. Table 7 shows the number of people living under the control of the Portuguese forces in the Lago District over the course of the conflict. It reveals that the colonial state, after having lost considerable ground at the beginning of the war, was able to gradually regain people, so that their number at the end of the war corresponded to about 50 percent of the pre-war census. On the other hand, the number of people under Frelimo's control shrank in the course of the war to the point that at its end probably less than five percent of the district's pre-war population was living under the nationalists' control.[165] Most others had fled to either Tanzania or Malawi (which was against the aims of both Frelimo and the colonial state). The death toll is very difficult to assess. But, given the Portuguese hunger policy against those outside the *aldeamentos*, it may have been considerable in certain areas of the war zone.[166]

---

164 Yussuf Adam, "Trick or Treat: The Relationship between Destabilisation, Aid and Government Development Policies in Mozambique 1975–1990" (PhD thesis, Roskilde University, 1996), 47. See as well: Munslow, *Mozambique*, 94–95.

165 In 1971, the Portuguese military estimated the number of Frelimo fighters living on the bases within and around Lago District to be about 365 and the number of civilians living around these bases to be about 1,630. When these numbers are added together this is about six percent of the district's pre-war census. However, these bases were only partly located within Lago District and also included a considerable number of "inhabitants" from other districts. Moreover, it can be expected that this number was further reduced in the last years of the war. See: AHMil, FO/63/13/950/17: José Azevedo, "Relatório Especial de Informações 01/71" (Metangula: Batalhão de Caçadores 2906, July 9, 1971).

166 The AHM's oral history crew was, for example, told in Mavago that many died of hunger, and that, in fact, the number of those who died of starvation was higher than the numbers of death from the proper war. See: AHM, Secção Oral, Transcrito NI 10: Germano Ntaula and Aly Saidy, N.° 162–163, Entrevista com o responsável da comissão de aldeias comunais (Mavago, Niassa), interview by José Negrão, 1980, 7. See as well: Deposito Museológico de Lichinga (DML), 1a Gaveta/N° 8: Samuel Raisse, "Pequeno episódio sobre a História da L.A.L. Nacional" (Mavago: Serviço Distrital de Cultura – Mavago, n.d.), 3.

1964	1965	1966	1967	1968	1969	1970	06/1971	1971	1972	12/1973	07/1974
32,161	9,828	10,946	13,660	14,556	15,013	15,246	15,408	15,539	15,943	16,292	16,495

Table 7: Population under Portuguese control, Lago District, 1964–1974.[167]

In the case of Nkholongue, the distribution was even more pronounced in favor of the Portuguese side. Portuguese statistics from 1972 put the population of Chingomanje's chiefdom at 486, compared with a pre-war census of 550.[168] Assuming there had been no natural population growth, this would mean that about 88 percent of Nkholongue's pre-war population lived in the *aldeamento*. However, these figures should be treated with caution. The information from my interviews suggests that the percentage of those who fled abroad must have been higher, namely about 25 to 30 percent of the original population. There are two possible explanations for reconciling the two sets of data: first, we can suppose that the pre-war census did not include the family of Chief Chingomanje VI. They had lived near Mtucula at the outbreak of the war and only came to Metangula during the war, where Chingomanje VI was then appointed successor to Chingomanje V.[169] Second, we can speculate whether the pre-war census excluded those who had migrated to M'chepa in the 1950s, most of whom fled to Malawi during the war.

My research clearly shows that the "liberated areas" did not correspond to what has been commonly written about them. In 1972, PIDE/DGS estimated the number of non-combatants living under the control of Frelimo in all of Niassa Province at only 2,900. The number of combatants was estimated at 920.[170] This compares to a population of 291,935 who lived under the control of Portuguese forces, which shows how critical we should be of Frelimo's version of history,

---

[167] Sources: AHM, GGM XX, cx. 2097: Nuno Egídio, "O Niassa: Relatório Anual de 1970" (Vila Cabral, February 28, 1971), 192; AHM, ISANI, cx. 99: Mário Freiria, "Relatório da Inspecção Ordinária à Circunscrição do Lago 1971" (Vila Cabral, July 4, 1971), 3; APGGN, 1 A: Mapa do Movimento da População da Circunscrição do Lago, Dezembro 1973 (Augusto Cardoso, January 12, 1974); APGGN, 1 A: Mapa do Movimento da População da Circunscrição do Lago, Julho 1974 (Augusto Cardoso, August 9, 1974); AHU, Biblioteca, L9560: José Guardado Moreira, "Governo do Distrito do Niassa: Relatório do ano de 1972" (Vila Cabral, May 31, 1973), 158.
[168] ANTT, SCCIM N.° 24 (folhas 247–253): Mapa comparativo da população do Distrito distribuída por regedorias e relacionada aos anos de antes da eclosão da subversão (1964/1965), e depois da subversão, para controle dos elementos refugiados (Vila Cabral, June 1972).
[169] PA, I043: interview with *P1148* (♂, 1960) (Malango, August 17, 2013).
[170] ANTT, SC-CI(2) GU, cx. 6, f. 18–33: Relatório Periódico de Informações – Grupo II: Niassa (Lourenço Marques, February 28, 1972), 9–10.

even if the situation in Cabo Delgado and Tete was different.[171] In Niassa, the exceptions were not those who lived in *aldeamentos* under Portuguese control, as is usually claimed,[172] but precisely those who lived in the areas controlled by Frelimo.

As I also highlight elsewhere,[173] daily life in many of the "liberated areas" of Niassa was in reality a precarious affair. The people there were busy ensuring their survival, rather than organizing the revolution. Living in Frelimo's "liberated areas" was no real option for most people in the long run, because in the case of Niassa these areas did not have the qualities attributed to them by Frelimo's propaganda. In practice, most people had only two options in the course of the war, either to live in the *aldeamentos* or to flee abroad.

Resettlement through Hunger: The Portuguese Scorched Earth Policy

The third point concerns the question of how people were actually resettled. Previous studies on the Mozambican case have not said much about this question. Evidence from the Lago District suggests that the way in which the majority of Nkholongue's population was resettled was not the norm. Rather, Portuguese sources show that a considerable portion of the district's population came to the *aldeamentos* on

---

171 PIDE/DGS reports from this period reveal great differences between the war situation in the different provinces. For examples, see: ANTT, PIDE, SC, CI(2), GU, cx. 33 (NT 8966), f. 209–243: Delegação de DGS em Lourenço Marques, "Situação Actual em Moçambique, Março de 1974," Secreto (Lourenço Marques, March 4, 1974); ANTT, PIDE, SC, CI(2), GU, cx. 13, f. 313–366: DGS SUBVC, "Relatório de Situação do Dist do Niassa: Período de 30NOV a 15DEZ" (Vila Cabral, December 19, 1972); ANTT, PIDE, SC, CI(2), GU, cx. 14, f. 583–595: DGS SUBVC, "Relatório de Situação do Dist do Niassa: Período de 31DEZ a 15JAN" (Vila Cabral, January 19, 1973); ANTT, SC-CI(2) GU, cx. 17, f. 32–49: DGS/SUBT, "Relatório de Situação N.° 8/73: Período de 16 a 30ABR73" (Tete, May 3, 1973), 1; ANTT, PIDE, SC, CI(2), GU, cx. 12, f. 520–545: DGS/SUBT, "Relatório de Situação N.° 20/72," November 2, 1972.
172 Helena Dolny for example began her description of the communal village of Lussanhando by saying: "Large areas of this northern province were liberated as the struggle for national independence advanced, but the inhabitants of this particular village had been grouped together by the Portuguese in an *aldeamento*, or strategic hamlet." See: Helena Dolny, "The Challenge of Agriculture," in *A Difficult Road: The Transition to Socialism in Mozambique*, ed. John S. Saul (New York: Monthly Review Press, 1985), 238.
173 Andreas Zeman, "Caught between the Guerrilla and the Colonial State: Refugee Life in Northern Mozambique During the Independence War (1964–1974)," in *On the Social History of Persecution*, ed. Christian Gerlach (Berlin: De Gruyter Oldenbourg, 2023), 115–138; Andreas Zeman, "Flag Independence without Flags? Mozambican Decolonization on the Periphery of the New Nation," *E-Journal of Portuguese History* 21, no. 2 (forthcoming 2023).

their "own" accord.[174] This is also confirmed by the research of Sayaka Funada-Classen.[175]

The Portuguese scorched earth policy played an important role in forcing people into the *aldeamentos*. One could now assume that this policy, because of its brutality, backfired on the Portuguese forces. However, this was not necessarily the case as it was Frelimo who had urged the people to leave their villages and fields in the first place. The available information suggests that most people expected a short war.[176] They were thus not prepared to subsist for long. In a rare critical account of the course of the war in Niassa, Barry Munslow highlighted these regional war hardships already in 1983, but still maintained that "the shared suffering appears to have promoted a firm bond between the people and the guerrillas."[177] This overlooks how few in fact stayed with Frelimo. My research points out that the lack of food led to considerable tensions among the people living on and near Frelimo's bases.[178] Many lost faith in the nationalist cause and abandoned Frelimo. As I have already mentioned, most of my interviewees who had joined Frelimo as fighters at the beginning of the war deserted in the first years of the war. They were no exceptions. Many of the inmates of Frelimo's post-colonial re-education camps were deserters.[179] In Niassa, Portuguese forces were undoubtedly fairly successful in creating discord among the nationalists and their supporters.[180]

---

174 Portuguese statistics show, for example, that of the 8,514 people "recuperated" by their forces throughout the Mozambican war zone in 1971, nearly 72 percent had "presented" themselves at the *aldeamentos*, and only 28 percent had been captured by Portuguese forces. These numbers have been put together from different documents from: AHMar, Coloredo, Pasta 060/MO. See as well: Zeman, "Caught between the Guerrilla and the Colonial State," 128.
175 Funada-Classen, *The Origins of War in Mozambique*, 322.
176 PA, I093: interview with *P0050* (♂, ~1922) (Nkholongue, January 19, 2016), min 01:29:58–01:30:33. See also the statements of Joanna Katto's interviewees: Katto, "Grandma Was a Guerrilla Fighter," 27, 33, 62. See as well: Munslow, *Mozambique*, 93.
177 Munslow, *Mozambique*, 94.
178 For evidence of such tensions in Niassa see for example: AHMar, Coloredo, Pasta 303-B/MO: DFE 5, "Ficha de Interrogatório de Pessoal Capturado ou Apresentado: Lufame Saide," September 5, 1967; AHMar, Coloredo, Pasta 047/MO: Kaúlza Arriaga, "Relatório de Acção Psicológica N.° 3/70" (Nampula, November 25, 1970), 18, 21; ANTT, PIDE, SC, CI(2), proc. 4276, NT 7336, pt. 1, f. 44–47: PIDE Subdelegação VC, "Auto de Perguntas: Momade Lezuani" (Vila Cabral, January 28, 1966); AHMar, Coloredo, Pasta 149/MO: Mário Tello Polléri, "Relatório de Acção Psicológica N.° 4/70" (Nampula, February 22, 1971), 20; AHMil, FO/63/12/947/9: Ficha de Interrogatório de Apresentados e Capturados: António Bonomar Namaumbo (Vila Cabral, November 13, 1973); AHMil, FO/63/12/947/9: Relatório de Interrogatório de Pessoal Capturado N.° 05/73 (Olivença, June 1, 1973).
179 Machava, "The Morality of Revolution," 105. 224–225. There are countless files on deserters at the APGGN, including "histories" of their desertion. See: APGGN, 1 A: Fichas dos Desertores: Inquérito Tipo B (Desertores), n.d.

Previous research has repeatedly highlighted that the colonial state exploited ethnic, regionalist and religious tension within Frelimo to its advantage.[181] The exploitation of such tensions certainly played some part in the Portuguese propaganda. However, as I also argue elsewhere, the actual operations by Portuguese forces mainly aimed at producing (economic) tensions over basic necessities among those siding with Frelimo.[182] The lack of food, rather than issues of religion or ethnicity, caused people—both Christians and Muslims and both Anyanja and Wayao—to lose faith in the nationalist cause. Initially, all of them had supported Frelimo in large numbers, even though Frelimo's main base of support had been in the Christian areas north of Metangula.

Examining the impact of the Portuguese scorched earth policy on social relations within Frelimo and its support base might also help explain similar developments on other war fronts. In his study on resettlement in Tete, for example, João Paulo Borges Coelho has provided several pieces of evidence of people who came to the *aldeamentos* on their "own" accord.[183] In one case, people who had been "freed" from an *aldeamento* by Frelimo evidently returned there as soon as they had the opportunity to do so.[184] However, a reflection on why people acted the way they did is not really provided by Borges Coelho.

"Social Progress": The Fallacy of the Seductive Propaganda Argument

To properly understand the reasoning of the people, we must consider a fourth point. The evidence shows that at least in Niassa the Portuguese forces were indeed anxious to provide a proper reception for those who came to the *aldeamentos*. They were received with clothing and food.[185] While the Portuguese forces initially tended to use mere repression to bring people to their side, they increasingly used incentives to do so in the course of the war. In fact, the Portuguese forces went surprisingly far in the realization of the "promotion of social progress," and not only around Metangula. In Mavago, for example, the AHM's oral history

---

180 On this point, see as well: Zeman, "Caught between the Guerrilla and the Colonial State," 132–135.
181 Margaret Hall and Tom Young, *Confronting Leviathan: Mozambique since Independence* (London: Hurst, 1997), 27; Edward A. Alpers, "Ethnicity, Politics, and History in Mozambique," *Africa Today* 21, no. 4 (1974): 39–52; Jundanian, "Resettlement Programs."
182 Zeman, "Caught between the Guerrilla and the Colonial State," 132.
183 Borges Coelho, "Protected Villages and Communal Villages," 269 (n. 89), 273, 313 (n. 55).
184 Borges Coelho, "Protected Villages and Communal Villages," 271.
185 See as well: Paul, *Memoirs of a Revolution*, 190–191.

project recorded a very similar pattern in an interview in the early 1980s, as one of the interviewees stated:

> The Portuguese came first. We, the [real] owners [of the land] were not considered, we were not people. So what happened then! When the armed struggle began, the Portuguese started to feel [for us]. [...] They began to join with us to eat at the same table, [to say] we are of the same type. They began to mobilize the people [and said that] you can come to the administration. They said that you should take the chalk to whiten your houses and that the unemployed could come to get employment so that they would receive money.[186]

The Portuguese propaganda to promote educational and health sectors was not just empty talk. In 1971, nine of Lago's ten *aldeamentos* had a school and seven a health post or hospital.[187] In the schoolyear 1971/1972, Niassa Province, previously the blank space of Portuguese education, had the highest schooling rate of all Mozambique. With 61 percent, it even exceeded by far the 41 percent of Mozambique's capital Lourenço Marques.[188] In Niassa, the number of children attending official government schools had risen at an annual rate of more than 50 percent since 1965.[189]

Repression: Lifecycles of Particular Types of Violence

Connected to this is a fifth point, namely that of repression. The growing importance of a policy of incentives did not mean that the Portuguese forces completely refrained from repression in the *aldeamentos*. People suspected of collaborating with Frelimo from the *aldeamentos* had to be prepared for anything. Such a fate befell, for example, the father of three of my interview partners. He had lived with his family in the *aldeamento* of Olivença, where he had worked as a privileged ivory carver already before the war. In 1969, he was suspected by the Portu-

---

[186] AHM, Secção Oral, Transcrito NI 11: Assumane Ntaúla and Chimanje Amido, N.° 119–125, Entrevista de Grupo em Nkalapa (Mavago, Niassa), interview by Gerhard Liesegang, Teresa Oliveira, and Mucojuane Mainga Vicente, July 13, 1981.
[187] AHMil, FO/63/13/950/17: José Azevedo, "Relatório Especial de Informações 01/71" (Metangula: Batalhão de Caçadores 2906, July 9, 1971), 15; AHM, ISANI, cx. 99: Mário Freiria, "Relatório da Inspecção Ordinária à Circunscrição do Lago 1971" (Vila Cabral, July 4, 1971), 9.
[188] APGGN, 1 A: Higino Carvalheira, "Relatório do Departamento do Ensino Primário 1971/1972" (Lourenço Marques, November 7, 1973), 95–96.
[189] AHU, Biblioteca, L9560: José Guardado Moreira, "Governo do Distrito do Niassa: Relatório do ano de 1972" (Vila Cabral, May 31, 1973), 37.

guese forces of being the ring leader of a clandestine Frelimo network.[190] He was taken into custody and sent away to Lourenço Marques. His family never heard from him ever again.[191] He was not the only who had disappeared: after the revolution in Portugal, at least 13 Mozambicans who lived in the Portuguese military sector "A" filed a complaint against the extinct PIDE/DGS for the "disappearance of a family member."[192]

However, certain repressive elements of the Portuguese strategy were dropped after the initial phase. While the Portuguese forces had acted ruthlessly against supposed enemies at the beginning of the war, they began to avoid collective arrests and killings as the war progressed.[193] As for the killings, this change was evident not only in the lakeshore area, but also, according to Sayaka Funada-Classen, in the district of Maúa.[194] To avoid the killing of people, the colonial state even began to pay its troops fixed bonuses for people brought alive to the *aldeamentos*. While according to the official guidelines of 1972 the bonus was only paid for armed combatants,[195] information from my interviews suggest that at least around Metangula the bonus was also paid for non-combatants.[196] One interviewee who

---

190 PA, I040: interview with P1030 (♀, 1965), P1009 (♀, 1958), P1029 (♂, ~1959) (Malango, August 16, 2013), min 00:11:37–00:24:28; PA, I041: interview with P0951 (♀, 1948), P0242 (♂, 1945) (Malango, August 16, 2013), min 00:21:37–00:22:44; AHD, MU/GM/GNP/RNP/0032/00342: PIDE Moçambique, "Informação N.° 996 – SC/CI(2)," September 30, 1969; AHD, MU/GM/GNP/RNP/0032/00342: D.G.S. Moçambique, "Informação N.° 1.169 – SC/CI(2)," November 14, 1969.
191 His daughters denied the "accusation" that he had helped Frelimo and claimed that other people living in the *aldeamento* envied him for his privileged position and had therefore accused him unjustly. See: PA, I040: interview with P1030 (♀, 1965), P1009 (♀, 1958), P1029 (♂, ~1959) (Malango, August 16, 2013), min 00:19:27–00:23:12.
192 The list of the complaints contains only the names of the complainants, but not those of the disappeared. We can speculate that case 1 is about the disappeared ivory carver since the name of the complainant is identical with the name of one of his sons-in-law. See: ANTT, PIDE, SC, CI(2), GU, cx. 35, pt. 37, f. 27–28: 2a Repartição, Região Militar de Moçambique, "Relação de processos e queixas referentes a pessoal da Ex-DGS oriundos de COM SEC 'A' e entregues para envio ao EMGFA com destino à Comissão de Apuramento de Responsabilidades dos crimes das extintas PIDE/DGS e LP," n.d.
193 For the avoidance of collective arrests, see: AHMil, DIV/2/7/55/4: Batalhão de Caçadores 2906. História de Unidade, n.d., II–97.
194 Funada-Classen, *The Origins of War in Mozambique*, 322–23.
195 Comissão para o Estudo das Campanhas de África (CECA), *Resenha histórico-militar das campanhas de África, Vol. 6: Aspectos da actividade operacional, Tomo III: Moçambique, Livro I* (Lisboa: Estado-Maior do Exército, 2012), 120, 197. For the internal discussions of the military about this bonus, see especially: AHMil, FO/63/21/961/2: COM SEC "A" ao CEM/QG/AV (3a.REP): Prémios por material capturado (N.° 2856/c-70, P.° 505.01.05), December 21, 1970.
196 PA, I117: interview with P1458 (♂, ~1945) (Micundi, April 20, 2016), min 01:09:05–01:10:45; PA, I115: interview with P0160 (♂, 1952) (Metangula, April 18, 2016), min 00:39:12–00:43:01.

accompanied the Portuguese troops as a guide during their operations put it this way:

> [T]hat government did not allow a soldier to kill people in the bush. It did not allow it. You must listen carefully here: once we had captured people, the soldiers took these people to the administration so that the administration would pay the company that had captured these people. This was done so that the soldiers would not kill people. For they were worth money.[197]

It must be emphasized that this does not mean that there were no more killings at all. One need only think of the Massacre of Wiriyamu, which was perpetrated not at the beginning but in the last third of the war.[198] However, as I have argued elsewhere, such massacres were certainly not the norm of an unchanging Portuguese warfare. Instead, they are best understood by taking into account the considerable temporal and regional dynamics of the war.[199]

In Niassa, the Portuguese policy began to change markedly from that employed and communicated at the beginning of the war. In January 1966, the Portuguese administrator of Lago District had still announced that "once the *aldeamentos* are in operation, any population encountered outside the planned area would simply be killed by the [Portuguese] troops, as the troops would be in no position to verify the origins of individuals in the bush!"[200] In contrast to this, reports of military operations show clearly how important it became for Portuguese troops to bring people back to the *aldeamentos* alive.[201] They also show that Portuguese troops doubtlessly tried to identify who was who in the area outside the *aldeamentos*.[202] My research points to the fact that the Portuguese resettlement scheme might have even been less repressive than its British counterparts in spite of

---

[197] PA, I115: interview with *P0160* (♂, 1952) (Metangula, April 18, 2016), min 00:39:12–00:39:52.
[198] Dhada, *The Portuguese Massacre of Wiriyamu*.
[199] Andreas Zeman, "Wiriyamu and the Colonial Archive: Reading It against the Grain? Along the Grain? Read It at All!," *History in Africa*, June 20, 2023.
[200] ANTT, SCCIM N.° 1639 (folhas 474–475): Boletim de Informação N.° 3/66 (Augusto Cardoso, January 14, 1966).
[201] AHMar, Coloredo 309/MO: António Tierno Bagulho, "Comando Naval de Moçambique ao Comando da Defesa Maritima dos Portos do Lago e ao Comando da Defesa Maritima do Porto de Porto Amélia" (Nampula, July 16, 1969); AHMar, Coloredo, Pasta 058/MO: Relatório de Comissão DFE N. 8. Anexo Hotel: Política Operacional, n.d.; AHMil, DIV/2/7, cx. 133, n.° 2, p.° 142: Comandante Fernando Augusto Lopes, "Comentário ao Relatório de Acção N.° 20/68 (BArt N.° 2838)" (Metangula, January 15, 1969). See as well: Zeman, "Caught between the Guerrilla and the Colonial State."
[202] AHMar, Coloredo, Pasta 303-A/MO: Comando do DFE 5, "Relatório de Missão de Intervenção do DFE5 N° 47: 'Operação Refractário,'" Confidencial (Augusto Cardoso, October 21, 1967), 4.

the Portuguese reputation to the opposite. For, in contrast to Kenya, there was no such thing as "punitive villages" in Mozambique.²⁰³

Pre-history: Taking an Empirical Look at Life before the *Aldeamento*

Sixth, the experiences of Nkholongue's population teach us to take a closer look at what happened before the resettlement, both in the short and long term. Relocations are often portrayed as moments that abruptly changed the previously stable life of people.²⁰⁴ Ideas of life before the resettlement are thereby frequently based more on generic expectations than on concrete empirical studies, and often characterized by notions of the Aboriginal Delusion (see my comments in Section 1.4). The previous chapter has shown that at least the life of the people of Nkholongue before their resettlement had not been as stable as one might expect. In fact, most people had given up their former homes in the decade before the war when they had migrated to Malango for economic reasons. Access to important ancestral graveyards had already been made impossible by the rising lake level in the 1930s. And shortly before their resettlement, many people had already left the village, but then returned there because of the difficult conditions they had found in the forests.

How fruitful it could be to start the analysis of resettlement earlier can also be demonstrated in the case of the book by the Isaacmans on the Cahora Bassa dam.²⁰⁵ Some of the interviews they conducted for their research are now available on Aluka. One conversation with a group of people who were resettled because of the flooding of the lake is especially revealing for my argument. It shows that these people had come to the area of the future lake only a short time before their resettlement, having fled the war and, in their case, the advance of Frelimo.²⁰⁶ Clearly, the resettlement experiences of these people differed from those of the "traditional" inhabitants of the Zambezi valley. But, unfortunately, the Isaacmans have not given space to the analysis of this dynamic in their book.

---

203 The British counter-insurgency campaign in Kenya made a distinction between so-called punitive and protective villages. See: Branch, *Defeating Mau Mau*, 107–108.
204 See for example: Isaacman and Isaacman, *Dams, Displacement, and the Delusion of Development*, 108–109; Henriksen, *Revolution and Counterrevolution*, 160–161; Cann, *Counterinsurgency in Africa*, 156–157; Castelo, "Colonatos e aldeamentos no Niassa," 488.
205 Isaacman and Isaacman, *Dams, Displacement, and the Delusion of Development*.
206 Aluka, The Isaacman Collection: Entrevista com Fernando Alberto Damião et al., July 17, 2001, accessed July 28, 2014, http://www.aluka.org/action/showMetadata?doi=10.5555/AL.SFF.DOCUMENT.ISAACMAN0004.

Preventive versus Improvised *Aldeamentos*

This brings me to my last point. Previous research has suggested that the experiences of resettlement were more painful and conflictual in areas where the war was already raging compared to areas where resettlement was carried out preventively.[207] The underlying assumption is that "preventive" *aldeamentos* could be better planned and equipped with the necessary infrastructure. In contrast, the *aldeamentos* in the war zones have been considered disadvantageous for their inhabitants, since their construction is said to have been dictated primarily by military needs. Undoubtedly, lack of time in their planning and construction often made these *aldeamentos* sites of improvisation that barely offered people the necessary or promised infrastructure.

The problem with this reasoned interpretation is that it tends to overlook the actual perspective of the resettled. The experiences of my interview partners point to the fact that people in war zones were more willing to accept resettlement because they had already experienced the deprivations of war.[208] In other words, people's attitude to resettlement depended heavily on their previous living conditions and less on what exactly they found in the *aldeamentos*. A very similar observation was made by the provincial government of Tete in 1967. Describing people's reluctance to go into the *aldeamentos* in Tete, the government compared the situation with Niassa and Cabo Delgado:

> The situation is completely different in this regard in Cabo Delgado and in Niassa. There the people have been suffering privation and lack for years, from the hut they left to the field they lack. They have taken refuge in the bush, where they have lived in precarious circumstances—and some have died—lacking everything, being constantly in a state of insecurity and fleeing both from the terrorists and the regular forces in a life that is no life, and which makes them look upon the *aldeamento* as a place of salvation to escape the suffering that they have been enduring.[209]

---

[207] This is for example suggested by: Isaacman and Isaacman, *Dams, Displacement, and the Delusion of Development*, 107. Similarily: Castelo, "Colonatos e aldeamentos no Niassa," 492; Clarence-Smith, *The Third Portuguese Empire*, 218.
[208] On this point, see as well: AHMil, DIV/2/7/55/4: Batalhão de Caçadores 2906. História de Unidade, n.d., II–53.
[209] ANTT, SCCIM N.° 1635 (f. 201–202): João Cecílio Gonçalves, "Governo do Distrito de Tete: Informação. Assunto: Aldeamentos," Secreto (Tete, February 15, 1967).

7.5 Conclusion

In this chapter, I have tried to analyze the Mozambican War of Independence from the perspective of the inhabitants of Nkholongue. I have highlighted the local dynamics of the war and tried to show how it became a viable option for people to go to and stay in the *aldeamentos* and to even support the Portuguese war effort. I have argued that the experiences of Nkholongue's population cannot just been extrapolated to other villages and/or regions, but that it still might contribute to our better understanding of the Mozambican War of Independence and other asymmetric wars in manifold ways.

In particular, my findings points to the fact that the effort of the Portuguese state to "win people's hearts and minds" should be taken more seriously than has been the case so far.[210] While there is no question that the state propaganda of minimum force and maximal modernization has hardly ever mirrored the realities, my findings show that the colonial state was regionally, in fact, ready to go quite far with its reforms, raising levels of for example schooling and health infrastructure to unprecedented heights. It must be emphasized that this does not mean that the Portuguese official mind suddenly acquired a desire to realize their myth of lusotropical racial harmony. Rather, as Cooper has argued for the late colonial reforms in French West Africa, Portuguese officials "were [also] acting for reasons of state," with the aim to "preserve [Portugal] as something more than a small state in Western Europe."[211] Violence and repression were not given up, as has been shown in relation to the scorched earth policy in the areas outside the *aldeamentos*. Still, the use of violence was re-calibrated in a way that was designed to facilitate blaming the nationalist and evading one's own responsibility.

One might fairly say that this decade of change could barely make up the previous long-lasting experiences of colonial exploitation. However, such a perspective fails to appreciate that, seen from the vantage point of a lifetime, ten years can be a lot. Furthermore, it fails to appreciate that, in this concrete case, the level of colonial exploitation before the war was not as intensive as elsewhere. Around Nkholongue, the peak of colonial presence occurred at a moment when the colonial state had reoriented its policies toward "development" and was no longer the

---

[210] Just recently, Alex Vines for example claimed that "[t]he Portuguese failed because they had neglected the far north and responded solely with violence." See: Alex Vines, "As Conflict in Cabo Delgado Increases, Will Frelimo Learn from Its Mistakes?," The Mail & Guardian, June 24, 2020, accessed June 29, 2020, https://mg.co.za/africa/2020-06-24-as-conflict-in-cabo-delgado-increases-will-frelimo-learn-from-its-mistakes/.
[211] Frederick Cooper, "Routes Out of Empire," *Comparative Studies of South Asia, Africa and the Middle East* 37, no. 2 (2017): 408.

often purely exploitative entity of the past. While little of the economic propaganda materialized in the case of Nkholongue, the growing colonial presence (especially of the military) still resulted in an increase of opportunities for people to raise their material standards of living, and thus influenced the way they currently look back on the whole colonial period.

The experiences of most of Nkholongue's inhabitants had little to do with global political or ideological divisions, but very much with the local and regional course of history and the war. Other scholars have referred to such constellations as non-ideological or localized contingencies.[212] In line with this, my research suggests that age was an important factor that contributed to which side one ended up living or fighting on.[213]

---

[212] MacMaster, "The 'Silent Native'"; Kalyvas, *The Logic of Violence in Civil War*.
[213] My three interviewees who entered the GE/Portuguese militias during the war were 20, 18, and 11 in 1965. Those interviewees who joined Frelimo were 38, 33, and 25 in 1965.

8 At the Margins of the Nation: Malawians at Heart in Mozambique

8.1 "Aah! Even I was afraid": Mozambican Independence on the Ground

"Aah! Even I was afraid," was the retrospective comment of one of my interviewees about his state of mind in the face of the "impending" moment of independence in 1975. This may be a startling reflection on what is by nature supposed to be a moment of joy for the formerly colonized. It may not be so surprising a comment if we consider the local history leading up to the moment of independence. We have seen in Chapter 7 that the majority of Nkholongue's inhabitants had ended up living in the Portuguese-controlled zone of the battle line, and many of them had begun to support the Portuguese counter-insurgency effort indirectly or directly. Above all for the latter, the revolution in Portugal and the subsequent recognition of Frelimo as the sole legitimate heir to the colonial state was a blow to their calculations. Once more, the Winds of History had changed the local situation abruptly and profoundly.

The idea of "ordinary people" being afraid of the moment of independence runs counter not only to popular imaginations but also to what has long been written by historians about independence. Historians initially tended to be pretty close allies of the newly independent nations in Africa. Not so differently from what had happened at the birth of historiography in Europe earlier, the resurgent historiography was to equip the new nations with their history. Historians took a comparatively uncritical stance towards the nation-building projects, being in many ways themselves part of them.[1] In relation to Mozambique, the Mozambican historian João Paulo Borges Coelho has aptly phrased this as "neighbourliness relations" that evolved between "Politics" and "History."[2] Undoubtedly, scholars became more critical of the new national elites in light of the political and economic developments after the end of the early euphoria.[3] At first, it was, however, primarily political scientists and not so much historians that addressed the history of

---

[1] Miles Larmer and Baz Lecocq, "Historicising Nationalism in Africa," *Nations and Nationalism* 24, no. 4 (2018): 11–12.
[2] Borges Coelho, "Politics and Contemporary History in Mozambique," 21.
[3] Thus, Malyn Newitt has recently offered a very critical and compelling overview of Frelimo's takeover in his *A Short History of Mozambique*: Malyn Newitt, *A Short History of Mozambique* (London: Hurst, 2017), chap. 7.

what has been called the post-colonial African malaise. The focus was thereby more on colonial legacies (authoritarianism, despotism, tribalization) than on proper processes of decolonization,[4] and more on external actors ("neo-colonialism," Cold War) and political elites ("neo-patrionalism," "politics of the belly") than on local outcomes and dynamics. Essentializations (including culturalist ones) had been rather popular.

Certainly, in line with Cooper's call to avoid teleological narratives of independence, historians have increasingly begun to analyze late-colonial alternative roads not taken. But, similar to the older national historiography, these analyses have usually had their end point at the moment of independence. Only later did Miles Larmer and Baz Lecocq highlight the need for empirical studies of competing nationalisms that transcended the moment of independence. Through their own studies they have contributed much to rejecting the independence myth of national unity.[5] Another important strand of historiography has examined continuities in colonial and post-colonial governance, highlighting for example the role of the developmental state.[6]

As for social history, there has been limited interest in the transition from the colonial to the post-colonial period. Alexander Keese argues that what little interest there was has recently even tended to recede.[7] This is where this chapter sets in

---

[4] On this point, see: Frederick Cooper, "Possibility and Constraint: African Independence in Historical Perspective," *The Journal of African History* 49, no. 2 (2008): 170–173.

[5] Larmer and Lecocq, "Historicising Nationalism in Africa"; Miles Larmer, *Rethinking African Politics: A History of Opposition in Zambia* (Farnham: Ashgate, 2011). See as well: Giacomo Macola, *Liberal Nationalism in Central Africa: A Biography of Harry Mwaanga Nkumbula* (New York: Palgrave Macmillan, 2010); Lucas Barnabé Ncomo, *Uria Simango: um homem, uma causa* (Maputo: Novafrica, 2003).

[6] For examples, see the issue on *Continuities in Governance in Late Colonial and Early Postcolonial East Africa* in *The International Journal of African Historical Studies* or Cooper's concept of the Gatekeeper State: Andrew Burton and Michael Jennings, "Introduction: The Emperor's New Clothes? Continuities in Governance in Late Colonial and Early Postcolonial East Africa," *The International Journal of African Historical Studies* 40, no. 1 (2007): 1–25; Frederick Cooper, *Africa since 1940: The Past of the Present* (Cambridge: Cambridge University Press, 2002). See as well: Christophe Bonneuil, "Development as Experiment: Science and State Building in Late Colonial and Postcolonial Africa, 1930–1970," *Osiris* 15, no. 1 (2000): 258–281.

[7] Alexander Keese, "Just like in Colonial Times? Administrative Practice and Local Reflections on 'Grassroots Neocolonialism' in Autonomous and Postcolonial Dahomey, 1958–1965," *The Journal of African History* 60, no. 2 (2019): 265. See as well: Alexander Keese, "Decolonisation, Improvised: A Social History of the Transfer of Power in Cabo Verde, 1974–1976," *Portuguese Studies Review* 25, no. 1 (2017): 294–297. Historians had already complained about the lack of such studies in the 2000s. See: Stephen Ellis, "Writing Histories of Contemporary Africa," *The Journal of African His-*

as it examines the social history of decolonization on the ground. Highlighting the experiences and perceptions of the inhabitants of Nkholongue across the moment of independence, this chapter hopes to make an important contribution to our understanding of what Arnold Temu once called "multiple meanings" of independence.[8] We will investigate how life changed locally and how official government policy translated into local practice.

With respect to Mozambique, there are few empirical studies about (a part of) society that cut across the moment of independence and explicitly ask about the effects of decolonization.[9] We have few if any inquiries into how Mozambicans actually experienced the transition from being subjects of an empire to being citizens of a nation. This is in line with the fact that Frelimo was one of the liberation movements that embarked on independence with the maximum of intellectual support. If there was an African hope on the scholarly horizon in the mid-1970s, this was definitely Mozambique, probably sidelined only by the intellectual attraction of Guinea-Bissau and especially Amílcar Cabral. In accordance with their own beliefs, scholars largely took Frelimo's popular support for granted. With few exceptions,[10] criticisms of certain policies began to rise only during the 1980s. It was only much later that such strong former party supporters like Allen Isaacman or John Saul admitted that they had been too confident of Frelimo.[11] Still, for many, Frelimo's post-independence project remains one of the "most principled and decent ever proposed for the continent."[12]

---

tory 43, no. 1 (2002): 1–26; M. Anne Pitcher, "Forgetting from Above and Memory from Below: Strategies of Legitimation and Struggle in Postsocialist Mozambique," *Africa* 76, no. 1 (2006): 106–108.
8 Arnold Temu, "Not Telling: African History at the End of the Millennium," *South African Historical Journal* 42, no. 1 (2000): 3.
9 Pamilla Gupta's article, which claims to examine the "multiple and sometimes contradictory experiences of decolonization," is based on anecdotal evidence only. See: Pamila Gupta, "Decolonization and (Dis)Possession in Lusophone Africa," in *Mobility Makes States: Migration and Power in Africa*, ed. Darshan Vigneswaran and Joel Quirk (Philadelphia: University of Pennsylvania Press, 2015), 173.
10 One of the earliest serious questionings of the myth of unity was made by Leroy Vail and Landeg White. See: Vail and White, *Capitalism and Colonialism in Mozambique*, 389–92. They were heavily criticized for it. See: Judith Head and David Hedges, "Problemas da história da Zambézia," *Estudos Moçambicanos*, no. 4 (1983): 127–139.
11 Allen Isaacman, "Legacies of Engagement: Scholarship Informed by Political Commitment," *African Studies Review* 46, no. 1 (2003): 1; John S. Saul, "Mozambique – Not Then but Now," *Review of African Political Economy* 38, no. 127 (2011): 93–101.
12 These are the words of Norrie MacQueen: Norrie MacQueen, *The Decolonization of Portuguese Africa: Metropolitan Revolution and the Dissolution of Empire* (London: Longman, 1997), 236. Despite his now more critical perspective, Saul remains generally positive in his appraisal of Frelimo. See: Saul, "Mozambique – Not Then but Now." For another recent positive appraisal, see: Anna

Nevertheless, important research complicating the social dynamics of Mozambique's post-colonial history has been accomplished. This includes for example the area of agricultural policies. In this respect, scholars criticized Frelimo from the early stages onward for its focus on state farms and its neglect of the country's numerous small peasants. The gigantic top-down plans for villagization and collectivization also came under scrutiny. The effects of the shortages of consumer and producer goods were repeatedly pointed out, even though many emphasized external rather than internal reasons as a cause of them.[13] These arguments were later explored more systematically by different scholars such as Merle Bowen in her impressive *The State against the Peasantry*, in which she argued that Frelimo's policies "proved to be as inimical to the peasantry as those of the Portuguese colonial regime,"[14] or such as Sérgio Chichava in his analysis of the failure of the "socialization of the countryside."[15]

In the mid-1980s, such arguments, coupled with a critical stance toward Frelimo's policies against everything "traditional," also began to animate the debate on the origins and drivers of the Mozambican Civil War. In a deviation from the previously dominant destabilization theory, it was argued that Frelimo's actions had alienated wide parts of the peasantry and thus provided Renamo with a social base (see Chapter 9). Consequentially, many works on the Civil War have included accounts of the experiences of the post-independence years by "ordinary" Mozambicans.

The arguments offered in this chapter support much of what has been previously said about the alienation of the peasantry from the party and state appara-

---

Maria Gentili, "'Queremos ser cidadãos': Citizenship in Mozambique from Frelimo to Frelimo," *Citizenship Studies* 21, no. 2 (2017): 182–195.
13 Aquino de Bragança et al., "A situação nas antigas zonas libertadas de Cabo Delgado" (Maputo: Oficina de História, 1983), accessed July 9, 2014, http://sas-space.sas.ac.uk/4503/1/a_situaco_nas_anti gas.pdf; Joseph Hanlon, *Mozambique: The Revolution under Fire* (London: Zed Books, 1990), 95–131; Rosemary E. Galli, "The Food Crisis and the Socialist State in Lusophone Africa," *African Studies Review* 30, no. 1 (1987): 19–44; Bertil Egerö, *Mozambique, a Dream Undone: The Political Economy of Democracy, 1975–84* (Uppsala: Nordiska afrikainstitutet, 1990); Lars Rudebeck, "Entwicklung und Demokratie – Notizen zur Volksmacht in Mozambique," in *Agrargesellschaften im portugiesisch-sprachigen Afrika*, ed. Peter Meyns (Saarbrücken: Breitenbach, 1988), 111–127; Meyns, "Zur Praxis ländlicher Entwicklungspolitik in Afrika"; Adam, "Trick or Treat."
14 Bowen, *The State Against the Peasantry*.
15 Sérgio Chichava, "'They Can Kill Us but We Won't Go to the Communal Villages!' Peasants and the Policy of 'Socialisation of the Countryside' in Zambezia," *Kronos* 39, no. 1 (2013): 112–130. See also Kathleen Sheldon's work on the impact of Frelimo's agricultural policies on women: Kathleen E. Sheldon, *Pounders of Grain: A History of Women, Work, and Politics in Mozambique* (Portsmouth: Heinemann, 2002), 165–179.

tus. Still, my contribution hopes to deepen our understanding of the social history of the period following Mozambican Independence in four respects.

First, what most analyses have in common is that the independence myth of national unity is still taken for granted. In the case of Mozambique, this view is especially strong, underpinned by the belief that the need for political mobilization in a war scenario was conducive to greater nationalist unity compared to other cases where decolonization was reached by more peaceful means.[16] In combination with what has been said in the previous chapter, this one hopes to show that the alienation of the peasantry was not a process setting in only some years after independence,[17] but that very different visions and predictions of the future existed already at the moment of independence. My argument is fully in line with that of Sayaka Funada-Classen, who has argued that the War of Independence produced not just unity but also disunity. But unlike Funada-Classen, I will try to analyze this disunity beyond the moment of independence.[18]

Connected to this is my second concern. Scholars writing about the post-independence history have suggested that the transition was easier in areas where Frelimo already had a presence during the War of Independence.[19] As this book hopes to show, this is an idea resulting from a romantic reading of the war, which, at least in the case of Niassa, barely captures the war's complex and dynamic realities.

Third, many analyses of Frelimo's economic policies have focused on cases where the government's plans were realized at least in design. Nkholongue was never made a communal village. Rather, Nkholongue was one of those places where many government policies were trickling down at best. Certainly, this chapter will show that the post-colonial state could be highly intrusive and authoritarian, but as in colonial times its presence was in many ways weak, and its leverage to enforce its policies limited. This left quite some room for local adaptations and state evasion.

Last but not least, many works have emphasized the crucial role of Frelimo's policies against tradition in alienating people from the party. This chapter shows

---

[16] On this point, see: Patrick Chabal, "Lusophone Africa in Historical and Comparative Perspective," in *A History of Postcolonial Lusophone Africa*, by Patrick Chabal (Bloomington: Indiana University Press, 2002), 20–22.
[17] Lubkemann captures the general tone of this argument, saying that "[w]ithin the first two years of independence the differences between the new government's vision of the postcolonial future and that imagined by the residents of Machaze became starkly—and consequentially—clear." See: Lubkemann, *Culture in Chaos*, 118.
[18] Funada-Classen, *The Origins of War in Mozambique*.
[19] For examples, see: Lubkemann, *Culture in Chaos*, 117; Newitt, *A Short History of Mozambique*, 153.

that these policies did indeed undermine Frelimo's local credibility, especially as Frelimo had used the "traditional authorities" as important means to recruit support at the beginning of the War of Independence. However, the chapter also underlines the importance of not falling prey to the Aboriginal Delusion (see my comments in Section 1.4). "Traditions" were not as static and communitarian values not as strong as is often suggested. Consequentially, this chapter also argues that the main reason for the local discontent with Frelimo was not its fight against "obscurantism," but the deterioration of the economic situation. This was especially pronounced as many Nkholongueans had seen a distinct rise of their standard of living in the last years of colonialism.

The chapter is divided into two main parts. In a first part, we will briefly focus on people's feelings and behavior after the end of the war when most people returned to the previous location of Nkholongue and Malango. In a second part, we will then analyze people's experiences of the first years of independence in the village.

8.2 "We even fled to Malawi": The Moment of Independence in the Biographies of People from Nkholongue

The moment of independence is usually associated with joy as far as it concerns the former colonized. But the dynamics analyzed in Chapter 7 allow us to understand that the end of the war and the anticipation of Frelimo rule could also generate quite different feelings among the villagers of Nkholongue. As we have seen, Nkholongue's population had initially supported Frelimo. But the course of the war had made them supporters of the Portuguese war effort. This made a lot of sense from a local perspective. For not only had the Portuguese state indeed made its policies more inclusive and less repressive, but there was also little to suggest that Frelimo could win this war.[20] The revolution in Portugal caught most of the former villagers quite unprepared: they had ended up on the wrong side of the conflict.

The expectation of having a Frelimo government was far from enjoyable for everybody. "Aah! Even I was afraid,"[21] were the words of one who had worked

---

20 On the latter point, see for example: PA, I115: interview with *P0160 (♂, 1952)* (Metangula, April 18, 2016), min 00:43:54–00:44:34; ANTT, PIDE, SC, CI(2), GU, cx. 18, f. 331–342: DGS SUBVC, "Relatório de Situação do Dist do Niassa: Período de 30ABR a 15MAI73" (Vila Cabral, May 19, 1973), 73; APGGN, 1 A: Relatório de Acção Psicológica N.° 3/74 do Posto Administrativo do Cóbuè, período de 01 a 31MAR74 (Cóbuè, April 1, 1974).
21 PA, I115: interview with *P0160 (♂, 1952)* (Metangula, April 18, 2016), min 00:57:45–00:57:50.

for the technical services of the navy base, and also served as a guide for the colonial troops. He was afraid of losing his job and afraid of suffering reprisals.[22] Rumors spread about Frelimo intending to kill the colonial "collaborators," and at least four men from Nkholongue, three of whom had joined the *Grupos Especiais*, fled to Malawi. One of these four put it like this:

> We were afraid when we heard it. We even fled to Malawi when we heard that Samora [Machel] said that they will kill all those who had worked for the Portuguese. We said: "they will kill us?" We were guilty of having done the job and that's why we fled to Malawi […][23]

The majority was certainly happy that the war was over as this finally ended the restrictions on free movement.[24] But to draw the conclusion that everybody was now celebrating and already had a clear-cut plan for the future would be misleading. This is also shown by a report from the representative of the UNHCR in Tanzania. Barely a month before Mozambican Independence in 1975, he visited the Mozambican refugee settlements along the border to explore people's intentions regarding a possible return to Mozambique. He reported that the "mass appear undecided and are following a policy of 'wait and see'."[25] Among the reasons for this lack of determination, he listed that people were uncertain "about the sort of reception they will receive from the authorities in Mozambique" and stated that people were afraid "that they may be treated harshly or as second-class citizens."[26] It cannot be forgotten in this respect that many people of the region had initially cooperated with Frelimo. It was against Frelimo's will and policy that they, then, fled either to the *aldeamentos* or abroad. Frelimo's policy had been one of keeping the people in the country under its control. Frelimo's resentment toward the people who had fled the country during the war and who had not supported the war effort to the end was also clearly evident in the speeches and statements that govern-

---

22 PA, I115: interview with *P0160* (♂, *1952*) (Metangula, April 18, 2016), min 00:57:33–00:58:54.
23 PA, I117: interview with *P1458* (♂, *~1945*) (Micundi, April 20, 2016), min 01:15:29–01:16:10. See as well: PA, I119: interview with *P0855* (♂, *1954*) (Malango, April 21, 2016), min 00:53:24–00:53:53; PA, I091: interview with *P0242* (♂, *1945*) (Malango, December 23, 2015), min 00:16:00–00:17:22. For people fleeing from other villages, see: PA, I095: interview with *P1453* (♂, *~1947*), *P1506* (♀, *~1950*) (Malango, January 28, 2016), 01:10:08–01:11:47.
24 PA, I145: interview with *P0284* (♂, *1966*), *P0273* (♀, *1950*) (Metangula, June 9, 2016), min 00:04:15–00:05:01; PA, I093: interview with *P0050* (♂, *~1922*) (Nkholongue, January 19, 2016), min 01:51:19–01:51:42.
25 AUNHCR, Box 1124, ARC-2/A48, 11/2/61–610.TAN.MOZ[a]: Robert Chambers, "Note on the Return of Refugees to Mozambique" (Dar-es-Salaam, June 9, 1975), 1.
26 AUNHCR, Box 1124, ARC-2/A48, 11/2/61–610.TAN.MOZ[a]: Robert Chambers, "Note on the Return of Refugees to Mozambique" (Dar-es-Salaam, June 9, 1975), 1.

ment officials made locally in the aftermath of the war.[27] In a speech in Chissindo near Metangula in October 1975, Armando Guebuza, Mozambique's new interior minister, accused returnees from Tanzania of having done nothing but dance and drink during the war.[28]

However, at the level of Nkholongue's former population, most of the worst fears did not come true. In fact, it was the permanent employees of the technical services of the navy base that could keep their jobs.[29] Far from suffering reprisals, they belonged to the group of late colonial social climbers that could sustain their privileges into independent Mozambique. Similarily, those who had fled to Malawi because of the aforementioned rumors had already returned to Mozambique after about a year, as there were no killings going on.[30]

Nobody from Nkholongue who had joined the colonial ranks during the war was sent to one of Frelimo's re-education camps.[31] But this is in fact no real surprise. For though one could be tempted to assume otherwise,[32] these camps were not built for colonial "collaborators" in the first place. Rather, the two main groups sent to these camps until 1976 were alleged prostitutes (more than 50 percent of the

---

27 For examples, see: Aurélio Valente Langa, *Memórias de um combatente da causa: O passado que levou o verso da minha vida* (Maputo: JV, 2011), 293–94; APGGN, 1 A: Assembleia Provincial VI Sessão: Síntese Final do estudo em grupos do discuros proferido por sua Excelencia Senhor Presidente do Partido Frelimo e Presidente da República Popular de Moçambique no comício popular realizado em Lichinga, durante a sua histórica visita a esta província (Lichinga, November 30, 1979), 2; APGGN, 1 A: 8a Sessão do Comité Geral: Resolução de Política Geral (Maputo, February 27, 1976), 20; APGGN, 1 A: Síntese do Relatório do Distrito de Amaramba, Primeira Reunião de Administradores, Comissários Políticos e Grupos Dinamizadores dos Distritos da Província do Niassa (Lichinga, May 20, 1976), 2.
28 AUNHCR, Box 1124, ARC-2/A48, 11/2/61–610.TAN.MOZ[b]: H. Idoyaga, "Memorandum HCR/MOZ/313/75: Excerpts Concerning Returned Mozambican Refugees from Speeches by Mozambican Minister of Interior, Mr. A. Guebuza" (Geneva, November 20, 1975). For more details, see: Zeman, "Caught between the Guerrilla and the Colonial State," 133–134.
29 PA, I115: interview with *P0160* (♂, *1952*) (Metangula, April 18, 2016), min 00:57:53–00:58:54; PA, I047: interview with *P0596* (♂, *~1950*) (Metangula, August 21, 2013), min 00:24:28–00:26:20; PA, I076: interview with *P1449* (♂, *~1948*) (Metangula, September 6, 2013), min 00:20:44–00:22:05; PA, I008: interview with *P0299* (♂, *1938*) (Nkholongue, September 1, 2010), min 00:57:18–01:00:09; AHMar, Coloredo, Pasta 066/MO: Relação do pessoal civil voluntário para receber instrução nas lanchas, n.d.
30 PA, I117: interview with *P1458* (♂, *~1945*) (Micundi, April 20, 2016), min 01:21:51–01:22:07.
31 PA, I115: interview with *P0160* (♂, *1952*) (Metangula, April 18, 2016), min 00:48:59–00:49:07; PA, I117: interview with *P1458* (♂, *~1945*) (Micundi, April 20, 2016), min 01:26:36–01:27:16.
32 For examples where this is suggested, see: João Paulo Borges Coelho, "Da violência colonial ordenada à ordem pós-colonial violenta: Sobre um legado das guerras coloniais nas ex-colónias portuguesas," *Lusotopie*, no. 10 (2003): 191; Oliveira, "Saved by the Civil War," 138; Rodrigues, "Vidas deslocadas pelo colonialismo e pela guerra," 52.

inmates) and former Frelimo fighters who had deserted during the war. Later, the number of those who Frelimo considered "drug addicts" grew more important.³³ In this light, it is very plausible that the danger of being sent to re-education contributed to the reasoning of two of my interviewees not to return to Mozambique after the war for very long periods as they had deserted Frelimo during the war.³⁴ One of them returned in 2007, and the other only in 2012.³⁵

While, thus, some were rather relieved at the way things were going, others were disappointed. These included the men who had stayed with Frelimo until the end of the war. Two who had probably done so now had to return to the village, obviously feeling robbed of the reward for their struggle. One of them complained that Frelimo had forgotten who had fought for them during the war. In his words:

> Now, at the end of the war, Frelimo made a little little little little bit an error. For, they only said: "the war is over." They did not pursue with whom they were. [...] This is called an error. [...] I went back where I came from. We went to Malango, there where we came from.³⁶

This quotation requires special attention with regard to the interviewee's emphasis on the smallness of the error committed by Frelimo. Quite certainly, the inter-

---

33 In 1976, there were 1,942 inmates in five re-education camps Niassa. The two largest camps were Msawizi and Ilumba. They were for alleged prostitutes and were guarded and run entirely by women. In 1976, they had together 1,101 inmates (plus an additional 76 children who were taken to the camps with their mothers). Mtelela and Chiputo, which were mainly for dissidents and deserters, had 131 and 315 inmates respectively. Naisseco hosted 395 people who were considered "drug addicts." See: APGGN, 1 A: Relatório Político-Militar da Província do Niassa (Lichinga, March 24, 1976), 4; APGGN, 1 A: Efectivos dos Campos de Reeducação, n.d.; APGGN, 1 A: Relação dos responsáveis e pessoal em serviço nos Campos de Reeducação, n.d.; APGGN, 1 A: Relação das crianças que se encontram nos campos com suas mães, n.d. See as well: PA, I115: interview with *P0160* (♂, 1952) (Metangula, April 18, 2016), min 00:49:07–00:49:28. See as well Machava who has shown that many inmates were detained for minor common law offenses: Machava, *The Morality of Revolution*, 218–219, 227.
34 One of them did explicitly deny that the fear to end up in a re-education camp had something to do with his staying in Malawi. See: PA, I120: interview with *P1102* (♂, 1932) (Malango, April 21, 2016), min 01:13:51–01:15:28. But there is some reason to doubt the credibility of this statement. See: PA, I115: interview with *P0160* (♂, 1952) (Metangula, April 18, 2016), min 00:50:39–00:52:04.
35 PA, I120: interview with *P1102* (♂, 1932) (Malango, April 21, 2016), 01:15:28–01:23:12; PA, I038: interview with *P1439* (♂, ~1940) (Malango, August 15, 2013), min 00:43:37–00:44:43.
36 "Agora, no fim da guerra, a Frelimo fez um pouco um pouco um pouco erro, porque só dizer: 'guerra acabou.' Não procurou, não procurou: estavam com quem? [...] Este chama-se erro. [...] Ia ficar onde que saía. Nos íamos para Malango, aí, onde saímos.", PA, I087: interview with *P1452* (♂, 1927) (Lichinga, September 10, 2013), min 00:43:33–00:44:36. For the fate of the other who had already passed away in 2006, see: PA, I105: interview with *P0242* (♂, 1945) (Malango, April 4, 2016), min 01:27:06–01:28:21.

viewee would have formulated his statement much more sharply 30 years ago. His emphasis on the negligibility of the error is most probably a consequence of the fact that he is a beneficiary of Frelimo's changed memory politics mentioned in the previous chapter (see Section 7.2). As a result of this, he was admitted to the *dinheiro dos antigos combatentes* in 1999, made a member of the provincial capital's parliament, and appointed a judge of a local court.[37] This is quite an astonishing late advancement for his deeds in the war.

It is quite certain that the lack of direct promotion after independence was linked to his lack of formal Portuguese education. It is true that the respective interviewee, despite being a Muslim, claimed to have visited the Anglican school in Messumba for some years. With this experience, he was a clear exception among the population of Nkholongue. But in light of his rather basic knowledge of Portuguese his formal education must have been limited. Furthermore, he himself pointed out that the only difference between him and Messumba-born Eduardo Mulémbwè, president of the national assembly from 1995 to 2009 and one of Frelimo's most influential politicians, was the fact that Mulémbwè had continued the school. My interviewee stopped it, as in order to continue he would have needed to convert to Christianity, according to his account.[38] This explanation is also in line with the analyses of Liazzat Bonate on the post-war experiences of (female) Muslim combatants and of Harry West on those of female combatants in general. They both came to the conclusion that many of their interviewees came away empty-handed after independence "due to their lack of formal Portuguese schooling."[39] Bonate put it like this:

> [G]uerrilla fighters and former political prisoners who completed at least two classes of the formal Portuguese schooling became party cadres, took government jobs or stayed in the military. But those who could neither write nor read in Portuguese [...] had no other options than to take up subsistence farming or take low-paying or symbolic jobs, like *Grupos Dynamizadores*, or return to the jobs they held before the war. Women were relegated to a domestic sphere and moved to live with their parents in villages until they married. Thus they could view their situation as unchanged or even having worsened.[40]

---

37 PA, I087: interview with *P1452 (♂, 1927)* (Lichinga, September 10, 2013), min 01:28:02–01:37:33.
38 PA, I087: interview with *P1452 (♂, 1927)* (Lichinga, September 10, 2013), min 00:16:09–00:21:42.
39 The quotation is from Bonate: Bonate, "Muslim Memories," 242. For West, see: Harry G. West, "Girls with Guns: Narrating the Experience of War of Frelimo's 'Female Detachment,'" *Anthropological Quarterly* 73, no. 4 (2000): 189. For the disappointment of female veterans about their fate after independence, see as well: Jonna Katto, "Emotions in Protest: Unsettling the Past in Ex-combatants' Personal Accounts in Northern Mozambique," *Oral History* 46, no. 2 (2018): 53–62.
40 Bonate, "Muslim Memories," 256.

We can observe that it was those who enjoyed higher levels of colonial education that now witnessed a further promotion.[41] In the case of Nkholongue's former population, this was Artur Tolohate. Tolohate was born in Nkholongue in 1943. Belonging to the village's Christian minority, he left the village with his mother and siblings to live in Messumba around 1952. There, he visited the school of the Anglican mission. In 1965, he joined Frelimo and quickly became one of the movement's most important photographers. After the war, he moved to Maputo, where he became the personal photographer of both Samora Machel and his successor Joaquim Chissano.[42] While a comparatively large number of the Messumba-educated Christians found their way into Mozambique's post-colonial elite in the manner of Tolohate,[43] the inhabitants of the predominantly Muslim villages south of Metangula had little "success" in this respect.

For the majority of Nkholongue's resettled population, independence meant a return to the village. However, many of those who had migrated to the hamlet of Malango in the years before the war did not return there but went again to Nkholongue proper.[44] In the case of the refugees staying in Tanzania, the governments

---

[41] See also Egerö's observations for the Mueda Plateau that Frelimo preferred educated *regressados* to war veterans when staffing local organs. See: Egerö, *Mozambique, a Dream Undone*, 157.

[42] Official sources give Messumba as his place of birth. My informants, including Tolohate's siblings, stated however that Tolohate was born in Nkholongue. While Tolohate's father was from Nkholongue, his mother was from Messumba. See: Hilário Matusse, "Artur Torohate: De guerrilheiro a homem da imagem," *Tempo*, no. 780 (September 22, 1985): 26–27; Teresa Sá Nogueira, "Cinema Moçambicano (3). Artur Torohate: Cineasta guerrilheiro," *Tempo*, n. 830 (September 7, 1986): 44–45; AIM, "Mozambique: Death of Leading Photographer," allAfrica, March 10, 2003, accessed October 21, 2016, http://allafrica.com/stories/200303100613.html; PA, I126: interview with *P1466 (♂, 1952)* (Chuangwa, April 28, 2016), min 00:01:02–00:06:02; PA, I165: interview with *P1467 (♀, 1948)* (Lichinga, June 27, 2016), min 00:01:41–00:05:49, 00:13:44–00:15:33; PA, I120: interview with *P1102 (♂, 1932)* (Malango, April 21, 2016), min 00:38:24–00:41:41.

[43] Another prominent figure in this respect is Brazão Mazula, president of the National Elections Commission (CNE) during Mozambique's first multi-party elections in 1994 and later vice-chancellor of the Eduardo Mondlane University in Maputo. The list also includes Mazula's younger brother Aguiar Mazula, who was Minister of Labor, Minister of State Administration and Minister of Defence. Huhn claimed that John Kachamila, Mozambique's former Minister of Natural Resources and later of Environmental Affairs, was equally among the graduates of Messumba. This is though not correct according to Kachamila's published memoirs. Therein, Kachamila stated that his family emigrated to Tanganyika when he was about four years old and that he did all his schooling in Tanganyika. See: Huhn, "Sustenance and Sociability," 52–53; John William Kachamila, *Do Vale do Rift ao sonho da liberdade: Memórias de Lissungo* (Maputo: Nachingwea, 2016).

[44] PA, I058: interview with *P1074 (♀, ~1940)* (Malango, August 28, 2013), min 02:18:30–02:22:39; PA, I049: interview with *P0267 (♀, 1949)* (Nkholongue, August 23, 2013), min 00:17:45–00:18:15; PA, I073: interview with *P1012 (♂, 1955)* (Malango, September 5, 2013), min 00:25:35–00:26:23; PA, I068: interview with *P0367 (♂, 1936)* (Nkholongue, September 2, 2013), min 00:50:48–00:52:31.

of Mozambique and Tanzania (in collaboration with the UNHCR) made official arrangements to repatriate the people, organizing transport by boat.[45] Several people from Nkholongue returned that way in October 1975, shortly before the rains.[46] In the case of the refugees living in Malawi, there was no comparable official coordination.[47] Rather, those who returned did so on their own.

While most people returned to Nkholongue and Malango, some stayed in Metangula and Malawi. In the case of Tanzania, I could identify only one person who did not return. But she had lived there with her husband already before the war.[48] It is rather difficult to deduce the reasons for people's decisions to return or to not return to the village from people's own statements. Most people who returned portrayed it as a rather obvious decision without any alternative.[49] The fact that others stayed shows, however, that there were certainly different factors at play. Those who stayed in Metangula were those who could keep their jobs or those who had married there.[50] But, for most others, it made more sense to return to Nkholongue or Malango, also because they could have bigger farms here.[51] One interviewee ex-

---

45 See various documents in: AUNHCR, Box 1124, ARC-2/A48, 11/2/61–610.TAN.MOZ.
46 PA, I145: interview with *P0284 (♂, 1966)*, *P0273 (♀, 1950)* (Metangula, June 9, 2016), min 00:01:10–00:03:33; PA, I115: interview with *P0160 (♂, 1952)* (Metangula, April 18, 2016), min 01:45:12–01:46:28. Some of the people are also included on the official list of those who returned. See: APGGN, 1 A: Pedro Chindandali, "Lista de regressados que desembarcam em Metangula em 8.10.975" (Metangula: Frelimo, October 11, 1975).
47 APGGN, 1 A: Relatório Político-Militar da Província do Niassa (Lichinga, March 24, 1976), 5.
48 For examples of those who stayed in Malawi, see: PA, I032: interview with *P1196 (♀, ~1955)*, *P0793 (♀, 1939)*, *P0792 (♂, 1917)* (Chipoka (Malawi), April 25, 2012), min 00:00:02–00:08:19; PA, I132: interview with *P1439 (♂, ~1940)*, *P1507 (♀, ~1930)*, *P1508 (♀)* (Ndegue (Salima), June 1, 2016); PA, I120: interview with *P1102 (♂, 1932)* (Malango, April 21, 2016), min 01:14:35–01:20:48. For the one who stayed in Tanzania, see: PA, I142: interview with *P0743 (♀, ~1930)* (Nkholongue, June 8, 2016).
49 PA, I041: interview with *P0951 (♀, 1948)*, *P0242 (♂, 1945)* (Malango, August 16, 2013), min 00:31:20–00:32:40; PA, I040: interview with *P1030 (♀, 1965)*, *P1009 (♀, 1958)*, *P1029 (♂, ~1959)* (Malango, August 16, 2013), min 01:08:57–01:09:20; PA, I054: interview with *P0554 (♀, 1949)* (Nkholongue, August 27, 2013), min 00:41:00–00:42:11; PA, I069: interview with *P0650 (♀, 1939)* (Nkholongue, September 2, 2013), min 00:26:54–00:28:04; PA, I078: interview with *P0258 (♂, 1953)* (Nkholongue, September 7, 2013), min 00:04:31–00:04:55; PA, I052: interview with *(♀, 1940)* (Nkholongue, August 26, 2013), min 00:24:24–00:25:23; PA, I044: interview with *P1081 (♀, 1945)* (Malango, August 17, 2013), min 00:17:15–00:18:23.
50 PA, I108: interview with *P1074 (♀, ~1940)* (Malango, April 6, 2016), min 00:39:40–00:40:59; PA, I074: interview with *P0160 (♂, 1952)* (Metangula, September 6, 2013), min 00:37:12–00:37:50; PA, I076: interview with *P1449 (♂, ~1948)* (Metangula, September 6, 2013), min 00:20:44–00:22:05; PA, I047: interview with *P0596 (♂, ~1950)* (Metangula, August 21, 2013), min 00:24:28–00:26:20.
51 PA, I040: interview with *P1030 (♀, 1965)*, *P1009 (♀, 1958)*, *P1029 (♂, ~1959)* (Malango, August 16, 2013), min 00:47:26–00:47:51; PA, I054: interview with *P0554 (♀, 1949)* (Nkholongue, August 27,

plicitly stated people needed money to stay in Metangula.⁵² However, the end of the war and the retreat of the Portuguese had gone hand in hand with the disappearance of many jobs.⁵³ We can also assume that the decision also depended on people's age. It seems that younger people were more willing to stay in Metangula than older people. The young had spent considerable parts of their lives in Metangula and preferred town to village life. One woman, born in 1960, for example, stated that she would have liked to stay in Metangula but that it was her mother who urged her to come back to the village to make her *machamba* and marry.⁵⁴

The decision to stay or leave, thus, depended heavily on one's prospects at the place of exile. This seems to have also been at stake in the case of those who had fled abroad. While the refugees in Tanzania had mostly lived in official refugee villages,⁵⁵ those in Malawi had apparently been integrated much more into local society. This integration was certainly also facilitated by the cultural commonalities (including the same language) that the refugees found in Malawi. It is also important to keep in mind that the end of the war in Mozambique coincided with a politically tense time in Tanzania as the country entered the coercive phase of its post-colonial villagization scheme.⁵⁶ This may have made staying in Tanzania far less attractive.

2013), min 00:41:00 – 00:42:11; PA, I062: interview with *P0713* (♂, *1944*) (Nkholongue, August 30, 2013), min 00:27:17 – 00:27:49, 00:36:47 – 00:38:27. One stated that her field in Metangula had been just as large as that in Malango: PA, I042: interview with *P1193* (♀, *1953*) (Malango, August 17, 2013), min 00:19:11 – 00:20:43.

52 PA, I085: interview with *P0147* (♀, *~1928*) (Nkholongue, September 9, 2013), min 00:19:21 – 00:20:39.

53 PA, I086: interview with *P0375* (♂, *1962*) (Nkholongue, September 9, 2013), min 00:15:54 – 00:16:54.

54 PA, I039: interview with *P0898* (♀, *1960*) (Malango, August 15, 2013), min 00:27:48 – 00:29:57, 00:32:45 – 00:33:43.

55 PA, I041: interview with *P0951* (♀, *1948*), *P0242* (♂, *1945*) (Malango, August 16, 2013), min 00:28:50 – 00:30:44.

56 Yusufu Qwaray Lawi, "Tanzania's Operation Vijiji and Local Ecological Consciousness: The Case of Eastern Iraqwland, 1974 – 1976," *The Journal of African History* 48, no. 1 (2007): 69 – 93; James C. Scott, *Seeing like a State: How Certain Schemes to Improve the Human Condition Have Failed* (New Haven: Yale University Press, 1998), 223 – 261.

8.3 From Taxing Natives to Taxing Citizens: The New Government on the Ground

Many of my interviewees were initially pretty reluctant to speak about the new government of independent Mozambique. An 81-year-old woman living in Malango answered "[m]aybe, the government knows,"[57] when I asked her about changes between the colonial and post-colonial government. Other interviewees made comparable statements to similar questions. One answered my question of what she thought of the new government in the following way:

> But we don't know anything of the government. We didn't go to school, did we? We don't know these things.[58]

The lack of enthusiasm for and the level of indifference towards this supposedly very important moment of Mozambican history is startling. There are different possible explanations for why people replied the way they did. Disappointment about the course of things after independence must certainly be considered an important factor in this respect. Or, as a former Frelimo fighter put it:

> We thought that, maybe, when the Portuguese leave, we will live well.[59]

But, as we have already seen, in the case of many people from Nkholongue, the disappointment about the course of the nationalist cause even preceded the moment of independence. Also, if the end of the war fueled new expectations and hopes for the future, they were not shared by everyone and not everyone had the same expectations. One interviewee answered the question of whether he was happy that Mozambique finally had its own independent government with the following words:

> We were happy that the war was over, but not because we will receive a new government. Yes, there were those who were saying this. But, I, myself, was just happy that the war was over.[60]

---

[57] PA, I046: interview with *P1045 (♀, 1932)* (Malango, August 20, 2013), min 00:35:58–00:36:04.
[58] PA, I101: interview with *P0316 (♀, ~1952)* (Nkholongue, February 22, 2016), min 00:38:36–00:38:59.
[59] PA, I038: interview with *P1439 (♂, ~1940)* (Malango, August 15, 2013), min 00:05:21–00:05:24.
[60] PA, I093: interview with *P0050 (♂, ~1922)* (Nkholongue, January 19, 2016), min 01:51:19–01:51:42.

It is, of course, difficult to assess the opinions and perspectives people held at the time through the means of oral history. But my interviews leave little doubt that if there was enthusiasm it was dampened rather quickly.

(Dis-)Continuities between the Colonial and Post-colonial Government

At first glance, the differences between Mozambique's colonial and post-colonial governments could not be much greater. While the *Estado Novo* has been characterized as a corporatist, authoritarian and even fascist regime, Frelimo saw itself as a progressive Marxist-Leninist vanguard. The party envisaged nothing less than a complete transformation of society and the creation of a "new man." Agriculture was to be collectivized and mechanized, and banks and other enterprises to be nationalized. People's lives were to be organized in communal villages, which ought to provide the health and education infrastructure that had previously been lacking. But Frelimo's socialist modernization course included not only the transformation of the economy and the promotion of the health and education sector but also the fight against "obscurantism." In what was to become known as the *abaixo* politics, Frelimo combated all so-called "vices" of both colonial and "traditional" society such as "tribalism," religion, prostitution, and witchcraft. The "traditional authorities" were denounced as colonial collaborators and not recognized by the state anymore. Instead, their place was taken by village and party secretaries and so-called *Grupos Dinamizadores* ("dynamizing groups"), consisting of local party loyalists.

But, as other scholars such as Anne Pitcher and Harri Englund have already argued, "the reality did not necessarily mirror the propaganda."[61] Frelimo's capacity to actually "implement in practice the changes promised in its rhetoric"[62] was in fact limited. This was, as we will now see, no different in the case of Nkholongue and is a valid assessment both for policies that were welcomed by the majority of the people and policies that were disapproved of by most people. But one has also to consider that while rhetoric alone did not change anything it could still be heard. So not only did it influence people's perceptions of what was going on, but it could also undermine Frelimo's political credibility in many different ways.

This is probably best demonstrated by looking at what happened to Nkholongue's political leadership. Nkholongue's chief was indeed deposed. He had no more

---

[61] Pitcher, "Forgetting from Above and Memory from Below," 90.
[62] Harri Englund, *From War to Peace on the Mozambique-Malawi Borderland* (Edinburgh: Edinburgh University Press, 2002), 13.

power in the state's eyes after independence. But it was his nephew and designated successor who was made the village secretary.⁶³ The sources leave little doubt that the two were very close. Such a constellation, where the secretary came from the same lineage as the former chief, has been reported from other places in Mozambique.⁶⁴ It can be assumed that such arrangements disappointed the followers of Frelimo's much more progressive propaganda. However, it seems that the followers of the progressive line were in fact in a minority in the case of Nkholongue. Here, Frelimo's modernizing discourse found little resonance.

In the case of the selection of the village secretary, then, Frelimo's credibility was most probably damaged not so much by the propaganda that was only half-realized but by the very propaganda itself, since this did not correspond to people's historical experiences. For as we have already seen in the previous chapter, Frelimo had relied extensively on chiefs to recruit people to their cause at the beginning of the armed struggle. To decry them now generally as colonial "collaborators" was somewhat inconsequential. Or, as one interviewee put it:

> In colonial times, the Portuguese condemned the chiefs, as Frelimo had used them as a means [to mobilize people]. [Frelimo's fighters] came here to speak to the chiefs, as they knew how to mobilize people and all this stuff. Now, when the government of Frelimo came, it turned out to be very bad for the chiefs. It was the chiefs who had to take the consequences.⁶⁵

---

63 Opinions differ as to how he was chosen. Some say that he was chosen by (the) people of the village, others claim that it was the government that selected him. In any case, this diversity of opinions suggests that the process was hardly fully transparent. See: PA, I118: interview with *P1218* (♀, *1930*) (Malango, April 21, 2016), min 00:33:34–00:34:11; PA, I062: interview with *P0713* (♂, *1944*) (Nkholongue, August 30, 2013), min 00:43:50–00:44:44; PA, I115: interview with *P0160* (♂, *1952*) (Metangula, April 18, 2016), min 02:18:13–02:18:35; PA, I124: interview with *P0376* (♂, *1968*) (Nkholongue, April 26, 2016), min 00:59:09–01:00:16; PA, I141: interview with *P0375* (♂, *1962*) (Nkholongue, June 6, 2016), min 00:42:45–00:43:29; PA, I144: interview with *P0411* (♂, *1965*) (Nkholongue, June 8, 2016), min 00:14:53–00:15:15; PA, I133: interview with *P1473* (♂ *~1938*), *P1504* (♀) (Limbi, June 1, 2016), min 00:55:43–00:58:29; PA, I119: interview with *P0855* (♂, *1954*) (Malango, April 21, 2016), min 00:59:54–01:00:55.
64 Pérez-Niño, "Post-Conflict Agrarian Change in Angónia," 165.
65 PA, I074: interview with *P0160* (♂, *1952*) (Metangula, September 6, 2013), min 00:25:59–00:26:48. For similar statements, see: PA, I123: interview with *P1460* (♀), *P1461* (♂, *~1935*), *P1462* (♂, *~1935*) (Meluluca, April 25, 2016), min 01:23:02–01:25:23; PA, I113: interview with *P0367* (♂, *1936*) (Nkholongue, April 13, 2016), min 02:17:00–02:19:52; PA, I077: interview with *P1489* (♂) (Metangula, September 6, 2013), min 00:12:22–00:14:00. See as well the work of Liazzat Bonate who has emphasized the importance of "traditional" and regional authorities for Frelimo in recruiting supporters in Cabo Delgado: Bonate, "Traditions and Transitions," chap. 6.

The interviews suggest that most villagers not only grappled to understand Frelimo's attitude towards the chiefs, but also had problems with the party's propaganda against religion and above all initiation rites.[66] People told me that they had to practice their rituals in hiding.[67] Furthermore, the government is said to have threatened to use the village mosque as a school if the people would not build one that was larger than the mosque.[68] However, it must also be emphasized that, within the village, the government's anti-traditionalism seems to have remained ambiguous.[69] This is shown by the fact that the new village secretary was himself a leading Muslim of the community and later even became the village's imam.

Furthermore, we should probably not overestimate people's general dissatisfaction with these policies.[70] "Traditions" are not as static as they are sometimes portrayed in the context of such questions.[71] This is best shown by looking at the history of these so-called "traditions": there is no doubt that, for example, initiation rites have remained very popular until the present. Nevertheless, we can also observe that these rites have changed considerably since independence. The initiation rites for girls, for example, previously had comprised four stages. Today, only one of these stages is practiced any longer. My interviewees point to the fact that this changed after independence, and that young women would nowa-

---

[66] PA, I087: interview with *P1452* (♂, *1927*) (Lichinga, September 10, 2013), min 01:06:19–01:08:43; PA, I094: interview with *P0727* (♂, *~1940*) (M'chepa, January 27, 2016), min 01:02:04–01:02:42; PA, I145: interview with *P0284* (♂, *1966*), *P0273* (♀, *1950*) (Metangula, June 9, 2016), min 00:05:25–00:06:30; PA, I133: interview with *P1473* (♂ *~1938*), *P1504* (♀) (Limbi, June 1, 2016), min 00:49:14–00:49:57. For the wider region, see: PA, I097: interview with *P1454* (♂, *~1951*) (Malango, February 5, 2016), min 01:36:40–01:40:20; PA, I099: interview with *P1420* (♂, *~1922*) (Ngongo, February 16, 2016), min 00:23:46–00:26:43; PA, I149: interview with *P1501* (♂, *1949*), *P1513* (♂, *1943*) (Chinuni, June 11, 2016), min 00:24:17–00:24:43.
[67] PA, I093: interview with *P0050* (♂, *~1922*) (Nkholongue, January 19, 2016), min 01:22:11–01:22:32; PA, I162: interview with *P0512* (♀, *1967*) (Nkholongue, June 22, 2016), min 00:54:22–00:55:12.
[68] PA, I086: interview with *P0375* (♂, *1962*) (Nkholongue, September 9, 2013), min 00:25:33–00:27:57.
[69] PA, I080: interview with *P0641* (♂, *1952*) (Nkholongue, September 7, 2013), min 00:33:27–00:35:30; PA, I158: interview with *P0764* (♂, *1962*) (Nkholongue, June 20, 2016), min 00:42:34–00:45:02.
[70] On this point, see as well: Bridget O'Laughlin, "Class and the Customary: The Ambiguous Legacy of the Indigenato in Mozambique," *African Affairs* 99, no. 394 (2000): 30.
[71] Olaf Juergensen, for example, portrayed it as very normal that people in the district of Angonia (Tete) were against Frelimo's anti-traditionalism. He asked: "But why should the peasantry not celebrate its 'traditionalism?,' particularly in isolated locations such as Angonia." See: Juergensen, "Peasants on the Periphery," 189.

days decline the other three stages.[72] Similarly, it is above all the old people and only very few young that still go to the mosque regularly today.[73] It is thus reasonable to assume that the opinions of different people and different generations were somewhat divided on the question of Frelimo's anti-traditionalism, even if this cannot be reconstructed with complete certainty with the available sources.

One should also be cautious with generalizing statements about the widespread unpopularity of Frelimo's *abaixo* politics since this issue was thoroughly explored by Renamo's propaganda after the Civil War. As we will see in the next chapter, Renamo was locally quite successful in spreading its version of history. On the other hand, it was certainly also people's experiences from the post-independence years that made it so easy for Renamo to convince people of its views.

While Frelimo's anti-traditionalism represented a clear break with the past, there were surprising continuities in another area, namely that of state employees. Following Nicolas Bancel, one could say that Frelimo in fact propagated a rupture less with the late colonial society than with the "traditional" order of peasant society.[74] We have already seen that the permanent employees of the Portuguese navy base could keep their jobs after independence. This is understandable, since they knew how to maintain the operation of the base (which now Frelimo intended to use), but it is still noteworthy since their duties during the war had included accompanying operations of Portuguese forces against Frelimo fighters as guides or carriers. Similarly, the first administrator of independent Lago District had been working for the colonial state since 1963.[75] Most of the colonial policemen

---

[72] PA, I156: interview with *P1478 (♀)* (Metangula, June 18, 2016), min 00:29:37–00:30:16; PA, I048: interview with *P1446 (♂, ~1945)* (Metangula, August 21, 2013), min 00:19:36–00:27:20; PA, I075: interview with *P1218 (♀, 1930)* (Metangula, September 6, 2013), min 00:11:18–00:14:39; PA, I054: interview with *P0554 (♀, 1949)* (Nkholongue, August 27, 2013), min 00:58:27–01:03:52; PA, I058: interview with *P1074 (♀, ~1940)* (Malango, August 28, 2013), min 00:05:01–00:11:12; PA, I059: interview with *P0090 (♀, ~1932)* (Metangula, August 29, 2013), min 01:06:04–01:08:49.
[73] However, more orthodox (Sunni) currents of Islam have recently begun to gain a foothold among younger people.
[74] Bancel formulated this idea in connection with the developments in French colonies in the 1950s. My thanks go to Christian Hadorn, who brought Bancel's argument to my attention. See: Hervé Sciardet, "De la colonisation à la décolonisation: les modes de constitution de la Françafrique. Une table ronde entre Nicolas Bancel et Jean-Pierre Dozon," *Mouvements*, no. 21–22 (2002): 23.
[75] He had previously been a deputy district administrator. It is, however, unclear whether in Metangula or elsewhere. See: APGGN, 1 A: Salomão Cossa, "Mapa com os elementos respeitantes aos trabalhadores dos Serviços de Administração Civil, em serviço nesta província" (Lichinga, June 2, 1977); APGGN, 1 A: Carta N.° 144/I/3 de Alfredo Lituri (Administração do Distrito de Lago) à Secretaria Provincial dos Serviços de Administração Civil do Niassa (Metangula, April 20, 1977).

could keep their jobs, at least in the beginning.[76] In their files we can read things like "[v]ery actively trying to adapt himself to the new political reality."[77]

Such continuities could do their part to provoke the view that government remained government, also after independence. The same is true for the question of taxation. In the district report of Metangula for July 1975, the first month after independence, the administrator in the state's services since 1963 wrote the following:

> In general, the people have been complying the directives transmitted directly or through the *Grupos Dinamizadores*. But they have not done so in the case of the payment of the tax, although insistent attempts have been made to explain to them the need and objective of its payment at this political moment of time.[78]

Similarly, the administrator of the locality of Cobué lamented two months later that only nine people had paid the tax, even though he had made every effort to "elucidate" the people about the difference between the current tax and the one they had paid in colonial times.[79] However, there is no doubt that even the administrators were well aware of the fact that, in many respects, taxation remained taxation. For as late as 1978 they used still the pre-printed forms from colonial times in order to report to the provincial administration the number of taxes collected.[80] In line with this, a provincial report of 1976 stated that many people were

---

[76] See: APGGN, 1 A: Carta N.º 144/I/3 de Alfredo Lituri (Administração do Distrito de Lago) à Secretaria Provincial dos Serviços de Administração Civil do Niassa (Metangula, April 20, 1977); APGGN, 1 A: Paulino C. Hamela (Comandante Provincial das Forças Policiais do Niassa), "Relatório" (Lichinga, October 22, 1978), 5.

[77] One of these policemen was from Malango. See: APGGN, QJ: Administração do Distrito de Metangula, "Relação dos elementos de identificação completa, dos Guardas Administrativos em serviço nesta área administrativa, conforme Cir. Conf. 29/MI/75, de 13 de Dezembro de 1975," March 10, 1976. See as well: APGGN, QJ: Alfredo Filimone Lituri, "Relatório da Administração do Distrito de Metangula, Julho 1975" (Metangula, August 4, 1975), 2.

[78] APGGN, QJ: Alfredo Filimone Lituri, "Relatório da Administração do Distrito de Metangula, Julho 1975" (Metangula, August 4, 1975), 2.

[79] APGGN, QJ: Acta da Reunião de todos os responsáveis das forças populares, dos grupos dinamizadores de círculo e localidade e ainda responsáveis da administração, realizada aos 12 de Outubro de 1975 (Cóbue, October 12, 1975).

[80] APGGN, QJ: Luciano da Fonseca Henriques, "Administração do Distrito de Metangula: Mapa comparativo da cobrança do Imposto Domciliário realizada no mês de Janeiro de 1978" (Metangula, February 10, 1978). On this point see as well Benedito Machava and Euclido Gonçalves, who have argued that "the format, form and style of bureaucratic documents continued almost unaltered" in general after independence: Machava and Gonçalves, "The Dead Archive," 555–556.

unwilling to pay taxes because "some administrators were still the same as the colonial ones."[81]

Health and Education

Frelimo is widely lauded for its successes in the sectors of health and education, both sectors that are usually said to have been widely ignored by the colonial government. This narrative needs some re-assessment from the perspective of Nkholongue. As we have seen in the previous chapter, it was precisely during the last decade of colonialism that the Portuguese state did indeed make an effort to spread educational and health facilities on an unprecedented scale. In the case of Nkholongue, the educational revolution thus did not start with independence, but rather with the Portuguese reaction to Frelimo's armed struggle. It is during the time in the *aldeamento* that the knowledge of the Portuguese language among the population of Nkholongue started to increase significantly. Independence witnessed a continuation of this process. More than 45 years after the closing of the Anglican missionary school, a school was re-opened in the village. Compared to the school in the *aldeamento*, there were now also more girls that visited this school.[82]

However, reports from different sources leave little doubt that the health and educational sector in Lago District faced a severe shortage of resources and personnel in the years following independence.[83] Even the administrations had to

---

81 APGGN, 1 A: Relatório Político-Militar da Província do Niassa (Lichinga, March 24, 1976), 5.
82 PA, I162: interview with *P0512 (♀, 1967)* (Nkholongue, June 22, 2016), min 00:00:59–00:01:42, 00:10:31–00:12:22; PA, I158: interview with *P0764 (♂, 1962)* (Nkholongue, June 20, 2016), min 00:05:41–00:06:43; PA, I015: interview with *P0367 (♂, 1936)* (Nkholongue, September 9, 2010), min 00:44:28–00:49:48. The Anglican school of Nkholongue was most probably closed in the early 1930s. See: "News from the Stations: IV. Msumba," *NDC*, no. 107 (April 1930): 7.
83 Moira Dick, "'If You Don't Know Niassa, You Don't Know Mozambique,'" in *Mozambique: Towards a People's Health Service*, ed. Gillian Walt and Angela Melamed (London: Zed Books, 1983), 56; AUNHCR, Box 1083, ARC-2/A48, 11/2/61–610.GEN.MOZ[b], f. 177: Sérgio Vieira de Mello, "Memorandum 460/MOZ/77: Report on Mission to the Provinces of Niassa and Cabo Delgado from 4 to 13 July 1977" (Maputo, July 14, 1977), 7; APGGN, 1 A: Júlio Reis and Alfredo Filimone Lituri, "Relatório do Distrito de Metangula," Primeira Reunião de Administradores, Comissários Políticos e Grupos Dinamizadores dos Distritos da Província do Niassa (Metangula, May 16, 1976); FMS, AMPA, Pasta 04331.009.001, f. 33–43: Método da pesquisa: A fase preparatória. Anexo N° 8: Experiência da vida professional dos informantes, A. Investigação Sociolinguística: O sistema nacional de educação e a situação multilingue do país (INDE, May 17, 1983); APGGN, QJ: Relatório Distrital de Lago, 3a Reunião do Conselho Provincial Coordenador de Saúde (Metangula, 1978).

fight with such banalities as lack of paper.[84] Evidence of this lack cannot just be found in the government reports of the time, but also remain visible on documents that I found at the administrative post of Maniamba. For among the few documents that were still "kept" from colonial times were those whose empty reverse side had been used for governmental affairs during the years after independence. In light of these facts, the quality of these services thus did not necessarily improve, but might also have worsened in some areas in those years.[85] A "community leader" in Tulo, for example, complained to an UNHCR official who visited the region in 1977 that "as refugees in Tanzania, his community [had] received more assistance than since they [had] returned to their country" and, thereby, explicitly referred to medical and educational facilities.[86] The respective official even commented that he was surprised that he had not heard more such complaints "given the indisputable readaptation difficulties faced in 1975/76."[87] The situation seems to have further worsened in the early 1980s. In March 1983, the provincial health direction complained that "the operation of our health facilities, particularly those on the periphery, has been limited to a few palliative actions" because of the lack of drugs. The requisitions for medical material had not been answered at all since the last trimester of 1982. Because of lack of suture, the provincial hospital in Lichinga was not able to carry out surgeries anymore.[88]

Time of Samora, Time of Lack

But, apart from these problems, the main reason for people's dissatisfaction with Frelimo was certainly the economic situation. The time of Samora (*nyengo ya Sa-*

---

[84] APGGN, QJ: Acta da Reunião de todos os responsáveis das forças populares, dos grupos dinamizadores de círculo e localidade e ainda responsáveis da administração, realizada aos 12 de outubro de 1975 (Cóbue, October 12, 1975), 2.

[85] One health report from 1978 put it like this: "The medical assistance in this district is not very glorious [...]". See: APGGN, QJ: Relatório Distrital de Lago, 3a Reunião do Conselho Provincial Coordenador de Saúde (Metangula, 1978), 1.

[86] AUNHCR, Box 1083, ARC-2/A48, 11/2/61–610.GEN.MOZ[b], f. 177: Sérgio Vieira de Mello, "Memorandum 460/MOZ/77: Report on Mission to the Provinces of Niassa and Cabo Delgado from 4 to 13 July 1977" (Maputo, July 14, 1977), 7.

[87] AUNHCR, Box 1083, ARC-2/A48, 11/2/61–610.GEN.MOZ[b], f. 177: Sérgio Vieira de Mello, "Memorandum 460/MOZ/77: Report on Mission to the Provinces of Niassa and Cabo Delgado from 4 to 13 July 1977" (Maputo, July 14, 1977), 7.

[88] APGGN, 1 A: Carta N.° 352/37/B: Director Provincial de Saúde do Niassa ao Central de Medicamentos e Artigos Medicos da Beira (Lichinga, March 21, 1983).

mora) is unambiguously remembered as a time of lack and hardship.[89] As I have already mentioned in Section 6.2 (see pp. 225–226), goods like salt, clothes, sugar, or cooking oil were barely available during those years. People had to revert to subsistence alternatives where possible.[90] One interviewee put it like this:

> Now, there was the 25 of June when Samora made our flag been hoisted. Then, the constitution of the republic, this People's Republic of Mozambique. That is when others began to say: "That's not it, that's not it." Now, as this one, Samora, was a cowboy, nobody could say "no." So, they began to isolate him economically. There was nudity here [...]! There was nudity! People washed their clothes with natural resources, trees, *njujo*, you know.[91]

The change was especially pronounced as many people had witnessed an improvement in the availability of precisely these goods in the years before independence. This fact even led some of my interviewees to openly prefer the late colonial to the early post-colonial time,[92] as evidenced by this dialogue:

> Q: Did the rule/leadership change between the time of the white people ('azungu') and the time of Samora?
> A: Of course, it changed.
> Q: What did change?
> A: Comparing the colonial time with the time of Samora, it was better during that of the white people. For, we lived well. They gave us salt.[93]

Another interviewee put it like this:

> [Life] changed. At that time when Frelimo entered, when they removed the whites, there were problems. There was no salt, there were no clothes.[94]

---

89 This lack is also very well documented in various government reports: APGGN, 1 A: Departamento de Política Económica do Niassa, "Relatório do Departamento da Política Económica do Partido em Niassa, para a Sede Nacional do Partido" (Lichinga, May 28, 1979), 8–9; APGGN, 1 A: Departamento da Política Económica do Partido, "Relatório sobre a situação sócio-económica na província" (Lichinga, February 27, 1980).
90 This was a common pattern in post-independence Mozambique. See: Newitt, *A History of Mozambique*, 555–57.
91 PA, I115: interview with *P0160* (♂, *1952*) (Metangula, April 18, 2016), min 02:14:12–02:15:34.
92 PA, I153: interview with *P1477* (♂, *~1940*) (Micucue, June 17, 2016), min 00:43:15–00:44:06; PA, I039: interview with *P0898* (♀, *1960*) (Malango, August 15, 2013), min 00:24:39–00:26:08; PA, I088: interview with *P0262* (♀, *~1940*) (Malango, December 23, 2015), min 00:02:14–00:04:02.
93 PA, I109: interview with *P1081* (♀, *1945*) (Malango, April 6, 2016), min 01:02:02–01:02:24.
94 PA, I055: interview with *P0639* (♀, *~1952*) (Nkholongue, August 27, 2013), min 00:21:51–00:22:02. For a similar type of nostalgia in the case of Tete, see: Harri Englund, "Waiting for the Portuguese: Nostalgia, Exploitation and the Meaning of Land in the Malawi-Mozambique Borderland," *Journal of Contemporary African Studies* 14, no. 2 (1996): 157–172. This kind of nostalgia can also be found in

These products were not just barely available. Many people also indicated that they lost purchasing power.[95] The new government set fixed prices, which were very unfavorable for most people of the region. This is shown by this excerpt from a party district report from 1977:

> As for the combat of speculation: the people understand very well [the objectives], but they admire that the structures of the party and the government just let the capitalists exploit them; even more they do not understand why the prices of the products of the people [(produced by the people)] should be lowered if these people also want to develop themselves. In the shops, everything is expensive [...] one fish is sold for 30$00 per kilo, while, in colonial times, the same fish was only 10$00 per kilo [...]. And, then, they want to buy at ours [(our products)] at very low prices. Why, don't they pursue to lower their prices? The same send sugar and flour to the fishing posts, where they sell it for very high prices. [...] The people call for having equality at the sales and for having reasonable prices. Otherwise, the combat against speculation will be very difficult. For, that what they mobilize for is not what they are doing.[96]

The evidence from Nkholongue illustrates the extent to which Frelimo's idea of economic transformation had been based on false premises, as the party looked at the agrarian structure through what Bridget O'Laughlin has called a "divided glass."[97] Frelimo believed that there was a traditional subsistence sector that could just continue to exist independently of the party's policies until the planned transformation would be ready to obliterate it. In doing so, the party underestimated the market integration, commodification and diversification of rural livelihoods, and thus the extent to which its policies would influence life in rural

---

government documents of the time. See for example: APGGN, QJ: Acta da Reunião realizada no Distrito de Majune aquando da visita de trabalho efectuada pelo Director Provincial do Comérico Interno (Lichinga, May 21, 1979), 2.

95 PA, I076: interview with *P1449* (♂, ~1948) (Metangula, September 6, 2013), min 00:22:05–00:23:45; PA, I037: interview with *P0855* (♂, 1954) (Malango, August 14, 2013), min 01:06:06–01:12:41; PA, I039: interview with *P0898* (♀, 1960) (Malango, August 15, 2013), min 00:26:08–00:26:49; PA, I156: interview with *P1478* (♀) (Metangula, June 18, 2016), min 00:23:13–00:23:45. This confirms the observations made by Juergensen in Tete's Angonia district and by the *Oficinia de História* in Cabo Delgado's "liberated areas." See: Juergensen, "Peasants on the Periphery," 222; Bragança et al., "A situação nas antigas zonas libertadas de Cabo Delgado," 55–56. On Frelimo's price policy in general, see: Steven Kyle, "Economic Reform and Armed Conflict in Mozambique," *World Development* 19, no. 6 (1991): 640.

96 APGGN, 1 A: Frelimo, "Relatório do Distrito de Metangula, por ocasião do Conselho Provincial" (Metangula, January 1, 1977), 3.

97 Bridget O'Laughlin, "Through a Divided Glass: Dualism, Class and the Agrarian Question in Mozambique," *Journal of Peasant Studies* 23, no. 4 (1996): 17. On this point, see as well: Bowen, *The State Against the Peasantry*, 55–57; Marc Wuyts, "Money, Planning and Rural Transformation in Mozambique," *The Journal of Development Studies* 22, no. 1 (1985): 180–207.

areas in general (on this point see also Chapter 6). The retreat to subsistence now came at a price of deteriorating standards of living and, connected to this, a growing anti-Frelimo sentiment.[98]

Socializing the Countryside

It was not only the lack of goods like salt or clothes and Frelimo's unfavorable price policy that alienated the people from the government, but also Frelimo's plan to "socialize" the countryside. One of the main complaints of my interviewees in this regard was Frelimo's demand to cultivate a *machamba de povo*, a collective maize field. With one exception, my interviewees were unanimous in condemning this policy.[99] One interviewee, who was still quite young at that time, put it like this:

> What concerns the *machamba de povo*, there was nobody who liked it. We saw that this was like slavery as we were made to do the work if we liked or not.[100]

While one of the village's older women said:

> We were against it, we were against Samora. We did not want these things here. Here, in this village, we did not want them. It was bad.[101]

It was not only the collective mode of production that people took exception to, but also the fact that it was required that the field was always watched over by one man and one woman who were not married to each other. This idea irritated at

---

[98] Helena Pérez-Niño made a similar observation in her study on tobacco farmers in Angónia (Tete). See: Pérez-Niño, "Post-Conflict Agrarian Change in Angónia," 162, 170.
[99] PA, I073: interview with *P1012 (♂, 1955)* (Malango, September 5, 2013), min 00:28:14–00:33:05; PA, I080: interview with *P0641 (♂, 1952)* (Nkholongue, September 7, 2013), min 00:49:46–00:50:45; PA, I078: interview with *P0258 (♂, 1953)* (Nkholongue, September 7, 2013), min 00:29:28–00:30:40; PA, I117: interview with *P1458 (♂, ~1945)* (Micundi, April 20, 2016), min 01:34:17–01:34:44; PA, I112: interview with *P0129 (♀, 1930), P0128 (♂, 1928)* (Nkholongue, April 12, 2016), min 01:58:35–02:00:30. The exception claimed that people simply did not understand the idea: PA, I118: interview with *P1218 (♀, 1930)* (Malango, April 21, 2016), min 02:01:02–02:06:22. In Lussefa, people even had to grow cotton in their collective field, as in colonial times. See: PA, I150: interview with *P1483 (♀, 1950), P1481 (♂, 1954)* (Lussefa, June 15, 2016), min 00:27:19–00:28:53.
[100] PA, I124: interview with *P0376 (♂, 1968)* (Nkholongue, April 26, 2016), min 01:11:15–01:11:27.
[101] PA, I106: interview with *P0262 (♀, ~1940)* (Malango, April 4, 2016), min 02:06:38–02:09:04.

least some villagers.¹⁰² Furthermore, people never saw anything of the produce.¹⁰³ One interviewee from a neighboring village described the *machamba de povo* at his village like this:

> It was a large field. But who ate that maize I don't know.¹⁰⁴

My interviewees' retrospective view of the economic situation fully corresponds to the assessment made at the time by Eileen and Ken Hamilton, two British missionaries working in Messumba:

> It was distressing to see the local people suffering due to lack of provisions—no soap, maize, sugar, salt, cooking oil—and forced to work on communal farms, the produce from which was destined for army use.¹⁰⁵

However, as in the case of the colonial government of the 1940s, the post-colonial government's capacity to enforce its policies was similarily limited. Like the fields of the Portuguese cotton regime (see pp. 168–171), the *machamba de povo* of Nkholongue's population was cultivated for only one or two years.¹⁰⁶ Similarly, Frelimo's plan to have people live in a "light version" of a communal village, that is, closer together on one and the same street (*nas linhas*, 'on the lines'), was not really implemented and abandoned rather quickly.¹⁰⁷

---

102 PA, I083: interview with *P1102 (♂, 1932)*, *P1074 (♀, ~1940)*, *P1141 (♂, 1932)* (Malango, September 8, 2013), min 01:05:01–01:10:25; PA, I119: interview with *P0855 (♂, 1954)* (Malango, April 21, 2016), min 01:03:09–01:04:54.
103 PA, I083: interview with *P1102 (♂, 1932)*, *P1074 (♀, ~1940)*, *P1141 (♂, 1932)* (Malango, September 8, 2013), min 01:10:25–01:13:21; PA, I085: interview with *P0147 (♀, ~1928)* (Nkholongue, September 9, 2013), min 00:24:54–00:25:39; PA, I117: interview with *P1458 (♂, ~1945)* (Micundi, April 20, 2016), min 01:34:44–01:35:00.
104 PA, I094: interview with *P0727 (♂, ~1940)* (M'chepa, January 27, 2016), min 01:10:37–01:10:41.
105 Ken Hamilton and Eileen Hamilton, "Flashback – Early Days of Independence," *Lebombo Leaves* 69, no. 19 (1978): 20.
106 PA, I073: interview with *P1012 (♂, 1955)* (Malango, September 5, 2013), min 00:28:14–00:33:05; PA, I080: interview with *P0641 (♂, 1952)* (Nkholongue, September 7, 2013), min 00:49:46–00:50:45; PA, I109: interview with *P1081 (♀, 1945)* (Malango, April 6, 2016), min 01:03:51–01:05:04; PA, I125: interview with *P1463 (♂, 1951)* (Ngala, April 27, 2016), min 00:47:11–00:47:17. For the government's limited capacity to enforce it against the will of the people, see as well: PA, I157: interview with *P1455 (♂, 1952)* (Tulo, June 18, 2016), min 00:36:21–00:38:29. In Chinuni, which is far from Metangula and difficult to reach, people obviously did not cultivate a *machama de povo* at all, even though they were ordered to do so. See: PA, I149: interview with *P1501 (♂, 1949)*, *P1513 (♂, 1943)* (Chinuni, June 11, 2016), min 00:24:32–00:25:11.
107 PA, I141: interview with *P0375 (♂, 1962)* (Nkholongue, June 6, 2016), min 00:44:16–00:46:35; PA, I164: interview with *P0375 (♂, 1962)* (Nkholongue, June 23, 2016), min 00:37:33–00:41:36; PA, I155:

Furthermore, it is important to not just portray the villagers of Nkholongue as helpless victims of the state's policies. First, we can expect that people's viewpoints were not as uniform as they might be presented now in retrospect. Some might have been initially more enthusiastic about certain policies than others. Also, the role of local state intermediaries was similarly ambiguous as in colonial times.[108] Second, people at times tried their own ways to bypass state policies or to adapt them to their needs. Smuggling was one way to do so,[109] misappropriating the goods obtained through consumer cooperatives another: consumer cooperatives had been introduced by the government as part of the attempt to socialize the retail trade system. No such cooperative was formed in Nkholongue, but at least two were in Metangula. During the time of the Samora they were one of the few places you could get at least some products. The information from the interviews show now that members of these cooperatives sometimes resold the products they had acquired through the cooperatives. Such sales also took place in Nkholongue.[110]

The Top-down Way of Governing

Frelimo continued with many policies from colonial times. This included the need to have a *guia de marcha*, a kind of travel permit for journeys. Such forms of pass laws had been introduced by both Frelimo and the Portuguese government during the war in order to better control the people. After the war they were continued by the new government. A person intending to travel needed to take a declaration

---

interview with *P0713* (♂, *1944*) (Nkholongue, June 18, 2016), min 00:13:23–00:15:25; PA, I158: interview with *P0764* (♂, *1962*) (Nkholongue, June 20, 2016), min 00:42:02–00:42:34; PA, I163: interview with *P0028* (♂, *1969*) (Nkholongue, June 22, 2016), min 00:21:51–00:22:54. The limited reach of this policy is also demonstrated by the fact that other interviewees denied that there was such a policy in the case of Nkholongue: PA, I153: interview with *P1477* (♂, *~1940*) (Micucue, June 17, 2016), min 00:46:07–00:46:58; PA, I161: interview with *P0160* (♂, *1952*) (Metangula, June 22, 2016), min 00:33:12–00:35:08.
108 On the role of intermediaries in post-colonial Mozambique, see: PA, I119: interview with *P0855* (♂, *1954*) (Malango, April 21, 2016), min 01:04:54–01:05:20; PA, I154: interview with *P0367* (♂, *1936*), *P0373* (♀, *1940*) (Nkholongue, June 18, 2016), min 00:27:02–00:28:57.
109 PA, I161: interview with *P0160* (♂, *1952*) (Metangula, June 22, 2016), min 00:19:13–00:23:50; PA, I158: interview with *P0764* (♂, *1962*) (Nkholongue, June 20, 2016), min 00:51:13–00:57:43; PA, I141: interview with *P0375* (♂, *1962*) (Nkholongue, June 6, 2016), min 00:51:10–00:56:05; PA, I163: interview with *P0028* (♂, *1969*) (Nkholongue, June 22, 2016), min 00:16:35–00:16:56.
110 PA, I162: interview with *P0512* (♀, *1967*) (Nkholongue, June 22, 2016), min 00:23:39–00:25:00; PA, I141: interview with *P0375* (♂, *1962*) (Nkholongue, June 6, 2016), min 00:15:07–00:16:43.

from the village secretary and apply for a *guia* at the district level. It seems that, in theory, it would even have been necessary to have a *guia* to travel from Nkholongue to Metangula. But as there was no permanent police checkpoint between the two places, people went without. There was, however, one checkpoint north of Metangula in the direction of Messumba, so that people traveling there were compelled to have a *guia*.[111] Harry West has argued that, by using the *guias*, Frelimo "marked its populations much as the colonial state that it had defeated had."[112] It is noteworthy that many scholars have depicted the *guia de marcha* system as one that was (re-)introduced only in the 1980s as a consequence of the Civil War.[113] Proper *guias* from the archives in Lichinga and information from my interviews show however that around Nkholongue this system was already in use in the 1970s, even if it might have been handled differently for different groups of people at different times.[114]

It was not only the type of policies that resembled much of the colonial precedents but also the way these policies were implemented. Frelimo's approach was very much a top-down approach in which the party promoted its policies in a high-handed and "triumphalist"[115] fashion. Various reports show that the post-colonial divide between Frelimo's urban elites (from the "south") and Niassa's population

---

111 PA, I161: interview with *P0160* (♂, *1952*) (Metangula, June 22, 2016), min 00:10:06–00:14:28; PA, I158: interview with *P0764* (♂, *1962*) (Nkholongue, June 20, 2016), min 00:10:19–00:12:33; PA, I160: interview with *P0727* (♂, *~1940*) (M'chepa, June 22, 2016), min 00:05:36–00:07:23; PA, I164: interview with *P0375* (♂, *1962*) (Nkholongue, June 23, 2016), min 00:05:24–00:09:35; PA, I163: interview with *P0028* (♂, *1969*) (Nkholongue, June 22, 2016), min 00:10:54–00:11:37; Litumbe, "Bishop Paulo Litumbe's Memoirs," 149.
112 West, "'Who Rules Us Now?,'" 107.
113 Corrado Tornimbeni, "'Isto foi sempre assim': The Politics of Land and Human Mobility in Chimanimani, Central Mozambique," *Journal of Southern African Studies* 33, no. 3 (2007): 489; Corrado Tornimbeni, "The Informalization of Formal Portuguese Controls on People's Movements and Identity in the Colony of Mozambique: The Heritage of Portuguese Colonialism in Current Local African Politics," *Portuguese Studies* 28, no. 2 (2012): 226; Hanlon, *The Revolution under Fire*, 262; West, "'Who Rules Us Now?,'" 107.
114 APGGN, 1 A: Administração do Distrito de Metangula, "Guia de Marcha N.° 65/977," August 14, 1977; APGGN, QJ: Administração do Distrito de Metangula, "Guia de Marcha N.° 18/I/6/1," March 27, 1976; APGGN, QJ: Governo da Província do Niassa: Gabinete do Governador, "Guia N. 86/79," March 31, 1979; PA, I160: interview with *P0727* (♂, *~1940*) (M'chepa, June 22, 2016), min 00:07:18–00:09:00; PA, I141: interview with *P0375* (♂, *1962*) (Nkholongue, June 6, 2016), min 00:07:39–00:08:54. See as well: AIMC, VIII-8, 4, N. 43: Acontecimentos da vida missionária no Niassa, 1977; AIMC, VIII-8, 4, N. 26: Comunicado aos missionarios da Diocese de Lichinga (Lichinga, September 29, 1978).
115 Bowen, *The State Against the Peasantry*, 53.

living in rural zones was huge.[116] For the people living in Nkholongue, these characteristics of Frelimo's style of governance might have been especially pronounced out of two reasons: first, because many people had hoped for a change for the better, and, second, because the Portuguese forces had indeed made a certain effort to win the people for their aims in the very last stage of colonialism (as argued in the previous chapter). It is probably one of the most tragic ironies of history that while the Portuguese forces thus finally showed an awareness for the fact that the continuation of their rule could not be taken for granted, most government representatives of post-independence Mozambique apparently had no doubts about being the natural rulers of the country.

Consequently, they did not "link" very much with the people, as one interviewee put it.[117] While, for example, the Portuguese soldiers were said to have given people a lift whenever possible, the same would not be done any more by the post-colonial forces.[118] A former Frelimo fighter (who did not desert) described Machel's high-handedness by contrasting him to Eduardo Mondlane, Frelimo's first president, who was killed during the war. He characterized Mondlane as a man of the people who ate together with them at the same table and played soccer with them. If we follow his words, this togetherness was lost with Machel.[119] In general, my interviewees portrayed Samora Machel as the opposite of the selfless, well-meaning, visionary leader he remains to certain circles in Maputo.[120]

As I highlight elsewhere, little of the alleged democratic content of Frelimo's revolution seems to have arrived in Niassa. Rather, Frelimo's ideas were transmit-

---

116 In an examination of the educational system, many of the teachers of the lakeshore area indicated, for example, how they felt left out by the developments. See: FMS, AMPA, Pasta 04331.009.001, f. 33–43: Método da pesquisa: A fase preparatória. Anexo N° 8: Experiência da vida professional dos informantes, A. Investigação Sociolinguística: O sistema nacional de educação e a situação multilingue do país (INDE, May 17, 1983), 1–2. For a description of how "urban elites" behaved in Niassa after independence see as well the statements of the Italian educationalist Lavinia Gasperini, who worked in Mozambique from 1977 to 1985: Lavinia Gasperini, *Moçambique: Educação e desenvolvimento rural* (Roma: Lavoro, 1989), 36.
117 PA, I078: interview with *P0258 (♂, 1953)* (Nkholongue, September 7, 2013), min 00:30:40–00:31:19.
118 PA, I097: interview with *P1454 (♂, ~1951)* (Malango, February 5, 2016), min 02:28:09–02:29:14; PA, I078: interview with *P0258 (♂, 1953)* (Nkholongue, September 7, 2013), min 00:25:38–00:26:24.
119 PA, I087: interview with *P1452 (♂, 1927)* (Lichinga, September 10, 2013), min 00:48:33–00:51:59. For Frelimo's post-colonial "high-handedness," see as well: Hanlon, *The Revolution under Fire*, 198–201, 262.
120 On Machel's status in modern-day Maputo, see: Jason Sumich, *The Middle Class in Mozambique: The State and the Politics of Transformation in Southern Africa* (New York: Cambridge University Press, 2018), 14.

ted in a decidedly authoritarian way.[121] Different interviewees answered the question of whether they were in favor of Frelimo's socialist policies that this was not a question of liking or not liking, but that this was an order.[122] To make people follow its orders, the party also did not shy away from using violence and fear.

Fanya Fujo or the Production of Fear

In the third quarter of 1979, the population of Nkholongue and the surrounding villages were all ordered to attend a gathering in Meluluca. The gathering is locally called *fanya fujo*, after the name given to the group that organized it. It is equally identified by the apparent aim of the gathering, which is given as *kuchapa mutu* or *lavar cabeça*, which translates as "brainwashing."[123] An identical gathering took place in Metangula for the villages north of the town.[124]

It is not entirely clear what kind of unit it was that "perpetrated" these gatherings. *Fanya fujo* is Kiswahili, and most probably derives from the name that was given by people in Tanzania to the Field Force Unit (FFU), which is a long-standing paramilitary unit of the Tanzanian police. Instead of FFU, people have been calling it the *Fanya Fujo Utaone* or *Fanya Fujo Uone*, which means "Make trouble, and you (will) see."[125] It is possible that the *fanya fujo* unit deployed to Meluluca was some sort of precursor of what was to become the Mozambican equivalent of the FFU,

---

121 Zeman, "Flag Independence without Flags?"
122 PA, I112: interview with P0129 (♀, 1930), P0128 (♂, 1928) (Nkholongue, April 12, 2016), min 01:58:35–01:59:22; PA, I148: interview with P1500 (♂, ~1946) (Bandeze, June 10, 2016), min 00:16:48–00:16:57.
123 PA, I086: interview with P0375 (♂, 1962) (Nkholongue, September 9, 2013), min 00:16:54–00:23:34; PA, I119: interview with P0855 (♂, 1954) (Malango, April 21, 2016), min 01:06:06–01:08:20, 01:13:57–01:18:01; PA, I124: interview with P0376 (♂, 1968) (Nkholongue, April 26, 2016), min 00:50:33–00:58:20; PA, I123: interview with P1460 (♀), P1461 (♂, ~1935), P1462 (♂, ~1935) (Meluluca, April 25, 2016), min 01:43:52–01:46:39; PA, I144: interview with P0411 (♂, 1965) (Nkholongue, June 8, 2016), min 00:15:57–00:16:57; PA, I152: interview with P1476 (♂, ~1935) (Milombe, June 16, 2016), min 01:02:23–01:04:56; PA, I156: interview with P1478 (♀) (Metangula, June 18, 2016), min 00:32:37–00:33:35; PA, I158: interview with P0764 (♂, 1962) (Nkholongue, June 20, 2016), min 00:43:43–00:44:58; PA, I115: interview with P0160 (♂, 1952) (Metangula, April 18, 2016), min 00:15:05–00:15:40; PA, I162: interview with P0512 (♀, 1967) (Nkholongue, June 22, 2016), min 00:20:17–00:21:22.
124 PA, I157: interview with P1455 (♂, 1952) (Tulo, June 18, 2016), min 00:08:52–00:11:47.
125 Roderick P. Neumann, *Imposing Wilderness: Struggles over Livelihood and Nature Preservation in Africa* (Berkeley: University of California Press, 1998), 147; Issa G. Shivji, *State Coercion and Freedom in Tanzania* (Roma, Lesotho: Institute of Southern African Studies, 1990), 19.

today commonly known as the anti-riot police *Força de Intervenção Rápida* ("Rapid Intervention Force," FIR).[126]

What was *fanya fujo*? In short, or in the words of one interviewee, "it was about beating the people."[127] At the gathering, people, and especially religious dignitaries, were humiliated. One interviewee described it as follows:

> Now, there, in Meluluca, they made it like this: [they asked:] "Who, who, is with Ramadan?" Pronto, this one was beaten. "You, you are with what?"—"I am an imam." He was beaten.[128]

A further central characteristic of the gathering was the dancing. People had to dance all night until daybreak. Those who fell asleep were punished. Some people were beaten, others tormented with the extremely itchy velvet bean (*mucuna pruriens, chitedze*).[129]

What was the purpose of *fanya fujo*? This question is somewhat more difficult to answer, at least in relation to the imminent reason for the gathering. Many people denied having gained much content from the gathering. As this meeting happened shortly before Samora Machel's visit to Metangula, several interviewees perceived that it was carried out in preparation of the president's visit, so that nobody would speak up at this occasion.[130] One said for example:

> They said that the president will come. That's the time of Samora, isn't it? Now, they wanted people to live with fear so that they don't make any confusion.[131]

---

126 Today, the official name of this police unit is *Unidade de Intervenção Rápida* ("Rapid Intervention Unit"). On the formation of the Mozambican FIR and the possible connection to the Tanzanian FFU, see: Renato Matusse, *Guebuza: A paixão pela terra* (Maputo: Macmillan Moçambique, 2004), 150–151.
127 PA, I156: interview with *P1478 (♀)* (Metangula, June 18, 2016), min 00:32:57–00:32:59.
128 PA, I158: interview with *P0764 (♂, 1962)* (Nkholongue, June 20, 2016), min 00:44:24–00:44:39.
129 PA, I133: interview with *P1473 (♂ ~1938), P1504 (♀)* (Limbi, June 1, 2016), min 00:49:57–00:52:35; PA, I124: interview with *P0376 (♂, 1968)* (Nkholongue, April 26, 2016), min 00:48:10–00:55:53; PA, I123: interview with *P1460 (♀), P1461 (♂, ~1935), P1462 (♂, ~1935)* (Meluluca, April 25, 2016), min 01:43:52–01:46:30; PA, I162: interview with *P0512 (♀, 1967)* (Nkholongue, June 22, 2016), min 00:20:17–00:21:22; PA, I141: interview with *P0375 (♂, 1962)* (Nkholongue, June 6, 2016), min 00:16:54–00:23:34; PA, I152: interview with *P1476 (♂, ~1935)* (Milombe, June 16, 2016), min 01:02:23–01:05:52.
130 PA, I119: interview with *P0855 (♂, 1954)* (Malango, April 21, 2016), min 01:06:53–01:07:04; PA, I155: interview with *P0713 (♂, 1944)* (Nkholongue, June 18, 2016), min 00:27:56–00:28:14; PA, I157: interview with *P1455 (♂, 1952)* (Tulo, June 18, 2016), min 00:11:13–00:11:47; PA, I133: interview with *P1473 (♂ ~1938), P1504 (♀)* (Limbi, June 1, 2016), min 00:52:57–00:54:32.
131 PA, I155: interview with *P0713 (♂, 1944)* (Nkholongue, June 18, 2016), min 00:27:56–00:28:14.

However, there are clear indications that the gathering's aim was not only to intimidate people into not speaking against the president, but also to prevent them from lending support to the armed opposition in Mozambique. Thus, another interviewee stated:

> They said that, "in this country, we don't want a plot/conspiracy. In this country, we don't want bandits. In this country, it is important to live in peace. For the bandits, there will be no excuse, there will be nothing."[132]

I was unable to encounter descriptions of comparable events in existing literature on Mozambican history, but a similar gathering was witnessed by the Italian missionary Adriano Severin in the town of Mecanhelas, in the southern part of Niassa, in the middle of 1980. According to Severin, the commander in charge of the gathering opened it by saying, "I have been given carte blanche by President Samora Moises Machel himself; I can do whatever I want, even kill."[133] In Severin's description of the event, which I found in the archives of the Consolata missionaries in Rome, he referred to the fact that the same commander had previously led an identical "operation" in Mandimba and Metangula.[134]

Meluluca, Metangula, Mandimba and Mecanhelas do have one important thing in common: they all lie in border regions to Malawi. It seems plausible that they were all targeted by the government exactly because of their proximity to Malawi. The years between 1978 and 1981 were characterized by the increasing activities of the *Partido Revolucionário de Moçambique* (Revolutionary Party of Mozambique, PRM). PRM was an armed opposition movement, operating mainly from Malawi. It merged with Renamo in 1982.[135] There is little evidence that PRM indeed pursued military activities in Niasssa at this moment in time. A police report from 1980 merely mentioned the presence of 80 armed enemies in Mepanhira near Mecanhelas. But the same police report leaves little doubt that the Mozambican authorities were highly concerned by the attitude of the people living along the border:

---

132 PA, I124: interview with *P0376* (♂, 1968) (Nkholongue, April 26, 2016), min 00:56:40–00:56:59.
133 "[H]o ricevuto carta bianca dallo stesso Signor Presidente Samora Moises Machel; posso fare quello che voglio, anche uccidere," AIMC, VIII-8, 5, N. 1: Adriano Severin, "Relazione degli avvenimenti accaduti a Mecanhelas nei giorni 21–22 Giugno 1980," n.d., 1.
134 AIMC, VIII-8, 5, N. 1: Adriano Severin, "Relazione degli avvenimenti accaduti a Mecanhelas nei giorni 21–22 Giugno 1980," n.d., 1.
135 PRM's history has been neglected so far. For an exception, see: Sérgio Chichava, "The Anti-Frelimo Movements & the War in Zambezia," in *The War Within: New Perspectives on the Civil War in Mozambique, 1976–1992*, ed. Eric Morier-Genoud, Michel Cahen, and Domingos Manuel do Rosário (Woodbridge: James Currey, 2018), 17–45.

8.3 From Taxing Natives to Taxing Citizens: The New Government on the Ground — 333

> [The situation as it concerns the enemy] is alarming as the enemy's infiltration can be noted, above all in the border regions to Malawi [...]. The elements in question infiltrate into our country, and aim at demobilizing the populations living along the borders by [politically] exploiting the lack of basic necessities.[136]

It seems that the government suspected the people living in these regions of not being true Mozambicans. One interviewee said that Aurélio Manave, the first governor of post-independence Niassa, had come to Meluluca about a year before the *fanya fujo* gathering to tell them that they were not full Mozambicans, but half Malawians.[137] What Manave meant by this becomes evident from an interview he gave to the Tempo magazine in 1976:

> [T]he enemy is also operating in the Province of Niassa. Because we have a border here with a country with which our relations are still very cold [Malawi]. We consider this border like a breach for the penetration of the enemy into our bosom. [...] The populations who were there [during the war] were not considered refugees.[138] Now, they are returning in an unorganized manner, using sinuous paths, and, thus, much the way as they left when they had to flee from the colonial repression [...]. We really have to ask: Is it that they are all Mozambicans? There, we doubt. In fact, one part is Mozambican, but the other is the proper enemy entering physically.[139]

The suspicion of the Mozambican authorities might also have been nurtured by the fact that the founder of PRM, Amós Sumane, was from the lakeside area. He had been a head teacher of the Anglican Mission of Messumba until 1963 when he disappeared to Tanzania to become one of the first members of Frelimo from the region.[140] He, however, deserted Frelimo after the beginning of the war, moved to Malawi where he was briefly a member of the *Comité Revolucionário de Moçambique* (COREMO) and then founded a new nationalist movement, the *União Nacional Africana de Rumbézia* (UNAR).[141] UNAR's objective was to achieve the inde-

---

136 APGGN, 1 A: Relatório sobre a reunião alargada com os Comandantes Distritais da P.P.M. do Niassa, de 27 a 29 de Março 1980 (Lichinga, March 29, 1980), 4.
137 PA, I086: interview with *P0375* (♂, *1962*) (Nkholongue, September 9, 2013), min 00:23:34–00:24:36.
138 This refers to the fact that most refugees to Malawi had not lived in official refugee camps like those in Tanzania. Rather, they were as a rule mostly integrated into existing villages.
139 "Entrevista com o Governador do Niassa: Aurélio Manave analisa problemas políticos da província," *Tempo*, no. 319 (November 14, 1976): 22–27.
140 Paul, *Memoirs of a Revolution*, 79, 97–98.
141 Frelimo and some scholars have claimed that UNAR was in fact a common project of PIDE/DGS, Jorge Jardim and the Malawian government. The PIDE files at the ANTT, however, give no real evidence to support such a theory even though PIDE/DGS seems to have seen the existence of UNAR as a welcome means to create further disharmony among Mozambique's nationalists.

pendence of northern Mozambique (the area between the Zambezi and Ruvuma river, so-called Rumbézia) by peaceful means. The name was later changed to *União Nacional Africana de Moçambique* (UNAMO) and the movement began to focus on achieving independence for the entirety of Mozambique, at least nominally.[142] PIDE/DGS reports show that Sumane and UNAR tried to mobilize support among the refugees from Lago District, remaining however ambiguous with regard to the success of this mobilization. According to PIDE/DGS, one of UNAR's supporters was Metangula's former chief Chilombe, who lived in Nkhotakota at the time.[143]

As we will see in the next chapter, the Mozambican government's fears were rather unfounded, at least as far as a possible "collaboration" with the armed opposition was concerned. Certainly, it is true that people were not very much in favor of Frelimo. But we have no indication that the PRM or Renamo were able to mobilize the people of the region in any significant way. Rather, the opposite was the case as people living in Nkholongue and Malango were to become major victims of attacks by Renamo. However, we can of course also assume that incidents like that of *fanya fujo* contributed to the fact that resistance to government policies and demands remained rather limited.

Manave's comment is interesting as it very much shows that, as in colonial times, people from Nkholongue again found themselves not viewed as true citizens in the state they were living in. Obviously, the new government considered them Malawians at heart. Certainly, this was not without historical and cultural foundation. It is telling that, around the same time, the "Malawiness" of the eastern lakeside was claimed by Henry Masauko Chipembere in his battle for the leadership of Malawian nationalism. Chipembere had been born in Messumba to an Anglican clergyman who later emigrated to Malawi with his family. Chipembere's "Mozambican" origins were welcome fodder for his opponents, who used them to claim

---

For the theory of UNAR being a plot by PIDE/DGS etc., see: Chichava, "The Anti-Frelimo Movements," 18–19.

142 ANTT, PIDE/DGS, 2ª Divisão de Informação, CI (2) 9713, f. 315–319: PIDE Delegação de Moçambique, "Informação N.º 416-SC/CI(2): Alteração da designação de 'UNAR' para 'UNAMO,'" April 16, 1969.

143 ANTT, SCCIM N.º 1165, f. 156: PIDE Delegação de Moçambique, "Relatório N.º 1328/69-GAB: Organização político-administrativa da UNAMO," August 4, 1969; ANTT, PIDE/DGS, 2ª Divisão de Informação, CI (2) 9713, f. 106: DGS Delegação de Moçambique, "Relatório Imediato N.º 1213/70/DI/2/SC: UNAMO – Dificuldades na área de Nkhotakota," June 20, 1970; ANTT, PIDE/DGS, 2ª Divisão de Informação, CI (2) 9713, f. 385–389: PIDE Delegação de Moçambique, "Relatório N.º 1704/68-GAB: UNAR – Actividades," October 2, 1968. The Anglican missionary John Paul met Sumane in Malawi in 1968 and wrote in his memoirs that UNAR attracted many Anyanja. See: Paul, *Memoirs of a Revolution*, 207.

that he was not a true Malawian. In response to this claim, Chipembere wrote a small booklet entitled *My Malawian Ancestors*. In it he stressed the common culture and origins of the people living on both sides of the lake and even explicitly singled out the inhabitants of Nkholongue as an example of the close affinities between the two shores, emphasizing their recent immigration and close ties to Nkhotakota.[144] The process of colonization and the success of colonial-border-nationalism on both sides of the lake had made such cultural and historical commonalities become problems for those affected.

In light of Frelimo's authoritarianism, the villagers of Nkholongue once again had to comply with the directives from above, rather than now belonging to the body of decision makers themselves. As throughout much of the colonial times, intimidation seemed to have played an important role for the state to be able to impose its rules. One interviewee commented rather unambiguously on the question of how they were convinced to cultivate maize:

> Q: And how did Samora convince the people to cultivate maize?[145]
> A: This one of *fanya fujo*. Yes, we were afraid of this group of *fanya fujo*.[146]

While different reports show that maize production began to be promoted before 1979, it is more than noteworthy that a district report of 1983 stated that it was Samora Machel who personally ordered the introduction of maize cultivation in the district during his 1979 visit.[147] It can, thus, be assumed that this interviewee reproduced people's perception of things of that time correctly, or that he at least reflected the atmosphere reigning in the years after independence pretty well.[148]

Frelimo's way of governing did, doubtlessly, not contribute to the fact that people felt part of Frelimo's nation-building project. How far, in fact, the ideas of the people of Nkholongue and Frelimo's elite were set apart is also shown by the way

---

144 Chipembere, *My Malawian Ancestors*, 11.
145 PA, I119: interview with P0855 (♂, 1954) (Malango, April 21, 2016), min 01:23:25–01:24:06.
146 PA, I119: interview with P0855 (♂, 1954) (Malango, April 21, 2016), min 01:25:34–01:25:53.
147 APGGN, 1 A: Relatório resumido da situação sócioeconómica e cultural do Distrito do Lago, 1983, July 20, 1983, 3.
148 For the importance of intimidation in the years after independence, see as well: PA, I094: interview with P0727 (♂, ~1940) (M'chepa, January 27, 2016), min 01:06:17–01:08:02; PA, I161: interview with P0160 (♂, 1952) (Metangula, June 22, 2016), min 00:13:37–00:15:28; PA, I068: interview with P0367 (♂, 1936) (Nkholongue, September 2, 2013), min 01:24:17–01:24:34; PA, I145: interview with P0284 (♂, 1966), P0273 (♀, 1950) (Metangula, June 9, 2016), min 00:05:25–00:06:30. This is also supported by observations from missionaries for other regions. See: David Bruno, "The Church in Moçambique Revisited," *Lebombo Leaves* 68, no. 23 (1980): 18; AIMC, X-406, N. 7: Diário de Unango, entry dated October 15, 1974.

various interviewees recalled the announcement by Samora Machel that the war against Renamo would be fought until the blood of the people formed a river and until the mothers stopped giving birth to boys. People's statements leave little doubt that what Machel probably meant as a stylistic device to strengthen people's morale had the opposite effect. For the people living in such areas like Nkholongue, the war, that will be discussed in the next chapter, was not about rhetoric but about bitter realities.[149]

8.4 Conclusion

The starting point of this chapter was the observation that we still know very little about how "ordinary" Mozambicans actually experienced the process of decolonization, and how they saw the moment of independence. Mozambique is no exception in this respect. Elsewhere, the social history of decolonization across the dividing point of the moment of independence has also been examined only unsatisfactorily.

The analysis of the experiences of decolonization in the case of the population of Nkholongue reveals two central points, first, that not everybody was looking forward to Mozambique's political independence, and, second, that the hopes for change were dampened rather quickly. The first point has to be explained by the fact that by the end of the war many of Nkholongue's inhabitants stood on the wrong side of the conflict. In this regard, the experiences of Nkholongue's inhabitants were not exceptional; rather, as has been shown in the previous chapter, only a few people lived inside Niassa under the control of Frelimo until the end of the war. From the perspective of Niassa, it did not appear so natural that Frelimo should take over the leadership of independent Mozambique. This is also suggested by the statements of several female Frelimo veterans from Niassa interviewed by Jonna Katto, who said that after independence they had "to organize meetings for the population to make them understand that Frelimo had liberated Mozambique."[150]

The causes for the second point are somewhat more complicated to examine. There is, however, no doubt that people's main complaint was the economic situa-

---

149 PA, I155: interview with *P0713* (♂, *1944*) (Nkholongue, June 18, 2016), min 00:28:52 – 00:29:31; PA, I083: interview with *P1102* (♂, *1932*), *P1074* (♀, *~1940*), *P1141* (♂, *1932*) (Malango, September 8, 2013), min 01:22:03 – 01:23:11; PA, I076: interview with *P1449* (♂, *~1948*) (Metangula, September 6, 2013), min 00:27:52 – 00:30:52; PA, I118: interview with *P1218* (♀, *1930*) (Malango, April 21, 2016), min 01:34:52 – 01:35:30.
150 Katto, *"Grandma Was a Guerrilla Fighter,"* 58. See as well: Katto, 68, 215.

tion. In the case of Nkholongue, the disappearance of such goods like salt, soap, or clothes was especially pronounced as the years before independence had been marked by a very good supply of these products. In this respect, my findings also confirm previous research on Tete and Cabo Delgado that have argued that many people lost purchasing power after independence.[151]

Another important reason for the alienation of Nkholongue's inhabitants from Frelimo was the party's highly authoritarian rule. The alleged "democratic content of Frelimo's reforms at the local level"[152] seems to have been limited in the case of Nkholongue, and, in fact, of the whole larger region. My research shows that Frelimo was readily prepared to use intimidation and violence to impose its policies. The gathering of *fanya fujo* is a telling example in this respect.

A third reason was the negative impact of the gap between propaganda and reality. One party report mirrored people's complaints in this regard by stating that "what [the leaders] mobilize for, is not what they are doing."[153] There is no doubt that this lack of political coherence heavily damaged Frelimo's credibility in manifold ways, and, thus, contributed to the party's unpopularity. In this respect, one also has to consider the many continuities from the colonial time that have been discussed in this chapter.

Seen from the perspective of Nkholongue, this was not the independence people had longed for. In many ways, the difference between Lisbon and Maputo proved to be pretty small. The emperor had just put on new clothes.[154] This also explains the indifference of many of my interviewees to this supposedly so important moment of Mozambican history: "Maybe, the government knows [what changed]."[155]

---

151 Juergensen, "Peasants on the Periphery," 222; Bragança et al., "A situação nas antigas zonas libertadas de Cabo Delgado," 55–56.
152 O'Laughlin, "Class and the Customary," 30.
153 APGGN, 1 A: Frelimo, "Relatório do Distrito de Metangula, por ocasião do Conselho Provincial" (Metangula, January 1, 1977), 2–3.
154 Burton and Jennings, "The Emperor's New Clothes?"
155 PA, I046: interview with *P1045 (♀, 1932)* (Malango, August 20, 2013), min 00:35:58–00:36:04.

9 From Victims to Voters: Renamo's Delayed Supporters

9.1 Renamo, or How to Evade the Blame

Few episodes of Mozambique's history have attracted as much scholarly attention as the Mozambican Civil War. At first, most narratives of the war were more or less congruent with the version presented by the Mozambican government. The war was depicted as a destabilization effort, orchestrated against Mozambique by the white minority governments of Rhodesia and South Africa. Renamo's soldiers were considered terrorists or—as Frelimo often referred to them—"armed bandits." This dominant version of the war was only challenged from the mid-1980s. The revisionists, led by the French scholars Christian Geffray and Michel Cahen, argued that Frelimo's authoritative modernization course had alienated the peasantry in many regions and thus allowed Renamo to gather a significant social base within Mozambique. According to this reasoning, Renamo had evolved "from foreign-backed Contras into one side in a genuine civil war."[1]

As a consequence of these claims there was a fierce debate about the origins and nature of Renamo.[2] Subsequent studies showed significant variations in how Renamo was received by people in different parts of the country. They also showed

---

[1] For the quotation, see: Georgi Derluguian, "Book Reviews: Revolution, Counter-Revolution and Revisionism in Postcolonial Africa: The Case of Mozambique, 1975–1994. By Alice Dinerman," *The International Journal of African Historical Studies* 40, no. 2 (2007): 307–308. For the early revisionist literature, see: Christian Geffray and Mögens Pedersen, "Transformação da organização social e do sistema agrário do campesinato no Distrito do Erati: Processo de socialização do campo e diferenciação social" (Maputo: Departamento de Arqueologia e Antropologia, Universidade Eduardo Mondlane, 1985); Michel Cahen, *Mozambique: La révolution implosée. Études sur 12 ans d'indépendance (1975–1987)* (Paris: L'Harmattan, 1987); Christian Geffray, *La cause des armes au mozambique: Anthropologie d'une guerre civile* (Paris: Karthala, 1990). It is noteworthy that Joseph Hanlon had already anticipated much of the argument of the coming debate in his 1984 monograph *Mozambique: The Revolution under Fire*, even if his conclusions were not drawn from genuine fieldwork but rather from his profound knowledge of the political situation in Mozambique, which he had acquired during his residence there as a journalist. See: Hanlon, *Mozambique: The Revolution under Fire*, 228–231.

[2] See especially: Michel Cahen, "Mozambique: The Debate Continues. Michel Cahen Writes …," *Southern Africa Report* 5, no. 4 (1990): 26–27; Claude Meillassoux et al., "Mozambique: The Debate Continues. The Cahen Document: Victory via Democracy for Socialism," *Southern Africa Report* 5, no. 4 (1990): 26–27; Otto Roesch, "Mozambique: The Debate Continues. Otto Roesch Replies," *Southern Africa Report* 5, no. 4 (1990): 28–29.

that Renamo evidently adapted its regional strategies according to this different level of receptivity, taking a much more brutal and terrorist-like approach in the country's south and a much more civilized and political approach in the country's center.³ In any case, the "revisionists" were certainly quite successful in arguing that Renamo had more sympathizers within the country than was previously assumed. According to analysts, this fact was also reflected in the results of the first multi-party elections of 1994 in which Renamo did much better than had been commonly expected.⁴

This chapter will explore the war experiences of Nkholongue's population. The central point of the chapter is that the alienated peasantry did not necessarily turn into supporters of Renamo's war effort: according to the argumentation laid out in Chapter 8, it seems evident that Nkholongue might have constituted a fertile recruiting ground for Renamo. Frelimo had few sympathizers here, mainly because of the economic situation, but also because of its authoritarianism. It would be of little surprise if Nkholongue had belonged to those places where Renamo was able to win the population for its war. This is, however, not what happened. Rather, it was the opposite: Nkholongue suffered badly under the repeated attacks by the South African-backed rebels. It was only after the war and, despite these attacks, that Renamo was able to gain considerable political support within Nkholongue and even to win the legislative elections of 1994 and both the presidential and legislative elections of 1999. To sum this up, many villagers of Nkholongue were delayed Renamo supporters. In the chapter, I will try to explain why the villagers did not become Renamo supporters in the first place when the chances for a symbiotic relationship looked rather promising, but did so in the second place when such a move seemed rather implausible at first glance. The chapter thus equally investigates the question of why Renamo's brutal past did not impact on the party's political attractiveness after the war.⁵

---

3 For a regional study of the war in the south, see: Otto Roesch, "Renamo and the Peasantry in Southern Mozambique: A View from Gaza Province," *Canadian Journal of African Studies/Revue Canadienne des Études Africaines* 26, no. 3 (1992): 462–84. See as well: Eric Morier-Genoud, Michel Cahen, and Domingos Manuel do Rosário, eds., *The War Within: New Perspectives on the Civil War in Mozambique, 1976–1992* (Woodbridge: James Currey, 2018); William Minter, *Apartheid's Contras: An Inquiry into the Roots of War in Angola and Mozambique* (Johannesburg: Witwatersrand University Press, 1994), 211–217.
4 Bernhard Weimer, "Mosambik hat gewählt: Analyse der Wahlergebnisse und Perspektiven des Wiederaufbaus (Mozambique Has Voted: Analysis of the Result and Perspectives for Reconstruction)," *Africa Spectrum* 30, no. 1 (1995): 12.
5 This question has been raised by others but been answered only unsatisfactorily. Vines mentions rather vague possibilities that contributed to this outcome, such as "informal amnesty," "traditional healing," and "forgiveness processes," without really examining these processes. See: Alex Vines,

The analysis of this chapter is also a contribution to the literature of political scientists who since the end of the Cold War have examined the "Rebel-to-Party Transformations" and the electoral performance by post-rebel parties around the globe.[6] It seems obvious that the use of indiscriminate violence is counterproductive in gaining popular support in civil wars.[7] Accordingly, the widespread use of indiscriminate violence is also generally seen as a negative factor in the electoral performance of rebel movements in the post-war period. Following a "vengeful voting logic,"[8] it is usually expected that electoral support for a party is suppressed in those areas where it committed human rights atrocities. Using broad quantitative data, various political scientists have attempted to evidence such correlations statistically. The results have thereby not been uniform. Thus, Michael Allison has claimed to have found such a correlation for the case of El Salvador, and John Ishiyama and Michael Widmeier for the cases of Tajikistan and Nepal respectively.[9] However, Sarah Daly has denied such a general correlation based on a broad cross-national database, and also offered calculations to reject Allison's findings, as he had ignored considering the direction of violence.[10] In contrast, Daly has argued that those belligerents who are militarily stronger at the time of the elections are usually able to appeal to swing votes, as the militarily stronger appear able to provide security. She has further highlighted the advantages of incumbents who usually "enjoy advantages through their control of the state apparatus and their experience in government,"[11] and, thus, also operate a "superior propaganda machine" that facilitates control over the writing of history and helps them "evade culpability for violence."[12] These are all factors that barely unambiguously apply

---

"Renamo's Rise and Decline: The Politics of Reintegration in Mozambique," *International Peacekeeping* 20, no. 3 (2013): 382.

6 For overviews of such research, see: Carrie Manning and Ian Smith, "Electoral Performance by Post-Rebel Parties," *Government and Opposition* 54, no. 3 (2019): 2; Katrin Wittig, "Politics in the Shadow of the Gun: Revisiting the Literature on 'Rebel-to-Party Transformations' through the Case of Burundi," *Civil Wars* 18, no. 2 (2016): 137–159.

7 Kalyvas offers an attempt to show when and why indiscriminate violence is nevertheless used, highlighting above all that it is cheaper than its selective counterpart. See: Kalyvas, *The Logic of Violence in Civil War*, 146–172.

8 Sarah Zukerman Daly, "Voting for Victors: Why Violent Actors Win Postwar Elections," *World Politics* 71, no. 4 (2019): 752–753.

9 Michael E. Allison, "The Legacy of Violence on Post-Civil War Elections: The Case of El Salvador," *Studies in Comparative International Development* 45, no. 1 (2010): 106; John Ishiyama and Michael Widmeier, "Territorial Control, Levels of Violence, and the Electoral Performance of Former Rebel Political Parties after Civil Wars," *Civil Wars* 15, no. 4 (2013): 534–535.

10 Daly, "Voting for Victors."

11 Daly, 768.

12 Daly, 749.

to Renamo's position in Nkholongue in 1994. Instead, my qualitative research points above all to the importance of having a story that resonates with people's grievances and pre-war experiences, something that might be difficult to capture by quantitative means.

By focusing on the history of the war in Nkholongue, this chapter also focuses on the history of the war in a province that has barely received any attention in this respect so far. While Niassa was one of the central theaters of the War of Independence and is also depicted as such in the existing superficial historiography, the province figures as a side-scene for the Civil War at best. Most synopses of the war totally ignore events in Niassa.[13] This ignorance is questionable if one looks at the statistics: Table 8 shows the share of schools that had been destroyed or closed as a consequence of the war per province since 1983. With 69 percent, Niassa ranks third. Figure 8 shows the number of demobilized soldiers as a share of the total population by province.[14] Here Niassa ranks first. In Yussuf Adam's "destabilization index," measuring the percentage of population out of government control, Niassa ranks fifth.[15] Certainly numbers need always to be treated with caution. But, in any case, the ignorance of the previous war literature on Niassa seems to be rather questionable and certainly not connected to the fact that the province was among the "least affected by the war" as claimed by Richard Synge.[16]

---

[13] One exception is Carolyn Nordstrom's brief ethnographic passage on the *The Quiet War of Two Villages in the Northern Hinterlands*. See: Carolyn Nordstrom, *A Different Kind of War Story* (Philadelphia: University of Pennsylvania Press, 1997), 98–101.
[14] Lago District had the second highest number of demobilized soldiers per inhabitants of all Mozambican districts according to this map: United Nations Office for Humanitarian Assistance Coordination, "Projected Density of 160,000 Demobilized Soldiers and Dependents (by District)," January 1994, accessed March 30, 2019, http://www.mozambiquehistory.net/history/peace_process/94/01/19940100_density_of_demobbed_soldiers.pdf. The sources of the data for the graph are the national census data of 1997 for the number of inhabitants per province and data provided by Sally Baden for the number of demobilized soldiers: Sally Baden, "Post-Conflict Mozambique Women's Special Situation, Population Issues and Gender Perspectives: To Be Integrated into Skills Training and Employment Promotion," BRIDGE Report, no. 44 (Brighton: Institute of Development Studies, June 1997), 72, accessed December 4, 2017, http://www.bridge.ids.ac.uk/bridge/Reports/re44c.pdf.
[15] Adam, "Trick or Treat," 103.
[16] Synge claimed that "Cabo Delgado and Niassa had been least affected by the war." See: Richard Synge, *Mozambique: UN Peacekeeping in Action, 1992–94* (Washington, D.C.: United States Institute of Peace Press, 1997), 87.

Tete	94.8
Zambezia	88.2
Niassa	69.3
Sofala	65.5
Maputo Province	60.2
Manica	48.4
Nampula	47.9
Inhambane	43.4
Gaza	30.9
C. Delgado	20.1

Table 8: Schools destroyed or closed because of the war by province (percentage of schools existing in 1983).[17]

The shift of focus to Niassa is equally interesting as the province was also a site of the previous War of Independence. To date, few studies have been conducted on regions that experienced both wars. Studies that have covered such areas have remained surprisingly silent about people's life during the 1964 to 1974 war and did little to contribute to compare the experiences of people in the two wars.[18] As this chapter attempts to show, a comparison through the prism of Nkholongue allows for a better understanding of the local characteristics of both wars.

9.2 The Local History of the War

The Mozambican Civil War is usually said to have lasted from 1976 to 1992. In Mozambique, the war is nowadays often called the 16-year war (*a guerra dos 16 anos*), the Frelimo way of avoiding calling it a civil war. From Nkholongue's perspective, such a delimitation makes little sense. It was not until 1985 that the first fighting occurred in Lago District. But it would also be mistaken to define the duration of the war according to the occurrence of local fighting, because wars can be felt and feared before they actually reach you directly.

---

17 Based on: Mario Joaquim Azevedo, *Tragedy and Triumph: Mozambique Refugees in Southern Africa, 1977–2001* (Portsmouth: Heinemann, 2002), 33.
18 For examples, see: Englund, *From War to Peace*; Juergensen, "Peasants on the Periphery."

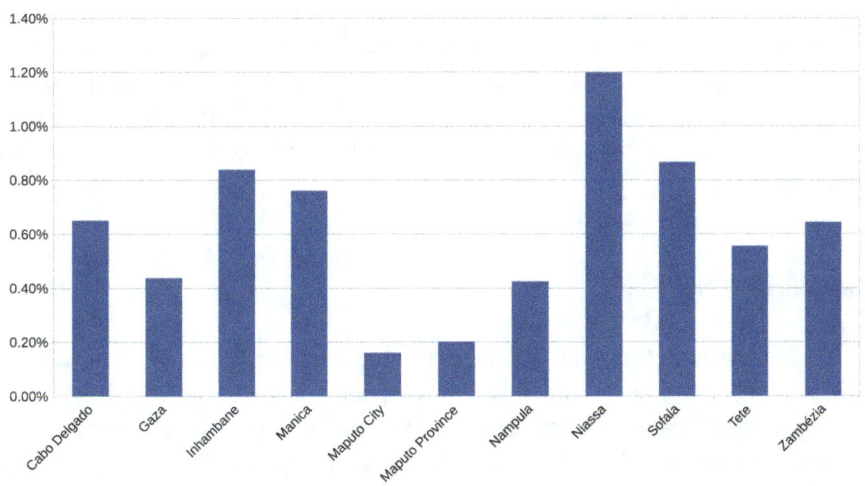

Figure 8: Number of demobilized soldiers as a share of the total population by province.

Recruitment Begins

The first clearly visible effect of the war in the region was certainly the beginning of the forced recruitment of men by government troops. Forced recruitment might sound extremely harsh in this respect. Most countries have some form of compulsory conscription, and rarely one speaks of "forced recruitment" in this context. Still, and apart from the fact that it is what it is, the "forced" nature of conscription in Mozambique probably needs to be emphasized for three reasons:

First, Mozambique was still a very young nation. People were not necessarily identifying themselves as much with the nation or the government as elsewhere. Second, the reach of the government's bureaucracy was very limited, the knowledge about the place of residence or age of its citizens often rudimentary or non-existent. Conscription was thus by nature a rather arbitrary process and, in the case of Mozambique, also included the recruitment of minors. Last but not least, Frelimo's recruitment practices differed markedly from those of the late colonial government which had set incentives to attract people to the military or militia service (see Chapter 7).

The experiences of Nkholongue's population allow us to assume that the effects of conscription on people's feelings have been rather underestimated so far. The evidence from my interviews shows that young men increasingly began to flee the country in the early 1980s because they were afraid of being recruited by the government.¹⁹ Two of my interviewees who were recruited had to serve very long conscription periods of nine years each.²⁰ The younger of them was recruited at an age of only 15 years. According to his testimony, he was just picked up off the street by the army. He managed to escape the first time but was caught again some time later.²¹ One interviewee lost her son who was conscripted and killed in fighting.²²

The Course of the War

As in other parts of the country, Renamo's attacks in the lakeshore area were directed to a large extent against the civilian population. Attacks on villages were used to sow general insecurity, destroy state infrastructure, and capture people and supplies such as food or clothes. Nkholongue's population was thereby attacked several times.²³ The exact course of the war in Nkholongue is difficult to reconstruct, since the war left many people traumatized and several people also declined to speak about it in detail, or about it at all. Furthermore, and in compar-

---

19 PA, I086: interview with *P0375* (♂, *1962*) (Nkholongue, September 9, 2013), min 00:29:35–; PA, I158: interview with *P0764* (♂, *1962*) (Nkholongue, June 20, 2016), min 00:13:01–00:13:54, 00:15:52–00:17:00; PA, I162: interview with *P0512* (♀, *1967*) (Nkholongue, June 22, 2016), min 00:32:32–00:30:43.
20 PA, I074: interview with *P0160* (♂, *1952*) (Metangula, September 6, 2013), min 00:19:46–00:22:10; PA, I115: interview with *P0160* (♂, *1952*) (Metangula, April 18, 2016), min 01:01:38–01:02:24; PA, I036: interview with *P0200* (♂, *1970*) (Nkholongue, August 4, 2012).
21 PA, I036: interview with *P0200* (♂, *1970*) (Nkholongue, August 4, 2012), min 00:16:06–00:23:52. For the arbitrary nature of recruiting practices by the government, see also: PA, I162: interview with *P0512* (♀, *1967*) (Nkholongue, June 22, 2016), min 00:35:06–00:36:27; PA, I133: interview with *P1473* (♂ ~*1938*), *P1504* (♀) (Limbi, June 1, 2016), min 00:39:44–00:42:22.
22 PA, I057: interview with *P0262* (♀, ~*1940*) (Malango, August 28, 2013), min 01:32:44–01:38:28.
23 The number of attacks that it is claimed to have taken place varies between four and seven. This discrepancy could be partly due to different definitions of the term "attack," but is also attributable to the fact that many villagers did not witness all of the attacks, having left the village after the first attacks. Four attacks were reported by: PA, I033: interview with *P0643* (♂, *1981*) (Nkholongue, June 9, 2012), min 00:04:39–00:12:06; PA, I069: interview with *P0650* (♀, *1939*) (Nkholongue, September 2, 2013), min 00:33:52–00:43:15; PA, I071: interview with *P0191* (♂, *1965*) (Nkholongue, September 4, 2013), min 00:17:28–00:20:15. Five attacks: PA, I052: interview with (♀, *1940*) (Nkholongue, August 26, 2013), min 00:25:23–00:29:21. Six attacks: PA, I067: interview with *P0236* (♂, *1975*) (Nkholongue, September 1, 2013), min 00:09:53–00:16:19. Seven attacks: PA, I078: interview with *P0258* (♂, *1953*) (Nkholongue, September 7, 2013), min 00:36:39–00:37:26.

ison to the War of Independence, we have almost no written evidence that could be balanced with the oral accounts of the war.[24]

Still, at least the sequence of the beginning of the war is more or less clear. The first time Renamo appeared on the local scene was in the course of 1986 when Nkholongue's chief Chingomanje VI and his wife were abducted by Renamo while staying at their maize fields in Mang'ombo (near Malo). The second time was about a week later, probably on October 4, 1986, when a group of about 30 armed Renamo soldiers entered Malango at dusk.[25] On that day, about 30 of Malango's inhabitants were abducted, 12 of which were subsequently shot near the Luchemanje river. After the attack on Malango, which will be discussed in detail below, most people fled to Metangula. Some, however, again returned to the village after some male villagers had received training and guns from the government to act as militia.[26] The information from my interviews suggests, however, that the militia was not capable of defending the village against further attacks.[27] Interviewees indicated that they as a rule ran away when Renamo attacked. And Renamo continued to attack. In another raid, this time on Nkholongue, Renamo's soldiers abducted six inhabitants, one of which died as a consequence of serious injuries that had been inflicted on her by one Renamo fighter.[28]

The general insecurity generated by these attacks had a deep impact on people's lives. People did not dare to sleep in their houses any more, as Renamo usually attacked in the evening hours. Instead, they slept in the reeds along the shores of the lake. Everyday activities such as collecting firewood had suddenly become

---

24 The records of the APGGN seem to be comparatively weak on the war period, and were, in any case, still mostly under "closure period" at the time of my research.
25 The exact date was given by one interviewee, see: PA, I074: interview with *P0160 (♂, 1952)* (Metangula, September 6, 2013), min 00:28:25–00:30:38. The date would fit with the fact that other interviewees stated that the attack happened on a Saturday. See: PA, I058: interview with *P1074 (♀, ~1940)* (Malango, August 28, 2013), min 02:23:41–02:40:28. On the duration between the two incidents, see: PA, I086: interview with *P0375 (♂, 1962)* (Nkholongue, September 9, 2013), min 01:11:01–01:11:33.
26 PA, I144: interview with *P0411 (♂, 1965)* (Nkholongue, June 8, 2016), min 00:07:41–00:09:46.
27 PA, I039: interview with *P0898 (♀, 1960)* (Malango, August 15, 2013), min 00:48:01–00:48:37; PA, I033: interview with *P0643 (♂, 1981)* (Nkholongue, June 9, 2012), min 00:14:32–00:15:17; PA, I055: interview with *P0639 (♀, ~1952)* (Nkholongue, August 27, 2013), min 00:34:24–00:36:40; PA, I040: interview with *P1030 (♀, 1965), P1009 (♀, 1958), P1029 (♂, ~1959)* (Malango, August 16, 2013), min 01:31:44–01:33:36.
28 PA, I068: interview with *P0367 (♂, 1936)* (Nkholongue, September 2, 2013), min 01:08:36–01:12:46; PA, I058: interview with *P1074 (♀, ~1940)* (Malango, August 28, 2013), min 02:23:41–02:40:28; PA, I055: interview with *P0639 (♀, ~1952)* (Nkholongue, August 27, 2013), min 00:25:57–00:39:15.

most dangerous.[29] Most people abandoned the village at some point. Some fled to Malawi.[30] But most went to Metangula. This time, life in Metangula was, however, difficult and many people remained dependent on their fields in the village. One interviewee who was still a child at the time put it like this:

> We always depended on here. Life in Metangula was very difficult. For we had no place to get soap, no place to get food. Therefore, whenever there was a calmer period without this movement of war no war, we came back here.[31]

One interviewee described how they paddled here on canoes, harvested their fields as quickly possible and then rushed back to Metangula.[32] Another described it like stealing from their own fields.[33] The risks that people were taking were considerable. The just-quoted interviewee recalled how they once came from Metangula to Nkholongue in order to fish. They had put out their nets and were playing soccer in the evening hours. At around 5.30 p.m., they heard a shot coming from the area where today Mbuna Bay is (see Map 4 on p. 374). They managed to escape, but Renamo was able to rob most of their belongings. They slept hidden behind big rocks and returned to Metangula the next day.[34] In another attack, the commander of Malango's militia was ambushed and seriously injured by Renamo as he was on his way to the village.[35]

---

29 PA, I033: interview with *P0643 (♂, 1981)* (Nkholongue, June 9, 2012), min 00:04:39–00:12:06; PA, I054: interview with *P0554 (♀, 1949)* (Nkholongue, August 27, 2013), min 00:11:47–00:13:59; PA, I067: interview with *P0236 (♂, 1975)* (Nkholongue, September 1, 2013), min 00:33:52–00:43:15; PA, I055: interview with *P0639 (♀, ~1952)* (Nkholongue, August 27, 2013), min 00:31:01–00:34:24; PA, I078: interview with *P0258 (♂, 1953)* (Nkholongue, September 7, 2013), min 00:33:16–00:35:19; PA, I069: interview with *P0650 (♀, 1939)* (Nkholongue, September 2, 2013), min 00:33:52–00:43:15.
30 PA, I007: interview with *P0298 (♀, ~1922)* (Nkholongue, September 1, 2010), min 01:02:56–01:04:18; PA, I035: interview with *P0743 (♀, ~1930), P0765 (♀, ~1932)* (Nkholongue, July 28, 2012), min 01:11:34–01:17:16.
31 PA, I033: interview with *P0643 (♂, 1981)* (Nkholongue, June 9, 2012), min 00:02:44–00:03:31. See as well: PA, I040: interview with *P1030 (♀, 1965), P1009 (♀, 1958), P1029 (♂, ~1959)* (Malango, August 16, 2013), min 01:17:12–01:17:53; PA, I057: interview with *P0262 (♀, ~1940)* (Malango, August 28, 2013), min 01:45:26–01:45:56; PA, I085: interview with *P0147 (♀, ~1928)* (Nkholongue, September 9, 2013), min 00:27:09–00:28:07; PA, I071: interview with *P0191 (♂, 1965)* (Nkholongue, September 4, 2013), min 00:20:15–00:22:21.
32 PA, I039: interview with *P0898 (♀, 1960)* (Malango, August 15, 2013), min 00:39:34–00:40:10.
33 PA, I046: interview with *P1045 (♀, 1932)* (Malango, August 20, 2013), min 00:39:41–00:40:35.
34 PA, I033: interview with *P0643 (♂, 1981)* (Nkholongue, June 9, 2012), min 00:04:39–00:12:06.
35 PA, I159: interview with *P0242 (♂, 1945)* (Malango, June 20, 2016), min 00:32:36–00:33:30.

The Two Wars in Comparison

It has been claimed that Frelimo reverted to very similar policies as the Portuguese in fighting the counter-insurgency, using the communal villages in a very similar way to how the Portuguese forces had used the *aldeamentos*.[36] However, it seems that the colonial and post-colonial government had quite different priorities. We have already seen in Chapter 7 that the Portuguese state began to follow a strategy that considered the promotion of "rural progress" as more important than the proper military actions. The post-colonial government was guided by different priorities. This is, for example, shown by an internal restricted manual for the communication of the Nkomati accord. It is true that it said that the war against the "bandits" can only be won by a combination of four actions: military, political, diplomatic, and economic. But it left no doubt whatsoever that "[t]he principal, decisive action is the military one."[37] In its guidelines and rhetoric, Frelimo was long convinced that "the armed bandits do not have and will never have a social base."[38]

Around the lakeshore, the post-colonial government seems to have never attempted to pursue any sort of counter-insurgency resettlement effort nor were there any comparable attempts to win "the hearts and minds" of the people. Help for refugees in Metangula was most limited.[39] Furthermore, there was no sud-

---

36 Lubkemann, *Culture in Chaos*, 145; Chichava, "'They Can Kill Us but We Won't Go to the Communal Villages!,'" 120, 127–128; Hanlon, *The Revolution under Fire*, 128–129; Christian Geffray and Mögens Pedersen, "Nampula en guerre," *Politique Africaine*, no. 29 (1988): 30; Cabrita, *The Tortuous Road*, 194. In contrast to these observations, Borges Coelho stated that the arrival of the war led to the decline of Frelimo's villagization scheme in Tete. See: João Paulo Borges Coelho, "State Resettlement Policies in Post-Colonial Rural Mozambique: The Impact of the Communal Village Programme on Tete Province, 1977–1982," *Journal of Southern African Studies* 24, no. 1 (1998): 86–91.
37 APGGN, 1 A: Guião para o trabalho de esclarecimento sobre as conversações entre Moçambique e África do Sul, Restrito (Maputo, October 7, 1984), 3.
38 APGGN, 1 A: Intervenção de sua Excelência o membro do Bureau Político do Comité Central do Partido Frelimo e Dirigente da Província na recepção dos membros do governo por ocasião do fim do ano de 1985, 7.
39 It seems that the system (*calamidade*) was only set up in the course of the war and remained limited in its extent: PA, I033: interview with P0643 (♂, *1981*) (Nkholongue, June 9, 2012), min 00:53:30–00:57:15; PA, I069: interview with P0650 (♀, *1939*) (Nkholongue, September 2, 2013), min 00:44:35–00:46:24; PA, I073: interview with P1012 (♂, *1955*) (Malango, September 5, 2013), min 00:48:03–00:48:45; PA, I067: interview with P0236 (♂, *1975*) (Nkholongue, September 1, 2013), min 00:09:53–00:16:19; PA, I071: interview with P0191 (♂, *1965*) (Nkholongue, September 4, 2013), min 00:20:15–00:22:21.

den rise in income possibilities as during the War of Independence.[40] One interviewee just laughed disparagingly when asked whether they received any support from the government, and his sister-in-law only groaned "those," shaking her head.[41]

Certainly, this lack of help was partly due to the government's limited capacity. This also becomes evident if one considers that the colonial government had paid militias comparatively high salaries. Frelimo did not pay them a salary at all.[42] Still, the evidence leaves no doubt that the post-colonial government indeed pursued quite a different war strategy. This is best demonstrated by the statement of the above-quoted interviewee who, with his friends, was caught by a surprise attack by Renamo while fishing on the beach of Nkholongue. He recalled that a navy boat patrolled the shores in the morning hours after the raid. They called the boat to the shore, told them of the attack, and begged for a ride to Metangula. But despite them being half-naked because Renamo had robbed part of their clothes, the navy soldiers did not take them.[43]

This incident shows not only that people were disappointed with the support they received from the government, but also that the Frelimo government cared much less about keeping civilians away from the enemy than the colonial government had done. While the Portuguese soldiers would have definitely returned the group to Metangula, the post-colonial government pursued a different strategy that imposed less control over the people, but equally offered them less protection. While the colonial government had tried to concentrate the whole population in a few well-defended locations, Frelimo applied a much more decentralized strategy that was barely able to prevent contacts between the population and the rebels.

This strategy was probably due not only to the fact that Frelimo's possibilities were much more limited than those of the Portuguese had been, but also to the fact that Renamo itself locally pursued a very different strategy than Frelimo had during the War of Independence. It is true that there were certain similarities,

---

40 PA, I040: interview with *P1030 (♀, 1965), P1009 (♀, 1958), P1029 (♂, ~1959)* (Malango, August 16, 2013), min 01:17:35–01:17:38.
41 PA, I040: interview with *P1030 (♀, 1965), P1009 (♀, 1958), P1029 (♂, ~1959)* (Malango, August 16, 2013), min 01:18:37–01:18:51. See as well: PA, I145: interview with *P0284 (♂, 1966), P0273 (♀, 1950)* (Metangula, June 9, 2016), min 00:42:33–00:43:00; PA, I054: interview with *P0554 (♀, 1949)* (Nkholongue, August 27, 2013), min 00:52:54–00:53:11; PA, I078: interview with *P0258 (♂, 1953)* (Nkholongue, September 7, 2013), min 00:36:39–00:37:26; PA, I033: interview with *P0643 (♂, 1981)* (Nkholongue, June 9, 2012), min 00:14:32–00:15:46.
42 PA, I105: interview with *P0242 (♂, 1945)* (Malango, April 4, 2016), min 01:35:00–01:35:42.
43 PA, I033: interview with *P0643 (♂, 1981)* (Nkholongue, June 9, 2012), min 00:04:39–00:12:06.

like for example the fact that Renamo had its bases in much the same areas as Frelimo during the previous war. But there is no doubt that, otherwise, their approaches could not have been much different.

We have seen in the previous chapter that Frelimo had tried to mobilize the people politically at the beginning of the War of Independence. Renamo's efforts in this respect were quasi non-existent. If politicization happened, then, it seems it was only after the abduction of people.[44] Or, as one of the survivors of Renamo's fatal attack on Malango put it:

> Nobody came saying, "We are now the group of Renamo," "We have the following program with the following objectives." No, that did not happen. It just came this day when they came to take us.[45]

Furthermore, Renamo's attacks were marked by a very high degree of violence. Even around Tulo, Renamo's local stronghold during the war, I was unable to find people who had not been first forcibly recruited by Renamo.[46] This perfectly fits with the general pattern that has been observed by scholars for most other regions of Mozambique.[47]

However, this does not mean that Renamo did not try to convince people politically once they had been abducted. This is demonstrated by the case of Nkholongue's chief, Chingomanje VI. As he was taken by Renamo while in his fields near Malo, we cannot be entirely sure whether the general assertion by interviewees that he was abducted is indeed correct. We also do not know whether the Renamo soldiers were aware of the fact that they had targeted a chief. In any case, the evidence clearly shows that Renamo was well aware of it later. This is because Chingomanje VI was "re-instated" as a chief at Renamo's base, first at Chilotochi and, later, at Tulo. If we follow my interviewees, he was highly esteemed by Rena-

---

[44] This difference has also been very well analyzed by one of my interviewees: PA, I115: interview with P0160 (♂, 1952) (Metangula, April 18, 2016), min 01:03:06–01:04:23.

[45] PA, I145: interview with P0284 (♂, 1966), P0273 (♀, 1950) (Metangula, June 9, 2016), min 00:22:54–00:23:48. See as well: PA, I083: interview with P1102 (♂, 1932), P1074 (♀, ~1940), P1141 (♂, 1932) (Malango, September 8, 2013), min 01:16:28–01:20:23.

[46] PA, I102: interview with P1509 (♂, 1972), P1510 (♀), P1511 (♀), P1512 (♀) (Tulo, February 22, 2016), min 00:05:03–00:09:20, 00:47:31–00:51:56.

[47] The results of Carrie Manning are especially interesting in this respect, as she shows that even among Renamo's later party cadres a high number was initially recruited against their will. See: Carrie Manning, "Constructing Opposition in Mozambique: Renamo as Political Party," *Journal of Southern African Studies* 24, no. 1 (1998): 161–89; Jessica Schafer, *Soldiers at Peace: Veterans and Society after the Civil War in Mozambique* (New York: Palgrave Macmillan, 2007), 58; William Minter, "Inside Renamo as Described by Ex-Participants," *Transformation*, no. 10 (1989): 5.

mo for his alleged spiritual powers. As such, he performed ritual ceremonies for the fighters and, according to one interviewee, also counseled them on military questions as he was said to have been capable of foreseeing the enemies' movements.[48] To sum up, Chingomanje VI served Renamo as a kind of personified demonstration of their political aim to reverse Frelimo's modernization policies.

Renamo's Fatal Attacks

Chingomanje's role with regard to the attacks on Malango and Nkholongue is controversial. While some considered or asserted that he sent the soldiers in order to bring "his people" to him,[49] others denied the possibility that the soldiers might have acted on his command in this respect.[50] One interviewee, an influential person from Metangula, accused him of having sent the soldiers to explicitly kill certain people.[51] Others, though, clearly defended him and said that he did what he could to save people. This included one of the few who spoke of Frelimo in appreciative terms.[52] One who was originally from Messumba but had married into Nkholongue, stated that Chingomanje helped his people, but simultaneously accused Chingomanje's wife of having sent Renamo to kill certain individuals.[53]

In any case, the version of Chingomanje having ordered specific killings seems rather implausible. This becomes clear if one looks at the course of Renamo's fatal attack on the village. According to my interviewees, Renamo gathered people indiscriminately, without regard to their age or sex.[54] It seems that Renamo's (non-)se-

---

[48] PA, I102: interview with *P1509 (♂, 1972), P1510 (♀), P1511 (♀), P1512 (♀)* (Tulo, February 22, 2016), min 00:38:47–00:43:09; PA, I068: interview with *P0367 (♂, 1936)* (Nkholongue, September 2, 2013), min 01:03:55–01:06:59; PA, I086: interview with *P0375 (♂, 1962)* (Nkholongue, September 9, 2013), min 00:39:45–00:40:45; PA, I036: interview with *P0200 (♂, 1970)* (Nkholongue, August 4, 2012), min 00:27:09–00:29:24, 00:34:13–00:40:42; PA, I075: interview with *P1218 (♀, 1930)* (Metangula, September 6, 2013), min 00:55:05–00:58:33.
[49] PA, I033: interview with *P0643 (♂, 1981)* (Nkholongue, June 9, 2012), min 00:21:56–00:23:22; PA, I145: interview with *P0284 (♂, 1966), P0273 (♀, 1950)* (Metangula, June 9, 2016), min 00:33:08–00:33:44; PA, I151: interview with *P1108 (♂, ~1973)* (M'chepa, June 15, 2016), min 00:15:12–00:16:30.
[50] PA, I072: interview with *P0262 (♀, ~1940)* (Malango, September 5, 2013), min 00:29:56–00:33:44; PA, I036: interview with *P0200 (♂, 1970)* (Nkholongue, August 4, 2012), min 00:29:30–00:30:42.
[51] PA, I077: interview with *P1489 (♂)* (Metangula, September 6, 2013), min 00:24:33–00:30:04.
[52] PA, I075: interview with *P1218 (♀, 1930)* (Metangula, September 6, 2013), min 00:55:05–00:58:33; PA, I078: interview with *P0258 (♂, 1953)* (Nkholongue, September 7, 2013), min 00:41:35–00:43:21.
[53] PA, I036: interview with *P0200 (♂, 1970)* (Nkholongue, August 4, 2012), min 00:40:51–00:43:47.
[54] PA, I145: interview with *P0284 (♂, 1966), P0273 (♀, 1950)* (Metangula, June 9, 2016), min 00:55:52–00:57:04; PA, I114: interview with *P1074 (♀, ~1940), P1141 (♂, 1932)* (Malango, April 15,

lection mainly depended on where they lived and what they owned rather than everything else. One has to imagine that it was already dark when Renamo arrived at the village.⁵⁵ One of the survivors of that night stated that most victims came from two specific zones in the village and explained it thus:

> Well, Sengenya was the place where they first arrived. And in the other place they heard the goats bleating. So then they went to Mr. X to the goat shed.⁵⁶

Renamo was not only interested in capturing people but above all food (including animals) and other goods. The people who were captured by Renamo had to carry these goods. This was no different on that night. As already stated, about 30 people including men, women and children were forced to go with Renamo into the forests.⁵⁷

After the Luchemanje river, the soldiers began to separate the captives. The reasoning behind this separation is not entirely clear, and, if we follow statements of survivors, there was no visible selection criteria. In any case, people were told by the soldiers that one group was to proceed to Renamo's base and the other to return to the village.⁵⁸ Meanwhile, the government had received information about Renamo's raid on Malango. One interviewee stated that a man cutting bamboo in the forest had sighted the group and alarmed the government's detachment at Mi-

---

2016), min 01:51:48–01:52:52. See as well: PA, I094: interview with *P0727 (♂, ~1940)* (M'chepa, January 27, 2016), min 01:17:43–01:18:09. One interviewee, however, guessed that her husband might have been killed because they found his Frelimo membership card in their house. She was, though, not in the village during the attack. See: PA, I075: interview with *P1218 (♀, 1930)* (Metangula, September 6, 2013), min 00:31:02–00:34:12, 00:43:04–00:49:20.

55 PA, I145: interview with *P0284 (♂, 1966), P0273 (♀, 1950)* (Metangula, June 9, 2016), min 00:22:54–00:23:48.
56 PA, I145: interview with *P0284 (♂, 1966), P0273 (♀, 1950)* (Metangula, June 9, 2016), min 00:40:18–00:40:27.
57 PA, I145: interview with *P0284 (♂, 1966), P0273 (♀, 1950)* (Metangula, June 9, 2016), min 00:25:53–00:26:22.
58 For the accounts of the survivors, see: PA, I145: interview with *P0284 (♂, 1966), P0273 (♀, 1950)* (Metangula, June 9, 2016), min 00:24:29–00:25:23; PA, I151: interview with *P1108 (♂, ~1973)* (M'chepa, June 15, 2016), min 00:10:33–00:18:40. For other accounts describing the incident, see: PA, I114: interview with *P1074 (♀, ~1940), P1141 (♂, 1932)* (Malango, April 15, 2016), min 01:51:48–01:59:02; PA, I115: interview with *P0160 (♂, 1952)* (Metangula, April 18, 2016), min 02:45:18–02:47:09; PA, I040: interview with *P1030 (♀, 1965), P1009 (♀, 1958), P1029 (♂, ~1959)* (Malango, August 16, 2013), min 01:10:36–01:12:41.

cucué. The government troops pursued the rebels and managed to intercept the one group that was still on its way to the base.⁵⁹

According to my interviewees, the captives from this group were all able to escape. It was the other group on its way back to the village that contained the victims.⁶⁰ One survivor of this group stated that it was shortly after they had heard shots, obviously coming from the fighting between the other group and the government troops, that the rebels began to kill them.⁶¹ At least 12 of Malango's inhabitants perished on that day.⁶² They were not only shot, but their bodies were apparently also mutilated. One interviewee stated that they had difficulties burying them properly.⁶³

Renamo's brutality was equally demonstrated during their attack on Nkholongue when they captured six people (four women, one man, and one baby). Again, we can observe a similar pattern: at some point in the forest, the group was separated. One woman, a niece of Nkholongue's chief in the matrilineal line, was said to be sent back to the village. The exact circumstances of what happened then are not entirely clear. But a rebel is said to have made her jump alive into a fire after they had some sort of argument. She initially survived, but later died of her injuries in Maniamba. Of the five others of this group, the man managed to escape at an unknown point of their journey. The three others (plus the baby) were carried up to Renamo's base at Chilotochi. Two of them (including the baby) managed to escape from Renamo after about a week when they had been sent to rob food from people's fields near Maniamba. The other stayed with Renamo until the end of the war.⁶⁴

---

59 For the interviewee who reported that the man cutting bamboo informed the troops, see: PA, I058: interview with *P1074* (♀, ~1940) (Malango, August 28, 2013), min 02:23:14–02:40:28. For other accounts, see: PA, I115: interview with *P0160* (♂, 1952) (Metangula, April 18, 2016), min 02:45:18–02:49:48; PA, I151: interview with *P1108* (♂, ~1973) (M'chepa, June 15, 2016), min 00:11:49–00:15:08.
60 PA, I145: interview with *P0284* (♂, 1966), *P0273* (♀, 1950) (Metangula, June 9, 2016), min 00:28:06–00:28:44.
61 PA, I145: interview with *P0284* (♂, 1966), *P0273* (♀, 1950) (Metangula, June 9, 2016), min 00:28:54–00:31:07. See as well: PA, I115: interview with *P0160* (♂, 1952) (Metangula, April 18, 2016), min 02:47:10–02:49:48.
62 PA, I145: interview with *P0284* (♂, 1966), *P0273* (♀, 1950) (Metangula, June 9, 2016), min 00:26:10–00:26:22; PA, I058: interview with *P1074* (♀, ~1940) (Malango, August 28, 2013), min 02:23:41–02:40:28.
63 PA, I058: interview with *P1074* (♀, ~1940) (Malango, August 28, 2013), min 02:23:41–02:40:28.
64 PA, I078: interview with *P0258* (♂, 1953) (Nkholongue, September 7, 2013), min 00:33:16–00:35:19; PA, I055: interview with *P0639* (♀, ~1952) (Nkholongue, August 27, 2013), min 00:36:40–00:39:15; PA, I080: interview with *P0641* (♂, 1952) (Nkholongue, September 7, 2013), min 00:05:15–00:07:35, 00:35:30–00:39:04; PA, I036: interview with *P0200* (♂, 1970) (Nkholongue,

These events show that the use of violence by Renamo against the villagers of Nkholongue was indiscriminate as far as the selection of victims is concerned but probably also calculated to demonstrate what could happen to those who opposed the rebels. They also provide an approximate idea of the atmosphere that prevailed at that time around Nkholongue. They allow us to understand that one interviewee, who had lost several family members during the attack on Malango, declined to talk to us about the history as he was understandably still left traumatized by this tragedy.[65] There is little doubt that Renamo's brutal behavior also included a high degree of sexual violence. One woman retold how in one attack her clothes were pulled away by a soldier so that she was naked, and related how she was beaten.[66] The one woman who stayed with Renamo until the end of the war also declined to speak with us on the grounds that she had seen too many sad things and was thus not willing to think about the past.[67]

It is difficult to understand that people, in the light of these events, would still return to the village during the war and rather not just stay in Metangula where Renamo never entered. But the fact that they returned nevertheless clearly suggests that the living conditions in Metangula must have been very difficult. Almost all villagers remembered the Civil War as having definitely been the worse war.[68] One man from M'chepa compared the two wars as follows in MLM's oral history project:

> The colonial war was somewhat normal because they did not kill. They did not have this law [of killing].[69]

August 4, 2012), min 00:05:59–00:16:06; PA, I005: interview with *P0641 (♂, 1952)* (Nkholongue, August 27, 2010), min 01:36:57–01:40:59.
65 This occurred on August 19, 2013, in Metangula, where the person had lived ever since.
66 PA, I052: interview with *(♀, 1940)* (Nkholongue, August 26, 2013), min 00:40:44–00:42:10.
67 She did not live in Nkholongue/Malango at the time of fieldwork, but in a neighboring village.
68 PA, I040: interview with *P1030 (♀, 1965), P1009 (♀, 1958), P1029 (♂, ~1959)* (Malango, August 16, 2013), min 01:18:03–01:18:37; PA, I052: interview with *(♀, 1940)* (Nkholongue, August 26, 2013), min 00:29:21–00:30:09; PA, I042: interview with *P1193 (♀, 1953)* (Malango, August 17, 2013), min 00:50:44–00:50:57; PA, I073: interview with *P1012 (♂, 1955)* (Malango, September 5, 2013), min 01:01:11–01:02:59; PA, I115: interview with *P0160 (♂, 1952)* (Metangula, April 18, 2016), min 01:02:47–01:03:04; PA, I054: interview with *P0554 (♀, 1949)* (Nkholongue, August 27, 2013), min 00:11:47–00:13:54.
69 MLM, 028: interview with A. A., Portuguese translation of the Chinyanja transcript (M'chepa, June 28, 2007). See as well: PA, I115: interview with *P0160 (♂, 1952)* (Metangula, April 18, 2016), min 01:03:06–01:04:23.

9.3 How Renamo Victims Became Renamo Supporters

Maybe one of the greatest surprises in Nkholongue's history is the fact that inhabitants of a village that had suffered several violent attacks by a rebel group became political supporters of this very group. Renamo's local political post-war success is visible in at least three different ways. First, Renamo performed surprisingly well in both the 1994 and the 1999 elections. Second, several men from the region became Renamo members after the war. And, third, it is Renamo's narrative of the war that clearly dominates people's perception of the course and causes of the war. Let us first have a look at the election results.

Mozambique's First Multi-Party Elections of 1994

Renamo's performance in Mozambique's first multi-party elections of 1994 was not only surprising on the local but also the national level. International observers were startled that this rebel group, above all known for its war atrocities, was able to win as much support as it did.[70] In the legislative elections, Renamo won 37.8 percent of the votes and thus not that significantly less than Frelimo with 44.3 percent. Renamo was able to win a majority in five of the countries' 11 provinces. The results were somewhat clearer in the presidential elections, where Mozambique's president Joaquim Chissano defeated Renamo's leader Afonso Dhlakama with 53.3 percent to 33.7 percent, but even here Dhlakama performed better than Chissano in five provinces. Renamo was able to further improve its results in the second elections of 1999 when the party secured 39 percent in the legislative and even 47.7 percent in the presidential elections.

Seen from a continental perspective, Renamo's political post-war performance is quite unique. Renamo performed clearly above average in the post-war elections in comparison to other former rebel movements like the RUF in Sierra Leone or UNITA in Angola.[71] In the 1990s, Renamo even temporarily became the largest opposition party of the whole continent.[72]

The results on the level of Niassa Province are especially interesting. Niassa was the only province that switched sides between the elections. While Frelimo

---

70 Carrie Manning, *The Politics of Peace in Mozambique: Post-Conflict Democratization, 1992–2000* (Westport: Praeger, 2002), 170; Vines, "Renamo's Rise and Decline," 383. The results probably surprised Vines himself. See: Alex Vines, *Renamo: Terrorism in Mozambique* (London: James Currey, 1991), 131–132.
71 Vines, "Renamo's Rise and Decline," 375, 390.
72 Vines, 383.

did better in the 1994 elections, Renamo won the 1999 elections. But on the level of the district of Lago, the situation was again different, with Frelimo winning both elections. If we, however, zoom further in we can see that while Frelimo won the district as a whole the party performed much worse in the predominantly Muslim areas of the district and thus also in Nkholongue's ward. There are no official results available on the village level for the first elections as it was only from 2009 onward that the village had its own polling station. In 1994, the villagers had to go to Meluluca, and in 1999 and 2004, to M'chepa.

	Chissano/ Frelimo	Dhlakama/ Renamo	Others	Blank votes	Invalid votes	Turnout	Voters registered
1994 Pres Meluluca	660 (36.9%)	553 (30.9%)	574 (32.1%)	102 (5.1%)	101 (5.1%)	1,990 (91.5%)	2,174
Country	53.3%	33.7%	13%				
1994 Leg Meluluca	439 (26.8%)	677 (41.3%)	525 (32.0%)	235 (11.8%)	110 (5.5%)	1,986 (91.4%)	2,174
Country	44.3%	37.8%	17.9%				

Table 9: Election results, 1994.

Table 9 shows the results of the 1994 elections of the polling station of Meluluca. A look at these elections results reveals some surprises. Renamo did not only perform unexpectedly well but was even able to beat Frelimo in the legislative elections. The biggest surprise and clearest deviation from national patterns, however, is the considerable success of third parties and their presidential candidates at the cost of a clearly below average Frelimo performance. Frelimo's bad performance in Meluluca was more pronounced in the 1999 elections and even more so if we zoom in to Nkholongue's polling station in M'chepa (see Table 10). Here, Dhlakama was able to win a landslide victory of almost 74 percent of the votes in the presidential elections. How can we explain the outcome of these elections?

	Chissano/ Frelimo	Dhlakama/ Renamo	Others	Blank votes	Invalid votes	Turnout	Voters registered
1999 Pres M'chepa	150 (26.1%)	424 (73.9%)	-	34 (5.5%)	11 (1.8%)	619 (72.6%)	853
1999 Leg M'chepa	116 (24.0%)	301 (62.2%)	67 (13.8%)	72 (12.1%)	39 (6.6%)	595 (69.8%)	853

Table 10: Election results, 1999.

If the 1994 elections showed anything, it was probably how unpopular Frelimo was in the region. The discrepancy between the presidential and legislative elections can probably be explained by three interrelated phenomena: first, we can ponder whether some people did not understand properly the aim and objective of the legislative elections or were pretty ignorant about them. This is somewhat supported by the relative high number of blank votes. Second, we can guess that the splitting of the vote was a deliberate strategy of some voters to ensure the continuation of the peace process.[73] Third, and probably most importantly, we can suppose that the popularity of the parties and their leaders differed. The information from my interviews suggests that Chissano was more popular than his party because he was credited with having ended the problems in the supply of goods such as salt and clothing, and with ending the war.[74] The results also suggest that Renamo's attraction was initially indeed somewhat limited, as it could only partly build on Frelimo's unpopularity, with such a high percentage of votes going to third parties. These votes were also not centered on one party, but rather distributed over many.

Renamo's Supporters

Still, in light of the war events just described, the question arises as to how Renamo could attract so much support in the 1994 elections and even more in the 1999 elections. Of course, one could consider that it was not Nkholongue's population who voted for Renamo but those of neighboring villages who voted at the same polling station. However, Renamo's local post-war success is not only suggested by the official results of the elections, but also very much supported by the statements of different interviewees. To make it clear: some of my interviewees categorically ruled out the possibility of ever voting for Renamo, saying that they could never

---

[73] Vines claimed that this happened in various parts of the country, but without providing evidence. See: Vines, 382.

[74] PA, I076: interview with *P1449* (♂, *~1948*) (Metangula, September 6, 2013), min 00:27:52–00:30:52; PA, I084: interview with *P1451* (♂, *1949*) (Nkholongue, September 9, 2013), min 00:40:12–00:43:02; PA, I118: interview with *P1218* (♀, *1930*) (Malango, April 21, 2016), min 01:34:49–01:35:30; PA, I124: interview with *P0376* (♂, *1968*) (Nkholongue, April 26, 2016), min 01:12:08–01:13:28; PA, I083: interview with *P1102* (♂, *1932*), *P1074* (♀, *~1940*), *P1141* (♂, *1932*) (Malango, September 8, 2013), min 01:20:23–01:22:03; PA, I161: interview with *P0160* (♂, *1952*) (Metangula, June 22, 2016), min 00:29:02–00:31:09. The fact that Chissano was more popular than Frelimo is also reflected in the countrywide results of the 1994 elections. This outcome was also anticipated by international media shortly before the elections. See: Bill Keller, "Mozambique Voting Today in First Free Election," The New York Times, October 27, 1994, accessed January 4, 2019, https://www.nytimes.com/1994/10/27/world/mozambique-voting-today-in-first-free-election.html.

vote for a group that had caused them that much suffering.[75] But others were less clear in this respect. One interviewee explicitly stated that a thing that is bad for somebody can be good for somebody else.[76] Some thought out loud that, maybe, those who had lost no direct relatives may have voted for Renamo.[77] While some, and these are the most interesting cases for the inquiry here in question, admitted their open support for Renamo. One of them had even been a survivor of Renamo's fatal attack on Malango. He was, however, not in the group that was sent back to the village and contained the victims, but in the other that was intercepted by the government troops.[78]

The interesting thing is that all Renamo supporters who I interviewed claimed that they only became supporters of the party after the war. The two villagers, who openly admitted their Renamo membership, claimed that they only joined Renamo in 1992/1993.[79] One of them, who had been in Malawi during the war, described his integration into Renamo like this:

> Then, in 1993, I came [back] here. [...] Now, it was when these gatherings of Renamo started that I finally began to realize: "aha, they were fighting for our liberty." Because for much of time here we did not live well with Frelimo. They prohibited the chief and the children's ceremony, this *jando*.[80]

Similarly, other interviewees who identified as Renamo supporters explained that they had not known what Renamo had actually been fighting for.[81] Even Renamo's district delegate at time of my fieldwork, living in the neighboring village of M'che-

---

75 PA, I052: interview with (♀, 1940) (Nkholongue, August 26, 2013), min 00:42:10–00:44:02. See as well: PA, I118: interview with *P1218* (♀, 1930) (Malango, April 21, 2016), min 01:57:40–02:00:22.
76 PA, I062: interview with *P0713* (♂, 1944) (Nkholongue, August 30, 2013), min 00:55:55–00:57:33.
77 PA, I080: interview with *P0641* (♂, 1952) (Nkholongue, September 7, 2013), min 00:50:45–00:53:14; PA, I118: interview with *P1218* (♀, 1930) (Malango, April 21, 2016), min 01:58:07–01:58:19; PA, I055: interview with *P0639* (♀, ~1952) (Nkholongue, August 27, 2013), min 00:41:17–00:42:59. Even a Renamo supporter indicated this: PA, I141: interview with *P0375* (♂, 1962) (Nkholongue, June 6, 2016), min 01:08:02–01:08:26.
78 PA, I151: interview with *P1108* (♂, ~1973) (M'chepa, June 15, 2016), min 00:10:33–00:20:37.
79 PA, I141: interview with *P0375* (♂, 1962) (Nkholongue, June 6, 2016), min 00:33:02–00:34:38; PA, I151: interview with *P1108* (♂, ~1973) (M'chepa, June 15, 2016), 00:18:40–00:18:53.
80 PA, I141: interview with *P0375* (♂, 1962) (Nkholongue, June 6, 2016), min 00:33:02–00:34:38. See as well his statement in the 2013 interview, when he did not yet reveal his membership but explained the population's support in very similar terms: PA, I086: interview with *P0375* (♂, 1962) (Nkholongue, September 9, 2013), min 00:35:31–00:36:46.
81 PA, I083: interview with *P1102* (♂, 1932), *P1074* (♀, ~1940), *P1141* (♂, 1932) (Malango, September 8, 2013), min 01:15:06–01:20:23; PA, I082: interview with *P1141* (♂, 1932) (Malango, September 8, 2013), min 00:42:18–00:48:37.

pa, only joined Renamo in 1993.⁸² When asked if he had not thought of joining Renamo during the war, he replied as follows:

> I didn't think that way because I actually didn't know what the motive, the objective of the war was.⁸³

Interestingly, another Renamo sympathizer argued not only that they did not know what Renamo was fighting for during the war, but also that Renamo may not have known how the people of Nkholongue and Malango were feeling about Frelimo.⁸⁴ She thus attempted to explain the indiscriminate violence Renamo had inflicted on them. In doing so, she perfectly reflected what Stathis Kalyvas has called the "identification problem," the "inability to tell friend from enemy" in irregular wars.⁸⁵ Certainly, such statements about lack of knowledge and involvement could also be interpreted as a deliberate (retrospective) strategy of evading responsibility.⁸⁶ However, I think that they were genuine, not only because they were generally consistent with the narratives presented as a whole but also given the fact that many who made them could just as easily have concealed their post-war allegiance to Renamo, especially since there seemed to be little objective advantage to being an overt Renamo supporter at the time of my fieldwork.

The Preponderance of Renamo's Version of History

All the evidence points to the fact that Renamo locally ran a quite successful election campaign that obviously perfectly resonated with people's grievances about Frelimo's post-colonial policies.⁸⁷ This success did not always necessarily translate into political support but is perfectly demonstrated by the fact that Renamo was

---

82 He had previously been a member of Frelimo. Furthermore, he had worked in a *loja de povo* ('people's shop') in Lichinga and, later, for the parastatal trading company Agricom. See: PA, I081: interview with *P1450 (♂, 1961)* (M'chepa, September 8, 2013), min 00:11:53–00:13:19, 00:40:49–00:42:55.
83 PA, I081: interview with *P1450 (♂, 1961)* (M'chepa, September 8, 2013), min 00:15:16–00:15:25.
84 PA, I083: interview with *P1102 (♂, 1932), P1074 (♀, ~1940), P1141 (♂, 1932)* (Malango, September 8, 2013), min 01:16:28–01:18:20.
85 Kalyvas, *The Logic of Violence in Civil War*, 89–91.
86 Similar statements about lack of knowledge and involvement have been gathered by other scholars. See for example: Sheldon, *Pounders of Grain*, 196.
87 See especially: PA, I144: interview with *P0411 (♂, 1965)* (Nkholongue, June 8, 2016), min 00:25:07–00:28:54; PA, I068: interview with *P0367 (♂, 1936)* (Nkholongue, September 2, 2013), min 01:18:37–01:23:10; PA, I072: interview with *P0262 (♀, ~1940)* (Malango, September 5, 2013), min 00:35:55–00:43:21.

most successful in spreading its version of history. Thus, my interviewees were pretty unequivocal in explaining the causes of the Civil War as a consequence of inner conflicts, as a split within Frelimo, or as some put it: "Renamo was born from Frelimo."[88] This is exactly what Renamo's propaganda was all about after the war.[89] Renamo's success in steering people's perception of the cause of the war is even more astonishing if one considers how much energy Frelimo had formerly put into their version of depicting Renamo as an externally driven terrorist movement. One interviewee answered my question of whether they did not learn Frelimo's external version at school by saying, "we learned it, but we forgot it."[90] Many interviewees credited Renamo or Dhlakama with having ended Frelimo's unpopular policies and having brought democracy to the country,[91] another of Renamo's often-made claims.[92]

Who are the people who have supported Renamo on the one and Frelimo on the other? There is no clear pattern recognizable. Equally, we cannot see too many ideological continuities. Rather, the evidence points to the fact that many people have adapted to new situations quite undogmatically and nominal membership does also not mean that people necessarily really identify with their party. The commander of Malango's militias during the Civil War was a former GE. Later, he even served as a village secretary for Frelimo.[93] One of two Renamo members who joined the party shortly after the war had been the head of Frelimo's youth

---

[88] PA, I115: interview with *P0160* (♂, *1952*) (Metangula, April 18, 2016), min 02:14:10–02:17:32; PA, I158: interview with *P0764* (♂, *1962*) (Nkholongue, June 20, 2016), min 00:45:08–00:46:15; PA, I037: interview with *P0855* (♂, *1954*) (Malango, August 14, 2013), min 01:04:36–01:06:06; PA, I067: interview with *P0236* (♂, *1975*) (Nkholongue, September 1, 2013), min 00:24:09–00:25:18; PA, I094: interview with *P0727* (♂, *~1940*) (M'chepa, January 27, 2016), min 01:08:02–01:09:25; PA, I113: interview with *P0367* (♂, *1936*) (Nkholongue, April 13, 2016), min 01:01:13–01:03:44. Even Frelimo supporters advocated for this theory. See: PA, I064: interview with *P1447* (♂, *1969*) (M'chepa, August 31, 2013), min 00:18:57–00:22:29. The story told very much resembled that heard by Juergensen in Angónia (Tete). See: Juergensen, "Peasants on the Periphery," 299.
[89] Manning, *The Politics of Peace in Mozambique*, 142.
[90] PA, I158: interview with *P0764* (♂, *1962*) (Nkholongue, June 20, 2016), min 00:46:23–00:00:46:50.
[91] PA, I033: interview with *P0643* (♂, *1981*) (Nkholongue, June 9, 2012), min 01:59:14–02:00:31; PA, I151: interview with *P1108* (♂, *~1973*) (M'chepa, June 15, 2016), 00:19:42–00:20:36; PA, I145: interview with *P0284* (♂, *1966*), *P0273* (♀, *1950*) (Metangula, June 9, 2016), min 00:44:44–00:45:43; PA, I071: interview with *P0191* (♂, *1965*) (Nkholongue, September 4, 2013), min 00:28:27–00:32:42; PA, I094: interview with *P0727* (♂, *~1940*) (M'chepa, January 27, 2016), min 01:02:35–01:02:42; PA, I127: interview with *P1468* (♂), *P1469* (♂), *P1470* (♂), *P1471* (♀) (Malo, May 2, 2016), min 02:00:05–02:01:06; PA, I160: interview with *P0727* (♂, *~1940*) (M'chepa, June 22, 2016), min 00:07:59–00:08:41.
[92] Manning, *The Politics of Peace in Mozambique*, 142, 209.
[93] PA, I105: interview with *P0242* (♂, *1945*) (Malango, April 4, 2016), min 01:30:08–01:35:00.

movement in the village after the war.⁹⁴ He explained his later membership in Renamo not only with Frelimo's unpopular socialist policies but also with the fact that the police had put him in jail for about a week as he had been caught smuggling.⁹⁵ His brother was a Frelimo party member at the time of fieldwork, flying Frelimo's flag. But he, too, was in fact very critical of Frelimo.⁹⁶ The other Renamo member claimed that he joined Renamo above all because the government did not help his family with the burial of his brother who had been conscripted by the government and killed in fighting.⁹⁷

It can certainly be assumed that Nkholongue's chief played some role in the post-war success of Renamo in the village. For he returned to the village after the war, and, obviously, remained a member of Renamo until his death from cholera in 1999.⁹⁸ His concrete role in the village and his influence on village politics after the war remains unclear. Statements from the interviews suggest that he indeed enjoyed some sort of political respect in the 1990s and that many did not blame him for his role during the war. We can assume in this regard that people's own awareness of their limited agency also facilitated local reconciliation after the war, at least to some degree.

In any case, it seems quite evident that Renamo's post-war success was owed in large part to the great lack of credibility that Frelimo had among Nkholongue's population as a consequence of its previous behavior that has been discussed in Chapters 7 and 8. This lack of credibility almost certainly also explains why Renamo was locally so successful in spreading its version of the history of the Civil War in spite of Frelimo's predominant position in national media and public discourse.

9.4 Conclusion

The aim of this chapter was to explore the question of why parts of Nkholongue's government-alienated population did not become Renamo supporters from the outset, but did so only after the war, when such a move seemed rather irrational at first glance. It has also examined the question of why Renamo's brutal war past did not affect its political appeal in the post-war period.

Although the results are not conclusive, some observations can be made. As for the first question, we have seen that Renamo locally did not appear very much like

---

94 PA, I141: interview with *P0375* (♂, *1962*) (Nkholongue, June 6, 2016), min 00:35:25–00:37:56.
95 PA, I141: interview with *P0375* (♂, *1962*) (Nkholongue, June 6, 2016), min 00:51:04–00:56:05.
96 PA, I124: interview with *P0376* (♂, *1968*) (Nkholongue, April 26, 2016).
97 PA, I151: interview with *P1108* (♂, *~1973*) (M'chepa, June 15, 2016), min 00:00:20–00:06:11.
98 I saw his Renamo membership card in 2010, which was then still kept by one of his relatives.

a political actor during the war. Most people did not know what Renamo was fighting for. Its recruitment practices totally differed from those Frelimo had used at the beginning of the War of Independence. As for the second question, I have argued that Renamo's post-war success must probably be explained with Frelimo's local unpopularity, its lack of credibility, and the lack of support that the government provided to people during the war. Conscription might also have played a role. In any case, my findings show that Renamo was locally pretty successful in blaming Frelimo (and above all Samora Machel) for the war.

My findings, even if not conclusive, can contribute to previous research on the war in at least four ways. First, they show that the revisionists' claim that Renamo gained a social base during the war cannot be transferred to every setting in (northern) Mozambique where people resented Frelimo, and also not to every setting where Renamo achieved political successes after the war. Second, and related to this first point, they show that in the case of the lakeshore area, Renamo made little attempt at political mobilization during the war. Chingomanje may have been re-instated as chief in Renamo's camp during the war, but he had also been forcibly recruited in the first place. Broad political mobilization began only after the war had ended. Third, my research has emphasized that the effects of state conscription on people's perceptions has so far most likely been underestimated. Finally, the various changes in political affiliation among individual villagers over the course of the two wars and beyond point to what might appear to be considerable ideological flexibility. In the end, however, they probably show above all that local perspectives had little to do with the dogmas and ideas being discussed among the national and international intelligentsia.

10 Tourism and the Return of Tradition and Custom: How to Find the Chief?

10.1 The Re-Emergence of the Customary Institutions

Daniel Immerwahr has recently highlighted the long-standing struggle between "thinking small" and "thinking big" in development theory and practice.[1] In Chapter 6, I have already discussed a similar struggle of ideologies in relation to the "agrarian question" and the disputed role of the "small peasantry" in agricultural development. While ideas of "thinking small" had been around for a long time, it was in the 1980s and 1990s that such ideas gained particular prominence in development thinking in sub-Saharan Africa. Previously, the focus of various international actors on "community development" had still been overshadowed by the intentions of the leaders of newly independent Africa to realize development from above in a "high-modernist" state fashion.[2] A variety of causes and pressures with different ideological backgrounds were responsible for the rise of "thinking smaller." These included the demise of political credibility of African leaders, the economic failure of various large-scale transformation projects, criticism of authoritarianism and, not least, the neo-liberal turn in international politics, all of which made concepts such as "decentralization" and "by-passing the state" widely acceptable across the political spectrum. Tobias Haller has called this an "ideological win-win situation—efficiency and the moral legitimacy of local participation, acting itself as an Anti-Politics Machine."[3]

The success of "thinking small" has resulted in the fact that "community participation" has become a commonplace in development theory and practice.[4] Interestingly, the call for greater "community participation" went hand in hand with a reiteration of what Tania Murray Li has called the "communal fix."[5] As in colonial

---

[1] Daniel Immerwahr, *Thinking Small: The United States and the Lure of Community Development* (Cambridge: Harvard University Press, 2015).
[2] On "high-modernism," see: Scott, *Seeing like a State*, 4–6.
[3] Tobias Haller, "The Different Meanings of Land in the Age of Neoliberalism: Theoretical Reflections on Commons and Resilience Grabbing from a Social Anthropological Perspective," *Land* 8, no. 7 (2019): 15.
[4] One that has arguably survived the recent revival of the development state. On the resurgence of the development state since the early 2000s, see for example: Didier Péclard, Antoine Kernen, and Guive Khan-Mohammad, "États d'émergence: Le gouvernement de la croissance et du développement en Afrique," *Critique internationale*, no. 89 (2020): 9–27.
[5] Li, "Indigeneity, Capitalism, and the Management of Dispossession."

times, many Africans were relegated to the sphere of collectivity, with their political channels seen in customary institutions.⁶ In many countries of Africa, it was the so-called "traditional authorities" who benefited from the increasing demand for grassroots participation in development schemes.⁷ The "communal fix" was thus also a "(neo-)traditional fix."

Because of its political significance and its multi-layered temporalities, the re-emergence of customary institutions has received considerable scholarly attention.⁸ This is especially true in the case of Mozambique as the changes that have taken place in much of sub-Saharan Africa since the 1990s have been particularly pronounced here. This is a consequence of Frelimo's previous very pronounced top-down approach to development and its very radical anti-traditional rhetoric after independence.

Scholarly opinions on how to assess the resurgence of the customary have varied widely but are probably best placed between two opposing ideal-type interpretations, one communitarian and one modernist: while the first has viewed customary institutions such as chiefs as a kind of timeless grassroots institutions who truly speak for their "communities," the second has branded them as "despots" who have their own interests at heart above all else. And while the first has celebrated the rise of legal pluralism as an opportunity to protect the rights of the "vulnerable" and "indigenous," the second has condemned this as a return or continuation of the legal dualism of colonial times.⁹

---

6 For the renewed importance of customary institutions, see: Peter Geschiere, "Epilogue: 'Seeing Like a State' in Africa – High Modernism, Legibility and Community," *African Studies* 66, no. 1 (2007): 130.
7 On this point in relation to Mozambique, see: Lars Buur and Helene Maria Kyed, "Introduction: Traditional Authority and Democratization in Africa," in *State Recognition and Democratization in Sub-Saharan Africa*, ed. Lars Buur and Helene Maria Kyed (New York: Palgrave Macmillan, 2007), 7. On this argument on a more general level, see: Geschiere, "Epilogue: 'Seeing Like a State' in Africa."
8 Juan Obarrio, *The Spirit of the Laws in Mozambique* (Chicago: University of Chicago Press, 2014); Lars Buur and Helene Maria Kyed, "Traditional Authority in Mozambique: The Legible Space between State and Community," in *State Recognition and Democratization in Sub-Saharan Africa*, ed. Lars Buur and Helene Maria Kyed (New York: Palgrave Macmillan, 2007), 105–27; Victor Igreja and Limore Racin, "The Politics of Spirits, Justice, and Social Transformation in Mozambique," in *Spirits in Politics: Uncertainties of Power and Healing in African Societies*, ed. Barbara Meier and Arne S. Steinforth (Frankfurt: Campus, 2013), 181–204.
9 For an overview of the spectrum of positions on this question, see: Olaf Zenker and Markus Virgil Hoehne, "Processing the Paradox: When the State Has to Deal with Customary Law," in *The State and the Paradox of Customary Law in Africa*, ed. Olaf Zenker and Markus Virgil Hoehne (Abingdon: Routledge, 2018), 9–14; Buur and Kyed, "Traditional Authority and Democratization in Africa," 4–12. A prominent example of the despot position is: Mahmood Mamdani, *Citizen and Subject: Contemporary Africa and the Legacy of Late Colonialism* (Princeton: Princeton University Press, 1996).

In this chapter, I join other scholars who have criticized the notion of traditional institutions as apolitical and timeless protectors of their homogeneous communities. However, I must also say that I find the term "despot" similarly inapplicable to the specific case of Nkholongue. On a personal note, I have to say that I had a high opinion of Chingomanje VIII. I think he was actually more concerned about social balance than some of the accusations leveled against him and cited in this chapter might suggest. The aim of this chapter is thus also not blame anyone personally for his possible "wrongdoing," but rather to highlight the myriad discrepancies and interactions between external conceptualizations and local realities.

Despite earlier criticisms, ideas of communitarian unity are still highly influential, chiefly among development professionals. Nkholongue's history vividly illustrates the unsuitability of these ideas. From the slave trade to the Civil War, we have come across numerous examples in which people from the same village were not on the same side but experienced history from very different perspectives. In this chapter, I will further elaborate on this heterogeneity. To this end, I will focus on the interplay of the resurgence of the customary institutions and the arrival of tourism projects in Nkholongue since the early 2000s. As I mentioned at the beginning of this book, I initially came to Nkholongue to work in a tourism project called Mbuna Bay. Mbuna Bay, however, was not the only tourism project in Nkholongue: over the past two decades, no less than seven tourism-related projects have either been planned or realized there.

The analysis of the arrival of these projects is of interest for the local history of the resurgence of the customary institutions and the rise of the concept of "community participation" for two reasons. First, all projects had to deal with the "community" and the customary institutions because of the Mozambican Land Law of 1997. This law introduced the concept of "community" into Mozambican legislation. It gave "local communities" a say in land requests and allowed them to use "customary norms and practices" to address land issues. It was thus also one of the first Mozambican laws to re-recognize customary laws. Second, the two largest of the tourism projects have pursued goals of fair tourism or ecotourism. "Community development" has therefore been an important aspect of their concepts.

In the chapter, I will make two main arguments. First, I will show that Nkholongue's population could not rely on a well-established system of political mechanisms to manage the challenges posed to Nkholongue by the changes in the Mozambican law and the numerous tourism projects. Rather, these challenges required new approaches that had to be negotiated and that have so far proven to be quite flexible and improvised. In this regard, my findings confirm other research that has shown that the state's recognition of the customary was hardly a re-recognition of what had already existed.[10] But while previous research has focused on the state's role in recognizing customary institutions and "community authorities," my own analysis is extended by asking how investors and initiators of the various tourism projects approached these authorities. This is interesting for two reasons. First, because some of these projects negotiated with chiefs before they were officially recognized by the government, and second, because the Mozambican law makes no distinction between chiefs and village secretaries. They are nominally on the same hierarchical level and have exactly the same duties and rights. It will be argued that external actors, through their usually unconscious "decision" to prefer either chief or secretary as a negotiating partner, had more influence on local power relations than they may have realized. This is particularly interesting since, as will be shown, many of Nkholongue's chiefs were anything but as "socially embedded" in their "community" as is often claimed for chiefs of Africa.[11]

The second point concerns the fact that what has been conceptualized as a "community" by both Mozambican legislation and external actors barely corresponds to the reality of such a "community." It will be shown that the village of Nkholongue is hardly as homogeneous a group as it is imagined by such concepts. Thus, I will try to show how both the law and tourism projects have not only contributed to re-configuring local notions of "community," but in some instances have also tended to produce tensions within what they or local actors have conceptualized as the "community."

If this chapter is critical of certain outcomes this is by no means to be interpreted as a blanket criticism of the land reform or of concepts such as "fair tourism" or "community participation." Of course, there is a broad and diverse literature that is highly critical of the sincerity of development agendas in general by assuming that hidden agendas are at work everywhere. This is certainly justified as there are many "sound reasons to be skeptical of some of the claims made in the name of [social] improvement."[12] Especially when it comes to a scheme as controversial as Mosagrius (more on this below), there is every reason to expect that "development" will primarily serve to secure the control of a particular class over other people and territory. There are certainly also many contradictions when it comes to combining ecology with tourism.[13] However, I agree with Tania Li's obser-

---

10 Buur and Kyed, "Traditional Authority in Mozambique."
11 See for example: Baldwin, *The Paradox of Traditional Chiefs in Democratic Africa*, 10.
12 Tania Murray Li, *The Will to Improve: Governmentality, Development, and the Practice of Politics* (Durham: Duke University Press, 2007), 9.
13 See for example: João Afonso Baptista, *The Good Holiday: Development, Tourism and the Politics of Benevolence in Mozambique* (New York: Berghahn, 2017).

vation that "the rush to identify hidden motives of profit or domination narrows analysis unnecessarily, making much of what happens in the name of improvement obscure."[14] Undoubtedly, there are also many instances of good faith that cannot be explained in terms of hidden agendas or motives. Therefore, this chapter, similar to Chapter 6 with regard to the "small peasant approach," hopes to show how fruitful it can be to consider the historical complexities on the ground in order to improve development practice.

Furthermore, this chapter should also be understood as a self-critical appraisal, which in many ways also concerns the project from which this book emerged. Undoubtedly, some of the processes analyzed in this chapter also apply to my study of Nkholongue's history, as this has also been drawn into the questions and struggles about what the "community" of Nkholongue actually is (or was) and who had the authority to speak about its history. Thus, my fieldwork also interacted with "community" conceptualizations.

The discussion of this chapter is mainly related to the Mozambican context, but links to analyses from elsewhere, with fair tourism and the question of community participation in land issues and land legislation being relevant across the continent and beyond. The chapter attempts to be a historically informed addition to the existing literature that has highlighted the existence of local inequalities, conflicts, and contestations behind the grassroots rhetoric of the customary.[15]

From a more regional perspective, this chapter follows to some extent in the footsteps of the anthropologist Elísio Jossias, who has explored issues of land tenure on the lakeshore further north in a similar interweaving of questions regarding the re-recognition of "traditional authorities," the new land law, and the arrival of a fair tourism project, in this case the award-winning Nkwichi Lodge.[16] In his study, however, Jossias was more concerned with the local notion of *dono de terra* ('landowner') than with how such local notions of and struggles over land

---

14 Li, *The Will to Improve*, 9.
15 Examples of this literature are: Jean-Philippe Platteau, "The Evolutionary Theory of Land Rights as Applied to Sub-Saharan Africa: A Critical Assessment," *Development and Change* 27, no. 1 (1996): 29–86; Christian Lund, *Local Politics and the Dynamics of Property in Africa* (Cambridge: Cambridge University Press, 2008); Richard Kuba and Carola Lentz, eds., *Land and the Politics of Belonging in West Africa* (Leiden: Brill, 2006); Sonja Vermeulen and Lorenzo Cotula, "Over the Heads of Local People: Consultation, Consent, and Recompense in Large-Scale Land Deals for Biofuels Projects in Africa," *The Journal of Peasant Studies* 37, no. 4 (2010): 899–916; Li, "Indigeneity, Capitalism, and the Management of Dispossession."
16 Jossias, "'O primeiro a chegar é o dono da terra'"; Elísio Jossias, "Renegociar a comunidade e disputar territórios: Posse e propriedade nas terras comunitárias na região do Lago Niassa," *Etnográfica* 26, no. 1 (2022): 5–27.

ownership have guided land consultation or been influenced by the new land law and the arrival of tourism companies.

Apart from this introduction, the chapter is divided into three parts. First, a brief look at the re-emergence of the customary in Mozambican legislation since the 1990s will be presented. The focus will be on the Mozambican Land Law of 1997 and the official re-recognition of the "traditional authorities" through Decree n.º 15/2000. In a second part, I will give an overview of the various tourism projects that have been planned or realized in Nkholongue since the early 2000s. The third and last part will then deal with the interactions of these projects with the population of Nkholongue and Malango.

10.2 Mozambican Legislation and the Customary

The re-emergence of the customary in Mozambican legislation since the 1990s must be understood in the context of Mozambique's transition from a socialist mono-party command economy to a capitalist-liberal multi-party democracy. Most of the laws that formed the legal basis for this transition were drafted under the auspices of the donors, the World Bank and the IMF. However, Frelimo was not content to simply accept the international recommendations and demands, but also strongly adapted these laws to its own political needs.

In the following, two sets of legal reforms shall be briefly discussed, as understanding them facilitates the analysis of the sequence of events that occurred when the first private investors came to Nkholongue in the 2000s. These are the Mozambican Land Law of 1997 and the recognition of the "traditional authorities" by Decree n.º 15/2000.

The Mozambican Land Law Reform of 1997

After independence, Frelimo nationalized all land. This certainly reflected Frelimo's socialist credentials but also the general importance of the land question in former settler colonies. Access to land was granted through a DUAT, which is the acronym for "Direito do Uso e Aproveitamento da Terra" ("Right of Use and Utilization of Land").[17]

---

[17] The first law regulating access to land in post-independence Mozambique was Law n.º 6/79. See: "Lei n.º 6/79 de 3 de Julho: Lei de Terras," *Boletim da República (I Série)*, no. 76 (July 3, 1979): 223–28.

The Mozambican Land Law Reform of 1997 did not abolish state ownership of land, but it did change the handling of DUATs significantly. From the perspective of Mozambique's rural population, four of these changes were crucial: first, unlike the previous law, the government now legally recognized the occupation of land by "local communities" and other good faith occupants, even if they had not formally acquired a DUAT (Article 12). Second, it guaranteed "local communities" a say in any future application for a DUAT, as each application was to be preceded by a consultation with the affected communities (Article 13). Third, the law now allowed joint title holding for "communities" as a collective group (Article 10). Last but not least, the new law granted "local communities" the right to use "customary norms and practices" to exercise the competences now conferred on them by the law (Article 24).[18]

Most observers have hailed the Mozambican Land Law of 1997 as a "progressive and innovative" improvement over the previous situation.[19] The political scientist Scott Kloeck-Jenson, who followed the reform process closely, called it "one of the most promising legal frameworks in sub-Saharan Africa with respect to strengthening smallholder land tenure security."[20] At last, the previously voiceless rural dwellers of Mozambique were given a stake in an issue that so crucially affected their livelihoods. Thus, most observers saw problems with the proper imple-

---

18 "Lei n.° 19/97 de 1 de Outubro: Lei de Terras," *Boletim da República (I Série)*, no. 40, 3° Suplemento (October 7, 1997).
19 The reform has also been celebrated by NGOs and donors as the most democratic and inclusive political process ever concluded in Mozambique. For positive appraisals, see: Robin L. Nielsen, Christopher Tanner, and Anna Knox, "Focus on Land in Africa: Mozambique's Innovative Land Law," January 2011, accessed April 20, 2019, http://www.focusonland.com/download/538ddd5cb3283/; Joseph Hanlon, *The Land Debate in Mozambique: Will Foreign Investors, the Urban Elite, Advanced Peasants or Family Farmers Drive Rural Development*, Research Paper Commissioned by Oxfam GB, Regional Management Center for Southern Africa (London, 2002); Christopher Tanner, "Law-Making in an African Context: The 1997 Mozambican Land Law," FAO Legal Papers Online, March 2002, accessed May 7, 2019, http://www.fao.org/fileadmin/user_upload/legal/docs/lpo26.pdf; Lídia Cabral and Simon Norfolk, "Inclusive Land Governance in Mozambique: Good Law, Bad Politics?," IDS Working Paper, no. 478 (Brighton, 2016), 44, accessed April 5, 2019, https://opendocs.ids.ac.uk/opendocs/bitstream/handle/123456789/12187/Wp478.pdf?sequence=1&isAllowed=y;
Aili Mari Tripp et al., *African Women's Movements: Transforming Political Landscapes* (Cambridge: Cambridge University Press, 2009), 134–136; Simon Hull, Kehinde Babalola, and Jennifer Whittal, "Theories of Land Reform and Their Impact on Land Reform Success in Southern Africa," *Land* 8, no. 11 (2019): 172.
20 Scott Kloeck-Jenson, "Locating the Community: Administration of Natural Resources in Mozambique," Land Tenure Center Working Paper, no. 32 (Madison, February 2000), 7. Scott Kloeck-Jenson was the leader of the Land Tenure Center programme in Mozambique until he and his family died tragically in a car accident in 1999.

mentation and enforcement of the law rather than with the law itself. Only a minority was less optimistic, warning that the law effectively meant a return to the legal dualism of colonial times and pointing to the danger of simplifying and romanticizing what the law called "local community."[21] This last concern was also shared by other scholars who were more sympathetic to the law.[22] For the new land law remained surprisingly vague on the question of what a "local community" actually is. It merely defined it as,

> a grouping of families and individuals, living in a territorial area that is at the level of a locality or smaller, which seeks to safeguard their common interests through the protection of areas for habitation or agriculture, whether cultivated or lying fallow, forests, places of cultural importance, pastures, water sources and areas for expansion.[23]

Even more importantly, the law itself failed to answer the crucial question of who is entitled to represent a community in political, legal, or economic negotiations.[24] Article 30 of the law just stated that "[t]he mechanisms for representation of, and action by, local communities, with regard to the rights of land use and benefit, shall be established by law."[25] Yet despite this legal announcement, this question has not really been answered to date.[26] Rather, Mozambican legislation on governance in "local communities" has remained a rather vague and at times even contradictory patchwork.[27]

---

21 Roland Brouwer, "The Risks of Repeating History: The New Land Law in Mozambique," *XII Congreso Internacional, derecho consuetudinario y pluralismo legal: Desafíos en el tercer milenio* (Arica (Chile), 2000), accessed April 2, 2019, http://dlc.dlib.indiana.edu/dlc/handle/10535/1461?show=full.
22 Kloeck-Jenson, "Locating the Community"; Scott Kloeck-Jenson, "Analysis of the Parliamentary Debate and New National Land Law for Mozambique" (Maputo: Land Tenure Center, 1997), 10, 16.
23 This translation is taken from: MozLegal, *Land Law Legislation* ([Maputo], 2004), 9.
24 Obarrio, *The Spirit of the Laws in Mozambique*, 52–53.
25 This translation is taken from: MozLegal, *Land Law Legislation*, 20.
26 The land law regulations of 1998 did not touch on this issue, and the technical annex to those regulations merely stated that, for the purpose of demarcating "community land" (this is for joint title holding), the local land office should work with both women and men and with different socio-economic and age groups of the "community" (Article 5) and that the three to nine "community representatives" required to sign the documents sealing the demarcation were to be chosen in public meetings (Article 6). This again rather vague description said nothing about "community representatives" in consultations for projects of investors. See: "Decreto n.° 66/98 de 8 de Dezembro: Regulamento da Lei de Terras," *Boletim da República (I Série)*, no. 48, 3° Suplemento (December 8, 1998); "Diploma Ministerial n.° 29-A/2000 de 17 de Março: Anexo Técnico ao Regulamento da Lei de Tarras [sic]," *Boletim da República (I Série)*, no. 50, Suplemento (March 17, 2000).
27 The regulations of the Law on Local State Organs (Decree n.° 11/2005) deal with "local communities" (Articles 104 to 122), but they clash with the land law, as they define the term "local community" differently than the land law, and, even worse, they remain surprisingly silent on the govern-

In practice, however, there is no doubt that a certain group of "community representatives" has gained considerable influence in land matters since the Land Law Reform of 1997. These are Mozambique's "traditional authorities."

Decree N.° 15/2000 and the (Re-)Recognition of Mozambique's "Traditional Authorities"

We have seen in the previous chapter that Frelimo's destabilization narrative of the Civil War was increasingly challenged from the mid-1980s onward. The most influential work in this respect was that of Christian Geffray, who argued that Frelimo's modernizing policies had alienated the peasantry and thus enabled Renamo to draw considerable support from it.[28] According to Geffray's initial hypotheses and later studies, it was primarily the "traditional authorities" and their followers who played a key role in supporting Renamo.[29]

Geffray's interpretation needs to be highlighted because it quickly gained currency among donors and NGOs. Consequently, it also had a strong influence on the mindset of the mediators of Mozambique's peace process.[30] As Harry West and Scott Kloeck-Jenson have put it, the "rarely articulated but even more rarely challenged" assumption was that "traditional authorities" would again have some place in the future political spaces.[31] This also explains why donors and NGOs supported research on their (re-)recognition. Thus, the Ford Foundation and USAID funded state-coordinated studies on Mozambique's "traditional authorities,"[32] and in Metangula, the NGO ACORD supported the local historian Chadreque Umali in compil-

---

ing role of the community authorities as defined in Decree n.° 15/2000, and also on the question of how the community is actually able to make decisions (see especially Article 105). See: "Decreto n.° 11/2005 de 10 de Junho: Regulamento da Lei dos Órgãos Locais do Estado," *Boletim da República (I Série)*, no. 23, 2° Suplemento (June 10, 2005). See as well: Gunilla Åkesson, André Calengo, and Christopher Tanner, "It's Not a Question of Doing or Not Doing It—It's a Question of How to Do It: Study on Community Land Rights in Niassa Province, Mozambique" (Uppsala: Institutionen för stad och land SLU, 2009), 23; Cabral and Norfolk, "Inclusive Land Governance in Mozambique," 24, 36–37.
28 Geffray and Pedersen, "Nampula en guerre."
29 Geffray, *La cause des armes au mozambique.*
30 Harry G. West and Scott Kloeck-Jenson, "Betwixt and Between: 'Traditional Authority' and Democratic Decentralization in Post-War Mozambique," *African Affairs* 98, no. 393 (1999): 460–461.
31 West and Kloeck-Jenson, 461.
32 Obarrio, *The Spirit of the Laws in Mozambique*, 57.

ing his history of the lakeshore's chiefdoms, which documents the succession of all former chiefs and their names.³³

The recognition of the "traditional authorities" must be understood in the context of the attempts to decentralize Mozambique's political apparatus in the 1990s. Frelimo was long divided over the form of decentralization and the role of "traditional authorities" in a more decentralized system. The first municipality law of 1994 would have provided for far-reaching democratic decentralization.³⁴ The emphasis is on "would," because the law was approved but never put into effect. It was rescinded in 1997 as part of Mozambique's second municipality law. Compared to the first version, the new law provided for a much more moderate form of decentralization and allowed Frelimo to limit its implementation to the urban areas.³⁵

The result of this process was that the question of how to organize politics in Mozambique's rural areas was left unanswered. Frelimo's hesitant attitude in this respect is also reflected in the Land Law of 1997, which, as mentioned above, included the concept of "local community" without specifying how these "communities" should be organized politically. A vague step toward solving this problem was only taken in 2000 when the government (re-)recognized the "traditional authorities" through Decree n.° 15/2000.³⁶

---

33 According to Brad Lester (ACORD's representative in Metangula), ACORD used Umali's history to engage with the communities and local leadership. ACORD also organized a meeting to bring together all "traditional leaders," "representatives of community groups," local business people, NGOs and the government. At this occasion, Umali's history of the Lago chiefdoms was also presented. This information was provided by Brad Lester in an email to Arianna Huhn on March 9, 2012, and shared with me as Arianna had contacted Brad Lester on our collective behalf. For Umali's history, see: PA, Chadreque Umali, *História de Nyanjas* (Metangula, 1996).
34 Einar Braathen, "Democratic Decentralisation in Mozambique?," in *Community & the State in Lusophone Africa: Papers Read at the Conference on New Research on Lusophone Africa Held at King's College London 16–17 May 2002*, ed. Malyn Newitt, Patrick Chabal, and Norrie Macqueen (London: King's College, 2003), 103–104.
35 Bernhard Weimer, "Para uma estratégia de descentralização em Moçambique: 'Mantendo a falta de clareza?': Conjunturas, críticas, caminhos, resultados," in *Moçambique: Descentralizar o centralismo. Economia política, recursos e resultados*, ed. Bernhard Weimer (Maputo: IESE, 2012), 84–89; Braathen, "Democratic Decentralisation in Mozambique?"; Salvador Cadete Forquilha, "O paradoxo da articulação dos órgãos locais do estado com as autoridades comunitárias em Moçambique: Do discurso sobre a descentralização à conquista dos espaços políticos a nível local," *Cadernos de Estudos Africanos*, no. 16/17 (2009): 89–114.
36 "Decreto n.° 15/2000, de 20 de Junho: estabelece as formas de articulação dos órgãos locais do estado com as autoridades comunitárias," *Boletim da República (I Série)*, no. 24, Suplemento (June 20, 2000).

It is noteworthy that the (re-)recognition did not take place through a separate law but through a ministerial decree. Most likely the sudden haste reflected Frelimo's shock at its poor performance in the 1999 elections, but also the desire of Frelimo's elite to decide for itself the terms of this recognition.[37] Obviously, Frelimo indeed began to believe that Renamo could rely on a sizable electorate because of its political proximity to the "traditional authorities," and that it therefore had to do something about it.

Decree n.° 15/2000 did not refer to "traditional authorities" exclusively but to what it called "community authorities." It defined them as "traditional chiefs, the *bairro* and village secretaries, and other leaders recognized as such by the respective local communities" (Article 1).[38] Thus, the decree recognized both the secretaries dating from Frelimo's socialist period and the "traditional authorities" as having equal status. The decree delineated several areas in which the local state organs were to cooperate with "community authorities," including the use and utilization of land. It also stipulated that "community authorities" would be responsible for collecting taxes. Their rights and duties were later specified in the Law of the Local State Organs (Law n.° 8/2003) and the related regulations (Decree n.° 11/2005).[39]

However, the process of the selection/election of "community authorities" was left virtually unaddressed by Decree n.° 15/2000 and also by subsequent legislation. The decree confined itself to stating that they must be legitimized by their "communities," without indicating how such legitimization should actually take place. Democratic approval was not mentioned.

10.3 Tourism and Leisure Projects in Nkholongue since 2000

Since the early 2000s, Nkholongue has become an important destination for initiators of projects in the recreation sector. Eight projects of international and national

---

[37] Astrid Blom, "Ambiguous Political Space: Chiefs, Land and the Poor in Rural Mozambique," in *In the Name of the Poor: Contesting Political Space for Poverty Reduction*, ed. Neil Webster and Lars Engberg-Pedersen (London: Zed Books, 2002), 124–25; Helene Maria Kyed, "The Politics of Legal Pluralism: State Policies on Legal Pluralism and Their Local Dynamics in Mozambique," *The Journal of Legal Pluralism and Unofficial Law* 41, no. 59 (2009): 93.
[38] "Decreto n.° 15/2000, de 20 de Junho: estabelece as formas de articulação dos órgãos locais do estado com as autoridades comunitárias."
[39] "Lei n.° 8/2003 de 19 de Maio: Lei dos Órgãos Locais do Estado," *Boletim da República (I Série)*, no. 20, Suplemento (May 19, 2003); "Decreto n.° 11/2005 de 10 de Junho: Regulamento da Lei dos Órgãos Locais do Estado."

investors have either reached an advanced planning stage or been realized, seven of which were related to leisure or tourism activities. Three of these eight projects were comparatively small and short-lived, including the weekend/holiday home of the former tourism director of Niassa Province (Manussa House, c. 2005–2008) and a similar project by two wealthy businessmen from Lichinga/Metangula that achieved only a rudimentary infrastructure around a large tent (Nkuti, c. 2014–2016).[40] However, the other five were comparatively large investments that employed a significant number of people. These were 1) the never fully realized Mtendele Estates/Lugala Forest Reserve (2003–2005), 2) the Swiss-owned Mbuna Bay (2006 to present) for which I worked for extended periods of time between 2010 and 2012, 3) the Lake Niassa Lodge, also known locally as the project of Marinela (open from 2012 to 2014), 4) a "recreational" research facility of the *Universidade Pedagógica de Moçambique* (Pedagogical University of Mozambique), whose building was completed in 2016 but has not yet been inaugurated,[41] and 5) a company founded by one of the owners of Mbuna Bay that produces dried organic mangoes and bananas for export to Europe (Global Farmers Market, 2013 to present). Map 4 provides an overview of the approximate locations of all these projects.[42]

This sudden increase in the planning and constructing of recreational facilities reflects two developments. First, it is a result of the increasing desire of Lichinga's growing middle and upper classes to spend their leisure time on the lakeshore. Second, it can be explained by the efforts of both government and donors to promote tourism as an important factor in the region's development. This is linked to a global trend through which the promotion of sustainable tourism has been gaining increasing importance among development experts, investors and tourists since the 1990s.[43] In line with this trend, the General Assembly of the United Nations decided in 1998 to declare 2002 the International Year of Ecotourism.[44]

---

40 The third project is locally called the "Akalengo" project and is located a little north of Malango. My interlocutors were not able to tell me the exact purpose of the project, apart from the fact that it had something to do with leisure/tourism. The bricks for the construction of its houses were made in 2010. Since then, however, no construction activity has taken place.
41 The site was described as "abandoned" by local media in August 2020. However, the university claimed it still planned to open the facility. See: Suizane Rafael, "Património da UniRovuma: 'Não abandonamos as nossas instalações em Sanga e Lago,'" *Faísca: O Jornal do Niassa*, no. 750 (August 3, 2020): 8–9.
42 For examples of how these projects are "listed" by locals, see: PA, I096: interview with *P1216 (♂, 1957)* (Malango, February 1, 2016), min 01:53:49–01:54:59; PA, I114: interview with *P1074 (♀, ~1940), P1141 (♂, 1932)* (Malango, April 15, 2016), min 00:49:12–00:50:59.
43 Baptista, *The Good Holiday*.

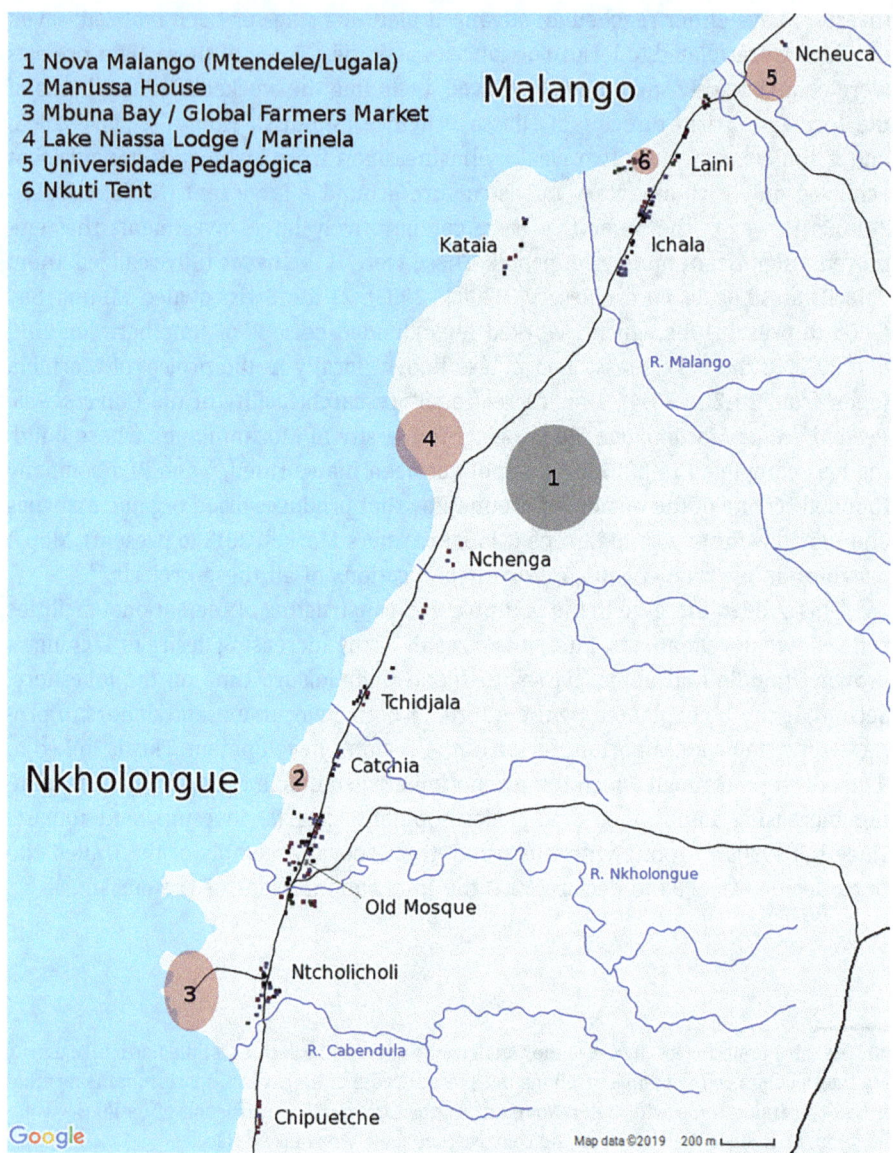

Map 4: Locations of the leisure and tourism projects in Nkholongue since 2000. Note that the Mtendele/Lugala project is not shown on the map as this would have encompassed the entire area of Malango. Instead, one can see the planned site of Nova Malango. Also not included on the map is the never realized "Akalengo" project, which would have been located north of Ncheuca/Malango. Map by the author using Map data©2019 from Google Maps.

Niassa Province, with its rather sparse population and comparatively "intact" wildlife and nature, has become an attractive destination for ecotourism initiatives. Jossias quotes the founder of Cobué's Nkwichi Lodge as saying, "[t]o do a project like this we needed a lot of land and not many people."[45] Over the past 25 years, the potential of the province's "unspoiled wilderness" to become one of Mozambique's most exclusive ecotourism destination has been cherished widely by government and donors.[46] A strategic starting point for the expansion of ecotourism on the lakeshore was the controversial Mosagrius agreement of 1996, which envisioned an area of 20,000 ha for ecotourism along the lake.[47] While no ecotourism projects were realized within the framework of Mosagrius, efforts to promote such projects have continued. In 2011, for example, the major part of the Mozambican lakeshore was declared a national nature conservation area under the international Ramsar convention, becoming the *Reserva Parcial do Lago Niassa*. The promotion of ecotourism has been one of the central goals of the WWF managed reserve.[48]

Given these promotional measures, tourism along the lakeshore has generally seen limited development.[49] With its high number of tourism projects, Nkholongue occupies a special role compared to other lakeside villages. There are several reasons for this. First, the village is comparatively easy to reach thanks to its proxim-

---

44 United Nations, "International Year of Ecotourism 2002 Launched at Headquarters Event," United Nations: Meetings Coverage and Press Releases, accessed May 8, 2019, https://www.un.org/press/en/2002/envdev607.doc.htm.

45 Jossias, "'O primeiro a chegar é o dono da terra,'" 29.

46 See for example the Strategic Plan for the Development of Tourism in Mozambique (2003–2014): Ministry of Tourism, "Strategic Plan for the Development of Tourism in Mozambique (2004–2013)," 2004, accessed April 8, 2019, http://www.portaldogoverno.gov.mz/por/content/download/1437/12142/version/1/file/plano+estrategico+desenvolvimento+turismo.pdf&usg=aovvaw382dc0-yzutxdc3lbtrp22.

47 Michel Chossudovsky, "'Exporting Apartheid' to Sub-Saharan Africa," *Review of African Political Economy* 24, no. 73 (1997): 389–98; Tomás Gaspar Mpate Decualanga, "A crise do programa Mosagrius na Província de Niassa e suas consequências sócio-económicas, 1996–2004" (Master thesis, Universidade Eduardo Mondlane, 2006); Carla Braga, "Matrilinearidade, desenvolvimento e terras no âmbito do programa Mosagrius em Issa Malanga, Niassa" (Master thesis, Maputo, Universidade Eduardo Mondlane, 2001), 63–69.

48 "Decreto n.° 59/2011 de 17 de Novembro: Reserva Parcial do Lago Niassa," *Boletim da República (I Série)*, no. 46, Suplemento (November 17, 2011); Valério Macandza, Robert K. Walker, and Jennifer Bisgard, "Performance Evaluation of Three Biodiversity and Ecotourism Activities in Mozambique," December 12, 2013, accessed April 8, 2019, https://pdf.usaid.gov/pdf_docs/PA00JKM6.pdf.

49 Ecotourism found its first materialization in the district in 1999 when two British Investors established the Manda Wilderness Community Trust with its award-winning Nkwichi Lodge near Mbueca south of Cobué.

ity to Metangula. This is especially true since the first of the Nkholongue-based projects, the Mtendele Estates/Lugala Forest Reserve, built a bridge over the Luchemanje river. The construction of this bridge made it possible to access the southern part of the Lago District by car and facilitated the construction of the road that allegedly opened this area to the world outside according to ORGUT's development consultants (see p. 41 in Section 1.4).[50] This brings us to a second point, which is that projects attract other projects. Third, the area around Nkholongue and Malango is more sparsely populated than the lakeshore north of Metangula and that of M'chepa to the south.

In what follows, two of the tourism projects will be described in more detail, Mtendele because it was the first, and Mbuna Bay because it proved to be the most durable of all.

The Mtendele Estates/ Lugala Forest Reserve

Launched in 2003, Mtendele (a Chinyanja word meaning "peace") was the first tourism project planned in Nkholongue. It was initiated by a South African businessman in collaboration with John Kachamila, then Mozambican Minister of Environmental Affairs and winner of WWF's Leaders for a Living Planet award for 2002. The two had previously worked together in the Vilanculos Coastal Wildlife Sanctuary near Inhambane[51] and intended to develop tourism in Niassa along similar lines. One of their projects, Lipilichi Wilderness, was established on Niassa's *planalto*, the other, Mtendele, was to be built along the lakeshore. The centerpiece of this second project was the Lugala Forest Reserve, a "game reserve" and "conservation area" extending inland from the lakeshore in Malango over an area that in its initial proposal covered about 22,000 hectares. The plan was to fence off part of the area and add game to it. The development of tourism was to be accomplished through three different concessions:

---

50 Access to Nkholongue was further improved in 2008 when the last part of the road from Lichinga to Metangula was asphalted.
51 The Vilanculos Coastal Wildlife Sanctuary has been discussed controversially. For a positive appraisal of this project, see: Anna Spenceley, "Tourism, Local Livelihoods, and the Private Sector in South Africa: Case Studies on the Growing Role of the Private Sector in Natural Resources Management," Sustainable Livelihoods in Southern Africa Research Paper 8 (Brighton: Institute of Development Studies, 2003), 40–49, accessed April 16, 2019, http://rgdoi.net/10.13140/RG.2.1.2266.8643. For a negative evaluation, see: Tamsyn Reynolds, "International Year of Ecotourism 2002 and a Case Study from Mozambique (Clearinghouse for Reviewing Ecotourism, No. 18)," Third World Network, accessed August 10, 2018, https://www.twn.my/title/eco18.htm.

1. The Mtendele Estates, consisting of 45 sites for private holiday houses along the shoreline between the villages of Micuio and Malango, including a "boat marina and jetty."
2. The Lugala Forest Lodge & Spa, consisting of a 20-bed lodge, a conference center and spa, located on a hill in the heart of the forest reserve.
3. The Wildlife Campus, consisting of a "bush campus with accommodation in traditional Niassa house design for 20 students, 4 lecturers and 3 admin persons" (this concession was applied for in collaboration with the Catholic University of Mozambique).[52]

According to the original concession application of 2003, 6.72 million dollars were to be invested and 326 people were to be employed for the construction phase.[53] Later, the plans were changed: priority was now given to the realization of the Mtendele Estates, which was now to include a five-star "Lake Lodge" with 40 beds, in addition to 50 private homes. The two other concessions were to be held back for a future proposal in the case of the Forest Lodge and considered for later realization in the case of the Wildlife Campus.[54] The investment for the realization of Mtendele Estates alone was now set at 14.59 million dollars.[55]

The project was never realized. The plans were abandoned in 2005 or 2006, mainly because the initiators were not able to raise enough money for the investments.[56] However, if realized, the project would have changed life in Nkholongue enormously. This was not only due to the high investment sum, but also because Malango stood in the project's way. The entire hamlet was to be relocated. The descriptive report of the project from 2005 stated:

---

[52] PA, Lugala Forest Reserve: A Forest Conservation and Eco Tourism Project. Concession Application, April 2003, 2–4.
[53] PA, Lugala Forest Reserve: A Forest Conservation and Eco Tourism Project. Concession Application, April 2003, 7.
[54] PA, Mtendele Estates. Lugala Forest Reserve: A Forest Conservation, Eco-Tourism and Premier Residential Project. Descriptive Report Including Land-Use Plan & Exploitation Plan. Final Report, June 2005, chap. 4.2 and 9.
[55] PA, Mtendele Estates. Lugala Forest Reserve: A Forest Conservation, Eco-Tourism and Premier Residential Project. Descriptive Report Including Land-Use Plan & Exploitation Plan. Final Report, June 2005, sec. Exploitation Strategy and Schedule, chap. 2.
[56] Personal communication by email, May 9, 2019.

On-going communications have been taking place over the past 18 months pertaining to the building of a new settlement to be known as Nova Malango 1500 m south of the current settlement. Chief Chingomanje and the community of Malango have identified the new site.[57]

One interviewee described this plan as follows:

[The representative of Mtendele Estates] asked the population to move a little bit ("pedia então a populaçao afastar um pouco") so that he could open houses there and make a big beach so that when the whites came, they could sleep there.[58]

The descriptive report of the project suggests that the population of Malango was in favor of the project and agreed to the resettlement. This is also indicated by the statements of Mtendele's local manager, who wrote to me that "nothing on the ground was cause for anything not going ahead."[59] However, testimonies from my interviews suggest that not everyone was ready to leave Malango. While some were in favor of the project, others opposed it.[60] There are two possible explanations for these different accounts of the circumstances. First, Mtendele (possibly in collaboration with the government) may have simply ignored or misrepresented local resistance to the project. Second, it seems plausible that Mtendele's local negotiating partners (the village representatives) were willing, at least initially, to accept the project without consulting all residents of the area. Although there is some evidence to support the latter explanation, I have not been able to confirm it with certainty. This is partly because of the political sensitivity of the issue,[61] but also because both the village's negotiators and the main opponent of the project had already passed away when I first learned about the details of the project.

---

57 PA, Mtendele Estates. Lugala Forest Reserve: A Forest Conservation, Eco-Tourism and Premier Residential Project. Descriptive Report Including Land-Use Plan & Exploitation Plan. Final Report, June 2005, chap. 5.3. See as well: PA, Mtendele Estate: A Forest Conservation and Wilderness Residential Project (Draft Version), n.d., 49–50.
58 PA, I141: interview with *P0375 (♂, 1962)* (Nkholongue, June 6, 2016), min 00:08:55–00:10:03.
59 Personal communication by email, May 9, 2019.
60 PA, I048: interview with *P1446 (♂, ~1945)* (Metangula, August 21, 2013), min 01:10:39–01:13:00; PA, I141: interview with *P0375 (♂, 1962)* (Nkholongue, June 6, 2016), min 00:00:26–00:22:02; PA, I144: interview with *P0411 (♂, 1965)* (Nkholongue, June 8, 2016), min 00:20:27–00:25:07; PA, I114: interview with *P1074 (♀, ~1940)*, *P1141 (♂, 1932)* (Malango, April 15, 2016), min 00:43:14–00:50:59; PA, I159: interview with *P0242 (♂, 1945)* (Malango, June 20, 2016), min 00:33:12–00:42:35; PA, I119: interview with *P0855 (♂, 1954)* (Malango, April 21, 2016), min 01:27:48–01:30:44.
61 One interviewee, for example, denied knowing anything about Mtendele, even though her son had been employed by the project and her husband had been the sub-chief at the time. See: PA, I042: interview with *P1193 (♀, 1953)* (Malango, August 17, 2013), min 00:55:25–00:56:49. On the fact that her son worked for the project, see: PA, I141: interview with *P0375 (♂, 1962)* (Nkholongue, June 6, 2016), min 00:16:46–00:17:33.

Echoing key concepts of earlier resettlement projects (see the Portuguese *aldeamentos* discussed in Chapter 7 and Frelimo's communal villages mentioned in Chapter 8), "community development" was presented as a central component of Malango's relocation. Nova Malango was to be built on a small elevation slightly inland from the lake. The former inhabitants of Malango were to be compensated for their "subsistence plots" and "scattered homesteads," which totaled 62 households according to a census completed in August 2003. The investors pledged to install a water-pipe system to pump water from the lake to the village. Furthermore, they promised the construction of a new school and health post ("clinic") in Nkholongue to serve both Nova Malango and Nkholongue, as well as the completion of a road to Nova Malango.[62] They also promised the initiation of "training and empowerment programs" that would "draw on the people of the villages of Malango and Nkholongue to enable them to secure employment at both the building and subsequent operational stages of the development."[63]

Although the project was abandoned, it did not remain a mere desk proposal. Rather, considerable preparatory works were carried out on the ground. Metangula's airstrip, built in colonial times, was restored and upgraded to accommodate the high-paying clientele. And, as already mentioned, a bridge was built across the Luchemanje river.[64] In addition, the project already hired several men from Nkholongue and Malango as "rangers" to prevent tree cutting in the designated area.[65] According to the probably inflated budget of the descriptive report, several hundred thousand dollars had already been invested by the time the project was abandoned.[66]

---

[62] PA, Mtendele Estates. Lugala Forest Reserve: A Forest Conservation, Eco-Tourism and Premier Residential Project. Descriptive Report Including Land-Use Plan & Exploitation Plan. Final Report, June 2005, chap. 5.3; PA, Mtendele Estate: A Forest Conservation and Wilderness Residential Project (Draft Version), n.d., 19–20.

[63] It is "Colongue" in the original. See: PA, Mtendele Estates. Lugala Forest Reserve: A Forest Conservation, Eco-Tourism and Premier Residential Project. Descriptive Report Including Land-Use Plan & Exploitation Plan. Final Report, June 2005, chap. 5.3.

[64] PA, Mtendele Estates. Lugala Forest Reserve: A Forest Conservation, Eco-Tourism and Premier Residential Project. Descriptive Report Including Land-Use Plan & Exploitation Plan. Final Report, June 2005, sec. Infrastructure and Development, chap. 1–3; PA, Mtendele Estate: A Forest Conservation and Wilderness Residential Project (Draft Version), n.d., 42–43.

[65] PA, I141: interview with *P0375 (♂, 1962)* (Nkholongue, June 6, 2016), min 00:00:17–00:06:23, 00:12:28–00:14:55.

[66] The figures presented should be viewed critically, as those responsible for the project were looking for investors and buyers of the concept and therefore may have intentionally inflated the money already spent. See: PA, Mtendele Estates. Lugala Forest Reserve: A Forest Conservation, Eco-Tourism and Premier Residential Project. Descriptive Report Including Land-Use Plan & Exploitation Plan. Final Report, June 2005, sec. Exploitation Strategy and Schedule, chap. 2.

Mbuna Bay

Mbuna Bay was initiated by a Swiss family in 2006. It had no connection to the Mtendele Estates/Lugala Forest Reserve and was much smaller, covering only a previously uninhabited[67] area of 4.5 hectares. On this area, the initiators started building a small lodge in 2007. It initially consisted of four small beach houses and a restaurant. The lodge started receiving tourists in 2009. Unlike Mtendele, Mbuna Bay has not been profit-oriented, but has been driven by the idea that tourism would one day finance the operation of the lodge and its employees.[68] Mbuna Bay has proven to be the most lasting project of all, and its initiators have continued to pay the salaries of its workers even during the recent pandemic, when tourism came to an almost complete standstill.

Despite its smaller size compared to Mtendele, Mbuna Bay has had a significant impact on village life since its arrival. This is mainly due to the fact that the company has employed a considerable number of villagers for both the construction phase and the operation of the lodge.[69] Furthermore, the lodge initiated and supported the construction of a well, a village school and, with the financial support from USAID, a health post.

10.4 Finding the "Community" (Representative)

We have already seen in Chapter 8 that Frelimo replaced the system of chiefdoms with party structures after independence. The chiefs were no longer recognized; their places were taken by secretaries. In the socialist administrative structure, Nkholongue became a party circle ("circulo") that included the subordinate party cell of Malango.[70] This hierarchical structure remained in place at least

---

[67] There were no houses in the area. Nevertheless, the beach was certainly used for various activities (washing clothes, dishes, bathing, fishing, etc.).

[68] See as well: Macandza, Walker, and Bisgard, "Performance Evaluation of Three Biodiversity and Ecotourism Activities in Mozambique," 18–20.

[69] When I worked for the company in 2011/2012, it had about 25 permanent employees.

[70] According to a party report from 1977, the circle of Nkholongue included not only the cell of Malango, but also that of M'chepa. This is noteworthy in that M'chepa had not actually belonged to the chiefdom of Nkholongue, but to that of the neighboring chiefdom of Ngolocolo. However, it is unclear whether this inclusion was an error in the report or in fact the result of an attempt by Frelimo to break up the old structures. Information from the interviews was contradictory on this issue. While some confirmed that M'chepa was indeed subordinate to Nkholongue at the time, the first secretary of Nkholongue denied that he had any say there. See: APGGN, 1 A: Frelimo, "Relatório do Distrito de Metangula, por ocasião do Conselho Provincial" (Metangula, January 1,

until the end of the Civil War. It was probably only the local implementation of Decree n.° 15/2000 that elevated the former undersecretary of Malango to the same hierarchical level as the secretary of Nkholongue.[71] Thus, while today both Nkholongue and Malango have their own "neighborhood secretary" ("secretário de bairro"), the system has not been adapted accordingly in the case of the "traditional authorities," since Malango's sub-chief continues to be subordinate to the chief of Nkholongue.[72]

It is very difficult to assess the intra-village role of the chief in Nkholongue in the years prior to the (re-)recognition of the "traditional authorities" in 2000. The information from the interviews suggests that Chingomanje VI, who had been appointed chief by the colonial government during the Mozambican War of Independence, continued to hold some political and ritual authority after independence, and probably even more so after his return from the Renamo base after the Civil War (see Chapter 9).[73] This is also supported by the fact that the first two secretaries of Nkholongue were both nephews of Chingomanje VI in the matrilineal line. The first of them held the office until about the end of the Civil War, the second until about 2005. Only then did a person unrelated to the chief became secretary.[74]

We can also assume that Chingomanje VI gradually resumed an unofficial intermediary role for the state after the Civil War. However, it needs to be empha-

---

1977), 1; PA, I160: interview with *P0727* (♂, ~1940) (M'chepa, June 22, 2016), min 00:02:43–00:05:36; PA, I154: interview with *P0367* (♂, 1936), *P0373* (♀, 1940) (Nkholongue, June 18, 2016), min 00:24:34–00:25:14; PA, I162: interview with *P0512* (♀, 1967) (Nkholongue, June 22, 2016), min 00:13:24–00:13:38; PA, I158: interview with *P0764* (♂, 1962) (Nkholongue, June 20, 2016), min 00:57:43–00:58:32.

71 PA, I159: interview with *P0242* (♂, 1945) (Malango, June 20, 2016), min 00:06:37–00:15:10; PA, I164: interview with *P0375* (♂, 1962) (Nkholongue, June 23, 2016), min 00:03:56–00:05:24; PA, I154: interview with *P0367* (♂, 1936), *P0373* (♀, 1940) (Nkholongue, June 18, 2016), min 00:25:53–00:27:02; PA, I163: interview with *P0028* (♂, 1969) (Nkholongue, June 22, 2016), min 00:07:02–00:08:57.

72 ADL, Governo do Distrito do Lago, "Matriz das Autoridades Tradicionais do 1° escalão reconhecidos e actualizados 2012: Posto Administrativo de Meluluca" (Metangula, February 23, 2012); ADL, Governo do Distrito do Lago, "Matriz das Autoridades Tradicionais segundo escalão reconhecidos e actualizados 2012 do Posto Administrativo de Meluluca" (Metangula, February 22, 2012).

73 PA, I033: interview with *P0643* (♂, 1981) (Nkholongue, June 9, 2012), min 00:31:43–00:37:51; PA, I062: interview with *P0713* (♂, 1944) (Nkholongue, August 30, 2013), min 00:41:32–00:44:13.

74 He was a former navigator in the Portuguese and later Mozambican navy and held the office until his death in 2013. See: PA, I124: interview with *P0376* (♂, 1968) (Nkholongue, April 26, 2016), min 01:01:00–01:02:47; PA, I164: interview with *P0375* (♂, 1962) (Nkholongue, June 23, 2016), min 00:41:07–00:44:16; PA, I008: interview with *P0299* (♂, 1938) (Nkholongue, September 1, 2010), min 01:01:55–01:04:07.

sized that, in the case of Nkholongue and the surrounding region, Decree n.° 15/ 2000 was not fully implemented until 2007, seven years after it was passed. The chiefs of region were officially recognized in June 2007, and the secretaries were only recognized in November of the same year.[75] Thus, when the first projects arrived in Nkholongue in the 2000s, the political structure provided for in the law had in fact not yet been constituted. To make matters more complicated, Chingomanje VI died shortly before Decree n.° 15/2000 was passed, most probably in 1999.[76] Elísio Jossias has described a very similar constellation where practice preceded full implementation of the legislation for the Cobué area. So, according to him, managers of Nkwichi Lodge entered into land negotiations with local chiefs before those had been officially recognized by the state.[77]

In the case of Nkholongue, the question of who was the legitimate chiefly authority was uncertain and disputed until the chiefs of the region were finally officially recognized in June 2007. The succession of Chingomanje VI was anything but straightforward. This was mainly due to the fact that the legitimate successor according to the inheritance rules of the chiefly family[78] was living in Malawi at the time of Chingomanje VI's death. Since the legitimate successor, a brother of Chingomanje VI, was not present, his position was assumed by his oldest nephew in the matrilineal line. This was the nephew who had been Frelimo's secretary in the socialist period.[79] In retrospect, this nephew said that he was the "interim

---

[75] The only exceptions were the chiefs of Meluluca and Lussefa, who had already been recognized in 2003 and 2005, respectively. See: ADL, Governo do Distrito do Lago, "Matriz das Autoridades Tradicionais do 1° escalão reconhecidos e actualizados 2012: Posto Administrativo de Meluluca" (Metangula, February 23, 2012); Ministério da Administração Estatal, "Perfil do Distrito de Lago, Província de Niassa," 50.

[76] He died of cholera. It is not entirely clear whether he died in 1999 or 2000. 1999 seems the more likely year, as Mozambique was hit by a severe cholera epidemic between 1997 and 1999. See: PA, I162: interview with *P0512* (♀, *1967*) (Nkholongue, June 22, 2016), min 00:44:31–00:44:59; PA, I033: interview with *P0643* (♂, *1981*) (Nkholongue, June 9, 2012), min 00:21:56–00:23:22; PA, I036: interview with *P0200* (♂, *1970*) (Nkholongue, August 4, 2012), min 00:44:00–00:45:56; José Paulo Langa et al., "Epidemic Waves of Cholera in the Last Two Decades in Mozambique," *The Journal of Infection in Developing Countries* 9, no. 6 (2015): 635–641.

[77] Jossias, "'O primeiro a chegar é o dono da terra,'" 47–48.

[78] As far as this can be reconstructed, chiefly succession in Nkholongue has always followed the materilineal line. Even though the system theoretically allows women to be chiefs, it has always been men in the case of Nkholongue. If one chief dies it is usually his younger brother that will take over. If there is no living brother, the office will go as a rule to the oldest son of the deceased's oldest sister.

[79] PA, I080: interview with *P0641* (♂, *1952*) (Nkholongue, September 7, 2013), min 00:55:01–00:55:32; PA, I033: interview with *P0643* (♂, *1981*) (Nkholongue, June 9, 2012), min 00:27:43–00:31:03; PA, I113: interview with *P0367* (♂, *1936*) (Nkholongue, April 13, 2016), min

chief" (*encarregado*) who only secured the position until the return of the legitimate successor from Malawi.[80]

This legitimate successor, who was to become Chingomanje VII, was in many ways a stranger when he arrived in Nkholongue as he had left Mozambique in 1950 "looking for employment" for Zambia and had not returned to the village since.[81] It is even possible that he had never really lived in Nkholongue before. To understand this, we have to go back to 1949 when Chingomanje IV died. It seems that by that time there was no more direct heir in the matrilineal line in the village. If we follow the statement of a member of the chief's family, it had therefore become necessary to call in a distant female relative who was connected to the kinship network going back to Unango. This relative was Amanhi N'gombe, the mother of Chingomanje V, Chingomanje VI, and Chingomanje VII. It is likely that these three sons of N'gombe spent most of their childhood and adolescence not in Nkholongue but in Mtucula where another part of the kinship network of the Chingomanjes lived.[82]

The details and exact chronology of the return of Chingomanje VII to Nkholongue are difficult to reconstruct. According to the interim chief, it was he who sent him a letter asking him to return to Mozambique to become Chingomanje. However, there is reason to suggest that the actual chain of events was more complex and conflictual as there is no doubt that the interim chief and his uncle became rivals, at the latest after the latter had returned to Mozambique.[83]

It is not entirely clear whether Chingomanje VII was indeed already present in the village when the representative of the Mtendele project first appeared there in 2003. If we follow his own statements about the year of his return, it is also pos-

---

01:51:14–01:53:53; PA, I013: interview with *P0367* (♂, *1936*) (Nkholongue, September 8, 2010), min 01:11:19–01:11:40.
80 PA, I113: interview with *P0367* (♂, *1936*) (Nkholongue, April 13, 2016), min 01:51:42–01:52:58.
81 For his biography, see: PA, I003: interview with *P0792* (♂, *1917*) (Nkholongue, August 20, 2010); PA, I010: interview with *P0792* (♂, *1917*) (Nkholongue, September 3, 2010).
82 Mtucula is the place where Saide Salimo had emigrated (see p. 203). According to archival records, Chingomanje VI lived there before being appointed chief during the Mozambican War of Independence. A son of a daughter of Amanhi N'gombe was also born there in 1952. See: AHM, GGM XX, cx. 902: Ficheiro dos regulados do Distrito de Niassa, 1954–1974; PA, I042: interview with *P1193* (♀, *1953*) (Malango, 17, 2013), min 00:20:43–03–00:23:11; PA, I043: interview with *P1148* (♂, *1960*) (Malango, August 17013), min 00:00:12–02–00:07:21; PA, I005: interview with *P0641* (♂, *1952*) (Nkholongue, August, 2010), min 00:06:44–04–00:07:36.
83 PA, I113: interview with *P0367* (♂, *1936*) (Nkholongue, April 13, 2016), min 01:51:14–01:53:53; PA, I033: interview with *P0643* (♂, *1981*) (Nkholongue, June 9, 2012), min 00:27:43–00:38:04; PA, I003: interview with *P0792* (♂, *1917*) (Nkholongue, August 20, 2010), min 01:39:11–01:43:43; PA, I005: interview with *P0641* (♂, *1952*) (Nkholongue, August 27, 2010), min 00:58:50–01:00:54; PA, I004: interview with *P0147* (♀, *~1928*), *P0129* (♀, *1930*) (Nkholongue, August 25, 2010), min 01:38:29–01:39:33.

sible that Chingomanje VII returned to the village only in 2004.[84] In any case, it was not at the house of Chingomanje VII in Nchenga (see Map 4 on p. 374), but at that of the interim chief where the representative of the Mtendele project first arrived. One of the interim chief's sons described this arrival as follows:

> [The representative of the project] wanted this place. So he came here, he and the chief Chilombe [from Metangula]. They came here to my father's. [...] The chief [Chingomanje VII] was living very far away in Nchenga at that time. So my father was here [next to the old mosque]. There was no road to get there [to Nchenga]. So, since Chilombe had always known my father and they had spent many years together, Chilombe said, "Let's talk to that one who is the second of the chief."[85]

Chingomanje VII was later indeed introduced to the representative of the Mtendele project as the chief of the village.[86] Nevertheless, the statement of the interim chief's son clearly suggests that the answer to the question of who was legitimized to negotiate with potential investors was not yet as clear as one might assume. This is also evident from the fact that when the initiators of Mbuna Bay first arrived in the village in the course of 2006, it was not Chingomanje VII, nor the interim chief, but a younger cousin of the interim chief who was introduced to them as the chief of the village. It was also this cousin—let us call him Interim Chief II—who acted as chief in the community consultation for Mbuna Bay's land request and signed the corresponding official community approval form as "chief" of the village.[87] That is how a son of Interim Chief II explained why his father acted as the chief at that time:

> [W]hen [Chingomanje VII] came [from Malawi], he and [the Interim Chief I] were enemies. You see? They were against each other. Because of this relationship, the village ("zona") was already living without coordination. People didn't know where to solve their problems or whatever. Then, other people from other villages came and chose a good person to stay here and live with the people. So they chose [the Interim Chief II], who is my father. From

---

84 Due to the timing, there is also reason to believe that Chingomanje VII returned to Nkholongue only because of the Mtendele project, as the chief's position had gained importance as a result. See: MLM, 019: interview with *M.S.*, transcript Chinyanja (Nkholongue, June 27, 2007); PA, I003: interview with *P0792* (♂, *1917*) (Nkholongue, August 20, 2010), min 00:53:10–00:54:30.
85 PA, I141: interview with *P0375* (♂, *1962*) (Nkholongue, June 6, 2016), min 00:06:35–00:07:26.
86 My thanks go to Mtendele's former on-site manager, who confirmed this to me in personal communication on May 9, 2019. See as well: PA, I010: interview with *P0792* (♂, *1917*) (Nkholongue, September 3, 2010), min 00:38:13–00:42:32.
87 PA, Ministério da Agricultura: Direcção Nacional de Geografia e Cadastro, "Modelo de Acta de Consulta as Comunidades Locais ao abrigo do N° 3 do Art°. 13 da Lei de Terras, conjugado com o N° 2 do Art°. 27 do respectivo regulamento" (Nkholongue, October 26, 2006).

that moment until the moment when [the owner of Mbuna Bay] came in the first days, she found whom? [The Interim Chief II]. You see?[88]

It was not until the initiators of Mbuna Bay returned in 2007 to begin the construction of their lodge that the old Chingomanje VII appeared at a village gathering and introduced himself as the real chief.

Between the death of Chingomanje VI in 1999 and the official recognition of Chingomanje VII by the Mozambican government in June 2007, Nkholongue had seen no fewer than three different individuals serve successively (or perhaps even simultaneously) as chiefs of the village. All of them were involved to some extent in official negotiations with investors. This demonstrates that the recognition of the "traditional authorities" in Nkholongue was hardly the re-recognition of that what had already existed. Rather, the changes in the law coincided with internal struggles over the chiefdom. Only the official recognition of Chingomanje VII in June 2007 ushered in a somewhat more stable phase as far as the position of the chief is concerned. Funnily enough, the state's recognition of Chingomanje VII as chief was immediately followed by his entry into "the books of history." For by pure coincidence, Chingomanje VII was interviewed as part of MLM's oral history project just nine days after his official recognition. In the interview, he mentioned nothing about the recent conflicts stating he had been chief for three years.[89] His explanation may have reflected his own perception of the way of things sincerely, but it flattened the local complexities of the (re-)cognition of "traditional authorities" to a smooth narrative of continuity.

However, in spite of his official recognition, the conflicts within the Chingomanje family continued after June 2007. In the years that followed, Chingomanje VII repeatedly turned to Mbuna Bay and at times to myself to complain about his position as an outsider and about the bad relationship with his relatives.[90] His complaints culminated in the accusation that one of his great-nephews had entered his house at night and tried to kill him in his sleep. Although we can doubt the truthfulness of this accusation it shows to what extent different members of the Chingomanje family were at odds with one another.

In December 2011, as a consequence of the never-ending disputes, Chingomanje VII decided to resign as chief and return to Malawi. I personally witnessed the ensuing events in the village as I was working for Mbuna Bay at the time. I was

---

88 PA, I033: interview with *P0643* (♂, *1981*) (Nkholongue, June 9, 2012), min 00:28:24–00:29:30.
89 MLM, 019: interview with *M.S.*, transcript Chinyanja (Nkholongue, June 27, 2007).
90 See as well: PA, I003: interview with *P0792* (♂, *1917*) (Nkholongue, August 20, 2010), min 02:05:16–02:11:31.

present at three of the meetings held to settle the succession. I had initially thought that this was mainly because they needed someone to drive the aging Chingomanje VII to the administrative post of Meluluca where the matter was presented to the government. However, contrary to what I had expected, the subsequent meetings at the chief's house were not attended by the bulk of the village's population but only by a small male-dominated circle of people.[91] This included Nkholongue's secretary, but most others belonged to the matrilineal family of the chief.[92] It is therefore remarkable that I was invited while the majority of Nkholongue's population was not. This may have been because I had expressed a great interest in being present at these occasions, but more likely also because the presence of a representative of such an important (economic) player in village affairs was considered significant to give the transfer of power its share of the necessary legitimacy.

In this context, it is noteworthy that during my stays in Nkholongue the authority and legitimacy of the chief within the village was in fact limited. When he called a village meeting, only a few people showed up. Also, when the district government announced a visit to the village, it was only the secretary who answered the chief's call to prepare the place of reception. From this perspective, both the chief and the secretary wielded limited authority among their fellow villagers and were viewed merely as part of the lowest part of the administrative structure of a state, with whom most villagers had a very ambivalent and also distant relationship. Many of my interviewees plainly stated that the chiefs no longer had the respect and authority they had enjoyed in earlier times.[93] Moreover, the legitimacy of the Chingomanjes was openly questioned by several interviewees. This also occurred with reference to history, something I already pointed at in Chapters 2 and 4 (see pp. 71, 84, 109–110). One interviewee from Malango, for example, advocated the secession of Malango from Nkholongue in chiefly affairs, saying:

> Our grandmother has left us the history that these chiefs we are with are not from among us. No, they just came here.[94]

---

91 There was just one woman in a group of about ten.
92 Of all the (village) meetings that I have attended, this was also the only meeting that was held inside a house and not outside.
93 PA, I043: interview with *P1148* (♂, *1960*) (Malango, August 17, 2013), min 01:06:08–01:07:40; PA, I053: interview with *P0189* (♀, *1940*) (Nkholongue, August 27, 2013), min 00:42:33–00:43:15; PA, I058: interview with *P1074* (♀, *~1940*) (Malango, August 28, 2013), min 00:13:47–00:15:30; PA, I038: interview with *P1439* (♂, *~1940*) (Malango, August 15, 2013), min 00:57:53–00:59:07; PA, I042: interview with *P1193* (♀, *1953*) (Malango, August 17, 2013), min 00:23:11–00:26:25.
94 PA, I096: interview with *P1216* (♂, *1957*) (Malango, February 1, 2016), min 01:14:09–01:14:29.

In his version, it was the Portuguese who had gone to Unango, brought Chingomanje to Nkholongue, and made him chief:

> This chief is chief because he came from the hands of the white men.⁹⁵

Questioning the legitimacy of the Chingomanjes in a similar vein, the following interviewee, who has lived in Malawi since 1945 explained his reasons for not returning to Nkholongue as follows:

> You have asked me, "You, why are you here? Why can't you go there? Have you ever been there in Nkholongue?" I said, "No." [The reason is that] I fear those fellows who say "ah, [that's] the owner of this village. Let's do something to finish him up." The one who is making this is Chingomanje because he knows that this village is not his but mine.⁹⁶

For Cobué, Jossias has highlighted the importance of "first-comer narratives" in connection with land claims, and related the competence to speak about such histories mainly to "traditional authorities" and some other recognized individuals, whom he calls "connoisseurs" of Anyanja history ("conhecedores da história dos Nyanja").⁹⁷ The latter diverges from my observations in Nkholongue, where the "first-comer narratives" of "traditional authorities" are widely disputed, and not only among different "traditional authorities."⁹⁸ This could be a result of Nkholongue's particular history but also of the fact that Jossias has relied heavily on "traditional authorities" as informants.⁹⁹

In the case of Nkholongue, the lack of intra-village authority of the chiefs, the questioning of their historical legitimacy by other villagers, the disputes over chiefly succession and the biography of Chingomanje VII show quite clearly that the Chingomanjes of recent times have barely fit the image of chiefs as a socially em-

---

95 PA, I096: interview with P1216 (♂, 1957) (Malango, February 1, 2016), min 01:24:48–01:24:53.
96 PA, I128: interview with P1426 (♂, 1929) (Malindi (Mangochi District, Malawi), May 28, 2016), min 00:30:46–00:31:32. See as well: PA, I128: interview with P1426 (♂, 1929) (Malindi (Mangochi District, Malawi), May 28, 2016), min 03:35:58–03:36:57.
97 Jossias, "'O primeiro a chegar é o dono da terra'."
98 My observations are more in line with those of Carola Lentz for Ghana, where most of her interlocutors had their own version of the local settlement history, regardless of their formal position, education, and age. See: Carola Lentz, *Land, Mobility, and Belonging in West Africa* (Bloomington, Indiana: Indiana University Press, 2013), 3–4.
99 Jossias' study defines the "traditional authorities" as historically and socially constructed, but they nevertheless appear as a fairly uncontested and in many ways also ahistorical institution. Thus, Jossias has almost completely ignored the role of secretaries and has said little about the changing role of the "traditional authorities" after independence.

bedded grassroots institution. Yet both state and investors (and myself) have tended to approach the political and social realities of Nkholongue with this image in mind. Thereby, the "community" has been seen as an entity whose members tend to share common interests and opinions, and who, in the rare case of conflict, possess the commonly accepted institution of the chief who is able to settle the dispute to everyone's satisfaction.

Let me illustrate the divergence between social realities in Nkholongue and external conceptualizations of these realities with two further examples. Both are evidence of external misconceptions about the role and function of the local community. The first example concerns an episode of a documentary by the Swiss TV broadcaster *Schweizer Fernsehen* (SF) filmed about Mbuna Bay in 2010. In this episode, the film crew visited the "traditional" "village healer."[100] The invocation of the concept of the "village healer" fits the notion of the village or community as a kind of self-contained unit with its own political, economic and, in this case, health institutions. But precisely in the case of the "traditional healer" or *curandeiro*, such a notion hardly corresponds to current village reality. The villagers of Nkholongue do not usually turn to the *curandeiro* resident in their village for "health issues." Rather, they travel elsewhere for medical advice, and in some cases go quite far. The healer resident in Nkholongue, on the other hand, usually receives his patients from elsewhere, in his case from places as far away as Nampula.[101]

The second example concerns the adaptation of the land law in Nkholongue. I was personally present at a community consultation on a land application by Mbuna Bay in early 2012. This consultation clearly revealed that the state's perception that local land management is in "communal" hands met a much more individualized reality, which included the existence of what has been called vernacular markets.[102] When the director of the Land Office of Lichinga asked for opinions on the first plot of land in question, only the person whom the other villagers considered the "owner" of the land was initially willing to give his opinion. At the direc-

---

100 "Dorfheilerin" in the German original. It is not mentioned in the documentary that in reality the film crew visited a village healer in the neighboring village of M'chepa, and not the one who runs his business in Nkholongue. See: Kurt Schaad, "Kairo-Kapstadt, Folge 5: Mosambik und Südafrika," June 4, 2010, min 06:52–08:07, accessed May 7, 2019, https://www.srf.ch/play/tv/sendung/kairo-kapstadt?id=c446dfa8-0d70-0001-aee6-9b2047301a80.
101 His rural rootedness serves him as an important marketing vehicle in urban areas. See: PA, I158: interview with *P0764 (♂, 1962)* (Nkholongue, June 20, 2016), min 00:18:38–00:24:28.
102 For vernacular markets, see: Admos Chimhowu and Phil Woodhouse, "Vernacular Land Markets and the Changing Face of Customary Land Tenure in Africa," *Forum for Development Studies* 32, no. 2 (2005): 385–414. Jossias has also observed such transactions in the region around Cobué. See: Jossias, "'O primeiro a chegar é o dono da terra,'" 201.

tor's insistence to hear other opinions on the same plot, someone took the floor and basically said:

> I cannot speak about someone else's land, and since the owner of that land has already spoken, there is no more reason to ask.

The rhetorical battle continued for some time until the state official finally convinced other villagers to give their consent to the plot in question by signing the required document. Various scholars have underlined how processes of community consultation are at risk of "elite capture," as chiefs and village elders alone decide the fate of their fellow villagers.[103] This was not the case in this consultation. Still, people were ignored in the sense that the state did not recognize that land was locally controlled and transacted differently than the regulations allowed.

The new challenges posed to Nkholongue by the changes in the law and the numerous tourism projects could not simply be met by a well-established system of widely accepted local political mechanisms. Rather, they required new approaches that had to be negotiated and that have so far proven to be flexible and improvised. This has given investors more influence on the political realities in the village than they might usually be aware of. The best example in this regard is the fact that Mozambican law does not provide for a hierarchy between secretaries and chiefs. They are nominally equal and have exactly the same duties and rights. Still, investors have generally not shown them the same respect and have tended to favor one of the two institutions. While, for example, Mtendele and Mbuna Bay (myself included) have at least initially preferred the chief to the secretary, the projects of Marinela and Nkuti have negotiated mainly with Malango's secretary. In the case of Mbuna Bay, I could see for myself how Nkholongue's former secretary kept complaining that he was just as important as the chief.

This is not meant as an accusation. At the beginning of my research, I was also quickly led to believe that the chief was a crucial player in the realization of my project. Thus, my first interviewee had at first refused to speak with me, stating that I first needed the chief's permission for my research. So I approached Chief Chingomanje VII, who initially refused this permission on the grounds that the village belonged to him and with it its history. This resonated perfectly with my own conception at the time of chiefs as a kind of timeless grassroots institution. Only in the course of my research did I realize that not everyone saw the need for a permission from the chief. On the contrary, some even refused to talk to me at first

---

103 Vermeulen and Cotula, "Over the Heads of Local People."

because they thought I was making common cause with the chief.[104] Furthermore, many of those who wanted to hear about the chief's approval apparently did so because they were only concerned to learn that the state had given its permission for the project, and because they viewed the chief as the state's key representative rather than as the respected institution that derives its power from the local community.

The question of whether the secretary or the chief is preferred is interesting for two reasons. First, this is because of different selection procedures of these institutions. While the chief is a hereditary position that has so far remained in the Chingomanje family, the secretary has for some time been determined by elections,[105] although to my knowledge the law itself still says nothing about the selection process of the secretaries. In Nkholongue, it seems to have become accepted practice for the chief to compile a list of two or three names, which are then voted on by the people in a secret ballot organized by staff of the government.[106] However, these elections only take place when a secretary dies or resigns.

Second, the choice between secretary and chief has far-reaching consequences, as it puts the respective person in a powerful position to appropriate and distribute resources. This is illustrated by the case of Mtendele's first arrival in the house of Interim Chief I as it was the interim chief who was first approached with a request for workers. A son of the interim chief described this occurrence as follows:

> So he began to talk with my father: "So I want a boy who can work with me there in the forest." Yes, he began like this. So my father accepted it.[107]

It was, thus, this son of Interim Chief I who was recruited as the first worker of the Mtendele project in Nkholongue and, if we follow his statement, kept his job despite the later resentment of Chingomanje VII against this arrangement.[108] Chingo-

---

104 This mainly concerned some residents of Metangula, who initially associated my project with the alleged efforts of Chingomanje VIII to persuade them to return to Nkholongue.
105 Information from my conversations about when they began electing secretaries is inconsistent but suggests that this occurred after the end of the Civil War.
106 This was also the case in the by-elections of October 2013. My thanks go to Maya Litscher, who informed me about the course of these elections. For information on how the election lists are compiled, see as well: PA, I096: interview with *P1216 (♂, 1957)* (Malango, February 1, 2016), min 01:50:47–01:51:42; PA, I041: interview with *P0951 (♀, 1948), P0242 (♂, 1945)* (Malango, August 16, 2013), min 00:44:43–00:47:03; PA, I118: interview with *P1218 (♀, 1930)* (Malango, April 21, 2016), min 00:26:41–00:34:11.
107 PA, I141: interview with *P0375 (♂, 1962)* (Nkholongue, June 6, 2016), min 00:07:26–00:08:20.
108 PA, I141: interview with *P0375 (♂, 1962)* (Nkholongue, June 6, 2016), min 00:07:26–00:08:20.

manje VII, on his part, himself began to receive some sort of salary from the Mtendele project when he was later regarded as the local negotiation partner of the project.[109] In the cases of two other projects, it was equally sons of the respective chiefs who were employed in important positions.[110] Mbuna Bay has hired workers from different families. However, if one interviewee's testimony is followed, this only happened because people from the village had protested in advance to the chief against favoring people from his family.[111] Similarly, in the cases of those projects that preferred to negotiate with the secretary of Malango rather than with the chief, it was often people from the social environment of this secretary that received jobs.

These examples already indicate that many villagers have recognized the tourism projects as a means of what Olivier de Sardan has called sidetracking, that is as a source of resources that they use to meet their own (immediate) needs (or those of their families and friends) rather than as development projects for the whole village.[112] This is also suggested by the way the already quoted son of the Interim Chief I answered my question about whether the sub-chief of Malango was one of the opponents to the Mtendele project:

> Q: And [the sub-chief of Malango] was he in favor of the project?
> A: You mean V.M.?
> Q: Yes?
> A: Yes.
> Q: So, he did not refuse it?
> A: He did not refuse anything.
> Q: This was done by other people?
> A: Yes, because even this one, his son. When I asked for his son [to work for the project]. This one, R.V..
> Q: Aha, yes.
> A: I asked him.[113]

---

109 PA, I010: interview with *P0792 (♂, 1917)* (Nkholongue, September 3, 2010), min 00:38:13–00:42:32.
110 This was so in the case of the Manussa house and in the case of the Lake Niassa Lodge. The latter demands some special attention in this respect as Marinela, the actual owner of the DUAT of the terrain had originally negotiated mainly with the secretary of Malango, and, thus, also employed people from his social environment. However, the two South African investors who came to develop the site in 2012 shifted their focus to the chief of Nkholongue and hired one of his sons as foreman.
111 This interviewee was a son of Interim Chief II. PA, I033: interview with *P0643 (♂, 1981)* (Nkholongue, June 9, 2012), min 01:25:29–01:40:30.
112 Olivier de Sardan, *Anthropology and Development*, 145. On this point, see as well: Emma Crewe and Elizabeth Harrison, *Whose Development? An Ethnography of Aid* (London: Zed Books, 1998), 157.
113 PA, I141: interview with *P0375 (♂, 1962)* (Nkholongue, June 6, 2016), min 00:17:15–00:17:33.

Although we can expect that not everyone was willing to give up his home just to have one of his sons employed, the naturalness with which this causality was presented in this dialogue is quite striking.[114]

This also points to the fact that both the changes in the law and the tourism projects, even though they were meant to develop and strengthen the "community," could at the same time contribute to growing tensions within it. We can be fairly certain that the struggles over the chiefdom described above were fueled by the arrival of the various investors, as their appearance increased the importance of the position of the chief. However, it is also evident that the intra-village authority of the institution of the chief tended to suffer from the arrival of the tourism projects.[115] This is because it has made this institution suspect for personal enrichment, even if this may in reality be limited, as in the case of Mbuna Bay. Thus, during my repeated stays in Nkholongue, several people complained that only the social entourage of the chief and especially his sons benefit from the projects' jobs.[116]

The authority of the institution of the chief suffered especially in the eyes of the people living in Malango. For, in the case of Mtendele, both Interim Chief I and Chingomanje VII negotiated the resettlement of the population of Malango while they themselves resided in Nkholongue proper. In the case of Mbuna Bay, the problem was different. For when Mbuna Bay spoke of the "community," it usually meant only Nkholongue proper. At least in the beginning, Malango was undoubtedly considered a different "community." It was from Nkholongue proper that most people were recruited, and it was there that the school and health post were built.

Malango has been largely left out of these developments.[117] Most projects that have been planned or realized in the vicinity of Malango have proven to be rather short-lived or have not followed aims of fair tourism as much (and I would argue as seriously) as Mbuna Bay. But not all of Malango's inhabitants see the chief's influence in this regard as being in reality limited. Rather, one interviewee explicitly blamed the chief for the fact that Malango had not yet received a school, asking

---

114 In this respect, see as well: PA, I144: interview with *P0411* (♂, *1965*) (Nkholongue, June 8, 2016), min 00:23:43–00:25:07.
115 PA, I038: interview with *P1439* (♂, *~1940*) (Malango, August 15, 2013), min 00:55:46–01:00:16.
116 Several did so in informal conversations. But, at times, such complaints were also voiced in interviews: PA, I075: interview with *P1218* (♀, *1930*) (Metangula, September 6, 2013), min 00:51:08–00:52:09; PA, I096: interview with *P1216* (♂, *1957*) (Malango, February 1, 2016), min 01:46:30–01:47:32.
117 At the time I worked for Mbuna Bay, there was only one employee from Malango.

why the chief did not fight to get the other projects to build a school in Malango as well.[118]

Figure 9: Still waiting for a "proper" building: the school of Malango during my fieldwork. Photograph taken by the author.

Such tensions have not just led to a questioning of the authority of the chief. The projects have in some instances also led to growing levels and feelings of inequality. This can be observed, for example, in the increasing fear of witchcraft and the rising number of witchcraft allegations. My interviewees all agreed that incidents of witchcraft had increased significantly in recent years.[119] Furthermore, inter-

---

118 PA, I096: interview with *P1216 (♂, 1957)* (Malango, February 1, 2016), min 01:57:28–01:57:44.
119 PA, I053: interview with *P0189 (♀, 1940)* (Nkholongue, August 27, 2013), min 00:17:24–00:21:38; PA, I054: interview with *P0554 (♀, 1949)* (Nkholongue, August 27, 2013), min 01:06:10–01:08:40; PA, I057: interview with *P0262 (♀, ~1940)* (Malango, August 28, 2013), min 01:47:47–01:51:10; PA, I078: interview with *P0258 (♂, 1953)* (Nkholongue, September 7, 2013), min 00:47:27–00:49:34; PA, I071: interview with *P0191 (♂, 1965)* (Nkholongue, September 4, 2013), min 00:32:42–00:36:38; PA, I059: interview with *P0090 (♀, ~1932)* (Metangula, August 29, 2013), min 00:10:56–00:13:03; PA,

viewees also suggested that the quality of magic had changed, in that charms were no longer focused on protection as in earlier times but increasingly used to inflict harm on others.[120] The increasing significance of witchcraft in daily life cannot be attributed solely to the projects realized in Nkholongue, but reflects broader developments in the region since the end of the Civil War, characterized by a general increase in external investment and social mobility, but also by growing inequality.

In this regard, it is also important not to over-emphasize the transformative role of formal investments. For, as pointed out in Chapter 6, an equally dynamic role in social change has been played by fishing, a sector that has so far evolved outside the formal procedures of land titling with only little state interference and no large investors involved. The growing capitalization of fishing has led to very similar conflicts in the case of Malango, ranging from internal struggles about resources to protests against the presence of fishermen from outside Malango on the hamlet's beach. This was evident, for example, in an incident in mid-2021 when a group of about seven policemen arrived in Malango, rounded up many young men, beat them up, extorted money, and eventually took several of them into custody. Afterwards, there were rumors that the policemen had been called by some inhabitants of Malango who were unhappy with various occurrences on Malango's beach, such as prostitution and noise nuisance.

Nevertheless, there is little reason to doubt that, through their influx of money, the tourism projects have locally also contributed to various examples of such conflicts. While I was working at Mbuna Bay, we had several cases of employees who were afraid they had been bewitched. Interestingly, these cases often involved workers from outside the village. Some villagers openly questioned the entitlement of those individuals to work at Mbuna Bay, arguing that since they were not from the community they were a poor choice for a project that placed so much emphasis on developing the "community." In this respect, my observations mirror the findings of Peter Geschiere who has shown how the decentralization through "community" in Cameroon's East Province in the 1990s triggered and intensified debates about belonging, exclusion and autochthony.[121]

I069: interview with *P0650* (♀, *1939*) (Nkholongue, September 2, 2013), min 00:49:53–00:51:05; PA, I082: interview with *P1141* (♂, *1932*) (Malango, September 8, 2013), min 00:48:37–00:51:04.

120 PA, I074: interview with *P0160* (♂, *1952*) (Metangula, September 6, 2013), min 00:46:19–00:47:49; PA, I062: interview with *P0713* (♂, *1944*) (Nkholongue, August 30, 2013), min 00:59:39–01:02:35; PA, I076: interview with *P1449* (♂, *~1948*) (Metangula, September 6, 2013), min 00:34:16–00:38:41.

121 Peter Geschiere, *The Perils of Belonging: Autochthony, Citizenship, and Exclusion in Africa and Europe* (Chicago: University of Chicago Press, 2009), chap. 3.

But accusations of witchcraft concerned both "outsiders" and "insiders." They were also used to explain deaths. This was, for example, the case during my fieldwork in August 2013. Shortly before my arrival, the village secretary of Nkholongue had died after an illness. It then turned out that several people accused the chief of having bewitched the secretary.[122] This example shows once more that Nkholongue has been anything but a conflict-free village characterized by solidarity, trust and communality, and even less so by Hydén's "economy of affection."[123]

10.5 Conclusion

In this chapter, I have analyzed the effects of the emergence of the development concept of "community participation" and the Mozambican (re-)recognition of customary laws and institutions at the level of the village of Nkholongue. Several findings can be presented.

First, my research clearly confirms the findings of Lars Buur and Helene Maria Kyed that the widespread mantra that Decree n.° 15/2000 was just "a formalization of what already exists" faced a much more complex reality on the ground.[124] The arrival of the various tourism and leisure projects in Nkholongue since the 2000s could not be managed by a well-versed existing system of political decision-making. Between the death of Chingomanje VI in 1999 and the official recognition of Chingomanje VII as chief by the government in 2007, Nkholongue had no fewer than three people serving as chiefs.

Second, the analysis has shown that the chiefs of Nkholongue have in recent times barely been as "socially embedded" in their "community" as is sometimes claimed. Rather, the example of the biography of Chingomanje VII demonstrates that even the opposite can be the case.

Third, it has been argued that the external investors can influence power relations within the village by favoring certain individuals and institutions as negotiation partners. This is particularly interesting since the institutions of the chief

---

122 Such claims also appeared in some of my interviews. See: PA, I078: interview with *P0258* (♂, *1953*) (Nkholongue, September 7, 2013), min 00:43:21–00:52:23; PA, I050: interview with *P1485* (♂, *1930*), *P1486* (♂, *1946*) (Metangula, August 25, 2013); PA, I059: interview with *P0090* (♀, *~1932*) (Metangula, August 29, 2013), min 00:04:17–00:13:03.
123 How inappropriate Hydén's terminology is (in relation to witchcraft) has also been pointed out by Peter Geschiere. See: Geschiere, "Witchcraft: The Dangers of Intimacy and the Struggle over Trust," 69. See as well: Peter Geschiere, "Witchcraft as the Dark Side of Kinship: Dilemmas of Social Security in New Contexts," *Etnofoor* 16, no. 1, (2003): 43–61.
124 Buur and Kyed, "Traditional Authority in Mozambique," 111–112.

and the secretary are actually equal under Mozambican law. In the case of Nkholongue, external actors have tended not only to capture already existing elites but also contributed to producing those elites.

Last but not least, we have seen again that the village of Nkholongue has not been as homogeneous a unit as "village communities" are often portrayed by external actors. In many ways, the legislative changes and tourism projects have contributed to redefining the meaning of "community." Furthermore, there is evidence that even projects that seek to strengthen the "community" can reinforce internal power struggles and weaken the sense of and for communality. Thus, this chapter has pointed out how the cooperation of chiefs with external investors can weaken the internal authority of those chiefs.[125] This observation also points to whether the understanding of development as an anti-politics machine is indeed accurate at all levels and from all perspectives. For in this case development has obviously triggered various political struggles at the village level. However, in my opinion, politicization through a full-scale democratization of Mozambique's rural areas would certainly be preferable, as this would—in spite of all possible shortcomings—probably be the best structural prerequisite for taking differing opinions and needs into account and thus also for mitigating the problems of elite preference and capture.

---

[125] Similar processes have been analyzed by Kaja Johansson for the case of large tree plantations in Niassa. In my eyes, however, Johansson has overestimated the social embeddedness of the institution of the chief for the time before the arrival of these external investments. See: Johansson, "Peasant Collective Action against Disembedding Land."

11 From Slave Trade to Tourism: Towards a Local History of Matriliny

11.1 Matriliny: Resilient, but Not Ahistorical

The purpose of this chapter is to trace the local history of matriliny in the long run. As pointed out in the introduction of this book, Nkholongue is located in what anthropologists used to call the "matrilineal belt" of Africa.[1] In this area, which includes parts of present-day Angola, Congo-Kinshasa, Zambia, Malawi, Tanzania, and Mozambique, property and social attributes have historically been transmitted through the female line rather than the male line. The Wayao and the Anyanja, who formed the original population of Nkholongue, are both considered matrilineal peoples, who "traditionally" marry uxorilocally, meaning that the husband moves to his wife's home village after marriage.

We have already considered processes that may have affected matrilineal principles and vice versa at various points in this book. In the introduction of the book, for example, I have emphasized that gender biases in sources may become particularly problematic in matrilineal contexts. In Chapter 2, we have reflected on the fact that the acquisition of slave wives enabled Nkholongue's male chief to rearrange his position in his lineage. In Chapter 3, we have considered that Islamization offered young men the opportunities to challenge the "bonds" of matriliny. In Chapter 6, we reflected on the gendered effects of the increase in subsistence production and labor migration. While, in Chapter 7, we have mentioned that the mixing of predominantly uxorilocal and virilocal populations in the *aldeamento* of Metangula may have influenced marriage practices.

Matriliny was long considered to be doomed. Colonial economists saw it as a backward stage of human development and an obstacle to economic development. Early scholars saw its demise as inevitable in the course of modernization.[2] The slave trade, the immigration of the patrilineal Angoni, the patriarchal ideologies of both Muslim and Christian missionaries, colonialism, and capitalism were all seen as factors detrimental to matriliny. Later research, especially on Malawi and Zambia, indeed highlighted various changes to the matrilineal landscape,

---

1 A.I. Richards, "Some Types of Family Structure amongst the Central Bantu," in *African Systems of Kinship and Marriage*, ed. A.R. Radcliffe-Brown and Daryll Forde (London: Oxford University Press, 1950), 207–251.
2 Johnson, "Matriliny."

even if some cautioned against generalizations.³ Thus, Kings Phiri underscored not only the impossibility of fully documenting the changes that had occurred since the mid-19th century, but also the unevenness with which they had taken place.⁴

Newer studies have in fact emphasized that matriliny has proven to be surprisingly resilient against the odds in different regions. Pauline Peters' anthropological research on southern Malawi has played a crucial role in this regard.⁵ As part of this trend, various scholars have also highlighted the need to historicize matriliny in general and its resilience in particular.⁶ Or, as Jessica Johnson has recently put it also in relation to southern Malawi, "[m]atriliny may be resilient, but it is not ahistorical."⁷ While such calls for a historicization of matriliny have been raised repeatedly, there have been few attempts to really examine its history in specific contexts over the long term, and such research that exists has often remained vague. Johnson's own statement that "changes come and go in ebbs and flows"⁸ may be a telling reflection of what we (do not) know for many places, but is an unsatisfying explanation from a social historical perspective. Even analyses of the current significance of matrilineal principles are lacking or remain vague for many sites. And Peters' observation that there is a dearth of research on such "basic issues" as variations in inheritance practices and residence patterns holds true to this day.⁹

The research patterns now described largely also apply to northern Mozambique. Thus, Signe Arnfred, Liazzat Bonate and Daria Trentini have recently high-

---

3 For examples, see: Gisela G. Geisler, *Die Politik der Geschlechterbeziehungen in einer ländlichen Gemeinde in Zambia: "Be quiet and suffer"* (Hamburg: Institut für Afrika-Kunde, 1990), 100–175; Kings M. Phiri, "Some Changes in the Matrilineal Family System among the Chewa of Malawi since the Nineteenth Century," *The Journal of African History* 24, no. 2 (1983): 257–274; Crehan, *The Fractured Community*, 106, 154.
4 Phiri, "Some Changes," 272.
5 Pauline Peters, "Against the Odds: Matriliny, Land and Gender in the Shire Highlands of Malawi," *Critique of Anthropology* 17, no. 2 (1997): 189–210; Pauline E. Peters, "'Our Daughters Inherit Our Land, but Our Sons Use Their Wives' Fields': Matrilineal-Matrilocal Land Tenure and the New Land Policy in Malawi," *Journal of Eastern African Studies* 4, no. 1 (2010): 179–199; Jessica Johnson, *In Search of Gender Justice: Rights and Relationships in Matrilineal Malawi* (Cambridge University Press, 2018).
6 Peters, "Revisiting," 134–135; Mary Jo Maynes et al., "Introduction: Toward a Comparative History of Gender, Kinship and Power," in *Gender, Kinship, Power: A Comparative and Interdisciplinary History*, ed. Mary Jo Maynes et al. (New York: Routledge, 1996), 1–23; Peters, "Against the Odds"; Katto, "'The *Rainha* Is the Boss!'"
7 Johnson, *In Search of Gender Justice*, 10.
8 Johnson, 10.
9 Peters, "Against the Odds," 207, no. 2.

lighted the resilience of matriliny and especially its coexistence with Islam.¹⁰ Other studies have focused on the interactions between matriliny and development policies, implying that matriliny is still the predominant lived reality.¹¹ However, most studies have remained vague about the current significance of matriliny in different spheres of life. Similarly, the need to historicize matriliny does not always seem to have been sufficiently considered.¹² Signe Arnfred, for example, in an article on Islam in matrilineal areas of northern Mozambique implied that Islam has a history while matriliny has none. Makua social structure is described in the present tense. It is matriliny that has implications for Islam. The fact that Islam may also have had implications for matriliny is not really taken into consideration.¹³

The general problem with researching the history of matriliny is that there is a significant lack of sources. As has already been pointed out in the introduction of this book and in Chapter 2, early European observers often tended to ignore or misrepresent social realities that diverged from their patriarchal worldviews. Oral history always faces the challenge that narratives about the past are shaped by current political and social realities. In this regard, Jonna Katto has recently highlighted the strengthening of what she calls "patriarchal storylines" in oral tra-

---

10 Signe Arnfred, *Sexuality & Gender Politics in Mozambique: Rethinking Gender in Africa* (Woodbridge: James Currey, 2011); Liazzat J.K. Bonate, "Islam and Matriliny along the Indian Ocean Rim: Revisiting the Old 'Paradox' by Comparing the Minangkabau, Kerala and Coastal Northern Mozambique," *Journal of Southeast Asian Studies* 48, no. 3 (October 2017): 436–451; Daria Trentini, "'I Am a Man of Both Sides': Female Power and Islam in the Life and Work of a Male Spirit Healer in Northern Mozambique," *International Feminist Journal of Politics* 23, no. 2 (2021): 198–220; Arnfred, "Implications of Matriliny."
11 Karin Lidström, "'The Matrilineal Puzzle' Women's Land Rights in Mozambique – Case Study: Niassa Province" (Master's thesis, Uppsala University, 2014), accessed October 24, 2014, http://www.diva-portal.org/smash/get/diva2:750207/FULLTEXT01.pdf; Anna G. Aradóttir, "Women's Land Rights under the Mozambican Land Law: An Ethnographic Study of the Matrilineal District of Majune, Niassa Province, Northern Mozambique" (Master's thesis, University of Gothenburg, 2016), accessed September 18, 2017, https://gupea.ub.gu.se/bitstream/2077/52902/1/gupea_2077_52902_1.pdf; ORGUT, "Sub-Report, District of Lago: Year One, 2011."
12 Braga's work on matriliny in Niassa remains a certain exception in this regard, since she has both tried to analyse the significance of matriliny in different spheres of life and also attempted to compare the situation of 1999/2000 with that of the 1960s. However, her observations are not very detailed. See: Carla Braga, "'They Are Squeezing Us!' Gender, Matriliny, Power and Agricultural Policies: Case Study in Issa Malanga," IASCP XIX Conference (Bloomington, 2000), accessed October 29, 2021, https://www.yumpu.com/en/document/view/40204615/gender-matriliny-power-and-agricultural-policies-case-study; Braga, "Matrilinearidade, desenvolvimento e terras"; Soila Hirvonen and Carla Braga, "Perfil de género: Província do Niassa" (Maputo: Agência Sueca de Cooperação Internacional para o Desenvolvimento, 1999).
13 Arnfred, "Implications of Matriliny."

ditions among the Wayao of Niassa.[14] In addition, I have encountered several moments where people's description of a (historical) norm of social practice did not match the real-life situation of these people. One male interviewee, for example, stated that "[m]arriage in earlier times was like this from the beginning: we married the women at their place and then took them to live at the men's place. That is how it was done even in earlier times."[15] However, when confronted with divergent experience of his parents—his father had moved to the place of his mother —he acknowledged that "some do it, and some don't do it,"[16] and thus suddenly suggested much more flexible conventions.[17]

This chapter hopes to deal with these challenges in two ways. First, the available information from qualitative sources will be combined with quantitative and genealogical data collected in the village surveys.[18] These data will allow us not only to describe the present reality of certain matrilineal principles in Nkholongue as accurately as possible, but also to make some statements about certain past practices. Second, the dense contextual knowledge of Nkholongue's history presented in the previous chapters should help us to narrow down and/or negate possible developments and causalities.

In analyzing the history of matriliny, this chapter is guided by the observation of newer research to understand matriliny as a set of characteristics rather than a fixed social structure that determines people's lives at every turn.[19] This is worth noting, since the study of matriliny received the most attention during the heyday of the social-structural approach to anthropology, and precisely in the form of village studies. These studies usually defined the villages of the larger region as matrilineal and ethnically homogeneous kinship units.[20] As other parts of this book

---

14 Katto, "'The *Rainha* Is the Boss!,'" 11. See as well: Megan Vaughan, "Which Family?: Problems in the Reconstruction of the History of the Family as an Economic and Cultural Unit," *The Journal of African History* 24, no. 2 (1983): 279.
15 PA, I117: interview with *P1458* (♂, ~1945) (Micundi, April 20, 2016), min 00:03:41–00:03:52.
16 PA, I117: interview with *P1458* (♂, ~1945) (Micundi, April 20, 2016), min 00:04:49–00:04:51.
17 For a similar example, see: PA, I105: interview with *P0242* (♂, 1945) (Malango, April 4, 2016), min 00:29:08–00:29:28.
18 Megan Vaughan suggested the use of genealogical data as "an independent check" on oral information concerning the history of social formations already in 1983. And Kiran Cunningham has demonstrated the usefulness of quantitative approaches to analyze the history of marriage practices in her study on a Mende village in Sierra Leone. See: Vaughan, "Which Family?," 279; Kiran Cunningham, "Let's Go to My Place: Residence, Gender and Power in a Mende Community," in *Gender, Kinship, Power: A Comparative and Interdisciplinary History*, ed. Mary Jo Maynes et al. (New York: Routledge, 1996), 335–349.
19 Peters, "Revisiting," 139. See as well: Johnson, *In Search of Gender Justice*, 10–11.
20 For examples, see: Mitchell, *The Yao Village*; Victor Witter Turner, *Schism and Continuity in an African Society: A Study of Ndembu Village Life* (Manchester: Manchester University Press, 1957).

have hopefully already demonstrated, there were in reality many other factors besides kinship that people used to negotiate their social statuses[21] and that informed everyday realities in Nkholongue. The clearest example in this regard is certainly the fact that the definition of the village as an ahistorical kinship unit is at odds with Nkholongue's formation in the slave trade.

Although the availability of sources makes the chapter focused on the present situation, and also limits the possibility of reconstructing historical developments, some insights on matriliny's history in Nkholongue can still be gained. The main section of this chapter is structured into four parts. The first will evidence the resilience of matrilineal descent in chiefly succession and inheritance. The second, however, will reveal a fairly recent shift from uxorilocality to virilocality which was preceded by similar developments in the Christian areas of the lakeshore. The third will highlight how the bond between fathers and children is currently, but also historically, more important than the matrilineal ideal would suggest. The fourth part will then try to analyze how the role of female authority has changed over time. The conclusion offers some reflections on possible causalities.

11.2 Matrilineal Resilience against the Virilocal Shift

The Resilience of Matrilineal Descent in Chiefly Succession and Inheritance

The picture of the significance of matrilineal principles in 21st-century Nkholongue is mixed. While there are several examples of apparent continuity there are also elements that deviate from the matrilineal ideal. One clear example of matrilineal resilience is chiefly succession. It is also one of those characteristics of matriliny which can be best traced over the long term. The missionary George Swinny had already observed matrilineal succession in 1886 after a trip from Nkholongue to Unango, noting that there "appears to be a general rule among the Yaos to exclude the sons of a deceased chief from the succession."[22] Missionary W.P. Johnson also wrote explicitly that Chingomanje's "kindred" was organized "by the mother."[23] Furthermore, two matrilineal successions of chiefs in colonial times are

---

21 On this point, see as well: Alexander H. Bolyanatz, "Matriliny and Revisionist Anthropology," *Anthropos* 90, no. 1/3 (1995): 175.
22 AUMCA, A1(VI)A, f. 1270–1293: Letter from George Swinny to W.H. Penney (Isle of Likoma, May 15, 1886), f. 1276.
23 Johnson, *African Reminiscences*, 145. For early successions, see also: PA, I032: interview with P1196 (♀, ~1955), P0793 (♀, 1939), P0792 (♂, 1917) (Chipoka (Malawi), April 25, 2012), min 00:17:32–00:29:15.

documented by records of the colonial administration.[24] As highlighted in the previous chapter, the chief's family even brought in a distant female relative from outside the village to ensure matrilineal succession when there was no direct heir in the matrilineal line after the death of Chingomanje IV in 1949. Recent successions have all followed the matrilineal line, and there is no indication that this might change in the near future.

	Male owners	Female owners	All owners
Maternal side	43 (46.2%)	78 (66.7%)	121 (57.6%)
Paternal side	22 (23.7%)	15 (12.8%)	37 (17.6%)
Others/Unknown	28 (30.1%)	24 (20.5%)	52 (24.8%)
Total	93	117	210

Table 11: Origin of farmland according to the 2016 survey.

When interviewees were asked about descent and belonging, the picture of responses varied. While several stated that children have belonged to the family of the mother,[25] some answers also remained vague or contradictory.[26] Several also suggested that this depended more on personal factors than on norms.[27] As we will see below, the historical importance of the relationships between fathers and children seems more important than the matrilineal ideal would allow. However, the data from the village surveys confirm the current importance of the maternal family in key spheres of people's daily lives. Thus, most people (58 percent) have obtained their farmland from the maternal side and only a minority (18 percent) from their paternal side (see Table 11). Furthermore, adult children tend to live closer to their maternal than their paternal family. This is illustrated by

---

24 AHM, GGM XX, cx. 902: Ficheiro dos regulados do Distrito de Niassa, 1954–1974.
25 PA, I165: interview with P1467 (♀, 1948) (Lichinga, June 27, 2016), min 00:21:50–00:22:30; PA, I112: interview with P0129 (♀, 1930), P0128 (♂, 1928) (Nkholongue, April 12, 2016), min 00:06:42–00:07:26. This was also the opinion of interviewees from the neighboring village of Malo: PA, I127: interview with P1468 (♂), P1469 (♂), P1470 (♂), P1471 (♀) (Malo, May 2, 2016), min 01:03:48–01:04:23. One interviewee suggested that there had been a shift from matrilineal to more patrilineal norms: PA, I111: interview with P0266 (♂, ~1932) (Metangula, April 11, 2016), min 00:19:08–00:20:09.
26 PA, I113: interview with P0367 (♂, 1936) (Nkholongue, April 13, 2016), min 01:06:59–01:20:22.
27 PA, I118: interview with P1218 (♀, 1930) (Malango, April 21, 2016), min 01:14:00–01:16:12; PA, I112: interview with P0129 (♀, 1930), P0128 (♂, 1928) (Nkholongue, April 12, 2016), min 00:06:24–00:08:51; PA, I048: interview with P1446 (♂, ~1945) (Metangula, August 21, 2013), min 00:48:22–00:51:40.

Table 12, which shows the number of adults living in a household 100 meters or less from households of their parents, uncles, or aunts (see also Figure 10 to understand the logic of this count).

	Total	Male child/nephew	Female child/niece
Mother – child	48	25	23
Maternal uncle – nephew/niece	29	18	11
Maternal aunt – nephew/niece	35	22	13
Father – child	25	14	11
Paternal uncle – nephew/niece	8	8	0
Paternal aunt – nephew/niece	5	5	0

Table 12: Number of adults living in a household 100 meters or less from households of their parents, uncles or aunts (according to the 2012 survey).

However, the two tables also underline some reservations about the matrilineal ideal. First, they reveal considerable diversity. Second, they demonstrate that these links to the maternal family extend not only to daughters but also to sons. Thus, there are a significant number of male owners of farms, the majority of whom has also received their land from the maternal side. Likewise, there are even more male than female children living near their mothers and maternal uncles and aunts. This clearly deviates from the matrilineal ideal described by Pauline Peters for southern Malawi, according to which daughters should own land, inherit it through their maternal family and live next to their maternal relatives.[28] Although a comparison over time is not possible, there is much to suggest that the number of sons inheriting land from and living next to their maternal family has grown in recent years in connection with the increasing importance of virilocal marriage.

The Virilocal Shift

Matriliny has usually been associated with uxorilocality, and the co-occurrence of elements of matriliny and virilocality has often been interpreted as a phase of

---

[28] Peters, "'Our Daughters Inherit Our Land, but Our Sons Use Their Wives' Fields'"; Peters, "Against the Odds."

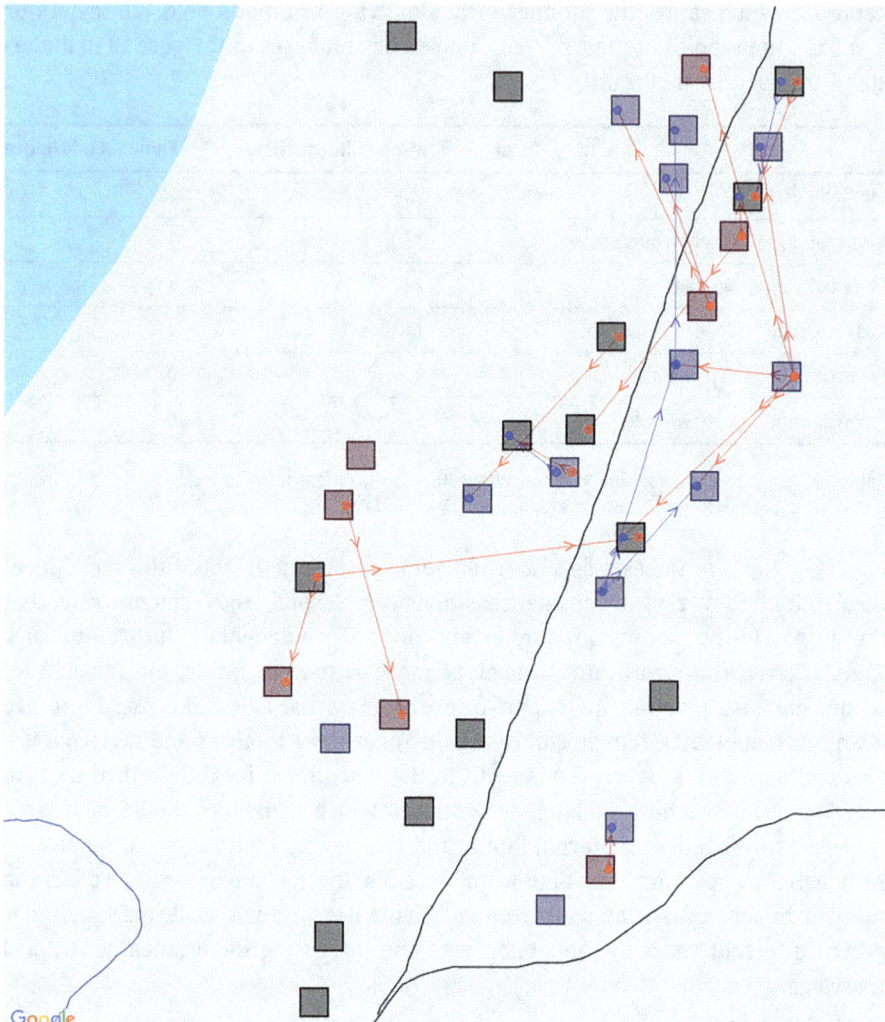

Figure 10: Visualization of adults living in a household 100 meters or less from the household of their parents in the center of Nkholongue proper. A red dot stands for a woman, a blue dot for a man. A red line represents a relationship to the maternal family, a blue one a relationship to the paternal family. The arrows point from parent to child. Figure by the author using Map data©2019 from Google Maps.

transition from a matrilineal to a more patrilineal or bilineal society.²⁹ Both Anyanja and Wayao are considered historically uxorilocal. The situation in Nkholongue in the 2010s deviated significantly from this uxorilocal ideal. Data on residence patterns from the surveys even show a prevalence of virilocal marriages. Table 13 shows the post-marital residences of exogamous marriages, while Table 14 attempts to classify endogamous marriages accordingly where possible.

Virilocal	59	33.3%
Uxorilocal	43	24.3%
Endogamous	41	23.2%
Neolocal	18	10.2%
Single and others	16	9.0%
Total	177	

Table 13: Residence patterns of households according to the 2012 survey.

Virilocal	25	61.0%
Uxorilocal	6	14.6%
Unclear	10	24.4%
Total	41	

Table 14: Classification of the residence patterns of endogamous households according to ownership of the house and/or proximity to the families of the households' inhabitants.

Again, there are no similar statistics for Nkholongue's past. Information from the interviews is contradictory with regard to the history of post-marital residence patterns. Some (women and men) claimed that the virilocal marriage had always been the standard,³⁰ while others stated that uxorilocality had been the norm in earlier

---

29 Phiri, "Some Changes"; A.I. Richards, "Review of Schism and Continuity in an African Society: A Study of Ndembu Village Life by Victor Turner," *Africa* 29, no. 1 (1959): 88; George Peter Murdock, *Social Structure* (New York: Macmillan, 1949), 207; Mary K. Shenk et al., "When Does Matriliny Fail? The Frequencies and Causes of Transitions to and from Matriliny Estimated from a de Novo Coding of a Cross-Cultural Sample," *Philosophical Transactions of the Royal Society B: Biological Sciences* 374, no. 1780 (2019): 1–15.
30 For such claims by women, see: PA, I112: interview with *P0129 (♀, 1930), P0128 (♂, 1928)* (Nkholongue, April 12, 2016), min 00:05:56–00:06:42; PA, I100: interview with *P0025 (♀, 1948)* (Nkholongue, February 22, 2016), min 00:12:02–00:12:21; PA, I116: interview with *P1457 (♀)* (Metangula, April

times.³¹ Even written sources are at times contradictory.³² Yet, taken together, the available sources allow us to identify a rather recent shift from uxorilocal to virilocal prevalence.

This change began in the Christian areas north of Metangula. Here, the European missionaries tried to actively intervene in marriage and family practices. For example, they propagated the payment of a bride price. Missionary Cox argued that this was primarily intended to combat a "traditional" payment that was due in the event of the premature death of a wife or her children.³³ According to Cox, however, this bride price, in connection with the introduction of the hut tax, above all had another effect. Thus, he wrote in 1943:

> But, unfortunately, while these payments at marriage soon became customary and are constantly rising, and have spread down to Msumba and even among the Yaos, the old payments at death are still maintained. And now there is another innovation. When the marriage payments have been made, the old custom of the husband going to live in the wife's village (matrilocal) is almost reversed. Among many of the Nyasas in Portuguese East Africa even the mere payment of hut tax generally carries with it the moving of the wife to the husband's village.³⁴

18, 2016), min 01:04:17–01:05:00; PA, I035: interview with *P0743 (♀, ~1930), P0765 (♀, ~1932)* (Nkholongue, July 28, 2012), min 00:03:51–00:05:33. For such claims by men, see: PA, I105: interview with *P0242 (♂, 1945)* (Malango, April 4, 2016), min 00:29:08–00:29:28; PA, I123: interview with *P1460 (♀), P1461 (♂, ~1935), P1462 (♂, ~1935)* (Meluluca, April 25, 2016), min 02:00:36–02:01:14; PA, I150: interview with *P1483 (♀, 1950), P1481 (♂, 1954)* (Lussefa, June 15, 2016), min 00:43:53–00:45:11.

31 PA, I128: interview with *P1426 (♂, 1929)* (Malindi (Mangochi District, Malawi), May 28, 2016), min 02:59:39–03:00:25; PA, I145: interview with *P0284 (♂, 1966), P0273 (♀, 1950)* (Metangula, June 9, 2016), min 00:12:59–00:13:29; PA, I113: interview with *P0367 (♂, 1936)* (Nkholongue, April 13, 2016), min 01:09:39–01:15:56.

32 Thus, the Portuguese geographer Raquel Soeiro de Brito, who visited the region in the early 1960s, described the marriage practices among the Anyanja indiscriminately as virilocal. It seems, however, plausible that Brito was overly guided in her statement by the experiences she had gathered in the Christian areas of the lakeshore. For at about the same time, the Portuguese anthropologist Manuel Gomes da Gama Amaral noted a difference between the Christian and Muslim areas, describing the former as virilocal and the latter as uxorilocal. See: Brito, *No trilho dos descobrimentos*, 207; Amaral, *O povo Yao*, 38–39.

33 H.A. Machell Cox, "Matrilineal and Patrilineal: Notes on Some African Tribal Relationships," *CA* 61, no. 723 (1943): 33–34. For the introduction of the bride price, see as well: Frank Winspear, "Some Reminiscences of Nyasaland," *The Society of Malawi Journal* 8, no. 2 (1960): 65–66. W.P. Johnson, for his part, claimed that it was an exaggeration to say that the mission had caused the spread of the bride price. In his view, the church had merely sanctioned its application. See: Johnson, *The Great Water*, 73.

34 Cox, "Matrilineal and Patrilineal," *CA* 61, no. 723 (1943): 33–34.

While Cox mentioned that the payments had also begun to spread among the Wayao, the Muslim areas were not yet affected by the change to virilocal marriage. This is confirmed by a short comment by the Portuguese anthropologist Manuel Amaral, who conducted research in the region in the 1960s. The focus of his work was on the Wayao of Niassa's *planalto*. Still, for the sake of comparison, he made a comment on the handling of inheritance and post-marital residence patterns in the lakeside villages:

> [T]he Anyanja population living north of the Anglican Mission of Messumba, which is heavily Christianized, is already predominantly patrilineal and virilocal; but the population living south of this mission [...], which is markedly Islamized and more in contact with the Wayao, still predominantly follows the matrilineal and uxorilocal system.[35]

While we do not know the basis on which Amaral reached this conclusion, his observation is consistent with the statements of several interviewees who indicated that the rise in virilocal marriage only began around the time of the War of Independence and followed the example of the Christian areas.[36] The recent nature of the shift in the Muslim areas is also confirmed by the fact that Christians from the region around Messumba still perceive Nkholongue as largely uxorilocal, despite the changed reality. Thus, one Christian interviewee from Chuanga, who was born in Nkholongue, stated:

> These Christians do not take the man to the woman's house. No. The man takes the woman to his house. [...] With the Muslims, as far as I have seen, it was always the man who left his house for the woman's house.[37]

While Amaral noted that the Anglican population was not only virilocal but also already patrilineal, missionary Cox had made a different observation 20 years earlier. According to him, the rise of virilocal marriage was not immediately followed by a decline of matrilineal principles in general. Cox stated:

---

35 Amaral, *O povo Yao*, 38–39.
36 PA, I058: interview with *P1074 (♀, ~1940)* (Malango, August 28, 2013), min 00:56:39–01:01:13; PA, I108: interview with *P1074 (♀, ~1940)* (Malango, April 6, 2016), min 02:47:16–02:48:27; PA, I118: interview with *P1218 (♀, 1930)* (Malango, April 21, 2016), min 01:12:41–01:13:13. For another statement endorsing the leading role of the Christian areas in this regard, see: PA, I128: interview with *P1426 (♂, 1929)* (Malindi (Mangochi District, Malawi), May 28, 2016), min 02:59:39–03:04:53.
37 PA, I126: interview with *P1466 (♂, 1952)* (Chuangwa, April 28, 2016), min 00:13:29–00:14:00. His sister made a more or less identical statement: PA, I165: interview with *P1467 (♀, 1948)* (Lichinga, June 27, 2016), 00:21:33–00:22:02.

> Yet it is curious how strong the power of the matrilineal system remains even when it has thus apparently broken down. For you will find that the children, as soon as they grow to any size, if asked where is their "kwao" (home), will almost always give the name of the village where their mother came from, and not of that where they may have grown up, their father's village where they actually live. Moreover, as they grow up the sons will always want to go to their mother's village.[38]

The situation Cox described for the Anglican areas in the 1940s mirrors the current situation in Nkholongue where ties to the maternal family are still important but virilocal marriage has overtaken uxorilocal.

The Long-Standing Importance of Bonds between Fathers and Children

While the matrilineal link definitely played an important role in people's everyday lives at the time of research in terms of inheritance and belonging, and also appears to have done so historically, much qualitative information points to an importance of fathers that departs from the matrilineal ideal according to which maternal uncles rather than fathers should play a major role in people's lives. We have already come across several episodes that indicate the historical importance of bonds between fathers and their children. In the 1890s, it was a son of the male chief who went to Quelimane to ratify his father's vassalage to the Portuguese king, and it was another son who went to the Anglican missionaries to ask for the British flag (see Chapter 4). While, in the 21st century, it was the sons of the village authorities who would work in the projects that came to Nkholongue (see Chapter 10). Moreover, fathers have often occupied rather prominent positions in the life biographies of many of my interviewees. This also holds true for the oldest interviewees.[39] Accordingly, the maternal family was often not as clearly the focus of my interviewees' narratives as one might have expected. Instead, many emphasized the conjugal family of mother and father.

The historical importance of men in family relationships can also be substantiated quantitatively. Table 15 shows the individuals with the highest number of descendants living in Nkholongue at the time of field research according to the vil-

---

38 Cox, "Matrilineal and Patrilineal," *CA* 61, no. 723 (1943): 34.
39 See for example: PA, I001: interview with *P0050* (♂, ~1922) (Nkholongue, August 17, 2010), min 00:00:00–00:06:31; PA, I002: interview with *P0128* (♂, 1928) (Nkholongue, August 18, 2010), min 00:08:15–00:15:33.

lage surveys.⁴⁰ The table shows that the ancestry of 172 inhabitants of Nkholongue can be traced to one couple, Dalia Lingamana and Tolohate Kancholochi. Several things can be said about the data of the table. First, male individuals are slightly more represented among the individuals with the highest number of descendants. This is especially due to polygamy (see cases 3, 4, and 5). While this alone might say little about people's sense of belonging, it must be noted that most of the men who appear in this table figured prominently in the historical narratives of my interviewees. Such a correlation is much less pronounced in the cases of the women who appear in the table. The table also shows that paternal links are important in most cases in establishing the connection of Nkholongue's inhabitants to these ancestors. This is because the number of descendants decreases significantly when only maternal links are followed. In this case, the first-ranked Dalia Lingamana and Tolohate Kancholochi do not have 172 descendants, but only 35. However, the number drops even more significantly when only paternal links are followed, underscoring the importance of maternal links in general.

It must be emphasized again that both the qualitative and quantitative information does not necessarily reflect the historical reality, but rather the way social connections were remembered and/or indicated at the time of fieldwork. Nevertheless, the overall findings regarding the historical importance of bonds to fathers appear to be solid. Part of this importance might be explained by older observations of anthropologists who argued that among the Wayao and Anyanja, male chiefs and other powerful men had been able to deviate from the uxorilocal and matrilineal norm.⁴¹ This is also in line with the figures from the table, according to which it is precisely the members of the chief's family (see cases 2 and 3) that have an above-average number of descendants who can be traced through paternal links only.

---

40 It is of course clear that this table does not represent the biological reality, but rather the "imagined kinship"—what can be traced from the social links people remember and/or indicated to remember in the survey.
41 Amaral, *O povo Yao*, 72; Mitchell, *The Yao Village*, 184.

	Name of ancestors	maternal links only	paternal links only	remarks
1	Dalia Lingamana ♀ Tolohate Kancholochi ♂	172	35	1
2	Amanhi N'gombe ♀ Astambuli Chiwaula ♂	130	18	(18)	parents of Muajuma Stambuli ♀ (80 descendants living in Nkholongue/16 maternal links only/35 paternal links only)
3	Cassimo Fiquilini ♂	128	(34)	36	husband of Muajuma Stambuli ♀ (80/16/35) and Dalini Omar ♀ (48/18/1)
4	Fazir Magaliwa ♂	100	(43)	6	husband of Ajalia Aissa ♀ (63/35/0), Azahabo Chipanga ♀ (38/9/3), and Zalia Panduarondua ♀ (3/0/3)[42]
5	Ginazar Ambali ♂	98	(37)	28	husband of Muanabibi Mbaia ♀ (55/0/26) and Dunia Rumasse ♀ (43/37/2)
6	Ricardo Guadani ♂ Mondoweni Sadi ♀	92	40	0	
7	Asanule Nsueca ♀ Bwana Azizi Chingomanje ♂	76	46	0	
8	Bolacuta Cacheula ♂	58	(29)	0	name of wife unknown
9	Azahabo Chipanga ♀	50	9	(3)	wife of Fazir Magaliwa ♂ (38/9/3) and Aissa Phulula ♂ (12/0/0)
10	Zamuda Amanze ♀ Tebro Njala ♂	37	8	10	

Table 15: Individuals with the highest number of descendants living in Nkholongue in 2012.[43]

---

[42] The sum of the descendants of the wives of Fazir Magaliwa is higher than his own total of descendants because a granddaughter of Azahabo Chipanga was married to a grandson of Ajalia Aissa. A total of four offspring of this relationship lived in Nkholongue at the time of research.
[43] The table does not include individuals who are descendants of another person with a higher number of descendants than themselves. The figure of "maternal links only" include the current male residents of Nkholongue although of course they constitute an end point if we follow the maternal links only. For male ancestors, the figure is given in brackets. The same in an analogous way is true for the figure of "paternal links only."

Female Authority

Recent research has challenged the old narrative that matriliny is just male authority in another guise and instead stated that matriliny goes hand in hand with women's greater autonomy and authority in society.[44] In fact, there is little doubt that uxorilocality contributes to women's position in society, since the husband is the outsider who needs to adapt to the new environment.[45] Furthermore, in the case of a uxorilocal marriage it is the husband who contributes to the development of the homestead with his work-power, and risks losing this work in the event of divorce. One male interviewee who was from Messumba and had come to Malango with his wife to work as a fisherman reflected this fact by highlighting the following differences between his Christianized and virilocal place of origin and Nkholongue, which he still perceived to be predominantly uxorilocal:

> Here, they don't do it [as in Messumba]. Here, the rule is that of the women. The women are the powerful ones in the house. For, here, the men who ask for marriage have to live in the women's house. That is what I can see here. But that doesn't exist in Messumba.[46]

Newer research has also highlighted cases where matriliny contributes to greater political authority. In this regard, my fieldwork experiences were more mixed. Certainly, some older women enjoyed considerable prestige, but village politics seemed to be dominated by men. All of the chiefs and village secretaries since my arrival in Nkholongue have been men. The sub-chief of Malango was a woman at the time of fieldwork,[47] but she was a very quiet person and her influence on day-to-day politics seemed limited. The talks about chiefly succession which I observed in 2012 were a male affair (see Chapter 10, p. 386). The current dominance of men in village politics also became apparent when Mbuna Bay want-

---

44 Johnson, "Matriliny"; Saidi, *Women's Authority and Society in Early East-Central Africa*; Arnfred, *Sexuality & Gender Politics in Mozambique*, 218–230.
45 On this point, see also Cunningham's compelling analysis of the influence of post-marital residence on the status of women in Mende village of Kpetema in Sierra Leone: Cunningham, "Let's Go to My Place."
46 "Kuno sachita. Kuno ordem ya chikazi. Wakazi ndeyawo apeleka pa nyumba ikhara ni mphamvu chifukwa si iphezekana unena kuti wamuna akapempha ukwati yofunika kuti wamuna achoke ukakhara kwa wakazi. Mwaona? Dela lakuno, tsono dela la uko, opande zimene.", PA, I097: interview with *P1454* (♂, ~1951) (Malango, February 5, 2016), min 00:22:03–00:22:24. For a similar statement of a former Christian from Messumba who had married a woman from Nkholongue, see: PA, I036: interview with *P0200* (♂, 1970) (Nkholongue, August 4, 2012), min 01:02:37–01:04:18, 01:14:04–01:17:22.
47 She is daughter of the former chief Chingomanje V.

ed to establish a community association to manage the money donated by tourists to "community projects." Mbuna Bay had proposed that both women and men be represented in the association. The chief shared this opinion only partially. While he readily accepted all male proposals, he stated that in the case of the women the consent of their husbands was required.[48]

Scholars such as Liazzat Bonate for the Macua and Jonna Katto for the Wayao have recently also highlighted the ritual power of the eldest sister of the chiefly lineage. Her role is said to have been complementary and parallel to the political role of the chief.[49] In fact, this position also existed and still exists in Nkholongue. It is usually held by the oldest female member of the chiefly lineage, who is the guardian of the sieve used in the *chiombo* ceremony, which takes place either at the grave of a former chief or the *nsolo* tree.[50] The historical importance of *chiombo* is difficult to reconstruct. Nowadays, it is hardly practiced in Nkholongue, and if it is, it is ignored by many villagers.[51] The role of the oldest female member of the chiefly lineage had generally been of limited significance in recent years, and she did not even live in the village during most of the time of my fieldwork.[52]

However, the limited significance of women in the chiefly lineage at the time of fieldwork might also simply have been a reflection of the reality that all the older members of the lineage were by coincidence men. In fact, Chingomanje VII was the only living member of the lineage of his generation during my stays in Nkholongue, all his sisters having already passed away. Two of his matrilineal nephews were still alive but no matrilineal nieces. Female members of the chiefly lineage only followed one generation further down.

With respect to Niassa's Wayao population, Jonna Katto has recently suggested that power and authority may have been more heavily feminized in earlier times,

---

48 In the end, village-wide elections were held. Three of the ten elected members were women. It is noteworthy that the chief's view also represented a clear departure from the matrilineal ideal, in which such authority was to be exercised by the wives' brothers rather than their husbands.
49 Bonate, "Traditions and Transitions," 57–58; Katto, *Women's Lived Landscapes of War and Liberation in Mozambique*, 21–22; Katto, "'The *Rainha* Is the Boss!'"
50 PA, I168: interview with *P0694* (♀, 1959) (Nkholongue, January 29, 2021).
51 PA, I068: interview with *P0367* (♂, 1936) (Nkholongue, September 2, 2013), min 01:05:21–01:06:59, 01:28:49–01:36:25; PA, I075: interview with *P1218* (♀, 1930) (Metangula, September 6, 2013), min 00:40:51–00:43:04; PA, I080: interview with *P0641* (♂, 1952) (Nkholongue, September 7, 2013), min 00:56:20–00:56:53; PA, I168: interview with *P0694* (♀, 1959) (Nkholongue, January 29, 2021). Similarly for Metangula: PA, I074: interview with *P0160* (♂, 1952) (Metangula, September 6, 2013), min 00:43:33–00:44:14; PA, I077: interview with *P1489* (♂) (Metangula, September 6, 2013), min 00:33:54–00:35:14.
52 PA, I168: interview with *P0694* (♀, 1959) (Nkholongue, January 29, 2021).

and especially before the slave trade.⁵³ The few available sources indeed provide some evidence to support this argument for Nkholongue, even if some doubts remain about the extent of this feminization of power.⁵⁴ We have already come across two such examples in Chapter 2. First, there is the migratory foundation myth, which involved not only five brothers (all with names), but also five sisters (without names) (see p. 70). Their presence could be interpreted as a sign of the historical complementarity of power between men and women, and their retrospective namelessness as a sign of the masculinization of power. Second, there is the visit of the Anglican bishop Smythies to Unango in 1887, during which he was obviously surprised to be received by a female figure of authority, so surprised indeed that he seems to have completely misinterpreted her role and position (see p. 78).

Most accounts of the early European visitors to the region, all of whom arrived after the slave and ivory trades had already long influenced local realities, indeed suggest rather patriarchal norms for the region as a whole. Or, as Jonna Katto has put it, they suggest that "the masculinisation of power was already a lived reality."⁵⁵ However, there are also some accounts that indicate that the complementarity of roles in different spheres of life was still clearly evident at the time. Thus, William Percival Johnson, one of the early Anglican missionaries who spent the longest time in the lakeshore region, emphasized the prominent role of women as heads of families, particularly among the Wayao and to a lesser extent among the Anyanja, noting that "they theoretically are the most important people"⁵⁶ in the villages. But he also observed that they usually kept a low profile in the public sphere and especially in contact with strangers. According to Johnson,

---

53 Katto, "'The *Rainha* Is the Boss!,'" 13–17. See as well: Liesegang, "A história do Niassa, ca. 1600–1920. Cap. VI."
54 A similar discussion has been led with regard to Malawi. Elias Mandala has for example argued that Mang'anja women in southern Malawi were the social equals of men prior to the expansion of the slave trade in the 1860s. John McCracken has doubted this argument. See: Mandala, *Work and Control in a Peasant Economy*, 21–25, 49, 72, 272–273; John McCracken, "Reviewed Work: Work and Control in a Peasant Economy: A History of the Lower Tchiri Valley in Malawi, 1859–1960 by Elias C. Mandala," *The American Historical Review* 97, no. 1 (1992): 261–262. For accounts that assume that Wayao and Anyanja women have long had limited political authority, see: Helen E.P. van Koevering, *Dancing Their Dreams: The Lakeshore Nyanja Women of the Anglican Diocese of Niassa* (Zomba: Kachere, 2005), 51; Molly Longwe, *Growing Up: A Chewa Girls' Initiation* (Zomba: Kachere, 2006), 20; Edward A. Alpers, "The Story of Swema: Female Vulnerability in Nineteenth-Century East Africa," in *Women and Slavery in Africa*, ed. Claire C. Robertson and Martin A. Klein (Madison: University of Wisconsin Press, 1983), 193.
55 Katto, "'The *Rainha* Is the Boss!,'" 13.
56 Johnson, *The Great Water*, 68.

the chiefs were usually men, stating that only "here and there in some small village there is a woman headman who acts for herself."[57]

In Nkholongue all chiefs have been male since the village's formation as a consequence of the slave trade. My informants stated that their culture would allow female chiefs but only if there were no suitable male heirs.[58] In the larger region, female chiefs have existed, even if they have usually constituted a minority. At the time of fieldwork, there were at least four chiefdoms in the region (Meluluca, Lussefa, Tulo, and Maniamba) ruled by women.[59] It is noteworthy that a development consultant who worked for the NGO ACORD in Lago District in the 1990s perceived the village-internal selection of Lussefa's female chief in 1996 as a new phenomenon, claiming that she was the first female chief in the history of Lussefa and suggesting that her NGO's activities may have contributed positively to this outcome.[60] In reality, however, she was not the village's first female chief, as cases of female chiefs are documented for Lussefa for 1919 and 1939.[61] Neighboring Meluluca also had a female chief in the first half of the 20th century.[62]

11.3 Conclusion

This chapter has attempted to analyze the local history of matriliny in the long run and to provide an overview of the current significance of matrilineal principles in Nkholongue. While the lack of sources has certainly limited the depth of the analysis, some developments could still be identified. Thus, we have seen that, as far as inheritance and chiefly succession are concerned, matriliny has proved to be resilient against all Winds of History. We, however, have also seen that the bond between fathers and children has long been more important than the matrilineal ideal would suggest. Furthermore, recent decades have been characterized by a shift to virilocal marriages. Although it is difficult to determine with certainty factors and causalities for these developments, five considerations seem possible:

---

57 Johnson, 68–69.
58 PA, I154: interview with *P0367* (♂, *1936*), *P0373* (♀, *1940*) (Nkholongue, June 18, 2016), min 01:53:53–01:54:54. On this point, see as well: Katto, "'The *Rainha* Is the Boss!,'" 9–10.
59 When interviewing the chiefs of Lussefa and Meluluca, both were assisted by male relatives who, in fact, spoke much more than the chiefs themselves. See: PA, I016: interview with *P1483* (♀, *1950*), *P1481* (♂, *1954*), *P1482* (♂, *1937*) (Lussefa, October 9, 2011); PA, I123: interview with *P1460* (♀), *P1461* (♂, *~1935*), *P1462* (♂, *~1935*) (Meluluca, April 25, 2016).
60 Lester, *Cassava Is the Root*, 59.
61 William Percival Johnson and H.A. Machell Cox, "News from the Stations: Station III," *NDC*, no. 64 (July 1919): 18–21; Cedric Frank, "The Darkness of Fear," *CA* 58, no. 695 (1940): 171–172.
62 Johnson, *The Great Water*, 68–69.

First, it can be asserted that the slave trade, as crucial an element it was in Nkholongue's early history, was obviously not able to "break" important matrilineal principles such as chiefly succession, belonging, and inheritance in the long run. However, given the importance of the virilocal marriage of slave wives, we can even assume that in the case of Nkholongue certain matrilineal principles regained strength after the end of the slave trade. This is noteworthy, as the possibility that matrilineal principles were strengthened at some point in recent history is rarely considered by scholars.[63]

Second, the same as for the slave trade applies to Islamization. Thus, matrilineal principles proved even more enduring in the Muslim areas of the region than in the Christian one. This is line with the observations of Jean Davison about Nyasaland, who has argued that Muslim missionaries were more eclectic than their Christian counterparts.[64] We can also expect that Christianity, with its emphasis on monogamous lifelong marriage, has produced more stable marriages than the version of Islam practiced in Nkholongue.[65] And at least at first glance, stable marriages seem to make patrilineal or bilinear principles more feasible.[66] Nevertheless, Islamization might have still contributed to a strengthening of the role of fathers. Missionary Cox had already written in the 1940s that the Muslims of the lakeshore very decidedly promoted the importance of the role of the father in the family.[67] One can also interpret the ubiquity of the patronym in the Muslim areas of the region as a sign of this importance.

---

[63] For an exception, see: Cynthia Brantley, "Through Ngoni Eyes: Margaret Read's Matrilineal Interpretations from Nyasaland," *Critique of Anthropology* 17, no. 2 (January 1, 1997): 147–169.
[64] Jean Davison, *Gender, Lineage, and Ethnicity in Southern Africa* (Boulder: Westview, 1997), 101. See as well: Bonate, "Islam and Matriliny along the Indian Ocean Rim."
[65] The village surveys clearly proved the instability of marriages. In 2012, nearly 29 percent of the village's married men had been married to more than one woman in their lifetime. This is only partly related to polygamy; the percentage was even slightly higher in the case of the women: 33 percent of them had at least one ex-husband, and almost 13 percent of the women had even two or more ex-husbands. This high incidence of relationships with different partners is also evident with regard to parenthood: 31 percent of women who had children in 2012 had children with at least two different partners, and nearly 10 percent had children with at least three different partners. For the men, it was 30.5 percent with at least two partners, and almost seven percent with at least three different partners. One piece of evidence that marriages in Muslim areas were already relatively unstable in the past can be found here: William Percival Johnson and H.A. Machell Cox, "News from the Stations: Station III," *NDC*, no. 67 (April 1920): 8.
[66] My reasoning is that infants and toddlers in particular are more likely to stay with their mothers in the event of a divorce.
[67] Cox, "Matrilineal and Patrilineal," *CA* 61, no. 723 (1943): 34.

Third, the shift to virilocality does not seem to have been related to labor migration as has been argued in some studies for other places.[68] Rather, in the case of Nkholongue, the shift began when labor migration lost its previous significance. Accordingly, the developments in Nkholongue seem to confirm the arguments of other scholars who have claimed for different settings that the long and repeated absence of men contributed to the preservation of matrilineal principles.[69] In this sense, one of my interviewees explained that children belonged very much to the family of their mother because the father could go abroad at any time.[70]

Fourth, Christian missionaries seem to have played an important role in initiating a change toward virilocal marriages. The transfer of this change from the Christian to the Muslim areas mirrors other post-colonial transfers described in other chapters, such as the construction of mud brick houses which had also begun earlier in the Christian areas (see Section 7.3, pp. 285–286). We can ponder whether the significant role of personalities from Christian areas in post-colonial Mozambique, described in Chapter 8, fostered such developments (see p. 312).

Fifth, as far as female authority is concerned, there is indeed evidence of a certain masculinization of power, but it is too sparse to reconstruct a real timeline of developments. Looking at recent developments in Lussefa, we can even reflect on whether there has not been a re-feminization of local power in some respects in recent years, not only because of the activities of NGOs but also as a result of the re-recognition of "traditional authorities" by the state described in Chapter 10. This is because Frelimo's emancipatory policies in the years after independence seem to have had limited impact on local politics. On the contrary, compared to female chiefs, I have never met a single female village secretary, neither in the sources nor during fieldwork.

---

[68] Margot L. Lovett, "From Sisters to Wives and 'Slaves': Redefining Matriliny and the Lives of Lakeside Tonga Women, 1885–1955," *Critique of Anthropology* 17, no. 2 (1997): 171–187; Phiri, "Some Changes," 271–72; Margaret Read, "Migrant Labour in Africa and Its Effects on Tribal Life," *International Labour Review* 45, no. 6 (1942): 628–629.

[69] They include Hirschmann and Vaughan for Malawi, Cunningham for Sierra Leone, and Pérez-Niño for Tete in Mozambique: David Hirschmann and Megan Vaughan, "Food Production and Income Generation in a Matrilineal Society: Rural Women in Zomba, Malawi," *Journal of Southern African Studies* 10, no. 1 (1983): 86–99; Cunningham, "Let's Go to My Place"; Pérez-Niño, "Post-Conflict Agrarian Change in Angónia," 247–248; Vaughan, "Which Family?," 279–280.

[70] PA, I105: interview with *P0242 (♂, 1945)* (Malango, April 4, 2016), min 00:26:47–00:27:47.

12 Conclusion: The World and a Really Small Place in Africa

Donald Wright has called his inspiring world-system analysis of the globalization of the Kingdom of Niumi in Gambia *The World and a Very Small Place in Africa*.[1] How small Niumi actually was with its over 40 villages and towns is debatable.[2] In comparison, my study has undoubtedly examined the history of a really small place in Africa. Estimations of Nkholongue's size include 300 inhabitants for the 1890s, 287 for 1940, 550 for 1964, and 948 for 2015. But why should we care about such a small place? What does it tell us about other places, and about the world? These are the three central questions this conclusion wants to reflect on.

In *Magomero*, Landeg White highlighted his attempt to recover the history of those "shut out of history or locked into their alternative history."[3] Certainly, a similar motive has been at work in this study in seeking to bring to the fore the experiences of the inhabitants of a seemingly insignificant out-of-the-way place in a corner of rural Africa. However, this book has not only been about the inclusion of a hitherto ignored stratum of world society, but also about the shift of perspective that enables us to question and challenge perceived wisdom of general history. In other words, this study has tried to show that Nkholongue can tell us something about the history that concerns us all.

With its focus on comparability and connections, this book has attempted to bridge the gap between an ever more abstract global history (focusing for example on objects and resources such as salt, rubber etc.) and the concrete lifeworlds of ordinary villagers in a corner of rural Africa. In this spirit, it has sought to offer analytical reflection while simultaneously remaining aware of people's voices and experiences.

Using Nkholongue as a microhistorical lens to examine general questions has allowed me to cast new light on a wide variety of topics. Thus, Chapter 2 has shown how the slave trade resulted in the formation of a small village and influenced the

---

[1] Donald R. Wright, *The World and a Very Small Place in Africa: A History of Globalization in Niumi, The Gambia*, 2nd ed. (New York, 2004).
[2] A European traveler estimated the number of inhabitants of Niumi at 200,000 in 1802. This seems to be an exaggeration. According to Charlotte Quinn, Niumi's "population was settled in over forty villages and towns, some with as many as 2,000 inhabitants." See: Charlotte A. Quinn, "Niumi: A Nineteenth-Century Mandingo Kingdom," *Africa* 38, no. 4 (1968): 444. Wright himself is surprisingly elusive when it comes to Niumi's actual size. See: Wright, *The World and a Very Small Place in Africa*, 3–4.
[3] White, *Magomero*, VII.

social structure of this village in such a way that its effects are still perceptible nowadays. In Chapter 3, I was able to show that, despite the claims of previous research, Nkholongue's chief had no key role in the initial spread of Islam. Rather, my findings point to the fact that Islamization was at least partly driven from below. Chapter 4 has highlighted the fact that colonization was perceived very differently by different actors, especially in a case like Nkholongue where the social hierarchies were highly pronounced at the moment of colonization. In Chapter 5, I have demonstrated how the experiences of colonialism changed significantly throughout the years. I have, thus, addressed the previous lack of periodization in studies on Portuguese colonialism. Chapter 6 has focused on the dynamic history of subsistence production in Nkholongue. It has, thus, put a big question mark on the still widespread perceptions of economies in rural Africa as being static or "uncaptured." In Chapter 7, the focus on people's experiences of the Mozambican War of Independence has allowed me to show how people who initially supported Frelimo later became supporters of the Portuguese war effort. Chapter 8 has highlighted the multiple meanings that independence could have for different people and pointed to the importance of examining the social history of decolonization on the ground. In Chapter 9, I was able to show that, in spite of Frelimo's local unpopularity, people from Nkholongue did not become Renamo supporters during the war but did so only after it. This suggests that the revisionists' claim of Renamo being capable of acquiring a social base during the war cannot be transferred to every setting in (northern) Mozambique where the party celebrated political successes after the conflict. Chapter 10 has demonstrated that the widespread picture of "traditional authorities" as a kind of grassroots institution barely corresponds to the complex realities in Nkholongue. While in Chapter 11 the combination of qualitative information and quantitative data has allowed me to provide evidence of a change in the local patterns of post-marital residence.

In contrast to many other history-from-below practitioners, I have also tried to emphasize that those "shut out of history" are not always only those standing on the "right side" of history, but can also include more ambiguous characters such as petty slave traders (Chapter 2), microcapitalists (Chapter 6), or colonial loyalists (Chapter 7). This book has highlighted the central role of structures in people's daily lives and decisions. It has emphasized that the frequently changing Winds of History repeatedly forced the villagers of Nkholongue to readapt their lives to new circumstances. It has thus underscored the global historicity of life in rural Africa, challenging notions of rural inertia or what I called the Aboriginal Delusion. Having done so for a concrete place over the *longue durée*, the book has attempted to improve our repertoire for historical reasoning, going beyond simplifying and abstract legacy explanations. Knowing, for example, people's experience of the War of Independence (Chapter 7) recalibrates the way we can look at the years after independence (Chapter 8). Or, knowing of Nkholongue's past in the slave trade (Chapter 2) reconfigures the way we can look at the re-recognition of the customary institutions (Chapter 10).

The longitudinal view has also enabled me to show that many developments in Nkholongue's history were not unidirectional, no one-way processes. This perspective also allows us to understand the seeming paradox that, despite the frequent and profound changes in Nkholongue's history, village life has also been marked by what might appear as considerable continuities. The longevity of Nkholongue as a village is in fact remarkable. Twice the village more or less ceased to exist. Twice, however, many people returned. Even though people from the same community were engaged on different sides in both wars, they found a way to come back together. However, the conflicts described in Chapter 10 and the ongoing separation of Malango and Nkholongue shows there is probably more reason to interpret Nkholongue as a whole as a community of fate rather than a community of will. Furthermore, this book has been biased in this respect as it has largely followed those who did return. My research has clearly shown how many people left the village at different occasions of history and did not return to it. Living in such distant places as Malawi or Nampula they often entertain only very loose if any connections to their village of origin. Even many "emigrants" living in Metangula are rarely if ever seen in Nkholongue.

Nevertheless, the seeming continuities cannot be so easily dismissed. In fact, they also reflect the perception of many Nkholongueans. One 64-year-old woman answered my question about how life changed throughout the years with the following comment:

> Nothing has changed. In the past, we ate and farmed, didn't we? And today we eat and farm.[4]

This book has hopefully shown that realities were somewhat more dynamic and complex. However, this woman's perspective points out that many daily routines in particular have remained (or become again) very similar over the long run. Furthermore, it hints at the fact that the repeated expectations of change, if not to use James Ferguson's "expectations of modernity,"[5] have not delivered what they promised. All too often the Winds of History interrupted developments on which people from Nkholongue were building, regardless of whether they did so

---

[4] "Vosasinthe nanga si kaleko timakhara sitimadya timalima, ni tsopano timadya timalima.", PA, I101: interview with *P0316* (♀, ~1952) (Nkholongue, February 22, 2016), min 00:51:36 – 00:52:05. For a similar statement, see: PA, I046: interview with *P1045* (♀, 1932) (Malango, August 20, 2013), min 00:51:45 – 00:51:47.
[5] Ferguson, *Expectations of Modernity*.

out of enthusiasm or constraint. These included widely visible disruptions such as the two wars, but also sudden breaks resulting from more silent processes such as the cessation of Nkholongue's role as a "firewood station" described in Chapter 6.

In this regard, the pace of life remained similar in the long run and continues to do so in recent years. The growth of the fishing sector, the arrival of tourism projects and the establishment of a small industry for dried fruits resulted in a previously unseen influx of money in the 2000s and early 2010s (see Chapters 6 and 10). But this process of growing market integration, whether good or bad for people in Nkholongue, has seen several setbacks during the last couple of years. The revival of the armed conflict between Renamo and Frelimo in Central Mozambique in 2013 once again made people in Nkholongue aware of their vulnerability. In 2016, the "secret loan scandal" led to a rapid devaluation of the *metical* and steeply rising prices for consumer goods such as sugar or cooking oil. Many small stores that had opened in Nkholongue and Malango in previous years have since then scaled down their range of goods or closed completely. The outbreak of the war between Islamist insurgents and the government in the neighboring province of Cabo Delgado in 2017 has left the future of Mozambique more uncertain than ever. All these events have resulted in making Mozambique an increasingly unattractive country for tourism. And the (economic) effects of the coronavirus pandemic and the war in Ukraine have also been felt in Nkholongue, as everywhere else in the world.

What does the history of Nkholongue tell us about the histories of other places in Mozambique, Africa or elsewhere? One has to be careful answering this question. This book has repeatedly highlighted the importance of microscopic and empirical analysis to understand the complexity of life in Nkholongue. I have tried to never claim certainty without the support of evidence. Nkholongue, like every other village, is undoubtedly a particular setting, and what is true for Nkholongue is not necessarily true for other places. I have already highlighted the village's location on the lake in relation to the question of global connections and the village's stability as a spatial settlement. Furthermore, not many villages in Africa have experienced a war of independence. This even applies to the majority of villages in Mozambique. In return, many places have felt the burden of exploitation of colonialism more heavily and longer than Nkholongue did.

Still, there are certainly also structural similarities between Nkholongue and other small places around the world in relation to various topics analyzed in this book. I have tried to think as much as possible about the generalizability of Nkholongue's experience and to link my findings to those by other scholars about other places. Some of my findings will hopefully also be able to inform analyses elsewhere in a fruitful way. Furthermore, this book has tried to provide an example of how it is possible to reconstruct the globally connected history of a seemingly undocumented and in many ways random village through the combination of intensive fieldwork and extensive archival research in different countries. Thus, I hope to have convincingly demonstrated how it is possible to effectively re-center our past and history to a small place, without losing track of the processes that have long connected and disconnected the entire world.

Figure 11: Sunset on the way to Nkholongue. Photograph taken by the author in 2016.

13 Bibliography

13.1 Archival Collections

Administração do Distrito de Lago (ADL), Metangula, Mozambique

I was able to consult only very few files. There is no inventory.

Administração do Posto Administrativo de Maniamba (APAM), Maniamba, Mozambique

The administration holds only a limited number of files. There is no inventory.

Aluka (www.aluka.org)

The Isaacman Collection

Archives de la Société des Missionnaires d'Afrique (AGMAfr), Rome, Italy

Dossiers personnels

Archives of the Society of Malawi (ASM), Blantyre, Malawi

Private Diary of A.M.D. Turnbull 1917–1918
Chauncy Maples Log 1914–1924
Colonel Barton's Diary 1915
Rangeley Papers

Archives of the Universities' Mission to Central Africa (AUMCA), Bodleian Library, Oxford, United Kingdom

A-F, Correspondence, pamphlets, some photographs and sketches
SF, Subject files
SF/FIN, Finance
TC, "Tin Chest series"
UX, Miscellaneous items

Archives of the United Nations High Commission for Refugees (AUNHCR), Geneva, Switzerland

Records of the Central Registry

Archives of the United Society Partners in the Gospel (AUSPG), London, United Kingdom

Diary of Philip Young, Engineer on the "Chauncy Maples", 1901–1903

Arquivo da Defesa Nacional (ADN), Paço de Arcos, Portugal

F. 002 Secretariado-Geral da Defesa Nacional 2ª Repartição, 1957–1974

Arquivo Geral Instituto Missionário da Consolata (AIMC), Rome, Italy

Membros do Instituto (VII)
Mozambico Niassa (VIII-7)
Diários das Missões IMC de Moçambique (X)

Arquivo Histórico Diplomático (AHD), Lisbon, Portugal

Ministério do Ultramar (MU)
Gabinete dos Negócios Políticos (GNP)
Repartição dos Negócios Políticos (RNP)

Arquivo Histórico da Marinha (AHMar), Lisbon, Portugal

Fundo Coloredo de Moçambique

Arquivo Histórico de Moçambique (AHM), Maputo, Mozambique

Governo Geral de Moçambique Séc. XX (GGM XX)
Direcção dos Serviços de Negócios Indígenas (SNI)
Inspecção dos Serviços Administrativos e dos Negócios Indígenas (ISANI)
Secção Especial
Secção da História Oral

Códice 11-2485: Documentos sobre as Missões Inglesas das Universidades na parte portuguesa da região do Lago Niassa depois da occupação pela Companhia em 1901, Vol. 1
Biblioteca

Arquivo Histórico Militar (AHMil), Lisbon, Portugal

Divisões, Colónias/Ultramar, Moçambique (DIV/2/7)
Quartel-General da Região Militar de Moçambique (FO63)

Arquivo Histórico Ultramarino (AHU), Lisbon, Portugal

Ministério do Ultramar (MU), Direcção-Geral de Obras Públicas e Comunicações (DGOPC)
Ministério do Ultramar (MU), Inspecção Superior de Administração Ultramarina (ISAU)
Missão Antropológica de Moçambique (MAM)
Biblioteca

Arquivo Nacional Torre do Tombo (ANTT), Lisbon, Portugal

Serviços de Centralização e Coordenação de Informações de Moçambique (SSCIM)
PIDE/DGS, Delegação de Moçambique, Subdelegação de Vila Cabral
PIDE/DGS, Direcção dos Serviços de Informação, Gabinete Ultramarino, Documentos da Província de Moçambique

Arquivo Permanente do Gabinete do Governador de Niassa (APGGN), Lichinga, Mozambique

These archives have no visible order. There is no classification and there are no inventories/catalogues. At the moment of research, the archives consisted of two parts, one on the first floor of the building of the provincial government (1 A) and the other in the changing and storage room of the government's gardeners (QJ).

Deposito Museológico de Lichinga (DML), Lichinga, Mozambique

Primeira Gaveta
Segunda Gaveta

Fundação Mario Soares (FMS) (www.casacomum.org)

Arquivo Mário Pinto d. Andrade (AMPA)
Documentos Bernardino Machado (DBG)

Malawian National Archives (MNA), Zomba, Malawi

Diocese of Malawi (145/DOM)
Universities' Mission to Central Africa (7/UMCA)
Kota Kota Mission (2/KOM)
Malindi Mission (25/MAM)
Provincial Commissioner, Central Province (NC)
District Commissioner, Dowa District (NCE)
District Commissioner, Kota-Kota (formerly Marimba) District (NCK)
District Commissioner, Fort Johnston (formerly South Nyasa) District (NSF)
Custodian of Enemy Property (LC)
Labour Office (LB)
Secretariat (S1-S2)
King African Rifles (KAR)

Museu Local de Metangula (MLM), Metangula, Mozambique

Projeto Património Arqueológico e Cultural, Oral History Interview Collection

Swiss Federal Archives (SFA), Bern, Switzerland

Schweizerische Vertretung, Lourenço-Marques (1922–1976)

The National Archives (TNA), Kew/London, United Kingdom

Foreign Office (FO)
Colonial Office (CO)
War Office (WO)
Records of the Board of Trade and of Successor and Related Bodies (BT)

13.2 Personal Archives (PA)

Interviews (includes only those used in this thesis)

In some cases, it has been very difficult to estimate the age of the interviewees. Most of the older people do not know their year of birth. The information on identity cards—if available—is not always correct. Some people also have different identity cards with different years of birth. If a year is preceded by a tilde (~), this means that the information is an estimate.

In general, all participants of the interviews are listed with their ID number, sex and age. There were, however, some interviews that were attended by other people who are not included in the information. These are mostly people who were present but said very little or people who joined the interview while this was already running, and, at times, left it again before it was over. Above all in interviews that were conducted outside of the village, it was not always possible for me to identify these people correctly.

I001: interview with P0050 (♂, ~1922). Nkholongue, August 17, 2010. 01:56:29.
I002: interview with P0128 (♂, 1928). Nkholongue, August 18, 2010. 01:12:27.
I003: interview with P0792 (♂, 1917). Nkholongue, August 20, 2010. 02:12:51.
I004: interview with P0147 (♀, ~1928), P0129 (♀, 1930). Nkholongue, August 25, 2010. 01:42:14.
I005: interview with P0641 (♂, 1952). Nkholongue, August 27, 2010. 01:52:05.
I006: interview with P1480 (♂, 1947). Nkholongue, August 30, 2010. 01:12:28.
I007: interview with P0298 (♀, ~1922). Nkholongue, September 1, 2010. 01:17:23.
I008: interview with P0299 (♂, 1938). Nkholongue, September 1, 2010. 01:12:31.
I009: interview with P0128 (♂, 1928). Nkholongue, September 1, 2010. 01:36:21.
I010: interview with P0792 (♂, 1917). Nkholongue, September 3, 2010. 00:52:39.
I011: interview with P0050 (♂, ~1922). Nkholongue, September 3, 2010. 00:33:11.
I012: interview with P0367 (♂, 1936). Nkholongue, September 3, 2010. 00:47:30.
I013: interview with P0367 (♂, 1936). Nkholongue, September 8, 2010. 01:43:55.
I014: interview with P0147 (♀, ~1928), P0129 (♀, 1930). Nkholongue, September 8, 2010. 00:30:38.
I015: interview with P0367 (♂, 1936). Nkholongue, September 9, 2010. 01:01:14.
I016: interview with P1483 (♀, 1950), P1481 (♂, 1954), P1482 (♂, 1937). Lussefa, October 9, 2011. 01:36:22.
I017: interview with P0792 (♂, 1917), P0793 (♀, 1939). Nkholongue, October 14, 2011. 01:26:03.
I019: interview with Chief Nampanda (♂). Unango, October 15, 2011. 00:15:51.
I030: interview with Chief Namtima (♀). Maniamba, April 6, 2012. 00:19:28.
I032: interview with P1196 (♀, ~1955), P0793 (♀, 1939), P0792 (♂, 1917). Chipoka (Malawi), April 25, 2012. 00:59:09.
I033: interview with P0643 (♂, 1981). Nkholongue, June 9, 2012. 02:27:00.
I035: interview with P0743 (♀, ~1930), P0765 (♀, ~1932). Nkholongue, July 28, 2012. 02:28:25.
I036: interview with P0200 (♂, 1970). Nkholongue, August 4, 2012. 01:36:53.
I037: interview with P0855 (♂, 1954). Malango, August 14, 2013. 01:21:42.
I038: interview with P1439 (♂, ~1940). Malango, August 15, 2013. 03:18:15.

I039: interview with P0898 (♀, 1960). Malango, August 15, 2013. 01:17:32.
I040: interview with P1030 (♀, 1965), P1009 (♀, 1958), P1029 (♂, ~1959). Malango, August 16, 2013. 01:37:52.
I041: interview with P0951 (♀, 1948), P0242 (♂, 1945). Malango, August 16, 2013. 00:49:49.
I042: interview with P1193 (♀, 1953). Malango, August 17, 2013. 01:06:12.
I043: interview with P1148 (♂, 1960). Malango, August 17, 2013. 01:17:00.
I044: interview with P1081 (♀, 1945). Malango, August 17, 2013. 00:36:46.
I045: interview with P0242 (♂, 1945). Malango, August 17, 2013. 00:24:38.
I046: interview with P1045 (♀, 1932). Malango, August 20, 2013. 01:10:07.
I047: interview with P0596 (♂, ~1950). Metangula, August 21, 2013. 00:51:53.
I048: interview with P1446 (♂, ~1945). Metangula, August 21, 2013. 01:14:35.
I049: interview with P0267 (♀, 1949). Nkholongue, August 23, 2013. 01:27:22.
I050: interview with P1485 (♂, 1930), P1486 (♂, 1946). Metangula, August 25, 2013. 02:52:27.
I051: interview with P0481 (♀, 1942). Nkholongue, August 26, 2013. 01:47:39.
I052: interview with P0240 (♀, 1940). Nkholongue, August 26, 2013. 00:44:02.
I053: interview with P0189 (♀, 1940). Nkholongue, August 27, 2013. 00:46:16.
I054: interview with P0554 (♀, 1949). Nkholongue, August 27, 2013. 01:13:27.
I055: interview with P0639 (♀, ~1952). Nkholongue, August 27, 2013. 00:44:51.
I056: interview with P1102 (♂, 1932). Malango, August 28, 2013. 00:49:51.
I057: interview with P0262 (♀, ~1940). Malango, August 28, 2013. 01:08:33.
I058: interview with P1074 (♀, ~1940). Malango, August 28, 2013. 02:46:44.
I059: interview with P0090 (♀, ~1932). Metangula, August 29, 2013. 01:20:07.
I060: interview with P0331 (♀, ~1948). Metangula, August 29, 2013. No audio.
I062: interview with P0713 (♂, 1944). Nkholongue, August 30, 2013. 01:05:04.
I063: interview with P1488 (♂, ~1930). M'chepa, August 31, 2013. 01:39:55.
I064: interview with P1447 (♂, 1969). M'chepa, August 31, 2013. 00:37:26.
I065: interview with P0583 (♂, 1972). Nkholongue, September 1, 2013. 00:55:21.
I066: interview with P0085 (♂, 1960). Nkholongue, September 1, 2013. 00:57:49.
I067: interview with P0236 (♂, 1975). Nkholongue, September 1, 2013. 00:31:55.
I068: interview with P0367 (♂, 1936). Nkholongue, September 2, 2013. 01:46:27.
I069: interview with P0650 (♀, 1939). Nkholongue, September 2, 2013. 00:54:17.
I070: interview with P1448 (♀, ~1935). Metangula, September 3, 2013. 00:28:59.
I071: interview with P0191 (♂, 1965). Nkholongue, September 4, 2013. 00:43:43.
I072: interview with P0262 (♀, ~1940). Malango, September 5, 2013. 01:15:43.
I073: interview with P1012 (♂, 1955). Malango, September 5, 2013. 01:02:59.
I074: interview with P0160 (♂, 1952). Metangula, September 6, 2013. 00:49:00.
I075: interview with P1218 (♀, 1930). Metangula, September 6, 2013. 01:04:00.
I076: interview with P1449 (♂, ~1948). Metangula, September 6, 2013. 00:46:46.
I077: interview with P1489 (♂). Metangula, September 6, 2013. 00:43:31.
I078: interview with P0258 (♂, 1953). Nkholongue, September 7, 2013. 00:53:41.
I079: interview with P0510 (♂, 1963). Nkholongue, September 7, 2013. 00:14:49.
I080: interview with P0641 (♂, 1952). Nkholongue, September 7, 2013. 00:58:34.
I081: interview with P1450 (♂, 1961). M'chepa, September 8, 2013. 00:42:54.
I082: interview with P1141 (♂, 1932). Malango, September 8, 2013. 01:00:21.
I083: interview with P1102 (♂, 1932), P1074 (♀, ~1940), P1141 (♂, 1932). Malango, September 8, 2013. 01:31:38.

I084: interview with P1451 (♂, 1949). Nkholongue, September 9, 2013. 00:55:56.
I085: interview with P0147 (♀, ~1928). Nkholongue, September 9, 2013. 00:32:28.
I086: interview with P0375 (♂, 1962). Nkholongue, September 9, 2013. 00:41:41.
I087: interview with P1452 (♂, 1927). Lichinga, September 10, 2013. 01:40:18.
I088: interview with P0262 (♀, ~1940). Malango, December 23, 2015. 00:33:02.
I091: interview with P0242 (♂, 1945). Malango, December 23, 2015. 00:19:10.
I093: interview with P0050 (♂, ~1922). Nkholongue, January 19, 2016. 02:05:05.
I094: interview with P0727 (♂, ~1940). M'chepa, January 27, 2016. 01:57:40.
I095: interview with P1453 (♂, ~1947), P1506 (♀, ~1950). Malango, January 28, 2016. 02:11:58.
I096: interview with P1216 (♂, 1957). Malango, February 1, 2016. 02:32:19.
I097: interview with P1454 (♂, ~1951). Malango, February 5, 2016. 02:29:46.
I099: interview with P1420 (♂, ~1922). Ngongo, February 16, 2016. 01:57:41.
I100: interview with P0025 (♀, 1948). Nkholongue, February 22, 2016. 00:57:26.
I101: interview with P0316 (♀, ~1952). Nkholongue, February 22, 2016. 01:28:36.
I102: interview with P1509 (♂, 1972), P1510 (♀), P1511 (♀), P1512 (♀). Tulo, February 22, 2016. 01:26:07.
I104: interview with P0298 (♀, ~1922). Nkholongue, March 1, 2016. 01:23:44.
I105: interview with P0242 (♂, 1945). Malango, April 4, 2016. 02:52:43.
I106: interview with P0262 (♀, ~1940). Malango, April 4, 2016. 02:50:13.
I107: interview with P1074 (♀, ~1940). Malango, April 5, 2016. 02:53:13.
I108: interview with P1074 (♀, ~1940). Malango, April 6, 2016. 01:52:45.
I109: interview with P1081 (♀, 1945). Malango, April 6, 2016. 01:25:08.
I111: interview with P0266 (♂, ~1932). Metangula, April 11, 2016. 01:57:49.
I112: interview with P0129 (♀, 1930), P0128 (♂, 1928). Nkholongue, April 12, 2016. 02:11:17.
I113: interview with P0367 (♂, 1936). Nkholongue, April 13, 2016. 02:59:35.
I114: interview with P1074 (♀, ~1940), P1141 (♂, 1932). Malango, April 15, 2016. 02:58:53.
I115: interview with P0160 (♂, 1952). Metangula, April 18, 2016. 03:26:47.
I116: interview with P1457 (♀). Metangula, April 18, 2016. 01:40:17.
I117: interview with P1458 (♂, ~1945). Micundi, April 20, 2016. 02:12:40.
I118: interview with P1218 (♀, 1930). Malango, April 21, 2016. 02:12:11.
I119: interview with P0855 (♂, 1954). Malango, April 21, 2016. 01:44:54.
I120: interview with P1102 (♂, 1932). Malango, April 21, 2016. 01:54:52.
I121: interview with P0527 (♂, ~1918). Maniamba, April 22, 2016. 01:22:14.
I122: interview with P1459 (♀, 1942), P1464 (♀, ~1974). Capi, April 22, 2016. 01:08:25.
I123: interview with P1460 (♀), P1461 (♂, ~1935), P1462 (♂, ~1935). Meluluca, April 25, 2016. 02:48:07.
I124: interview with P0376 (♂, 1968). Nkholongue, April 26, 2016. 01:45:06.
I125: interview with P1463 (♂, 1951). Ngala, April 27, 2016. 01:38:02.
I126: interview with P1466 (♂, 1952). Chuangwa, April 28, 2016. 01:16:39.
I127: interview with P1468 (♂), P1469 (♂), P1470 (♂), P1471 (♀). Malo, May 2, 2016. 02:49:36.
I128: interview with P1426 (♂, 1929). Malindi (Mangochi District, Malawi), May 28, 2016. 04:00:37.
I129: interview with P1426 (♂, 1929). Malindi (Mangochi District, Malawi), May 29, 2016. 03:02:09.
I130: interview with P1472 (♀, ~1955). Mangochi (Malawi), May 29, 2016. 00:45:53.
I131: interview with P1434 (♂, 1942). Lifuwu (Salima District, Malawi), May 31, 2016. 03:02:27.
I132: interview with P1439 (♂, ~1940), P1507 (♀, ~1930), P1508 (♀). Ndegue (Salima District, Malawi), June 1, 2016. 02:47:25.

I133: interview with P1473 (♂ ~1938), P1504 (♀). Limbi (Salima District, Malawi), June 1, 2016. 02:02:14.
I134: interview with P1490 (♀, 1944). Nkhotakota, June 2, 2016. 00:22:11.
I135: interview with P1494 (♂, 1942). Nkhotakota, June 2, 2016. 01:31:42.
I137: interview with P1496 (♀, 1950), P1497 (♂, 1964). Nkhotakota, June 2, 2016. 00:22:43.
I138: interview with P1498 (♂, 1940). Nkhotakota, June 2, 2016. 00:28:00.
I139: interview with P1475 (♀, 1960), P1474 (♂, 1972). Nkhotakota, June 2, 2016. 00:17:01.
I141: interview with P0375 (♂, 1962). Nkholongue, June 6, 2016. 01:16:37.
I142: interview with P0743 (♀, ~1930). Nkholongue, June 8, 2016. 01:22:31.
I144: interview with P0411 (♂, 1965). Nkholongue, June 8, 2016. 00:33:39.
I145: interview with P0284 (♂, 1966), P0273 (♀, 1950). Metangula, June 9, 2016. 01:01:14.
I148: interview with P1500 (♂, ~1946). Bandeze, June 10, 2016. 00:31:54.
I149: interview with P1501 (♂, 1949), P1513 (♂, 1943). Chinuni, June 11, 2016. 01:03:00.
I150: interview with P1483 (♀, 1950), P1481 (♂, 1954). Lussefa, June 15, 2016. 00:45:20.
I151: interview with P1108 (♂, ~1973). M'chepa, June 15, 2016. 00:42:16.
I152: interview with P1476 (♂, ~1935). Milombe, June 16, 2016. 01:23:52.
I153: interview with P1477 (♂, ~1940). Micucue, June 17, 2016. 01:02:47.
I154: interview with P0367 (♂, 1936), P0373 (♀, 1940). Nkholongue, June 18, 2016. 01:21:30.
I155: interview with P0713 (♂, 1944). Nkholongue, June 18, 2016. 00:35:06.
I156: interview with P1478 (♀). Metangula, June 18, 2016. 00:38:21.
I157: interview with P1455 (♂, 1952). Tulo, June 18, 2016. 00:23:55.
I158: interview with P0764 (♂, 1962). Nkholongue, June 20, 2016. 01:08:03.
I159: interview with P0242 (♂, 1945). Malango, June 20, 2016. 00:58:17.
I160: interview with P0727 (♂, ~1940). M'chepa, June 22, 2016. 00:15:44.
I161: interview with P0160 (♂, 1952). Metangula, June 22, 2016. 00:48:57.
I162: interview with P0512 (♀, 1967). Nkholongue, June 22, 2016. 00:57:38.
I163: interview with P0028 (♂, 1969). Nkholongue, June 22, 2016. 00:31:38.
I164: interview with P0375 (♂, 1962). Nkholongue, June 23, 2016. 00:43:14.
I165: interview with P1467 (♀, 1948). Lichinga, June 27, 2016. 00:31:56.
I166: interview with P1479 (♀, ~1922), P1505 (♂, 1957). Nampula, June 28, 2016. 01:26:03.
I168: interview with P0694 (♀, 1959). Nkholongue, January 29, 2021. 00:40:49.

Other Sources

Amanze, James. "Nkholongue Village, Niassa," email, May 5, 2018.
Lugala Forest Reserve: A Forest Conservation and Eco Tourism Project. Concession Application, April 2003.
Ministério da Agricultura: Direcção Nacional de Geografia e Cadastro, "Modelo de Acta de Consulta as Comunidades Locais ao abrigo do N° 3 do Art°. 13 da Lei de Terras, conjugado com o N° 2 do Art°. 27 do respectivo regulamento" (Nkholongue, October 26, 2006).
Mtendele Estate: A Forest Conservation and Wilderness Residential Project (Draft Version), n.d..
Mtendele Estates. Lugala Forest Reserve: A Forest Conservation, Eco-Tourism and Premier Residential Project. Descriptive Report Including Land-Use Plan & Exploitation Plan. Final Report, June 2005.
Umali, Chadreque. *História de Nyanjas* (Metangula, 1996).

13.3 Published Primary Sources

Periodicals

Central Africa (CA), 1883–1964
African Tidings
Mtenga Watu, 1892–1894
The Nyassa News (TNN), 1893–1895
Likoma Diocesan Quarterly Paper (LDQP), 1903–1908
Nyasaland Diocesan Quarterly Paper (NDQP), 1909–1911
Nyasaland Diocesan Chronicle (NDC), 1911–1960
Lebombo Leaves, 1959–1980
Tempo, 1970–1980

Autobiographical Sources and Travel Journals

Ambali, Augustine. *Thirty Years in Nyasaland*. Westminster: UMCA, 1931.
Antcliff, Joan. *Living in the Spirit*. Herefordshire: Orphans, 2004.
Bellingham, William. *The Diary of a Working Man (William Bellingham) in Central Africa, December, 1884, to October, 1887*. Edited by J. Cooke Yarborough. London: Society for Promoting Christian Knowledge, 1888.
Chipembere, Henry B.M. *My Malawian Ancestors*, 1969.
Desmore, Abe J.B. *With the 2nd Cape Corps Thro' Central Africa*. Cape Town: Citadel, 1920.
Elton, James Frederick. *Travels and Researches among the Lakes and Mountains of Eastern & Central Africa*. Edited by H.B. Cotterill. London: John Murray, 1879.
Gomes e Sousa, Alice. "O Lago Niassa (excerptos dum diário)." *Portugal Colonial: Revista de Propaganda e Expansão Colonial* 4, no. 50 (1935): 13–16.
Hetherwick, A. "Notes of a Journey from Domasi Mission Station, Mount Zomba, to Lake Namaramba, August 1887." *Proceedings of the Royal Geographical Society and Monthly Record of Geography* 10, no. 1 (January 1888): 25.
Hine, J.E. *Days Gone by: Being Some Account of Past Years Chiefly in Central Africa*. London: John Murray, 1924.
Howard, Robert. *Five Years Medical Work on Lake Nyasa: A Report to the Medical Board of the Universities' Mission on the Health of the European Missionaries in the Likoma Diocese*. London: UMCA, 1904.
Johnson, William Percival. *My African Reminiscences 1875–1895*. Westminster: UMCA, 1924.
Johnson, William Percival. *Nyasa. The Great Water*. 1922. Reprint, New York: Negro Universities Press, 1969.
Kachamila, John William. *Do Vale do Rift ao sonho da liberdade: Memórias de Lissungo*. Maputo: Nachingwea, 2016.
Kida, Mateus. "A abertura das frentes de combate em Niassa." In *Simpósio 50 anos da Frelimo (1962–2012): Fontes para a nossa história*, edited by Carlos Jorge Siliya, Benigna Zimba, and Páscoa Themba, 112–17. Colecção Memórias do Combatente. Maputo: Centro de Pesquisa da História da Luta de Libertação Nacional, 2012.

Langa, Aurélio Valente. *Memórias de um combatente da causa: O passado que levou o verso da minha vida*. Maputo: JV, 2011.
Laws, Robert. "Voyage on Lake N'yassa." *The Free Church of Scotland Monthly Record*, no. 189 (April 1, 1878): 83–87.
Lester, Rodah Namwalizi. *Cassava Is the Root: Community Development with Women. Recipes for Africa*. Toronto: lulu.com, 2010.
Lettow-Vorbeck, Paul von. *Meine Erinnerungen aus Ostafrika*. Leipzig: Koehler, 1920.
Lima, Pedroso de. "8.000 quilómetros através de Moçambique." *Boletim Geral das Colónias* 11, no. 118 (Abril de 1935): 42–66.
Litumbe, Paulo. "Appendix 4: Bishop Paulo Litumbe's Memoirs." In *Dancing Their Dreams: The Lakeshore Nyanja Women of the Anglican Diocese of Niassa*, by Helen E.P. van Koevering, 145–70. Malawi, 2005.
Livingstone, David. *The Last Journals of David Livingstone in Central Africa*. Edited by Horace Waller. New York, 1875.
Livingstone, David. "Field Diary IV, 1 July – 5 September 1866." Livingstone Online. Accessed October 29, 2021. http://livingstoneonline.org/in-his-own-words/catalogue?query=liv_000004&view_pid=liv%3A000004.
Livingstone, David. "Unyanyembe Journal, 28 January 1866–5 March 1872." Livingstone Online. Accessed January 10, 2018. https://livingstoneonline.org/in-his-own-words/catalogue?view_pid=liv%3A000019.
Livingstone, David, and Charles Livingstone. *Narrative of an Expedition to the Zambesi and Its Tributaries*. New York: Harper, 1866.
Paul, John. *Mozambique: Memoirs of a Revolution*. Harmondsworth: Penguin, 1975.
Pelembe, João Facitela. *Lutei pela pátria: Memórias de um combatente da luta pela libertação nacional*. Maputo, 2012.
Richter, Julius. *Evangelische Mission im Nyassa-Lande*. Berlin: Evangel. Missionsgesellschaft, 1892.
Sim, Arthur Fraser. *The Life and Letters of Arthur Fraser Sim*. Westminster: UMCA, 1897.
Steere, Edward. *A Walk to the Nyassa Country*. Zanzibar: UMCA, 1876.
Stewart, James. "The Second Circumnavigation of Lake Nyassa." *Proceedings of the Royal Geographical Society and Monthly Record of Geography, New Monthly Series* 1, no. 5 (1879): 289–304.
Sutherland, James. *The Adventures of an Elephant Hunter*. London: Macmillan, 1912.
Tazama, Osvaldo. "Osvaldo Assahel Tazama." In *Protagonistas da Luta de Libertação Nacional*, edited by Ana Bouene Mussanhane, 617–629. Maputo: Marimbique, 2012.
Vilhena, Ernesto Jardim de. *Companhia de Nyassa: Relatorios e memorias sobre os territorios pelo governador*. Lisboa: Typographia da "A Editora," 1905.
Webb, Robert. *A Visit to Africa 1896*. Westminster: UMCA, 1897.
Whiteman, Ralph J. "A Traveller's Letter Home: Jubilee Voyage of the 'SS Chauncy Maples' (Written in October 1951)." June 2011. Accessed August 9, 2011. http://www.chauncymaples.org/newsletter/chauncy_maples_jubilee_voyage.pdf.
Winspear, Frank. "Some Reminiscences of Nyasaland." *The Society of Malawi Journal* 8, no. 2 (1960): 35–74.
Young, Edward D. *Nyassa, a Journal of Adventures: Whilst Exploring Lake Nyassa, Central Africa, and Establishing the Settlement of "Livingstonia."* London: John Murray, 1877.
Young, Edward D. "On a Recent Sojourn at Lake Nyassa, Central Africa." *Proceedings of the Royal Society of London* 21, no. 4 (1877): 225–233.

Zilhão, Sérgio. "Depoimento de Comandante de Mar e Guerra Sérgio Zilhão." In *Combater em Moçambique: Guerra e descolonização 1964–1975*, by Manuel A. Bernardo, 335–354. Lisboa: Préfacio, 2003.

Legislation

Conselho de Ministros. "Resolução n.° 37/2001: Política sobre os assunto dos antigos combatentes e estratégia de sua implementação." *Boletim da República. Publicação Oficial da República de Moçambique*, no. 20 (May 22, 2001).
"Decreto n.° 3/86 de 25 de Julho." *Boletim da República (I Série)*, no. 30, 3.° Suplemento (July 26, 1986).
"Decreto n.° 11/2005 de 10 de Junho: Regulamento da Lei dos Órgãos Locais do Estado." *Boletim da República (I Série)*, no. 23, 2° Suplemento (June 10, 2005).
"Decreto n.° 15/2000, de 20 de Junho: estabelece as formas de articulação dos órgãos locais do estado com as autoridades comunitárias." *Boletim da República (I Série)*, no. 24, Suplemento (June 20, 2000).
"Decreto n.° 59/2011 de 17 de Novembro: Reserva Parcial do Lago Niassa." *Boletim da República (I Série)*, no. 46, Suplemento (November 17, 2011).
"Decreto n.° 66/98 de 8 de Dezembro: Regulamento da Lei de Terras." *Boletim da República (I Série)*, no. 48, 3° Suplemento (December 8, 1998).
"Diploma Ministerial n.° 29-A/2000 de 17 de Março: Anexo Técnico ao Regulamento da Lei de Tarras [sic]." *Boletim da República (I Série)*, no. 50, Suplemento (March 17, 2000).
"Lei N.° 3/2002, de 17 de Janeiro: Estatuto do Combatente da Luta de Libertação Nacional," *Boletim da República (I Série)*, no. 3, Suplemento (January 17, 2002).
"Lei n.° 6/79 de 3 de Julho: Lei de Terras." *Boletim da República (I Série)*, no. 76 (July 3, 1979): 223–228.
"Lei n.° 8/2003 de 19 de Maio: Lei dos Órgãos Locais do Estado." *Boletim da República (I Série)*, no. 20, Suplemento (May 19, 2003).
"Lei n.° 19/97 de 1 de Outubro: Lei de Terras." *Boletim da República (I Série)*, no. 40, 3° Suplemento (October 7, 1997).

Various Published Sources

AIM. "Mozambique: Death of Leading Photographer." allAfrica, March 10, 2003. Accessed October 21, 2016. http://allafrica.com/stories/200303100613.html.
"A New Zealander's Investments." *The Press (Christchurch)*. March 7, 1914.
Anlagen zum Jahresbericht über die Entwicklung der deutschen Schutzgebiete in Afrika und der Südsee im Jahre 1905/1906. Berlin: Mittler, 1907.
Annuário de Moçambique 1908. Lourenço Marques: Imprensa Nacional, 1908.
Anuário de Lourenço Marques. Lourenço Marques: A. W. Bayly, 1946.
Anuário de Lourenço Marques. Lourenço Marques: A. W. Bayly, 1947.
Augusto, António. "Medições de inteligência de algumas tribos indígenas das Zambézia e do Niassa, Moçambique." *Anais da Junta das Missões Geográficas e de Investigações Coloniais* 3, no. 5 (1948).

Cardoso, Antonio M. "Documento N.° 38: O Sr. Antonio Maria Cardoso ao Ministro da Marinha, telegramma, transmitido por Lourenço Marques, 10 de Abril de 1889." In *Negocios externos: Documentos apresentados ás cortes na sessão legislativa de 1890*, 19. Lisboa: Imprensa Nacional, 1890.
Companhia do Nyassa. "Boletim N.° 60." 1903.
Companhia do Nyassa. "Relatório e Contas apresentados a Assembleia Geral Ordinária em 30 de Julho de 1906." Lisboa, 1906.
Companhia do Nyassa. "Relatório e Contas apresentados à Assembleia Geral Ordinária em 9 de Dezembro de 1912." Lisboa, 1912.
Companhia do Nyassa. "Boletim N.° 169." 1912.
Companhia do Nyassa. "Boletim N.° 190." 1913.
Companhia do Nyassa. "Boletim N.° 189." 1913.
Companhia do Nyassa. "Relatório e Contas apresentados à Assembleia Geral Ordinária em 30 de Dezembro de 1915." Lisboa, 1915.
Companhia do Nyassa. "Relatório e Contas apresentados à Assembleia Geral Ordinária em 4 de Dezembro de 1916." Lisboa, 1916.
Companhia do Nyassa. "Relatório e Contas apresentados à Assembleia Geral Ordinária em 3 de Dezembro de 1918." Lisboa, 1918.
Companhia do Nyassa. "Relatório e Contas apresentados à Assembleia Geral Ordinária ia em 2 de Dezembro de 1919." Lisboa, 1919.
Companhia do Nyassa. "Relatório e Contas apresentados à Assembleia Geral Ordinária em 2 de Dezembro de 1920." Lisboa, 1920.
Companhia do Nyassa. "Report of the Council of Administration to Be Presented to the Ordinary General Meeting of Shareholders to Be Held in Lisbon, on Monday, December 3, 1912." Lisbon, 1923.
Companhia do Nyassa. *A Companhia do Nyassa: Facts e documentos*. Lisboa, 1928.
"Entrevista com o Governador do Niassa: Aurélio Manave analisa problemas políticos da província." *Tempo*, no. 319 (November 14, 1976): 22–27.
"Exhibition @ Museu Local: Metangula, Mozambique." Accessed June 8, 2019. http://www.ariannahuhn.info/museu-local-exhibition.html.
FAO and IFAD. "United Nations Decade of Family Farming 2019–2028 – Global Action Plan." Rome: FAO, 2019.
Instituto Hidrográfico. *Roteiro da costa portuguesa do Lago Niassa*. Lisboa, 1963.
Instituto Nacional de Estatística. "Recenseamento Geral da População e Habitação 2007. Indicadores socio-demográficos distritais: Província de Niassa." Maputo, 2010.
Instituto Nacional de Estatística (Portugal). *Anuário Estatístico do Ultramar*. Lisboa, 1942.
Johnson, William Percival. "Inclosure 2 in No. 2: Mr. Johnson to Commissioner Johnston." In *Africa. No. 5 (1893). Papers Relative to the Suppression of Slave-Raiding in British Central Africa*, 6–8. London, 1893.
Keller, Bill. "Mozambique Voting Today in First Free Election." The New York Times, October 27, 1994. Accessed January 4, 2019. https://www.nytimes.com/1994/10/27/world/mozambique-votingtoday-in-first-free-election.html.
"Livingstone's Reisen in Inner-Afrika, 1866–1873." *Mittheilungen aus Justus Perthes' Geographischer Anstalt über wichtige neue Erforschungen auf dem Gesamtgebiete der Geographie* 21 (1875): 86–109.
Mário, Tomás Vieira. "Unango: Nasce uma cidade." *Tempo*, no. 506 (June 22, 1980): 7.

Matusse, Hilário. "Artur Torohate: De guerrilheiro a homem da imagem." *Tempo*, no. 780 (September 22, 1985): 26–27.

Ministério da Administração Estatal. "Perfil do Distrito de Lago, Província de Niassa." Maputo, 2005. http://www.portaldogoverno.gov.mz/por/content/download/2837/23237/version/1/file/Lago.pdf.

Ministry of Tourism. "Strategic Plan for the Development of Tourism in Mozambique (2004–2013)." 2004. Accessed April 8, 2019. http://www.portaldogoverno.gov.mz/por/content/download/1437/12142/version/1/file/plano+estrategico+desenvolvimento+turismo.pdf&usg=aovvaw382dc0-yzutxdc3lbtrp22.

"Moçambique lembrou-se de Kajika." *Faísca: O Jornal do Niassa*, no. 644 (June 14, 2014): 8–10.

Mondlane, Eduardo. *The Struggle for Mozambique*. Harmondsworth: Penguin, 1969.

MozLegal. *Land Law Legislation*. [Maputo], 2004.

"Nachrichten von Dr. Roscher in Inner-Afrika." *Mittheilungen aus Justus Perthes' Geographischer Anstalt über wichtige neue Erforschungen auf dem Gesamtgebiete der Geographie* 6 (1860): 280–81.

"Novo Regime do Imposto Indígena." *Moçambique: Documentário Trimestral*, no. 45 (1946): 172–76.

Notícias Online. "Combatentes homenageados." May 21, 2014. Accessed August 3, 2014. http://www.jornalnoticias.co.mz/index.php/politica/16120-combatentes-homenageados.

Notícias Online. "Mais 33 mil combatentes vão beneficiar de pensões – Jornal Notícias." January 2, 2014. Accessed August 3, 2014. http://www.jornalnoticias.co.mz/index.php/politica/9366-mais-33-mil-combatentes-vao-beneficiar-de-pensoes.

Notícias Online. "MICO regista perto de 166.800 combatentes." June 14, 2014. Accessed July 16, 2014. http://www.jornalnoticias.co.mz/index.php/politica/17594-mico-regista-perto-de-166-800-combatentes.

Notícias Online. "PR sobre a fixação de pensões: Reduz insatisfação do combatente." March 14, 2016. Accessed July 18, 2019. https://www.jornalnoticias.co.mz/index.php/politica/51279-pr-sobre-a-fixacao-de-pensoes-reduz-insatisfacao-do-combatente.

"Nyasaland and the Slave Traffic." *The Anti-Slavery Reporter* 14, no. 5 (September 1894): 281–286.

"O processo eleitoral no Niassa: Entrevista com Aurélio Manave, Primeiro Secretário Provincial." *Tempo*, no. 376 (December 18, 1977): 36–40.

OECD and FAO, eds. *OECD-FAO Agricultural Outlook 2016–2025. Special Focus: Sub-Saharan Africa*. Paris: OECD Publishing, 2016.

O'Neill, Henry. "Document No. 131: Consul O'Neill to the Marquis of Salisburgy, Mozambique, 13 December 1879." In *Slave Trade No. 1 (1881): Correspondence with British Representatives and Agents Abroad, and Reports from Naval Officers and the Treasury, Relative to the Slave Trade*, 165–67. London: Houses of Parliament, 1881.

O'Neill, Henry. "Paper No. 38: Consul O'Neill to Earl Granville, Mozambique, 30 April 1883." In *Slave Trade No. 1 (1884). Correspondence with British Representatives and Agents Abroad, and Reports from Naval Officers and the Treasury, Relative to the Slave Trade: 1883–1884*, 25. London: Houses of Parliament, 1884.

Overseas Club and Patriotic League. "List of Subscribing Members 1918–19." London, n.d.

Overseas Club and Patriotic League. "List of Subscribing Members 1919–20." London, n.d.

Rafael, Suizane. "Património da UniRovuma: 'Não abandonamos as nossas instalações em Sanga e Lago.'" *Faísca: O Jornal do Niassa*, no. 750 (August 3, 2020): 8–9.

República de Moçambique. "Balanço do Plano Económico e Social 2006," 2007. Accessed April 20, 2019. http://www.portaldogoverno.gov.mz/por/content/download/1767/14380/version/1/file/pes+2006+balan%25c3%25a7o+anual+2006.pdf.

Rigby, C.P. "Proceedings No. 43 of 1860." *Transactions of the Bombay Geographical Society* 16 (1863): xlvi–lii.

Roscher, Gerd. *Kurze Schatten*. 2013. 58 min.

Royal Commission on Fugitive Slaves. *Report of the Commissioners, Minutes of the Evidence, and Appendix, with General Index of Minutes of Evidence and Appendix: Presented to Both Houses of Parliament by Command of Her Majesty*. London, 1876.

Sá Nogueira, Teresa. "Cinema Moçambicano (3). Artur Torohate: Cineasta guerrilheiro." *Tempo*, no. 830 (September 7, 1986): 44–45.

Schaad, Kurt. "Kairo-Kapstadt, Folge 5: Mosambik und Südafrika," June 4, 2010. Accessed May 7, 2019. https://www.srf.ch/play/tv/sendung/kairo-kapstadt?id=c446dfa8-0d70-0001-aee6-9b2047301a80.

Serrano, António de Melo. "Um reconhecimento no Distrito do Lago." *Anais do Instituto de Medicina Tropical* 8, no. 4 (1951): 645–687.

Ssentongo, G.W., and Nfamara J. Dampha. "Report of the Technical Consultation between Malawi and Mozambique on the Development and Management of the Fisheries of Lakes Malawi, Chilwa and Chiuta." UNDP/FAO IFIP Project. Bujumbura, March 1992. http://www.fao.org/docrep/014/am851e/am851e.pdf.

Swann, Alfred J. "Summary of 1895 Report on the Marimba District." *British Central Africa Gazette*, April 15, 1896.

Termos de Vassallagem nos territorios de Machona, Zambezia e Nyassa 1858 a 1889. Lisboa: Imprensa Nacional, 1890.

The Earth Institute (Columbia University), Millennium Promise, and UNDP. "The Millennium Villages Project: 2009 Annual Report." Accessed October 27, 2021. https://irp-cdn.multiscreensite.com/6fae6349/files/uploaded/MVP%202009%20Annual%20Report%20-%20EIMPUNDP%20-%20General%20Public%20Version%20-%20FINAL.pdf.

UN Millennium Project. "Millennium Villages: A New Approach to Fighting Poverty." Accessed December 10, 2014. http://www.unmillenniumproject.org/mv/.

United Nations. "International Year of Ecotourism 2002 Launched at Headquarters Event." United Nations: Meetings Coverage and Press Releases. Accessed May 8, 2019. https://www.un.org/press/en/2002/envdev607.doc.htm.

United Nations Office for Humanitarian Assistance Coordination. "Projected Density of 160,000 Demobilized Soldiers and Dependents (by District)," January 1994. Accessed March 30, 2019. http://www.mozambiquehistory.net/history/peace_process/94/01/19940100_density_of_demobbed_soldiers.pdf.

"War News for Darkest Africa: German Message to a Nyasa Notable." *The Times*, January 14, 1916.

Wikipedia. "MV Chauncy Maples." Accessed April 20, 2019. https://en.wikipedia.org/w/index.php?title=MV_Chauncy_Maples&oldid=881783935.

"Zonas Libertadas: Berço da revolução." *Tempo*, Número especial: Dedicado à viagem presidencial à Província do Niassa (December 26, 1979): 91–95.

13.4 Secondary Sources

Abdallah, Yohanna B. *The Yaos: Chiikala Cha Wayao*. Edited by Meredith Sanderson. 2nd ed. London: Frank Cass, 1973. First edition published 1919.

Abu-Lughod, Lila. "The Romance of Resistance: Tracing Transformations of Power through Bedouin Women." *American Ethnologist* 17, no. 1 (1990): 41–55.
Achebe, Chinua. *Things Fall Apart*. 1958. Reprint, London: Penguin, 2006.
Adam, Yussuf. "Trick or Treat: The Relationship between Destabilisation, Aid and Government Development Policies in Mozambique 1975–1990." PhD thesis, Roskilde University, 1996.
Åkesson, Gunilla, André Calengo, and Christopher Tanner. "It's Not a Question of Doing or Not Doing It—It's a Question of How to Do It: Study on Community Land Rights in Niassa Province, Mozambique." Uppsala: Institutionen för stad och land SLU, 2009.
Akyeampong, Emmanuel, and Hippolyte Fofack. "The Contribution of African Women to Economic Growth and Development in the Pre-Colonial and Colonial Periods: Historical Perspectives and Policy Implications." *Economic History of Developing Regions* 29, no. 1 (2014): 42–73.
Alexopoulou, Kleoniki, and Dácil Juif. "Colonial State Formation without Integration: Tax Capacity and Labour Regimes in Portuguese Mozambique (1890s–1970s)." *International Review of Social History* 62, no. 2 (2017): 215–252.
Allina, Eric. "Resistance and the Social History of Africa." *Journal of Social History* 37, no. 1 (2003): 187–198.
Allina, Eric. *Slavery by Any Other Name: African Life under Company Rule in Colonial Mozambique*. Charlottesville: University of Virginia Press, 2012.
Allison, Michael E. "The Legacy of Violence on Post-Civil War Elections: The Case of El Salvador." *Studies in Comparative International Development* 45, no. 1 (2010): 104–124.
Alobo Loison, Sarah. "Rural Livelihood Diversification in Sub-Saharan Africa: A Literature Review." *The Journal of Development Studies* 51, no. 9 (2015): 1125–1138.
Alpers, Edward A. "The Story of Swema: Female Vulnerability in Nineteenth-Century East Africa." In *Women and Slavery in Africa*, edited by Claire C. Robertson and Martin A. Klein, 185–219. Madison: University of Wisconsin Press, 1983.
Alpers, Edward A. "Trade, State, and Society among the Yao in the Nineteenth Century." *The Journal of African History* 10, no. 3 (1969): 405–420.
Alpers, Edward A. "The Yao in Malawi: The Importance of Local Research." In *The Early History of Malawi*, edited by Bridglal Pachai, 168–78. London: Longman, 1972.
Alpers, Edward A. "Towards a History of the Expansion of Islam in East Africa: The Matrilineal Peoples of the Southern Interior." In *The Historical Study of African Religion*, edited by Terence O. Ranger and Isaria N. Kimambo, 172–201. London: Heinemann, 1972.
Alpers, Edward A. "Ethnicity, Politics, and History in Mozambique." *Africa Today* 21, no. 4 (1974): 39–52.
Alpers, Edward A. *Ivory & Slaves in East Central Africa*. Berkeley: University of California Press, 1975.
Alpers, Edward A. "Africa Reconfigured: Presidential Address to the 1994 African Studies Association Annual Meeting." *African Studies Review* 38, no. 2 (1995): 1–10.
Alpers, Edward A. "East Central Africa." In *The History of Islam in Africa*, edited by Nehemia Levtzion and Randall L. Pouwels, 303–25. Athens: Ohio University Press, 2000.
Amaral, Manuel Gomes da Gama. *O povo Yao = Mtundu Wayao: Subsídios para o estudo de um povo do noroeste de Moçambique*. Lisboa: IICT, 1990.
Anderson, David. *Eroding the Commons: The Politics of Ecology in Baringo, Kenya, 1890–1963*. Oxford: James Currey, 2002.
Anderson, David, and Daniel Branch. "Allies at the End of Empire—Loyalists, Nationalists and the Cold War, 1945–76." *The International History Review* 39, no. 1 (2017): 1–13.

Andrade, Tonio. "A Chinese Farmer, Two African Boys, and a Warlord: Toward a Global Microhistory." *Journal of World History* 21, no. 4 (2011): 573–591.
Aradóttir, Anna G. "Women's Land Rights under the Mozambican Land Law: An Ethnographic Study of the Matrilineal District of Majune, Niassa Province, Northern Mozambique." Master thesis, University of Gothenburg, 2016. https://gupea.ub.gu.se/bitstream/2077/52902/1/gupea_2077_52902_1.pdf.
Arnfred, Signe. *Sexuality & Gender Politics in Mozambique: Rethinking Gender in Africa*. Woodbridge: James Currey, 2011.
Arnfred, Signe. "Implications of Matriliny: Gender and Islam in Northern Mozambique." *International Feminist Journal of Politics* 23, no. 2 (2021): 221–42.
Arrighi, Giovanni "Labour Supplies in Historical Perspective: A Study of the Proletarianization of the African Peasantry in Rhodesia." *The Journal of Development Studies* 6, no. 3 (1970): 197–234.
Asch, Michael, Colin Samson, Ulf Dahre, and Adam Kuper. "More on the Return of the Native." *Current Anthropology* 47, no. 1 (2006): 145–149.
Asch, Michael, Colin Samson, Dieter Heinen, Justin Kenrick, Jerome Lewis, Sidsel Saugestad, Terry Turner, and Adam Kuper. "On the Return of the Native." *Current Anthropology* 45, no. 2 (2004): 261–267.
Atieno-Odhiambo, E.S. "The Movement of Ideas: A Case Study of Intellectual Responses to Colonialism among the Liganua Peasants." In *History & Social Change in East Africa*, edited by Bethwell A. Ogot, 165–185. Nairobi: East African Literature Bureau, 1976.
Austin, Gareth. *Labour, Land, and Capital in Ghana: From Slavery to Free Labour in Asante*. Rochester: University of Rochester Press, 2005.
Austin, Gareth. "The 'Reversal of Fortune' Thesis and the Compression of History: Perspectives from African and Comparative Economic History." *Journal of International Development* 20, no. 8 (2008): 996–1027.
Austin, Gareth. "The Return of Capitalism as a Concept." In *Capitalism: The Reemergence of a Historical Concept*, edited by Jürgen Kocka and Marcel van der Linden, 207–234. London: Bloomsbury, 2016.
Austin, Gareth. "Slavery in Africa, 1804–1936." In *The Cambridge World History of Slavery*, edited by David Eltis, Stanley L. Engerman, Seymour Drescher, and David Richardson, 4: 174–196. Cambridge: Cambridge University Press, 2017.
Austin, Gareth, and Stephen Broadberry. "Introduction: The Renaissance of African Economic History." *The Economic History Review* 67, no. 4 (2014): 893–906.
Axelson, Eric. *Portugal and the Scramble for Africa: 1875–1891*. Johannesburg: Witwatersrand University Press, 1967.
Azevedo, Mario Joaquim. *Tragedy and Triumph: Mozambique Refugees in Southern Africa, 1977–2001*. Portsmouth: Heinemann, 2002.
Baden, Sally. "Post-Conflict Mozambique Women's Special Situation, Population Issues and Gender Perspectives: To Be Integrated into Skills Training and Employment Promotion." BRIDGE Report, no. 44. Brighton: Institute of Development Studies, June 1997. http://www.bridge.ids.ac.uk//bridge/Reports/re44c.pdf.
Badiane, Ousmane, and Tsitsi Makombe. "Agriculture, Growth, and Development in Africa." In *The Oxford Handbook of Africa and Economics. Volume II: Policies and Practices*, edited by Célestin Monga and Justin Yifu Lin, 307–324. Oxford: Oxford University Press, 2015.
Baêna, Luís S. de. *Fuzileiros: Factos e feitos na guerra de África. 1961/1974*. Vol. 4: Crónica dos feitos de Moçambique. 4 vols. Lisboa: INAPA, 2006.

Baldwin, Kate. *The Paradox of Traditional Chiefs in Democratic Africa*. New York: Cambridge University Press, 2016.

Baptista, João Afonso. *The Good Holiday: Development, Tourism and the Politics of Benevolence in Mozambique*. New York: Berghahn, 2017.

Barley, Nigel. *Adventures in a Mud Hut: An Innocent Anthropologist Abroad*. New York: Vanguard Press, 1984.

Barnard, Alan. "Kalahari Revisionism, Vienna and the 'Indigenous Peoples' Debate." *Social Anthropology* 14, no. 1 (2007): 1–16.

Barnes, Herbert. *Johnson of Nyasaland: A Study of the Life and Work of William Percival Johnson*. Westminster: UMCA, 1933.

Bashir Salau, Mohammed. *The West African Slave Plantation: A Case Study*. New York: Palgrave Macmillan, 2011.

Bayly, Christopher A. *The Birth of the Modern World, 1780–1914: Global Connections and Comparisons*. Malden: Blackwell, 2004.

Becker, Felicitas. *Becoming Muslim in Mainland Tanzania 1890–2000*. Oxford: Oxford University Press, 2008.

Becker, Felicitas, Salvatory S. Nyanto, James Giblin, Ann McDougall, Alexander Meckelburg, and Lotte Pelckmans. "Researching the Aftermath of Slavery in Mainland East Africa: Methodological, Ethical, and Practical Challenges." In *Slavery & Abolition* 44, no. 1 (2023): 131–156.

Beckett, Ian F.W. "The Portuguese Army: The Campaign in Mozambique, 1964–1974." In *Armed Forces and Mordern Counterinsurgency*, edited by Ian F.W. Beckett and John Pimlott. London: Croom Helm, 1985.

Bellagamba, Alice, Sandra E. Greene, and Martin A. Klein, eds. *African Voices on Slavery and the Slave Trade*. New York: Cambridge University Press, 2013.

Bellagamba, Alice, Sandra E. Greene, and Martin A. Klein. "Introduction. When the Past Shadows the Present: The Legacy in Africa of Slavery and the Slave Trade." In *The Bitter Legacy: African Slavery Past and Present*, edited by Alice Bellagamba, Sandra E. Greene, and Martin A. Klein, 1–28. Princeton: Markus Wiener, 2013.

Bellagamba, Alice, Sandra E. Greene, and Martin A. Klein. *African Slaves, African Masters: Politics, Memories, Social Life*. Trenton: Africa World Press, 2017.

Bernstein, Henry. "Taking the Part of Peasants?" In *The Food Question: Profits versus People?*, edited by Henry Bernstein, Ben Crow, Maureen Mackintosh, and Charlotte Martin, 69–79. London: Routledge, 1990.

Bernstein, Henry. "Considering Africa's Agrarian Questions." *Historical Materialism* 12, no. 4 (2004): 115–144.

Berry, Sara. *No Condition Is Permanent: The Social Dynamics of Agrarian Change in Sub-Saharan Africa*. Madison: University of Wisconsin Press, 1993.

Berry, Veronica, and Celia Petty, eds. *The Nyasaland Survey Papers 1938–1943: Agriculture, Food, and Health*. London: Academy Books, 1992.

Bertocchi, Graziella. "The Legacies of Slavery in and Out of Africa." *IZA Journal of Migration* 5, no. 1 (2016): 24.

Beusekom, Monica van. *Negotiating Development: African Farmers and Colonial Experts at the Office Du Niger, 1920–1960*. Portsmouth: Heinemann, 2002.

Bissell, William Cunningham. "Engaging Colonial Nostalgia." *Cultural Anthropology* 20, no. 2 (2005): 215–248.

Blaser, Thomas. "Africa and the Future: An Interview with Achille Mbembe." Africa is a Country. Accessed January 27, 2021. https://africasacountry.com/2013/11/africa-and-the-future-an-interview-with-achille-mbembe/.
Blom, Astrid. "Ambiguous Political Space: Chiefs, Land and the Poor in Rural Mozambique." In *In the Name of the Poor: Contesting Political Space for Poverty Reduction*, edited by Neil Webster and Lars Engberg-Pedersen, 104–128. London: Zed Books, 2002.
Blood, A.G. *The History of the Universities' Mission to Central Africa*. Vol. 2: 1907–1932. 3 vols. London: UMCA, 1957.
Bolyanatz, Alexander H. "Matriliny and Revisionist Anthropology." *Anthropos* 90, no. 1/3 (1995): 169–180.
Bonate, Liazzat. "Traditions and Transitions: Islam and Chiefship in Northern Mozambique ca. 1850–1974." PhD thesis, University of Cape Town, 2007.
Bonate, Liazzat. "Islam in Northern Mozambique: A Historical Overview." *History Compass* 8, no. 7 (2010): 573–593.
Bonate, Liazzat. "Muslim Memories of the Liberation War in Cabo Delgado." *Kronos* 39, no. 1 (2013): 230–256.
Bonate, Liazzat. "Islam and the Yao." Oxford Islamic Studies Online. Accessed May 22, 2018. http://www.oxfordislamicstudies.com/article/opr/t343/e0055?_hi=0&_pos=1.
Bone, David S. "Islam in Malawi." *Journal of Religion in Africa* 13 (1982): 126–138.
Bone, David S. "Towards a History of Islam in Malawi." In *History Seminar Papers 1982/83*. Chancellor College, Zomba, 1983.
Bone, David S. "An Outline History of Islam in Malawi." In *Malawi's Muslims: Historical Perspectives*, edited by David S. Bone, 13–26. Blantyre: CLAIM, 2000.
Bonneuil, Christophe. "Development as Experiment: Science and State Building in Late Colonial and Postcolonial Africa, 1930–1970." *Osiris* 15, no. 1 (2000): 258–281.
Bontinck, François. "Un explorateur infortuné: Albrecht Roscher (1836–1860)." *Africa: Rivista Trimestrale di Studi e Documentazione dell'Istituto Italiano per l'Africa e l'Oriente* 44, no. 3 (1989): 403–412.
Borges Coelho, João Paulo. "Protected Villages and Communal Villages in the Mozambican Province of Tete (1968–1982): A History of State Resettlement Policies, Development and War." PhD thesis, University of Bradford, 1993. http://www.saber.ac.mz/bitstream/10857/3221/1/HTP-018.pdf.
Borges Coelho, João Paulo. "State Resettlement Policies in Post-Colonial Rural Mozambique: The Impact of the Communal Village Programme on Tete Province, 1977–1982." *Journal of Southern African Studies* 24, no. 1 (1998): 61–91.
Borges Coelho, João Paulo. "African Troops in the Portuguese Colonial Army, 1961–1974: Angola, Guinea-Bissau and Mozambique." *Portuguese Studies Review* 10, no. 1 (2002): 129–150.
Borges Coelho, João Paulo. "Da violência colonial ordenada à ordem pós-colonial violenta: Sobre um legado das guerras coloniais nas ex-colónias portuguesas." *Lusotopie*, no. 10 (2003): 175–193.
Borges Coelho, João Paulo. "Politics and Contemporary History in Mozambique: A Set of Epistemological Notes." *Kronos* 39, no. 1 (2013): 20–31.
Bowen, Merle L. *The State Against the Peasantry: Rural Struggles in Colonial and Postcolonial Mozambique*. Charlottesville: University Press of Virginia, 2000.
Bozzoli, Belinda. *Women of Phokeng: Consciousness, Life Strategy, and Migrancy in South Africa, 1900–1983*. Portsmouth: Heinemann, 2002.
Bozzoli, Carlos, and Tilman Brück. "Agriculture, Poverty, and Postwar Reconstruction: Micro-Level Evidence from Northern Mozambique." *Journal of Peace Research* 46, no. 3 (2009): 377–397.

Braathen, Einar. "Democratic Decentralisation in Mozambique?" In *Community & the State in Lusophone Africa: Papers Read at the Conference on New Research on Lusophone Africa Held at King's College London 16 – 17 May 2002*, edited by Malyn Newitt, Patrick Chabal, and Norrie Macqueen, 99 – 126. London: King's College, 2003.

Braga, Carla. "'They Are Squeezing Us!' Gender, Matriliny, Power and Agricultural Policies: Case Study in Issa Malanga." IASCP XIX Conference. Bloomington, 2000. Accessed October 29, 2021. https://www.yumpu.com/en/document/view/40204615/gender-matriliny-power-and-agricultural-policies-case-study.

Braga, Carla. "Matrilinearidade, desenvolvimento e terras no âmbito do programa Mosagrius em Issa Malanga, Niassa." Master thesis, Universidade Eduardo Mondlane, 2001.

Bragança, Aquino de, Yussuf Adam, Jacques Depelchin, Anna Maria Gentili, Gary Littlejohn, and Vladimir Zamparoni. "A situação nas antigas zonas libertadas de Cabo Delgado." Maputo: Oficina de História, 1983. http://sas-space.sas.ac.uk/4503/1/a_situaco_nas_antigas.pdf.

Branch, Daniel. *Defeating Mau Mau, Creating Kenya: Counterinsurgency, Civil War, and Decolonization*. Cambridge: Cambridge University Press, 2009.

Brass, Tom. *Peasants, Populism and Postmodernism: The Return of the Agrarian Myth*. London: Frank Cass, 2000.

Brass, Tom. "Weapons of the Week, Weakness of the Weapons: Shifts and Stasis in Development Theory." *Journal of Peasant Studies* 34, no. 1 (2007): 111 – 153.

Brass, Tom. *Class, Culture and the Agrarian Myth*. Leiden: Brill, 2014.

Brass, Tom. "Who These Days Is Not a Subaltern? The Populist Drift of Global Labor History." *Science & Society* 81, no. 1 (2017): 10 – 34.

Brass, Tom. *Marxism Missing, Missing Marxism: From Marxism to Identity Politics and Beyond*. Leiden: Brill, 2021.

Braudel, Fernand. *La méditerranée et le monde méditerranéen à l'époque de Philippe II*. 2nd ed., 2 vols. Paris: Armand Colin, 1966. First edition published 1949.

Bravo, Nelson Saraiva. *A cultura algodeira na economia do norte de Moçambique*. Lisboa: Junta de Investigações do Ultramar, 1963.

Brennan, James R. "Book Review of Africa, Empire and Globalization: Essays in Honor of A.G. Hopkins." *Britain and the World* 8, no. 2 (2015): 254 – 257.

Brito, Raquel Soeiro de. *No trilho dos descobrimentos: Estudos geográficos*. Lisboa: Comissão Nacional para as Comemorações dos Descobrimentos Portugueses, 1997.

Brouwer, Roland. "The Risks of Repeating History: The New Land Law in Mozambique." XII Congreso Internacional, derecho consuetudinario y pluralismo legal: Desafíos en el tercer milenio. Arica (Chile), 2000. Accessed April 2, 2019. http://dlc.dlib.indiana.edu/dlc/handle/10535/1461?show=full.

Brown, Richard D. "Microhistory and the Post-Modern Challenge." *Journal of the Early Republic* 23, no. 1 (2003): 1 – 20.

Brownhill, Leigh, and Terisa E. Turner. "Ecofeminism at the Heart of Ecosocialism." *Capitalism Nature Socialism* 30, no. 1 (2019): 1 – 10.

Bruijn, Mirjam de, Rijk van Dijk, and Jan-Bart Gewald, eds. *Strength beyond Structure: Social and Historical Trajectories of Agency in Africa*. Leiden: Brill, 2007.

Bryceson, Deborah F. "Deagrarianization and Rural Employment in Sub-Saharan Africa: A Sectoral Perspective." *World Development* 24, no. 1 (1996): 97 – 111.

Bryceson, Deborah F. "Multiplex Livelihoods in Rural Africa: Recasting the Terms and Conditions of Gainful Employment." *The Journal of Modern African Studies* 40, no. 1 (2002): 1 – 28.

Bryceson, Deborah F. "The Scramble in Africa: Reorienting Rural Livelihoods." *World Development* 30, no. 5 (2002): 725–739.

Bryceson, Deborah F. "Domestic Work." In *General Labour History of Africa*, edited by Stefano Bellucci and Andreas Eckert, 301–332. Woodbridge: James Currey, 2019.

Bundy, Colin. *The Rise and Fall of the South African Peasantry*. London: Heinemann, 1979.

Burbank, Jane, and Frederick Cooper. *Empires in World History: Power and the Politics of Difference*. Princeton: Princeton University Press, 2010.

Burton, Andrew, and Michael Jennings. "Introduction: The Emperor's New Clothes? Continuities in Governance in Late Colonial and Early Postcolonial East Africa." *The International Journal of African Historical Studies*, 40, no. 1 (2007): 1–25.

Buur, Lars, and Helene Maria Kyed. "Introduction: Traditional Authority and Democratization in Africa." In *State Recognition and Democratization in Sub-Saharan Africa*, edited by Lars Buur and Helene Maria Kyed, 1–28. New York: Palgrave Macmillan, 2007.

Buur, Lars, and Helene Maria Kyed. "Traditional Authority in Mozambique: The Legible Space between State and Community." In *State Recognition and Democratization in Sub-Saharan Africa*, edited by Lars Buur and Helene Maria Kyed, 105–127. New York: Palgrave Macmillan, 2007.

Bwalya, Donald H. "Agricultural Change in the Northern Province of Zambia, 1948–1978: A Case Study of Maize Production in Kasama District." Master thesis, University of Zambia, 1989. http://dspace.unza.zm/bitstream/handle/123456789/1950/BwalyaDHJ0001.PDF?sequence=2&isAllowed=y.

Byres, Terence J. "Neo-Classical Neo-Populism 25 Years On: Déjà Vu and Déjà Passé. Towards a Critique." *Journal of Agrarian Change* 4, no. 1–2 (2004): 17–44.

Cabral, Lídia, and Simon Norfolk. "Inclusive Land Governance in Mozambique: Good Law, Bad Politics?" IDS Working Paper, no. 478. Brighton, 2016. https://opendocs.ids.ac.uk/opendocs/bitstream/handle/123456789/12187/Wp478.pdf?sequence=1&isAllowed=y.

Cabrita, João M. *Mozambique: The Tortuous Road to Democracy*. Basingstoke: Palgrave, 2000.

Cahen, Michel. *Mozambique: La révolution implosée. Études sur 12 ans d'indépendance (1975–1987)*. Paris: L'Harmattan, 1987.

Cahen, Michel. "Mozambique: The Debate Continues. Michel Cahen Writes …" *Southern Africa Report* 5, no. 4 (1990): 26–27.

Cahen, Michel. "The Mueda Case and Maconde Political Ethnicity: Some Notes on a Work in Progress." *Africana Studia*, no. 2 (1999): 29–46.

Cahen, Michel. "Notes de lecture: Les Africains et la ville." *Le Mouvement Social*, no. 204 (2003): 149–160.

Cahen, Michel. "Slavery, Enslaved Labour and Forced Labour in Mozambique." *Portuguese Studies Review* 21, no. 1 (2013): 253–265.

Candido, Mariana P. *An African Slaving Port and the Atlantic World: Benguela and Its Hinterland*. Cambridge: Cambridge University Press, 2013.

Cann, John P. *Counterinsurgency in Africa: The Portuguese Way of War, 1961–1974*. Westport: Greenwood, 1997.

Cann, John P. *Brown Waters of Africa: Portuguese Riverine Warfare 1961–1974*. 2007. Reprint, Solihull: Helion, 2013.

Carswell, Grace. "Livelihood Diversification: Increasing in Importance or Increasingly Recognised? Evidence from Southern Ethiopia." *Journal of International Development* 14, no. 6 (2002): 789–804.

Castelo, Cláudia. "Colonatos e aldeamentos no Niassa, Moçambique: Processos e impactos sociais em tempo de guerra (1964–1974)." *Tempo* 27, no. 3 (2021): 478–500.

Castryck, Geert. "'My Slave Sold All of Kigoma': Power Relations, Property Rights and the Historian's Quest for Understanding." In *Sources and Methods for African History and Culture: Essays in Honour of Adam Jones*, edited by Geert Castryck, Silke Strickrodt, and Katja Werthmann, 317–335. Leipzig: Leipziger Universitätsverlag, 2016.

Chabal, Patrick. "Lusophone Africa in Historical and Comparative Perspective." In *A History of Postcolonial Lusophone Africa*, by Patrick Chabal, 1–134. Bloomington: Indiana University Press, 2002.

Chabatama, Chewe M. "Peasant, Farming, the State, and Food Security in the North-Western Province of Zambia, 1902–1964." PhD thesis, Unversity of Toronto, 1999.

Chanock, Martin. "A Peculiar Sharpness: An Essay on Property in the History of Customary Law in Colonial Africa." *The Journal of African History* 32, no. 1 (1991): 65.

Chen, Joyce, Kumbukani Chirwa, and Sonia Ehrlich Sachs. "Fortification with Micronutrient Powder to Address Malnutrition in Rural Kenya." *Sight and Life* 29, no. 1 (2015): 129–131.

Chibber, Vivek. *Postcolonial Theory and the Specter of Capital*. London: Verso, 2013.

Chibber, Vivek. *The Class Matrix: Social Theory after the Cultural Turn*. Cambridge: Harvard University Press, 2022.

Chichava, Sérgio. "'They Can Kill Us but We Won't Go to the Communal Villages!' Peasants and the Policy of 'Socialisation of the Countryside' in Zambezia." *Kronos* 39, no. 1 (2013): 112–130.

Chichava, Sérgio. "The Anti-Frelimo Movements & the War in Zambezia." In *The War Within: New Perspectives on the Civil War in Mozambique, 1976–1992*, edited by Eric Morier-Genoud, Michel Cahen, and Domingos Manuel do Rosário, 17–45. Woodbridge: James Currey, 2018.

Chimhowu, Admos, and Phil Woodhouse. "Vernacular Land Markets and the Changing Face of Customary Land Tenure in Africa." *Forum for Development Studies* 32, no. 2 (2005): 385–414.

Chitonge, Horman. "Capitalism in Africa: Mutating Capitalist Relations and Social Formations." *Review of African Political Economy* 45, no. 155 (2018): 158–167.

Chossudovsky, Michel. "'Exporting Apartheid' to Sub-Saharan Africa." *Review of African Political Economy* 24, no. 73 (1997): 389–398.

Clarence-Smith, William G. *The Third Portuguese Empire, 1825–1975: A Study in Economic Imperialism*. Manchester: Manchester University Press, 1985.

Clarence-Smith, William G. "'Thou Shalt Not Articulate Modes of Production.'" *Canadian Journal of African Studies/Revue Canadienne des Études Africaines* 19, no. 1 (1985): 19–22.

Cobbing, Julian. "The Mfecane as Alibi: Thoughts on Dithakong and Mbolompo." *The Journal of African History* 29, no. 3 (1988): 487–519.

Coghe, Samuël. *Population Politics in the Tropics: Demography, Health and Transimperialism in Colonial Angola*. Cambridge: Cambridge University Press, 2022.

Cohen, David William. "Doing Social History from Pim's Doorway." In *Reliving the Past: The Worlds of Social History*, edited by Olivier Zunz, 191–235. Chapel Hill: University of North Carolina Press, 1985.

Cohen, David William, and E.S. Atieno-Odhiambo. *Siaya: The Historical Anthropology of an African Landscape*. London: James Currey, 1989.

Cole-King, P.A. *Lake Malawi Steamers*. Limbe: Department of Antiquities, 1987.

Collier, Paul. "On the Economic Consequences of Civil War." *Oxford Economic Papers* 51, no. 1 (1999): 168–183.

Comissão para o Estudo das Campanhas de África (CECA). *Resenha histórico-militar das campanhas de África, Vol. 4: Dispositivo das nossas forças Moçambique*. Lisboa: Estado-Maior do Exército, 1989.

Comissão para o Estudo das Campanhas de África (CECA). *Resenha histórico-militar das campanhas de África, Vol. 6: Aspectos da actividade operacional, Tomo III: Moçambique, Livro I*. Lisboa: Estado-Maior do Exército, 2012.

Cooper, Frederick. *Plantation Slavery on the East Coast of Africa*. New Haven: Yale University Press, 1977.

Cooper, Frederick. "The Problem of Slavery in African Studies." *The Journal of African History* 20, no. 1 (1979): 103–125.

Cooper, Frederick. *From Slaves to Squatters: Plantation Labor and Agriculture in Zanzibar and Coastal Kenya, 1890–1925*. New Haven: Yale University Press, 1980.

Cooper, Frederick. "Conflict and Connection: Rethinking Colonial African History." *The American Historical Review* 99, no. 5 (1994): 1516–1545.

Cooper, Frederick. *Decolonization and African Society: The Labor Question in French and British Africa*. Cambridge: Cambridge University Press, 1996.

Cooper, Frederick. "Mahmood Mamdani, Citizen and Subject: Contemporary Africa and the Legacy of Late Colonialism. Princeton: Princeton University Press, 1996. xii + 353pp." *International Labor and Working-Class History* 52 (1997): 156–160.

Cooper, Frederick. "Africa in a Capitalist World." In *Crossing Boundaries: Comparative History of Black People in Diaspora*, edited by Darlene Clark Hine and Jacqueline McLeod, 391–418. Bloomington: Indiana University Press, 1999.

Cooper, Frederick. "What Is the Concept of Globalization Good for? An African Historian's Perspective." *African Affairs* 100, no. 399 (2001): 189–213.

Cooper, Frederick. *Africa since 1940: The Past of the Present*. Cambridge: Cambridge University Press, 2002.

Cooper, Frederick. *Colonialism in Question: Theory, Knowledge, History*. Berkeley: University of California Press, 2005.

Cooper, Frederick. "Postcolonial Studies and the Study of History." In *Postcolonial Studies and Beyond*, edited by Ania Loomba, Suvir Kaul, Matti Bunzl, Antoinette Burton, and Jed Esty, 401–431. Durham: Duke University Press, 2005.

Cooper, Frederick. "Possibility and Constraint: African Independence in Historical Perspective." *The Journal of African History* 49, no. 2 (2008).

Cooper, Frederick. "How Global Do We Want Our Intellectual History to Be?" In *Global Intellectual History*, edited by Samuel Moyn and Andrew Sartori, 283–294. New York: Columbia University Press, 2013.

Cooper, Frederick. "Routes Out of Empire." *Comparative Studies of South Asia, Africa and the Middle East* 37, no. 2 (2017): 406–411.

Cooper, Frederick. "From Enslavement to Precarity? The Labour Question in African History." In *The Political Economy of Everyday Life in Africa*, edited by Wale Adebanwi, 135–156. Woodbridge: James Currey, 2017.

Cooper, Frederick. "Decolonization in Tropical Africa." In *The Oxford Handbook of the Ends of Empire*, edited by Martin Thomas and Andrew S. Thompson, 316–332. Oxford: Oxford University Press, 2018.

Cooper, Frederick. "The 'Labour Question' in Africa and the World." In *General Labour History of Africa*, edited by Stefano Bellucci and Andreas Eckert, 617–636. Woodbridge: James Currey, 2019.

Coquery-Vidrovitch, Catherine. *Afrique noire: permanences et ruptures*. 2. éd. rév. Paris: L'Harmattan, 1992.

Corbin, Alain. *Le monde retrouvé de Louis-François Pinagot: sur les traces d'un inconnu, 1798–1876*. Paris: Flammarion, 1998.
Correia, Milton. "Os Yao e o contexto da luta armada de independência nacional em Moçambique (1964–1974)." PhD thesis, Universidade de São Paulo, 2017.
Correia, Milton. "História e textualização: A historiografia da frente do Niassa (Moçambique) 1964–1974." *Revista de História*, no. 178 (2019): 1–33.
Costa, Camilo Silveira de. "O Niassa visto por dentro." *Boletim Geral do Ultramar* 35, no. 411–412 (1959): 147–228.
Crehan, Kate A. *The Fractured Community: Landscapes of Power and Gender in Rural Zambia*. Berkeley: University of California Press, 1997.
Crewe, Emma, and Elizabeth Harrison. *Whose Development? An Ethnography of Aid*. London: Zed Books, 1998.
Cunningham, Kiran. "Let's Go to My Place: Residence, Gender and Power in a Mende Community." In *Gender, Kinship, Power: A Comparative and Interdisciplinary History*, edited by Mary Jo Maynes, Ann Waltner, Birgitte Soland, and Ulrike Strasser, 335–349. New York: Routledge, 1996.
Curtin, Philip. "The European Conquest." In *African History: From Earliest Times to Independence*, by Philip Curtin, Steven Feierman, Leonard Thompson, and Jan Vansina, 398–422, 2nd ed. Harlow: Longman, 1995.
Daly, Sarah Zukerman. "Voting for Victors: Why Violent Actors Win Postwar Elections." *World Politics* 71, no. 4 (2019): 747–805.
Dasgupta, Biplab, ed. *Village Studies in the Third World*. Delhi: Hindustan, 1978.
Davis, Mike. *Planet of Slums*. London: Verso, 2006.
Davis, Natalie Zemon. *The Return of Martin Guerre*. Cambridge: Harvard University Press, 1983.
Davison, Jean. *Gender, Lineage, and Ethnicity in Southern Africa*. Boulder: Westview, 1997.
Decualanga, Tomás Gaspar Mpate. "A crise do programa Mosagrius na Província de Niassa e suas consequências sócio-económicas, 1996–2004." Master thesis, Universidade Eduardo Mondlane, 2006.
Derluguian, Georgi. "Book Reviews: Revolution, Counter-Revolution and Revisionism in Postcolonial Africa: The Case of Mozambique, 1975–1994. By Alice Dinerman." *The International Journal of African Historical Studies* 40, no. 2 (2007): 307–308.
Deutsch, Jan-Georg. *Emancipation without Abolition in German East Africa, c. 1884–1914*. Oxford: James Currey, 2006.
Dhada, Mustafah. *The Portuguese Massacre of Wiriyamu in Colonial Mozambique, 1964–2013*. London: Bloomsbury, 2016.
Dick, Moira. "'If You Don't Know Niassa, You Don't Know Mozambique.'" In *Mozambique: Towards a People's Health Service*, edited by Gillian Walt and Angela Melamed, 45–58. London: Zed Books, 1983.
Dietsche, Evelyn, and Ana Maria Esteves. "Local Content and the Prospect for Economic Diversification in Mozambique." In *Mining for Change: Natural Resources and Industry in Africa*, edited by John Page and Finn Tarp, 209–213. Oxford: Oxford University Press, 2020.
Dirlik, Arif. "Is There History after Eurocentrism? Globalism, Postcolonialism, and the Disavowal of History." *Cultural Critique*, no. 42 (1999): 1–34.
Dirlik, Arif. "How the Grinch Hijacked Radicalism: Further Thoughts on the Postcolonial." *Postcolonial Studies* 2, no. 2 (1999): 149–163.
Dolny, Helena. "The Challenge of Agriculture." In *A Difficult Road: The Transition to Socialism in Mozambique*, edited by John S. Saul, 211–252. New York: Monthly Review Press, 1985.

Domingos, Nuno, Miguel Bandeira Jerónimo, and Ricardo Roque, eds. *Resistance and Colonialism: Insurgent Peoples in World History*. Cham: Palgrave Macmillan, 2019.
Drayton, R.S. "Variations in the Level of Lake Malawi." *Hydrological Sciences Journal* 29, no. 1 (1984): 1–12.
Droessler, Holger. "Copra World: Coconuts, Plantations and Cooperatives in German Samoa." *The Journal of Pacific History* 53, no. 4 (2018): 417–435.
Dunaway, Wilma A. "Nonwaged Peasants in the Modern World-System: African Households as Dialectical Units of Capitalist Exploitation and Indigenous Resistance, 1890–1930." *Journal of Philosophical Economics* 4, no. 1 (2010): 19–57.
Dusinberre, Martin. *Hard Times in the Hometown: A History of Community Survival in Modern Japan*. Honolulu: University of Hawai'i Press, 2012.
Eckert, Andreas. "Scenes from a Marriage: African History and Global History." *Comparativ: Zeitschrift für Globalgeschichte und vergleichende Gesellschaftsforschung* 29, no. 2 (2019): 36–51.
Eckert, Andreas, and Adam Jones. "Historical Writing about Everyday Life." *Journal of African Cultural Studies* 15, no. 1 (2002): 5–16.
Egerö, Bertil. *Mozambique, a Dream Undone: The Political Economy of Democracy, 1975–84*. Uppsala: Nordiska afrikainstitutet, 1990.
Eile, Lena. *Jando: The Rite of Circumcision and Initiation in East African Islam*. Lund: Plus Ultra, 1990.
Ellis, Frank. "Household Strategies and Rural Livelihood Diversification." *Journal of Development Studies* 35, no. 1 (1998): 1–38.
Ellis, Stephen. "Writing Histories of Contemporary Africa." *The Journal of African History* 43, no. 1 (2002): 1–26.
Elwert, Georg, and Diana Wong. "Subsistence Production and Commodity Production in the Third World." *Review (Fernand Braudel Center)* 3, no. 3 (1980): 501–522.
Englund, Harri. "Waiting for the Portuguese: Nostalgia, Exploitation and the Meaning of Land in the Malawi-Mozambique Borderland." *Journal of Contemporary African Studies* 14, no. 2 (1996): 157–172.
Englund, Harri. "The Self in Self-Interest: Land, Labour and Temporalities in Malawi's Agrarian Change." *Africa* 69, no. 1 (1999): 139–159.
Englund, Harri. *From War to Peace on the Mozambique-Malawi Borderland*. Edinburgh: Edinburgh University Press, 2002.
Epple, Angelika. "Globale Mikrogeschichte: Auf dem Weg zu einer Geschichte der Relationen." In *Im Kleinen das Grosse suchen: Mikrogeschichte in Theorie und Praxis*, edited by Ewald Hiebl and Ernst Langthaler, 37–47. Innsbruck: StudienVerlag, 2012.
Epple, Angelika. "Lokalität und die Dimensionen des Globalen: Eine Frage der Relationen." *Historische Anthropologie* 21, no. 1 (2013): 4–25.
Etherington, Norman. "A Tempest in a Teapot? Nineteenth-Century Contests for Land in South Africa's Caledon Valley and the Invention of the Mfecane." *The Journal of African History* 45, no. 2 (2004): 203–219.
Feichtinger, Moritz. "'A Great Reformatory': Social Planning and Strategic Resettlement in Late Colonial Kenya and Algeria, 1952–63." *Journal of Contemporary History* 52, no. 1 (2017): 45–72.
Feichtinger, Moritz. "'Villagization': A People's History of Strategic Resettlement and Violent Transformation. Kenya & Algeria, 1952–1962." PhD thesis, Universität Bern, 2016.
Feichtinger, Moritz, and Stephan Malinowski. "'Eine Million Algerier lernen im 20. Jahrhundert zu Leben': Umsiedlungslager und Zwangsmodernisierung im Algerienkrieg 1954–1962." *Journal of Modern European History* 8, no. 1 (2010): 107–135.

Ferguson, James. *The Anti-Politics Machine: "Development," Depoliticization, and Bureaucratic Power in Lesotho*. Cambridge: Cambridge University Press, 1990.
Ferguson, James. *Expectations of Modernity: Myths and Meanings of Urban Life on the Zambian Copperbelt*. Berkeley: University of California Press, 1999.
Finnegan, William. *A Complicated War: The Harrowing of Mozambique*. Berkeley: University of California Press, 1992.
Fischer-Tiné, Harald. "Marrying Global History with South Asian History: Potential and Limits of Global Microhistory in a Regional Inflection." *Comparativ: Zeitschrift für Globalgeschichte und vergleichende Gesellschaftsforschung* 29, no. 2 (2019): 52–77.
Forquilha, Salvador Cadete. "O paradoxo da articulação dos órgãos locais do estado com as autoridades comunitárias em Moçambique: Do discurso sobre a descentralização à conquista dos espaços políticos a nível local." *Cadernos de Estudos Africanos*, no. 16/17 (2009): 89–114.
French, David. *The British Way in Counter-Insurgency, 1945–1967*. Oxford: Oxford University Press, 2011.
Frieden, Jeffry A. *Global Capitalism: Its Fall and Rise in the Twentieth Century*. New York: W.W. Norton, 2006.
Funada-Classen, Sayaka. *The Origins of War in Mozambique: A History of Unity and Division*. Translated by Masako Osada. Somerset West: African Minds, 2013.
Galli, Rosemary E. "The Food Crisis and the Socialist State in Lusophone Africa." *African Studies Review* 30, no. 1 (1987): 19–44.
Galli, Rosemary E. *Peoples' Spaces and State Spaces: Land and Governance in Mozambique*. Lanham: Lexington, 2003.
Galli, Rosemary E., and Jocelyn Jones. *Guinea-Bissau: Politics, Economics and Society*. London: Pinter, 1987.
Galligan, Thomas. "The Nguru Penetration into Nyasaland." In *From Nyasaland to Malawi: Studies in Colonial History*, edited by Roderick J. Macdonald, 108–123. Nairobi: East African Publishing House, 1975.
Gasperini, Lavinia. *Moçambique: Educação e desenvolvimento rural*. Roma: Lavoro, 1989.
Geffray, Christian. *La cause des armes au mozambique: Anthropologie d'une guerre civile*. Paris: Karthala, 1990.
Geffray, Christian, and Mögens Pedersen. "Transformação da organização social e do sistema agrário do campesinato no Distrito do Erati: Processo de socialização do campo e diferenciação social." Maputo: Departamento de Arqueologia e Antropologia, Universidade Eduardo Mondlane, 1985.
Geffray, Christian, and Mögens Pedersen. "Nampula en guerre." *Politique Africaine*, no. 29 (1988): 28–40.
Geisler, Gisela G. *Die Politik der Geschlechterbeziehungen in einer ländlichen Gemeinde in Zambia: "Be quiet and suffer."* Hamburg: Institut für Afrika-Kunde, 1990.
Gentili, Anna Maria. "'Queremos ser cidadãos': Citizenship in Mozambique from Frelimo to Frelimo." *Citizenship Studies* 21, no. 2 (2017): 182–195.
Gerlach, Christian. *Extremely Violent Societies: Mass Violence in the Twentieth-Century World*. Cambridge: Cambridge University Press, 2010.
Gerstenberger, Debora, and Joël Glasman. "Globalgeschichte mit Maß: Was Globalhistoriker von der Akteur-Netzwerk-Theorie lernen können." In *Techniken der Globalisierung*, edited by Debora Gerstenberger and Joël Glasman, 11–40. Bielefeld: transcript Verlag, 2016.

Geschiere, Peter. "Witchcraft as the Dark Side of Kinship: Dilemmas of Social Security in New Contexts." *Etnofoor* 16, no. 1, (2003): 43–61.
Geschiere, Peter. "Epilogue: 'Seeing Like a State' in Africa – High Modernism, Legibility and Community." *African Studies* 66, no. 1 (2007): 129–134.
Geschiere, Peter. *The Perils of Belonging: Autochthony, Citizenship, and Exclusion in Africa and Europe.* Chicago: University of Chicago Press, 2009.
Geschiere, Peter. "Witchcraft: The Dangers of Intimacy and the Struggle over Trust." In *Trusting and Its Tribulations: Interdisciplinary Engagements with Intimacy, Sociality and Trust*, edited by Vigdis Broch-Due and Margit Ystanes, 60–83. New York: Berghahn, 2016.
Ghobrial, John-Paul A. "Introduction: Seeing the World like a Microhistorian." *Past & Present* 242, Supplement 14 (2019): 1–22.
Ginzburg, Carlo. *The Cheese and the Worms: The Cosmos of a Sixteenth Century Miller.* Translated by John Tedeschi and Anne Tedeschi. Baltimore: Johns Hopkins University Press, 1980.
Glasman, Joël. "Penser les intermédiaires coloniaux: Note sur les dossiers de carrière de la police du Togo." *History in Africa* 37 (2010): 51–81.
Gleave, Michael B. "Hill Settlements and Their Abandonment in Western Yorubaland." *Africa: Journal of the International African Institute* 33, no. 4 (1963): 343–352.
Gomes e Sousa, António. "Elementos para uma monografia agrícola do Distrito do Niassa (conclusão)." *Portugal Colonial: Revista de Propaganda e Expansão Colonial* 4, no. 51 (1935): 7–12.
Good, Charles. *The Steamer Parish: The Rise and Fall of Missionary Medicine on an African Frontier.* Chicago: University of Chicago Press, 2004.
Good, Kenneth. "The Reproduction of Weakness in the State and Agriculture: Zambian Experience." *African Affairs* 85, no. 339 (1986): 239–265.
Gooding, Philip. "Islam in the Interior of Precolonial East Africa: Evidence from Lake Tanganyika." *The Journal of African History* 60, no. 2 (2019): 191–208.
Gottschalk, Sebastian. *Kolonialismus und Islam: Deutsche und britische Herrschaft in Westafrika (1900–1914).* Frankfurt: Campus Verlag, 2017.
Gower, R.H. "Swahili Borrowings from English." *Africa: Journal of the International African Institute* 22, no. 2 (1952): 154–157.
Green, Erik. "Diversification or De-Agrarianization? Income Diversification, Labor, and Processes of Agrarian Change in Southern and Northern Malawi, Mid-1930s to Mid-1950s." *Agricultural History* 82, no. 2 (2008): 164–192.
Greenstein, Robert. "The Nyasaland Government's Policy Towards African Muslims, 1900–25." In *From Nyasaland to Malawi: Studies in Colonial History*, edited by Roderick J. Macdonald, 144–68. Nairobi: East African Publishing House, 1975.
Greenstein, Robert. "Shayks and Tariqas: The Early Muslim 'Ulama' and Tariqa Development in Malawi, c.1885–1949 (CC/H/429/76)." In *History Seminar Papers 1976/77*. Chancellor College, Zomba, 1976.
Guenther, Mathias, Justin Kenrick, Adam Kuper, and Evie Plaice. "The Concept of Indigeneity." *Social Anthropology* 14, no. 1 (2006): 17–32.
Guerreiro, António. "Achille Mbembe: 'África é a última fronteira do capitalismo.'" Público, December 9, 2018. Accessed December 10, 2018. https://www.publico.pt/2018/12/09/mundo/entrevista/africa-ultima-fronteira-capitalismo-1853532.
Gulliver, P.H. "Political Evolution in the Songea Ngoni Chiefdoms, 1850–1905." *Bulletin of the School of Oriental and African Studies* 37, no. 1 (1974): 82–97.

Gupta, Pamila. "Decolonization and (Dis)Possession in Lusophone Africa." In *Mobility Makes States: Migration and Power in Africa*, edited by Darshan Vigneswaran and Joel Quirk, 169–193. Philadelphia: University of Pennsylvania Press, 2015.

Guthrie, Zachary Kagan. "Labor, Mobility and Coercion in Central Mozambique, 1942–1961." PhD thesis, Princeton University, 2014.

Guthrie, Zachary Kagan. *Bound for Work: Labor, Mobility, and Colonial Rule in Central Mozambique, 1940–1965*. Charlottesville: University of Virginia Press, 2018.

Guyer, Jane I. "Wealth in People and Self-Realization in Equatorial Africa." *Man (New Series)* 28, no. 2 (1993): 243–265.

Guyer, Jane I., and Samuel M. Eno Belinga. "Wealth in People as Wealth in Knowledge: Accumulation and Composition in Equatorial Africa." *The Journal of African History* 36, no. 1 (1995): 91–120.

Hack, Karl. "'Devils That Suck the Blood of the Malayan People': The Case for Post-Revisionist Analysis of Counter-Insurgency Violence." *War in History* 25, no. 2 (2018): 202–226.

Hafkin, Nancy. "Trade, Society, and Politics in Northern Mozambique, c.1753–1913." PhD thesis, Boston University, 1973.

Hall, Margaret, and Tom Young. *Confronting Leviathan: Mozambique since Independence*. London: Hurst, 1997.

Haller, Tobias. "The Different Meanings of Land in the Age of Neoliberalism: Theoretical Reflections on Commons and Resilience Grabbing from a Social Anthropological Perspective." *Land* 8, no. 7 (2019): 104.

Hanlon, Joseph. *Mozambique: The Revolution under Fire*. London: Zed Books, 1990.

Hanlon, Joseph. *The Land Debate in Mozambique: Will Foreign Investors, the Urban Elite, Advanced Peasants or Family Farmers Drive Rural Development*. Research Paper Commissioned by Oxfam GB, Regional Management Center for Southern Africa. London, 2002.

Hanlon, Joseph, ed. "Mozambique News Reports & Clippings," no. 492 (June 28, 2020).

Harrison, Elizabeth. "'People Are Willing to Fight to the End': Romanticising the 'Moral' in Moral Economies of Irrigation." *Critique of Anthropology* 40, no. 2 (2020): 194–217.

Havik, Philip. "Public Health and Tropical Modernity: The Combat against Sleeping Sickness in Portuguese Guinea." *História, Ciências, Saúde-Manguinhos* 21, no. 2 (2014): 641–666.

Head, Judith, and David Hedges. "Problemas da história da Zambézia." *Estudos Moçambicanos*, no. 4 (1983): 127–139.

Hebinck, Paul. "Post-Apartheid Land and Agrarian Reform Policy and Practices in South Africa: Themes, Processes and Issues." In *In the Shadow of Policy: Everyday Practices in South Africa's Land and Agrarian Reform*, edited by Paul Hebinck and Ben Cousins, 3–28. Johannesburg: Wits University Press, 2013.

Hedges, David, Aurélio Rocha, Eduardo Medeiros, and Gerhard Liesegang. *História de Moçambique Vol. 3: Moçambique no auge do colonialismo, 1930–1961*. Maputo: UEM, 1993.

Henriksen, Thomas H. *Revolution and Counterrevolution: Mozambique's War of Independence, 1964–1974*. Westport: Greenwood, 1983.

Hill, Polly. *Rural Hausa: A Village and a Setting*. Cambridge: Cambridge University Press, 1972.

Hill, Polly. "Problems with A. G. Hopkins' Economic History of West Africa." *African Economic History*, no. 6 (1978): 127–133.

Hill, Polly. *The Migrant Cocoa-Farmers of Southern Ghana: A Study in Rural Capitalism*. Cambridge: Cambridge University Press, 1963. Reprint, Hamburg: Lit-Verlag, 1997.

Hirschmann, David, and Megan Vaughan. "Food Production and Income Generation in a Matrilineal Society: Rural Women in Zomba, Malawi." *Journal of Southern African Studies* 10, no. 1 (1983): 86–99.
Hirvonen, Soila, and Carla Braga. "Perfil de género: Província do Niassa." Maputo: Agência Sueca de Cooperação Internacional para o Desenvolvimento, 1999.
Hobsbawm, Eric J. *The Age of Extremes: The Short Twentieth Century, 1914–1991*. Michael Joseph, 1994. Reprint, London: Abacus, 1995.
Hodge, Joseph Morgan. "Writing the History of Development (Part 1: The First Wave)." *Humanity: An International Journal of Human Rights, Humanitarianism, and Development* 6, no. 3 (2015): 429–463.
Hopkins, Antony G. *An Economic History of West Africa*. Harlow: Longman, 1973.
Hopkins, Antony G. "Making Poverty History." *The International Journal of African Historical Studies* 38, no. 3 (2005): 513–531.
Hopkins, Antony G. "The New Economic History of Africa." *The Journal of African History* 50, no. 2 (2009): 155–177.
Hubbell, Andrew. "A View of the Slave Trade from the Margin: Suroudougou in the Late Nineteenth-Century Slave Trade of the Niger Bend." *The Journal of African History* 42, no. 1 (2001): 25–47.
Huhn, Arianna. "Sustenance and Sociability: Foodways in a Mozambican Town." PhD thesis, Boston University, 2013.
Huhn, Arianna. "The Tongue Only Works Without Worries: Sentiment and Sustenance in a Mozambican Town." *Food and Foodways* 21, no. 3 (2013): 186–210.
Huhn, Arianna. "Enacting Compassion: Hot/Cold, Illness and Taboos in Northern Mozambique." *Journal of Southern African Studies* 43, no. 2 (2017): 299–313.
Huhn, Arianna. *Nourishing Life: Foodways and Humanity in an African Town*. New York: Berghahn Books, 2020.
Hull, Simon, Kehinde Babalola, and Jennifer Whittal. "Theories of Land Reform and Their Impact on Land Reform Success in Southern Africa." *Land* 8, no. 11 (2019): 172.
Hunt, Nancy R. "Whither African History?" *History Workshop Journal* 66, no. 1 (2008): 259–265.
Hurst, Ellen. "Local Villages and Global Networks: The Language and Migration Experiences of African Skilled Migrant Academics." *Globalisation, Societies and Education* 15, no. 1 (2017): 50–67.
Hydén, Göran. *Beyond Ujamaa in Tanzania: Underdevelopment and an Uncaptured Peasantry*. Berkeley: University of California Press, 1980.
Hydén, Göran. "Governance and Poverty Reduction in Africa." *Proceedings of the National Academy of Sciences* 104, no. 43 (2007): 16751–16756.
Hydén, Göran, Kazuhiko Sugimura, and Tadasu Tsuruta, eds. *Rethinking African Agriculture: How Non-Agrarian Factors Shape Peasant Livelihoods*. London: Routledge, 2020.
Hynd, Stacey. "Small Warriors? Children and Youth in Colonial Insurgencies and Counterinsurgency, ca. 1945–1960." *Comparative Studies in Society and History* 62, no. 4 (2020): 684–713.
Iggers, Georg G., and Q. Edward Wang. *A Global History of Modern Historiography*. London: Routledge, 2008.
Igreja, Victor, and Limore Racin. "The Politics of Spirits, Justice, and Social Transformation in Mozambique." In *Spirits in Politics: Uncertainties of Power and Healing in African Societies*, edited by Barbara Meier and Arne S. Steinforth, 181–204. Frankfurt: Campus, 2013.
Immerwahr, Daniel. *Thinking Small: The United States and the Lure of Community Development*. Cambridge: Harvard University Press, 2015.

Inikori, Joseph, and Stanley Engerman, eds. *The Atlantic Slave Trade: Effects on Economies, Societies, and Peoples in Africa, the Americas, and Europe.* Durham: Duke University Press, 1992.

Isaacman, Allen. *Cotton Is the Mother of Poverty: Peasants, Work, and Rural Struggle in Colonial Mozambique, 1938–1961.* Portsmouth: Heinemann, 1996.

Isaacman, Allen. "Legacies of Engagement: Scholarship Informed by Political Commitment." *African Studies Review* 46, no. 1 (2003): 1.

Isaacman, Allen, and Arlindo Chilundo. "Peasants at Work: Forced Cotton Cultivation in Northern Mozambique, 1938–1961." In *The Rise and Fall of Modern Empires*, edited by Owen White, 1: Social Organization: 69–102. Farnham: Ashgate, 2013.

Isaacman, Allen, and Barbara Isaacman. "Resistance and Collaboration in Southern and Central Africa, c. 1850–1920." *The International Journal of African Historical Studies* 10, no. 1 (1977): 31–62.

Isaacman, Allen, and Barbara Isaacman. *Mozambique: From Colonialism to Revolution.* Boulder: Westview, 1983.

Isaacman, Allen, and Barbara Isaacman. *Dams, Displacement, and the Delusion of Development: Cahora Bassa and Its Legacies in Mozambique, 1965–2007.* Athens: Ohio University Press, 2013.

Isaacman, Allen, Michael Stephen, Yussuf Adam, Maria Joao Homen, Eugenio Macamo, and Augustinho Pililao. "'Cotton Is the Mother of Poverty': Peasant Resistance to Forced Cotton Production in Mozambique, 1938–1961." *African Studies* 13, no. 4 (1980): 581–615.

Ishiyama, John, and Michael Widmeier. "Territorial Control, Levels of Violence, and the Electoral Performance of Former Rebel Political Parties after Civil Wars." *Civil Wars* 15, no. 4 (2013): 531–550.

Israel, Paolo. "A Loosening Grip: The Liberation Script in Mozambican History." *Kronos* 39, no. 1 (2013): 10–19.

Iwuagwu, Obi. "The Spread of Cassava (Manioc) in Igboland, South-East Nigeria: A Reappraisal of the Evidence." *Agricultural History Review* 60, no. 1 (2012): 60–76.

Jerónimo, Miguel Bandeira, and António Costa Pinto. "The International and the Portuguese Imperial Endgame: Problems and Perspectives." *Portuguese Studies* 29, no. 2 (2013): 137–141.

Jerónimo, Miguel Bandeira, and António Costa Pinto. "A Modernizing Empire? Politics, Culture, and Economy in Portuguese Late Colonialism." In *The Ends of European Colonial Empires*, edited by Miguel Bandeira Jerónimo and António Costa Pinto, 51–80. Basingstoke: Palgrave Macmillan, 2015.

Jerven, Morten. "A Clash of Disciplines? Economists and Historians Approaching the African Past." *Economic History of Developing Regions* 26, no. 2 (2011): 111–124.

Jerven, Morten. *Africa: Why Economists Get It Wrong.* London: Zed Books, 2015.

Jerven, Morten, Gareth Austin, Erik Green, Chibuike Uche, Ewout Frankema, Johan Fourie, Joseph Inikori, Alexander Moradi, and Ellen Hillbom. "Moving Forward in African Economic History: Bridging the Gap between Methods and Sources." African Economic History Working Paper Series, no. 1. Lund: Lund University, 2012.

Johansson, Kajsa. "Peasant Collective Action against Disembedding Land: The Case of Niassa Province, Mozambique." In *Social Movements Contesting Natural Resource Development*, edited by John F. Devlin, 21–41. London: Routledge, 2019.

Johnson, Jessica. "Matriliny." Cambridge Encyclopedia of Anthropology, September 1, 2016. Accessed May 17, 2019. http://www.anthroencyclopedia.com/entry/matriliny.

Johnson, Jessica. *In Search of Gender Justice: Rights and Relationships in Matrilineal Malawi.* Cambridge University Press, 2018.

Jones, Sam, and Inge Tvedten. "What Does It Mean to Be Poor? Investigating the Qualitative-Quantitative Divide in Mozambique." *World Development* 117 (2019): 153–166.
Jordan, Stefan. *Theorien und Methoden der Geschichtswissenschaft*. Paderborn: Ferdinand Schöningh, 2009.
Jossias, Elísio. "'O primeiro a chegar é o dono da terra': Pertença e posse da terra na região do Lago Niassa." PhD thesis, Universidade de Lisboa, 2016.
Jossias, Elísio. "Renegociar a comunidade e disputar territórios: Posse e propriedade nas terras comunitárias na região do Lago Niassa." *Etnográfica* 26, no. 1 (2022): 5–27.
Joyce, Patrick. "What Is the Social in Social History?" *Past & Present* 206, no. 1 (2010): 213–248.
Juergensen, Olaf Tataryn. "Peasants on the Periphery: A Geohistory of Rural Change in Mozambique, c.1960–1992." PhD thesis, Queen's University, 1996.
Jundanian, Brendan F. "Resettlement Programs: Counterinsurgency in Mozambique." *Comparative Politics* 6, no. 4 (1974): 519–540.
Kaiwar, Vasant. *The Postcolonial Orient: The Politics of Difference and the Project of Provincialising Europe*. Leiden: Brill, 2014.
Kalyvas, Stathis N. *The Logic of Violence in Civil War*. Cambridge: Cambridge University Press, 2006.
Kalyvas, Stathis N., and Matthew Adam Kocher. "How 'Free' Is Free Riding in Civil Wars? Violence, Insurgency, and the Collective Action Problem." *World Politics* 59, no. 2 (2007): 177–216.
Kankpeyeng, Benjamin W. "The Slave Trade in Northern Ghana: Landmarks, Legacies and Connections." *Slavery & Abolition* 30, no. 2 (2009): 209–221.
Katto, Jonna. *"Grandma Was a Guerrilla Fighter": Life Memories of the Women Who Fought for Mozambique's Independence in Northern Niassa*. Tallinna: Tallinna Raamatutrükikoda, 2018.
Katto, Jonna. "Emotions in Protest: Unsettling the Past in Ex-combatants' Personal Accounts in Northern Mozambique." *Oral History* 46, no. 2 (2018): 53–62.
Katto, Jonna. *Women's Lived Landscapes of War and Liberation in Mozambique: Bodily Memory and the Gendered Aesthetics of Belonging*. London: Routledge, 2019.
Katto, Jonna. "'The *Rainha* Is the Boss!': On Masculinities, Time and Precolonial Women of Authority in Northern Mozambique." *Gender & History*, January 7, 2022, 1–23. https://doi.org/10.1111/1468-0424.12590.
Katzenellenbogen, Simon E. *South Africa and Southern Mozambique: Labour, Railways, and Trade in the Making of a Relationship*. Manchester: Manchester University Press, 1982.
Keese, Alexander. "'Proteger os pretos': Havia uma mentalidade reformista na administração portuguesa na África Tropical (1926–1961)?" *Africana Studia*, no. 6 (2003): 97–125.
Keese, Alexander. *Living with Ambiguity: Integrating an African Elite in French and Portuguese Africa, 1930–61*. Stuttgart: Franz Steiner, 2007.
Keese, Alexander, ed. *Ethnicity and the Long-Term Perspective: The African Experience*. New York: Peter Lang, 2010.
Keese, Alexander. "Forced Labour in the 'Gorgulho Years': Understanding Reform and Repression in Rural São Tomé e Príncipe, 1945–1953." *Itinerario* 38, no. 1 (2014): 103–124.
Keese, Alexander. "Tax in Practice: Colonial Impact and Renegotiation on the Ground." In *Administration and Taxation in Former Portuguese Africa, 1900–1945*, by Philip Havik, Alexander Keese, and Maciel Santos, 82–97. Newcastle upon Tyne: Cambridge Scholars, 2015.
Keese, Alexander. "Taxation, Evasion, and Compulsory Measures in Angola." In *Administration and Taxation in Former Portuguese Africa, 1900–1945*, by Philip Havik, Alexander Keese, and Maciel Santos, 98–137. Newcastle upon Tyne: Cambridge Scholars, 2015.

Keese, Alexander. *Ethnicity and the Colonial State: Finding and Representing Group Identifications in a Coastal West African and Global Perspective (1850–1960)*. Leiden: Brill, 2016.
Keese, Alexander. "Decolonisation, Improvised: A Social History of the Transfer of Power in Cabo Verde, 1974–1976." *Portuguese Studies Review* 25, no. 1 (2017): 291–312.
Keese, Alexander. "Just like in Colonial Times? Administrative Practice and Local Reflections on 'Grassroots Neocolonialism' in Autonomous and Postcolonial Dahomey, 1958–1965." *The Journal of African History* 60, no. 2 (2019): 257–276.
Keese, Alexander, and Brice I. Owabira. "Rescuing, Interpreting, and, Eventually, Digitizing Regional Postcolonial Archives: Endangered Archives and Research in Pointe-Noire, Republic of Congo." *History in Africa* 47 (2020): 143–165.
Kinyanjui, Wanjiru. "Über Filme und Dörfer." In *Filmwelt Afrika: Retrospektive des panafrikanischen Filmfestivals FESPACO in Ouagadougou, Burkina Faso*, edited by Haus der Kulturen der Welt, 17–22. Berlin, 1993.
Kirscht, Holger. *Ein Dorf in Nordost-Nigeria: Politische und wirtschaftliche Transformation der bäuerlichen Kanuri-Gesellschaft*. Münster: LIT Verlag, 2001.
Kitching, Gavin. *Development and Underdevelopment in Historical Perspective: Populism, Nationalism, and Industrialization*. London: Routledge, 1982.
Klein, Martin A. "The Study of Slavery in Africa." *The Journal of African History* 19, no. 4 (1978): 599–609.
Klein, Martin A., ed. *Peasants in Africa: Historical and Contemporary Perspectives*. Beverly Hills: Sage, 1980.
Klein, Martin A. "Studying the History of Those Who Would Rather Forget: Oral History and the Experience of Slavery." *History in Africa* 16 (1989): 209–217.
Klein, Martin A. *Slavery and Colonial Rule in French West Africa*. Cambridge: Cambridge University Press, 1998.
Kloeck-Jenson, Scott. "Analysis of the Parliamentary Debate and New National Land Law for Mozambique." Maputo: Land Tenure Center, 1997.
Kloeck-Jenson, Scott. "Locating the Community: Administration of Natural Resources in Mozambique." Land Tenure Center Working Paper, no. 32. Madison, February 2000.
Kocka, Jürgen. "Sozialgeschichte zwischen Strukturgeschichte und Erfahrungsgeschichte." In *Sozialgeschichte in Deutschland: Entwicklungen und Perspektiven im internationalen Zusammenhang. Band 1: Die Sozialgeschichte innerhalb der Geschichtswissenschaft*, edited by Wolfgang Schieder and Volker Sellin, 67–88. Göttingen: Vandenhoeck & Ruprecht, 1986.
Kocka, Jürgen. "Perspektiven für die Sozialgeschichte der neunziger Jahre." In *Sozialgeschichte, Alltagsgeschichte, Mikro-Historie*, edited by Winfried Schulze, 33–39. Göttingen: Vandenhoeck & Ruprecht, 1994.
Koevering, Helen E.P. van. *Dancing Their Dreams: The Lakeshore Nyanja Women of the Anglican Diocese of Niassa*. Zomba: Kachere, 2005.
Kohl, Karl-Heinz. "Der 'Ureinwohner' kehrt zurück." Welt-Sichten, May 19, 2017. Accessed April 9, 2020. https://www.welt-sichten.org/artikel/32756/der-ureinwohner-kehrt-zurueck.
Komlosy, Andrea. "Work and Labor Relations." In *Capitalism: The Reemergence of a Historical Concept*, edited by Jürgen Kocka and Marcel van der Linden, 33–69. London: Bloomsbury, 2016.
Korieh, Chima J. *The Land Has Changed: History, Society, and Gender in Colonial Eastern Nigeria*. Calgary: University of Calgary Press, 2010.
Kuba, Richard, and Carola Lentz, eds. *Land and the Politics of Belonging in West Africa*. Leiden: Brill, 2006.

Kuper, Adam. "The Return of the Native." *Current Anthropology* 44, no. 3 (2003): 389–402.
Kwaule, Fabiano. "Kanyenda, the Mwale Expansion into Nkhota-Kota and the Swahili Challenge, 1750–1890." In *History Seminar Papers 1978/79*. Chancellor College, Zomba, 1979.
Kwaule, Fabiano. "Kanyenda and the Swahili Challenge." In *Malawi's Muslims: Historical Perspectives*, edited by David S. Bone, 64–68. Blantyre, 2000.
Kyed, Helene Maria. "The Politics of Legal Pluralism: State Policies on Legal Pluralism and Their Local Dynamics in Mozambique." *The Journal of Legal Pluralism and Unofficial Law* 41, no. 59 (2009): 87–120.
Kyle, Steven. "Economic Reform and Armed Conflict in Mozambique." *World Development* 19, no. 6 (1991): 637–649.
Landry, Jennifer, and Praxie Chirwa. "Analysis of the Potential Socio-Economic Impact of Establishing Plantation Forestry on Rural Communities in Sanga District, Niassa Province, Mozambique." *Land Use Policy* 28, no. 3 (2011): 542–551.
Langa, José Paulo, Cynthia Sema, Nilsa de Deus, Mauro Maria Colombo, and Elisa Taviani. "Epidemic Waves of Cholera in the Last Two Decades in Mozambique." *The Journal of Infection in Developing Countries* 9, no. 6 (2015): 635–641.
Langworthy, Harry W. "Swahili Influence in the Area between Lake Malawi and the Luangwa River." *African Historical Studies* 4, no. 3 (1971): 575–602.
Langworthy, Harry W. "Central Malawi in the 19th Century." In *From Nyasaland to Malawi: Studies in Colonial History*, edited by Roderick J. Macdonald, 1–43. Nairobi: East African Publishing House, 1975.
Larmer, Miles. *Rethinking African Politics: A History of Opposition in Zambia*. Farnham: Ashgate, 2011.
Larmer, Miles, and Baz Lecocq. "Historicising Nationalism in Africa." *Nations and Nationalism* 24, no. 4 (2018): 893–917.
Laumann, Dennis. *Colonial Africa, 1884–1994*. New York: Oxford University Press, 2012.
Law, Robin, ed. *From Slave Trade to "Legitimate" Commerce: The Commercial Transition in Nineteenth-Century West Africa*. Cambridge: Cambridge University Press, 1995.
Law, Robin. *Ouidah: The Social History of a West African Slaving "Port" 1727–1892*. Athens: Ohio University Press, 2004.
Lawi, Yusufu Qwaray. "Tanzania's Operation Vijiji and Local Ecological Consciousness: The Case of Eastern Iraqwland, 1974–1976." *The Journal of African History* 48, no. 1 (2007): 69–93.
Lawrance, Benjamin N., Emily Lynn Osborn, and Richard L. Roberts, eds. *Intermediaries, Interpreters, and Clerks: African Employees in the Making of Colonial Africa*. Madison: University of Wisconsin Press, 2006.
Lazarus, Neil. "'Third Worldism' and the Political Imaginary of Postcolonial Studies." In *The Oxford Handbook of Postcolonial Studies*, edited by Graham Huggan, 324–339. Oxford: Oxford University Press, 2013.
Le Roy Ladurie, Emmanuel. *Montaillou, village occitan de 1294 à 1324*. Paris: Gallimard, 1975.
Lentz, Carola. "First-Comers and Late-Comers: Indigenous Theories of Landownership in West Africa." In *Land and the Politics of Belonging in West Africa*, edited by Richard Kuba and Carola Lentz, 35–56. Leiden: Brill, 2006.
Lentz, Carola. *Land, Mobility, and Belonging in West Africa*. Bloomington, Indiana: Indiana University Press, 2013.
Levi, Giovanni. "On Microhistory." In *New Perspectives on Historical Writing*, edited by Peter Burke, 93–113. Cambridge: Polity Press, 1991.

Levi, Giovanni. "Globale Mikrogeschichte als 'Renaissance'? Ein Kommentar zu Hans Medick." *Historische Anthropologie* 25, no. 1 (2017).
Li, Tania Murray. *The Will to Improve: Governmentality, Development, and the Practice of Politics.* Durham: Duke University Press, 2007.
Li, Tania Murray. "Indigeneity, Capitalism, and the Management of Dispossession." *Current Anthropology* 51, no. 3 (2010): 385–414.
Li, Tania Murray. *Land's End: Capitalist Relations on an Indigenous Frontier.* Durham: Duke University Press, 2014.
Lidström, Karin. "'The Matrilineal Puzzle' Women's Land Rights in Mozambique – Case Study: Niassa Province." Master thesis, Uppsala University, 2014. http://www.diva-portal.org/smash/get/diva2:750207/FULLTEXT01.pdf.
Liebst, Michelle. "African Workers and the Universities' Mission to Central Africa in Zanzibar, 1864–1900." *Journal of Eastern African Studies* 8, no. 3 (2014): 366–381.
Liesegang, Gerhard. "Guerras, terras e tipos de povoaçoes: Sobre uma 'tradiçao urbanística' do norte de Moçambique no século XIX." *Revista Internacional de Estudos Africanos*, no. 1 (1984): 169–184.
Liesegang, Gerhard. "A First Look at the Import and Export Trade of Mozambique, 1800–1914." In *Figuring African Trade: Proceedings of the Symposium on the Quantification and Structure of the Import and Export and Long Distance Trade in Africa 1800–1913*, edited by Gerhard Liesegang, Helma Pasch, and Adam Jones, 452–523. Berlin: Dietrich Reimer, 1986.
Liesegang, Gerhard. "The Arquivo Histórico de Moçambique and Historical Research in Maputo." *History in Africa* 27 (2000): 471–477.
Liesegang, Gerhard. "A história do Niassa, ca. 1600–1920. Cap. VI: A estrutura politica, a estratificação social e o lugar dos chefes na estrutura económica e religiosa antes da conquista colonial." 2014. Accessed January 11, 2018. https://www.academia.edu/8133173/Hist%C3%B3ria_do_Niassa_precolonial_Ch._VI_Estrutura_Politica.
Liesegang, Gerhard. "Sobre telescopação e de-telescopação: Como a tradição dinástica dos Tembe e Khosa." September 2014. Accessed January 18, 2018. https://www.academia.edu/8441504/Sobre_Telescopa%C3%A7%C3%A3o_e_De-Telescopa%C3%A7%C3%A3o_Como_a_tradi%C3%A7%C3%A3o_din%C3%A2stica_dos_Tembe_e_Khosa.
Linden, Ian. "Mponda Mission Diary, 1889–1891. Part III: A Portuguese Mission in British Central Africa." *The International Journal of African Historical Studies* 7, no. 4 (1974): 688.
Linden, Ian. *Catholics, Peasants, and Chewa Resistance in Nyasaland: 1889–1939.* Berkeley: University of California Press, 1974.
Linder, Adolphe. *Os Suíços em Moçambique.* Maputo: AHM, 2001.
Lindsay, Lisa A. "Biography in African History." *History in Africa* 44 (2017): 11–26.
Lindsay, Lisa A. "Slavery, Absorption, and Gender: Frederick Cooper and the Power of Comparison." *History in Africa* 47 (2020): 65–74.
Lobato, Alexandre. "Augusto Cardoso e o Lago Niassa." *Stvdia. Revista Quadrimestral*, no. 19 (1966): 7–91.
Longwe, Molly. *Growing Up: A Chewa Girls' Initiation.* Zomba: Kachere, 2006.
Lonsdale, John. "Agency in Tight Corners: Narrative and Initiative in African History." *Journal of African Cultural Studies* 13, no. 1 (2000): 5–16.
Lovejoy, Paul E. *Transformations in Slavery: A History of Slavery in Africa.* Cambridge: Cambridge University Press, 1983.

Lovett, Margot L. "From Sisters to Wives and 'Slaves': Redefining Matriliny and the Lives of Lakeside Tonga Women, 1885–1955." *Critique of Anthropology* 17, no. 2 (1997): 171–187.
Lubkemann, Stephen. *Culture in Chaos: An Anthropology of the Social Condition in War.* Chicago: University of Chicago Press, 2008.
Lund, Christian. *Local Politics and the Dynamics of Property in Africa.* Cambridge: Cambridge University Press, 2008.
LUSA. "British Historian Malyn Newitt Calls for More Studies on Northern Mozambique." Club of Mozambique, June 21, 2018. Accessed June 10, 2019. https://clubofmozambique.com/news/british-historian-malyn-newitt-calls-for-more-studies-on-northern-mozambique/.
Macandza, Valério, Robert K. Walker, and Jennifer Bisgard. "Performance Evaluation of Three Biodiversity and Ecotourism Activities in Mozambique," December 12, 2013. Accessed April 8, 2019. https://pdf.usaid.gov/pdf_docs/PA00JKM6.pdf.
MacDonald, Duff. *Africana; or the Heart of Heathen Africa: Vol. I—Native Customs and Beliefs.* London: Simpkin Marshall, 1882.
Machava, Benedito, and Euclides Gonçalves. "The Dead Archive: Governance and Institutional Memory in Independent Mozambique." *Africa* 91, no. 4 (2021): 553–574.
Machava, Benedito. "The Morality of Revolution: Urban Cleanup Campaigns, Reeducation Camps, and Citizenship in Socialist Mozambique (1974–1988)." PhD thesis, University of Michigan, 2018.
MacKenzie, John. "The Naval Campaigns on Lakes Victoria and Nyasa, 1914–18." *The Mariner's Mirror* 71, no. 2 (1985): 169–182.
MacMaster, Neil. "The 'Silent Native': Attentisme, Being Compromised, and Banal Terror during the Algerian War of Independence, 1954–1962." In *The French Colonial Mind, Vol. 2: Violence, Military Encounters, and Colonialism,* edited by Martin Thomas, 283–303. Lincoln: University of Nebraska Press, 2011.
Macola, Giacomo. *Liberal Nationalism in Central Africa: A Biography of Harry Mwaanga Nkumbula.* New York: Palgrave Macmillan, 2010.
Macpherson, Fergus. *Anatomy of a Conquest: The British Occupation of Zambia, 1884–1924.* Harlow: Longman, 1981.
MacQueen, Norrie. *The Decolonization of Portuguese Africa: Metropolitan Revolution and the Dissolution of Empire.* London: Longman, 1997.
Mamdani, Mahmood. *Citizen and Subject: Contemporary Africa and the Legacy of Late Colonialism.* Princeton: Princeton University Press, 1996.
Mandala, Elias C. *Work and Control in a Peasant Economy: A History of the Lower Tchiri Valley in Malawi, 1859–1960.* Madison: University of Wisconsin Press, 1990.
Mandala, Elias C. *The End of Chidyerano: A History of Food and Everyday Life in Malawi, 1860–2004.* Portsmouth: Heinemann, 2005.
Mann, Kristin. *Slavery and the Birth of an African City: Lagos, 1760–1900.* Bloomington: Indiana University Press, 2007.
Manning, Carrie. "Constructing Opposition in Mozambique: Renamo as Political Party." *Journal of Southern African Studies* 24, no. 1 (1998): 161–189.
Manning, Carrie. *The Politics of Peace in Mozambique: Post-Conflict Democratization, 1992–2000.* Westport: Praeger, 2002.
Manning, Carrie, and Ian Smith. "Electoral Performance by Post-Rebel Parties." *Government and Opposition* 54, no. 3 (2019): 415–453.
Martin, Susan M. *Palm Oil and Protest: An Economic History of the Ngwa Region, South-Eastern Nigeria, 1800–1980.* Cambridge: Cambridge University Press, 1988.

Massari, Augusto. *Gli italiani nel Mozambico portoghese: 1830–1975.* Torino: L'Harmattan Italia, 2005.
Massinga, Alfredo V. R., and Patricio Contreras. "The Fishing Centres of Lake Niassa (Mozambique)." *Revista de Investigação Pesqueira (Maputo)*, no. 17 (1988): 1–43.
Matusse, Renato. *Guebuza: A paixão pela terra.* Maputo: Macmillan Moçambique, 2004.
Maynes, Mary Jo, Ann Waltner, Birgitte Soland, and Ulrike Strasser. "Introduction: Toward a Comparative History of Gender, Kinship and Power." In *Gender, Kinship, Power: A Comparative and Interdisciplinary History*, edited by Mary Jo Maynes, Ann Waltner, Birgitte Soland, and Ulrike Strasser, 1–23. New York: Routledge, 1996.
Mbembe, Achille. "The Subject of the World." In *Facing up to the Past: Perspectives on the Commemoration of Slavery from Africa, the Americas and Europe*, edited by Gert Oostindie, 21–28. Kingston, Jamaica: Ian Randle Publishers, 2001.
Mbembe, Achille. *Out of the Dark Night: Essays on Decolonization.* New York: Columbia University Press, 2021.
McArthur, John W, and Jeffrey D. Sachs. "A General Equilibrium Model for Analyzing African Rural Subsistence Economies and an African Green Revolution." *Africa Growth Initative Working Paper*, no. 12 (June 2013).
McCaskie, Tom C. *Asante Identities: History and Modernity in an African Village 1850–1950.* Edinburgh: Edinburgh University Press, 2000.
McCracken, John. "Coercion and Control in Nyasaland: Aspects of the History of a Colonial Police Force." *The Journal of African History* 27, no. 1 (1986): 127–147.
McCracken, John. "Reviewed Work: Work and Control in a Peasant Economy: A History of the Lower Tchiri Valley in Malawi, 1859–1960 by Elias C. Mandala." *The American Historical Review* 97, no. 1 (1992): 261–262.
McCracken, John. *A History of Malawi 1859–1966.* Woodbridge: James Currey, 2012.
Medeiros, Eduardo. *As etapas da escravatura no norte de Moçambique.* Maputo: AHM, 1988.
Medeiros, Eduardo. *História de Cabo Delgado e do Niassa (c. 1836–1929).* Maputo: Central Impressora, 1997.
Medick, Hans. "Mikro-Historie." In *Sozialgeschichte, Alltagsgeschichte, Mikro-Historie*, edited by Winfried Schulze, 40–53. Göttingen: Vandenhoeck & Ruprecht, 1994.
Medick, Hans. *Weben und Überleben in Laichingen 1650–1900: Lokalgeschichte als allgemeine Geschichte.* Göttingen: Vandenhoeck & Ruprecht, 1996.
Medick, Hans. "Turning Global? Microhistory in Extension." *Historische Anthropologie* 24, no. 2 (2016): 241–252.
Meillassoux, Claude, ed. *L'esclavage en Afrique précoloniale.* Paris: François Maspero, 1975.
Meillassoux, Claude, Christine Messiant, Michel Cahen, and Jorge Derluguian. "Mozambique: The Debate Continues. The Cahen Document: Victory via Democracy for Socialism." *Southern Africa Report* 5, no. 4 (1990): 26–27.
Meyns, Peter. "Zur Praxis ländlicher Entwicklungspolitik in Afrika – Anmerkungen zu Mozambique und Tanzania." In *Agrargesellschaften im portugiesisch-sprachigen Afrika*, edited by Peter Meyns, 39–59. Saarbrücken: Breitenbach, 1988.
Miers, Suzanne, and Martin A. Klein, eds. *Slavery and Colonial Rule in Africa.* Portland: Frank Cass, 1999.
Miers, Suzanne, and Igor Kopytoff, eds. *Slavery in Africa: Historical and Anthropological Perspectives.* Madison: University of Wisconsin Press, 1977.

Mihanjo, Eginald. "Transformation of the Kisi Pottery Enterprise in Southwest Tanzania." In *Negotiating Social Space: East African Microenterprises*, edited by Patrick O. Alila and Poul O. Pedersen, 273–290. Trenton: Africa World Press, 2001.

Miller, Joseph C. "Breaking the Historiographical Chains: Martin Klein and Slavery." *Canadian Journal of African Studies/Revue Canadienne des Études Africaines* 34, no. 3 (2000): 512–531.

Minter, William. "Inside Renamo as Described by Ex-Participants." *Transformation*, no. 10 (1989): 1–27.

Minter, William. *Apartheid's Contras: An Inquiry into the Roots of War in Angola and Mozambique*. Johannesburg: Witwatersrand University Press, 1994.

Mitchell, J. Clyde. "The Yao of Southern Nyasaland." In *Seven Tribes of British Central Africa*, edited by Elizabeth Colson and Max Gluckman, 292–353. London: Oxford University Press, 1951. Reprint, Manchester: Manchester University Press, 1959.

Mitchell, J. Clyde. *The Yao Village: A Study in the Social Structure of a Malawian People*. 1956. Reprint, Manchester: Manchester University Press, 1971.

Moore, Henrietta L., and Megan Vaughan. *Cutting Down Trees: Gender, Nutrition, and Agricultural Change in the Northern Province of Zambia, 1890–1990*. Portsmouth: Heinemann, 1994.

Moore-Gilbert, Bart. "Spivak and Bhabha." In *A Companion to Postcolonial Studies*, edited by Henry Schwarz and Sangeeta Ray, 451–466. Malden: Blackwell, 2007.

Morier-Genoud, Eric, Michel Cahen, and Domingos Manuel do Rosário, eds. *The War Within: New Perspectives on the Civil War in Mozambique, 1976–1992*. Woodbridge: James Currey, 2018.

Morris, Brian. *The Power of Animals: An Ethnography*. Oxford: Berg, 1998.

Morris, Brian. *An Environmental History of Southern Malawi: Land and People of the Shire Highlands*. Cham: Palgrave Macmillan, 2016.

Motta, Helena. "Processamento artesanal de pescado em Moçambique." Instituto de Investigação Pesqueira, Boletim de Divulgação, no. 30. Maputo, 1990.

Msiska, Augustine W.C. "The Spread of Islam in Malawi and Its Impact on Yao Rites of Passage, 1870–1960." *The Society of Malawi Journal* 48, no. 1 (1995): 1995–1995.

Mteti, Shakila Halifan. "Engendering Pottery Production and Distribution Processes among the Kisi and Pare of Tanzania." *International Journal of Gender and Women's Studies* 4, no. 2 (2016): 127–141.

Mueller, Bernd E.T. "The Agrarian Question in Tanzania: Using New Evidence to Reconcile an Old Debate." *Review of African Political Economy* 38, no. 127 (2011): 23–42.

Munslow, Barry. *Mozambique: The Revolution and Its Origins*. London: Longman, 1983.

Munslow, Barry. "State Intervention in Agriculture: The Mozambican Experience." *The Journal of Modern African Studies* 22, no. 2 (1984): 199–221.

Murdock, George Peter. *Social Structure*. New York: Macmillan, 1949.

Murton, James Ernest, Dean Bavington, and Carly A Dokis. "Introduction: Why Subsistence?" In *Subsistence under Capitalism: Historical and Contemporary Perspectives*, edited by James Ernest Murton, Dean Bavington, and Carly A Dokis, 3–36. Montreal: McGill-Quenn's University Press, 2016.

Mussanhane, Ana Bouene, ed. *Protagonistas da Luta de Libertação Nacional*. Maputo: Marimbique, 2012.

Muto, Megumi, and Takashi Yamano. "The Impact of Mobile Phone Coverage Expansion on Market Participation: Panel Data Evidence from Uganda." *World Development* 37, no. 12 (2009): 1887–1896.

Mutongi, Kenda. *Worries of the Heart: Widows, Family, and Community in Kenya*. Chicago: University of Chicago Press, 2007.

Naiene, Ângelo José, and Arlindo Langa. "Atribuição de pensão aos antigos combatentes desmobilizados: O impacto na reintegração social no centro de produção dos antigos combatentes 25 de Setembro, em Umbeluzi, Distrito de Boane, Província de Maputo, no período 1986–2001." PhD thesis, Universidade Eduardo Mondlane, 2002. http://www.saber.ac.mz/bitstream/10857/2172/1/Ap-025.pdf.

Ncomo, Lucas Barnabé. *Uria Simango: um homem, uma causa*. Maputo: Novafrica, 2003.

Ndegue, David F. *A Luta de Libertação na Frente do Niassa*. Vol. 1. Maputo: JV, 2009.

Neil-Tomlinson, Barry. "The Nyassa Chartered Company: 1891–1929." *The Journal of African History* 18, no. 1 (1977): 109–128.

Neto, Maria da Conceição. "In Town and Out of Town: A Social History of Huambo (Angola), 1902–1961." PhD thesis, SOAS, University of London, 2012. http://eprints.soas.ac.uk/13822/1/Neto_3375.pdf.

Neumann, Roderick P. *Imposing Wilderness: Struggles over Livelihood and Nature Preservation in Africa*. Berkeley: University of California Press, 1998.

Neuparth, Augusto. "A Fronteira Luso-Allemã de Moçambique VI." *Revista Portugueza Colonial e Maritima* XIX, no. 138 (1908): 8–20.

Neves, Jaime. "A tripanossomíase rodesiense na região do Meluluca." *Moçambique: Documentário Trimestral*, no. 76 (1953): 35–48.

Newitt, Malyn. *Portugal in Africa: The Last Hundred Years*. London: Longman, 1981.

Newitt, Malyn. *A History of Mozambique*. Bloomington: Indiana University Press, 1995.

Newitt, Malyn. *A Short History of Mozambique*. London: Hurst, 2017.

Newitt, Malyn. "Michel Cahen's Review of a Short History of Mozambique: Some Thoughts." *Lusotopie* 17, no. 1 (2018): 168–173.

Nielsen, Robin L., Christopher Tanner, and Anna Knox. "Focus on Land in Africa: Mozambique's Innovative Land Law," January 2011. Accessed April 20, 2019. http://www.focusonland.com/download/538ddd5cb3283/.

Nordstrom, Carolyn. *A Different Kind of War Story*. Philadelphia: University of Pennsylvania Press, 1997.

Northrup, Nancy. "The Migrations of Yao and Kololo into Southern Malawi: Aspects of Migrations in Nineteenth Century Africa." *The International Journal of African Historical Studies* 19, no. 1 (1986): 59–75.

Nunn, Nathan. "The Long-Term Effects of Africa's Slave Trades." *Quarterly Journal of Economics* 123, no. 1 (2008): 139–176.

Nunn, Nathan, and Leonard Wantchekon. "The Slave Trade and the Origins of Mistrust in Africa." *American Economic Review* 101, no. 7 (2011): 3221–3252.

Nweke, Felix I., John K. Lynam, and Dunstan S.C. Spencer. *The Cassava Transformation: Africa's Best-Kept Secret*. East Lansing: Michigan State University Press, 2002.

Obarrio, Juan. *The Spirit of the Laws in Mozambique*. Chicago: University of Chicago Press, 2014.

O'Laughlin, Bridget. "Through a Divided Glass: Dualism, Class and the Agrarian Question in Mozambique." *Journal of Peasant Studies* 23, no. 4 (1996): 1–39.

O'Laughlin, Bridget. "Class and the Customary: The Ambiguous Legacy of the Indigenato in Mozambique." *African Affairs* 99, no. 394 (2000): 5–42.

O'Laughlin, Bridget. "Proletarianisation, Agency and Changing Rural Livelihoods: Forced Labour and Resistance in Colonial Mozambique." *Journal of Southern African Studies* 28, no. 3 (2002): 511–530.

Oliveira, Pedro Aires. "Saved by the Civil War: African 'Loyalists' in the Portuguese Armed Forces and Angola's Transition to Independence." *The International History Review* 39, no. 1 (2017): 126–142.

Olivier de Sardan, Jean-Pierre. *Anthropology and Development: Understanding Contemporary Social Change*. London: Zed Books, 2005.

Onselen, Charles van. *The Seed Is Mine: The Life of Kas Maine, a South African Sharecropper 1895–1985*. New York: David Philip, 1996.

Oppen, Achim von. "Village Studies: Zur Geschichte eines Genres der Sozialforschung im südlichen und östlichen Afrika." *Paideuma* 42 (1996): 17–36.

Oppen, Achim von. "Cassava, 'The Lazy Man's Food'? Indigenous Agricultural Innovation and Dietary Change in Northwestern Zambia (ca. 1650–1970)." In *Changing Food Habits: Case Studies from Africa, South America and Europe*, edited by Carola Lentz, 43–71. Amsterdam: Harwood, 1999.

Oppen, Achim von. "The Village as Territory: Enclosing Locality in Northwest Zambia, 1950s to 1990s." *The Journal of African History* 47, no. 1 (2006): 57–75.

ORGUT. "Inception Report." Reality Checks in Mozambique: Building Better Understanding of the Dynamics of Poverty and Well-Being. ORGUT Consulting, 2011. http://www.cmi.no/publications/file/4508-reality-checks-in-mozambique.pdf.

ORGUT. "Sub-Report, District of Lago: Year One, 2011." Reality Checks in Mozambique: Building Better Understanding of the Dynamics of Poverty and Well-Being. ORGUT Consulting, 2011.

ORGUT. "Sub-Report, District of Lago: Year Four, 2014." Reality Checks in Mozambique: Building Better Understanding of the Dynamics of Poverty and Well-Being. ORGUT Consulting, 2014.

ORGUT. "1st Reality Check in Mozambique: Brief." Accessed December 4, 2020. https://www.sida.se/globalassets/global/countries-and-regions/africa/mozambique/brief-1st-reality-checks-final.pdf.

Ortner, Sherry B. "Resistance and the Problem of Ethnographic Refusal." *Comparative Studies in Society and History* 37, no. 1 (1995): 173–193.

Ortner, Sherry B. *Anthropology and Social Theory: Culture, Power, and the Acting Subject*. Durham: Duke University Press, 2006.

Osborn, Emily Lynn. "Work and Migration." In *The Oxford Handbook of Modern African History*, edited by John Parker and Richard J. Reid, 189–207. Oxford: Oxford University Press, 2013.

Overbeek, Winfridus. *O avanço das monoculturas de árvores em Moçambique: Impactos sobre as comunidades camponesas na Província de Niassa. Um relatório de viagem*. Montevideo: World Rainforest Movement, 2010.

Page, Melvin E. "Up from the Farm: A Global Microhistory of Rural Americans and Africans in the First World War." *Journal of Global History* 16, no. 1 (2021): 101–121.

Palmer, Hilary C., and Malyn Newitt. *Northern Mozambique in the Nineteenth Century: The Travels and Explorations of H.E. O'Neill*. Leiden: Brill, 2016.

Parker, John, and Richard Rathbone. *African History: A Very Short Introduction*. Oxford: Oxford University Press, 2007.

Parker, John, and Richard J. Reid. "Introduction. African Histories: Past, Present, and Future." In *The Oxford Handbook of Modern African History*, edited by John Parker and Richard J. Reid, 1–18. Oxford: Oxford University Press, 2013.

Péclard, Didier, Antoine Kernen, and Guive Khan-Mohammad. "États d'émergence: Le gouvernement de la croissance et du développement en Afrique." *Critique internationale*, no. 89 (2020): 9–27.

Pélissier, René. *História de Moçambique: Formação e oposição 1854–1918*. Vol. 1. 2 vols. Lisboa: Estampa, 2000.

Pélissier, René. *História de Moçambique: Formação e oposição 1854–1918*. Vol. 2. 2 vols. Lisboa: Estampa, 2000.

Penvenne, Jeanne. *African Workers and Colonial Racism: Mozambican Strategies and Struggles in Lourenço Marques, 1877–1962*. Portsmouth: Heinemann, 1995.

Pérez-Niño, Helena. "Post-Conflict Agrarian Change in Angónia: Land, Labour and the Organization of Production in the Mozambique-Malawi Borderland." PhD thesis, SOAS, University of London, 2014.

Peša, Iva. "'Cassava Is Our Chief': Negotiating Identity, Markets and the State through Cassava in Mwinilunga, Zambia." In *Transforming Innovations in Africa: Explorative Studies on Appropriation in African Societies*, edited by Jan-Bart Gewald, André Leliveld, and Iva Peša. Leiden: Brill, 2012.

Peša, Iva. *Roads through Mwinilunga: A History of Social Change in Northwest Zambia*. Leiden: Brill, 2019.

Peters, Pauline. "Revisiting the Puzzle of Matriliny in South-Central Africa: Introduction." *Critique of Anthropology* 17, no. 2 (1997): 125–146.

Peters, Pauline. "Against the Odds: Matriliny, Land and Gender in the Shire Highlands of Malawi." *Critique of Anthropology* 17, no. 2 (1997): 189–210.

Peters, Pauline. "Land Appropriation, Surplus People and a Battle over Visions of Agrarian Futures in Africa." *Journal of Peasant Studies* 40, no. 3 (2013): 537–562.

Peterson, Brian. *Islamization from Below: The Making of Muslim Communities in Rural French Sudan, 1880–1960*. New Haven: Yale University Press, 2011.

Peterson, Derek R. "Culture and Chronology in African History." *The Historical Journal* 50, no. 2 (2007): 483–497.

Phillips, Kristin. *An Ethnography of Hunger: Politics, Subsistence, and the Unpredictable Grace of the Sun*. Bloomington: Indiana University Press, 2018.

Phiri, Kings M. "Some Changes in the Matrilineal Family System among the Chewa of Malawi since the Nineteenth Century." *The Journal of African History* 24, no. 2 (1983): 257–274.

Piot, Charles. *Remotely Global: Village Modernity in West Africa*. Chicago: University of Chicago Press, 1999.

Pitcher, M. Anne. "Sowing the Seeds of Failure: Early Portuguese Cotton Cultivation in Angola and Mozambique." *Journal of Southern African Studies* 17, no. 1 (1991): 43–70.

Pitcher, M. Anne. "From Coercion to Incentives: The Portuguese Colonial Cotton Regime in Angola and Mozambique, 1946–1974." In *Cotton, Colonialism, and Social History in Sub-Saharan Africa*, edited by Allen Isaacman and Richard Roberts, 119–146. Portsmouth: Heinemann, 1995.

Pitcher, M. Anne. "Review of Cotton Is the Mother of Poverty: Peasants, Work, and Rural Struggle in Colonial Mozambique, 1938–1961 by Allen Isaacman." *Journal of Southern African Studies* 22, no. 4 (1996): 689–691.

Pitcher, M. Anne. "Forgetting from Above and Memory from Below: Strategies of Legitimation and Struggle in Postsocialist Mozambique." *Africa* 76, no. 1 (2006): 88–112.

Platteau, Jean-Philippe. "The Evolutionary Theory of Land Rights as Applied to Sub-Saharan Africa: A Critical Assessment." *Development and Change* 27, no. 1 (1996): 29–86.

Pletcher, Jim. "Ecological Deterioration and Agricultural Stagnation in Eastern Province, Zambia." *The Centennial Review* 35, no. 2 (1991): 369–388.

Porter, Andrew. "'Commerce and Christianity': The Rise and Fall of a Nineteenth-Century Missionary Slogan." *The Historical Journal* 28, no. 3 (1985): 597–621.

Pössinger, Hermann. *Bericht über eine Reise nach Angola und Moçambique*. München: IFO, 1964.

Pössinger, Hermann. *Landwirtschaftliche Entwicklung in Angola und Moçambique*. München: IFO, 1968.

Pritchett, James A. *Friends for Life, Friends for Death: Cohorts and Consciousness among the Lunda-Ndembu*. Charlottesville: University of Virginia Press, 2007.

Purtschert, Patricia, Barbara Lüthi, and Francesca Falk, eds. *Postkoloniale Schweiz: Formen und Folgen eines Kolonialismus ohne Kolonien*. Bielefeld: transcript, 2012.
Quinn, Charlotte A. "Niumi: A Nineteenth-Century Mandingo Kingdom." *Africa* 38, no. 4 (1968): 443–455.
Raidone, Assumail, Manuel Vene, and Laurindo Malimusse. *Vida e obra de Francisco Orlando Magumbwa*. Lichinga: ARPAC, 2013.
Raidone, Assumail, Manuel Vene, Sérgio Patrício, and Laurindo Malimusse. *Vida e obra de Bernabé Adison Kajika (1938–1974)*. Lichinga: ARPAC, 2014.
Raimundo, José A. "La place et le rôle des villageois dans le processus de mise en oeuvre de la politique agraire au Mozambique: le cas des communautés Ajaua de la Province de Nyassa (1975 à 2005)." PhD thesis, Université de Paris VIII, 2008.
Randolph, B.W. *Arthur Douglas: The Story of His Life*. Westminster: UMCA, 1912.
Rangeley, W.H.J. "The Ayao." *The Nyasaland Journal* 16, no. 1 (1963): 7–27.
Ranger, Terence O. "Towards a Usable African Past." In *African Studies Since 1945: A Tribute to Basil Davidson*, edited by Christopher Fyfe, 17–30. London: Longman, 1976.
Ranger, Terence O. *Peasant Consciousness and Guerilla War in Zimbabwe: A Comparative Study*. London: James Currey, 1985.
Read, Margaret. "Migrant Labour in Africa and Its Effects on Tribal Life." *International Labour Review* 45, no. 6 (1942): 605–631.
Redmond, Patrick M. "A Political History of the Songea Ngoni from the Mid-Nineteenth Century to the Rise of the Tanganyika African National Union." PhD thesis, University of London, 1972. https://eprints.soas.ac.uk/29676/1/10752648.pdf.
Reid, Richard. "Past and Presentism: The 'Precolonial' and the Foreshortening of African History." *The Journal of African History* 52, no. 2 (2011): 135–155.
Reid, Richard. "States of Anxiety: History and Nation in Modern Africa." *Past & Present* 229, no. 1 (2015): 239–269.
Reusch, Richard. *Der Islam in Ost-Afrika mit besonderer Berücksichtigung der muhammedanischen Geheim-Orden*. Leipzig: Adolf Klein, 1931.
Revel, Jacques, ed. *Jeux d'échelles: La micro-analyse à l'expérience*. Paris: Gallimard, 1996.
Revel, Jacques. "Micro-analysis et construction du social." In *Jeux d'échelles: La Micro-Analyse à l'expérience*, edited by Jacques Revel, 15–36. Paris: Gallimard, 1996.
Reynolds, Tamsyn. "International Year of Ecotourism 2002 and a Case Study from Mozambique (Clearinghouse for Reviewing Ecotourism, no. 18)." Third World Network. Accessed August 10, 2018. https://www.twn.my/title/eco18.htm.
Richards, A.I. "Some Types of Family Structure amongst the Central Bantu." In *African Systems of Kinship and Marriage*, edited by A.R. Radcliffe-Brown and Daryll Forde, 207–251. London: Oxford University Press, 1950.
Richards, A.I. "Review of Schism and Continuity in an African Society: A Study of Ndembu Village Life by Victor Turner." *Africa* 29, no. 1 (1959): 88–90.
Robertson, Claire C., and Martin A. Klein. "Women's Importance in African Slave Systems." In *Women and Slavery in Africa*, edited by Claire C. Robertson and Martin A. Klein, 3–25. Madison: University of Wisconsin Press, 1983.
Robinson, David. *Paths of Accommodation: Muslim Societies and French Colonial Authorities in Senegal and Mauritania, 1880–1920*. Athens: Ohio University Press, 2000.
Robinson, David. *Muslim Societies in African History*. Cambridge: Cambridge University Press, 2004.
Rodney, Walter. *How Europe Underdeveloped Africa*. London: Bogle-L'Ouverture, 1972.

Rodrigues, Fatima da Cruz. "Vidas deslocadas pelo colonialismo e pela guerra." *Estudos Ibero-Americanos* 45, no. 2 (2019): 49–63.
Roesch, Otto. "Mozambique: The Debate Continues. Otto Roesch Replies." *Southern Africa Report* 5, no. 4 (1990): 28–29.
Roesch, Otto. "Renamo and the Peasantry in Southern Mozambique: A View from Gaza Province." *Canadian Journal of African Studies/Revue Canadienne des Études Africaines* 26, no. 3 (1992): 462–484.
Ross, Robert. "Transcending the Limits of Microhistory." *The Journal of African History* 42 (2001): 126–127.
Rudebeck, Lars. "Entwicklung und Demokratie – Notizen zur Volksmacht in Mozambique." In *Agrargesellschaften im portugiesisch-sprachigen Afrika*, edited by Peter Meyns, 111–127. Saarbrücken: Breitenbach, 1988.
Sachs, Jeffrey. *The End of Poverty: Economic Possibilities for Our Time*. New York: Penguin, 2005.
Sachs, Jeffrey. "The End of Poverty: Economic Possibilities for Our Time." *European Journal of Dental Education* 12, Special Issue: Global Congress on Dental Education III (2008): 17–21.
Sachs, Jeffrey. "Africa's Demographic Transition and Economic Prospects." In *The Oxford Handbook of Africa and Economics*, edited by Célestin Monga and Justin Yifu Lin, 2: Policies and Practices: 873–94. Oxford: Oxford University Press, 2015.
Sackley, Nicole. "The Village as Cold War Site: Experts, Development, and the History of Rural Reconstruction." *Journal of Global History* 6, no. 3 (2011): 481–504.
Saidi, Christine. *Women's Authority and Society in Early East-Central Africa*. Rochester: University of Rochester Press, 2010.
Sandwell, Ruth W. "History as Experiment: Microhistory and Environmental History." In *Method and Meaning in Canadian Environmental History*, edited by Alan MacEachern and William J. Turkel, 124–138. Toronto: Nelson, 2009.
Santos, Ana Margarida. "The Past in the Present: Memories of the Liberation Struggle in Northern Mozambique." 7° Congresso Ibérico de Estudos Africanos. Lisboa, 2010. Accessed October 30, 2019. http://www.observatori.org/paises/pais_70/documentos/_Mozambbique_The%20past%20in%20the%20present.pdf.
Santos, Ana Margarida. "Resistance and Collaboration: Conflicting Memories of the Liberation Struggle (1964–1974) in Northern Mozambique." *Social Evolution & History* 13, no. 2 (2014): 151–175.
Santos, Maciel. "The Peasant Tax in Northern Mozambique (1929–1939): Forced Cultivation, a Growth Factor?" In *Administration and Taxation in Former Portuguese Africa*, by Philip Havik, Alexander Keese, and Maciel Santos, 138–166. Newcastle upon Tyne: Cambridge Scholars, 2015.
Santos, Nuno. *O desconhecido Niassa*. Lisboa: Junta de Investigações do Ultramar, 1964.
Sarkar, Sumit. "The Decline of the Subaltern in Subaltern Studies." In *Writing Social History*, 82–108. Delhi, 1997.
Saul, John S. "Mozambique – Not Then but Now." *Review of African Political Economy* 38, no. 127 (2011): 93–101.
Saul, John S., and Colin Leys. "Sub-Saharan Africa in Global Capitalism." *Monthly Review: An Independent Socialist Magazine* 51, no. 3 (1999).
Saunders, Christopher. "Conference Report: Mfecane Afterthoughts." *Social Dynamics* 17, no. 2 (1991): 171–177.

Schafer, Jessica. *Soldiers at Peace: Veterans and Society after the Civil War in Mozambique*. New York: Palgrave Macmillan, 2007.
Schär, Bernhard C. "Rösti und Revolutionen: Zur postkolonialen Re-Lektüre der Schweizer Geschichte." *Widerspruch*, no. 72 (2018): 9–19.
Scheuzger, Stephan. "Global History as Polycentric History." *Comparativ: Zeitschrift für Globalgeschichte und vergleichende Gesellschaftsforschung* 29, no. 2 (2019): 122–153.
Schlumbohm, Jürgen, ed. *Mikrogeschichte – Makrogeschichte: Komplementär oder inkommensurabel?* Göttingen: Wallstein, 1998.
Schmied, Doris. *Subsistence Cultivation, Market Production and Agricultural Development in Ruvuma Region, Southern Tanzania*. Bayreuth: Eckhard Breitinger, 1989.
Schumacher, E.F. *Small Is Beautiful: Economics as If People Mattered*. London: Blond & Briggs, 1973.
Sciardet, Hervé. "De la colonisation à la décolonisation: Les modes de constitution de la Françafrique. Une table ronde entre Nicolas Bancel et Jean-Pierre Dozon." *Mouvements*, no. 21–22 (2002): 15–27.
Scott, James C. *The Moral Economy of the Peasant: Rebellion and Subsistence in Southeast Asia*. New Haven: Yale University Press, 1976.
Scott, James C. *Weapons of the Weak: Everyday Forms of Peasant Resistance*. New Haven: Yale University Press, 1985.
Scott, James C. *Seeing like a State: How Certain Schemes to Improve the Human Condition Have Failed*. New Haven: Yale University Press, 1998.
Scott, James C. *The Art of Not Being Governed: An Anarchist History of Upland Southeast Asia*. New Haven: Yale University Press, 2009.
Seibert, Julia. *In die globale Wirtschaft gezwungen: Arbeit und kolonialer Kapitalismus im Kongo (1885–1960)*. Frankfurt: Campus Verlag, 2016.
Sewell, William Hamilton. *Logics of History: Social Theory and Social Transformation*. Chicago: University of Chicago Press, 2005.
Sharkey, Heather J. "African Colonial States." In *The Oxford Handbook of Modern African History*, edited by John Parker and Richard J. Reid, 151–170. Oxford: Oxford University Press, 2013.
Sheldon, Kathleen E. *Pounders of Grain: A History of Women, Work, and Politics in Mozambique*. Portsmouth: Heinemann, 2002.
Shenk, Mary K., Ryan O. Begley, David A. Nolin, and Andrew Swiatek. "When Does Matriliny Fail? The Frequencies and Causes of Transitions to and from Matriliny Estimated from a de Novo Coding of a Cross-Cultural Sample." *Philosophical Transactions of the Royal Society B: Biological Sciences* 374, no. 1780 (2019): 1–15.
Shepperson, George. "The Jumbe of Kota Kota and Some Aspects of the History of Islam in British Central Africa." In *Islam in Tropical Africa*, edited by I. M. Lewis, 193–207. London: Oxford University Press, 1966.
Sheriff, Abdul. *Slaves, Spices, & Ivory in Zanzibar: Integration of an East African Commercial Empire into the World Economy, 1770–1873*. London: James Currey, 1987.
Sheriff, Abdul. "Localisation and Social Composition of the East African Slave Trade, 1858–1873." *Slavery & Abolition* 9, no. 3 (1988): 131–145.
Shivji, Issa G. *State Coercion and Freedom in Tanzania*. Roma, Lesotho: Institute of Southern African Studies, 1990.
Sicard, S.V. "The Arrival of Islam in Malawi and the Muslim Contribution to Development." *Journal of Muslim Minority Affairs* 20, no. 2 (2000): 291–311.

Sikainga, Ahmad. *Slaves into Workers: Emancipation and Labor in Colonial Sudan*. Austin: University of Texas Press, 1996.

Silberfein, Marilyn. "Cyclical Change in African Settlement and Modern Resettlement Programs." In *Rural Settlement Structure and African Development*, edited by Marylin Silberfein, 47–72. New York: Routledge, 1998.

Silverman, Marilyn, and P.H. Gulliver. "Historical Anthropology through Local-Level Research." In *Critical Junctions: Anthroplogy and History beyond the Cultural Turn*, edited by Don Kalb and Herman Tak, 152–167. New York: Berghahn, 2005.

Simão, Jaime, João Paulo Borges Coelho, and Gerhard Liesegang. "Collection and Administration of Oral History Records in the Arquivo Histórico de Moçambique and Problems with Research and Publication Encountered with Projects in the Social and General History of the War of Liberation (1964–1975) and the Post-Liberation Wars (1975–1992) in Mozambique." *Esarbica* 21 (2002): 91–104.

Siméant, Johanna. "Three Bodies of Moral Economy: The Diffusion of a Concept." *Journal of Global Ethics* 11, no. 2 (2015): 163–175.

Sketchley, Peter. "Fishing Co-operatives on Lake Niassa: Seeds of a New Socialist Society or New Roots for an Old Exploiting Class?" *Review of African Political Economy* 9, no. 24 (1982): 85–95.

Souto, Amélia Neves de. *Caetano e o ocaso do "Império": Administração e guerra colonial em Moçambique durante o Marcelismo (1968–1974)*. Porto: Afrontamento, 2007.

Souto, Amélia Neves de. "Memory and Identity in the History of Frelimo: Some Research Themes." *Kronos* 39, no. 1 (2013): 280–296.

Spear, Thomas. "Neo-Traditionalism and the Limits of Invention in British Colonial Africa." *The Journal of African History* 44, no. 1 (2003): 3–27.

Spenceley, Anna. "Tourism, Local Livelihoods, and the Private Sector in South Africa: Case Studies on the Growing Role of the Private Sector in Natural Resources Management." Sustainable Livelihoods in Southern Africa Research Paper, no. 8. Brighton: Institute of Development Studies, 2003. http://rgdoi.net/10.13140/RG.2.1.2266.8643.

Spivak, Gayatri Chakravorty. "Can the Subaltern Speak?" In *Marxism and the Interpretation of Culture*, edited by Cary Nelson and Lawrence Grossberg, 271–312. Urbana: University of Illinois Press, 1988.

Stanley, Brian. "'Commerce and Christianity': Providence Theory, The Missionary Movement, and the Imperialism of Free Trade, 1842–1860." *The Historical Journal* 26, no. 1 (1983): 71–94.

Stannus, Hugh. "The Wayao of Nyasaland." In *Varia Africana III*, edited by E. A. Hooton and Natica I. Bates, 229–372. Cambridge: The African Department of the Peabody Museum of Harvard University, 1922.

Stapleton, Timothy J. *No Insignificant Part: The Rhodesia Native Regiment and the East Africa Campaign of the First World War*. Waterloo, Canada: Wilfrid Laurier University Press, 2006.

Stuart, Richard. "Christianity and the Chewa: The Anglican Case 1885–1950." PhD thesis, University of London, 1974.

Stuart, Richard. "Os Nyanja, o U.M.C.A. e a Companhia do Niassa, 1880–1930." *Revista Internacional de Estudos Africanos* 3 (1985): 9–44.

Stucki, Andreas. *Aufstand und Zwangsumsiedlung: Die kubanischen Unabhängigkeitskriege 1868–1898*. Hamburg: Hamburger Edition, 2012.

Stucki, Andreas. "Frequent Deaths: The Colonial Development of Concentration Camps Reconsidered, 1868–1974." *Journal of Genocide Research* 20, no. 3 (2018): 305–26.

Stucki, Andreas. *Violence and Gender in Africa's Iberian Colonies: Feminizing the Portuguese and Spanish Empire, 1950s–1970s*. Cham: Palgrave Macmillan, 2019.
Sumich, Jason. *The Middle Class in Mozambique: The State and the Politics of Transformation in Southern Africa*. New York: Cambridge University Press, 2018.
Sweden Abroad. "Poverty Monitoring – Niassa Reality Check." Accessed November 21, 2018. https://www.swedenabroad.se/en/about-sweden-non-swedish-citizens/mozambique/development-and-aid-mozambique/poverty-monitoring--niassa-reality-check/.
Synge, Richard. *Mozambique: UN Peacekeeping in Action, 1992–94*. Washington, D.C.: United States Institute of Peace Press, 1997.
Tanner, Christopher. "Law-Making in an African Context: The 1997 Mozambican Land Law." FAO Legal Papers Online, March 2002. Accessed May 7, 2019. http://www.fao.org/fileadmin/user_upload/legal/docs/lpo26.pdf.
Tembe, Joel Das Neves, ed. *História da Luta de Libertação Nacional*. Vol. 1. Maputo: Ministério dos Combatentes, 2014.
Temu, Arnold. "Not Telling: African History at the End of the Millennium." *South African Historical Journal* 42, no. 1 (2000): 2–10.
Thomas, Lynn M. "Historicising Agency." *Gender & History* 28, no. 2 (2016): 324–339.
Thomas, Martin, Bob Moore, and L.J. Butler. *Crises of Empire: Decolonization and Europe's Imperial States, 1918–1975*. London: Bloomsbury, 2008.
Thomas, Martin, Bob Moore, and L.J. Butler. "Contrasting Patterns of Decolonization: Belgian and Portuguese Africa." In *Crises of Empire: Decolonization and Europe's Imperial States, 1918–1975*, edited by Martin Thomas, Bob Moore, and L.J. Butler, 385–410. London: Bloomsbury, 2008.
Thomas, Martin, and Andrew S. Thompson. "Rethinking Decolonization: A New Research Agenda for the Twenty-First Century." In *The Oxford Handbook of the Ends of Empire*, edited by Martin Thomas and Andrew S. Thompson, 1–26. Oxford: Oxford University Press, 2018.
Thorold, Alan. "Yao Conversion to Islam." *Cambridge Anthropology* 12, no. 2 (1987): 18–28.
Thorold, Alan. "The Yao Muslims: Religion and Social Change in Southern Malawi." PhD thesis, Churchill College (Cambridge), 1995.
Thorsen, Anne Kristine. "Reducing Social Vulnerabilities through Foreign Investments: A Case-Study of Niassa Green Resources in Northern Mozambique." Master thesis, Universitetet i Stavanger, 2017.
Tilley, Helen. *Africa as a Living Laboratory: Empire, Development, and the Problem of Scientific Knowledge, 1870–1950*. Chicago: University of Chicago Press, 2011.
Tiquet, Romain. "Challenging Colonial Forced Labor? Resistance, Resilience, and Power in Senegal (1920s–1940s)." *International Labor and Working-Class History* 93 (2018): 135–150.
Tornimbeni, Corrado. "'Isto foi sempre assim': The Politics of Land and Human Mobility in Chimanimani, Central Mozambique." *Journal of Southern African Studies* 33, no. 3 (2007): 485–500.
Tornimbeni, Corrado. "The Informalization of Formal Portuguese Controls on People's Movements and Identity in the Colony of Mozambique: The Heritage of Portuguese Colonialism in Current Local African Politics." *Portuguese Studies* 28, no. 2 (2012): 216.
Torrão, Nazaré. "Entrevista com Lídia Jorge." *Língua-Lugar: Literatura, História, Estudos Culturais*, no. 1 (2020): 168–197.
Tosh, John. "The Cash-Crop Revolution in Tropical Africa: An Agricultural Reappraisal." *African Affairs* 79, no. 314 (1980): 79–94.

Trentini, Daria. "'I Am a Man of Both Sides': Female Power and Islam in the Life and Work of a Male Spirit Healer in Northern Mozambique." *International Feminist Journal of Politics* 23, no. 2 (2021): 198–220.

Tripp, Aili Mari, Isabel Casimiro, Joy Kwesiga, and Alice Mungwa. *African Women's Movements: Transforming Political Landscapes*. Cambridge: Cambridge University Press, 2009.

Trivellato, Francesca. "Is There a Future for Italian Microhistory in the Age of Global History?" *California Italian Studies* 2, no. 1 (2011).

Turner, Victor Witter. *Schism and Continuity in an African Society: A Study of Ndembu Village Life*. Manchester: Manchester University Press, 1957.

Tvedten, Inge, and Rachi Picardo. "'Goats Eat Where They Are Tied Up': Illicit and Habitual Corruption in Mozambique." *Review of African Political Economy* 45, no. 158 (2018): 541–557.

Vail, Leroy. "Mozambique's Chartered Companies: The Rule of the Feeble." *The Journal of African History* 17, no. 3 (1976): 389–416.

Vail, Leroy, and Landeg White. *Capitalism and Colonialism in Mozambique*. London: Heinemann, 1980.

VandenBroek, Angela. "Agency and Practice Theory." In *21st Century Anthropology: A Reference Handbook*, edited by H. James Birx, 480–487. Thousand Oaks: SAGE, 2010.

Vansina, Jan. *Oral Tradition as History*. Madison: University of Wisconsin Press, 1985.

Vaughan, Megan. "Which Family?: Problems in the Reconstruction of the History of the Family as an Economic and Cultural Unit." *The Journal of African History* 24, no. 2 (1983): 275–283.

Velsen, Jaap van. *The Politics of Kinship: A Study in Social Manipulation among the Lakeside Tonga of Malawi*. Manchester: Manchester University Press, 1964.

Vermeulen, Sonja, and Lorenzo Cotula. "Over the Heads of Local People: Consultation, Consent, and Recompense in Large-Scale Land Deals for Biofuels Projects in Africa." *The Journal of Peasant Studies* 37, no. 4 (2010): 899–916.

Vines, Alex. *Renamo: Terrorism in Mozambique*. London: James Currey, 1991.

Vines, Alex. "Renamo's Rise and Decline: The Politics of Reintegration in Mozambique." *International Peacekeeping* 20, no. 3 (2013): 375–393.

Vines, Alex. "As Conflict in Cabo Delgado Increases, Will Frelimo Learn from Its Mistakes?" The Mail & Guardian, June 24, 2020. Accessed June 29, 2020. https://mg.co.za/africa/2020-06-24-as-conflict-in-cabo-delgado-increases-will-frelimo-learn-from-its-mistakes/.

Vries, Jan de. "Changing the Narrative: The New History That Was and Is to Come." *The Journal of Interdisciplinary History* 48, no. 3 (2017): 313–334.

Vries, Jan de. "Playing with Scales: The Global and the Micro, the Macro and the Nano." *Past & Present* 242, Supplement 14 (2019): 23–36.

Waane, Sac. "Pottery-Making Traditions of the Ikombe Kisi, Mbeya Region, Tanzania." *Baessler-Archiv* 25 (1977): 251–317.

Walraven, Klaas van. "Prologue: Reflections on Historiography and Biography and the Study of Africa's Past." In *The Individual in African History: The Importance of Biography in African Historical Studies*, edited by Klaas van Walraven, 1–50. Leiden: Brill, 2020.

Wand, Karl. *Albrecht Roscher: Eine Afrika-Expedition in den Tod*. Darmstadt: Roether, 1986.

Ward, Stuart. "Whirlwind, Hurricane, Howling Tempest: The Wind of Change and the British World." In *The Wind of Change*, edited by L.J. Butler and Sarah Stockwell, 48–69. London: Palgrave Macmillan, 2013.

Waters, Tony. *The Persistence of Subsistence Agriculture: Life beneath the Level of the Marketplace*. Lanham: Lexington, 2006.

Watson-Franke, Maria-Barbara. "Masculinity and the 'Matrilineal Puzzle.'" *Anthropos* 87, no. 4/6 (1992): 475–488.
Webster, J.B. "From Yao Hill to Mulanje Mountain: Ivory and Slaves and the Southwestern Expansion of the Yao (CC/H/142/77)." In *History Seminar Papers 1977/78*. Chancellor College, Zomba, 1977.
Wehler, Hans-Ulrich. "Aus der Geschichte lernen?" In *Aus der Geschichte lernen? Essays*, by Hans-Ulrich Wehler, 11–18. München: Beck, 1988.
Wehler, Hans-Ulrich. "Alltagsgeschichte: Königsweg zu neuen Ufern oder Irrgarten der Illusion?" In *Aus der Geschichte lernen? Essays*, by Hans-Ulrich Wehler, 130–151. München: Beck, 1988.
Weimer, Bernhard. "Para uma estratégia de descentralização em Moçambique: 'Mantendo a falta de clareza?': Conjunturas, críticas, caminhos, resultados." In *Moçambique: Descentralizar o centralismo. Economia política, recursos e resultados*, edited by Bernhard Weimer, 76–102. Maputo: IESE, 2012.
Weimer, Bernhard. "Mosambik hat gewählt: Analyse der Wahlergebnisse und Perspektiven des Wiederaufbaus (Mozambique Has Voted: Analysis of the Result and Perspectives for Reconstruction)." *Africa Spectrum* 30, no. 1 (1995): 5–33.
Wenzlhuemer, Roland. "Connections in Global History." *Comparativ: Zeitschrift für Globalgeschichte und vergleichende Gesellschaftsforschung* 29, no. 2 (2019): 106–121.
West, Harry G. "Girls with Guns: Narrating the Experience of War of Frelimo's 'Female Detachment.'" *Anthropological Quarterly* 73, no. 4 (2000): 180–194.
West, Harry G. "'Who Rules Us Now?' Identity Tokens, Sorcery, and Other Metaphors in the 1994 Mozambican Elections." In *Transparency and Conspiracy: Ethnographies of Suspicion in the New World Order*, edited by Harry G. West and Todd Sanders, 92–124. Durham: Duke University Press, 2003.
West, Harry G. *Kupilikula: Governance and the Invisible Realm in Mozambique*. Chicago: University of Chicago Press, 2005.
West, Harry G., and Scott Kloeck-Jenson. "Betwixt and Between: 'Traditional Authority' and Democratic Decentralization in Post-War Mozambique." *African Affairs* 98, no. 393 (1999): 455–484.
Whatley, Warren, and Rob Gillezeau. "The Impact of the Transatlantic Slave Trade on Ethnic Stratification in Africa." *American Economic Review* 101, no. 3 (2011): 571–576.
White, Landeg. *Magomero: Portrait of an African Village*. Cambridge: Cambridge University Press, 1987.
Whitfield, Harvey Amani, and Bonny Ibhawoh. "Problems, Perspectives, and Paradigms: Colonial Africanist Historiography and the Question of Audience." *Canadian Journal of African Studies/Revue Canadienne des Études Africaines* 39, no. 3 (2005): 582–600.
Whyte, Christine. "'Freedom but Nothing Else': The Legacies of Slavery and Abolition in Post-Slavery Sierra Leone, 1928–1956." *The International Journal of African Historical Studies* 48, no. 2 (2015): 231–250.
Wiegink, Nikkie. *Former Guerrillas in Mozambique*. Philadelphia: University of Pennsylvania Press, 2020.
Wiener, Martin J. "The Idea of 'Colonial Legacy' and the Historiography of Empire." *Journal of The Historical Society* 13, no. 1 (2013): 1–32.
Willis, Justin. "Chieftaincy." In *The Oxford Handbook of Modern African History*, edited by John Parker and Richard Reid, 208–223. Oxford: Oxford University Press, 2013.
Wilson, Japhy. "Paradoxical Utopia: The Millennium Villages Project in Theory and Practice." *Journal of Agrarian Change* 17, no. 1 (2017): 122–143.

Wilson, Monica. *For Men and Elders: Change in the Relations of Generations and of Men and Women among the Nyakyusa-Ngonde People, 1875–1971.* New York: Africana, 1977.

Wittig, Katrin. "Politics in the Shadow of the Gun: Revisiting the Literature on 'Rebel-to-Party Transformations' through the Case of Burundi." *Civil Wars* 18, no. 2 (2016): 137–159.

Wolpe, Harold. "Capitalism and Cheap Labour-Power in South Africa: From Segregation to Apartheid." *Economy and Society* 1, no. 4 (1972): 425–456.

Wright, Donald R. *The World and a Very Small Place in Africa: A History of Globalization in Niumi, The Gambia.* 2nd ed. New York, 2004.

Wuyts, Marc. "Money, Planning and Rural Transformation in Mozambique." *The Journal of Development Studies* 22, no. 1 (1985): 180–207.

Yoshida, Masao. "African Economic History: Approaches to Research." In *Writing African History*, edited by John Edward Philips, 308–328. Rochester: University of Rochester Press, 2005.

Young, Sherilynn. "Fertility and Famine: Women's Agricultural History in Southern Mozambique." In *The Roots of Rural Poverty in Central and Southern Africa*, edited by Robin Palmer and Neil Parsons, 66–81. London: Heinemann, 1977.

Zeleza, Paul Tiyambe. *A Modern Economic History Africa.* Vol. 1: The Nineteenth Century. Dakar: Codesria, 1993.

Zeleza, Paul Tiyambe. "Review of Cutting Down Trees: Gender, Nutrition, and Agricultural Change in the Northern Province of Zambia, 1890–1990." *The International Journal of African Historical Studies* 28, no. 2 (1995): 404–406.

Zeleza, Paul Tiyambe. "The Troubled Encounter between Postcolonialism and African History." *Journal of the Canadian Historical Association* 17, no. 2 (2007): 89–129.

Zeman, Andreas. "Caught between the Guerrilla and the Colonial State: Refugee Life in Northern Mozambique During the Independence War (1964–1974)." In *On the Social History of Persecution*, edited by Christian Gerlach, 115–138. Berlin: De Gruyter Oldenbourg, 2023.

Zeman, Andreas. "Wiriyamu and the Colonial Archive: Reading It against the Grain? Along the Grain? Read It at All!" *History in Africa*, June 20, 2023, 1–31. https://doi.org/10.1017/hia.2023.2.

Zeman, Andreas. "Flag Independence without Flags? Mozambican Decolonization on the Periphery of the New Nation." *E-Journal of Portuguese History* 21, no. 2 (forthcoming 2023).

Zenker, Olaf, and Markus Virgil Hoehne. "Processing the Paradox: When the State Has to Deal with Customary Law." In *The State and the Paradox of Customary Law in Africa*, edited by Olaf Zenker and Markus Virgil Hoehne, 1–40. Abingdon: Routledge, 2018.

Zimba, Benigna. "Slave Trade and Slavery in Southeastern Africa: Interviews and Images." In *Slave Routes and Oral Tradition in Southeastern Africa*, edited by Benigna Zimba, Edward Alpers, and Allen Isaacman, 295–335. Maputo: Filsom, 2005.

Zimba, Benigna, ed. *A mulher moçambicana na Luta de Libertação Nacional: Memórias do Destacamento Feminino.* Maputo: Centro de Pesquisa da História da Luta de Libertação Nacional, 2012.

List of Maps

Map 1:	Nkholongue and the larger region including the borders of the modern day district of Lago —— **XIX**
Map 2:	The lakeshore area around Nkholongue —— **XX**
Map 3:	Modern-day Nkholongue and the previous location of the village around Linga —— **216**
Map 4:	Locations of the leisure and tourism projects in Nkholongue since 2000 —— **374**

List of Figures

Figure 1: *Arquivo Permanente do Gabinete do Governador do Niassa*: the ground floor room —— **33**
Figure 2: CM during its "Golden Jubilee Voyage" in 1951 —— **208**
Figure 3: Aerial view of Nkholongue showing the plain between the creeks of Nkholongue and Cabendula —— **215**
Figure 4: Level of Lake Malawi, 1900–1980 —— **217**
Figure 5: Fishing *ussipa*: dugout canoe with car battery and LED light bulbs —— **242**
Figure 6: The *aldeamento* of Metangula in 1973 —— **285**
Figure 7: Mozambique and the "liberated areas" in 1969 according to Frelimo's propaganda —— **289**
Figure 8: Number of demobilized soldiers as a share of the total population by province —— **343**
Figure 9: Still waiting for a "proper" building: the school of Malango during my fieldwork —— **393**
Figure 10: Visualization of adults living in a household 100 meters or less from the household of their parents in the center of Nkholongue proper —— **404**
Figure 11: Sunset on the way to Nkholongue —— **421**

List of Tables

Table 1:	Tax levels 1903–1961 —— **155**
Table 2:	Number of inhabitants by chiefdom of the P.A. Metangula, 1940 and 1964 —— **160**
Table 3:	Stops of the Anglican steamboats in Nkholongue —— **205**
Table 4:	Order of Sailing S.S. Chauncy Maples, 1949 —— **206**
Table 5:	Tax censuses of the administrative post of Metangula, 1957–1958 —— **222**
Table 6:	Number of births at home and at hospital ordered by age cohorts —— **283**
Table 7:	Population under Portuguese control, Lago District, 1964–1974 —— **291**
Table 8:	Schools destroyed or closed because of the war by province (percentage of schools existing in 1983) —— **342**
Table 9:	Election results, 1994 —— **355**
Table 10:	Election results, 1999 —— **355**
Table 11:	Origin of farmland according to the 2016 survey —— **402**
Table 12:	Number of adults living in a household 100 meters or less from households of their parents, uncles or aunts (according to the 2012 survey) —— **403**
Table 13:	Residence patterns of households according to the 2012 survey —— **405**
Table 14:	Classification of the residence patterns of endogamous households according to ownership of the house and/or proximity to the families of the households' inhabitants —— **405**
Table 15:	Individuals with the highest number of descendants living in Nkholongue in 2012 —— **410**

Index

Abdallah, Yohanna B.   60, 62, 77f., 98, 111, 119f., 125, 133, 149, 153, 155f., 162–164, 166, 173, 178–181, 186, 205
Aboriginal Delusion   37, 39–43, 106–108, 202, 257, 298, 307, 418, see also substantivism
administration see also Companhia do Nyassa, government, men on the spot
– colonial 38, 106, 130, 143–146, 153, 158, 161, 165, 181–186, 284, 287, 297, 402
– post-colonial 316–322
age   24, 27, 43, 45, 99f., 102, 111, 202, 221, 233, 240, 272, 283, 301, 314, 319, 343, 344, 350, 369, 387, 426
agency   2, 4f., 18–23, 35, 39, 44, 51, 58, 108, 222, 360
agriculture   XVII, 19, 28, 40f., 48, 80, 133–135, 149–151, 153, 165, 192–202, 211–218, 224f., 227–239, 241, 248–251, 276f., 287, 305, 311, 313, 316, 325f., 346, 362, 369, 419, see also cassava, cotton, farmland, maize, rice, sorghum
aldeamentos   228, 252–258, 270–287, 290–300, 308, 321, 347, 379, 397, see also resettlement
Angoni (people)   62f., 66f., 72, 98, 112–114, 121, 132, 397
Anyanja (people)   60f., 70f., 81, 91, 97, 104, 134, 174, 221, 294, 334, 387, 397, 405–407, 409, 413
archives   3, 16, 23f., 29–34, 36, 108f., 328, 332
askaris   122–125, 162, 178

barter   201, 211f., 218, 243
Botmann, Leonhard   148–150, 153

capitalism   146–151, 163–166, 194–201, 239–248, 250, 324, 367, 397, 418
cassava   148, 202, 211, 214, 218, 229–239, 249
– spread of   229–232
chidulo (salt)   208f., 225
chiefs   see also Chilombe, Chingomanje, Kalanje, Mataka, Nampanda

– and colonialism   157, 165, 178f., 183–186, 243, 284
– and colonization   39, 49f., 102f., 106, 109–130, 135f., 172f.
– and decolonization   264, 273, 316–318, 349f., 357, 360f., 380f.
– and Islamization   49, 85–99, 101–103, 418
– and matriliny   397, 409–416
– and the slave trade   1, 38, 49, 54, 56f., 60, 64, 67–81, 84, 131, 135, 235, 397
– re-recognition of   9, 52, 362–367, 370–372, 380–393, 395f.
– succession of   52, 78, 371, 382–387, 401f., 411, 414f.
Chikoka, Isa   99f., 175–177
children   77, 79, 119, 157, 164f., 194, 207, 209, 221f., 235, 241, 272, 278, 282f., 295, 310, 351, 357, 401–403, 406, 408, 414–416
Chilombe (chief of Metangula)   70f., 113, 160, 218, 263, 334, 384
Chingomanje, Azizi   101, 119, 129, 410
Chingomanje (chief of Nkholongue)   V, XVII, 1, 27f., 52f., 65, 67–78, 80–82, 91–98, 100f., 109–121, 123–130, 135, 146, 160, 172f., 183f., 186, 204, 206, 209, 214, 273, 291, 345, 349f., 361, 364, 378, 381–387, 389–392, 395, 401f., 411f., see also Kingomanga
Chingomanje, Salimo   97f., 117, 134, 214
Chinyanja (language)   8, 25, 30, 54, 59, 96, 119, 131, 152, 211, 229, 376
– dialects   55, 285
chiombo (ceremony)   412
chiwondo (bark cloth)   207f., 226
Chipembere, Henry M.   210, 334f.
Chissano, Joaquim   312, 354–356
Chiyao (language)   25, 59f., 157
Christianity   29, 52, 85–95, 97, 101f., 122, 129, 176f., 219, 269, 285f., 294, 311f., 397, 401, 406–408, 411, 415f.
– and matriliny   52, 285f., 397, 401, 406–408, 411, 415f.
cipaios   145, 159, 165, 182–184, 267

Civil War (1976–1992)   1 f., 28, 38, 47 f., 51 f., 54, 113, 177, 234, 236, 245, 305, 319, 328, 332 f., 338–361, 364, 370, 381, 390, 394, 418
– compared to the War of Independence   342 f., 347–350, 353, 360 f.
clothes   93, 113, 154, 164, 202, 207 f., 218 f., 222 f., 225 f., 248, 279, 294, 323, 325, 337, 344, 348, 353, 356, 380, *see also* chiwondo (bark cloth), consumer goods (shortages of), tailoring
CM   *see* S.S. Chauncy Maples (steamship)
Cobué   XIX f., 115, 126, 145, 158, 164, 237, 241, 243, 264, 320, 375, 382, 387 f.
colonialism   5, 32, 37, 44 f., 50, 58, 104–108, 138–191, 196, 203, 253, 256, 266 f., 303, 307, 321, 328 f., 363, 397, 418, 420
colonization   2, 7, 34 f., 38–40, 42 f., 45, 47–50, 62, 84, 88, 93, 101, 103–138, 141, 152, 172, 176, 189, 192, 204, 213, 240, 335, 418
Companhia do Nyassa   31, 96 f., 101, 105 f., 108–111, 118, 121–130, 132 f., 141–154, 159 f., 162–167, 170, 172–174, 176, 179, 181–185, 190, 205
conflicts (intravillage)   19, 22, 26, 52, 102, 258, 260 f., 350, 356 f., 366, 382–396, 419
consumer goods   38, 182, 202 f., 218 f., 223, 225, 245, 279, 420, *see also* clothes, salt, soap
– prices of   279, 281, 324 f., 420
– replacing subsistence goods   207–209, 225–227
– shortages of   38, 225–227, 279, 305, 323–327, 336 f., 346, 356
continuities   48, 109–111, 134, 200, 213 f., 316, 319 f., 337, 359, 419
cotton   38, 50, 138–140, 142, 148–151, 163–172, 186, 189 f., 199, 203, 220, 230 f., 250, 267, 288, 325 f.
counter-insurgency   2, 39, 225, 252–257, 255 f., 298, 302, 347–349, *see also* aldeamentos, Civil War, resettlement, War of Independence
Cox, Machell H. A.   124, 133, 144, 155, 162–166, 169, 176, 180, 184, 192, 205, 230–232, 235 f., 406–408, 414 f.

decolonization   2, 51, 140 f., 252, 255, 262, 302–337, 418, *see also* War of Independence
descent   *see* matriliny
Deuss, Ludwig   100 f., 128, 148–150
Dhlakama, Afonso   354 f., 359
dhows   71, 73, 75, 81, 90, 93, 96, 119–121, 126 f., 148
dinheiro dos antigos combatentes   26, 258–261, 311
diseases   110, 126, 146, 163, 186–189, 251, 265, 269, 360, 382
drought   63, 107, 230, 238, 251
dualism
– economic   202, 324 f., *see also* substantivism
– epistemic   19, 43, 104
– legal   161 f., 363, 369

economy of affection   195, 197, 395, *see also* substantivism
education   *see also* schools
– after independence   288–290, 316, 321 f., 329
– during colonialism   282 f., 295, 311 f.
elections   39, 51, 312, 339 f., 354–356, 372, 390, 412
Estado Novo   50, 142, 146 f., 157, 167, 185, 187, 190, 262, 316
everyday life   3 f., 10, 22 f., 28, 34, 36, 38, 48, 53, 59, 79, 80, 109, 132, 136, 167, 199, 207, 226, 280, 283–286, 292, 345 f., 394, 401 f., 418–421
exploitation   50, 55, 109, 123 f., 128, 138, 141–143, 147, 151–171, 189 f., 201, 224, 243 f., 266 f., 294, 300 f., 324–326, 420, *see also* labor
Eyre, C.B.   101, 123 f., 126–129, 153, 163 f., 166, 173, 180, 184, 226

famine   *see* hunger
farming   *see* agriculture, farmland
farmland   28, 80, 132 f., 135, 193, 198, 202, 215, 217, 228 f., 231–236, 256, 272 f., 276 f., 287, 313, 402 f., *see also* machamba
firewood
– for home consumption   133, 211, 228, 273, 284, 345 f.

- for steamships 48, 125f., 153–155, 175f., 201, 204–213, 219, 240, 420
fishing XVII, 25, 37, 41, 79, 110, 151, 153, 192, 194, 202f., 208, 213, 227, 234, 239–248, 250, 265, 324, 346, 348, 380, 394, 411, 420
Frelimo 18, 21, 46, 51, 142, 158, 172, 190, 247, 253, 255–261, 263–270, 272–275, 281f., 286, 288–296, 298, 300–302, 304–313, 315–319, 321–330, 332–339, 342f., 347–351, 354–361, 363, 367, 370–372, 379f., 382, 416, 418, 420

gender relations 24, 34–35, 43, 76–78, 98f., 102, 153, 155f., 162, 164f., 188f., 211, 219–224, 226–228, 231, 238, 240, 271f., 278, 282f., 397–416
global history 2f., 5, 10–15, 46f., 417
globalization 13, 37, 46f., 192, 198, 249, 417
- processes of decreasing 46f., 143–147, 212f., 249, see also subsistence production (reversal to)
government see also administration, Companhia do Nyassa
- British (of Nyasaland) 92, 95, 119, 205
- colonial 7, 30, 32, 144, 150, 153f., 157, 162, 165, 167, 170f., 184, 186f., 205, 231, 238f., 253–255, 262f., 272, 295, 297, 299, 316, 343, 347f., 381
- post-colonial 7, 9, 26, 31, 46, 184, 226, 233–235, 245, 258–261, 304, 306f., 311, 315–338, 341, 343–345, 347f., 351f., 357, 360f., 365, 368, 371, 373, 375, 378, 385f., 390, 395, 420
Grupos Especiais (GE) 261, 281f., 308, 359

handicraft 39, 194, 210, 219, 228, see also ivory carving, pottery
health see also diseases
- after independence 288, 316, 321f., 379f., 388, 392
- and colonialism 186–189, 204, 253, 282f., 295, 300
history from below 4f., 18–21, 418
hunger
- because of drought 63, 107, 230, 238
- because of environmental issues 211f., 215–218
- because of forced labor 38, 162–167, 169f., 189f., 203, 230
- because of market disruptions 215–218
- during wars 63, 79, 107, 162f., 179f., 256, 269–271, 274, 276f., 290, 292–294, 344, 346, 351f.
- Portuguese hunger policy 274f., 290, 292–294
- seasonal 166

inequality 20, 42f., 188, 192, 239–241, 366, 393f., see also racism, stratification
initiation rites 95, 97, 318f., 357, see also jando (initiation dance)
intermediaries 19, 107f., 172, 183–186, 188–190, 197, 327, see also askaris, chiefs, cipaios
Islam
- and matriliny 98, 102, 397, 399, 406f., 415f.
- its role in colonial Mozambique 39, 87, 101, 128f., 136, 152, 172, 174–181, 190, 285, 294, 311
- its role in post-colonial Mozambique 1, 41, 311f., 318f., 355, 420
- spread of 2, 35, 39, 49, 84–103, 136, 418
ivory carving 210f., 219f., 240f., 246, 295

jando (initiation dance) 97, 357
Johnson, William Percival 30, 66, 71f., 74–76, 79–82, 89–91, 93–100, 112–114, 116–120, 124, 128, 133f., 148, 151f., 155f., 163, 176f., 184, 210, 229, 237, 243, 401, 406, 413–415
Jumbe (of Nkhotakota) 64–67, 70, 72–75, 92f., 95, 99f., 112, 120f., 132

Kalanje (chief of Unango) 53, 70, 72, 74–78, 93f., 98, 110, 115, 117–121, 123–125, 173, 179
Kingomanga 67–69, 112
Kiswahili 67, 90, 120, 129, 177, 202, 330

labor see also agriculture, labor migration, subsistence production
- communal 235–237, 325f.
- forced 38, 133, 136, 139, 141, 151, 154, 161–171, 182, 189f., 196, 199, 203, 325f.
- slave 55, 58, 62, 78–80

– wage   148 f., 154, 156, 182, 188, 194, 225, 227 f., 242 – 247, 266, 272, 278 f., 282, 295, 309, 313 f., 373, 377, 379 f., 391 f., 394
labor migration   35, 47, 50, 52, 147, 154, 156, 182 f., 194, 196, 202, 219 – 224, 226, 231, 233, 240, 248 f., 272, 383, 397, 416
– and gender relations   156, 219 – 224, 226, 397, 416
– and subsistence production   224
Lago District   XIX, 53, 95, 97, 144 – 146, 159, 171, 184, 259, 263, 268, 277, 282, 290 – 292, 297, 319, 321, 334, 341 f., 355, 376, 414
land see farmland, land law
land law   364, 366 – 371, 388 f., 392
language   XVII, 25, 28, 42, 49, 53, 56, 90, 100, 128, 256, 283, 314, 321, see also Chinyanja, Chiyao, Kiswahili, Portuguese, translation
Legacy Mode   37, 44 – 46, 58
legislation   141, 247, 364 – 372, 382, see also dualism (legal), land law
Lichinga   XVII, XIX f., 24, 31, 41, 143, 228, 234, 241, 278, 322, 328, 358, 373, 376, 388, see also Vila Cabral
Likoma   XIX, 30, 118, 175, 206
Litumbe, Paulo   104, 167, 171, 174, 266, 328
Lourenço Marques   XIX, 185, 288 f., 295 f., see also Maputo
Lussefa   XIX f., 27, 64 – 74, 93 f., 99, 112, 124, 152, 160, 164, 167, 175 – 177, 220, 284, 325, 382, 414, 416

machamba   202, 314
– machamba de povo   325 f.
Machel, Samora   65, 308, 312, 322 f., 325, 327, 329, 331 f., 335 f., 361
Magomero   4 f., 7 f., 11, 29, 89, 417
maize   227, 229, 231 – 239, 243, 325 f., 335, 345
– consumption   235, 239
– cultivation   229, 231 – 239
– promotion after independence   227, 233 – 236, 238, 325 f., 335
Makanjira   57, 60, 64 f., 73 f., 78, 86, 93 – 95, 99 f., 112, 115, 118 f., 121, 128, 132
Malango   XVII, XX, 9, 24 f., 37 f., 53, 125, 134, 201, 212 – 218, 223, 225, 232 – 234, 244, 260, 270 f., 298, 307, 310, 312 – 315, 320, 334, 345 f., 349 – 353, 357 – 359, 367, 373 f., 376 – 381, 386, 389, 391 – 394, 411, 419 f.
– 1st formation   97, 134, 214 f.
– 2nd formation   38, 201, 212 – 218, 232, 298
– possible separation from Nkholongue   XVII, 9, 380 f., 386, 392 f., 419
Malawi   XVII, XIX, 7, 24 f., 29 f., 41, 51, 54, 63, 86, 88, 171, 210, 213, 219, 223, 228, 235, 241 f., 244, 247, 249, 260, 265, 271, 273, 279 f., 290 f., 307 – 310, 313 f., 332 – 335, 346, 357, 382 – 385, 387, 397 f., 403, 413, 416, 419, see also Nyasaland
Malinganile   111, 134, 172 f., 183
Malo   XX, 173, 187 f., 213, 345, 349, 402
Manave, Aurélio   333 f.
Maniamba   XIX f., 38, 144, 158, 168, 184, 188, 267, 322, 352, 414
Maniamba (chief of Ngolocolo)   70 f., 115
Maputo   XVII, XIX, 240, 312, 329, 337, 342, see also Lourenço Marques
Maravi   59 – 62, 77, see also Anyanja
Marimba   54, 66, 69, 77, 96, 98, see also Nkhotakota
market   47, 50, 165 f., 194 – 199, 202, 207 – 213, 218 f., 224 – 228, 233 – 235, 237 f., 241 – 248, 250, 279, 324, 388, 420
– disruptions   166, 212 f., 219, 224 – 227, 250, 279, 322 – 325
– production for the   47, 194 – 199, 207 – 213, 226 f., 233, 241 – 248, 235, 238, 241 – 248, 250
marriages   52, 77, 79, 134, 155, 188 f., 223, 285, 311, 313 f., 325, 350, 397, 400, 403, 405 – 408, 410 f., 414 – 416, see also uxorilocality, virilocality
Mataka (chief of Cobué)   126
Mataka (chief of Muembe)   57, 64 f., 68 f., 74, 78, 86, 111 f., 121, 126, 134, 172 – 174, 179, 183
matriliny   2, 34 f., 41 f., 47, 52, 77 f., 98, 102, 352, 381 – 383, 386, 397 – 416, see also uxorilocality
Mbemba   66, 68 f., 112
Mbuna Bay   XVII f., 23, 202 f., 228, 346, 364, 373 f., 376, 380, 384 f., 388 f., 391 f., 394, 411 f.

M'chepa   XX, 157, 214f., 218, 271, 284, 291, 353, 355, 376, 380, 388
MCT (Mission for the Combat of the Trypanosomiasis)   146, 172, 186–188, 214f.
means of production   241–245
Meluluca   XIXf., 40f., 53, 70–73, 94, 115, 123, 160, 165, 192, 271, 284f., 330–333, 355, 382, 386, 414
memory politics   46, 258–262, 265, 288–292, 311, 342, see also dinheiro dos antigos combatentes
men on the spot   130, 141, 152f., 157–159, 266
Messumba   XIXf., 53, 81, 93, 97, 115, 119, 122, 129, 158, 160, 165, 169, 182, 186, 204, 206, 218f., 232, 237, 264, 266, 269f., 311f., 326, 328, 333f., 350, 407, 411
Metangula   XVII, XIXf., 17, 24f., 32, 38, 41, 53f., 70f., 95, 100, 113, 122f., 125–128, 130, 138, 143–151, 153–156, 158–160, 164, 166, 169, 178–180, 182, 184, 188, 190, 192, 204f., 211f., 218–222, 225, 228, 232, 234, 240–242, 245f., 258, 263, 265, 268–288, 291, 294, 296, 309, 312–314, 319f., 327f., 330–332, 334, 345–348, 350, 353, 370f., 373, 376, 379, 384, 390, 397, 406, 412, 419
microhistory   1–23, 46, 49, 85, 89, 96, 117, 190, 417
– and global history   10–14
migration   9, 43, 50, 61–63, 66, 70, 72, 97, 105, 133f., 160f., 172, 181–183, 187f., 190, 200f., 203, 214f., 218, 224, 228, 247, 271, 276, 291, 298, 312, 334f., 383, 412f., 419, see also labor migration, mobility, refugees, resettlement
militias   255, 281, 301, 343, 345f., 348, 359
Millennium Villages   7f., 200
Mkwanda, Abdallah   100f., 128, 130, 148, 173
mobility   13, 47, 89, 194, 200, 209, 220, 224, 249
– social   79, 102, 279, 309, 394
moral economy   194, see also economy of affection, substantivism
Mtucula   203, 214, 275, 291, 383
Muembe   XIX, 64f., 68, 126, 179f.

Nampanda (chief of Unango)   70, 72, 123

nationalism   39, 46f., 50f., 190f., 254–256, 258, 261f., 267, 269, 290, 293f., 300, 302f., 306, 315, 332–335
Ngolocolo   XX, 115, 160, 164, 167, 187, 220, 229, 232, 271, 284, 380
N'gombe, Amanhi   383, 402, 410
Niassa (province)   XVII, XIX, 17f., 27, 31, 34, 40f., 53, 60, 77, 86, 142–144, 147, 168, 172, 192, 224, 234, 239, 243, 253, 258, 262f., 275, 287–295, 297, 299, 306, 322, 328–330, 332f., 336, 341–343, 354f., 373, 375f., 399f., 407, 412
njujo (soap)   226, 323
Nkhotakota   XIX, 1, 54, 64–67, 69, 72f., 75, 80–83, 86, 92, 96, 99f., 112, 119–121, 130, 133f., 148, 177, 204, 206f., 210, 219, 230, 236, 280, 334f., see also Marimba
nostalgia   21, 323
Nyasaland   30, 87, 105, 119, 147, 149f., 154, 156, 161, 178, 181–183, 190, 219–223, 267, 272, 415, see also Malawi

One-Way-Analysis   13, 37, 46–49, 56, 142, 250, 419
oral history   4, 17, 23, 31f., 35f., 89, 91, 104, 111, 143, 160f., 167, 171, 174, 179, 184, 207, 218, 221, 232, 244, 254, 258, 262, 290, 294, 316, 353, 385, 399
– project of the AHM   31f., 104, 167, 171, 174, 179, 221, 244, 290, 294f.
– project of the MLM   XIII, 32f., 221, 223, 254, 262, 353, 385
ORGUT (consulting firm)   40f., 47, 192, 200–202, 229, 376

Partido Revolucionário de Moçambique (PRM)   332–334
Paul, John   158f., 184, 263, 266, 269, 277, 281, 294, 333f.
PIDE/DGS   32, 104, 138, 269, 291f., 296, 333f.
police   101, 152f., 159, 168, 181, 183f., 186, 269, 280, 287, 319f., 328, 330–332, 360, 394, see also cipaios, PIDE/DGS
postcolonial studies   42–45, 58
pottery   50, 154, 201–203, 209–212, 218, 220, 224, 228, 243, 248f.

racism 146, 181, 247, 256, 266
railway 146 f., 171, 213, 289
religion 56, 85 f., 95, 98, 102, 176, 285, 294, 316, 318, *see also* Christianity, chiombo (ceremony), Islam
Renamo 1, 38, 51, 234, 246, 287, 305, 319, 332, 334, 336, 338–341, 344–346, 348–361, 370, 372, 381, 418, 420
refugees 38, 41, 54, 113, 128, 183, 228, 247, 249, 254, 268–275, 279 f., 290–292, 298 f., 307–309, 312–314, 322, 333 f., 343–347, 352
resettlement *see also* villagization
– because of sleeping sickness 187 f., *see also* MCT
– during the War of Independence 1, 13 f., 35 f., 38 f., 39, 42, 50 f., 214, 225, 228, 232, 246 f., 252–254, 256–258, 270–273, 275–277, 284 f., 287, 292, 294, 297–299, 312, *see also* aldeamentos
– for tourism projects 377–379, 392
– socialist 305, 316, 326, 347
resistance 18 f., 39, 50, 83 f., 102–106, 125, 134, 169, 172, 174–181, 185, 188, 190, 195, 250, 266 f., 271, 334, 378
rice 170 f., 229, 232, 239
roads XVII, XIX, 41, 154, 156, 158, 160–162, 171, 192, 213, 269, 376, 379, 384
romanticization 18 f., 288–292, 306, 369, *see also* substantivism
Roscher, Albrecht 27, 63, 66–69, 72, 79, 112
ruptures 3, 38 f., 42 f., 61, 150, 199, 224, 226, 234, 245, 247, 250, 257, 420, *see also* Winds of History

sailing *see* dhows
Salimo, Saide 134, 203, 214, 383
salt 38, 69, 203, 207–209, 219, 225 f., 248, 279, 323, 325 f., 337, 356, 417, *see also* chidulo
schools 9, 25, 91, 120, 123, 129, 153, 164, 204, 240 f., 253, 256, 258, 263, 282 f., 295, 300, 311 f., 315, 318, 321, 341 f., 359, 379 f., 392 f., *see also* education
– in Nkholongue 9, 91, 120, 129, 204, 318, 321, 379 f., 392 f.
scorched earth 274–276, 290, 292–294, 300

secretaries (village/neighborhood/party) 9, 316–318, 328, 359, 365, 372, 380–382, 386 f., 389–391, 395 f., 411, 416
settlement patterns 7–9, 14, 47 f., 50, 109, 130–136, 200, 203, 213–216, *see also* resettlement, urbanization
slavery 1, 38, 45, 49, 54–59, 74, 76–84, 106, 108, 130, 135 f., 325, *see also* labor (slave)
– abolition of 56, 57, 98–100, 102, 106, 121, 130–136
slave trade 1 f., 13, 29, 35, 38, 42–45, 47–49, 52, 54–84, 87, 90, 92 f., 95, 102, 107, 109, 111 f., 119, 131, 133–136, 196, 199 f., 203, 235, 239 f., 248, 364, 397, 401, 413–415, 417, 419
– and matriliny 35, 52, 77 f., 397, 401, 412–415
soap 38, 226, 279, 326, 337, 346, *see also* njujo
social history 4 f., 12, 21–23, 36, 51, 56, 184, 252, 303 f., 306, 336, 418
socialism 28, 104, 225, 245, 247, 305, 316, 325–327, 330, 360, 367, 372, 380, 382
soldiers 101, 122 f., 159, 173, 178, 183 f., 270, 277 f., 297, 329, 338, 341, 343, 345, 348–351, 353 *see also* askaris, Grupos Especiais (GE)
– fighters of Frelimo 21, 257–262, 264–268, 272, 275, 290, 293, 310, 311, 315, 317, 319, 329
sorghum 229, 231–233, 236
sources 3 f., 15 f., 18, 23–36, 42 f., 52 f., 56 f., 59, 67, 75 f., 78, 85 f., 100, 108 f., 111, 116 f., 130, 134, 142, 149, 152, 155, 160, 162 f., 174, 178 f., 186, 189, 200 f., 213, 217, 242, 252, 264, 268, 279, 282, 286, 291 f., 312, 317, 319, 321, 328, 332, 341, 397, 399–401, 406, 413 f., 416, 422–426, *see also* archives, oral history, surveys
– lack of 16, 23, 34, 42, 52, 57, 59, 78, 130, 142, 162, 186, 189, 200, 345, 399, 401, 414
– problems/biases of 15, 24, 26, 28, 34–36, 63, 130, 152, 258–262, 279, 397, 406
South Africa 1, 38, 62, 148 f., 154, 156, 199, 220–222, 249, 267, 272, 338 f., 376, 391
S.S. Chauncy Maples (steamship) 38 f., 138, 163, 166, 204–220, 225, 228, 232

steamships   1, 38f., 48, 50, 72, 89–91, 93, 97, 125, 134, 146–148, 153, 175, 178, 190, 201, 204–213, 220, 225, 240, 248, *see also* S.S. Chauncy Maples
stratification (social)   22, 47, 80f., 107, 133, 239–247, *see also* inequality, racism
subsistence production   2, 38, 41, 47, 50f., 192–194, 196f., 199, 201–203, 213, 218, 224–238, 241, 246, 248, 250f., 276f., 311, 323–325, 379, 397, 418
– disappearance of   192, 207–209, 225–227, 241–243, 250, 277
– reversal to   38, 47, 50f., 194, 201, 203, 213, 218, 224–226, 228, 250, 311, 323, 325, 397
substantivism   194–198, 251, *see also* economy of affection
surveys   16, 23f., 26, 28f., 52, 71, 76, 82, 202f., 229, 234f., 244f., 283, 400, 402f., 405, 408–410, 415
– village survey of 2012   26, 28, 71, 202f., 403, 405, 410, 415
– village surveys of 2016   28, 202f., 229, 234f., 243, 283, 402
Swahili   47, 64, 76, 80, 86, 88, 90, 93, 113, *see also* Kiswahili
Swinny, George   V, 53, 67–69, 73–76, 79f., 90–92, 95f., 113f., 229, 401

tailoring   219, 240
Tanganyika   154, 182, 219, 221, 262f., 312
Tanzania   34, 76, 97, 210, 244, 251, 273, 290, 308f., 312–314, 322, 330f., 333, 397
taxation
– pre-colonial   76, 80
– colonial   133, 138, 151–161, 164, 166, 172, 174, 181–183, 185–187, 189, 203, 207, 218–222, 243, 406
– post-colonial   315, 320f., 372
Thubiri   100f., 128f., 176
tourism   XVII, 1f., 38, 52, 202, 228, 234, 362, 364–367, 372–380, 389, 391f., 394–397, 412, 420, *see also* Mbuna Bay
trade   27, 48, 60f., 72f., 76, 87, 100–102, 120f., 128, 146–150, 209, 212, 218f., 240, 246, 287, 327, 413, *see also* market, slave trade

traders   25, 45, 60, 62, 64f., 75f., 78, 80f., 83, 90, 92f., 95f., 100f., 112f., 120f., 128, 132, 147f., 219, 229, 240, 246, 287, 418
traditional authorities   *see* chiefs
translation   8f., 25, 46, 53, 69, 119, 127, 175, 211
transport   48, 121, 127, 147, 151, 171, 204, 213, 232, 243, 271f., 287, 313, *see also* dhows, railway, roads, steamships

Umali, Chadreque   69, 77, 97, 99, 110, 134, 203, 370f.
Unango   XIX, 1, 28, 32, 47, 54, 57, 65–72, 74–76, 78, 81, 83, 90, 107, 110, 112, 116, 119–121, 123, 125, 131f., 149, 158f., 162, 164, 167, 169, 173f., 178–180, 186, 335, 383, 387, 401, 413, 426
urbanization   37, 48, 282, *see also* settlement patterns
uxorilocality   52, 285, 397, 401, 403, 405–409, 411

veterans   26, 157f., 258–262, 264, 266, 311f., 336, *see also* dinheiro dos antigos combatentes
Vila Cabral   XIX, 147, 159, 168, 240f., 263, 289, *see also* Lichinga
village (concept and definition)   XVII, 5–9, 200, 400f., 419, *see also* settlement patterns, villagization, village studies
villagization   7, 15, 305, 314, *see also* aldeamentos, resettlement
village studies   6, 8, 28, 200, 400
virilocality   52, 285, 397, 401, 403–409, 411, 414–416

war *see also* Civil War, War of Independence, World War One
– colonization wars   110f., 126f., 134, 172f., 183
– pre-colonial wars   55, 59, 62–66, 72–74, 98, 104, 109, 113, 131, 133, 135f.
War of Independence   21, 26, 28, 32, 34, 48, 50f., 54, 104, 157, 161, 177, 183, 214, 220, 228, 232, 236, 246f., 252–301, 306f., 341f., 345, 348f., 361, 381, 383, 407, 418, 420, *see also* Civil War (compared to the War of Independence)

Wayao (people)   1, 47, 57, 59–68, 70–78, 82–84, 86–88, 92 f., 95, 98, 102 f., 111 f., 121, 125, 134, 172, 174, 207 f., 243, 294, 397, 400, 405, 407, 409, 412 f.
Winds of History   3, 21, 36–39, 45, 48, 52, 59, 107, 121 f., 302, 414, 418–420, *see also* ruptures

World War One   39, 148–150, 156, 162, 172, 174–181, 189 f., 226, 230

Yao *see* Wayao

Zanzibar   29, 61 f., 67, 79, 86, 90, 99, 112

www.ingramcontent.com/pod-product-compliance
Lightning Source LLC
Chambersburg PA
CBHW051533230426
43669CB00015B/2585